NAHUM–MALACHI
A Commentary in the Wesleyan Tradition

NAHUM–MALACHI
A Commentary in the Wesleyan Tradition

Laurie J. Braaten
and Jim Edlin

BEACON HILL PRESS
OF KANSAS CITY

Beacon Hill Press of Kansas City
PO Box 419527
Kansas City, MO 64141
www.BeaconHillBooks.com

ISBN 978-0-8341-3563-5

Printed in the United States of America

Cover Design: J.R. Caines
Interior Design: Sharon Page

Unless otherwise indicated, all Scripture quotations are from the Holy Bible, New International Version® (NIV®). Copyright © 1973, 1978, 1984, 2011 by Biblica, Inc.™ Used by permission of Zondervan. All rights reserved worldwide. www.zondervan.com. *Emphasis indicated by underlining in boldface quotations and italic in lightface quotations.*

The following version of Scripture is in the public domain:

The King James Version (KJV)

The following copyrighted versions of Scripture are used by permission:

The Holy Bible, English Standard Version® (ESV®). Copyright © 2001 by Crossway Bibles, a publishing ministry of Good News Publishers. All rights reserved.

Holman Christian Standard Bible® (HCSB), copyright © 1999, 2000, 2002, 2003, 2009 by Holman Bible Publishers, Nashville, Tennessee. All rights reserved.

The New American Standard Bible® (NASB®), copyright © 1960, 1962, 1963, 1968, 1971, 1972, 1973, 1975, 1977, 1995 by The Lockman Foundation. www.Lockman.org.

The New JPS Hebrew-English Tanakh (NJPS), © 2000 by The Jewish Publication Society. All rights reserved.

The New King James Version® (NKJV). Copyright © 1982 by Thomas Nelson, Inc. All rights reserved.

The Holy Bible, New Living Translation (NLT), copyright © 1996, 2004, 2015 by Tyndale House Foundation. Used by permission of Tyndale House Publishers, Inc., Carol Stream, IL 60188. All rights reserved.

The New Revised Standard Version Bible (NRSV), copyright © 1989 National Council of the Churches of Christ in the United States of America. All rights reserved.

The Revised English Bible (REB). copyright © 1989 by Oxford University Press and Cambridge University Press. All rights reserved.

The Revised Standard Version (RSV) of the Bible, copyright 1946, 1952, 1971 by the Division of Christian Education of the National Council of the Churches of Christ in the USA. All rights reserved.

Library of Congress Cataloging-in-Publication Data

Names: Braaten, Laurie J., 1951- author. | Edlin, Jim, 1950- author.
Title: Nahum-Malachi : a commentary in the Wesleyan tradition / Laurie J. Braaten and Jim Edlin.
Other titles: Nahum to Malachi.
Description: Kansas City : Beacon Hill Press of Kansas City, 2020. | Series: New Beacon Bible commentary | Includes bibliographical references. |
 Summary: "A Bible commentary in the Wesleyan tradition, on the books of Nahum, Habakkuk, Zephaniah, Haggai, Zechariah, and Malachi"— Provided by publisher.
Identifiers: LCCN 2019043036 (print) | LCCN 2019043037 (ebook) | ISBN 9780834135635 (paperback) | ISBN 9780834136854 (ebook)
Subjects: LCSH: Bible. Minor Prophets—Commentaries.
Classification: LCC BS1560 .B725 2020 (print) | LCC BS1560 (ebook) | DDC 224/.907—dc23
LC record available at https://lccn.loc.gov/2019043036
LC ebook record available at https://lccn.loc.gov/2019043037

The Internet addresses, email addresses, and phone numbers in this book are accurate at the time of publication. They are provided as a resource. Beacon Hill Press of Kansas City does not endorse them or vouch for their content or permanence.

10 9 8 7 6 5 4 3 2 1

COMMENTARY EDITORS

General Editors

Alex Varughese
Ph.D., Drew University
Professor Emeritus of Biblical
Literature
Mount Vernon Nazarene University
Mount Vernon, Ohio

George Lyons
Ph.D., Emory University
Professor Emeritus of New Testament
Northwest Nazarene University
Nampa, Idaho

Section Editors

Robert Branson
Ph.D., Boston University
Professor Emeritus of Biblical
Literature
Olivet Nazarene University
Bourbonnais, Illinois

Alex Varughese
Ph.D., Drew University
Professor Emeritus of Biblical
Literature
Mount Vernon Nazarene University
Mount Vernon, Ohio

Kent Brower
Ph.D., The University of Manchester
Vice Principal
Senior Lecturer in Biblical Studies
Nazarene Theological College
Manchester, England

George Lyons
Ph.D., Emory University
Professor Emeritus of New Testament
Northwest Nazarene University
Nampa, Idaho

CONTENTS

GENERAL EDITORS' PREFACE

The purpose of the New Beacon Bible Commentary is to make available to pastors and students in the twenty-first century a biblical commentary that reflects the best scholarship in the Wesleyan theological tradition. The commentary project aims to make this scholarship accessible to a wider audience to assist them in their understanding and proclamation of Scripture as God's Word.

Writers of the volumes in this series not only are scholars within the Wesleyan theological tradition and experts in their field but also have special interest in the books assigned to them. Their task is to communicate clearly the critical consensus and the full range of other credible voices who have commented on the Scriptures. Though scholarship and scholarly contribution to the understanding of the Scriptures are key concerns of this series, it is not intended as an academic dialogue within the scholarly community. Commentators of this series constantly aim to demonstrate in their work the significance of the Bible as the church's book and the contemporary relevance and application of the biblical message. The project's overall goal is to make available to the church and for her service the fruits of the labors of scholars who are committed to their Christian faith.

The *New International Version* (NIV) is the reference version of the Bible used in this series; however, the focus of exegetical study and comments is the biblical text in its original language. When the commentary uses the NIV, it is printed in bold. The text printed in bold italics is the translation of the author. Commentators also refer to other translations where the text may be difficult or ambiguous.

The structure and organization of the commentaries in this series seeks to facilitate the study of the biblical text in a systematic and methodical way. Study of each biblical book begins with an **Introduction** section that gives an overview of authorship, date, provenance, audience, occasion, purpose, sociological/cultural issues, textual history, literary features, hermeneutical issues, and theological themes necessary to understand the book. This section also includes a brief outline of the book and a list of general works and standard commentaries.

The commentary section for each biblical book follows the outline of the book presented in the introduction. In some volumes, readers will find section *overviews* of large portions of scripture with general comments on their overall literary structure and other literary features. A consistent feature of the commentary is the paragraph-by-paragraph study of biblical texts. This section has three parts: *Behind the Text*, *In the Text*, and *From the Text*.

The goal of the *Behind the Text* section is to provide the reader with all the relevant information necessary to understand the text. This includes specific historical situations reflected in the text, the literary context of the text, sociological and cultural issues, and literary features of the text.

In the Text explores what the text says, following its verse-by-verse structure. This section includes a discussion of grammatical details, word studies, and the connectedness of the text to other biblical books/passages or other parts of the book being studied (the canonical relationship). This section provides transliterations of key words in Hebrew and Greek and their literal meanings. The goal here is to explain what the author would have meant and/or what the audience would have understood as the meaning of the text. This is the largest section of the commentary.

The *From the Text* section examines the text in relation to the following areas: theological significance, intertextuality, the history of interpretation, use of the Old Testament scriptures in the New Testament, interpretation in later church history, actualization, and application.

The commentary provides *sidebars* on topics of interest that are important but not necessarily part of an explanation of the biblical text. These topics are informational items and may cover archaeological, historical, literary, cultural, and theological matters that have relevance to the biblical text. Occasionally, longer detailed discussions of special topics are included as *excursuses.*

We offer this series with our hope and prayer that readers will find it a valuable resource for their understanding of God's Word and an indispensable tool for their critical engagement with the biblical texts.

Roger Hahn, Centennial Initiative General Editor

Alex Varughese, General Editor (Old Testament)

George Lyons, General Editor (New Testament)

ABBREVIATIONS

With a few exceptions, these abbreviations follow those in *The SBL Handbook of Style* (Alexander 1999).

General

→	See the commentary at
AD	anno Domini (precedes date)
BC	before Christ (follows date)
BT	Book of the Twelve
ca.	*circa*, around
ch(s)	chapter(s)
cp.	compare
ed(s).	editor(s)
e.g.	*exempli gratia*, for example
etc.	*et cetera*, and the rest
HB	Hebrew Bible
Heb.	Hebrew
i.e.	*id est*, in other words, that is
lit.	literally
LXX	Septuagint
MT	Masoretic Text
n.	note
NT	New Testament
OAN	Oracles Against Nations
OT	Old Testament
repr.	reprint, reprinted
v(v)	verse(s)
vol(s).	volume(s)

Modern English Versions

ESV	English Standard Version
HCSB	Holman Christian Standard Bible
KJV	King James Version
NASB	New American Standard Bible
NCV	New Century Version
NIV	New International Version
NJPS	Tanakh: The Holy Scriptures: The New Jewish Publication Society Translation
NKJV	New King James Version
NLT	New Living Translation
NRSV	New Revised Standard Version
REB	Revised English Bible
RSV	Revised Standard Version

Print Conventions for Translations

Bold font	NIV (bold without quotation marks in the text under study; elsewhere in the regular font, with quotation marks and no further identification)
Bold italic font	Author's translation (without quotation marks)

Behind the Text:	Literary or historical background information average readers might not know from reading the biblical text alone
In the Text:	Comments on the biblical text, words, phrases, grammar, and so forth
From the Text:	The use of the text by later interpreters, contemporary relevance, theological and ethical implications of the text, with particular emphasis on Wesleyan concerns

Ancient Sources

Old Testament

Gen	Genesis
Exod	Exodus
Lev	Leviticus
Num	Numbers
Deut	Deuteronomy
Josh	Joshua
Judg	Judges
Ruth	Ruth
1—2 Sam	1—2 Samuel
1—2 Kgs	1—2 Kings
1—2 Chr	1—2 Chronicles
Ezra	Ezra
Neh	Nehemiah
Esth	Esther
Job	Job
Ps/Pss	Psalm/Psalms
Prov	Proverbs
Eccl	Ecclesiastes
Song	Song of Songs/ Song of Solomon
Isa	Isaiah
Jer	Jeremiah
Lam	Lamentations
Ezek	Ezekiel
Dan	Daniel
Hos	Hosea
Joel	Joel
Amos	Amos
Obad	Obadiah
Jonah	Jonah
Mic	Micah
Nah	Nahum
Hab	Habakkuk
Zeph	Zephaniah
Hag	Haggai
Zech	Zechariah
Mal	Malachi

(Note: Chapter and verse numbering in the MT and LXX often differ compared to those in English Bibles. To avoid confusion, all biblical references follow the chapter and verse numbering in English translations, even when the text in the MT and LXX is under discussion.)

New Testament

Matt	Matthew
Mark	Mark
Luke	Luke
John	John
Acts	Acts
Rom	Romans
1—2 Cor	1—2 Corinthians
Gal	Galatians
Eph	Ephesians
Phil	Philippians
Col	Colossians
1—2 Thess	1—2 Thessalonians
1—2 Tim	1—2 Timothy
Titus	Titus
Phlm	Philemon
Heb	Hebrews
Jas	James
1—2 Pet	1—2 Peter
1—2—3 John	1—2—3 John
Jude	Jude
Rev	Revelation

Modern Journals and Reference Works

AB	Anchor Bible
ABD	Anchor Bible Dictionary (see Freedman)
ACCS	Ancient Christian Commentary on Scripture
ANEP	The Ancient Near East in Pictures Relating to the Old Testament
ANESTP	The Ancient Near East: Supplementary Texts and Pictures Relating to the Old Testament
ANET	Ancient Near Eastern Texts Relating to the Old Testament (see Pritchard 1969a)
AOTC	Abingdon Old Testament Commentaries
BDB	A Hebrew and English Lexicon of the Old Testament (see Brown, Driver, Briggs)
BHK	Biblia Hebraica
BHS	Biblia Hebraica Stuttgartensia
BHQ	Biblia Hebraica Quinta
BibOr	Biblica et orientalia
BQMP	Biblia Qumranica Minor Prophets
BSac	Bibliotheca Sacra
BT	The Bible Translator
BWANT	Beiträge zur Wissenschaft vom Alten und Neuen Testament
BZAW	Beihefte zur Zeitschrift für die alttestamentliche Wissenschaft
CBC	Cambridge Bible Commentary
CC	Continental Commentaries
EBC	Expositor's Bible Commentary
EDB	Eerdmans Dictionary of the Bible
EvQ	Evangelical Quarterly
FOTL	Forms of the Old Testament Literature
GKC	Gesenius' Hebrew Grammar (see Gesenius)
HALOT	The Hebrew and Aramaic Lexicon of the Old Testament (see Kohler)
HBD	HarperCollins Bible Dictionary
HBT	Horizons in Biblical Theology
HSM	Harvard Semitic Monographs
IBC	Interpretation: A Bible Commentary for Teaching and Preaching
IBHS	An Introduction to Biblical Hebrew Syntax (see Waltke)

ICC	International Critical Commentary
IDB	*Interpreter's Dictionary of the Bible*
IDBSup	*Interpreter's Dictionary of the Bible: Supplementary Volume*
Int	*Interpretation*
ITC	International Theological Commentary
JAOS	*Journal of the American Oriental Society*
JBL	*Journal of Biblical Literature*
JBQ	*Jewish Biblical Quarterly*
JNSL	*Journal of Northwest Semitic Languages*
JR	*Journal of Religion*
JSOT	*Journal for the Study of the Old Testament*
JSOTSup	Journal for the Study of the Old Testament: Supplement Series
JSS	*Journal of Semitic Studies*
JTS	*Journal of Theological Studies*
KTU	*Die keilalphabetischen Texte aus Ugarit*
LEH	Lust, Eynikel, and Hauspie, *Greek-English Lexicon of the Septuagint.* Revised ed.
LSJ	Liddell, Scott and Jones, *A Greek- English Lexicon*
NAC	New American Commentary
NCB	New Century Bible
NIB	*New Interpreter's Bible*
NIBCOT	New International Bible Commentary on the Old Testament
NIDB	*New Interpreter's Dictionary of the Bible*
OTE	*Old Testament Essays*
OTG	Old Testament Guides
OTL	Old Testament Library
OTP	*Old Testament Pseudepigrapha*
SBLSymS	Society of Biblical Literature Symposium Series
SJOT	*Scandinavian Journal of the Old Testament*
SVT	*Supplements to Vetus Testamentum*
TBC	Torch Bible Commentaries
TDOT	*Theological Dictionary of the Old Testament* (see Botterweck)
TLOT	*Theological Lexicon of the Old Testament*
TOTC	Tyndale Old Testament Commentaries
TWOT	*Theological Wordbook of the Old Testament* (see Harris)
VT	*Vetus Testamentum*
WBC	Word Biblical Commentary
YLT	Young's Literal Translation
ZAW	*Zeitschrift für die alttestamentliche Wissenschaft*

Greek Transliteration

Greek	Letter	English
α	alpha	a
β	bēta	b
γ	gamma	g
γ	gamma nasal	n (before γ, κ, ξ, χ)
δ	delta	d
ε	epsilon	e
ζ	zēta	z
η	ēta	ē
θ	thēta	th
ι	iōta	i
κ	kappa	k
λ	lambda	l
μ	mu	m
ν	nu	n
ξ	xi	x
ο	omicron	o
π	pi	p
ρ	rhō	r
ρ	initial rhō	rh
σ/ς	sigma	s
τ	tau	t
υ	upsilon	y
υ	upsilon	u (in diphthongs: au, eu, ēu, ou, ui)
φ	phi	ph
χ	chi	ch
ψ	psi	ps
ω	ōmega	ō
ʼ	rough breathing	h (before initial vowels or diphthongs)

Hebrew Consonant Transliteration

Hebrew/ Aramaic	Letter	English
א	alef	ʼ
ב	bet	b
ג	gimel	g
ד	dalet	d
ה	he	h
ו	vav	v or w
ז	zayin	z
ח	khet	ḥ
ט	tet	ṭ
י	yod	y
כ/ך	kaf	k
ל	lamed	l
מ/ם	mem	m
נ/ן	nun	n
ס	samek	s
ע	ayin	ʻ
פ/ף	pe	p; f (spirant)
צ/ץ	tsade	ṣ
ק	qof	q
ר	resh	r
שׂ	sin	ś
שׁ	shin	š
ת	tav	t; th (spirant)

NAHUM, HABAKKUK, ZEPHANIAH

Laurie J. Braaten

DEDICATION

This work is dedicated to
Jay Powell (AKA "Dr. Jay").
Your encouragement and comments on this project,
breadth of knowledge, service to humanity,
and love of the outdoors have been a constant inspiration.
I bless the path that led you and Vickie to our door.
Thank you for being, as you like to say,
"a failure at retirement."

ACKNOWLEDGMENTS

I would like to thank the steering committees of the Book of the Twelve and Ecological Hermeneutics Sections of the Society of Biblical Literature, and the Chicago Society of Biblical Research where many of the ideas found in this work were first presented and discussed. Although many were involved, I particularly acknowledge Jim Nogalski, Paul Redditt, Norm Habel, Peter Trudinger, and Troy Martin. A special word of appreciation is due to Robert Haak, who kindly supplied me with copies of some of his important, yet unpublished works on Zephaniah. The constant nudging and editorial comments of Jay Powell (to whom this volume is dedicated) were vital for completion of this work. I continue to be grateful for my early teachers of biblical texts whose influence continues, especially Robert Branson and Charles D. Isbell. Of course, I must take final responsibility for whatever errors or oddities might be contained on these pages. Thanks is also due to Beacon Hill Press for undertaking this commentary project and for inviting me to participate in it, and particularly for the patience and tireless and prompt editorial work of Alex Varughese. As always, without the understanding, support and keen insight of Brenda, none of this would have been possible.

Laurie J. Braaten

BIBLIOGRAPHY FOR NAHUM-ZEPHANIAH

Achtemeier, Elizabeth. 1962. "Righteousness in the Old Testament." *IDB* 4:80-85.

———. 1986. *Nahum—Malachi.* IBC. Atlanta: John Knox.

Aharoni, Yohanan, and Avi-Yonah, Michael. 1977. *The Macmillan Bible Atlas.* Revised Edition. New York: Macmillan.

Albright, W. F. 1950. "The Psalm of Habakkuk." Pages 1-18 in *Studies in Old Testament Prophecy: Presented to Theodore H. Robinson.* Edited by H. H. Rowley. Edinburgh: T & T Clark.

Allis, O. T. 1955. "Nahum, Nineveh, and Elkosh." EvQ 27:67-80.

Andersen, Francis I. 2001. *Habakkuk. A New Translation with Introduction and Commentary.* AB 25. New York: Doubleday.

Armerding, Carl E. 1985a. "Nahum." *EBC.* Vol. 7. Grand Rapids: Zondervan.

———. 1985b. "Habakkuk." *EBC.* Vol. 7. Grand Rapids: Zondervan.

Avigad, N. 1976. "The Excavations in the Jewish Quarter of the Old City, 1969-71." Pages 41-51 in *Jerusalem Revealed: Archaeology of the Holy City 1968-1974.* Edited by Yigael Yadin. New Haven: Yale.

Baker, David W. 1988. *Nahum, Habakkuk, Zephaniah.* TOTC. Vol 23b Downers Grove: InterVarsity.

Ball, Edward. 1999. "'When the Towers Fall:' Interpreting Nahum as Christian Scripture." Pages 211-30 in *In Search of True Wisdom: Essays in Old Testament Interpretation in Honour of Ronald E. Clements.* Edited by E. Ball. JSOTSup 300. Sheffield: Sheffield Academic.

Becking, Bob. 1995. "Divine Wrath and the Conceptual Coherence of Nahum." SJOT 9:277-96.

Bennett, Harold V. 2008. "Justice, OT." *NIDB* 4:476-77.

Bennett, Robert A. 1996. "The Book of Zephaniah." *NIB* 7:659-704.

Ben Zvi, Ehud. 1991. *A Historical-Critical Study of Zephaniah.* BZAW 198. Berlin: Walter de Gruyter.

Bergmann, Claudia D. 2008. *Childbirth as a Metaphor for Crisis.* BZAW 382. Berlin: Walter de Gruyter. Berlin, Adele. 1994. *Zephaniah. A New Translation with Introduction and Commentary.* AB 25A. New York: Doubleday.

Blenkinsopp, Joseph. 1996. *A History of Prophecy in Israel.* Revised and Enlarged. Louisville: Westminster John Knox.

Botterweck, G. Johannes and Helmer Ringgren, eds. 1974-2016. *Theological Dictionary of the Old Testament.* Translated by John T. Willis. 15 Volumes. Revised Edition. Grand Rapids: Eerdmans.

Braaten, Laurie J. 2000. "Love." *EDB*, 825-26.

———. 2001. "Earth Community in Hosea 2." Pages 185-203 in Habel, 2001.

———. 2003a. "God Sows: Hosea's Land Theme in the Book of the Twelve." Pages 104-32 in Redditt and Schart, *Thematic Threads in the Book of the Twelve.*

———. 2003b. "May the Glory of the LORD Endure Forever! Biblical Reflections on Creation Care." Pages 414-34 in *Perspectives on an Evolving Creation.* Edited by Keith B. Miller. Grand Rapids: Eerdmans.

———. 2006. "All Creation Groans: Romans 8:22 in Light of the Biblical Sources." HBT 28 (2006): 131-59.

Branson, Robert D. 1990. "*yāsar; mûsār.*" *TDOT* 6:127-134.

Bright, John. 1981. *A History of Israel.* 3rd ed. Philadelphia: Westminster.

Brown, Francis, S. R. Driver, and Charles A Briggs. 1907. *A Hebrew and English Lexicon of the Old Testament. With an Appendix Containing the Biblical Aramaic.* London: Oxford.

Brown, William P. 1996. *Obadiah through Malachi.* Westminster Bible Companion. Louisville: Westminster John Knox.

———. 1999. *The Ethos of the Cosmos. The Genesis of Moral Imagination in the Bible.* Grand Rapids: Eerdmans.

Brownlee, William H. 1959. *The Text of Habakkuk in the Ancient Commentary from Qumran.* Journal of Biblical Literature Monograph Series, vol. 11. Philadelphia, Society of Biblical Literature.

———. 1963. "The Placarded Revelation of Habakkuk." *JBL* 82:319-25.

Bruce, F. F. 1993. "Habakkuk." In McComiskey (1992-98) Vol 2:831-96.

Calvin, John. 1847. *Jonah, Micah, Nahum*. Vol III. of *Commentaries on the Twelve Minor Prophets*. Translated by John Owen. Edinburgh: Calvin Translation Society. Repr. in *Calvin's Commentaries*. Vol. XIV. Grand Rapids: Baker, 1979.

———. 1848. *Habakkuk, Zephaniah, Haggai*. Vol IV. of *Commentaries on the Twelve Minor Prophets*. Translated by John Owen. Edinburgh: Calvin Translation Society. Repr. in *Calvin's Commentaries*. Vol. XV. Grand Rapids: Baker, 1979.

Carr, G. Lloyd. 1980. "*shālôm*." *TWOT* 2:931.

Cathcart, Kevin J. 1973. *Nahum in the Light of Northwest Semitic*. BibOr 26. Rome: Biblical Institute Press.

———. 1979. "More Philological Studies in Nahum." *JNSL* 7: 1-12.

Cathcart, Kevin J and Gordon, Robert P. 1990. *The Targum of the Minor Prophets. Translated, with a Critical Introduction, Apparatus, and Notes*. The Aramaic Bible, 14. Collegeville: Liturgical Press.

Christensen, Duane L. 2009. *Nahum: A New Translation with Introduction and Commentary*. The Anchor Yale Bible, 24F. New Haven: Yale University Press.

Clark, David J. 1981. "Wine on the lees (Zeph 1.12 and Jer 48.11)." *BT* 32, 241-43.

Clarke, Adam. 1823. Isaiah - Malachi. Vol. 4 of *The Holy Bible Containing the Old Testament*. New Corrected edition. New York: Eaton & Mains.

Coggins, Richard J. 1985. "In Wrath Remember Mercy. A Commentary on the Book of Nahum." Pages 1-63 in *Israel Among the Nations. A Commentary on the Books of Nahum and Obadiah and Esther*. ITC. Grand Rapids: Eerdmans.

Cohen, A., ed. 1948. *The Twelve Prophets. Hebrew Text and English Translation with Introduction and Commentary*. London: Soncino Press.

Coppes, Leonard J. 1980. "*nûd*, wander, have compassion on." *TWOT* 2:560-61.

Dangl, Oskar. 2001. "Habakkuk in Recent Research." *Currents in Research: Biblical Studies*. 9:131-68.

Davidson, A. B. 1896. *The Books of Nahum, Habakkuk and Zephaniah*. The Cambridge Bible for Schools and Colleges. Cambridge: Cambridge University Press.

De Roche, Michael. 1980. "Zephaniah I 2-3: The Sweeping of Creation." *VT* 30:104-109.

Driver, Godfrey Rolles. 1976. *Semitic Writing: From Pictograph to Alphabet*. The Schweich Lectures of the British Academy. Revised ed. Edited by S. A. Hopkins. London: Oxford.

Driver, S. R. 1906. *The Minor Prophets: Nahum, Habakkuk, Zephaniah, Haggai, Zechariah, Malachi*. NCB. New York: Henry Frowde.

Eaton, J. H. 1961. *Obadiah, Nahum, Habakkuk, and Zephaniah. Introduction and Commentary*. TBC. London: SCM.

Eising, H. 1980. "*chayil*." *TDOT* 4:348-55.

Everson, A. Joseph. 1974. "The Days of Yahweh." *JBL* 93:329-37.

Ferreiro, Alberto, ed. 2003. *The Twelve Prophets*. ACCS, Vol XIV. Edited by Thomas C. Oden. Downers Grove: InterVarsity.

Floyd, Michael H. 1994. "The Chimerical Acrostic of Nahum 1:2-10." *JBL* 113:421-37.

———. 2000. *Minor Prophets, part 2*. FOTL XXII. Grand Rapids: Eerdmans.

Freedman, D. N. 1992. *The Anchor Bible Dictionary*. 6 Vols. New York: Doubleday.

Fretheim, Terence E. 2000. *The Earth Story in Jeremiah 12*. Pages 96-110 in Habel, 2000.

García-Treto, Francisco O. 1996. "The Book of Nahum." In *NIB*, 7:593-619.

Gerstenberger, Erhard S. 1988. *Psalms, part 1, With an Introduction to Cultic Poetry*. FOTL XIV. Grand Rapids: Eerdmans.

Gesenius, W. E. Kautzsh, and A. E. Cowley. 1910. *Gesenius' Hebrew Grammar*. Second English Edition. London: Oxford.

Glasson, T. Francis. 1969/70. "The Final Question - in Nahum and Jonah. *Expository Times* 81:54-55.

Goldingay, John, and Scalise, Pamela J. 2009. "Nahum, Habakkuk, Zephaniah and Haggai." Pages 1-175 in *Minor Prophets II*. NIBCOT. Peabody, Mass: Hendrickson, 2009.

Gordon, Robert P. 1990. "Nahum - Malachi" in Cathcart and Gordon, 1990.

Haak, Robert D. 1992. *Habakkuk*. SVT XLIV. Leiden: Brill.

———. 2003. "Conversations with Zephaniah." Unpublished paper supplied by author.

Habel, Norman C., ed. 2000. *Readings from the Perspective of Earth*. The Earth Bible, Vol. 1. Sheffield: Sheffield Academic.

———, ed. 2001. *The Earth Story in the Psalms and the Prophets*. The Earth Bible, Vol. 4. Sheffield: Sheffield Academic.

Habel, Norman C., and Peter Trudinger, eds. 2008. *Exploring Ecological Hermeneutics*. SBLSymS 46. Atlanta: Society of Biblical Literature.

Hare, D. R. A. 1985. "The Lives of the Prophets. A New Translation and Introduction." *OTP* 2:379-99.

Harris, R. Laird, Gleason L. Archer, and Bruce K. Waltke, eds. 1980. *Theological Wordbook of the Old Testament*. 2 vols. Chicago: Moody Press.

Hayes, John H. 1968. "The Usage of Oracles Against Foreign Nations in Ancient Israel." *JBL* 87:81-92.

Hayes, Katherine M. 2002. *"The Earth Mourns:" Prophetic Metaphor and Oral Aesthetic*. Academia Biblica, 8. Atlanta: Society of Biblical Literature.

Hiebert, Theodore. 1986. *God of My Victory: The Ancient Hymn of Habakkuk 3*. HSM 38. Atlanta: Scholars Press.

———. 1992. "Theophany in the Old Testament." *ABD* VI:505-11.

———. 1996. "The Book of Habakkuk." *NIB* 7:623-55.

Holladay, William L. 2001. "Reading Zephaniah with a Concordance." *JBL* 120:671-84.

Jørgensen, K. E. Jordt. 1980. *Fauna and Flora of the Bible*. 2nd ed. Helps for Translators. New York: United Bible Society.

Keck, Leander. 1994-2002. *The New Interpreter's Bible*. 12 vols. Nashville: Abingdon.

Keil, C. F. 1868. *Minor Prophets*. Vol. X/2 of *Commentary on the Old Testament* by C. F. Keil and F. Delitzsch. Translated by James Martin. Repr., Grand Rapids: Eerdmans, 1986.

Kellermann, D. 1975. "*gā'ah*, etc." *TDOT* 2:344-50.

Kim, Uriah Y. 2008. "Josiah." *NIDB* 3:413-15.

King, Greg A. 1994. "The Remnant in Zephaniah." *BSac* 151, 414-27.

———. 2000. "Day of the Lord." *EDB*, 324-25.

Koehler, L., W. Baumgartner, and J.J. Stamm. 1994-2000. *The Hebrew and Aramaic Lexicon of the Old Testament*. Translated and under the supervision of M.E.J. Richardson. Leiden: Brill.

Köhler, Ludwig. 1956. "Justice in the Gate." Pages 149-75 in *Hebrew Man*. Trans. by Peter R. Ackroyd. London: SCM.

Lambdin, Thomas O. 1962. "Thebes." *IDB* 4:615-17.

Lehrman, S. M. 1948. "Nahum, Habakkuk, Zephaniah." Pages 191-251 in Cohen 1948.

Levenson, Jon D. 1984. "The Temple and the World. *JR* 64:275-98.

Liddell, Henry George, Robert Scott, Henry Stuart Jones. 1996. *A Greek-English Lexicon*. 9th ed. with revised supplement. Oxford: Clarendon.

Liedke, G. 1997. "*ykḥ* hi. to determine what is right." *TLOT* 2:542-44.

Longman, Tremper, III. 1993. "Nahum." In McComiskey (1992-98) Vol 2:765-829.

Luckenbill, Daniel David. 1926-27. *Ancient Records of Assyria and Babylon*. Two vols. Chicago: University of Chicago Press.

Luther, Martin. 1525a. "Lectures on Habakkuk." Pages 107-48 of *Lectures on the Minor Prophets, II: Jonah, Habakkuk*. [Lectures on Habakkuk delivered 1525]. Vol. 19 of *Luther's Works*. Edited by H. C. Oswald. Translated by Charles D. Froehlich. Saint Louis: Concordia Publishing House, 1974.

———. 1525b. "Lectures on Nahum." Pages 279-315 of *Lectures on the Minor Prophets, I: Hosea, Joel, Amos, Obadiah, Micah, Nahum, Zephaniah, Haggai, Malachi*. [Lectures on Nahum delivered 1525]. Vol. 18 of *Luther's Works*. Edited by H. C. Oswald. Translated by Richard J. Dinda. Saint Louis: Concordia Publishing House, 1975.

———. 1525c. "Lectures on Zephaniah." Pages 319-64 of *Lectures on the Minor Prophets, I: Hosea, Joel, Amos, Obadiah, Micah, Nahum, Zephaniah, Haggai, Malachi*. [Lectures on Zephaniah delivered 1525]. Vol. 18 of *Luther's Works*. Edited by H. C. Oswald. Translated by Richard J. Dinda. Saint Louis: Concordia Publishing House, 1975.

———. 1526. "Lectures on Habakkuk." Pages 151-237 of *Lectures on the Minor Prophets, II: Jonah, Habakkuk*. [Lectures on Habakkuk delivered 1526]. Vol. 19 of *Luther's Works*. Edited by H. C. Oswald. Translated by Martin H. Bertram. Saint Louis: Concordia Publishing House, 1974.

Machinist, Peter. 1983. "Assyria and Its Image in First Isaiah." *JAOS* 103:719-37.

Maier, Walter A. 1959. *The Book of Nahum - A Commentary*. Grand Rapids: Baker.

Margulis, Baruch. 1970. "The Psalm of Habakkuk: A Reconstruction and Interpretation." *ZAW* 82:409-42.

Marzouk, Safwat. 2008. "Libya, Libyans." *NIDB* 3:654.

Mason, Rex. 1994. *Zephaniah, Habakkuk, Joel*. OTG. Sheffield: Sheffield Academic.

May, H. G., ed. 1984. *Oxford Bible Atlas*. 3rd Edition. New York: Oxford University Press.

McBride, S. Dean. 2007. "Deuteronomy, Book of." *NIDB* 2:109-17.

McComiskey, Thomas Edward, ed. 1992-98. *The Minor Prophets. An Exegetical and Expository Commentary*. Three vols. Grand Rapids: Baker.

McLean, John A. 2000. "Leopard." *EDB*, 801.

Miller, J. Maxwell, and Hayes, John H. 2006. *A History of Ancient Israel and Judah*. 2nd Edition. Louisville: Westminster John Knox.

Motyer, J. Alec. 1998. "Zephaniah." In McComiskey (1992-98) Vol 3:897-962.

Muraoka, T. 2009. *A Greek-English Lexicon of the Septuagint*. Louvain, Belgium: Peeters.

Murphy-O'Connor, Jerome. 2008. "Jerusalem." *NIDB* 3:246-59.

Nogalski, James. 2003. "The Day(s) of YHWH in the Book of the Twelve." Pages 192-213 in Redditt and Schart.

Nogalski, James D. 2011. *The Book of the Twelve: Micah - Malachi*. Smyth & Helwys Bible Commentary. Macon: Smyth & Helwys.

Nogalski, James D., and Marvin A. Sweeney, eds. 2000. *Reading and Hearing the Book of the Twelve*. SBLSymS. Atlanta: Society of Biblical Literature.

Noth, Martin. 1928. *Die israelitichen Personennamen im Rahmen der gemeinsemitischen Namengegung*. BWANT III. Stuttgart: Kohlmammer.

O'Brien, Julia M. 2004. *Nahum, Habakkuk, Zephaniah, Haggai, Zechariah, Malachi*. AOTC. Nashville: Abingdon.

Otzen, Benedikt. 1975. "*bĕliyyā'āl*." *TDOT* 2:131-36.

Patterson, Richard D. 1991. *Nahum. Habakkuk, Zephaniah*. Wycliffe Exegetical Commentary. Chicago: Moody.

Petersen, David L. 2009. "Prophets, Prophecy." In *NIDB* 4:622-48.

Pinker, Aron. 2000. "The Book of Zephaniah: Allusions to the Tower of Babel." *JBQ* 28:3-11.

———. 2005. "Nahum - The Prophet and his Message." *JBQ* 33:81-90.

Pritchard, James B., ed. 1958. *The Ancient Near East. An Anthology of Texts and Pictures*. Princeton: Princeton University Press.

———, ed. 1969a. *Ancient Near Eastern Texts Relating to the Old Testament*. 3rd ed. with Supplement. Princeton: Princeton University Press.

———, ed. 1969b. *The Ancient Near East in Pictures Relating to the Old Testament*. Princeton: Princeton University Press.

Pusey, E. B. 1860. *Micah, Nahum, Habakkuk, Zephaniah, Haggai, Zechariah and Malachi*. Vol. 2 of *The Minor Prophets: A Commentary Explanatory and Practical*. 1860. Repr., Grand Rapids: Baker, 1950.

Rad, Gerhard von. 1959. "The Origin of the Concept of the Day of Yahweh." *JSS* 4:97-108.

Redditt, Paul L. and Schart, Aaron, eds. 2003. *Thematic Threads in the Book of the Twelve*. BZAW 325. Berlin: Walter de Gruyter.

———. 2008. "Locust." *NIDB* 3:684-85.

Roaf, Michael. 1990. *Cultural Atlas of Mesopotamia and the Ancient Near East*. New York: Facts on File.

Roberts, J.J.M. 1991. Nahum, *Habakkuk, and Zephaniah*. OTL. Louisville: Westminster John Knox.

———. 2009. "Zion Tradition." *NIDB* 5:987-88.

Robertson, O. Palmer. 1990. *The Books of Nahum, Habakkuk, and Zephaniah*. NICOT. Grand Rapids: Eerdmans.

Rosenberg, A. J. 1988. *The Twelve Prophets. A New English Translation of the Text, Rashi and Commentary*. Vol. 2. New York: Judaica Press.

Sadler, Rodney S., Jr. 2006. "Cushan-Rishathaim," "Cush, Cushite," "Cushan," and "Cushite Wife." *NIDB* 1:812-15.

Saggs, H. W. F. 1962. *The Greatness that was Babylon. A sketch of the ancient civilization of the Tigris-Euphrates valley*. New York: Mentor.

———. 1969. "Nahum and the Fall of Nineveh." *JTS* 20:220-25.

Sakenfeld, Katharine Doob. 2006-09. *The New Interpreter's Dictionary of the Bible*. 5 vols. Nashville: Abingdon.

Sanders, James A. "Torah." *IDBSup.*, 909-11.

Schmitt, John J. 1983. "The Gender of Ancient Israel." *JSOT* 26:115-25.

Schottroff, W. 1997. "*pqd*." *TLOT* 2:1018-31.

Scott, James M. 1985. "A New Approach to Habakkuk II 4-5A." *VT* 3:330-40.

Sellin, Ernst. 1968. *Introduction to the Old Testament*. Thoroughly revised and rewritten by Georg Fohrer. Translated by David E. Green. Nashville: Abingdon.

Sheppard, Gerald T. 1992. "Theology and the Book of Psalms." *Int* 46:143-55.

Simian-Yofre. 1998 *"nḥm." TDOT* 9:340-55.

Smith, George Adam. 1906. *Zephaniah, Nahum, Habakkuk, Obadiah, Haggai, Zechariah I.-VIII., Malachi, Joel, Zechariah IX.-XIV and Jonah.* Vol 2 of *The Book of the Twelve Prophets, Commonly Called Minor.* New York: Armstrong.

Smith, J. M. P. 1911. "A Critical and Exegetical Commentary on Nahum." Pages 267-360 in *Micah, Zephaniah, Nahum, Habakkuk, Obadiah, Joel.* J. M. P. Smith, William Hayes Ward, and Julius A. Bewer. ICC. New York: Scribner's.

Smith, R. L. 1984. *Micah-Malachi.* WBC 32. Waco: Word.

Smith-Christopher, Daniel L. 2000. "Peace." *EDB,* 1021-22.

Spronk, Klaas. 1997. *Nahum.* Historical Commentary on the Old Testament. Kampen: Kok Pharos.

Stolz, F. 1997. *"nś' to lift, bear." TLOT* 2:769-74.

Sweeney Marvin A. 1992. "Concerning the Structure and Generic Character of the Book of Nahum." *ZAW* 104:364-77.

———. 2000a. "Structure, Genre, and Intent in the Book of Habakkuk." *VT* 41 (1991):63-83. Repr. pages 224-44 in *Prophecy in the Hebrew Bible: Selected Studies from* Vetus Testamentum. Compiled by David E. Orton. Brill's Readers in Biblical Studies, Vol. 5. Leiden: Brill.

———. 2000b. *The Twelve Prophets,* Vol. 2. Berit Olam. Collegeville: Liturgical Press.

———. 2003. *Zephaniah: A Commentary.* Hermeneia. Minneapolis: Augsburg Fortress.

Swete, Henry Barclay. 1905-1909. *The Old Testament in Greek: According to the Septuagint.* Three volumes. Third and Fourth Editions. London: Cambridge University Press.

Szeles, Maria Eszenyei. 1987. "Watchtower Theology. A Commentary on the Book of Habakkuk." Pages 1-57 in *Wrath and Mercy. A Commentary on the Books of Habakkuk and Zephaniah.* Translated by George A. F. Knight. ITC. Grand Rapids: Eerdmans.

Tsumura, David Toshio. 1982. "Hab 2:2 in the light of Akkadian Legal Practice." *ZAW* 94:294-95.

Tucker, Gene M. 1977. "Prophetic Superscriptions and the Growth of a Canon." Pages 56-70 in *Canon and Authority: Essays in Old Testament Religion and Theology.* Edited by George W. Coats and Burke O. Long. Philadelphia: Fortress.

Van Leeuwen, Raymond. 1993. "Scribal Wisdom and Theodicy in the Book of the Twelve." Pages 31-49 in *In Search of Wisdom: Essays in Memory of John G. Gammie.* Edited by Leo G. Perdue, Bernard Scott, and William Wiseman. Louisville: John Knox.

Vaux, Roland de. 1965 *Ancient Israel.* 2 Vols. New York: McGraw Hill.

Vlaardingerbroek, Johannes. 1999. *Zephaniah.* Historical Commentary on the Old Testament. Leuven, Belgium: Peeters.

Vollmer, J. 1997a. *"'śh to make, do." TLOT* 2:944-51.

———. 1997b. *"p'l to make, do." TLOT* 2:1014-18.

Waltke, Bruce K. and O'Connor, M. 1990. *An Introduction to Biblical Hebrew Syntax.* Winona Lake: Eisenbrauns.

Ward, William Hayes. 1911. "A Critical and Exegetical Commentary on Habakkuk." Pages 3-28 in *Micah, Zephaniah, Nahum, Habakkuk, Obadiah, Joel.* J. M. P. Smith, William Hayes Ward, and Julius A. Bewer. ICC. New York: Scribner's.

Watts, John D. W. 1975. *The Books of Joel, Obadiah, Jonah, Nahum, Habakkuk and Zephaniah.* CBC. Cambridge: Cambridge University Press.

Weber, Carl Philip. 1980a. *"ḥag feast." TWOT* 1:261-63.

———. 1980b. *"ḥayil might." TWOT* 1:271-72.

Weis, R. D. 1992. "Oracle." *ABD* 5:28-29.

Wendland, E. R. 1998. "What's the 'Good News' - Check out the 'feet'! Prophetic rhetoric and the salvific centre of Nahum's 'vision'." *OTE* 11:154-81.

Wesley, John. 1754. *Explanatory Notes upon the New Testament.* Reprinted by London: Epworth, 1976.

———. 1765. *Explanatory Notes Upon the Old Testament.* Vol. III. Bristol: William Pine.

———. 1984. "Awake, Thou that Sleepest, Sermon 3." Pages 142-58 in *The Works of John Wesley,* Vol 1. Edited by Albert C. Outler. Nashville: Abingdon.

Westermann, Claus. 1967. *Basic Forms of Prophetic Speech.* Trans by Hugh Clayton White. Philadelphia: Westminster.

———. 1981. *Praise and Lament in the Psalms.* Translated by Keith R. Crim and Richard N. Soulen. Atlanta: John Knox.

Westermann, C., and R. Albertz. 1997. *"glh to uncover." TLOT* 1:314-20.

Williams, Matthew. 2014. "Winemaking Lees." [cited 22 February 2014]. Online: http://www.ehow.com/about_5390908_winemaking-lees.html.

Wilson, Robert R. 1984. *Prophecy and Society*. Philadelphia: Fortress.

Wineland, John D. 2000. "Fishing." *EDB*, 463.

Wiseman, Donald J. (1980). "*hālal wound (fatally), bore through, pierce*." *TWOT* 1:288-89.

Yadin, Yigael. 1963. *The Art of Warfare in Biblical Lands in the Light of Archaeological Study*. Translated by M. Pearlman. 2 Vols. New York: McGraw-Hill.

Young, Robert. 1997. *Young's Literal Translation*. Oak Harbor: Logos Research Systems.

Zalcman, Lawrence. 1986. "Ambiguity and Assonance at Zephaniah II 4." *VT* 36:365-71.

Zohary, Michael. 1982. *Plants of the Bible*. Cambridge: Cambridge University Press.

TABLE OF SIDEBARS

NAHUM

INTRODUCTION

A. The Prophet

The book of Nahum tells us nothing specific about the prophet except that he is an Elkoshite (1:1). The location of the town of Elkosh is unknown, despite early attempts to identify it. The name of NT Capernaum (Mark 1:21), "Village of Nahum," suggests that tradition associated this town with the prophet. It is uncertain when and how this Judean prophet became associated with Capernaum, located in northern Israel. The prophet's name, *nāḥûm* (from the root *nḥm*), is usually translated as "Comfort."

B. Historical Setting and Date of the Book

Since Nahum mentions the fall of Thebes (3:8), which occurred in 663 BC, his prophecy, most likely, belongs to a period after that event. The book also assures Judah that Nineveh will fall, which places it before 612 BC. It is possible that the prophet pronounced judgment against Assyria during the general decline of the empire in the seventh century BC. Rebellion broke out in Babylon and in the eastern and western part of the empire in 652 BC. The Assyrian king, Ashurbanipal, eventually regained control, first taking action against Babylon (648 BC), then against the remaining offenders to the east and west, including Palestine (ca. 640 BC). This would place Nahum somewhere during or shortly after these events, in the reign of either Manasseh (r. 687-642), Amon (r. 642-640), or early Josiah (r. 640-609; see 2 Kgs 21:1-23:30, the dates and background are found in Bright, 1981, 311, 313-22; cp. Miller and Hayes 2006, 421-38).

Manasseh was among the 22 kings mentioned by Assyria as supplying Assyrian building materials; he also aided Assyria on Egyptian campaigns (Luckenbill 1927, 2:771, 876; *ANET*, 294). Josiah came to power as Assyria was weakening and began to assert control over Israelite territory, which had been in Assyrian hands (see 2 Kgs 23:15-23). Though the book could be placed during the pro-Assyrian days of Manasseh or Amon or the anti-Assyrian days of Josiah, the likelihood is that it belongs to the former period when Judah was a loyal vassal of Assyria. Nahum warns Judah and other nations not to continue to depend on Assyria, since Assyria and its allies were slated for divine judgment.

C. Literary Structure and Canonical Context

The book of Nahum falls into three major divisions corresponding to the current English divisions of chapters. The second and third divisions are characterized by irony, and often employ the literary form of a taunt song against the once invincible power of Assyria. See the outline of the book above in Contents.

The book of Nahum is part of a greater literary work, commonly called the Minor Prophets, but more anciently known as the Book of the Twelve (henceforth BT). Although each of the twelve books in this collection might be read and understood in isolation, there is a growing consensus that they can also be read and interpreted as a single work in their own right.

In the Hebrew and English order of BT (the Greek canon differs), Nahum follows Micah. Micah ends with a prayer for deliverance and Nahum supplies the answer. Judah can take comfort in the fact that God's actions toward them has changed from judgment to deliverance. God will fulfill the promises of Isaiah and will deliver Judah from Assyria. But Nahum also warns Judah that nations who act like Assyria, or who rely on Assyria, will be judged.

D. Message of Nahum

The book of Nahum is devoted to the announcement of divine judgment on Assyria. God's destructive wrath is emphasized throughout the book. Therefore, it is often dismissed by conscientious believers who see such violence as incompatible with God's love for the entire creation. Rather than characterize Nahum as a book about divine punishment for sin, it is more helpful to read it as a message about God's justice—properly understood as restorative or loving justice. Several aspects of this message will be discussed below. For a more detailed discussions of Nahum's message see From the Text sections of the commentary.

The good news announced by Nahum is that the Lord will free the weak of the world from their violent oppressors. Although "good news" terminology does not appear until about a third of the way through the book (Nah 1:15 [2:1 HB]; cp. 1:7), the Lord's deliverance of the downtrodden and oppressed (e.g., 1:13; 2:2 [2:3 HB]; 3:1-4, 19c) is the necessary background for the threats of destructive wrath found throughout the book. When the weak have no way of freeing themselves from abusive oppressors, it is nothing short of good news when someone offers to intervene to help them; it is the promise of freedom from violence and oppressive conditions.

In Nahum, as elsewhere in the Bible, when such help is promised from God it is often expressed in military imagery: God is a conquering hero who rescues the oppressed (cp. 1:3b-6, 8; 2:13[14 HB]; Exod 15:3). The manifestations of the Divine Warrior's wrath, hot anger, and sweeping judgment are welcomed by those who need a Savior who will use these forces to free them from oppression. It is a mistake to read such imagery as coming from a primitive culture which revels in violence for its own sake. It is an even more severe error to interpret such imagery as sanctioning our use of violence in the name of God.

The ultimate goal of God's wrath is to free a broken creation from evil and redeem it for divine purposes. This is another way of looking at the point made above. God is good (Nah 1:7) and ultimately wills the best for creation. Rhetoric that might be interpreted otherwise functions to show that God is the creator whose power exceeds the strongest elements of nature (e.g., Nah 1:3b-6). But the point is not that God is destructive, rather that this power is used for good. That is to say, the Lord has the resources to offer refuge to those in need (v 7).

The scriptures indicate that God's aim is *shalom*, the wellbeing of creation as it is supposed to function according to God's ultimate intentions (e.g., Carr 1980, 931; Smith-Christopher 2000, 1021-22). The corrective justice announced in Nahum aims to restore *shalom* by setting right a creation that has been corrupted by human violence and therefore fails to accomplish God's redemptive purposes. The Lord's judgment against Assyria is this type of corrective justice against a nation whose wickedness and abuses were well-known (e.g., Nah 3:1-4).

A related point is that *the aim of divine judgment is restoration, not retribution or revenge for wrongs committed against people.* Nahum uses a term for God's work that is sometimes misunderstood as revenge (*nāqam*, see 1:2). A more helpful understanding of the term and Nahum's point is that God is *vindicating*, that is, setting right creation and delivering oppressed peoples. The point is not that God is getting even for sins committed against a divine law, rather, that sometimes God finds it necessary to remove those who commit violence in order to vindicate or restore creation (→ Nah 1:2). Revenge is not commended here, nor elsewhere in Scripture.

God's concern for vindication is global. Nahum is primarily addressed to Judah and Jerusalem as the oppressed who need God's vindicating work. Yet, the prophet also makes it clear that others benefit from God's liberating action (e.g., 2:13 [2:14 HB]; 3:4; 19c). Nahum's message offers an occasion for believers to rejoice in this good news of God's salvation (1:15-2:1 [2:1-2 HB]). But it is not a time for God's people to gloat over revenge for wrongs committed against them, although others may be tempted to do just that (see 3:7, 19b). The presupposition behind this global work is that God is the Creator and cares for the entire creation, not just for the chosen or those who acknowledge the Lord. That leads us to the next point.

If we rephrase and develop some of the discussion above, we see in Nahum that *the Creator's wrath is revealed against those whose wickedness disrupts creation's shalom* (1:2-6; see above). The Lord wills to be worshipped and served. Those who worship and serve themselves rather than God, and who harm God's creatures will ultimately be judged by the Creator (1:9; 11, 14). The Creator holds all nations accountable for their deeds. Nahum indicates, however, that this is God's work. Nowhere does the prophet use his oracle against Assyria as a call to arms by God's people.

Two interesting subjects develop from the points made here. First, Nahum makes it clear that the Lord holds accountable those who benefit from the wickedness of others. The Assyrians are likened to a pride of lions (Nah 2:11-13 [12-14 HB]). While only some of them go out and bring in the prey, the whole lion family benefits from the actions of the hunters. Likewise, all Assyrians are held accountable for the violence of their leaders (2:13 [2:14 HB]). Those in Assyria who profit from the country's imperialism will be held accountable for Assyrian violence, even if they are not part of the royal family or the Assyrian army.

Second, by extension, this corporate accountability could be applied also to the powerful in Judah whose alliances, treaties, and trade agreements made them complicit in Assyria's evil deeds (see discussions above and in the commentary). If Judeans prosper due to Assyrian imperialism, then Judah's leaders, and even Judah's population, are at risk of being judged for Assyrian sins. Yet the Lord does not hastily execute divine judgment, and that is the final point.

The Lord is patient and slow to execute anger against sin (1:3). God's failure to act quickly to deliver from hardships may cause some frustration among believers and the oppressed, as we will see explicitly in the commentary on Habakkuk. But God loves the entire world and is willing to give time for all to repent (cp. 2 Pet 3:9). Furthermore, we have seen that those who benefit from the sins of others may be liable to divine judgment. Consequently, God's patience also grants sufficient time for those who are praying for deliverance to repent of their own personal and corporate sins (1:3*ab*; see Rom 2:4). God's patient waiting and withholding judgment in the face of rampant and destructive sin is nothing short of an act of divine grace.

In the final analysis, if we scratch below the surface of the threats of destructive wrath we find in Nahum a message about a loving God who cares about creation. It is a further question whether or not it is helpful or appropriate in today's world to continue to adopt Nahum's imagery of violence in the service of the Good News. If Nahum's image of a Divine Warrior delivering the world from sin is used to justify individual or corporate violence, then the interpreter has missed the point of the prophet's message.

COMMENTARY

I. THE LORD THE VINDICATOR: NAHUM 1:1-15 [1:1—2:1 HB]

BEHIND THE TEXT

The opening division of Nahum prepared the seventh century BC audience for the Lord's deliverance of Judah from Assyrian domination (→ Introduction). Since the backdrop for this message is found in the book of Isaiah, it is difficult to examine the first chapter of Nahum without making frequent references to Isaiah's message. In the latter third of the eighth century, Isaiah announced that the Lord was going to use Assyria to discipline Israel and Judah for their disobedience to God. Since the Assyrians themselves were violent, boastful, and idolatrous, however, Isaiah announced that God would later punish Assyria for its sins and deliver the remnant of Israel (see especially Isa 8:5-8; 10:5-34). As we will see below, the first chapter of Nahum makes frequent allusions to Isaiah's prophecies concerning Assyria, and it appears that Nahum expects his audience to be familiar with Isaiah's message (see Spronk 1997, 7-8).

It is also instructive to interpret Nahum 1 in its immediate context after Micah. The book of Nahum is identified as an oracle from God and a vision (1:1), both of which could contain a prophetic answer to a prayer for guidance (Lam 2:9, see v 14). In its context in the BT, Nahum functions as the oracular answer to Micah's prayer of Lament (Mic 7:1-20). Micah, identifying with the community of God's people (i.e., Jerusalem) who have fallen under God's judgment, now awaits the light of the Lord's salvation in darkness. In Nahum, God promises that deliverance for which Judah had longed through the intercession of Micah would soon be fulfilled. Jerusalem and Judah will be delivered from Assyrian oppression, represented by Nineveh.

Most interpreters identify a partial alphabetic poem (acrostic) within the first chapter of Nahum. In an acrostic, the first word in each verse, or section, begins with a successive letter of the Hebrew alphabet. Some observe that if there is an acrostic in Nah 1 it is fragmentary and incomplete, so it is questionable whether the text can still qualify as an acrostic (for more details see Floyd 1994, 421-30; and others).

Although not strictly a hymn (see Floyd 1994, 430-37), Nahum 1:2-8 contains imagery similar to the biblical hymns found elsewhere. The hymnic style serves as an appropriate introduction to Nahum's prophecy. The opening line (1:2a), extolling God as *zealous . . . a vindicator and Lord of wrath*" (NIV "a jealous and avenging God . . . and is filled with wrath"), functions as the theme to the book of Nahum (Maier 1959, 152-53; Patterson 1991, 21-25).

In its present form Nah 1 (1:1-15 in English, 1:1-2:1 in Hebrew) contains a superscription (or heading, v 1), a hymnic celebration of the Lord's power as vindicator (vv 2-8), followed by warnings of judgment toward God's enemies and assurances of salvation for God's people (vv 9-15).

IN THE TEXT

A. Superscription (1:1)

■ 1 The superscription provides basic information about the prophecy of Nahum. Nahum is among six of the books of the Minor Prophets whose superscription in v 1 does not include a dating formula identifying the time of the prophecy according to Israelite, Judean, or Persian era kings (see Joel 1:1; Obad 1:1; Jonah 1:1; Hab 1:1; and Mal 1:1; see Tucker 1977, 60-61).

The superscription identifies the book as **a prophecy *against*** (or concerning) Nineveh; the Hebrew term for **prophecy** (*maśśā'*) is often translated *oracle* (e.g., NRSV; see also Hab 1:1; Mal 1:1). Generally, the term indicates a message from God in a time of crisis. The exact meaning of the term *maśśā'* as it relates to prophecy is not clearly known. Based on its possible origin from the verb root *nś'* ("lift up"), scholars think the word means "burden," "something lifted," hence "a load," etc. A longstanding view is that in prophecies the word means "burden," or a prophecy that is difficult, since it often contains a word of judgment. However, not all "oracles" are judgment prophecies (Maier 1959, 145-47; Stolz 1997, 773-74). It is more likely that the origin of the word is in the "lifting up" of the prophetic voice; hence, it is more appropriate to render the word as **pronouncement,** although sometimes the traditional translation "oracle" is used below.

The phrase **a pronouncement against** (concerning) Nineveh (v 1) identifies the book of Nahum as an "Oracle Against the Nations" (OAN). These oracles are found in nearly every prophetic book and serve to assure Israel that God is watching out for them.

Oracles against the Nations

Oracles against the Nations condemn a nation's violence or idolatry by denouncing their capital or chief cities. The existence of these OAN assumes that the nations are accountable to Israel's God as the Creator. OAN are almost always addressed to the people of God who are suffering under the nations' violent acts rather than directly to the guilty nations (see 2 Kgs 19:20-28). The prophet may have turned or looked in the direction of the nation, or a present representative, to indicate a word against a non-Israelite group (see Num 24:20-21). OAN serve to assure God's people that God will deliver them, and so they are a source of comfort during a time of suffering or crisis (see Hayes 1968, 81-92; and others).

The subject of Nahum's oracle is **Nineveh**. As the capital of Assyria, Nineveh represents the entire Assyrian nation. When this city fell in 612 BC it brought to a close the once mighty Assyrian empire. The mention of the city at the beginning of the book indicates that the general statements concerning God's enemy in Nah 1:1-8 apply to Assyria.

A **vision** is a form of prophetic reception of God's word that revealed God's will to the prophet (Isa 6:1-13; Jer 1:11-19; Amos 7:1, 7; 8:1; 9:1) and was then later communicated to humans as spoken or written prophecy. Like Nahum, other prophetic books are identified as a **vision** when either they are labeled as a **vision** (ḥĕzôn, Isa 1:1; Obad 1:1) or it is stated that the prophet "saw [it] in a vision," (ḥāzâ, Amos 1:1; Hab 1:1).

Nahum's prophecy is called **the book of the vision** (sēper ḥĕzôn), indicating that the content of the prophetic revelation has been recorded as a written document. Since the book or codex form was not invented until the second century AD, the term sēper actually indicates any document, usually a scroll. Another reference to a written vision is found in Hab 2:2-3, where the prophet is commanded to take the Lord's answer and "Write the vision; make it plain on tablets" (NRSV, → Hab 2:2-3). Other books make references to written documents within the prophetic book that became part of it (e.g., Isa 30:8; Jer 29:1-23; 30:2-3; 36:2-4; 32; Mal 3:16), but only Nahum is identified entirely as a written document.

The name **Nahum**, Hebrew naḥûm, from the root nḥm, is usually explained as meaning "comfort." There are other meanings for the word group formed by the Hebrew root nḥm, however. These include "compassion," "change," and "relent," and their meanings are interrelated (see Simian-Yofre 1998, 342). It is possible that all of these terms may offer information about the function of the book of Nahum. In the context of Micah's prayer of mourning in Mic 7, Nahum is a book of "change," "compassion" and "comfort." First, the book indicates a *change* in God's treatment of Judah: the time of judgment under Assyria will soon come to an end. Second, this change is grounded in God's *compassion* toward Judah, which is greater than God's former determination to punish. Third, God's word of change and compassion offers *comfort* to a people still under Assyrian domination (cp. Isa 40:1-2). Finally, the book indicates that God has *relented* regarding the forgiveness offered Nineveh in Jonah and will now hold Nineveh accountable for its evil deeds (→ Nah 3:19).

Verse 1 identifies Nahum as an **Elkoshite** (*'lqšy*), the resident of an unknown village. The Hebrew term *'lqšy* could be read as "God (El) is Severe," or "God is My Severe One." Perhaps its main function is to present Nahum's prophecy as an announcement of vindication against Nineveh by the Lord who is "a zealous and avenging God" or a "Severe God" (see 1:2; Allis 1955, 76; Spronk 1997, 28, 31-33).

B. Praise for the Lord as Vindicator (1:2-8)

1. Attributes of the Vindicator (1:2-3*a*)

■ **2-3*a*** The hymn begins with an assertion of the attributes of the Lord as a powerful vindicator (vv 2-3*a*). Nahum's confessions about God's character as *a zealous God*, **slow to anger but great in power,** and **the LORD will not leave the guilty unpunished,** are found elsewhere in the OT in the context of God's dealings with Israel (Exod 20:5; 34:6*b*-7,14; Num 14:18; Ps 103:8-9). The prophet adapts this material by applying it to the punishment of God's enemies.

The phrase *a zealous* (jealous) *God* (*'el qannô'*) is often found in the OT in the context of a warning to Israel to worship only the one true God (Exod 20:5; 34:14; Deut 4:24; Josh 24:19). According to Becking, "this designation is one of the oldest definitions of Israelite monotheism" (1995, 295). God's zealousness (*qen'â*) can be a consuming judgment set in motion by God's idolatrous people (1:18; 3:8). The use of this designation in a prophecy against Nineveh indicates that the Creator God holds the nations accountable for the worship of the true God, just as Israel is held responsible (1:14). In this context, the root *qn'* also connotes the divine *zeal* for God's people; Nineveh's judgment means God's saving compassion is at work on behalf of God's people. Therefore, a *zealous God* is a fitting translation of *'el qannô'* in 1:2 (see Joel 2:18; Zech 1:14, 8:2).

Verse 2 continues the description of God with *and a vindicator* (*noqēm*) *is the Lord*. This is a key idea in the passage. The phrase *noqēm yhwh* appears three times in v 2. (The NIV translates the term once as **avenging** and twice as **vengeance.**) The term *nqm* connotes here God's saving or vindication of God's people from Assyrian cruelty and oppression. For God's vindication to be effective it is necessary for God to act in judgment, which is often God's work of setting things right. In this case, it is for Israel that has been injured by the oppressive measures of Assyria.

The Lord is also called *a Lord of wrath* (ba'al ḥēmâ) *. . . and a keeper of anger . . . toward . . . enemies* (v 2). Divine wrath is the negative side of God's salvation or vindication; it is God's action against those who work against God's purposes. The term *Lord* (ba'al) here may simply connote that God "owns" or possesses this characteristic (see NIV **filled with wrath**) (Cathcart 1979, 2). The term ba'al also had other uses in Israel's history, including being a title and proper name for a Canaanite god.

The word nôṭēr (**keeper of anger**) (NIV **vents his wrath**), when applied to humans, can be translated "bear a grudge" (Lev 19:18, NIV and NRSV). It has a different connotation when applied to God, however. The term nôṭēr suggests the idea that God does not resort to divine wrath quickly, but only acts when it is deemed absolutely necessary. The Lord's **foes . . . enemies** are those who stand in opposition to God's plans and purposes for the creation. In this context they are the oppressive Assyrians.

Verse 3a alludes to a well-known formula that extols the Lord's attributes of mercy, forgiveness and judgment after God threatened to destroy the sinners of the wilderness generation (Exod 34:6-7). This formula, adapted in several biblical hymns and prayers, is a unifying thread throughout the BT (van Leeuwen 1993, 31-49). Nahum begins the citation of this formula with the phrase: **the LORD is slow to anger.** In Exod 34:6-7, this formula includes the phrases "abounding in love" and "forgiving wickedness." Nahum, however, omits these phrases and adds **but great in power** before concluding with *and the Lord by no means clears the guilty* (cp. Exod 34:7b). While God is not going to forgive Assyria, neither does God rush to judgment against this nation. However, slow to anger does not mean that Assyria will escape God's judgment; Nahum emphasizes the eventual certainty of the Lord's judgment. This emphasis on the Lord's judgment is good news to an oppressed people: God's judgment will free Judah from Assyrian bondage.

2. Theophany of the Lord the Creator (1:3b-6)

■ **3b-6** This unit describes a theophany of the Lord the Creator. The passage presents the Lord as a Divine Warrior who marches forth to rectify creation and vindicate the people of God (see Exod 15:2-18; Judg 5:4-5; Pss 18:6-19; 68:7-10). This reinforces God's attributes of power (vv 2-3a), whose appearance causes an upheaval in the forces of nature. Verse 3b presents the appearance of the Lord in the might of the storm. God's **way is in the whirlwind and the storm**. God's sovereignty is revealed in the **whirlwind**, and out of it the Lord can teach humans the divine way (see Job 38:1; 40:6 and the divine discourse that follows). In the OT God is Israel's warrior by acting through the force of the storm to save Israel and to judge God's enemies (Isa 29:5-6; 66:13-16; Jer 23:19-20; Zech 9:14-15).

The Lord's transcendence and power are expressed in terms of God's exalted stature: **clouds are the dust of his feet**. God riding or being manifest in the clouds is traditional ancient West Asian imagery associated with the storm god, who is also typically the warrior god. This was especially applied to Baal in the Ugaritic texts (see Cathcart 1973, 47-48). Since Israel's God takes up the function of all the gods, this imagery could be applied to the Lord (e.g., Pss 18:9-14 [18:10-15 HB]; 68:4 [68:5 HB]; 69:33 [34 HB]; 83:15 [16 HB]; 104:3). Here the **clouds** are likened to **dust** stirred up as God travels in the ***path*** (way) of the **storm**.

Although different Hebrew terms are used, clouds are often associated with God and divine action. Clouds are also depicted as surrounding God's throne (Ps 97:2; Isa 14:14; Ezek 1:4, 28), and manifest God's power and guidance (Exod 13:21-22; Ps 77:17 [18 HB]); etc.). In the BT, the day of the Lord's judgment is described twice as ***a day of clouds and rainclouds*** (Joel 2:2; Zeph 1:15; → sidebar Day of the Lord below). In Nahum the storm and dust connote the march of the Divine Warrior to execute judgment; the storm imagery here further emphasizes God's power and ability to act according to divine plans. As Luther says, no power can "resist the vengeance of the Lord, because the Lord moves like a whirlwind and storm" (Luther 1525b, 287).

The statement the Lord **rebukes the sea and dries it up** (v 4) alludes to the foundational saving acts of the Lord. First, God created the dry earth to provide living space for plant and animate life (Gen 1:2, 9). Second, Israel was saved when the Lord dried up the sea in the Exodus (Exod 15:8-10). Third, God's future acts of salvation, particularly the homecoming from exile, are depicted as a new creation and new Exodus events by use of water imagery (Isa 43:1-2; 50:2). Some of the passages cited above, like Nahum, complete the poetic parallelism by speaking of the drying of **the rivers**. The term **rebukes** (*go'ēr*) here does not have the negative connotation of the sea as the Lord's enemy, as in the Ba'al cycle (cp. Hab 3:8). The Creator's authoritative speech to the creation is intended here. Moreover, the water of the sea and rivers are often clearly portrayed positively in the Bible (Pss 24:2; 46:4 [5 HB]; 93:4-5).

In v 4 **Bashan, Carmel** and **Lebanon** are places noted for their fertility (e.g., Jer 50:9; Mic 7:14). These places, all located in the northern regions of Israel, fell under Assyrian control in the eighth century. Nahum suggests that these mountainous areas, known for their forests, tall trees, and rich pasture lands, will **wither and . . . fade** or ***languish*** (*'umlal* found twice in this verse) because of God's drying up of the rivers. When humans sin, or God judges human sin, or both, the Bible often speaks of the adverse effects on creation.

The Interconnections of the Moral and Natural Orders

According to the biblical way of thinking the moral order is tied together with the natural order of creation, comprising one unified system (these two orders are depicted side by side in Ps 19, vv 1-6 [2-7 HB] and 7-14 [8-15 HB]. When the moral order is disrupted by sin, the natural order suffers as well (see Hos 4:1-3 and Isa 24:4-6). In such cases the earth and its inhabitants are stricken with infertility and languish, and the whole created order mourns their plight (see Braaten 2006, 131-59; Fretheim 2000, 96-110).

In a theophany it is common to declare that **mountains** (or the earth) **quake before** God (v 5; see Ps 46:2-3 [3-4 HB]; Hiebert 1992, 505-11). This trembling or shaking of the earth is often associated with the shaking of the cosmos when the Lord appears as the Divine Warrior (e.g., Judg 5:4-5; Ps 18:7 [8 HB]; Isa 13:13, and elsewhere). The meaning of the verb *hitmogāgû*, translated here as **melt away**, is uncertain. Other possibilities are "waver," "flow" (from melt, see Amos 9:13), or "break apart." **The earth trembles at his presence** is literally "the earth lifts up before" God. The response of the inhabitants of the world is the same; they too tremble before the Divine Warrior. If the literal reading is followed, then the text may be dealing with the lifting of the voice as in mourning or crying; in that case, the text indicates the mourning of the earth and its inhabitants in response to the theophany of the Lord.

Verse 6 mentions the Lord's anger again, and so returns to the judgment theme which opened the passage. The awesome power of the Lord in nature (vv 3*b*-5) leads naturally to a (rhetorical) question that returns to the initial references to God's wrath: **Who can *stand before* his indignation?** The word translated **indignation** (*za'am*) is literally "curse." The word has the nuance of anger, and it is parallel to *ḥarôn 'appô*, "anger," in the next line. The second line, ***and who can arise against the heat of his*** [God's] ***anger***, thus conveys a similar idea. The Hebrew idiom for God's **anger** (*ḥarôn 'appô*) is literally "the heat of the nose," perhaps like the current expression "red in the face." The heat imagery continues when God's **wrath *gushes*** out like fire. God's judgment against Israel or the nations is sometimes depicted as the fire of wrath or zeal (Deut 4:24; and elsewhere).

The final line in v 6 is a contrast to the opening lines: **the rocks are *torn down* before** the Lord. Not only can no one arise against the Lord's judgment (v 6*a*), what is already established and ostensibly invincible—rock cliffs—can be torn down by the Lord. There is also a pun here: if the Lord can tear apart rocks (*ṣûrîm*, v 6), then God's adversaries (*ṣārîm*, v 2, → above) do not stand a chance! The strength of a rock mountain probably matched what many Judeans felt about the seemingly invincible Assyrian Empire backed by its conquering gods. The formidable power of Assyria, however, is no match for the Lord, the Creator of the earth!

3. The Lord as Refuge (1:7-8)

■ **7-8** The third unit (vv 7-8) offers the first unmistakably positive side to God's power. The words of the prophet in vv 2-6 might be disturbing to the reader since the images of judgment found here have a history of being spoken against the disobedient among God's people. So the prophet now clarifies that from the perspective of God's people, **the Lord is good, a refuge in *the day of adversity, and a knower of the one who seeks shelter in*** God (v 7). God is called **good** often, especially in hymnic or liturgical texts, and sometimes in close connection with

God's *ḥesed* ("steadfast love"; e.g., see Ps 100:5). The Lord's goodness provides hope for those who take refuge in God. This does not exempt God's people from trials, however, sometimes under the divine hand (Lam 3:21-39; cp. Job 2:10; Ps 119:71). Nahum's message is that the time of trial will soon end for the faithful, and the Lord's goodness will once more be evident.

The phrase **a refuge in** *the day of adversity* may be linked to the reference to rock in v 6, since the Lord is sometimes praised as a rock stronghold, or rock of refuge (Deut 32:37; Ps 18:2 [3 HB]; Isa 17:10). *Adversity* or **trouble** (*ṣarâ*) is from the same root as adversary (→ v 2 about this as a key term). In the OT, (the) day(s), or time(s) of adversity (or "distress") often connotes times of community or personal hardship, during which the Lord is expected to provide protection (Pss 9:9 [10 HB]; 10:1; Isa 33:2; Jer 14:8). In Nahum *the day of adversity* is also probably related to the Day of the Lord, which is a central idea in the BT (e.g., Joel 1:14-15; Amos 5:18-20; etc.).

The Day of the Lord

References to the Day of the Lord ("on that day," etc.) are scattered throughout the prophets, especially in the BT (e.g., Isa 2:12, 17, 20; Jer 46:10; Ezek 13:5; Joel 1:15; 2:1; Amos 5:18, 20; Obad 1:15; Zeph 1:7-10; Zech 14:1; Mal 3:2; 4:1,5). This is a day when God judges the wicked and restores divine order to creation. It appears to be rooted in the ancient concept that in the creation of the world, the Exodus, and the conquest of the Promised Land, the Lord, the Divine Warrior, established divine rule by conquering powers that threaten the cosmos and God's people (e.g., Exod 15:1-18; Judg 5:3-5; Pss 89:5-18 [6-19]; 114:1-8). The celebration of these victories in worship gave people hope that the Lord would also defeat present and future enemies (Cross 1973, 91-111). The earliest reference to the day is in Amos, where it already appears to be a widely held concept (Amos 5:18).

In the BT, the Day of the Lord is a day of adversity when God's people are persecuted by the nations (Obad 12, 14) or judged by the Lord (Zeph 1:14-15). It is also the day of salvation that God's people await after the Lord's judgment has run its course (Hab 3:16; see Nogalski 2003, 209-210). The Judeans had experienced "days of the Lord" or adversity when they went through judgment by the Lord (Everson 1974, 329-37). These include the Assyrian crisis with the downfall of the northern kingdom, and the Babylonian conquest of Judah and Jerusalem (Isa 2:6-22; Zeph 1:2-18, Lam 2:21-22; Ezek 13:5). Nah 1:7 offers continued hope during present and future troubles. Later in Judean history the day, or the Day of the Lord, was envisaged as a great final act of judgment against evil and salvation for the faithful (texts mentioned above in Joel and Isaiah were later interpreted in this manner, see also Mal 4:5-6 [3:23-24 HB] and Zech 14:1-21).

In v 7 the Lord is called a *knower* (*yodēaʿ*), a term difficult to translate directly (NIV **cares for**). In Hebrew, to know someone is to have a close relationship with that person. When the Lord knows someone, that person is granted salvation and life. For example, at the end of Exod 2:25, the statement **God knows** signals

48

that God's saving work is about to begin. The word "know" may connote God's care, election, and protection of the covenant people, and may also describe the people's relationship to God (see Schottroff 1997, 515-21).

God knows *the one who seeks shelter in* God (NIV those who trust in him (*ḥōsê bô*). In the psalms this is sometimes expressed as God's people finding in the Lord a rock or fortress. Finding refuge in God, or God being a refuge from troubles or enemies, is a common theme in the psalms, and it is sometimes associated with confessions of God's goodness, as here (see Pss 2:12; 5:11 [12 HB]; etc.). In the BT, a remnant of God's people will take refuge in the Lord in Zion after divine judgment against Judah and Jerusalem is complete (Joel 3:16 [4:16 HB]; Zeph 3:12-13). After the fall of Assyria, Nah 1:7 continued to inspire the faithful to take refuge in the Lord as Judah continued to face crises with the nations and unbelievers in their midst.

Though the opening words of v 8, *but with a passing* (NIV overwhelming) *flood*, may function as the second half of the last line in v 7, the phrase also makes sense as the beginning of a new poetic line. Nahum uses the image of a flood to announce the destruction of Nineveh (see also Isa 30:27-28; see God's judgment through Assyria as overwhelming Judah and Israel like a flood in Isa 8:7-8). Since Assyrian kings also claimed they or their gods could destroy their enemies "like a flood" (see Machinist 1983, 726-28, and others), Nahum's hearers would have perceived here an ironic reversal, or a case of poetic justice. In v 8 Nahum assures the people that although they had experienced God's judgment through Assyria, God continues to care for and provide protection for those who find refuge in their God. The Lord would soon completely reverse the situation and work deliverance.

The next half line reads God **will make an end of Nineveh**, or literally, *will make a full end of her place*. This is another case of poetic justice: what Nineveh has done to others will now be done to her. God will hold the king and his subjects accountable for the political and military policies that have wreaked havoc in the ancient world.

The last line in v 8 asserts that the Lord *will pursue enemies (into) darkness.* **Darkness** may connote a lack of the Lord's light, that is, God's salvation (Pss 18:28 [29 HB]; 27:1; Job 18:18). Here it may also refer to Sheol, the realm of the dead (Job 10:21; see Cathcart 1973, 58-59). Isaiah depicted the Assyrian invasion and subjugation of the northern tribes of Israel as a time of great darkness, after which God's salvation would shine as a dawning light (Isa 8:21—9:2). Darkness is also a motif connoting the prospect of judgment in the Day of the Lord (Joel 2:1-2, Amos 5:18, 20, etc.; see Spronk 1997, 50). Nahum's announcement of Assyria experiencing darkness would have given hope to the Judeans, who sit in the darkness of the Lord's judgment. The light of God's salvation will soon shine on them (see Mic 7:8-9).

C. The Lord's Vindication in Action (1:9-15 [1:9—2:1 HB])

I. The Plotters Will Be Consumed (1:9-11)

■ **9** Verse 9 indicates the futility of resisting the Lord by posing a rhetorical question: *Why do you plot against the Lord?* The first word (*mah*), is usually translated "what" (niv **whatever**), but also occasionally means "why." The unnamed **you** probably refers to the Assyrians (the NIV translates it as **they**). Watts narrows down this reference to Nineveh's leaders and military officers, whom he sees as departing from Nineveh (and the city's patron goddess, Ishtar) to harm Jerusalem (Watts 1975, 106). Later readers would apply the references to the Babylonians and other peoples who resisted God's will or opposed God's people.

The verb translated as **plot** (*ḥšb*) has a variety of related meanings, including "think, consider, reckon or regard as," etc. Here the context, especially v 11, makes it clear that the verb has a negative connotation. The response found in the next line indicates the Lord *is making a full end*. *Full end* (*kālâ*) connotes the total destruction of Nineveh (see v 8).

The last line, *an adversary will not rise up a second time*, is most likely a reference to Nineveh, the capital that represents the Assyrian empire. *Adversary* (*ṣārâ*) is from the root *ṣr* which connotes "adversity" or "trouble" in v 7. The NIV translates the term in v 9 as **trouble**, since it is a homograph of (i.e., has the same consonants as) the word found in v 7. Nineveh has been the source of trouble for Judah since the middle of the eighth century. So the NIV **trouble** in v 9 does not alter the meaning of the text. Nahum promises that Assyria will not rise up again to assert itself against Judah.

■ **10** Verse 10 is difficult to interpret (see Cathcart 1973, 60; for a summary of interpretations see Spronk 1997, 53-56). A careful reading, however, will yield understandable results. The verse begins with *kî*, "because," which provides the reason why Nineveh, the "adversary," will not rise up a second time (end of v 9). The Hebrew of the first line could be rendered literally as *because unto (or upon) thorns they are entangled*. The NIV **they will be entangled among thorns** conveys this meaning though it does not translate the particle *kî*. This rendering would mean that the Assyrians will not rise up a second time because they have been blocked by God's judgment.

The next phrase is the most widely discussed in the verse. We translate it as *and like their beer they are guzzled* by taking the term *sĕbû'îm* as a passive participle of *sb* ("to be drunk down, imbibed, or guzzled") (cp. Sweeney 1992, 370 n. 26). This reading indicates the swift destruction of the Assyrians, who are swallowed quickly like the voracious imbibing of beer. The NIV **and drunk from their wine** suggests that the Assyrians will be incapacitated—entangled (as if) in thorns, drunk from excessive drinking.

The next phrase, *they are* consumed like *thoroughly* dry stubble, presents a similar picture. The Hebrew word for **consumed** (*'ukkĕlû*) is literally "eaten."

The burning of **stubble** sometimes refers to God's consuming judgment (e.g., see Exod 15:7). Stubble is easily burned. This picture is "doubly heightened" by the concluding phrase, ***thoroughly* dry** (Maier 1959, 192).

■ **11** The references in v 11 are obscure and have occasioned much debate. The Hebrew reads: ***from you one departed* who plots evil against the** LORD. The "you" is feminine singular; Jerusalem or Nineveh is intended here. The one who ***departed*** is probably a king. So either the Assyrian king left **Nineveh** (added by the NIV) on his way to battle Judah, or a king left the city of Jerusalem, after opposing the Lord. In the latter case, the king who left Jerusalem could have been either an Assyrian king or a Judean King who behaved wickedly. One ancient suggestion is that it was the wicked king Manasseh (2 Kgs 21:1-18) who left Jerusalem to go into Assyrian exile (2 Chr 33:11-13; see Rosenberg 1988, 244; Pinker 2005, 85). This commentator accepts another older view that fits the context well, that this is a reference to the Assyrian King Sennacherib who withdrew from Jerusalem after attacking the city in 701 BC. The verse would thus be Nahum's reference to Sennacherib's inability to completely subjugate Jerusalem as he planned (2 Kgs 18:13-16; 19:35-36; see Ball 1999, 223).

Nahum offers two descriptions of this king. First, he is ***one . . .* who plots evil against the** LORD. Sennacherib's attempt to take control of Jerusalem, the chosen city where God dwells, is his evil plot against the Lord. Second, Nahum describes this king as ***one who counsels worthlessness*** (devises wicked plans). He opposes or works against the Lord's purposes. Nahum suggests that Sennacherib's conquest of Jerusalem was ultimately not complete due to his resistance to God's plans (cp. Isa 10:7-15). The word translated as ***worthlessness*** (*bĕlîyyā'āl*) connotes what is opposed to social or religious order. People designated as *bĕlîyā'āl* are unprincipled troublemakers; they are idolaters (Deut 13:13 [14 HB]), have no respect for law or social order (Jud 19:22), and can be easily hired as false witnesses in a legal action (1 Kgs 21:10, 13). By NT times "Belial" (alternatively "Beliar") was used as an alternate name for Satan (2 Cor 6:15; see Otzen 1975, 131-36).

2. Assurances of Salvation for Jerusalem (1:12-13)

■ **12** **This is what the** LORD **says** is a messenger formula introducing the speech of the Lord. It is the only place it occurs in Nahum.

Although they *are complete* describes the seemingly unconquerable state of the Assyrian troops. The Hebrew adjective *šĕlēmîm*, related to the term *shalom*, connotes "whole," "full," or "perfect." In this context it connotes "maximum potential," hence "full strength" (NRSV; see Cathcart 1973, 63). Luther describes the sense of the word well: they are "well armed . . . most resourceful and wise, so that they lack nothing that belongs to a well-equipped army" (Luther 1525b, 293). The word can sometimes be translated as **allies**, as the NIV does here.

The next phrase, although difficult to translate, may be rendered ***as numerous as they are, so will they*** be destroyed and pass away. We might compare this phrase to the expression "the bigger they are, the harder they fall." The Hebrew word translated **pass away** (*'ober*) appears in v 8 in the expression ***passing flood*** (NIV "overwhelming flood"). This verse reinforces what was said there; the ***passing flood*** of divine judgment will result in the seemingly superior tyrant "passing away."

The next words of v 12 are spoken directly to God's people; ***although I oppressed you, I will not oppress you again*** (v 12). The word for ***oppressed*** (NIV **afflicted**), from the stem *'nh*, occurs often in the OT. The word (and its cognates) can also be translated "humbled, bowed down, afflicted, poor, or destitute." God may oppress (or "humble, afflict") Israel as punishment for sin (Deut 8:2-3 and elsewhere). The word **you** is feminine singular and refers to Jerusalem (NIV adds **Judah**). The oppression is a reference to God using Assyria as an instrument of judgment against sinful Jerusalem (see the description of the city in Isa 1:21-23). In the past Jerusalem has been ***oppressed*** by the Lord, but her affliction will soon come to an end. However, it is not an unconditional promise never to discipline the people of God when they become disobedient and work against divine purposes.

■ **13** The Lord continues to describe Jerusalem's deliverance in v 13. ***I am about to break his yoke bar from upon you and your bonds I will tear away***. The opening Hebrew word *wĕ'attâ (*and now*)* connotes impending action. Subjugation to God or a foreign power was sometimes described as submitting to the yoke (see Lev 26:13; Jer 2:20; 27:6-8). Here **his** refers to the king of Assyria. Assyrian kings boasted about imposing their yoke on West Asian countries. In the eighth century BC Sennacherib claimed, "I laid waste the large district of Judah and put the straps . . . of my (yoke) upon Hezekiah, its king." (*ANET* 288). This yoke, Nahum promises, will soon be removed.

3. Vile Kings Forgotten, the Lord's Shalom Celebrated (1:14-15 [1:14—2:1 HB])

■ **14** This section contains words of judgment toward the Assyrian king and salvation for Judah. The prophet addresses someone, **the Lᴏʀᴅ *has commanded concerning you***. Since ***you*** is masculine singular it probably refers to the king (→ v 13) and not **Nineveh** (added by the NIV). The Assyrian king is explicitly mentioned in 3:18 and is probably the unnamed subject of 1:11.

The verse mentions three things important to royal status: posterity or name, temple, and tomb (Floyd 2000, 49). The phrase, **you will have no descendants to bear your name**, reads literally, "there will not be sown (anyone) from your name again." In other words, this is the end of the king's dynasty, and his name will not be preserved for posterity.

In the next line of v 14, the Lord also announces judgment against the king's idols that are in the temple of his gods: ***I will cut off from the house of your gods the carved and cast image*** (cp. NRSV). Nahum no doubt has Assyrian idolatry in mind. Assyrian kings prided themselves on restoring the images of ancient gods after their temples had been destroyed. One of the kings' (especially Sennacherib's and Esarhaddon's) self-attributions was "maker" or "restorer" of divine images (e.g., Luckenbill 1927, 2:435, 441, 444). The act of cutting off or destroying the images would not only attack the king's idolatry and image making, it would also be an affront to the Assyrian gods. These gods cannot do anything to stop or save themselves from destruction by the Lord, Israel's God and the supreme God over creation.

Since the king has no offspring to attend to a proper burial, God will dispose of the body (Roberts 1991, 54). The phrase *I will appoint your grave* is unusual. The term *appoint* (*'āśîm*), which means to "put, place, set up," in this context suggests the Lord's verdict of the king's death. The grave is the future that the Lord has appointed for him. Nahum's oracle may have been influenced by the fate of Sennacherib, who after blaspheming the Lord outside Jerusalem fled to Assyria and was murdered by his sons in the temple of his god (Isa 10:5-34; 36-37; see Sweeney 2000b, 2:433).

Moreover, the Lord states that all this king deserves is a grave because he is **vile** or *insignificant* (v 14). The word *qallôtâ* is literally "small." This term may be understood in light of the way Assyrian kings sometimes had themselves depicted on stone monuments as larger than life (see Pritchard 1958, picture #121). In v 14, the king is cut down to size when the Lord declares him to be "small." "Because [the king], in contrast to his self-estimate, is actually of little consequence, God will provide a grave suitable for his true importance" (Smith 1984, 79).

■ **15 [2:1 HB]** God's people are now addressed with promises of salvation in v 15. *Look! Upon the mountains are* **the feet of one who brings good news,** *one who announces wellbeing.* Isaiah 52:7 opens with a phrase that is nearly identical to Nah 1:15. The word *mbśr* means "bearer of news," usually **good news**, but occasionally the news could be bad (e.g., 1 Sam 4:17). In the OT **good news** could be the birth of a child (Jer 20:15), the report of victory in a battle (1 Sam 31:9; Ps 68:11 [12 HB]), or the proclamation of deliverance (Isa 40:9; 41:27) by God's anointed prophetic messenger (Isa 61:1). In the NT the Greek equivalent terms of the root *bśr*, the verb *euangelizō* and the noun *euangelion*, connote Jesus' proclamation of the good news (or gospel) of the Kingdom of God (Matt 11:5; Mark 1:1, 14).

Though Isaiah may have borrowed this announcement from Nahum or vice versa, another possibility is that it was a popularly known expression that both prophets employed for their own purposes. Since people are always eager to get good news, especially during times of crisis, it is easy to see how a phrase like this could be a common saying. It suggests the welcomed sight of an approaching messenger running over the surrounding mountains and toward the beleaguered city of Jerusalem (Robertson 1990, 81). The parallel passage, Isa 52:7-8, explicitly mentions sentinels as sharing in the proclamation of the good news. Floyd suggests that Nahum is using the metaphor of the prophet as sentinel (see Ezek 3:17-21 and Hab 2:1), who from his watch post announces and interprets the significance of the approach of various persons (Floyd 2000, 56-47). Watts observes that Nahum directs the people's attention to the surrounding hills for a herald in anticipation of the fulfillment of the prophecy (Watts 1975, 109). In the context of the book, however, Nahum may have in mind either himself or the Lord; the latter is more likely in light of the Lord's theophany in vv 3-5. It is interesting to note that in Isa 52, the image

53

of the approaching messenger as the *bearer* of the good news (v 7) quickly gives way to the depiction of the approach of the Lord, the *content* of the good news (vv 8-10).

The bearer of good news is further described as **one who announces wellbeing**. The Hebrew word for **wellbeing** (*šālôm*) is often translated **peace** (see NIV), but its meaning is much more comprehensive (see *HALOT*). It connotes the "wellbeing" or "wholeness" (or even "prosperity") granted by God that is necessary for creation to flourish according to the Creator's intentions (see Ezek 34:25; 37:26). So it is often found in blessings (e.g., Num 6:24-26). Thus, this message of *shalom* is more than that there will be peace after the defeat of an enemy; it would also assure Judah that the Lord is at work setting right a damaged situation. It is worthy of note that there is an expectation in the prophets that true *shalom* can only be brought by the Lord and the faithful leader whom the Lord sends (Isa 9:6-7 [5-6 HB]; 32:1, 14-20, etc.; see Spronk 1997, 79).

The next line in v 15 contains two commands. The first command is **celebrate your festivals, Judah.** The occasions in view are probably the three pilgrimage **festivals** where the Israelites celebrated God as Creator and sustainer of the harvest and Redeemer in the Exodus (Exod 23:14; Num 28:16-39; Deut 16:16-17; 26:11). It appears that these observances had been hindered during the time of Assyrian subjugation—either due to the interference of Assyria or the faithlessness of the Judean kings (2 Kgs 23:21-24, see Calvin 1847, 450). The **festivals** could not only be observed freely after Assyria was removed from interference in Judean life, but these celebrations also *anticipated* the Lord's future work as the Creator and Redeemer God who could deliver Judah from all hostile powers. The festivals were also occasions to extend God's redemptive love by sharing one's bounty with the less fortunate (Deut 16:11). This is essentially a way of extending the Lord's liberating salvation to others. With the resumption of the festivals, therefore, the Judeans were given a renewed opportunity to fulfill God's calling to be a source of blessing to all the families in the land (Gen 12:3).

The second command is **fulfill your vows**. A vow (*nēder*) could be a communion or thanksgiving offering expressing gratitude for answered prayer (Lev 7:16; Pss 50:14-15; 61:5 [6 HB]; etc.; see Sweeney 2000b, 2:434). Such vows were sometimes made during prayers of affliction when people prayed for deliverance from a problem or enemy (e.g., Gen 28:20-21). The vows referred to here may have been made in connection with petitions for deliverance from Assyria. The word **fulfill** is another key word in this section. It is from the root *šlm*, which is the basis for the word "wellbeing" or "peace" appearing earlier in the verse. Judah will experience the promised *well-being* as they thankfully worship the Lord by *fulfilling* their vows.

The last line of v 15 begins with the particle *kî* (**because**) which introduces the reason for the commands stated in the previous line: ***worthlessness will no longer pass over you.*** The term **worthlessness** (*bĕlîyā'āl* or Belial, → 1:11) connotes the **wicked** Assyrian empire. ***Pass over*** (*'br*) conveys the image of the ***pass-***

ing flood (→ v 8) or the threat of military invasion (see Isa 8:7-8). Judah receives the promise that Assyria will no longer be a military threat to the nation.

The last line, **they will be completely destroyed (*all of it will be cut off*)**, asserts the demise of the Assyria, its people, its king and its gods. The destruction of Assyria will be complete; *cut off* conveys the idea of complete demise. This is good news to all who suffered under Assyria's oppressive policies (see Nah 3:19).

FROM THE TEXT

Nahum opens with a depiction of God that is bound to make the average Christian cringe: God is described as vengeful and wrathful. Although one might choose, with some interpreters, to categorize the contents of the book as nationalistic and sub-Christian, another course would be to attempt to take the book seriously as Scripture. Perhaps we could not only learn about the proper context of God's wrath, but why we tend to neglect or avoid this theological concept. When we read Nah 1 on its own terms, we discover not only several important truths about God's vindicating wrath, but an enduring and comforting message regarding God's work of *shalom* for the creation.

First, *God's saving work includes vindication* (Nah 1:2). It is important to God that the creation be vindicated, that is, *set right*. God's vindication is not to be compared with petty human revenge or "getting even" because someone has not respected one's legitimate authority. Rather, God's will is that the entire creation be set right: that God's people and all peoples live in *shalom* according to God's creation intentions. This positive goal of vindication often entails the negative action of removing an evil agent who works against God and creation's *shalom*. But it is much more than this, and the final goal of restoration must always be kept in view.

Therefore, *God's saving work of vindication includes divine wrath* (Nah 1:2, 6). God's wrath is the power that removes what hinders God's purposes and destroys *shalom* in God's creation and between all of earth's inhabitants. Understood in this manner, divine wrath is an aspect of God's love. Divine love motivates God to seek *shalom* for the entire created order. Divine wrath is God's love in action correcting what is wrong for the sake of the Creator's purposes for creation. The Lord is not quick to anger (v 3*a*), but only acts with destructive wrath as a last resort. However, the Lord's slowness to anger is not a sign of God's weakness or lack of concern, but of patient love (v 3*a*). The Bible is filled with examples of God's patience as the warnings of prophets are repeatedly ignored. In the biblical narrative, it is usually only when God's warnings have gone unheeded—*sometimes for centuries*—that the Lord resorts to wrathful destruction.

The Lord's awesome revelation of power by the disruption and sovereign control of the creation is a danger signal to all peoples of the earth (vv 3*b*-6). It is only when one has stood before this powerful display of divine power that one can hear what God has to say (cp. Job 38-42; see Brown 1999, 338-40). While God's enemies have much to fear due to their disobedience, the Lord's people need to remember that their position, gifts, calling, and privileges are granted by God's grace and not given due to intrinsic merit. When the prophet threatens that God will disrupt the cosmic elements of creation to show Assyria the power of divine judgment, it is a warning to all peoples who aspire to Assyria's power or position. This includes leaders among God's people who compromise with Assyria or who adopt Assyria's policies, as well as the nations that God would use to judge Assyria. All creation stands at a distance before the God of judgment.

The Lord's triumph over evil is certain (see especially 1:6, 8, 9, 10, 13, 14, 15c [2:1c HB]). Evil is "unnatural"; it is incongruent with God's purposes. Therefore, evil will be consumed by divine judgment as certainly as thorns and stubble are cleared from the land and burned by the farmer (1:10)—there is no room for the good crops and the thorns to grow side by side. On the other hand, this can be a disruptive process, and some evil will remain in the world until the end of this age (Matt 13:24-30).

Yet, God is good, and a refuge to those who trust in God and not their own resources (vv 7-8). When the Lord is slow to anger toward evil doers, then God's people often suffer in the interim (v 12b). God is a refuge of strength during such times. We have hope that eventually God will set things right (vv 12-13), and the forces of evil will be swept away just as surely as they swept away others.

The good news of the Lord's promised work in creation is the beginning of the restoration (v 15 [2:1 HB]). First, as God's people respond to the good news that there will be a deliverance from evil, God's past and future salvation are celebrated in worship. This worship looks back to what God has done before as an assurance that God will continue the work into the future. Second, this future gives hope that since God's kingdom will come, a small piece of it can be enacted on earth as the word of hope is proclaimed and God's *shalom* is implemented through love of God and neighbor. Third, while vestiges of worthlessness continue to be evident in the world, God's people are assured that there will be a day when evil will no longer disrupt God's creation.

Finally, *the God of Nah 1 has been revealed to creation through the revelation of Jesus Christ*. Through Jesus the good news of the dawning of God's kingdom is announced (Mark 1:14-15; Matt 7:10). This announcement has two outcomes. On the one hand, this kingdom consists in the offer of repentance for all creation (Matt 4:17) and healing (Matt 4:23-25). This is the dawning of God's *shalom* (Luke 2:14) offered through the Holy Spirit (John 14:25-31; 20:19-23, 26). God grants forgiveness and the *shalom* of life to those who respond to Jesus (Mark 2:5-10; John 3:16; 10:10). On the other hand, those who choose the path of evil and resist God's work through the Son become objects of God's wrath and judgment (Matt 12:35-37; Rom 2:4-8; Rev 6:15-17).

Nahum reminds those who follow Jesus that their enemies are in reality God's enemies and that God will vindicate them by vanquishing the powers of evil (1 John 3:8; Heb 2:14-15; Matt 12:28; Luke 10:18). Yet those who take refuge in the Son of God during crises will find a yoke that provides rest and relief from the yoke of slavery to this present evil age (Matt 11:29-30).

II. THE LORD'S VINDICATION OVER NINEVEH ANTICIPATED: NAHUM 2:1-13 [2-14 HB]

BEHIND THE TEXT

The historical situation of Nahum 2 is best understood in the background of the international unrest against Assyria and the general decline of the Assyrian empire in the seventh century BC. After Babylon led a rebellion against Assyria in 652 BC, the Assyrian king, Ashurbanipal, eventually regained control, first taking action against Babylon (648 BC), then against the remaining offenders to the east and west, including Palestine (ca. 640 BC). The Assyrian resurgence was short-lived, however; when Ashurbanipal died in 627 BC, rival parties within Assyria soon vied for control, leaving Assyria weak in the face of attacks. Beginning in 626 BC the Babylonians, now joined by the Medes, once again rebelled. Within two decades the mighty Assyrian empire would collapse, with Nineveh falling in 612.

Even within a few years after the rebellion of 652, news of such events would have convinced many within Judah that Isaiah's prophecies of Assyria's fall were about to be fulfilled. The prophet Nahum announced that the Lord would soon initiate attacks against Nineveh which would lead to its demise. Nahum 2:1-10 portends the type of events that would precede the fall of Nineveh with 2:11-12 anticipating the aftermath when the Assyrian forces were stranded without a base of operations. For a summary of the events surrounding the final days of Assyria see Bright 1981, 313-16.

Nahum 2:11-13 employs the West Asian and biblical lion motif. This imagery was especially popular with Assyrian kings, who depicted themselves and their troops as mighty lions conquering their prey (see Robertson 1990, 95). When Assyrian kings likened themselves to lions they also sometimes depicted themselves as striking their enemy like a windstorm or flood (see Luckenbill 1927, 2: 561, 925)—suggesting they were manifesting the power of a storm deity. The dread caused by a possible lion attack is a fitting analogy to the terror occasioned by Assyrian cruelty (see the numerous references to Assyrian cruelty in *ANET* 284-300).

Nahum's vivid descriptions of the battle scene, his acquaintance with the environs of Nineveh, and frequent ironic allusions to Assyrian propaganda suggest that the prophet was at least indirectly aware of some aspects of Assyrian geography, administration and literary tradition (discussed in Machinist 1983, 736).

Since the whole book of Nahum was probably composed to be recited in a single setting (→ Introduction and 1:1), the book coheres as a unified piece and perceived literary divisions are not major structural breaks. In other words, there are literary connections between the divisions proposed here, so other possible structural partitions are possible (e.g., Floyd 2000, 59-62). While the entire book can be classified as an OAN (→ sidebar Oracles Against the Nations), this division of the book (2:1-13 [2:2-14 HB]) exhibits a characteristic of this genre not found in the first division (1:1-15 [1:1-2:1 HB])—a detailed portrayal of an impending attack against the doomed nation.

Nahum 2:1-13 [2:2-14 HB] has two separate, but related literary sections. The first section, 2:1-10 [2:2-11 HB], anticipates the fall of Nineveh in the classical style of an OAN. As an OAN, this section depicts the fall of a country or city not as a detailed prediction of exactly how events will unfold, but as an imaginative depiction of likely scenarios in the context of ancient West Asian practices of war. Nahum's Judean audience takes on the role of onlookers who overhear God's proclamation of judgment against their formidable foe. As supposed bystanders they "witness" the Lord giving notice to the enemy that their end is near.

The second section, 2:11-13 [2:12-14 HB], is a taunt song, which compares Nineveh's former glory to what it will soon be under God's judgment. It is marked by a change of imagery: Nineveh is compared to a den of lions whose lair is filled with prey (vv 11-12 [12-13 HB]). This section concludes with an oracle of the Lord announcing that the situation is about to be reversed—the Lord will cut off the prey from the lions who will now become the object of attack (v 13 [14 HB]). Although implied throughout the chapter, here the attack against Nineveh is explicitly described as coming from the Lord. This picks up the motif of the Divine Warrior, which is implied in the theophoric description of the Lord in 1:3*b*-6.

This prophecy concerning the downfall of Nineveh and the Assyrian empire, although addressed specifically to the context of the mid to late seventh century BC, was probably soon applied to other contexts where God's people yearned for deliverance from oppressive powers. After the Assyrian deliverance took place—in a manner portended by 2:1-13 [2:2-14 HB]—the people of God found strength to believe that God could deliver them again from the Egyptians, Babylonians, Persians, Greeks, or Romans.

IN THE TEXT

A. Nineveh's Certain Fall (2:1-10 [2-11 HB])

I. Nineveh Called to Prepare for Battle (2:1-2 [2-3 HB])

■ **I [2 HB]** This unit opens with a warning to Assyria concerning an impending onslaught by **an attacker**. The title **attacker** (*mēpîṣ*) is literally "a disperser, scatterer." Cathcart claims that in battle contexts the term indicates "putting the enemy in confusion and routing them" (1973, 80). A *scatterer will come up* against . . . **Nineveh** has military connotations. There are strong contextual arguments for identifying the Lord as the *scatterer*. The Lord is not only identified as the attacker in 2:13 [2:14 HB] and depicted as the Divine Warrior in Nah 1, but the Lord is also celebrated elsewhere as the one who scatters Israel's (and God's) enemies (Num 10:35; Ps 18:14 [15 HB]).

The Hebrew lacks the word **Nineveh** (supplied by the NIV), although it is the implied antecedent of the second person feminine pronoun *you*. As God's judgment, Nineveh's army will be defeated and its citizens dispersed like those involved in building a tower at Babel (Gen 11:8-9).

In the remainder of this verse, the prophet articulates a series of four concise commands imploring Assyrian readiness for the impending battle. The commands address a masculine singular subject, probably Assyria, the Assyrian army, or the Assyrian king.

Since ancient cities were fortified for protection against enemy attack, the command to **guard the fortress** would focus on the protection of Nineveh. The call to **guard** includes the idea of the sentinel standing guard on the city wall, watching for an approaching enemy (Patterson 1991, 572; 2 Kgs 9:17-20). **Brace yourselves** is literally *strengthen (your) loins.* This is the only place in the OT where this phrase occurs. An equivalent phrase today would be "roll up your sleeves." The command **marshal all your strength** is literally *strengthen your power greatly.*

The verse as a whole underscores that Assyria has been adequately warned to prepare for battle. Even if Assyria has been fully warned and is in top battle readiness (see 1:12), God's judgment is inescapable (→ From the Text).

■ **2 [3 HB]** This verse is a word of promise that seems to fit awkwardly in the context of warnings to Nineveh of an impending attack. The verse begins with the motive for God's judgment on Assyria: *For* the LORD **will restore the splendor.** Compare the NRSV; the NIV leaves *kî, for,* untranslated. The phrase **restore the splendor** (*šāb ga'ôn*) is similar in meaning and usage to God's promise to "restore (the) fortunes" (*šāb šĕbût*) of Israel (→ Zeph 2:8). It often connotes a restoration or homecoming after judgment. The word *ga'ôn,* though it elsewhere means "to be high" or "exalted," probably connotes here Israel's fertile land (see Kellermann 1975, 344-50). The reference to the destruction of **their vines** leads us to think that restoration of agricultural fertility is intended here. Since the Assyrians had annexed Israelite territory, beginning in 734 BC, God promises to reverse the effects of Assyrian destruction and exploitation of Israelite soil.

The NIV's translation, **the splendor of Jacob like the splendor of Israel,** could be understood to mean that Jacob represents Judah, and Israel refers to the old northern kingdom. The problem with this interpretation is that it suggests that Judah *will be restored* just as Israel *has been restored.* Israel, of course, had been destroyed in the eighth century BC and had *not* been restored in Nahum's day (Longman 1993, 802). A more probable view is that **Jacob** and **Israel** are both names for the northern kingdom which was conquered and exiled by the Assyrians in 722 BC (this usage is found in Amos 6:8; 7:2; see Spronk 1997, 86). Thus it is possible to see here the promise of the restoration of the old northern kingdom (see Jer 31:15-22).

The motivation for God's restoration is expanded in the next line, ***because (kî)* destroyers have laid them waste and have ruined their vines.** The Hebrew root *bqq,* "lay waste," usually indicates destruction of land (Isa 24:1, 3, Jer 51:2) by God's judgment. The word **destroyers** (*boqĕqîm*) is from the same root as **laid . . . waste.** So the phrase could be literally translated as "the wasters laid them waste" (or "the destroyers destroyed them"). The destruction that Nahum is referring to is the Assyrian onslaught against the northern kingdom in the years 734-722 BC. The Assyrian campaigns during this time resulted in the destruction of land, the exile of the people, and the annexation of the territory by Assyria (2 Kgs 15-17; see Bright 1981, 273-76). The word translated **vines** (*zĕmûrâ*) only appears a few times in the OT. It is used literally or figuratively for grape vines or their branches (Num 12:23). The expression **their vines** probably represents all of Israel's agriculture (by *pars pro toto*).

In summary, this part of the verse indicates God will restore the exiled northern kingdom to its former glory. It is likely that Nahum's Judean audience included refugees from the fallen northern kingdom who have settled in and around Jerusalem after 722 BC (see Avigad 1976, 44). Nahum's prophecy would have been especially relevant to those whose families had been displaced by the Assyrian empire.

2. The Advancing Army and the Troops of Nineveh (2:3-5 [4-6 HB])

■ **3 [4 HB]** The next three verses, vv 3-5 [4-6 HB], describe the respective armies of the "scatterer" (→ 2:1) and of Nineveh. The advancing army of the "scatterer" is composed of elite troops, probably God acting through the heavenly army (→ 2:13). The **soldiers** are literally ***mighty men*** or "war heroes" (*gibbōrîm*). The Hebrew phrase *'anšê ḥayil*, translated **warriors,** is literally "men of valor" or ***valiant men*** (Weber 1980b, 271-72). The **reddened** shields may connote shields of leather dyed red. The **scarlet** garments probably indicate the red garments uniforms worn by Babylonian warriors (Ezek 23:14).

The description of the advancing army now turns to the chariots in vv 3*b*-4 [4*b*-5 HB]. The opening phrase literally reads "as the fire of *peladot is the chariot*" (*bĕ'ēš pĕlādôt hārekeb*). The singular *rekeb*, "chariot," often functions as a collective, and thus could be rendered **the chariots** (see Gen 50:9, etc.; *HALOT*). This is the only occurrence of the word *pĕlādôt*. Some scholars connect it with a Persian word for "steel." This understanding is reflected in many contemporary translations, including the NIV's **the metal on the chariots flashes.** Some ancient versions read here *bĕ' ēš lĕppādôt* (see *BHS*), which assumes the switching of the consonants *p* and *l* at an early stage of the copying of the text. The Hebrew root *lpd*, "torch," is sometimes found with the word fire (*'ēš*), as here (see Ezek 1:13; Dan 10:6). Based on ancient versions, the opening phrase could be translated, ***like fiery torches are the chariots***, which fits the context here (see KJV, RSV, NKJV).

The next phrase, *bĕyôm hākînô*, can be rendered **on the day** *of his preparation* or "readiness." This refers to the time of battle and preparation of the troops for battle (see Driver 1906, 30). *His* probably refers to the "scatterer" (see v 1 [2 HB]). The NIV translation, **on the day they are made ready,** refers this phrase to the **soldiers**. The word **day** in a judgment context would also evoke thoughts of the Day of the Lord (→ 1:7 and sidebar The Day of the Lord).

The final phrase in the verse mentions a specific type of tree that has been made to "reel" (*wĕhabbĕrōšîm hor'ālû*). The trees (*bĕrōšîm*) may refer to several types of evergreens including cypresses, junipers and pines (Zohary 1982, 106-107). For convenience sake the term will be translated as ***cypress***. One ancient view, mentioned by the medieval Jewish commentator Kimchi (or Redak, AD 1160-1235) is that this tree is a reference to spears of cypress (cp. NIV's **spears of juniper**), that is, spears with cypress shafts (cited by Rosenberg 1988, 2:245). The root (*r'l*) of the verb *hor'ālû* (**brandished**) is rare (→ Hab 3:9). In its few appearances outside of this passage it means to "stagger, reel" because of too much wine—always in a figurative sense after one drinks the cup of God's judgment (Ps 60:3 [5 HB]; Isa 51:17, 22). Thus the phrase may be interpreted literally: ***even the cypresses are made to sway*** (see KJV; O'Brien 2004, 60). The storm imagery in this translation fits the immediate and broader contexts of Nah 1-2. The imagery of swaying of the trees fits well with the upheaval and shaking of nature at the appearance of the Divine Warrior in 1:3b-6 (see also 2:4).

■ **4 [5 HB]** Since this verse refers to **chariots,** it could be either a *continuation* of the description of the advancing troops of the Lord or the *beginning* of a portrayal of the defending troops. The vocabulary of this line supports the view that the chariots belong to Nineveh and that they are under divine judgment. The word translated **storm** (*yithôllû* from *hthll*) is a verb that means "pretend or act as mad, or insane" (see 1 Sam 21:13 [14 HB]). A literal translation of the phrase would be **the chariots *drive madly* through the streets** (see Jer 46:9; 2 Kgs 9:20; cp. the contemporary expression "he drives like a mad man"). The next half line continues the description with the phrase ***they rush* back and forth through the squares.** Even before the attackers breach the walls and enter the city (see v 6), chaos overtakes the troops of Nineveh within the city. Nineveh's predicament is already gloomy before the attackers enter the city!

The next line employs lightning imagery to describe the chariots: ***their appearance is like flashes.*** The word *lappîdîm* (translated ***flashes***) often means torches (→ v 3). The last line, **they dart *back and forth* like lightning,** conveys the confusion within city wall. The verb **dart,** *yerôṣēṣû,* is literally "run, run swiftly." The word **lightning** (*bārāq*) does not describe an enemy elsewhere; it is possible that Nahum uses this word to paint a contrast here. While the flashing chariots of the "scatterer" are steadily advancing toward Assyria with the objective of destroying Nineveh, the city's chariots are rushing around madly, darting back and forth in a state of panic and confusion. Even before the "scatterer" strikes a physical blow, the Lord's forces have begun to weaken the enemy.

■ **5 [6 HB]** This verse continues to depict the reactions of the defending troops in Nineveh. It opens with ***he remembers his officers*** (*yizkor 'addîrrāyw*). The word **officers** is literally "nobles" (2 Chron 23:20). Since the same word (*'addîrrêkā,* "your nobles") is associated with the king of Assyria in 3:18, ***he*** and ***his*** most likely refers to the king here also (see Spronk 1997, 93; NIV inexplicably supplies **Nineveh** and changes the verb and pronouns to feminine; **Nineveh summons her picked troops**). As the confusion and chaos continues, the king "remembers" to summon the **officers** to check the defense status of the city walls. However, the ineptitude of the defenders continues. In the officers' haste, **they stumble on their way.** This reference to officers who **stumble** further supports the view that the troops of the "scatterer" are no longer being described. Stumbling usually connotes weakness or divine judgment. Nineveh's troops stumble while the troops of the "scatterer" are getting ready for the attack.

The next phrase is literally **they *hurry* to *her* city wall.** As elsewhere in Nahum, when ***her*** refers to the enemy it denotes Nineveh. **But the protective shield is put in place.** This is the only occurrence of the word *sōkēk* (**shield**). Recently this word has been translated as ***mantelet*** (see RSV and NRSV), a domed shield placed against the outside of the wall to protect from a sapper undermining a city wall

(Yadin 1963, 2:316, 462-63). The rush to the wall is too little, too late. Before the Assyrians can mount a counter attack or even an effective defensive maneuver, the "scatterer" already has offensive and defensive implements of war in place. This is the beginning of the end for Nineveh. The verses which follow portray a swift end for the city.

3. Nineveh's Rapid Fall Anticipated (2:6-10 [7-11 HB])

■ **6 [7 HB]** Two verses, vv 6 [7 HB] and 8 [9 HB], depict the fall of Nineveh with water imagery. The first verse implies the opening of **the river gates**, which results in the collapse of **the palace**. However, the precise meaning of this verse is not clear. Rashi interprets the **gates** as the city gates next to the river, which were opened (or breached), allowing the attackers to penetrate the city (Rosenberg 1988, 2:246). More recent interpreters see here a reference to the flooding of the city by the attackers. However, Nahum elsewhere likens the Lord's judgment to a sweeping flood (see 1:8). Here Nahum announces that the city of Nineveh and its palace-temple complex will be irreparably damaged by the judgment of the Lord.

■ **7 [8 HB]** This verse describes the action taken against an unnamed female subject. Interpreters from ancient to modern period have attempted to see here a reference to the Assyrian queen or the goddess Ishtar (see Rosenberg 1988, 2:247). In its context, however, it is more natural to assume that this verse refers to **Nineveh** (added by NIV) who has been consistently personified as a woman.

The Lord has **decreed** that all the inhabitants of the city **be exiled and carried away**. The verb *gullet* (from *glh*), translated **exiled**, could also be rendered *stripped*. In either case, there may be a word play on the two meanings of the homograph. On the one hand, Assyria had exiled many populations, so Nineveh receives its due by being exiled by God's decree. On the other hand, there could also be an allusion to publicly shaming the city, who is stripped of her glory as the capital city.

The second part of the verse anticipates mourning rituals in the city when it is destroyed by God's judgment. The **female slaves** are mentioned here because the city is being lamented by its inhabitants, and it was customary for women to lead in the wailing and ceremonial actions of mourning (see Jer 9:17-22 [16-21 HB]). Here the women **moan like doves** (see Isa 38:14; Ezek 7:16). The expression has an old history in Mesopotamian lament scenes (*ANET* 650). The custom of women who **beat upon their breasts** is also mentioned in Isa 32:12 (cp. Luke 18:13; 23:48), but with different vocabulary. The usual word for **breasts** is not used here, instead the text reads literally ***their heart(s)*** (*lebbēhen*). This use of the inner for the outer (i.e., the "heart" for the "chest") may connote the strong inner emotion and sincerity of the outer actions (cp. Joel 2:13).

■ **8 [9 HB]** **Nineveh** is mentioned by name for the first time since the opening verse of Nahum. In the second half of this verse through verse 9 [10 HB], the prophet conveys the gravity of the situation by articulating the voices and thoughts of those present at the rout of Nineveh.

First, the prophet states that the city **is like a pool**. This verse picks up the flooding imagery of 2:6 [2:7 HB]; only now the flood is not of the attacking forces, but of the fleeing defenders. Nineveh was located on two rivers; the likening of the city to a pool may also be an allusion to the literal meaning of Nineveh as "house of fishes" (see Spronk 1997, 99-100). According to the vocalization of MT, the next phrase is literally "from her days" (*mîmêhî*). If this reading is retained then this is a reference to the reputation of Nineveh's water works (see Spronk, who translates this phrase "as it existed," 1997, 99). The NIV accepts a common alternate vocalization of the text as *mêmêhî*, **whose waters** (or "her waters"). We follow the alternative vocalization and render the phrase literally as **whose waters *indeed are fleeing***. The waters of Nineveh here represent the city's armies and other citizens who desperately flee before the flood waters of the Lord's troops.

To the fleeing troops another course of action is advised, however: "Stop! Stop!" The word is ʿ*ămôdû*, literally "stand, take a stand." The phrase **they cry** (NIV) is lacking in the Hebrew text. So the question is open: Who would issue such a command? It could be the king or a commander of the Assyrian troops trying to gain control of the fleeing troops. The attempt to stop the panicked troops is futile, **but no one turns back**. The city will fall quickly, with barely a sword lifted in defense. This dramatic portrayal of a quick fall emphasizes the certainty of God's promised action.

■ **9 [10 HB]** Another double set of commands is found at the beginning of this verse, matching the command in v 8 [9 HB] to stop (see Cathcart 1973, 102). The commands in this verse are depicted as either from the Lord or the commander of the attacking troops. The city has been left defenseless, so the troops are exhorted to **Plunder the silver! Plunder the gold!** The wealth of the Assyrian empire is at their disposal, **the supply is endless**. The term **supply** (*těkûnā*) indicates stored valuables (see *HALOT*).

The wealth is further described as ***the riches of every valuable object*** (the wealth from all its treasures). The word ***riches*** is from the root *kbd*, which is often translated as "glory, honor." This wealth included items plundered from other nations. Assyria's glory was in its riches and army, both of which are now gone. The empire that once boasted of plundering the nations will now be plundered (see Achtemeier 1986, 21).

■ **10 [11 HB]** The panic of the city is described here in chilling detail. The opening of the verse connotes Nineveh's downfall in concise and abrupt terms: ***Desolation! Destruction! Devastation!*** (cp. Roberts 1991, 55). The three terms *bûqâ ûměbûqâ ûměbullāqâ* forcefully emphasize the point with strong alliteration, or paronomasia (repetition of syllables). The first two terms occur only here and are probably related to the term *bqq* in 2:2 [2:3 HB], which describes Assyria as the destroyer who laid waste the lands of other nations (→ 2:2). What this nation has done to others is now done to it, the destroyer is being destroyed.

The rest of the verse describes the physiological effects of fear upon Nineveh's residents. The terms here could all be translated as abrupt interjections.

First, **Hearts melt!** (*lēb nāmēs*). Although singular ("heart melts"), this phrase is a collective and so is translated as a plural. The expression connotes extreme discouragement, terror, and failing courage (see Josh 2:11 5:1; Isa 13:7; Ezek 21:12). The second indicator of fear is **Shaking of knees!** The term translated **shaking,** *pîq,* is from a root which sometimes means to "reel, totter." Weakening or shaking of knees commonly occurs in reaction to fear (see Isa 35:3; Job 4:4).

Next, there is **Trembling of all loins!** The term "loins" functions at the beginning of the section to call Assyria to be strong against the attack (→ 2:1). Here it connotes that Assyria fails; it is weak with panic when the attack occurs. Finally, **every face grows pale**. The expression means either that the face is flush or hot with fear, or that the glow leaves the face. Hence, it grows pale (see *HALOT*).

In summary, it is evident that the Assyrians' pride of empire and their boasting in riches and power have been replaced by overwhelming terror and the loss of bodily control. The "scatterer" (2:1 [2 HB]) has effectively brought forward the judgment of the Lord.

B. The Lion Will Prey No More (2:11-13 [2:12-14 HB])

I. The Great Lions' Den—Once Filled with Prey (2:11-12 [12-13 HB])

■ **11 [12 HB]** This short unit concludes this section of Nahum. This passage is a taunt song mocking Assyria's fall from military prowess in ancient West Asia. The rhetorical question, **Where now is the lions' den . . . ?,** suggests that it has been destroyed, probably another use of the prophetic perfect (see the appropriate comments of Longman 1993, 810). With the fall of Nineveh, which Nahum declares is imminent, the hiding place of the lions will soon be destroyed. The **place where they fed their young** is literally *the pasture of the young lion. Pasture* would not be the normal haunt of a lion, and its use here changes the imagery in this passage from the hiding place of the lion to its hunting grounds.

The next poetic line in the verse assumes the subject of lion's den and continues the rhetorical question. Here we find two additional terms for lion: the terms **lioness** and *lion cub*. The line reads literally, *where the lion goes the* **lioness** *is there, and the lion cub, and there is* **nothing to fear**. This piling on of lion terms suggests a pride of lions whose appetite is insatiable (→ next verse; cp. Job 38:38-39). While the den was intact, the lions were protected, so they had **nothing to fear**. The lions can act with impunity as long as they have the safety of their lair.

So it is with the king of Assyria and his troops; Nineveh provides a safe haven of retreat from their aggression and violence. Once Nineveh falls, however, the Assyrian military forces will be left without a refuge. This is ultimately what took place—when Nineveh fell and its king died in the battle in 612, what was left of the army came to a quick end (Bright 1981, 314-16).

■ **12 [13 HB]** The lion *tears* [*ṭōrēp*] for his whelps, *and strangles for his lion-esses*. This verse continues the portrayal of Nineveh as the lions' den. Here the former strength of the Assyrian king (and troops) is portrayed as a lion providing prey for his family. In Assyrian sources the kings frequently boast of the plunder they brought home from their conquests (see the multiple references in *ANET*, 274-301). The result of the lion's hunting is a den filled with carcasses: *he fills his lairs with prey* (*ṭerep*) *and his dens* *with torn prey* (*ṭērēpâ*). Since the appetite of the lions must be satisfied, the lion is driven to constant hunting. Nahum's depiction of the lion filling his dens is a grim allusion to the Assyrian kings' distribution of the ill-gotten gains of war. Nahum's depiction of the lions awaiting this prey thus suggests that the citizens of Assyria, who directly benefited from the violence of the king and his troops, are held accountable for the violence of their leaders.

2. The Predator Will Become the Lord's Prey (2:13 [14 HB])

■ **13 [14 HB]** This verse serves to conclude the entire section (2:1-13 [2-14 HB]). "*Look*, I am against you" is directed at Nineveh (**you** is feminine). This phrase occurs first in Nahum, and then often in Jeremiah and Ezekiel (e.g., Nah 3:5; Jer 21:13; 50:31; Ezek 13:8, 20; 21:8). It is sometimes called the "challenge formula" since by it God calls out an opponent for a battle or judgment (see Sponk 1997, 107). Because the Assyrians have plotted "*against* the LORD" (Nah 1:9), the Lord is about to act *against* Assyria in judgment. This use of the challenging formula "Look, I am against you" (*hnny 'lyk*) can be contrasted with the more common promise of presence to God's people, "I will be (or I am) with you" (see Exod 3:12 and elsewhere; see Achtemeier 1986, 22).

The next phrase, **declares the LORD Almighty**, is literally *an utterance of the LORD of hosts*. The expression LORD *of hosts* probably has its origin in the depiction of the Lord as the Divine Warrior who heads the heavenly army. The Divine Warrior is sometimes depicted bringing down the heavenly hosts to aid in a battle against God's enemies (Judg 5:20-23; 2 Kgs 6:17; see Sponk 1997, 108). If this meaning of the title is still current with Nahum, then this picks up the Divine Warrior theme of ch 1. This is first time that the Lord is explicitly named as the one directing the campaign against Nineveh.

The remainder of the verse applies God's actions against Nineveh, again indicated by feminine pronouns. The pronouns alternate between "your" and "her" (the NIV translates all pronouns as second person). By referring to the destruction of **chariots** and **young lions**, this verse ties together the battle imagery of the first section (2:1-10 [2-11 HB]) with the lion imagery of the second section (2:11-13 [12-14 HB]).

There is no doubt a bit of irony in the phrase **I will burn up in smoke** *her chariotry*. The fiery and flashy chariots of the "scatterer's" troops (2:3 [4 HB]) are contrasted with the smoke-obscured chariots of Assyria. The chariots of the "scatterer," likened to flaming torches and lightening, have set fire to the chariots of Nineveh. Nahum later mentions that fire consumes the city (Nah 3:13, 15, see Maier 1959, 286).

The next phrase, **the sword will devour your young lions**, implies that Assyrians will be destroyed by the weapon with which they have destroyed other nations, including Israel. Here **young lions** are probably viewed as capable of preying (see Ezek 19:6), and so probably represent the Assyrian troops (see Cathcart 1973, 106 and 109). The use of **devour** is also ironic; the devourers—the young lions—will be devoured. In Hos 11:6, Assyrian swords consume Israel; in Nahum, the sword is turned against Assyria. Once again we have a case of poetic justice.

The word **prey** ties the two sections together. **I will leave you no prey on the earth** is literally "I will cut off from the earth your prey." The NIV's rendering probably captures the meaning of the Hebrew phrase. The earth and its inhabitants may now rest in peace because the God of Israel has stopped the violence of the aggressor.

Nahum continues with the results of the conquest of Nineveh, **the voices of your messengers will no longer be heard**. The Hebrew word translated **voices** is singular and could also be translated literally as "sound." The Hebrew phrase provides a contrast with the close of the previous section, which alludes to messengers of good news. Assyria's messengers have frequently brought good news to the city about successful military campaigns against other nations (see Ashurbanipal's report in *ANET* 296). Nahum's announcement signifies that Nineveh will not only stop preying on the world through violence, but also that no last-minute good news will be conveyed to the city by messengers. Jerusalem, on the other hand, expectantly awaits the messenger proclaiming the good news of *shalom* (1:15 [2:1 HB]), which is not only the end of Assyrian oppression, but the restoration of wellbeing and proper worship. In one sense the role of messenger is being played by Nahum, whose prophecies are the announcement both of good news to Judah and bad news for Assyria.

FROM THE TEXT

Nahum's message of judgment against the oppressive Assyrian empire contains some significant theological themes that are worth pondering today. Several are included below.

The Lord's judgment against oppressors is certain and just. This is the cumulative effect of the commands for Assyria to be prepared for the battle. First, the commands underscore once again the nearness of God's judgment. It is just around the corner; it could happen at any moment—Assyria must start preparing now!

Second, as in the plagues against Egypt in the Exodus narrative (Exod 4:21-13:36), God announces in advance through a spokesperson that divine judgment is coming. Although as an OAN the warning is more rhetorical than actual, the effect on the hearer is threefold: it demonstrates God's fairness, heightens the responsibility (and guilt) of the warned nation, and glorifies God to a watching world.

The reader of the BT also knows that Assyria was once before warned of God's judgment and was able to avoid it by repentance (Jonah 3:1-10). The net effect is to heighten Nineveh's responsibility for its sins, and therefore the justice of God in acting against the city. The Aramaic Targum to Nahum emphasizes this when it adds an interpretive comment to Nah 1:1: "Previously Jonah . . . prophesied against her and she repented of her sins; and when she sinned again there prophesied once more against her Nahum . . ." (Gordon 1990, 131). Since the judgment was publicly announced in advance, God's righteous purposes are revealed to a world which often wonders why unrighteousness and suffering so often gain the upper hand. Those who take note of God's vindicating action are invited to acknowledge God's work and join the people of God, as did Rahab and her family of old (Josh 2:8-14).

Third, all of Assyria's preparations will be futile, however, since the Lord's intentions to judge Nineveh have been made clear since the opening words of Nahum's prophecy. Assyria can be fully prepared and ready for battle, but God's judgment will still prevail (→ 1:12).

Likewise today, Nahum's prophecy testifies to the fact that there will be certain judgment for oppressive nations and groups. It may be slow in coming and the oppressed of the earth may ask "how long" suffering will endure, but in God's broader purposes we can be certain that God's justice will prevail. Ample warning has been provided in scripture and in the positive example of God's people when they respond correctly to God's grace and foster communities of divine fellowship and justice through the workings of the Holy Spirit.

What this nation has done to others is now done to it; the destroyer is being destroyed, the plunderer will be plundered. As Achtemeier observes, this section of Nahum is filled with irony: what Assyria does to others, the Lord will return to it, and what Assyria seeks falsely, Judah will receive as a gift of God (Achtemeier 1986, 21-22; see also Maier 1959, 278). As elsewhere in the Bible, Nahum's depiction of poetic justice is a warning that the sins of the oppressors will eventually consume them. The old adage is still true: "those who live by the sword will die by the sword." The Bible would add "and God will make sure they do!"

The Lord brings under judgment both the lion and his family. The Assyrians of Nineveh benefited from the imperial policies of the king, enforced by the violence of Assyrian troops. While they did not commit the acts that secured this wealth, their enjoyment of these goods rendered them guilty of the predatory practices that acquired them.

In today's global society, it is difficult not to be involved indirectly in the violent or dishonest practices of others. Yet, that does not absolve us of the responsibility of demanding that our goods be obtained justly. It is our responsibility to ensure that what we purchase cheaply does not damage the physical, social, or spiritual wellbeing of others, or cause unjustifiable damage to the creation. This constant desire for more is greed, which is named as sin throughout the NT (Matt 23:25; Luke 12:15; 1 Cor 6:10 and elsewhere), as is its close companion, covetousness (Rom 1:28; 7:7-8; 13:9; James 4:2). Yet these are seldom mentioned in today's consumer cultures.

It is important that we live sustainably and that our greed—often disguised as "need" by the propaganda of the powerful—not drive us to take from creation more than is necessary, thereby robbing weaker nations or future generations of God's gifts. Unfortunately, it is easy to mistake our *ability* to amass goods as God's will and a sign of divine blessing. Yet, it is obvious that not all who are wealthy are children of God. Therefore, it is important that we pray for the ability to discern between genuine blessing and excessive, and therefore immoral, consumption.

Those who oppose God's purposes will be opposed by God. The Lord's general message of assurance in the Bible is (do not fear, for) "I am with you" (→ In the Text above). But to those who hardheartedly resist God and cruelly oppress humankind and creation, God says "I am against you" (2:13 [14 HB]; 3:5; see also Jer 51:25; Ezek 13:8; 21:3 and elsewhere; see Achtemeier 1986, 22).

This is not an easy message to hear, and certainly it is not what God's people have come to expect from a God who through the ages promised to be with and protect those who have been called, and whose nature has been ultimately revealed as love (1 John 4:8). But being a God of love does not exclude God from proclaiming opposition to those who cruelly resist God's purposes. Indeed, sometimes the Lord's love for the many *demands* that God act against the few. While God's people can take comfort that their Savior will oppose those who oppress them, the promises of protection for God's people are not absolute. *Any* who oppose God's purposes are in danger of being opposed by God. Therefore, God's people must be cautious that they do not take on the characteristics or methods of those whom God is against, and thus be joined with them in their judgment (see Jer 21:13; 50:31).

God's message of peace (shalom or wellbeing) will prevail over the propaganda of the powerful. This chapter ends with the announcement of the end of "the voices of (Assyria's) messengers" (2:13 [14 HB]). The Assyrian propaganda machine struck terror in their world. By intimidation, threats, false promises and force they coerced peoples to submit to their rule.

Today we live with a constant barrage of propaganda: whether in the form of commercials in the various mass media, slogans of special interest groups, or the boastful assertions of nations. While it is sometimes helpful to encapsulate ideas or goals in short memorable sayings, it is also possible by such words to promote a group's self-interest at the expense of others and to exclude, demonize, and oppress.

Unfortunately, the appeal of oppressive words can be powerful and seductive, for it promises the good life through status, acceptance, wealth or power. But surrendering to the alluring claims of propaganda rarely satisfies. It often comes at the price of the suffering of others, and ultimately the loss of one's soul. The only ones who truly "benefit" are the powerful, since their propaganda is in reality only a thinly veiled guise to promote *their* own interests and power.

The groans of those who suffer under such propaganda reach God (cp. Exod 2:23-24), and God will surely hear and act to deliver. The prophet Nahum declares that the messengers of such oppressive policies will be silenced (2:13 [14 HB]). Instead, the message of good news of *shalom* will be proclaimed (1:15 [2:1 HB]). God's glorious presence, inhabiting the worship of God's people (see Ps 22:3 [4 HB]), will create a just community characterized by God's wellbeing. When God is thus glorified, creation is being restored, and the emptiness that cannot be filled by the propaganda of the powerful is filled by the peace of God.

The Lord has the final word when it comes to divine judgment against a sinful world. Finally, it must be borne in mind that Nahum's prophecy has a specific setting and announces divine judgment against a specific nation. While we have gleaned from this prophecy some general truths about the Lord's purposes regarding setting the creation right and punishing oppressive powers, we cannot be certain when or how God will act in every circumstance. As Job discovered, sometimes God's justice is slow in coming, and we cannot understand why suffering is so pervasive. Sometimes it does appear that cheaters are the winners and the faithful are the losers. At these times it is important not to lose one's faith in a just God, who, for reasons unknown, is delaying action. It may also be the time to renew a healthy eschatological perspective. God's people are called to live as though God's justice prevails *now,* and trust that if not now, then in the *final judgment* the oppressors will receive their deserved punishment and the people of God will be vindicated.

III. THE LORD'S VINDICATION OVER NINEVEH CELEBRATED: NAHUM 3:1-19

BEHIND THE TEXT

For the historical background of this section see Behind the Text on Nahum 2. This section of Nahum still partakes in the larger literary category of an Oracle Against the Nations (OAN), which has characterized the book as a whole. Since the entire book shares a single genre and setting, it is difficult to determine distinct sections for this division. The prophet takes up a new thought in 3:1, the dominant lion imagery at the close of Nahum 2 having been dropped (although there is a link back to it in v 1). The passage begins by addressing Nineveh in the third person, pronouncing a woe against the city (vv 1-4). It continues by addressing the city directly in the second person (vv 5-17) and concludes with a direct address to the king of Assyria (vv 18-19).

The certainty of Nineveh's demise is a major theme in this final division of the book. It is conveyed by the use of three sets of rhetorical questions (vv 7, 8, 19), whose implied answers underscore the certainty of Nineveh's impending fall (cp. Robertson 1990, 99). These questions also serve as one set of markers that divide this unit into two sections: verse 1-7 and 8-19.

The first section, vv 1-7, is a woe oracle, and like the concluding section of 2:11-13 [2:12-14 HB], it is also a taunt song mocking the downfall of a once mighty and oppressive empire. In Nahum 3 the woe oracle concludes with additional funeral language in v 7, the announcement of Nineveh's impending devastation and the ironic notice that "she" will be abandoned and left without sympathizers.

The concluding section, vv 8-19, begins and ends with rhetorical questions. The first question in v 8 invokes the historical precedent of the fall of Thebes as an indication of the certainty of Nineveh's demise. The final verse with its concluding question bears some resemblance to the questions concluding the previous section (v 7). Both verses express how unlikely it would be for Nineveh to find any last-minute aid due to Assyria's past cruelty. The final question also emphasizes for one final time that Assyria deserves to suffer divine judgment and also functions as the conclusion of the book.

IN THE TEXT

A. Nineveh's Funeral Anticipated—A Taunt Song (3:1-7)

1. Quick Destruction of Bloody City Anticipated (3:1-3)

■ 1 The opening taunt song of 3:1-7 is Nineveh's mock funeral. The initial interjection **Woe!** (*hôy*) is a prophetic adaptation of funeral language to divine judgment, otherwise known as a woe oracle. By celebrating a funeral in advance the prophet underscores the certainty of the Lord's judgment—Nineveh is as good as dead! Nineveh's funeral has already been anticipated by the mourning of its female citizens in 2:7 [2:8 HB].

Nineveh is called a **city of blood**, literally "bloods" (*dāmîm*), better translated as *bloodshed* (see this label for Jerusalem in Ezek 22:2; 24:6, 9). Bloodshed and whoredom (*zĕnûnîm*, see Nah 3:4) are found together as sins defiling the land (of Israel) at the beginning of the BT (see Hos 1:2, 4; 2:4). Since Assyria's violence was perpetrated throughout West Asia, the Assyrian bloodshed that Nahum condemns here is probably violence against many peoples and not just Israel and Judah (cp. Isa 10:12-14).

The phrase **full of lies** is literally "the whole of it is a lie" (*kullâ kaḥaš*), perhaps meaning "everyone in it is lying, deceitful." Many commentators point to the deceit of the Assyrian officials in their dealings with nations, especially with Judah in the eighth and seventh centuries BC (2 Chr 28:16-20; 2 Kgs 18:13-37; e.g., see Robertson 1990, 101-102).

The next poetic line, **full of plunder, never without victims!** picks up the lion motif of 2:11-13 [2:12-14 HB]. The phrase **full of plunder** (*pereq mĕlē'â*) conveys an idea similar to that of *wayĕmallē' ṭerep* in 2:12 [2:13 HB], which can be rendered as *he (the lion) has filled with prey his lair.* The noun form of the word translated **plunder** (*pereq*) is rare; in Ps 7:2 [3 HB] the verbal form *pāraq* is used with the term prey (*ṭerep*), as in this verse (see Spronk 1997, 118). The psalm likens an enemy to a preying lion.

The second phrase is literally "prey does not cease" (*lō' yāmîš ṭārep*), which can be rendered **endless prey.** The Hebrew word *ṭerep* (NIV **victims**) is the same term rendered "prey" in 2:12 [2:13 HB]. One possible interpretation of this part of the verse is that Nineveh is full of plunder for the taking by the invading troops (→ 2:9). Since this poetic line appears to be parallel with the previous line, it is more likely, however, that this **plunder** and **prey** are what have been amassed violently and deceitfully by Nineveh (→ 2:12). The message of the prophet is that the wealth of the city is not enough to save it. Indeed, since it was immorally amassed, it will only bring the city under God's judgment.

■ **2-3** The next two verses portray in staccato cadence the sounds and sights of the invasion of Nineveh. The terseness of the Hebrew adds to its gripping effect (the NIV translation is a good attempt to capture the poetic imagery in these verses). This depiction of the invading troops as they pass through the city complements the portrayal of the troops as they approach the city in 2:3 [2:4 HB]. One of the ironies of this scene is that its brutality matches that practiced by Assyria itself, and so interpreters are divided as to whether this is a portrayal of the invasion of Nineveh or an account of Nineveh's past cruelties! (see Spronk 1997, 119).

Verse 2 and the beginning of verse 3 depict the equine troops: those driving chariots and riding on horses. Noises are emphasized by repetition of the Hebrew word *qôl*, which literally means "sound," but which takes on different meanings according to its context. The air is filled with **the crack of whips** (Hebrew *qôl šôṭ*) of the charioteers and **the clatter of wheels** (*qôl ra'aš 'ôpān*) of the chariots. The last phrase is literally "sound of shaking of wheel" perhaps better translated as *sound of rumbling wheel* (see NRSV). "Shaking" is often connected with the tumult of war (see Jer 8:16; 10:22)). Since the troops attacking Nineveh have been sent by the Lord, the reference to shaking here may be another hint that Nineveh's fall is ultimately due to the action of the Divine Warrior vindicating the cosmos.

The reference to **galloping horses** (*wĕsûs dōher*) may connote a full charge of the attackers through the city, indicating that the defenders are retreating instead of engaging their enemy (→ 2:8). Spronk observes that the root for gallop is only found elsewhere in Judg 5:22, where God is depicted as fighting against Israel's enemies through cosmic forces (Spronk 1997, 118).

The final phrase is literally *dancing chariots* (*merĕkkābâ mĕraqqēdâ*). The expression has a poetic ring, the two words have equal syllables and exhibit alliteration, assonance and rhyme. The participle *mĕraqqēdâ* means literally "to skip, dance." In the only other use of the word in the BT, Joel 2:5 employs it in a poetic description of the locust army led by the Lord to judge Judah (see also Joel 2:11). The verbal root *rqd* also appears twice in theophany contexts, where it connotes the response of creation to the redemptive actions of the Creator (Pss 29:6; 114:4, 6). Both of these passages could be interpreted as appearances of the Divine Warrior.

The staccato-like description of the enemy continues in v 3. The phrase, **charging cavalry**, is literally "horsemen bring up" (*pārāš maʿāleh*), which is not easy to interpret. The form of the verb *maʿāleh* is a *hiphil* participle, which means "cause to go up." This would presumably be a more fitting action for a rider than for a horse. But what does the rider "cause to go up"? The word for horse is lacking in the text. The NIV reading is a reasonable interpretation (see also NRSV, NASB). An imminent attack is intended here.

The text next describes the weapons as **flashing swords and glittering spears**. The word *lahab*, translated **flashing**, is literally "flaming." The spears are literally described as "lightning spears" (*ûbēraq ḥānît*; see the imagery of fire and flashing 2:3 [2:4 HB]; also the weapons of the Divine warrior in Hab 3:11 and Zech 9:14). The lightening imagery may be seen as another allusion to the Divine Warrior acting through these earthly events (→ 1:3 and 5).

The remainder of v 3 details the carnage left by the attacking troops. **Many casualties** is literally *a multitude of pierced* (*rōb ḥālāl*). Since the ancient West Asian weapons of warfare were primarily arrows, spears, and swords, this is a very descriptive term (see Wiseman 1980, 1:288). The NIV's rendering of **casualties** recognizes that the word sometimes denotes the wounded and not just of the dead—although the rest of the verse suggests that Nahum might have the fatally wounded in mind here.

The phrase **piles of dead** is literally *heavy with carcasses*. The word *heavy* (from the root *kbd*) connotes here abundance (see 2:9 [2:10 HB]) though often it is translated as "glory" or "honor." The next short phrase, **bodies without number**, is literally *endless corpses*. The Hebrew phrase *wēʾēn qēṣeh*, "endless" (like the root *kbd*), connotes the endless supply of riches in 2:9 [2:10 HB]. Ironically, the city whose glory was its "heaviness" of endless riches is now filled with the "heaviness" of its endless dead (cp. Wendland 1998, 173). The path of riches has become the pursuit of death for Nineveh.

Finally, the dead are so deep on the streets that there are **people stumbling over the corpses**. The Hebrew contains only two words, (*yikšēlû bigwîyātām*), literally *there is stumbling over their corpses*. In 2:5 [2:6 HB], the word "stumble" connotes the hasty attempt of the Assyrians to defend their city. Here, Assyrians are fleeing before their attackers and stumbling over their own dead (see Maier 1959, 298). The ironic impact of this verse in the context of Nahum is evident. Nineveh has fallen, a victim to the same violence it once employed against others. Once again, poetic justice is served.

2. Punishment of the Idolatrous City, No Comforters (3:4-7)

■ **4** The description of the battle scene now gives way to God's threats of punishment directly against Nineveh. The NIV translation, **all because of** (*mērōb*, literally "from many") **the wanton lust of a prostitute**, interprets the attack of the city (vv 2-3) as a punishment for Nineveh's **prostitution**. Verse 5 then starts a new sentence in the NIV. It is also possible to read vv 4 and 5 as a single sentence, with v 4 introducing new charges against Nineveh and v 5 (continuing to v 7) announcing God's punishment (see NRSV). In that case *mērōb* would be translated as **on account of the abundance of**. Since the imagery and subject change in v 4, the latter reading is preferable.

The phrase **the wanton lust of a prostitute** is literally *the whoredoms of the whore* (*zĕnûnê zônâ*). The phrase **wanton lust** might suggest that Nineveh's *inner character* is in view; the word ***whoredoms*** focuses on the *actions* of the subject.

Whoredom as a Figure of Speech

With one exception (Gen 38:24), the term ***whoredoms*** is employed as a figure of speech and describes all manner of defections from the Lord (e.g., 2 Kgs 9:22; see NRSV). The BT opens with a command for Hosea to ***marry a woman of whoredoms and have children of whoredoms***, which is a symbol that ***the land commits great whoredom away from the Lord*** (Hos 1:2, cp. NRSV). This figure of speech continues in Hosea, with the land accused of further acts of whoredom because the people participate in Baal worship and other condemned practices, mostly connected with worship (Hos 2:2 [2:4 HB], 4[6 HB], 5[7 HB], etc.; see Braaten 2003a, 105-125). When "whoredom" is applied to the nations, it sometimes connotes (greedy) profiteering through trade (Isa 23:17-18; cp. Rev 17:1-5; 18:2-3), excessive violence, abuse of and failure to acknowledge God-given power (Isa 47:1-7), and idolatrous self-sufficiency (Isa 47:8-13; cp. Rev 18:7). Most of these charges have already been raised against Assyria in Isaiah and Nahum, and profiteering is evidently in view in Nah 3:16.

The remainder of the poetic line is in apposition to the first phrase. That is, it expands on the description of Nineveh personified as a prostitute. The two words in the Hebrew phrase that follows, *ṭôbat ḥēn*, literally "good of grace," are sometimes used separately to connote attractive appearance or agreeable personality (see *HALOT*). Since the words are found in the context of the words "whore" and "sorcerer," **alluring** is a suitable translation of the phrase (see NRSV's "gracefully alluring"). Another phrase which would be appropriate in this context and at the same time convey the ambiguity of the Hebrew is ***charmingly attractive***. The power and wealth of Nineveh made the city, despite its history of violence, seductively attractive to those who strove for the same affluence.

Next, Nineveh is called **the mistress of sorceries** (*ba'ălat kĕšāpîm*). The term **mistress** can be misleading, since it often connotes an illicit lover in English. A *ba'ălâ* is the female equivalent of a *ba'al* ("lord"). A more suitable term such as "ruler, sovereign," or "her highness" would be appropriate here (thus **sovereign of sorceries**).

The root *kšp* is usually understood as "sorcery," which is one of the many forms of soothsaying, divination, and magic practiced throughout ancient West Asia. Assyria was known to practice various types of divination, and it is feasible that is in view here in v 4 (see Maier 1959, 302-303). It is also possible that the term is used in a generalized way to connote worship of gods other than the Lord (Sweeney 2000b, 2:443). Nineveh, representing the seat of Assyria's power, is charged with relying on powers other than the Lord, and the result is oppressive violence. As indicated above, this poetic line is the beginning of a sentence which will be completed by the next half of the verse.

In the next poetic line Nineveh is described as the one **who sells nations through her whoredoms and families through her sorceries**. The literal translation would be "who sells nations for the price of her whoredoms, etc." In Nineveh's case, the "payment" for its immoral actions is the subjugation and enslavement of nations and families (hence the NIV's paraphrastic translation, **who enslaved nations . . . and peoples**). The expression is used ironically; while prostitutes and sorcerers usually sell their services to their clients, here it is the *clients*—nations and families—who are being sold by the whore/sorcerer. In other words, even the appealing advantages offered by Nineveh brought a quick demise to her clients. They allied themselves with Assyria because of its power and were betrayed; Nahum announces that they will soon fall under the tyranny of Assyrian imperialism.

■ **5** In vv 5-7 the prophet announces Nineveh's punishment in terms of the prostitute imagery introduced in v 4. The opening phrase, "**Look, I am against you,**" **an utterance of** the LORD **of hosts** appears in 2:13 [2:14 HB] to announce God's punishment against Nineveh. The following words are a first person divine speech, which continues through the end of v 7.

God's first action of punishment is **I will lift your skirts over your face.** The word translated **lift** is from the Hebrew root *glh*, which means "uncover, reveal." In the ancient context of war, this phrase suggests the exposure of nakedness to publicly humiliate captives of war (e.g., Isa 20:3-4). For the shaming of those who were caught in adultery, see Hos 2:3 [5 HB], 10 [12 HB]. The remainder of the verse develops the warning of public shame and humiliation (**I will show the nations your nakedness and the kingdoms your shame**).

■ **6** The public shaming continues in graphic detail, and many contemporary readers may feel uncomfortable with too much information (→ sidebar Feminine Personification and Violence).

The word translated **filth**, *šiqqūṣîm*, is plural, and could be translated literally as "abominations" or **detestable things**. The term is also employed to depict other gods or idols, sometimes due to the detestable practices of their worshipers (e.g., see Deut 7:25-26). The point of the throwing of **detestable things** at Nineveh may once again be to show how poetic justice will be rendered for Assyria's sins. The empire that practiced detestable customs in the name of its gods, including cruelty in warfare, and idolatry, will now be stoned (see Lev 20:2) with detestable things. This includes the images representing Assyrian gods. God's judgment is implied in the threat of treating Nineveh with **contempt**. The shaming of Nineveh by God is made worse because the actions will be a public display: God will **make** it **a spectacle**. This is essentially already stated in v 5 and is repeated here for emphasis.

Feminine Personification and Violence

Nahum 3:1-7 contains many graphic images that contemporary audiences may find disturbing. This is especially the case for the portrayal of violence against Nineveh, personified as a woman punished by God in vv 5-6—a punishment which by today's standards is clearly abusive. If this action were to be portrayed dramatically in current film it would be rated R for graphic nudity and violence.

Although the contemporary reader correctly finds the punishment described in vv 5-6 as morally objectionable and inappropriate in today's contexts, much of it appears to be based on clan law as it was practiced in the ancient world. One of the problems of the informal legal practices characteristic of family law, however, is that it is easy for matters to get out of hand, and for mob violence to break out. Such especially appears to be the case for the actions depicted in v 6, which look more like a lynching than a sanctioned and acceptable legal procedure. Therefore, this practice would be revolting even to ancient readers who were fair-minded or sensitive.

Whether or not invoking disgust in his audience is the prophet's rhetorical intention, one can only speculate. Perhaps Nahum was trying to remind the reader of the extent of the revolting and senseless violence and public shaming formerly practiced by Assyria. Even if that is the case, however, readers have good cause to be uncomfortable with such a portrayal. They have legitimate concerns that the violence in the text may become a contributing factor for some people to justify or accept the demeaning of or physical abuse of women today.

■ **7** This verse concludes the section by anticipating the reaction of those who will be "present" at the judgment of Nineveh. **All who see you** (*kl r'ayk*) contains a link with the previous verses since "spectacle" (v 6) and **see** are from the same Hebrew word and contain the same consonants (*r'y*). Onlookers will **flee**, probably due to the horror of the scene. The city that many found appealing is now appalling. The expression **in ruins** (*šoddēdâ*) is literally *devastated*. The verb appears often in OAN to depict the destruction of a nation or its capital city.

The verse concludes with two rhetorical questions whose implied answer is "no one." The first question is **who will mourn for her?** The word translated here as **mourn** (*yānûd*) is literally "sway, move back and forth, or shake" (the head; see Coppes 1980, 560-61). In similar contexts it indicates a sympathetic action, and so the phrase could be translated *who will sympathize with her*.

The second question, **Where can I find *comforters for* you?**, also implies a negative response. Sympathy and comfort are actions expected from friends in the context of loss and mourning in the ancient West Asian world. Comfort from others not only consoles the sufferer, but also provides the individual with a supportive community during this time of isolation. Nahum anticipates Assyria as an abandoned nation without anyone to come alongside as its comforters. Nahum (*naḥûm*, derived from the root *nḥm*, meaning "comfort"), who announces God's comfort for Judah by saving them from Assyria, sees no comforters for Assyria. Ironically, Nineveh's *lack of comforters* for Assyria signals *God's comfort* for Jerusalem and the people of Judah.

B. Nineveh's Survival Is Hopeless (3:8-19)

1. Like Thebes, You Will Fall! (3:8-12)

■ **8-9** The taunt song of vv 1-7 now gives way to more traditional oracles of judgment. Verses 8 and 9 comprise a unit which initiates a comparison between Nineveh and Thebes, presenting Thebes as well protected and defended city. The comparison begins with the rhetorical question: **Are you better than Thebes?** It is apparent that the prophet expects a negative answer; what the prophet is actually asking is **Will you fare better than** Thebes? Thebes is literally *No Amon*, *nô' 'āmôn*, which is a Hebrew rendering of an Egyptian phrase meaning "City of Amon." Thebes was the primary worship site of the chief god Amon, and the capital of Egypt during several important eras of Egyptian history. Despite its greatness, Thebes fell, ironically, to the Assyrians in ca. 663 BC (see Lambdin 1962, 615-17).

Like Nineveh, Thebes is **situated on** a river (**the Nile**). The Nile, its channels, together with the moats and irrigation ditches of Thebes lend themselves to the picture of the city **with water around her** (Maier 1959, 316). The first half of the next line is literally *so that (her) rampart is sea* (**The river was her defense**). The Nile is called here *sea*, which would be a fitting description of the river at flood stage (Keil 1868, 33). The next half line reads literally, "from the sea (*miyyām*) was her wall." The LXX and other ancient versions vocalized the consonants *mym* as *mayim* (**waters**; MT *miyyām*; see NIV). The resulting phrase, **the waters (were) her wall**, parallels (repeats) the idea found in the first half line, in good Hebrew poetic style.

While v 8 mentions Thebes' strategic defensive advantage, v 9 recounts her many allies. The NIV has conflated the first line, which reads literally, **Cush was her might and Egypt—without end!** Cush (often translated "Ethiopia," see NIV note), located south of Egypt, was the ruling dynasty over Egypt when Thebes was its capital. The country is well known for supplying warriors to various ancient countries, including Judah and Egypt (Sadler 2006, 813-14). The phrase *without end* (→ 2:9 and 3:3) seems to connote the seemingly endless military resources of Thebes' Egyptian allies.

Put and Libya are often interpreted as the same country, since the LXX often translates Put as Libya (e.g., Spronk 1997, 130). It is possible that **Put** is an alternate spelling of Punt, which was located southeast of Egypt (see Maier 1959,

321-22). **Libya** is the area northwest of Egypt. It is mentioned with Cush among the allies aiding Egypt in a battle against Rehoboam (2 Chron 12:3; see Marzouk 2008, 654; for the locations of Punt and Libya see the map in May 1984, 66-67).

The line ends with the phrase **were among *your* allies.** The last word in Hebrew, *b'zrtk*, is literally "your (fem. sing.) help, helpers." Thebes' strong allies virtually surrounded her, which would have given the city a sense of security. Although Thebes was surrounded with water and encircled with formidable defensive forces, none of these advantages were able to save her from defeat. How much more will Nineveh fall, against whom the Lord has declared divine judgment?

■ **10** While v 10 continues to focus on the sack of Thebes, in vv 10-11 the comparison between Thebes and Nineveh becomes direct. The first line in v 10 reads literally ***Even she into exile (went), she went into captivity.*** The verb "went" (*hlkh*) is found in the second half of the line, and implied for the first. Despite Thebes' strength and allies, she was still defeated and her population was taken captive and sent into exile.

The second line of v 10 articulates one of the atrocities of ancient warfare; ***Even*** **her infants were dashed to pieces at every street corner.** This horrific act is mentioned elsewhere in Scripture (e.g., see Ps 137:9). The act was conducted **at every street corner**, perhaps prominent locations in order to horrify and subjugate the defeated citizens (Spronk 1997, 131).

The next line reads, ***over her honored ones* lots were cast.** The ***honored ones*** would be the leading citizens, or **nobles**. These would include the educated, whose skills could be employed in the royal court and elsewhere (note the biblical example of Daniel). For nations casting lots for the possession of captives see Joel 3:3 [4:3 HB] and Obad 11 (see Maier 1959, 326).

The following line completes the picture, ***and all her great ones were bound in fetters***. The **great ones** would be the distinguished citizens, and are probably the same as the **nobles** in the previous line. The custom of binding captives is mentioned often in scripture (see Maier 1959, 326; for binding kings and nobles with fetters see Ps 149:8; see Cathcart 1973, 137). The events depicted here are commonly portrayed in Assyrian literature and on reliefs in the royal palace. The Assyrian relief depicting the capture of Thebes shows men, women, and children being led captive out of the city (see Yadin 1963, 2:462).

■ **11** At this point the prophecy begins to explicitly compare the fate of Nineveh to that of Thebes. There are two comparisons, each introduced with **you too** (*gm't*, the NIV and NRSV do not translate the second one). To bring out the similarity of this expression to the double expression in v 10, the first line of v 11 can be translated as ***even you* will become drunk,** which is a figure of speech for judgment (see elsewhere drinking the cup of God's wrath, which will result in "staggering," or a humiliating (down)fall; e.g., Isa 51:17; Jer 13:12-14 etc.).

The next phrase is difficult to interpret. It is literally ***you will become concealed***. The NIV translation **you will go into hiding** (cp. NRSV) is questionable.

Maier suggests that the expression means that Nineveh will be hidden or "buried" "beneath ruins" (Maier 1959, 330).

The next line reads *even you will* **seek refuge from the enemy.** Nineveh is depicted as a refugee seeking shelter. The population of the city will not be able to rely on the fortifications of Nineveh, but will instead need to find protection elsewhere. Nahum 1:7 uses the word for **refuge,** *mā'ôz,* to describe the security found in the Lord by those seek protection from God on the day of adversity. Reliance upon God would be Nineveh's only hope, but Nineveh will continue in her violence and self-sufficient idolatry to the bitter end. In 1:2 and 8 God's enemies are those whom God pursues in judgment. Since Nineveh is God's enemy it cannot depend on God and will not find refuge from its own enemies.

■ **12** If it is not already evident to the reader from what has been said thus far in Nahum, v 12 states it unequivocally: the demise of Nineveh will be the fall of the entire Assyrian nation. All Assyrian strongholds (**All your fortresses**) will share Nineveh's fate. Although it is possible to interpret the meaning of the term **fortresses** (*mṣbrym*) to be Nineveh's defense system, the context suggests that these are fortified cities spread throughout the land (→ v 13; the Targum translates *mṣbrym* as "cities" both here and in v 14). The **fortresses** are likened to **fig trees with their first ripe fruit.** This first ripe fruit or yield (*bekkûrîm*) of the early season is especially desirable. Because early fruit receives more of the tree's strength, it is often larger and tastier. Maier observes that first ripened fruit usually falls more easily from a tree, and so might be obtained by shaking the tree rather than picking. In this passage the extended figure of the **shaken** tree, the falling of choice **figs,** and the eager **eater** suggests the instability or quick fall of Assyrian fortresses and their resources. This includes their wealth, fortifications, provisions, armaments, and troops (cp. Maier 1959, 332-33).

2. Your Preparations Will Fail, You Will Be Consumed! (3:13-17)

■ **13** This verse begins a new literary unit with the prophet mockingly taking the role of a Ninevite sentinel (vv 13-17). Some interpreters regard the line, **your troops** *are women in your midst,* as a statement about the population literally being **women,** the men having been dispersed or killed in war (e.g., Floyd 2000, 74). The alternative view is that the phrase indicates military weakness, since women were not typically war heroes—Deborah and Jael being notable exceptions (see Judg 4). The translation **weaklings** is a contemporary equivalent. For unknown reason the NIV omits the words *in your midst.*

The words in the next poetic line are literally *to your enemies are wide open* the gates of your land. The phrase **gates of your land** is a figure of speech for access to the land or especially the approaches to Nineveh (Keil 1868, 36-37). Some interpret this as referring to the gates of Nineveh; Robertson suggests the gates were left open by fleeing citizens (Robertson 1991, 119-20). Most countries protected accessible approaches to their territory with fortified outposts. City walls were protected by an elaborate gate complex. For these gates to be **wide open to your enemies** indicates the country and capital city's vulnerability to attack.

The final poetic line in the verse continues references to weakened defenses through accessible gates; **fire has consumed *your gate* bars**. As is often the case in prophecy, the certainty of the event is underscored by presenting it as if it had already occurred (the prophetic perfect). The gates themselves were usually made of wood, although the bars that secured them were sometimes made of iron or bronze (e.g., 1 Kgs 4:13; Isa 45:2). Since the gate is usually the last barrier holding back an invading army, having a gate or its bars burned is a sign of weakness and defeat (see Jer 17:27; Neh 1:3; 2:3). Ironically, the Assyrians are depicted as burning the gates of Thebes when they conquered it (Yadin 1963, 462). The image of consumption by fire indicates God's judgment against adversaries in 1:6, and specifically against Nineveh in 1:10.

■ **14** Verses 14-15a taunt Nineveh to prepare for a battle that will ultimately be futile (cp. 2:1-9 [2:2-10 HB]). Verse 14 contains a series of commands addressing Nineveh. The first recognizes one of the most important preparations for a battle, **Draw water for the siege**. This command is emphatic, it reads literally, "water for the siege draw for yourself." Note Ahaz's apparent concerns over an insecure water supply when Jerusalem was facing an impending attack (Isa 7:1-3) and his son Hezekiah's resolution of the water supply problem by constructing a water tunnel into the city (2 Kgs 20:20). Nineveh's water supply was dependent upon canals which could easily be cut off by an enemy; and not all the water that ran through the city was potable (Maier 1959, 339-40).

The next phrase, *ḥzqy mbṣryk*, is literally **strengthen your *fortresses*** (or possibly "fortifications"). When the Assyrians marched against Jerusalem in the eighth century they systematically attacked and destroyed the fortified cities that could possibly come to Jerusalem's aid, Lachish being the most well-known (Aharoni and Avi-Yonah 1977, #154). Perhaps the prophet envisions a similar scenario for the march on Nineveh. In view of v 12, the translation *fortresses* is preferable, although in this verse "fortifications" or **defenses** is possible.

The next two parallel lines read literally, ***Go into the mire and tread on the clay***. Potters and brick makers would sometimes work clay with their feet (see the Egyptian depiction of brick making in *ANEP* 115). The verse ends with the command, ***Seize the brick mold***. The term translated *seize* (*ḥḥzyqy*) is literally "make strong, strengthen," and is from the same root as **strengthen** (*ḥzyqy*) at the beginning of the verse. Nineveh is told to strengthen the country's fortresses by working clay into the bricks that will be used to repair and strengthen the defensive structures. The irony is that Nineveh's efforts to strengthen itself will prove futile in the face of God's judgment.

■ **15** The irony of the call for defensive measures is underscored by the next phrase, **There the fire will consume you**. The word **there** indicates that where Nineveh should be the strongest, that is, at the very place where it is strengthening defenses, would be the point at which the defenses would be breached (similarly

Kimchi, cited in Rosenberg 1988, 2:254; Keil 1868, 37). Judgment by **fire** is very common in the prophets and is found often in the BT (e.g., see Amos chs 1-2). The verb **consume**, from the root *'kl*, usually connotes eating food. But it is also employed figuratively of either the burning of **fire** or destruction by the sword (e.g., Deut 32:42; Nah 1:10; 2:13 [14 HB]). **Consume** is a key term in this section. It appears in vv 13 and 15, and underlies one aspect of the locust imagery that continues through v 17.

The next phrase, **the sword will cut you down,** continues the depiction of war against Nineveh. While swords may literally **cut,** there is probably a pun on the verb since it often connotes the "cutting off" of a people, name, etc., from existence and memory (cp. Nah 1:14, 15 [2:1 HB]). So the translation **cut you *off*** is probably required here (cp. NRSV). It is noteworthy that references to burning, consumption by sword, and being cut off are also found in 2:13 [2:14 HB].

The following phrase is in apposition, literally translated, **the sword will cut you *off, it will consume you* like *the young locust.*** Locust imagery appears several times in this and the following verses, but the figure of speech seems to change. The destructive nature of large swarms of locusts and grasshoppers renders them, like fire, an apt symbol of God's consuming judgment (e.g., Exod 10:3-20; Joel 1-2; Amos 7:1-6; cp. Rev 9:1-12). Like the **fire** mentioned above, *locusts* will completely destroy what they **devour.** The NIV translates the root *'kl* as both **consume** and **devour** in this verse, emphasizing the complete consumption or destruction of the city.

Although the locust imagery continues, it is common to assume that v 15*b* introduces a new section. The prophet once again taunts Nineveh regarding the futility of its preparations; *Increase* **yourself** like *the young locust.* The verb *increase* (NIV **multiply**) is found twice in this verse. The Hebrew verb *hitkabbēd* (from *kbd*) literally means "make yourself heavy". The root often has the extended meaning of "honor, glory, wealth" (→ 2:9 and 3:3). Here, the prophet taunts Nineveh to try to resist the enemy that would consume the city like locusts by multiplying like young locusts and thus match the enemy's resources.

The next phrase repeats the taunting command: *increase yourself* like the *migratory locust.* The exhortation is ironic; usually large swarms of locusts cannot be resisted. In the context of this judgment oracle, v 15*b* conveys the idea that Nineveh's *kābôd*, neither her past wealth or greatness, nor her future attempts to "increase" her defensive resources, will save her.

■ **16** The locust imagery continues into vv 16-17. Nineveh's possible future efforts to save herself through "increase" are shown to be futile by a comparison to past efforts and results. **You have multiplied your merchants till they are more than the stars of the sky.** The phrase **you have multiplied** (*herbēt*) is possibly a pun on locusts (*'arbeh*) in the previous line. There is alliteration and assonance by repetition of *r, b* and the *e* in the final syllable (BDB lists the two words as related to the root for the word *rbb*, "to multiply"). The prophet has moved to a description of Nineveh's *past* multiplication of resources and present situation. Due to its limited resources, the Assyrians had two means of sustaining themselves, either through trade or war. **Merchants**, therefore, were as necessary for the country's survival as were soldiers. **The stars of the sky** is a standard phrase for an uncountable multitude (see e.g., Gen 15:5). The imagery indicates Assyria's merchants literally spread out like stars in the sky throughout the empire to conduct trade to benefit their country.

The next phrase is difficult to interpret; literally it reads, "a young locust strips and flies away." The NIV understands this phrase as an implicit comparison, so it inserts the word **like** at the beginning for clarification. The NIV also clarifies the meaning of the phrase by inserting the words **the land.** Nineveh's merchants are like **locusts** or an invading army that greedily **strip** the resources of other countries; then when everything is gone, they **fly away** with the resources they amassed to enrich Nineveh. Verse 16 implies that Nineveh's wealth would not stave off God's judgment; in fact, it only hastens God's judgment because of her impoverishing of other countries by removing their resources.

■ **17** This verse concludes the series of images relating to locusts that began in v 15. The word translated **guards** (*mennezārîm*) is found only here. In the parallel phrase the word **officials** (*ṭpsrym*) appears only here and Jer 51:27. Verse 17*a* compares Nineveh's guards and officials to **swarms of locusts that settle *on* the walls on a cold day.** They **settle in**, literally "encamp on" (*ḥnh b-*), stone walls on an overcast day since the rocks would absorb heat and would be warmer than the ambient temperature. Once the **sun appears** through the clouds, *they flee*. Here the reader expects the locusts to hop or **fly**, but the imagery applies more to the royal officials than the locusts. Indeed, as Luther observes, one expects an army to encamp against an enemy, but here the officials camp in a convenient warm place only to flee in fear (Luther 1525b, 314).

Nineveh is warned here that the government system that Assyria relied upon in the past—whether part of the organizational infrastructure or associated with the military—would disintegrate at the first sign of trouble for the city. As soon as it seems more advantageous for the officials to be elsewhere they will *flee* from the city and disappear without a trace. The tables will once again be turned, for Assyria had often boasted that their enemies fled at the approach of the Assyrian troops (see Maier 1959, 345).

3. You Will Have No Helpers, the King's Wounds Are Mortal! (3:18-19)

■ **18** Verses 18-19 are a mock dirge that concludes this section and the entire book of Nahum. Although there are grounds for interpreting this unit as depicting the aftermath of the fall of Nineveh, the position taken here is that this passage continues to deal with the same issue taken up in vv 8-17, that is, any defensive preparations taken by Nineveh and Assyria will be futile.

Verse 18 offers some problems to translators. The opening line is literally, **Your shepherds slumber, O *king of Assyria, your nobles stay put*"** (NIV rearranges the word order). The phrase **your shepherds slumber** is clear, although its meaning is disputed. The term **shepherds** is commonly used metaphorically to connote protection, and thus connotes leaders and rulers (e.g. Isa 44:28; Jer 3:14). Since "sleep" is sometimes a euphemism for death in the OT, some see here a reference to the death of the leaders in battle (e.g., see Maier 1959, 357). The view adopted here is that the **shepherds** are lax in their responsibilities; that is, they are asleep at the job.

The **king of Assyria** has been addressed earlier in Nahum (1:14), although this is the first time he has been explicitly mentioned. The word translated here as **nobles** occurs in 2:5 [2:6 HB]. The verb in the last line is *yiškēnû*, which means "they reside, inhabit, dwell, stay put" (see *HALOT*). Since it is parallel to "they slumber," this verb is interpreted in the NIV as (they) **lie down to rest** (see *BHS*). The LXX understands the verb in this way, and reads *you [the king of Assyria] have put to sleep your mighty ones*. The issue is that Assyrian leaders are failing to execute important tasks.

The second half of v 18 indicates that the people of Assyria (**Your people**) **are scattered on the mountains** because of the failure of their leaders. **Your people** (*'mk*) probably has the more specialized sense of *your troops*, as in v 13. The NIV **scattered** is based on reading the Hebrew *nāpošû* (from a rare verb *pûš*) as *nāpoṣu*, "they are scattered, dispersed" (see *BHS* and *HALOT*). The image of an absent shepherd and scattered flock is common in the OT (1 Kgs 22:17; Jer 23:1-2; Ezek 34:5; Zech 10:2; 13:7). If the officers were not asleep on the job, they could have acted to prevent this situation. Instead, *there is* **no one to gather** the irresponsible troops. The picture developed here is similar to 2:5 [2:6 HB]. In both passages the king of Assyria is unable to defend the city because of the ineptness of his military. In this verse the officers have fallen asleep on the job while their troops have gone AWOL, seeking refuge in the mountains. The city is in trouble both from her enemies without and weakness from within (Floyd 2000, 75). The king is left alone to defend his city, and its fate is sealed.

■ **19** This verse continues to address the king of Assyria (see v 18, and **your** and **you** in v 19). The first phrase in the opening line seems to read literally, "there is no quenching your wound." While the meaning of the verbal root *khh* is usually connected with extinguishing a flame, in this context the unique noun form (*kēhâ*) could mean "alleviation, relief, assuagement, lessening." It is probably best to translate the line as *there is no relief* for your wound. The word for **wound**, *šeber*, often appears in lament contexts where the wound is identified as the judgment of God (e.g., Jer 10:19; Lam 2:11; 3:48; cp. Longman 1993, 828).

The next half of the line is literally, *incurable is your blow*. The word *blow* (*makâ*) often occurs with the term **wound** and with similar meanings (e.g., Jer 10:19; Mic 1:9). In summary, the situation for the Assyrian king, and by extension Nineveh and Assyria, is likened to a fatal injury (see NIV **your wound is fatal**). As elsewhere in Nahum, this blow is referred to as if it were a past event, underscoring the certainty of its fulfillment. There will be no recovery after God's judgment, the prophetic word announces with certainty the beginning of the end.

The next phrase, **All who hear the news about you** reminds the reader of 3:7, "everyone who sees you." However, v 19 is directed to the king of Assyria and v 7 toward Nineveh. Others will now spread the news of the Assyrian king's downfall, and the hearers will *clap hands over you*. This indicates rejoicing, often at a victory over or release from an enemy by God (see Ps 47:1 [2 HB]). As the Judeans would resume proper worship of the Lord in Jerusalem at the news of Nineveh's fall (2:1 [2:2 HB]), so the nations would rejoice over their freedom at the news of the king's (and Nineveh's) demise.

We have already noted how the previous line reminds the reader of 3:7. Likewise, the rhetorical question in the last line is contextually similar to the question in v 7. *For over whom has not passed your evil continually?* The implied answer is, of course, "no one." The statement supplies the reason why all will clap their hands in celebration. Just as there will be no one to lament the fallen city (v 7), so will there be no one who will not rejoice over the fall of the Assyrian king. The intergenerational evil deeds of the Assyrian monarchy have caught up with the king. There will be no allies in his time of need; on the contrary, everyone will rejoice at the demise of his wicked reign, for it means freedom from his constant evil.

Before closing this section of the commentary, one more observation should be made. It has been observed that only two books of the Bible end with a rhetorical question, Nah 3:19 and Jonah 4:11 (Glasson 1969/70, 54-55). Both are in the BT, and both focus on Nineveh; but their meanings contrast greatly. In Jonah, the prophet has been *unjustifiably angry* because God spared Nineveh when **they turned from their evil ways** (Jonah 3:8)—a repentance led by the king of Nineveh (Jonah 3:5-9) and based on the possibility that God might **turn and relent** (Jonah 3:9). In response, **God relented regarding the evil** God planned to do to them (Jonah 3:10) and instead showed mercy, compassion, and relentless love (Jonah 4:1-2). The book ends with God responding to angry Jonah by asking the prophet (and the reader!) whether or not *God should be compassionate toward Nineveh* since it contains so many people and animals.

In Nahum, where the subject has been the fall of Nineveh, the prophet Nahum (speaking on behalf of God) *justifies universal rejoicing at God's judgment on the Assyrian king* because of the *unceasing evil* that he and Assyria (Nineveh) have been perpetrating. In Nahum it is clear that the judgment is deserved; indeed one meaning of the name "Nahum" is "relent, change" and could signal that God has again relented concerning the fate of Nineveh. While Nineveh did fall under God's judgment for its relentless evil, Jonah asks readers of the BT to consider the divine alternative: this is not God's only response to sin—God may choose to act out of relentless love and spare sinners, even toward a Middle Eastern empire and its great tyrant.

We conclude with a few implications from the text. First, *violence is ultimately disturbing to the Creator, whose ultimate goal is shalom.* As much as God's people would like to revel with Nahum in the vindication of creation and the overthrow of the tyrant, they must not dwell too long on that thought. The violence depicted in Nahum is contextual—it does not reveal God's ultimate plan, nor is it to be imitated by God's people. There remains something sad and disturbing in the demise of a people and even the overthrow of a tyrant; and that must not be forgotten as Nahum is appropriated as scripture.

God is the Creator who judges all peoples equally. God's people must examine themselves and not be content to congratulate themselves that they are not Nineveh (Goldingay 2009, 40). In the Scriptures, the judgment threatened against Nineveh by one prophet is a mere echo of the judgments threatened against Jerusalem in others. Nineveh is called a city of blood and a prostitute, an imperial power that preyed on *outsiders*; yet Jerusalem is portrayed in similar terms as its rich and powerful prey on the weaker among *its own people* (e.g., Isa 1:21-31; Zeph 1:4-18; see Goldingay 2009, 37-38.) It should be noted that Nineveh is condemned for its sins, not for its lack of election. Likewise, the election of God's people will not save them when they practice the same type of greed, oppression, and disregard for others that the non-elect practice.

As later onlookers of God's judgment on Nineveh, we should have the same reaction of horror and disgust when we see such sins practiced, no matter who commits them. Whether it is a matter of actions perpetrated by nations, godless sinners or God's people, all are ultimately accountable to the Creator for injustices against God's creatures. *God is not pleased with those who prey on others; it does not matter who the predator is.* No amount of past good deeds or heartfelt experiences will atone for abuse of power against the weak of God's creation.

God calls people to bring divine blessing on creation, not enrich themselves at the expense of their neighbors. God called Israel to be source of blessing for the families and nations of the world. Its multiplication "as the stars of the heaven" was to enrich others with God's blessing (Gen 12:3; 18:18; 22:17-18; 26:4; 28:14). By contrast, Assyria's multiplication of troops and merchants (3:15-17) preyed upon Earth's creatures and deprived others of the Creator's gifts (3:4; see also 2:12 [2:13 HB]). Instead of a blessing they brought a curse upon the world. Such multiplication not only preyed upon others, but eventually hurt Assyria as its merchant class took only for themselves and consumed their own country (3:16). It is the same today; excessive consumption or hoarding of global goods not only hurts others, but will hurt the nations and economic systems that perpetrate such injustice. As in Nahum's day, such activity stands under divine judgment.

God must remove unrelenting evil because of the damage it does to others (3:19, etc.); but God's unrelenting love is always an option open to God (Jonah 4:11). Nahum and Jonah should be read side by side for a balanced perspective on God's mercy and judgment. It is interesting to note that in the Greek canon Nahum is found immediately after Jonah. The historical critical view is that the prophecies of Jonah were written later than Nahum and were meant to offer a corrective to Nahum's judgment oracles (e.g., Glasson 1969-70, 54). This is an important point to consider, for while the believer is often quick to rejoice when divine justice is served, the same believer hopes that God will be merciful in times of personal and community need. There is hope for all who repent, even the perpetrators of unthinkable evil.

Regardless of which book was composed first, from a canonical perspective Nahum appears *after* Jonah (in both the Hebrew and Greek canons), and when read this way a different message must be considered. God can be merciful to the repentant sinner, but even then, the sinner who relentlessly continues to perpetrate evil (Nah 3:19) frustrates even the mercy and patience of God (Nah 1:2-3). While Jonah is a testimony that God may "relent" regarding judgment (Jonah 3:10), Nahum is a warning that God may also relent regarding formerly granted mercy. Divine grace is always unmerited, yet it demands human transformation as its result. The individual or community that receives pardon then continues to live destructively has taken God's grace for granted and is in danger of incurring the full weight of divine judgment.

As mentioned often in this study, Nahum's warnings of judgment against Nineveh and Assyria are tacit warnings to those who imitate Assyrian policies—including those most accountable to God, God's people. Those who bask in God's grace can easily take God for granted and forget that if they produce the works of the flesh rather than the fruit of the Spirit that they have no part in God's kingdom (Gal 5:16-26). In other words, one message for the believer who reads Jonah and Nahum together is that the possibility of divine grace is always there, even to the most wicked outsiders, but the prospect of divine judgment is also present, even for the closest insiders.

HABAKKUK

INTRODUCTION

A. Historical Setting and Date of the Book

The book of Habakkuk can be placed historically by its reference to the Chaldean threat (→ 1:6-17). This is our only clue for its date since the book lacks the customary formula dating the prophecy to one or more king's reign (e.g., Hos 1:1; Zeph 1:1). The Chaldeans were a Neo-Babylonian tribe, which in 626 BC exerted enough pressure on Assyria to weaken its control over its West Asian vassals, including Judah (→ Introduction to Nahum). During this time King Josiah of Judah was able to gain some independence from his Assyrian overlord and institute a series of religious and social reforms based on Deuteronomy (2 Kgs 22-23).

In 612 BC the Neo-Babylonians, under Nabopolassar, defeated the Assyrian capital of Nineveh, thus fulfilling the prophecies of Nahum. But now this new world power began threatening the West. In 609 BC Josiah was killed in his attempt to stop Pharaoh Neco II of Egypt from defending what was left of Assyria from Babylon (2 Kgs 23:29-30). Neco was not successful, although he retained enough power to temporarily hold sway over Judah to appoint Jehoiakim as king (r. 609-598 BC; see 2 Kgs 23:31-37).

The Neo-Babylonians dealt Egypt a crushing blow at Carchemish in 605 BC and Babylon (now under Nebuchadnezzar) quickly gained complete control over the West the following year. Nebuchadnezzar asserted sovereignty over Judah and its neighbors in several campaigns. Jehoiakim initially submitted to Babylon, but after a few years rebelled, hoping for help from Egypt. This was a mistake and shortly afterwards Babylon plundered Jerusalem (597 BC), deposed the Judean King Jehoiachin (son of the recently deceased Jehoiakim), and placed his uncle Zedekiah (r. 597-586 BC) on the throne (2 Kgs 24:1-20; briefly recounted in the Babylonian Chronicle, see *ANET* 563-64). At this time the first deportation of Judean citizens to Babylon occurred (2 Kgs 24:10-17). A second, much more comprehensive deportation took place in 586 BC when the Babylonians destroyed Jerusalem after Zedekiah rebelled (2 Kgs 25:1-21; Bright 1981, 313-331).

This was an era of hardship for Judeans, as the corrupt Judean leaders oppressed their subjects while Babylon imposed a heavy tribute. The events outlined above also coincide with the activity of Jeremiah, who confirms that this was a time of syncretism and mistreatment of the weak.

As we will see in the commentary, Habakkuk is familiar with the ruthless nature of the Chaldeans (i.e., Neo-Babylonians, see Hab 1:5-8, 12-17), which would probably place the prophet after 609 BC when they began to threaten the West. Where Habakkuk is specifically dated among the events outlined above depends on the identity of the wicked of 1:4 (see a summary of various views in Dangl 2001, 139-44). Another factor is whether the entire prophecy is an extended dialogue that takes place at a single time, or whether the book follows the usual pattern for the formation of prophetic writings and represents prophecies delivered over a more extensive period.

For reasons that will be more fully developed at various points in this commentary, it appears that the wicked in ch 1 are initially powerful individuals in Judah, but after God reveals to him that the Chaldeans will be agents of divine judgment, the prophet condemns both wicked Judeans and Babylonians. The unjust situation condemned in 1:2-4 and 2:6-19 is, at times, not only similar to those perpetrated under Jehoiakim but also resembles those committed under Nebuchadnezzar (2 Kgs 23:36-37; see Jer 7:5-10; cp. 7:1 and 26:1). Although one cannot be certain, it is possible that the prophecies found in 1:2-11 were originally uttered in Jehoiakim's reign and shortly after, probably with time gaps between prophetic address and divine response. In these words the prophet is fulfilling his role as intercessor, asking God for relief from injustices under corrupt Judean leaders.

Once the Babylonians began to assert increased pressure on Judah, the second complaint and response in 1:12-2:5 and the woes of 2:6-19 may have been added to the collection of prophecies, with the first two chapters serving as a liturgy for a public fast. According to the Hebrew text of Jer 36:9, such a fast occurred during the ninth month (December) in the fifth year of Jehoiakim (the LXX reads the eighth year, → below). This fast would have taken place in 604 BC, as Nebuchadnezzar began to invade Palestine, moving Jehoiakim to switch allegiance from Egypt to Babylon (2 Kgs 24:1). This would be an appropriate setting for uttering these oracles, although it does not preclude them from being repeated later under Zedekiah.

The background of 3:17-19 indicates agrarian losses, which can be partially attributed to the abuses noted in the rest of the book, including oppressive policies of corrupt leaders and a Babylonian invasion. But the agricultural problems appear to have been worsened by a drought (Margulis 1970, 438-39), which may be the same one mentioned in Jer 14:1-13. Jeremiah 14:11-12 presumes that the people have called a fast in response to the drought. It is conceivable that the lament comprising Hab 3, or even much of Hab 1-3, was recited (again) by the prophet at that time. Jeremiah does not give a date for this fast, but it might have taken place in 601 BC, while Jehoiakim was a Babylonian vassal. This date is derived from the LXX dating of the fast of Jer 36:9 (the Hebrew places it in the fifth year, → above), which places a fast in the eighth year of Jehoiakim.

Alternatively, it is possible that the two textual readings reflect two fasts, the Hebrew giving the date for the first, and the LXX the date for the second. The LXX might have incorrectly associated a later fast with the events recounted in Jer 36. For the views presented here see especially Holladay, although he argues for only one fast, which he determines occurred on the eighth year, according to the LXX date (Holladay 2001, 123-130).

It is possible that ch 3 may have originally been spoken before some of the material in chs 1-2. Since most laments end with a vow to praise God, the hymnic motifs and vow to praise of ch 3 commended it as a fitting conclusion to the prophecy, whose first two chapters contain the prophet's complaints and intercessory laments with divine responses. The final form of Habakkuk contains material dated before 586 BC since there is no indication in it that Nebuchadnezzar had already destroyed Jerusalem, nor any mention of the exile. Habakkuk was probably compiled before that date, although nothing precludes a final version drawn up shortly afterwards. For more on the historical context see the final section of this introduction and the commentary.

B. The Prophet

As mentioned earlier, the book of Habakkuk, like Nahum, lacks a customary dating formula in the first verse. Nor does the book mention anything about the prophet's background. Unfortunately, the prophet's name sheds no light on the identity or function of the prophet. It is unlikely that the name can be traced to a Hebrew root, despite past attempts to do so (Andersen 2001, 88-89). Habakkuk is probably derived from an Akkadian (Assyrian) word for a plant (Noth 1928, 230-31). Since the seventh century BC was a time of Assyrian vassalage and influence, it would not be unusual to find Assyrian names among Judean citizens.

The earliest reference we have to the Prophet is in one of the second century BC Greek Apocryphal additions to Daniel—Bel and the Dragon (see 1:33-39). The superscription of one textual tradition of that book reads, **From the Prophet**

Habakkuk, son of Joshua, from the tribe of Levi. The first century AD Jewish work, *The Lives of the Prophets*, retells the story with some additions in 12:1-13, but states that Habakkuk was from the tribe of Simeon. It also identifies him as coming from Bethzouchar, probably a village near Bethlehem (see Hare 1985:393-94). The sources of these authors' information are unknown.

C. Habakkuk's Prophetic Role

The prophet's role can only be reconstructed from the contents of the book. The author of Bel (→ above) may have ascribed a priestly lineage to the prophet by an ancient independent tradition, or it may have been an educated guess based on the contents of the book.

Many interpreters associate Habakkuk with the temple priests or cultic prophets due to the complaint and divine response sequences in 1:2-2:5, Habakkuk's call for silence before the Lord in the temple (2:20), and the hymnic conclusion in ch 3, which resembles temple liturgical material. The latter also contains a psalm-like superscription (3:1) and postscript (3:19*b*), which includes directions for playing it on stringed instruments (see Keil 1868, 48). Chronicles refers to temple singers whose activities were sometimes called prophetic (1 Chr 16:4-6; 25:1-9). Furthermore, it is not unusual for prophets to have a priestly background, as is the case for Jeremiah, Ezekiel, and possibly Joel and Zechariah (Jer 1:1; Ezek 1:3; Joel 1-2; Zech 1:1).

D. Literary Features of Habakkuk

The book of Habakkuk, in its final form, is a unified composition. The superscription identifies the book as a *maśśā'*, commonly translated "oracle," but perhaps better translated "pronouncement" (→ Nah 1:1). Pronouncements or oracles are prophetic answers to people in the community who raise questions concerning God's actions. The prophet attempts to clarify God's activity in current events and instructs how humans should respond to God's acts (see Weis 1992, 28-29). Three prophetic books are designated as oracles in their superscriptions—Nahum, Habakkuk, and Malachi. That oracles can take a number of forms or genres is evident in Nahum, which is predominately an Oracle against the Nations, a form only faintly attested in Habakkuk.

As mentioned above, the book of Habakkuk may have evolved over the course of several years. Yet at the final stage of development it is an extended lament. Although it does not strictly follow the usual structural elements of a self-contained psalm of lament (or complaint, see Gerstenberger 1988, 12), the prophecy functions in a similar manner. Since prophets used a number of forms to serve their rhetorical purposes, it is possible Habakkuk borrowed from temple literature to convey his message. However, that does not mean that all (or even any) of the book was performed as a lament in the temple (Petersen 2009, 641). Yet, the abundance of material at home in a ritual setting and the nature of the prophecy as a whole suggest otherwise. The situation reflected in the prophecy implies that the way through the crises at hand is a public response in the form of a lament, in which the faithful follow the example of the prophet in ch 3.

We suggest that the prophecy may have served as a liturgy during the early stages of the Babylonian crisis, which was exacerbated by a drought. The lament elements include complaints (1:2-17; 3:2-19; see Floyd 2000, 85). Within the complaints we find reports of divine oracles (1:5-11; 2:2-5); there are also expressions of confidence (2:6-20; see Sellin-Fohrer 1968, 454; also → 3:3-15) and anticipation of praise (3:17-19). For another proposal regarding the lament form of the entire book see Haak 1992, 11-22.

Since the final written form of the prophecy appears to be a unity, divisions are somewhat artificial. But for literary purposes, it is helpful to split the prophecy into three major divisions comprising the Dialogues, Woes, and Psalm. First, the prophecy begins with an interchange between the prophet and God. Habakkuk's struggle over the apparent injustices of God (1:2-2:1) comes to a turning point when God promises to reveal a vision which will resolve the matter and assures that the current oppression by the wicked over the righteous will ultimately be corrected (2:2-5). Second, the prophet then expresses his confidence that the wicked will fail in a series of woes (2:6-20). Finally, he concludes with a lament psalm (3:1-19), which has strong hymnic characteristics with its extended expression of confidence and anticipation of praise.

E. Reading Habakkuk in Its Historical Literary Contexts

The message of Habakkuk is derived not only from its historical context, but also from its literary context in BT. There is an important interplay between these contexts. Looking at the historical context, we see that Judah's submission to Egypt and then Babylon came quickly upon the heels of an optimistic age. Under Josiah, an early version of Deuteronomy was rediscovered in the temple and he attempted to lead the nation in a wholehearted commitment to the Mosaic Torah. Idolatry was suppressed, worship was centralized in the Jerusalem temple, and justice was pursued for the oppressed (2 Kgs 22-23; Jer 22:15-16; see Deut 12). According to the precepts of Deuteronomy, Josiah's reform had promised the Judeans that those who lived by Torah would be blessed by God (e.g., Deut 7:12-16; 11:26-28).

Yet, Judah's hopes were quickly dashed when Josiah was killed in 609 BC (2 Kgs 23:28-30). Why didn't God allow such a righteous person to continue to promote the Torah of God? Where was the long life he was promised (2 Kgs 22:18-20)? To make matters worse, under Jehoiakim the righteous were oppressed by the wicked (e.g., Jer 22:13-17). Why did not God, according to the Deuteronomic Torah, curse the wicked and bless the righteous? (see Deut 28). These questions, which challenge the justice of God, seem to lie behind the first section of Habakkuk. But the divine response seems worse than the problem: God will use the

Chaldeans to deal with the wicked! This seems to raise more questions than it answers and furthers the perception that the God of Israel is arbitrary and unjust.

Reading Habakkuk after Nahum only sharpens the problem. It seems that Judah has hardly any time to celebrate their liberation from Assyrian oppression promised by Nahum before God communicates through Habakkuk that Judah will now be conquered by Babylon! For further discussion on the canonical and historical interplay between Nahum, Habakkuk, and Zephaniah see Introduction to Zephaniah.

Another context to consider for the message of Habakkuk is the prophecies of Jeremiah, whose ministry overlapped Habakkuk's. A key element in Jeremiah's message was that God was bringing a nation from the north, identified as Babylon, to punish Judah for their persistent sin (e.g., Jer 1:14-16 and elsewhere). Judah's best course was to submit to Babylon for God's discipline until their time of release was granted by God (Jer 21:8-10; 27:1-22; 29:1-14). This was not a popular message, and Jeremiah received opposition for it (e.g., Jer 1:16-19; 28:1-4). Jeremiah sometimes prophesied in Jerusalem, at times in the vicinity of the temple (e.g., Jer 7:1-14). It is possible that Habakkuk's revelation concerning God bringing Babylon against Judah was influenced by encounters with Jeremiah.

The two prophets offer an important contrast in their message regarding judgment. Jeremiah emphasized how much Judah deserved this judgment due to their lack of repentance and the sovereign right of the Lord to do this. Habakkuk, on the other hand, was concerned about God being implicated with an evil nation and knew that when God's judgment took place many innocents would suffer—some of the same folk on behalf of whom the prophet was interceding in 1:2-5. It would be easy to picture Habakkuk as being among those who challenged Jeremiah's message! Although these two prophetic viewpoints appear worlds apart, the fact that both prophecies have been preserved in the canon testifies to the contextual suitability of each message. While it is appropriate to affirm the need for God to judge evildoers and evil structures in society, God's people must never forget that the guilty and innocent are inextricably bound together in communities, and it may not be possible to judge the wicked without harming the innocent. That being the case, God's judgment should not be too quickly requested or celebrated without concern and intercession for the inevitable demise of the innocent. Habakkuk is testimony to the appropriateness for God's people to challenge such divine judgment—no matter how deserved it may appear to be for some. These themes will be further developed throughout the commentary.

F. Message of Habakkuk

The overarching theme of Habakkuk is the enduring faithfulness of God despite all circumstances. The Lord is faithful, even when God's beneficence is not evident in contemporary events (2:4; 3:16-19). The entire book is built on the prophet's attempt to come to grips with this and accept that God is not neglecting the suffering people of God. We will look at a few of the important themes that emerge out of this struggle. For a more detailed discussion of Habakkuk's message see From the Text sections in the commentary.

Habakkuk teaches that *sometimes God does not match our expectations and the usual human solutions or easy answers may not work.* Habakkuk relies on time honored *torah* traditions (→ 1:4) that indicate that the Lord hears the cries of the oppressed and marginalized and will act on their behalf (1:2-4; see Exod 22:21-27 [20-26 HB]; Deut 24:14-15). The prophet finds out that these traditions do not always guarantee that the Lord will act immediately for suffering individuals. People are caught up in larger social networks and communities, and their lives are often intertwined with the lives of others. Sometimes widespread harm will occur if God were suddenly to deal with the powerful few who are causing others to suffer. God's work often has a more comprehensive aim that individuals or small communities may not perceive.

Another aspect of this is that God's faithfulness does not depend on the moment by moment blessings of earthly prosperity for God's people (3:17). Rather, God's faithfulness is the assurance that God has in view a positive outcome for all of creation (as indicated by the prophet's invective against its abusers in 2:8 and 17).

Related to the discussion above is the fact that sometimes God's ways of dealing with evil are difficult to understand and may even contradict what the faithful perceive as being appropriate for a holy God (1:13). God seldom intervenes directly in human affairs. Rather, the Lord often works through processes and human activities that are already at work. Consequently, God's actions are conveyed through weak and sinful humans. Stated even more boldly, God's works are often caught up in the ambiguous, evil, and even idolatrous ways of the world (1:5-11, 15-17).

This appears inconsistent to the human mind, which wants to jump to the conclusion that if God does not stop evil deeds, or if the Lord's works somehow result through them, that God must therefore somehow approve of evil and evil doers—as the prophet implies in 1:12-17. Yet, that is not the case; the Lord is not pleased with evil doers and they are still liable for their conduct. They may get away with their misdeeds and may even prosper now, or perhaps unwittingly accomplish God's will when they intend otherwise (cp. Isa 10:5-7). Yet, Habakkuk's woes (2:6-19) and final petition (3:16) indicate that ultimately evil doers will be held accountable, despite the fact that the Lord seems to be doing nothing about them now, nor in the immediate future (cp. 1:5).

Finally, it is evident that the book of Habakkuk emphasizes *the importance of prayer and praise* (→ Literary Features of Habakkuk above). From beginning to end Habakkuk is a book of prayer. The book opens with the prophet addressing the Lord, while referring back to his past prayers (1:2-4). The book closes with a lament (3:1-19); in fact, as indicated earlier, the entire book can be characterized as a prayer of lament or complaint.

The book is therefore instructive for the prayer life of later believers. In Habakkuk, prayer is presented as a way to address God in times of uncertainty. Habakkuk's prayers are a dialogue with God as the prophet struggles to understand the ways of the Creator. God answers the prophet's protests (1:5-11; 2:2-5) and the prophet questions God's ways (1:2-4, 12-17) and awaits further responses (2:1; 3:1, 16). The book concludes with the prophet trusting in God's faithfulness based on traditional teaching (or *torah*, → 1:4) about God's past faithfulness (→ 3:2-15).

In other words, prayer is characterized as a give and take dialogue that alternates between addressing God, listening to God, arguing with God, and accepting what appear to be partial answers for the present and delayed promises for a brighter future. The book of Habakkuk shows that prayer affirms faith in God, a trust in God's faithfulness even when God is seemingly absent or is doing things that make little sense on a human level.

Habakkuk also offers insight regarding *the appropriateness of praise during challenging times.* We have seen above that prayer during difficult times is not a blind trust, which too quickly assents to heartbreaking suffering. Similarly, genuine praise of God is difficult in the midst of a harsh present with the prospect of a bleak future. The prophet's honesty and struggle to understand and accept God's will indicate that sometimes such conflict is the unavoidable path to praise. We learn from Habakkuk that often genuine praise is possible only after such conflict is addressed. Only then can the child of God praise God for what is promised (e.g., Hab 2:4) by affirming God's commitment to deliver the world from evil (2:6-20) and by exalting the Lord in the midst of disappointment (3:3-15). In summary, Habakkuk exemplifies that prayer and praise often entail a struggle to understand and accept that the Lord's intentions for the entire creation are gracious.

COMMENTARY

I. WHY IS LIFE SO UNFAIR? COMPLAINTS AND RESPONSES: HABAKKUK 1:1—2:5

BEHIND THE TEXT

This division of the book likely reflects events from the reign of Jehoiakim (609-598 BC), who rejected the Deuteronomic reforms of his father Josiah (2 Kgs 22-23; cp. Jer 26:1-6 and 7:1-16). The prophet's cries against injustices (1:2-5) fit this era. After Josiah was defeated and killed by Pharaoh Neco, the latter imposed taxes of gold and silver under Jehoahaz (who reigned for three months), then under Jehoiakim, whom the pharaoh placed on the throne as a puppet king (2 Kgs 23:31-37). No doubt the poor and small land owners bore the brunt of these taxes as local leaders bled them dry to pay their assessed portion. Furthermore, Jeremiah indicates that Jehoiakim was condemned for costly building projects funded by fraud and withheld wages, for ignoring justice for the poor, and for oppression, violence and bloodshed (Jer 22:11-17).

99

It is possible that some of the prayers in Habakkuk may also be dated, or were reused, after Nebuchadnezzar invaded Judah (598 BC) and conquered Jerusalem (597 BC). The prophet's protest that God has not responded to his prayers (see 1:2) suggests that the complaints included here are samples or extracts from previous prayers. Such persistent prayers may suggest that the prophet was performing a regularly appointed prophetic duty in the Jerusalem temple. This is supported by observation that the contents of this division are similar to complaints found in the psalms, which were uttered on behalf of others by priests or cultic prophets. Some of these psalms include divine responses, like those reported in Habakkuk (e.g., Pss 12, 14, 50, 60, 85).

Although the present form of this division appears to be a dialogue, in its original life setting there were likely gaps between God's response in 1:5-11 and the prophet's complaint in 1:12-2:1. In the latter passage it appears that the prophet has a clearer view of Babylonian atrocities and that he is disappointed that God's promise to work through them (1:5-11) does not mean executing selective judgment on the wicked among Judah. Indeed, it appears that the whole nation, wicked and innocent, suffers under Babylonian policies. It is therefore possible that Habakkuk's second complaint (1:12-2:1) could be dated as late as the reign of Zedekiah (597-586), after Babylon's initial intervention in Jerusalem and the deportation of some of its citizens (cp. Hiebert 1996, 638).

This continuing dialogue testifies to an extended complaint process different from what might be suggested by a quick reading of the lament psalms in the book of Psalms. It is likely that many of these psalms are compact stylized representations of an extended process of seeking God's help and waiting faithfully for a satisfactory answer. While these prayers often include complaint, petition, confession of trust in past divine help, confession of confidence, a divine response, and anticipated thanksgiving in a compact form (Gerstenberger 1988, 12), it is likely that this sequence did not always occur in one prayer, but developed over an extended period. This is the case in Habakkuk, where after repeated complaints the prophet is exasperated over God's apparent unresponsiveness to his earlier prayers. That the entire book of Habakkuk could be conceived as a lament, or complaint form (→ Introduction to Habakkuk), suggests that in some cases the prayers of complaint went on for years before coming to a divine resolution.

This literary unit falls naturally into the following parts. The superscription (1:1) constitutes the title of the book. The remainder of this section is made up of two prophetic complaints and God's (reported) response. The prophet's first complaint focuses on the injustices of the wicked against the righteous within Judah, for which he considers the Lord responsible (1:2-4). The divine response to Habakkuk's complaint is an announcement that God is beginning to raise up the Babylonians as a means of judgment (1:5-11). God's answer occasions a second complaint, in which the prophet essentially protests that this is theologically inconsistent since it implicates a holy God in wrongdoing (1:12-2:1). Behind this complaint is almost certainly the prophet's awareness of the many innocent lives that suffer under such a sweeping judgment.

IN THE TEXT

A. Superscription (1:1)

■ 1 The first verse is the superscription, which serves as a title and identifies the contents of the book. Some recent interpreters claim that this superscription identifies only the first two chapters as an "oracle" (traditional translation of *maśśā'*, see NRSV; NIV **prophecy**), with the third chapter having its own superscription (e.g., Sweeney 2000b, 2:459-60). Yet such a partial coverage for a superscription would be unusual, even though the term oracle is sometimes used within a prophetic book to delineate a section (e.g., Isa 13-17; Zech 9, 12).

The books of Nahum and Malachi are also identified as an "oracle" in their superscriptions. Even the double superscriptions (1:1 and 3:1), each containing the prophet's name, is not unusual—Isaiah has three! (Isa 1:1; 2:1; and 13:1). A comparison to other prophetic superscriptions suggests that Hab 1:1 serves to introduce the entire book (see Tucker 1977, 57-68). (→ Nah 1:1 for comments on *maśśā'*, which is translated "oracle," **prophecy**, "burden," *pronouncement,* etc.)

The *pronouncement* is further described as one that Habakkuk . . . *saw* (**received**) (cp. Isa 13:1). Although the word *saw* (*ḥāzâ*) sometimes connotes a prophetic vision, here it more likely indicates a revelation from God. The term *ḥāzâ* and its cognate noun, *ḥāzôn*, "vision, revelation," designates something that can be written down (see Hab 2:2, "revelation").

For the name **Habakkuk** see Introduction. Habakkuk is called **the prophet** (*nābî'*); this is the first time the term *nābî'* occurs in a prophetic superscription. This is one of several terms that described prophetic individuals in ancient Israel. The term most likely means "called one" (see Blenkinsopp 1996, 26-30). The term "prophet" also designated paid professionals who mishandled God's word (e.g., Isa 9:15 [14 HB]; Jer 5:13; Ezek 13; Hos 9:7; Mic 3:11, etc.). Authentic prophets often adopted the term "visionary, seer," suggested by the root *ḥzh* in the superscriptions (v 1). Hence, the reference to Habakkuk's **prophecy** as something *he saw* is meant to undergird the divine authority of his message.

B. Why, O Lord, Do You Tolerate Injustice? (1:2-11)

1. Habakkuk's Complaint Concerning Success of the Wicked in Judah (1:2-4)

■ 2 In this unit, the prophet raises a complaint regarding community injustices and the Lord's failure to act (vv 2-4). **How long?** (*'ad-'ānâ*) expresses frustration over a refusal of another party to respond. Psalm 13:1-2 [2-3 HB] uses the phrase four times as a cry against God for his failure to respond to previous pleas. However, such cries are primarily rhetorical; the faithful are not necessarily requesting a specific timetable, rather, they are attempting to secure divine assurance that God hears the cries of the faithful and will soon act to deliver them when it seems that God has failed to respond for too long (see Andersen 2000, 108-109).

Here Habakkuk complains directly to the LORD because he has persistently called **for help** but God does **not listen**. The prophet is crying on behalf of others who are victims of violence, oppression, and injustice (→ vv 3-4 and Behind the Text). It is generally expected throughout the Bible that the Lord hears and answers prayers of the distressed (Pss 34:15 [16 HB]; 145:19). But at times it seems that God does not respond to one's prayers and it is a cause for complaint against God (v 2*a*; see Job 24:12; Ps 18:41 [42 HB]; Lam 3:8). The Hebrew verb for **listen**, or "hear" (*šm'*), like its English counterpart, often carries the meaning of response, such as "listen, obey, pay attention, etc." Here **listen** is clarified by its parallel term **save** (→ below).

This second part of the verse is still governed by the phrase **How long?** found at the beginning, so Habakkuk essentially says *(How long) will I cry out to you?* The term **cry out** (*z'q*) is sometimes found on the lips of the suffering as they pray to God (Lam 3:8; Pss 107:13; 19; 142:1 [2 HB]). Habakkuk cries out to God "**Violence!**" This is a key term in the book; the prophet uses it six times (1:2, 3, 9; 2:8, 17 [twice]; Armerding 1985b, 500). Although the word *ḥāmās* can mean a "wrong" in general (e.g., see Gen 16:5), here it probably connotes physical violence, since Habakkuk uses it with that sense elsewhere (1:3, 9; 2:8; 17(twice)).

The prophet complains that the Lord does **not save** though he cries out for help. The Hebrew verb for **you . . . save** (*tôšîaḥ*) connotes rescue or deliverance from enemies or other external troubles, and should not be interpreted as salvation in a spiritual sense. Habakkuk hopes to motivate God to put an end to the **violence** he is decrying (Sweeney 2000b, 2:462-63).

■ **3** The prophet here begins a second set of questions introduced by **Why?** (*lāmmâ*)—a term often used to introduce accusations in individual complaints (e.g. Pss 10:1; Jer 15:18; see Roberts 1991, 89). **Why do you make me look at injustice?** The prophet here accuses God of making him **look at** crimes. The verbal root *r'h*, used in **you make me look at** (or *you show me tar'ēnî*), is sometimes found in prophetic vision reports (see Amos 7:1-9; 8:1-4; 9:1-4). But Habakkuk is not reporting a vision, rather he uses *you show me* ironically; he does not think that God is responding according to expectations. The fact that God can *show* Habakkuk **injustice** and yet do nothing to stop it is incomprehensible to the prophet. The term *'āwen* (**injustice**), can also be translated as "iniquity, wickedness, trouble." Those who destroy community through their unjust practices incur God's judgment (e.g., see Isa 10:1; Prov 6:12-15). Once again, since the situation is counter to conventional expectations, the prophet is essentially challenging the Lord concerning why the expected divine judgment has not appeared.

The prophet continues the interrogation of the Lord with **Why** (implied, see Roberts 1991, 89) **do you tolerate wrongdoing?** The word translated **you tolerate**

102

(*tabbîṭ*) is literally "you look at." The word sometimes has the nuance **regard favorably** (e.g., 1 Sam 16:7). Once again, when the Lord looks upon an unjust situation it is expected that God will act to set it right (e.g., Ps 33:13), *not* regard it favorably, as the prophet accuses.

In the second line of the verse the prophet gives examples of the **wrongdoing** that he sees. The terms **destruction and violence** are also found together in Jer 6:7; 20:8; Ezek 45:9; and Amos 3:10 (Keil 1868, 56). **Destruction** (*šōd*) in this context denotes oppressive actions committed by the powerful against the weak and poor (see also Prov 21:7; Jer 6:7; Ezek 45:9). Habakkuk has already declared that he is shouting out **violence** without any response from God (v 2). By saying they are **before me**, the prophet reiterates here that **destruction and violence** are unavoidably a part of his regular experience.

The prophet now gives more specific examples of how the violence takes place, **there is strife, and conflict abounds. Strife** is a translation of *rîb*, which could also be rendered "dispute, quarrel." **And conflict abounds** translates the difficult phrase *ûmādôn yiśśā'*. The verbal root *nś'* usually means "lift up"; this phrase could be translated here as **and disputation arises. Disputation** can be interpreted as quarrelling or contentiousness (e.g., Prov 6:14), but it is also found in lawsuit contexts (e.g., Jer 15:10). The context here suggests that the powerful use corrupt legal processes to exploit the weak.

■ **4** In this verse the final statements by the prophet in this unit characterize the general situation. **Therefore *torah* is paralyzed.** The Hebrew idiom *'al- kēn*, **therefore** (see also 1:16, 17), indicates a result of a previous situation; because God is failing to answer cries for help and correct community injustices (see vv 2-3), the situation is getting worse (Roberts 1991, 90).

The word **torah** (*tôrâh*), is often translated **law**, but *tôrâh* is a much more comprehensive term. It literally means "teaching, instruction" and includes both oral and written teaching about God's acts of salvation (God's gracious deeds) and instruction in how to live as a result of God's acts. Commandments and warnings concerning the consequences of disobedience are only one aspect of *torah* (see Sanders 1976, 909-11). Habakkuk was active shortly after the rediscovery of Deuteronomic Torah (→ Introduction to Habakkuk), which clearly tells Israel that their obedience to God's commandments are motivated out of God's prior love for Israel (e.g., Deut 24:17-22; see Braaten 2000, 825-26). Habakkuk is concerned here about the degeneration of Judean society after the death of Josiah, when other gods were once again worshiped and, consequently, the Lord's commandments concerning how to treat others were forgotten (cp. Jer 7:5-7; 22:13-19). Because leaders do not implement the justice commanded in Torah (→ below) and the Lord fails to respond to violence, corrupt lawsuits, and disregard for God's commandments, **torah** is ineffective or **paralyzed**.

One reason **torah** is ineffective is because **justice never prevails. Justice,** *mišpāṭ*, often connotes the restoration of social relationships and is applied primarily to protecting the innocent and marginalized from powerful oppressors (e.g.,

Deut 16:18-20; see Bennett 2008, 476-77). The phrase **never prevails** is literally "continually does not come forth"; the last phrase *(lō-yēṣēʻ)* could be rendered as *not issued*. The **justice** expected of God's redeemed people in everyday activities and court cases (v 3) is lacking. Injustices would also be one form of the violence that Habakkuk decries in vv 2-3.

The next phrase is literally *because* the wicked *surround* the righteous *(be-cause, kî*, is untranslated in the NIV). The terms **wicked** *(rāšāʻ)* and **the righteous** *(hāṣṣaddîq)* often connote the **guilty** and **innocent** in a dispute or court case. Habakkuk portrays a situation where **the wicked**, or *the guilty*, have control of the community, so that **the righteous** do not have a chance for a fair hearing. The image of the wicked surrounding the righteous occurs several times in the psalms (e.g., Pss 17:9, 11; 22:12 [13 HB]). The expectation of the faithful, however, is that they will be protectively surrounded by God (Pss 32:7; 125:2).

The last line, *therefore (so that)* justice is perverted, states the negative consequence of the power the wicked have over the righteous. The last phrase is literally "comes out bent/crooked." The term "comes out" (omitted in the NIV) is a translation of the same term rendered *issued* above. The prophet states that **justice is *continually not issued* (*lō-yēṣēʻ*);** but when it *is*, it is *issued* (*yēṣēʻ*) **crooked.** Although this may be the same thing stated in different ways, it is also possible that the prophet is envisaging two situations: one in which the innocent request justice and they are ignored, and the other would be the rare instance that a complaint is actually heard in court and then corrupt judges automatically rule in favor of the wicked.

When justice is lacking in the gates where courts were typically held (see Amos 5:10-15), cases could be appealed to higher courts. Such **justice** was to be administered by God through the king, appointed judges and Levitical priests (Deut 16:18-19; 17:8-11). Israel was assured that if human justice was withheld, that the Lord would uphold it and punish the guilty (Deut 10:18; 16:20). Again, the irony of the situation is that not only is the Lord not intervening to uphold justice as expected, but also that this lack of intervention has apparently emboldened the wicked and made the situation worse (cp. Ps 94:3-7).

It appears from vv 2-4 that the prophet has first-hand experience with the injustices of Judean society. Moreover, he seems to hold the Lord accountable for putting him in such a position, for God has "**made**" him "**look at**" them (v 3). It seems that one of the prophet's assigned roles puts him in a position to directly see injustices and a corrupt legal system. If Habakkuk were a Levitical priest (→ Introduction), he would be responsible for teaching *torah* and justice (Deut 17:8-11; 33:10) and, perhaps, assist in court cases. When called upon to do this the prophet found a completely corrupt system that he was apparently powerless to change.

2. The Lord's Response: Horrible Events Will Challenge Judah's Faithfulness! (1:5-11)

■ **5** The next unit (vv 5-11) contains the Lord's response to Habakkuk's complaint in vv 2-4. Some interpreters claim that this is closer to an oracle of judgment, and so does not function as an answer to the prophet's lament in vv 2-4 (e.g., Hiebert 1996, 634-35). Admittedly, this is not the usual oracle of salvation, or expected type of response, as indicated by Habakkuk's complaint in vv 12-17. It must be noted, however, that nearly every oracle of salvation includes an element of judgment since deliverance of the righteous necessarily means judgment of the wicked. Habakkuk had petitioned for God's judgment on the wicked, and that is what God promises to do here. Ironically, God's salvation, or judgment on the wicked, will have negative consequences for the whole community, and this is one of the issues the prophet will continue to engage through the end of the book.

God begins to answer the prophet's complaint with some of the same words Habakkuk directed at God. The entire response uses plural verbs and pronouns, indicating it is addressed to the people and not just the prophet. **Look . . . watch** are the two terms used by the prophet in v 3 when the prophet asked why the Lord showed him injustice and tolerated wrong. These two verbs are plural imperatives, which might be literally translated "you all look . . . you all watch." **Look at the nations** suggests that the people are to consider what is happening on the international scene to answer their questions about God's response to local issues. What the people will see will be so completely unexpected that they are commanded to **be utterly amazed** (or **utterly horrified**) literally *horrify yourself (and) be horrified* (*whtmhw tmhw*). Isaiah 29:9 uses the same expression to describe a people who are incapable of understanding the Lord's work (see Andersen 2001, 142-43). The verbal sequence *see . . . be horrified* is also found in Ps 48:5 [6 HB] to describe the consternation of kings who are unable to besiege the divinely protected Zion (Jerusalem). Here the situation will be reversed (Robertson 1990, 145), with Judah *horrified* at how easily Babylon defeats kings and fortified cities, which would presumably include Jerusalem (see v 10).

For (*kî*) introduces the reason for the people's horror. **I am going to do something** can be literally translated either as "a work is working" or *[I am] working a work*; the LXX adopts the latter. The similar expression in Ps 44:1 [2 HB] supports the LXX. Either way, it is understood from the context that the work is God's (cp. Floyd 2000, 104). The Lord's work (*p'l*) can either bring benefit or judgment (→ 3:2), depending on what God deems is needed at the time. The words **in your [plural] days** connote that the divine action that Habakkuk and the righteous have been awaiting is about to break forth.

The final phrase of this verse expands the thought of the first line: *you will not respond in faith when you are told* (*l' t'mnynw ky yspr*). In worship and instruction God's people are **told** about the Lord's past remarkable deeds of salvation, which inspires faith in God's ability to save in the present and a continuing faithful response by the hearers (e.g., Pss 9:1 [2 HB]; 44:2 [2 HB]; 73:28). The situation is reversed here; the prophet tells the people that the Lord's future work will *not* inspire faith! Unfortunately, if the Lord is going to act swiftly against the wicked as the prophet demands (see vv 2-4), then innocent bystanders will be caught up in the aftermath, only further weakening their faith in God (→ From the Text).

In summary, this verse challenges the faithful to look among the nations as an example of what God is doing there and will soon be doing among the Judeans. As the following verses unfold the nature of this work, it becomes evident why it would be problematic to attribute it to the Lord (→ sidebar God's Judgment through Foreign Nations) and subsequently result in a loss of faith. The correction for this unintended consequence will be taken up in 2:2-5, but first the people must prepare for the impending crises (1:6-11, 15-17).

■ **6** Why God's work will not inspire faith is now revealed: ***For* I am raising up the Babylonians** (literally ***Chaldeans***). This people established the Neo-Babylonian empire that quickly displaced the Assyrians and conquered West Asia and Northern Africa (→ Introduction). The opening phrase could also be translated ***For I am about to raise up*** (*ky hnny mqym*). When dealing with Israel, God usually raises up (*mqym*) or appoints judges, priests or prophets within Israel (see Goldingay 2009, 57). Habakkuk announces God's work is about to be accomplished by outsiders, **the *Chaldeans***. This is unexpected, but not unheard of.

God's Judgment through Foreign Nations

Jeremiah, a contemporary of Habakkuk, also announced God's use of a northern invader, eventually identified as Babylon (Jer 4:6; 5:15-17; 25:9; 27:6). Earlier, Amos 6:14 spoke of God "raising up (*mqym*) against you a nation" (NRSV), which proved to be the Assyrians, something also announced by Isaiah (see 5:26-30; 10:5-6). The use of other nations or foreign rulers to accomplish divine purposes for God's people is directly related to the notion that God is the Creator who governs the whole creation (Jer 27:5-15). It would be wrong, however, to understand that God is *causing* any nation to carry out earthly destruction. In this world, nation will always rise up against nation (Mark 13:8)—they do not need divine motivation. A more appropriate view is that God can at any point declare any present or impending destructive act as working divine judgment (→ From the Text).

The next phrase is in apposition to the previous phrase, and further defines their character: **that ruthless and impetuous *nation***. This literally reads, "the bitter and hastily acting nation." "Bitter" (*hammar*) can also be translated here as *fierce* (*BDB*, see 2 Sam 17:8). To be **impetuous**, or to ***act hastily***, suggests that the Babylonians act quickly, before their anger or fierceness subsides.

The phrase **who sweep across the whole earth** is literally ***who walks the broad places of the land***. The Hebrew word for **broad places** is *mrhbym*, which elsewhere figuratively indicates "safe pasture(s)" (e.g., Hos 4:16; Ps 18:19 [20 HB]).

Ironically, here it means the opposite, since it is where the Chaldean nation *seizes* **dwellings not their own**. The word *seizes* (from *yrš*) sometimes has the connotation of "take possession, dispossess" of an inheritance or an enemy's land (see BDB). The Israelites dispossessed the Canaanites when they occupied the land, Babylon will do the same to Judah. This may suggest that Judah has forfeited their use of God's land like the Canaanites of old.

Dwellings (*miškānôt*) often poetically represents tents or houses (Num 24:5), or the pasturage of wild animals (Job 39:6). But it can also connote the space(s) that the Lord inhabits in the temple (Pss 43:3; 84:1 [2 HB]]). Since it is not specified which **dwellings** are being dispossessed, perhaps all are in view here. The words *not his own* form a wordplay; they are homophones in Hebrew (*lō' lô*). The phrase indicates that the Chaldeans are overstepping their assigned boundaries (Deut 32:8). Although occupied by various peoples, technically all lands and everything within them belong to the Lord (Ps 24:1). The Creator is free to redistribute creation to whomever God wills—even to a fierce conqueror like Babylon (see Jer 27:4-8). This is certainly a horrible work in the eyes of God's people! (v 5).

■ **7** The description of the Chaldean (Babylonian) nation, begun in v 6, continues throughout the remainder of this section, ending in v 11. What is said here indicates that they are already conquering other lands, so that the "raising up" of them that God is about to do (v 6) relates chiefly to how this empire will deal with Judah.

This nation is *dreadful and awe-inspiring* (*'āyōm wĕnôrā'*). The term translated *dreadful* (NIV feared) is rare. The second term **dreaded** is literally "feared, fearful" and can connote something that inspires life-threatening terror (as the desert in Deut 1:19). But it sometimes expresses the awe or respect due the Lord's person or works (e.g., Exod 34:10; Deut 7:21).

The next phrase picks up some vocabulary that appears in the prophet's complaint in 1:3-4. Translated literally, it reads "from himself his justice and his lifting up come forth." *His justice . . . comes* (*mšpṭ ... yṣ'*) duplicates the expression found twice in v 4, there translated *justice . . . issued*. The meaning of the second term, *śĕ'ētô*, "his lifting up," is difficult. It is usually understood as connoting self-promotion (**promote their own honor**; e.g., Gen 49:3). The term used here could be shorthand for the expression "lifting up the voice," or *pronouncement* (→ 1:1 and 1:3). If *pronouncement* is understood as "legal decree(s)," then it forms a hendiadys with *justice* at the beginning of the line and is also a link with the prophet's complaint about the broken legal system in vv 3-4. The Israelite understanding of justice and law originated with God. By contrast, Babylonian justice is self-determined; it is *from himself* (*mimmennû*)—placed at the beginning of the sentence for emphasis in the Hebrew. The NIV **they are a law to themselves** conveys this idea.

Although God has designated Babylon to accomplish divine purposes, Babylon seems to know nothing of this and only serves its own interests (see the similar situation with Assyria in Isa 10:5-14). Yet, if God has chosen the nation to promote justice, Habakkuk's audience may rightly wonder how this divine oracle or "pronouncement" (v 1) addresses the concerns raised in vv 3-4 and hope for further clarification. But it does not come; the negative portrayal of Babylon only worsens as the description further unfolds.

■ **8** This verse compares the Babylonian cavalry to animals of prey—only the Babylonians are worse! The images in this verse share the idea of sudden, swift attack from a great distance. Their "dreadful and awe-inspiring" nature mentioned in the previous verse is developed here. The horses they ride are **swifter than leopards,** *and quicker* than wolves—animals proverbial noted for their fierceness. **Leopards,** like other large felines, are feared for their swiftness and stealth. They are sometimes used to symbolize nations who quickly conquer large territories (Dan 7:6; Rev 13:2; McLean 2000, 801). West Asian **wolves** attack their animal prey at night (NIV **dusk**).

The term translated **cavalry** (*pāršû*) appears twice in this passage and can connote either horses attached to chariots, riders, or horsemen (as below, see *HALOT*). The word for **gallops** (*pāšû*) is literally "frisk," which connotes unrestrained joy in Mal 4:2 [3:20 HB]. Here it might be interpreted as celebration of victories in the battlefield (see Jer 50:11). The term **headlong** is an interpretive addition in the NIV; it is not found in the Hebrew.

The next phrase probably begins a new sentence (cp. NRSV). *His* **horsemen come from afar** is congruent with the following imagery of the **eagle**, which circles high above, **swooping** quickly on its prey. The text literally reads *he flies* like an eagle, *quickly* to devour. Like **an eagle** Babylon will attack swiftly, plundering the land and leaving very little behind. This imagery occurs elsewhere as a figure of God's judgment against nations (Jer 48:40; 49:22) or of divine judgment against God's people through other nations (Deut 28:49).

■ **9** **They all come intent on violence** indicates Babylon's objective, which is literally *for violence he comes* (*lḥms ybw'*). See the similar depiction of the Assyrians in Isa 10:7. The prophet had earlier complained about the **violence** (*ḥms*) that he saw among his own people (Hab 1:2, 3), now the Lord tells him that the nation being sent to correct the situation is thoroughly committed to **violence**! This is certainly not what the prophet and the oppressed among Judah are waiting to hear. Since the Lord is raising them up, then it would be hoped that they would come to correct injustices.

The imagery for the destructive Babylonian troops now shifts from animals of prey to a windstorm. The next phrase (*mgmt pnyhym qdymh*) contains problems and is difficult to translate (see NIV note and the commentaries). The word **hordes** (*mgmt*) appears only here and is sometimes translated as *all of.* One possible literal rendering of the remainder of the expression is "their faces are forward" (cp. NRSV). The translation *their faces* **like a desert wind** is a plausible rendering with strong support from the versions (see *bhq*, Brownlee 1959, 19-20). The versions and Qumran commentary understood the word *qdymh* to be *qdym*, "east wind" (without the final -*h*). God's judgment, or agent of judgment, is depicted as an east wind elsewhere (e.g., Jer 18:13).

108

The verse concludes with *he* [Babylon] ***gathers captives like the sand,***
which means they are innumerable. Those who survive the "animals of prey" are
carried away captive, like sand picked up by the desert winds (cp. Luther 1525a,
113). The possibility of Judah becoming "captives like sand" is ironic—the sign of
Israel's promised blessing to become like the "sand of the sea" (e.g. Gen 32:12 [13
HB]; 41:49) now signifies judgment (cp. Baker 1988, 54).

■ **10** This verse emphasizes the fearlessness and invincibility of Babylon. ***He
mocks kings, and rulers are laughable to him***. The NIV uses plural subjects **they**
to clarify that the Babylonians are in view. ***Laughable*** is a translation of the noun
miśḥāq, "object of laughter, derision." The verbal form is found in the next line, ***at
every fortified city he laughs*** (*yiśḥāq*). A walled city is no barrier, Babylon simply
piles up dirt and conquers it, as the text literally reads. The feminine pronoun *it*
probably refers to ***fortified city*** (*mṣbr*).

This verse attests the well-known practice of attacking armies, who **by
building earthen [siege] ramps** approach and batter down or scale high city walls
(e.g., 2 Sam 20:15; 2 Kgs 19:32; for Assyrian ramps see *ANET* 288). The image
of piling up dirt is probably connected to the wind-swept sand depositing dunes.
Since captors often forced prisoners of war to build siege ramps (as noted by Sweeney 2000b, 2:466), the picture begun in v 9 is completed: the captives, swept up
like dust by the wind, are deposited at city walls where they become (builders of)
siege ramps, perhaps against their own people.

Powerful rulers and massive fortifications present no challenge for Babylon.
While the verse is making a general statement about the strength of the Babylonian troops, the prophet and his audience would not have failed to make an
application to their own community, for Jerusalem was a fortified city where the
king resided. Furthermore, since the policies of the Jerusalemite king and his officials were responsible for the violence and injustices about which the prophet
complains (→ vv 2-4), a conquest of Jerusalem is apparently God's answer to their
prayers. But this can hardly be the solution that they had envisioned!

■ **II** The first part of this verse is difficult to interpret. It could be translated
literally as ***then he sweeps past, a wind, and he passes through***. The expression ***a wind*** is probably to be understood as a metaphor, that is, **like a wind**. This
continues the wind imagery begun in v 9. The use of *ḥālap*, ***sweeps past***, perhaps
suggests the image of a gusty windstorm (Isa 21:1) that passes through quickly. In
other words, Babylon conquers a city, then quickly moves on to its next victim.

The verb for ***passes through*** (*wayya'ābōr*) often connotes passing through a
land and is also found with *ḥālap* in Isa 7:8 to depict Assyrian troops like a flood
sweeping over Judah. The root *'br* also sometimes carries the meaning of "pass
beyond a boundary," in the sense of "overstep, transgress," and may have a double
meaning here. The Masoretic editors of the Hebrew text may have had this in
mind when they punctuated the text so that the first half of the verse reads ***and he
crosses over he transgresses and he becomes guilty*** (*wē'šm*). The MT makes good

contextual sense. The verb *wĕ'šm* can also be taken with the next phrase, however, and read *he becomes guilty, whose strength becomes his god.*

Verses 10-11 bear some resemblance to Isaiah's description of the proud Assyrians who self-sufficiently scoffed at world powers (Isa 10:8-14, see Roberts 1991, 97). The dialogue has now come full circle, the prophet began by calling on the Lord, the covenant God of Israel; it concludes with reference to a nation whose God is its own might. What is implicit in the description of Babylon as a violent nation determining their own "justice" is now made explicit: they are guilty of self-worship, or idolatry. This immediately raises a theological problem with the recipients of this word: how can the God of Israel use such a blatantly sinful, un-just and idolatrous nation to correct injustices among God's own people? Are not the agents of judgment guiltier than those being judged?

C. Why, O Lord, Are You Inconsistent with Yourself? (1:12—2:5)

1. Habakkuk's Complaint Regarding Success of Babylon (1:12—2:1)

■ 12 This verse begins a new section. The first unit of this section (1:12-2:1) contains a further complaint by the prophet, possibly occasioned by God's contro-versial response to the first complaint (1:5-11). But it is likely that there has been an intervening period during which the predicted judgment has occurred through Nebuchadnezzar's intrusions into Palestine and Jerusalem, and that the prophet is reacting to its effect on the innocent of the land. The prophet is attempting to persuade the Lord to find another way to settle problems among God's people that is more consistent with the divine character and purposes. This section concludes with the prophet's report of the Lord's response (2:2-5).

The opening rhetorical question, **Are you not from everlasting?** (or *from days of old?*), is not just an abstract theological confession about God's eternal nature. Rather, it evokes the long history of God's salvific purposes for Israel, of-ten rehearsed during temple worship (e.g., Pss 74:12; 77:5 [6 HB]; cp. Hab 3:2). Habakkuk appeals to his relationship with God as prophetic intercessor by the personal references to the LORD as **My God, my Holy One. Holy One** is a com-mon epithet for God, and is especially popular in Isaiah (e.g., Isa 1:4; 5:19 40:25 and elsewhere). As the **Holy One,** God is categorically different from humans and has the power to deliver from trouble when humans are helpless (see Hab 3:3). Because of God's holy character and covenantal relationship to Israel (**my God**)—which includes God's saving purposes for Israel—Habakkuk asserts that *we* **will never die** (NIV note). Though the ruthlessness of the divinely appointed Babylonians makes the extinction of Israel a distinct possibility, the prophet finds hope for the future of the nation in the holy character of God. The NIV "**you** [God] **will not die**" (also NRSV) follows an old scribal tradition that lacks ancient and contextual support.

The next line is literally, LORD, *for justice you* have appointed *him*. This refers to the Chaldeans (i.e., Babylonians), who are referred to with a collective singular ("him") throughout 1:6-11. Habakkuk uses the word *justice* (*mšpṭ*) in his complaint in 1:4, where he twice decried the lack of fairness in Judean society. God's answer in 1:7 occasions a problem since it suggests that Chaldean violence is its own brand of self-serving justice. Habakkuk is apparently articulating here what he thinks is implied in God's troublesome response: that the violence of Babylon is being used by God to correct injustices in the world, including among God's people.

Rock, like **Holy One**, is an ancient title for God (various Hebrew terms are used). It suggests divine protection and deliverance (Deut 32:4; 1 Sam 2:2; Ps 18:3 [4 HB]; see Patterson 1991, 163). **You** and **my** before **Rock** are not in the Hebrew text, although they may be implied from the previous lines. This last line of the verse repeats the thought of the previous line. Literally, it reads *for correction you have established him*. *Correction* (*hôkîaḥ*) can also be rendered "rebuke, chasten, mediate justice" (see BDB and *HALOT*). In legal contexts it can connote the determination of what is right (Amos 5:10; Isa 29:21; see Liedke 1997, 542-44). **Justice** and *correction* suggest that God's work would put Judah back on the right path. But instead it appears that it is about to make Judah **die** (→ above). It seems to Habakkuk either that the goal of God's use of Babylon to "correct" Judah will be their destruction or that Babylon has gone beyond its charge (see Isa 47:5-6; Driver 1906, 73; Bruce 1993, 853, and others).

■ **13** The first part of this verse bears a resemblance to Habakkuk's complaint in 1:3. The phrase **to look on evil** (*mr'wt*) probably suggests *to look favorably upon* or *accept evil* (see Amos 5:22). The prophet continues, **and to look at trouble** (NIV **wrongdoing), *you are not able***. The first half of this expression is found in 1:3 in nearly identical words (*'āmāl hābbîṭ*). As mentioned there, the verb can have the meaning of **tolerate**, *regard favorably*. In this context, the prophet is saying that as the Holy One who has determined to save Israel, God is **too pure** (*ṭĕhôr*) to tolerate either the Judean powerful or Chaldean *evil* against the faithful—to do so would suggest that God is impure or unethical.

By saying that God is **too pure** to look favorably upon *evil* and *trouble*, of course, implies that it seems like this is exactly what God is doing! This is now made explicit with the question **why then do you tolerate** or *regard favorably* the **treacherous?** —another use of the verb *hābbîṭ* (→ above). **Treacherous** is literally *treacherous ones*, the plural may indicate that Habakkuk has both the wicked in Judah and the Babylonians in view.

In the next line the why is implied, it is carried over from the previous line. **Why are you silent while the wicked swallow up *the [one] more righteous than himself?*** The singular is used again suggesting that the Chaldeans are in view. When the faithful suffer, God is expected to act and not be **silent** (e.g., Pss 35:22; 39:12 [13 HB]). As mentioned above (→ v 4), the term **righteous** can have the connotation of *innocent* in a legal proceeding. The picture is similar here and little has changed since the first complaint. Whether it be unrighteous Judean leaders or Babylon, the **wicked** still *surround* (v 4) or **swallow up** (v 13) the **righteous.**

It is possible to interpret this verse as the prophet's protest that even sinful Judah is *more righteous than* wicked Babylon, or that all nations that Babylon oppresses are righteous by comparison (Andersen 2001, 183). But it makes better contextual sense to view this as congruent with his earlier complaints: since Babylon will not bring selective justice against the sinful in Judah, the **righteous** within Judah will still suffer, only now under Babylon (→ 2:4). God's action through Babylon may bring an end to unjust Judeans, but it will still **swallow up** the **righteous** on whose behalf Habakkuk is praying. Like Abraham of old, Habakkuk appeals to God's sense of justice on behalf of the innocent ("righteous") who will perish in God's sweeping judgment against the wicked (Gen 18:23-33). **Swallow up** (*bl'*) is ironic since Israel confesses that the Lord's actions swallow up God's and Israel's enemies (Exod 15:12; Ps 21:8-10 [9-11 HB]; Isa 25:7-8; see Robertson 1990, 161). Unless God reverses the present course of events, the opposite is about to happen (see Jer 51:34).

■ **14** In vv 14 through 17 the prophet likens the nations (see v 17) to fish, who are helpless against skilled anglers. The comparison is perhaps developed from the idea of the righteous being a meal swallowed by the wicked (v 13, see Andersen 2001, 183). The prophet's concern for innocent sufferers is now extended to the nations.

You have made people is an allusion to the creation narratives found in Genesis. The term **made** (*ta'āśeh* from the root form *'āśâ* means "to make") is one of the most common terms for God's creating activity in the OT (see Vollmer 1997a:949-51), although Genesis 1-2 also uses "create" (*bārā'*) and "form" (*yāṣar*) for humankind (*'ādām*, → following). **People** is literally Adam (*'ādām)* or **humankind** (see NRSV on Gen 1:26-27; cp. Gen 2:7). Habakkuk compares **humankind** to the **fish** *of* the sea (vv 14-17). This extended comparison seems to be based more on human observation than Israel's creation traditions regarding human dominion over the animals.

The term **sea creatures** (*remeś*) is literally "creeping," or *moving things*, sometimes translated "teems, swarms, gliding" when applied to aquatic life (see Gen 1:20-22). While certain creatures function well without a leader (Prov 6:6-8; 30.27), the schooling behavior of fish makes them easy prey for human nets. Humans, on the other hand, rely upon either God, or divinely appointed rulers for protection. The statement that they **have no ruler** may be ironic, since Israel confessed that the Lord rules over them (Judg 8:23; 1 Sam 8:7) and the nations (Pss 22:28 [29 HB]; 47:2-9 [3-10 HB]). Instead of exercising the Lord's beneficent rule, however, Babylon is exploiting its charge for its own luxury (see Hab 1:16).

In summary, as the prophet surveys the social and political climate of his day, he concludes that the Creator has left humans to fend for themselves, much like the creatures of the sea. Therefore, injustices and evil reign where the powerful are free to assert their control over the weak (cp. Ps 82:2-3; Isa 63:19).

■ **15** The fish imagery continues here, with references to some of the most common methods used to catch fish in the ancient world (see Wineland 2000, 463). The term **wicked foe** is inserted by the NIV to clarify the subject; the Hebrew simply reads *he*. The passage uses singular verbs of the Babylonians, presented as a fisherman. The prey is Adam, or humankind (→ v 14), which is connoted by the singular *him*.

The passage begins with the words **all of them** (literally *him*), emphasizing the plight of the "fish." Fish **hooks** were tied to a line held directly by hand. They were either baited or dragged quickly to snag fish. The phrase reads literally *he drags him with his* net (cp. NRSV). The **net** was used for both hunting (see Mic 7:2) and fishing.

The parallel line continues; **he gathers them up in his dragnet**. The word **gathers** connotes the gathering of prisoners in v 9 (Anderson 2000, 185). In the ancient world, war captives were sometimes depicted as being gathered in nets (Haak 1992, 51). The word translated **dragnet** is from a Hebrew formation *mkmr*, which is also applied to hunting and fishing nets. The outcome after a successful day of fishing is indicated by two *therefore* (*'al kēn*) clauses, one at the end of this verse, the other at the beginning of v 16 (see also v 17). The first response is understandable; the angler **rejoices and is glad** at the good catch.

■ **16** The second response to the abundant catch is clearly idolatrous: the angler **sacrifices** and **burns incense** to his fishing gear. Although not an allegory, it is clear that the fishing gear represents Babylonian implements of war and ultimately their military might. So essentially, this is self-idolatry.

The beginning of the second line is literally, *For by them his portion is fat.* The term *portion* can indicate a food portion, but it also sometimes connotes a share of plunder (e.g., Gen 14:24; 1 Sam 30:24). A *fat* or *rich* portion may suggest more than enough, hence the NIV's **he lives in luxury.** The line concludes with a parallel phrase, literally *and his food is rich* (and enjoys the choicest food). In other words, the Babylonians are living affluently at the expense of the nations. Their rich food is comprised of war captives, along with their land and resources (→ v 13).

■ **17** The prophet's complaint about Babylonian cruelty comes to an end with a question. The text reads literally *Will he therefore* (a third use of *'al kēn*, → vv 15-16) *empty his net, to kill nations continually without compassion?* Habakkuk's question is apparently rhetorical. Although it appears as if the Babylonians will not cease their compassionless killing (see Haak 1992, 52), the question suggests it should be otherwise (Sweeney 2000b, 2:468-69).

This brings us full circle from the prophet's opening statement (v 12), where it is observed that according to the faithful's expectations, God's people will not die. Yet, by appointing the Babylonians as agents of justice (v 12), that is exactly what is happening. Their global violence does not selectively spare God's people, nor does it set right the social disorders behind the complaints of 1:2-4. From Habakkuk's perspective, this justice is not corrective; it does not set things right for the oppressed, nor has it restored righteous leaders to Judah. Rather, it makes no distinction between the righteous and wicked among God's people. Habakkuk has laid out this obviously inconsistent situation in his second complaint, expecting the Lord to act according to traditional theological expectations and do something to spare Judah from Babylonian atrocities.

■ **2:1** The report of Habakkuk's actions in this verse is similar to Isaiah's (Isa 21:6-9). The verb (*'e'ĕmōdâ*) in the opening statement is a cohortative, which signifies the resolve of the prophet, **Let me stand**. The term **watch** indicates sentinels, guards (e.g., 2 Sam 20:3), or a priestly post (e.g., Num 1:5). It may be metaphorical for the prophet as a sentinel who warns of God's coming judgment (e.g., Ezek 3:16-21). Or it may be a combination of these.

The verbal root of **station myself** (*yṣb*), often connotes people waiting on the Lord to perform some mighty deed of salvation (e.g., Exod 14:13). The term *mṣwr may* indicate **ramparts**, siege works, or a fortified city (see Deut 20:20; Zech 9:3; 2 Chron 11:5), or according to the context here, *watchtower*. Whether the word refers to a priestly post or the prophet's role as sentinel, it may be metaphorical here.

I will look (*wa'ăṣappeh*) is from another word that literally means *I will keep watch*. It sometimes connotes a prophet awaiting divine revelation (e.g., Hos 9:8; Jer 6:17 Ezek 3:17; Haak 1992, 53; and others). The mighty deed, which the prophet stations himself **to see,** is a word from the Lord, that is, **what [God] will say to me** (for "seeing" God's word → 1:1 and 2:2). The latter is literally **what [God] will say in** or *through* me (*dbr b-*, see Hos 1:2; Eaton 1961, 94, and others).

The next phrase explains the purpose of the divine word; it is **what answer** Habakkuk is **to give** (*mâ 'āšîb*), literally, *what I will return* to the (righteous) Judeans, some of whom have possibly inquired for God's response to their suffering (see the NIV note on the last line: *and what to answer when I am rebuked*). The term *tôkaḥtî*, translated **this complaint**, is difficult to interpret because of the first person suffix *my* in Hebrew (see the discussion in Patterson 1991, 161-62). It usually means something like "my reproof, rebuke, or correction" for someone who is in danger of going astray (e.g. Prov 3:11). The key to its meaning is found in the use of the same root in 1:12 to connote God's use of the Babylonians for *correction*. Here it is possible to interpret *my correction* as Habakkuk's anticipation of God's *correction* of himself for his bold complaints (Floyd 2000, 111, 120). However, the tone of the passage suggests otherwise, that Habakkuk's complaints are *his correction* of God, as in Job's argument (or case) against God (Job 13:3, 6; 23:4; Robertson 1990, 167; Sweeney 2000b, 2:470). The irony is obvious; God has purportedly used the Babylonians for the *correction* of Judah, but the prophet reports the results as a failure; in other words, he offers his *correction* of God! The prophet now anticipates that God will take this to heart, and that the Lord will either reveal to the prophet a new course of action or explain the inconsistencies in the divine character that Habakkuk has pointed out. It is clear that the prophet hopes for the former.

2. The Lord's Reported Response: Wait, Live by Faithfulness! (2:2-5)

■ **2 Then the LORD replied** indicates Habakkuk's report of the Lord's final response in vv 2-5. This passage is full of textual and interpretive difficulties. The prophet is commanded to **write down the revelation.** The word for **revelation** (*ḥāzôn*) is literally **vision,** the word used to describe the contents of Nahum (→ Nah 1:1). The book of Habakkuk is identified as a "pronouncement" which the prophet "saw" or "had a vision of" (*ḥāzâ*) (→ Hab 1:1). The exact content of Habakkuk's written **vision** is widely debated, but it probably includes at least v 4 (Sweeney 2000b, 2:471).

The **tablets** could have been made of wood or clay (see Driver 1976, 79-80, 239-40). The command **make it plain** (*ûbā'ēr*) is similar to the instructions God gives to Moses to write the Deuteronomic Torah plainly on stone (Deut 27:8). The root *b'r* could simply mean "incise" here (Andersen 2001, 204). Some interpret the word to connote large and clear characters (**plain,** as NIV and NRSV) so that a running herald may easily read it (e.g., Brownlee 1963, 320-21). But the word *b'r* is also employed with the sense of *expound* (Deut 1:5), and that is probably the meaning here (Roberts 1991, 109-110, accepts both meanings), since neither the significance nor the time of fulfillment of the **vision** are evident (v 3). The fact that multiple **tablets** are needed suggests that the revelation (and its explication) is not brief (Tsumura 1982, 294). The use of the word **tablets** also brings to mind the writing of the Mosaic Torah (see e.g., Exod 24:12; 31:18).

The **vision** and its interpretation comprise God's new instruction (*torah*), intended to comfort the oppressed and warn the wicked. Certainty is impossible, but it seems natural to assume that the **vision** follows immediately after these instructions, with 2:4-5 being the basic revelation and 2:6-20 the prophetic explication (see Nogalski 2011, 2:669).

The purpose for writing the message is **so that a herald** (literally "reader, proclaimer," see NIV note) **may run with it.** This refers to the prophetic dissemination of the message, which is often referred to as "running" (e.g., Jer 23:21; 2 Chron 30:6, 10; 2 Sam 18:19). The concern here is for Habakkuk's interpreted **vision** to be prophetically announced to the righteous sufferers beyond the walls of Jerusalem.

■ **3** Despite its lack of specificity, this verse intends to give hope about the certainty of the fulfillment of the vision. The first phrase literally says *there is still a vision* for *the* appointed time. **Appointed time** (*mô'ēd*) can connote an appointment made between two parties (e.g., 1 Sam 13:8), the time for the work of God to be accomplished (Ps 102:13 [14 HB]), or the time for God's promise to be fulfilled (Gen 17:21; 18:14). Here, as elsewhere, the exact time of fulfillment seems to be known only by God.

The verbal root in the phrase **it speaks** (*yāpēaḥ*) has been traditionally identified as *pûaḥ,* "to puff, breathe" (see BDB). It can also be read as a noun meaning "witness" (see *HALOT*). The term **end** can connote a limited or set number of days, either definite (e.g., Gen 8:6) or indefinite (e.g., Neh 13:6). Here it means at the end of a short intervening time and not the end times. This awaited **end** is the **appointed time** when God's work on behalf of the righteous will be evident. Sweeney is no doubt correct to identify the fulfillment of this oracle as the fall of Babylon (Sweeney 2000b, 2:471). In this context, **prove false** (*yĕkazzēb*) may have the nuance of *disappoint* (see BDB).

God further reiterates that the Judeans should not give up on the fulfillment of the revelation. *If it lingers, wait for it.* The last phrase is a purpose clause reassuring the hearers of its fulfillment: *For* it will certainly come (*kî bō' yābō'*) and will not delay. The seeming contradiction between the lingering and the not delaying of the revelation probably suggests that although there would be a seemingly long delay, one should not give up certainty of its fulfillment.

■ **4** Verses 4 and 5 are the main content of the revelation or vision communicated to the prophet. These verses appear to answer Habakkuk's concerns regarding the dominance of the wicked (vv 4*a*, 5) and offer hope for the suffering righteous (v 4*b*). In other words, this is an oracle of salvation (or word of assurance) similar to those found (or implied) in many psalms of lament (see Haak 1992, 15).

The vision begins by pointing out the interconnected character and fate of the wicked. **See, the enemy is puffed up; his desires are not upright.** The NIV adds the word **enemy** for clarification. A literal translation for the line would be *(Being) puffed up, his appetite within (bô) is not upright.* Responding to the prophet's earlier complaints, God says the wicked among the Babylonians (and Judeans) are arrogant or proud; their motivation is distorted and results in harmful actions, not only to others but to themselves (→ v 5).

Contrasted with the proud and wicked are the **righteous** or the innocent among the Judeans, on behalf of whom the prophet has been inquiring of God (→ 1:4). As in Hab 1, the singular term **righteous**, is used as a collective for "righteous (ones)." The addition of the word **person** by the NIV obscures this fact. The text literally reads **the righteous . . . will live by his faithfulness.** Although **faithfulness** (*'ĕmunâ*) is sometimes translated faith (see NRSV and NIV note), it connotes an outer commitment and not just an inner belief. The pronoun **his** could refer back to the singular (collective) noun **righteous**, thereby connoting the righteous people's **faithfulness** toward God. Yet since the reader expects a statement about how *God* is going to help the righteous, a better option is to understand **his** to refer to God; that is, the **righteous live by** (or because of) God's **faithfulness** toward them. This is probably the understanding of the LXX which reads "the righteous live by *my* faithfulness."

Faithfulness is an important divine characteristic: it describes the divine governance of creation; it moves God to act for the sake of Israel (e.g., Hos 2:20 [22 HB]; Ps 33:4; 36:5-6 [6-7 HB]; Lam 3:23). It is noteworthy that when the NT cites the verse the pronoun is omitted (with some minor LXX manuscripts). They read "the righteous shall live by faith" (Rom 1:17b; Gal 3:11; cp. Heb 10:38), so that multiple meanings are possible. The righteous rely on God to **live**, which, in the context of the suffering and oppression mentioned in Hab 1, means first to survive the threat of an unjust death (Andersen 2001, 215-16).

■ **5** This verse begins with *furthermore,* indicating that it is a continuation and expansion of v 4. The text continues **indeed, wine betrays him,** literally "the wine is a betrayer." We follow the reading *wealth is a betrayer* (supported by the Qumran *pesher,* see NRSV), which the context favors. The words *wealth* (*hwn*) could be misread as *wine* (*hyyn*) since the consonants *yod* and *waw* are often confused in Hebrew writing. Ultimately, unjust gain of the wicked will fail, since those who live for it are never satisfied (as the verse goes on to say).

The text continues, *the arrogant person will therefore not succeed* (the prefixed *w-* indicates here consequence, *therefore*), which is a contrast to the righteous who will live (v 4, see Brownlee 1959, 132). The *arrogant person* (*gbr yhyr*) is a collective expression that applies both to the Judean rulers and Babylonian conquerors (cp. Roberts 1991, 117). The NIV translation **rest** is based on an emendation of the difficult term *yinweh,* which recently has been understood as reaching a goal (*succeed,* see *HALOT*).

The *arrogant* who amass unjust *wealth* certainly seem to succeed, at least for the time being, but the prophet explains why ultimately this is not the case. **He is as greedy as the grave** is literally *he enlarges his appetite like sheol.* The term *appetite* (*nepeš*) is also found in v 4 to connote improper motivation. *Sheol* is the dwelling place of the dead in Israelite thinking. The next line restates the thought, **and like death is never satisfied** or *satiated.* The imagery is ironic. Death is a fitting figure of endless appetite, since "death" never stops demanding more victims. But while the pursuits of the arrogant wealthy may appear to be gratifying and successful, it is never satisfied. Ultimately the endless desires of the wicked will lead to self-destruction, which is God's judgment (cp. Isa 5:11-14).

The concluding poetic lines are no doubt another use of irony. On the surface, it appears to describe the successful exploits of the Babylonians. This is the understanding of the Qumran *pesher* which renders the verbs as plurals. But the terms **gathers** and *collects* also connote the gathering of bones for final burial (e.g., Gen 25:8). So this sentence probably contains a double entendre; the apparently successful plundering of the nations is outmatched by the inescapable exploits of death, who also **gathers to himself all the nations** and *collects to himself* **all the peoples.** In other words, the arrogant empire builders will in the end die; they will fall victim to an even more powerful conqueror, death. Ultimately this is God's judgment, which is also sometimes depicted as the gathering or harvest of the wicked (e.g., Zeph 3:8; Hos 4:3, see Hayes 2002, 59, n 86). On the other hand, God's righteous ones, the innocent sufferers, will continue to live (v. 4*b*)

FROM THE TEXT

A prominent theme underlying this text is *God's concern for justice in human relations.* This is evident in several ways.

First, *God is concerned about the suffering of the oppressed.* This is the basis of Habakkuk's intense complaint (1:2-4), for he knew from his tradition God hears and responds to the cries of the marginalized and abused of society (Exod 22:21-27 [20-26 HB]; Deut 24:10-22). This is what the OT commonly calls "salvation" or God's saving help. This same concern is found throughout the ministry of Jesus and in the admonitions of the early church (e.g., James 5:27). The text reminds its readers that God expects them to act out of concern for the oppressed, and that it should extend beyond the bounds of God's people (e.g., Exod 22:21 [20 HB]; 23:9; Lev 19:34; Deut 5:14). Jesus is the savior of all people (1 Tim 4:10) and his blood was shed for all things (Col 1:20). Thus, the God of the Bible cares about the earthly condition of *all* peoples, and even God's creation, and not just about believing souls going to heaven.

Second, *God's timetable for justice does not always match human expectations.* Habakkuk expresses his deep concern that God does not act quickly and decisively to stop injustices he sees around him. However, he continues to seek justice and urges God to act. We cannot always know why God delays setting things right, but the Bible hints at some. (1) *Social injustices have human causes and God wills that they be addressed by humans living according to divine purposes.* Prayers of complaint (or lament) such as Habakkuk's (1:2-4) were prayed in public ceremonies (e.g., 2 Chr 20:3-19; Joel 1:14). Though directed to God, such prayers would have confronted those who were guilty of injustices in the community and challenged them to repent of their evil (e.g., Ps 55:12-13 [13-14 HB]; Sheppard 1992, 145-47). When we pray for God's justice, it is also important to ask ourselves if we are implicated in the suffering we find in our world. Taking responsibility for our unjust actions certainly hastens God's work of restoring justice in our world. (2) *God often delays justice in order to extend divine mercy for all* (see 2 Pet 3:9; Rom 2:4-5). One of Habakkuk's aims may have been to bring the guilty to repentance (Luther 1526, 159). The perpetrators of injustice are sometimes God's disobedient people who might bring great glory to God if they repent (think of the Apostle Paul!).

Third, *God is free to use any means to carry out divine purposes.* Habakkuk struggled with the idea that a wicked nation like Babylon could be used by God. But the passage reveals a perplexing aspect of the way God often works. God does not usually intervene directly in human affairs, but God may "join in" processes that are already at work in creation, whether they be aimed at accomplishing good or evil. Babylon was already intent on world domination; yet God declares their actions as divine judgment against sinful Judeans. But that does not mean that God commends Babylonian arrogant abuse of power. Babylon is still an evil nation and eventually God will judge Babylon for their exploitative deeds (Hab 2:4-5). Despite the fact that God uses them, their evil deeds are not the actions of God, nor do they or their deeds somehow become "good." It is important to keep this in mind when some bad event or catastrophe occurs that may somehow indirectly further God's purposes. It is sometimes correct to say in retrospect that God finds a way to bring some good out of an evil act (see Gen 50:20). But it is usually (if not always) wrong to say that God did something evil to accomplish something good. This essentially makes God the author of sin and holds the Lord accountable for all wrongdoing (Calvin 1848, 28).

Fourth, *when God acts in the world, God often gets dirty in the process.* Habakkuk has difficulty believing that a pure God could even look upon sin (1:13), much less participate in the sinful processes of the world. We sometimes assume that God wants to keep a distant and detached moral purity that would be corrupted by contact with sin. But that is an abstract idea about God that has little support from the scriptures. Habakkuk reminds us that God gets involved in a world filled with evil, so God's people can expect to see God at work there.

It is interesting how interpreters over the centuries quote the passage about God's pure eyes (1:13) with approval, stating that it shows how God cannot look upon sin or tolerate sinners (e.g., various rabbis in Neusner 2007, 18, 23, 25; Chrysostom in Ferreiro 2003, 188; Wesley 1984, 1:148-49 [Ser 3.II.6]). It escapes their notice that this expression is the prophet's short-sighted theological assessment of God's work in the world. Such inadequate theology can also make it difficult to read and understand scripture, since we tend to ignore or explain away whatever is inconsistent with our views. We can easily miss what the Bible says about God when it does not fit our preconceived theological notions.

Yet, Habakkuk's protest preserves an important point. The faithful are bound in community to the faithless, and any action against one is going to affect the other. A quick divine intervention against a few demanded by the prayers of the faithful is bound to bring significant collateral damage on the many. The question is whether such an intervention ultimately serves God's purposes for the world. Perhaps the ultimate answer is for God's people to avoid hasty prayers for deliverance. Instead they should wait and trust the Lord during times of crises and allow God to determine the best course of action (Hab 3:16-19).

Fifth, *believers must wrestle with God in prayer when they have difficulty seeing God at work in the world.* Habakkuk directly challenges God because he knows that justice is a divine concern, and justice is lacking in Judean society. We find similar confrontations between humans and God in the Psalms, Job, and Jeremiah (to name just a few). Such conflicts are not a sign of weakness or doubt, rather they come from a deep faith in God and a knowledge concerning God's intended order for creation. They indicate a desire to see God's will be done on earth as it is in heaven (cp. Achtemeier 1986, 36).

Habakkuk may think that God is too slow to act or disagree with God's method of acting, but his concerns are justifiable in light of the biblical tradition. Furthermore, God's responses indicate that Habakkuk's protests are proper (Goldingay 2009, 55). Most importantly, Habakkuk would probably never have come to a proper understanding, acceptance, and articulation of God's will without these confrontational prayers. Sometimes struggling in dialogue with God may be the only way that God can get through to us and reveal the divine will.

This passage ends on a few notes of hope. First, although the situation may seem urgent, *God's people are often told to wait for God's work* (2:3-5). Habakkuk is given a certain vision to address the crises of his day, and that vision required waiting for its complete fulfillment. God tells Habakkuk to wait for God's certain (appointed) intervention (2:3). For Habakkuk's generation, this communicated hope that God's work of justice through Babylon would be completed within a foreseeable future. Later generations such as the Qumran covenanters (1QpHab vii.4-ix.2), the early Church (Rom 1:17; Gal 3:11, Heb 10:38), and the Rabbis (Neusner 2007, 48-49) picked up Habakkuk's prophecy and found hope that they would see God at work within their own generation and beyond ("the end"). Most notably, NT writers such as Paul testified that through Christ God's final work is beginning to be brought to completion in this age. Although it is always possible to see how far this present age falls short of God's purposes, God's people are challenged to wait and always be hopeful that God's faithfulness will be evident soon. We can be assured that God will act to correct earthly injustices. It may not be according to our timetable, during our lifetime, or even in the near future, but God will act. All we may have in the meantime is to wait and live by God's word (Calvin 1848, 67-69).

Second, *by God's faithfulness, the righteous will live.* Although it may not be apparent at the moment, Habakkuk is assured that God is still faithful, and that God's faithfulness will set Habakkuk's world in order. Throughout the scriptures we read that God is and will be faithful to the creation, and particularly to believers. All personal, social, institutional, or global problems will not be solved satisfactorily in this present evil age. But God does promise believers life (cp. John 10:10), which could be equated with *shalom*—wholeness or wellbeing. God's promised life may be as simple as having our daily bread or enduring hardships with our faith intact. It may be the confidence that while our own lot is one of hardship that the intergenerational body of Christ will endure and thrive by God's faithfulness. It may only be the awareness that we are planting seeds that will surely grow, although we do not see evidence now. It may be the faith that we will share in the resurrection of the dead and in God's eternal kingdom through Christ (cp. Rom 8:12-25).

God's faithfulness enables believers to live righteously, that is, to live in right relationship with God and others. To live by God's faithfulness involves not only deriving *one's life from God,* but also *entails ordering one's life by the faithfulness of God.* In other words, God's faithfulness always entails a faithful response from God's people. This response extends God's grace and works into the world. This is the purpose of the stipulations in the Mosaic Torah (e.g., Lev 19:33-34) as well as the Christian commandment to love one another. Indeed, just as Jesus summarized the Torah in the commands to love God and neighbor (Mark 12:29-31) by citing two passages from the Torah (Deut 6:5 and Lev 19:18), Rabbi Simelai said that Habakkuk summarized *torah* in one saying: "the righteous shall live by his faith" (Neusner 2009, 49-52).

God will vindicate the righteous; the arrogant oppressors will not have the last word (2:4-5). It is difficult for God's people to hold their faith and confidence in a just God when we see the powerful arrogantly trampling the innocent with impunity. It is even more distressing when those appointed to maintain justice are unjust (Szeles 1987, 12), especially when God-appointed church leaders mistreat their flock. In Habakkuk, the punishment fits the crime: the Judeans who perpetrate injustice because they reject God's order will fall victim to the same injustices under a nation who also rejects God's order (Achtemeier 1986, 38; see 1:6-12).

Today we are not always certain that evil will be so swiftly redressed. Though we hope for justice, there seems to be no end to human greed and exploitation of the weak both in the public and private sectors of our world. Yet, Habakkuk reminds us that apparently endless desire always has an inevitable end. Since it imitates death in its insatiable quest, death will be its fate (2:4a, 5, 6-19). The old German saying is appropriate: "Greed can be satisfied only with a load of earth" (Luther 1526, 202). Wealth or power is not endless, and arrogant insatiable evildoers will fail, whether the legal system finally holds them accountable, their greed consumes them in this lifetime, or they are ultimately held accountable in the final judgment. In the meantime, God's people must not become despondent, cynical, or imitate evil (as the way to conduct business in "the real world"); rather, they must maintain their trust in a faithful God and be an example of faithful living before a righteous God. We must wait. The vision is certain. God's faithfulness will be revealed (Hab 2:3-4).

II. CONFIDENCE THAT THE LORD WILL JUDGE THE WICKED: FIVE WOES: HABAKKUK 2:6-20

BEHIND THE TEXT

For the general historical context see the discussion in the Introduction. The specific background reflected here is the imperialistic policies of Babylon. It reflects Babylonian conquest of peoples and lands, particularly their great building projects supported by plundering nations through looting, tribute, and forced labor (for a general background of the Neo-Babylon empire see Saggs 1962, 146-57; Roaf 1990, 198-204). Yet some oracles also apply to oppressive Judean leaders (→ Behind the Text for Hab 1:1-2:5).

The passage is a clarification of the judgment awaiting the wicked, which is threatened in general terms in the vision of Hab 2:4-5. As such, it is the initial expounding of that vision (→ 2:3) and was probably included with vv 4-5 at a very early time. The oracles probably circulated with the original vision, which was to be delivered by prophetic messengers (→ 2:2). But they could have also been used as part of a ritual observance announcing doom on God's enemies (cp. Num 22-24; see Eaton 1961, 101; Westermann 1967, 198), composed shortly after the circulation of the vision.

123

These oracles function as a more specific answer to the complaints of Habakkuk and so serve to comfort the oppressed; that is, they confirm that the prophet's (people's) prayers have been heard and God will remove oppressive powers from their midst. As such the foreign oppressor (Babylon) would not have heard the oracles (see Goldingay 2009, 70; and the discussion of the purpose of woe oracles in Gowan 1976, 58-67). Yet, it may have been a different matter for local Judean oppressors, whose offenses were similar, and who may even have aided the Babylonians for their own personal advancement. They would have the knowledge of God's instruction and so would be more directly accountable for injustices than the outside oppressors.

Although these oracles are cast as a taunt song of the nations (v 6), it would miss the point to search for a historic occasion where non-Judean nations would have uttered them. Rather, this taunt functions more like an ideal script of the Lord's concerns placed in the mouth of the nations. The positive values presumed therein attests to the righteous or just order reflected in God's instruction (torah), which all nations would recognize if they would submit to the sovereignty of Israel's God (Isa 2:2-4; Mic 4:1-4). A similar idea is found in many of the Psalms, where all creation is called upon to worship the Lord (e.g., Pss 97:6-9; 98:2-3, 7-9; 148:1-14; cp. Phil 2:9-11). Babylon's crimes are not just against Judah; they are against all peoples, nations, all creation, and ultimately they are a defiance of God (see Floyd 2000, 115-118). The oracles show the reader that when God acts to save Judah it is on behalf of all creation, and that the Lord should be given glory for it (Hab 2:14, 18-20).

After a brief introduction in v 6a, the text contains a series of five woe oracles, each characterized by the use of woe! (see Gowan 1976, 51-67; → sidebar Woe Oracles at Nah 3:1). Although there is some variation, the typical features of woe oracles are found here including the pronouncement of woe on a named subject, usually combined with accusations against the subject (vv 6b, 9, 12, 15, 18-19), and the announcement of God's judgment (vv 8a, 10, 16-17, 18-19).

The offenses enumerated in the oracles are usually cast in terms of proverbial maxims applicable to individuals, generally recognized as important for maintaining various social relationships and obligations (cp. Robertson 1990, 187-88; Andersen 2001, 233-34). The list of offenses is climactic; that is, each one builds on and is more serious than the previous. Usually the maxim is given as a figure of speech, which is dropped when the oracle is restated or interpreted in terms of the corporate offense. Two oracles conclude with the same refrain, underscoring the creation-wide significance of the oppressor's sins (vv 8, 17). In fact, each oracle ends with a creation motif (vv 8, 11, 14, 17, 20), and the fifth oracle also begins with one (vv 18-19). Verse 20 offers a positive contrast to the woe against idolaters and also serves as both a fitting conclusion for the series and a transition to Hab 3.

124

IN THE  TEXT

A. Woe to Greedy Plunderers! (2:6-8)

■ **6** Verse 6*a* introduces the oracles that follow as a **taunt** song of all the nations (**all of them**) that Babylon has oppressed. The introduction is formulated as a question (**will not**), which implies an affirmative answer. **Taunt him** is literally "raise up a parable over someone" (*'lyw mšl yś'w*), an expression found in the prophets connoting a mocking song directed toward those slated for divine judgment (see Isa 14:4; Mic 2:4). Babylon is again referred to collectively as **him**, as in ch 1.

The words **ridicule** (*mlyṣh* means "allusive expression" or *satire*) and **scorn** (*hydwt* means *riddles*) also occur in Prov 1:6. Both convey the proverbial nature of the woe oracles in vv 6-19. These terms suggest that at least some of the woe oracles may not be fully understood without further reflection, since they are given in figures of speech applied to individual offenders (Floyd 2000, 135-36). Specifically, these oracles may also apply to the Judean oppressors who are guilty of the same offenses as the Babylonians. In that case the people raising the taunt (**all of them**) would include the righteous Judeans suffering under Judean oppressors (1:2-4).

Woe to him (v 6*b*) is an expression which articulates anguish over the recently departed (e.g., 1 Kgs 13:10; Jer 22:18), but is adapted by the prophets into "woe oracles" connoting divine judgment. The offender (depicted as a collective individual representing the Babylonian and Judean oppressors) *amasses* (*hmrbh*, literally "makes many, multiplies") *what does not belong to him* (cp. NRSV). The Hebrew has an abrupt **How long?** that is an interjection interrupting the objects of the woe. The NIV rearranges the text by moving **How long** to the end of the verse with the addition of the implied phrase **must this go on?** This harkens back to the similar "How long?" of 1:2. The prophet (and the righteous) seems to implore God for an end to suffering (Pss 6:3 [4 HB]; 90:13).

The initial "woe to" applies to the last phrase in the verse in Hebrew, which is literally *and enriches himself with pledged goods*. The word *'bṭyṭ* (*pledged goods*), which occurs only here, means items taken as a security deposit for loans (see Deut 24:11, 13) or as tribute or plunder from other nations (Deut 15:6, see Sweeney 2000b, 2:474). On the surface the charge is a figure of speech; Babylon's plundering of the nations is compared to a creditor taking and refusing to return pledged goods or make good on the loan (see vv 7-8). But it could also be applied literally to oppressive Judean creditors who are taking advantage of the poor (see Amos 2:8).

■ **7** The loan imagery continues in this verse. The question beginning with **will not** implies an affirmative response. **Your creditors** refer to the nations conquered by Babylon. Since Babylon took "pledges" from the nations (tribute and plunder, v 6) and never actually returned them, it is now "indebted" to the nations; ironically these nations become Babylon's creditors. These will **suddenly arise** against their oppressors. The tables will be turned; the former oppressors will become the oppressed.

The NIV rearranges the next phrase to make better sense; it literally begins *will not those who make you tremble awaken?*, suggesting that Babylon had previously been in fear of nations it conquered. No matter how powerful a person or group becomes, there is often a nagging fear that the subjects (who usually out number their oppressors!) will one day wake up and rise against them. Babylon should have been very aware of this possibility since they themselves had gained power by overthrowing Assyrian rule. The loan imagery is now dropped and the ill gained goods are presented as *spoils* of war; the takers of spoil will become *spoils* for others (see v 8; cp. Jer 30:16).

■ **8 Because** (*kî*) introduces the reason for divine judgment, which is the charge restated here without the loan imagery of vv 6-7. Specifically, **you have plundered many nations.** Babylon has enriched itself through plunder and tribute from other nations. Likewise, powerful Judeans have enriched themselves through exploiting their own people.

The judgment of v 7 is restated in terms of the punishment fitting the crime (see Obad 1:15; Zech 2:8-9 [12-13 HB]; Ezek 39:10). The oppressor will be plundered by **the peoples who are left** or *all the remnant of the peoples*. The term *remnant* (*ytr*) refers to those who are the survivors after warfare (Josh 13:12; 2 Kgs 25:11). It is also one of the terms that connotes the remnant of Israel that will be restored by God after hardships (Mic 5:2 [1 HB]). Both meanings are suitable here. In regard to the Judean oppressors, the oppressed righteous remnant is the true Israel. The people left after Babylonian and Judean oppression will **plunder** their oppressors (see v 6). It is a descriptive statement; it does not suggest divine causation or approval of the plundering, any more than God approves of the horrendous actions of Babylon articulated in 1:6-11.

The conclusion of the verse restates the punishable offenses underlying the crimes. The first is the shedding of **human blood** by Babylon (*on account of human bloodshed*). *Human bloodshed* is first condemned in Gen 4:6-12 and is one of the universal prohibitions promulgated by God after the flood (Gen 9:5-6).

The following offenses are all dependent on the preceding *on account of*, so the next phrase could read *on account of violence to the earth* (or **lands**, both translations are possible for *'rṣ*). Andersen argues that this is a reference to Babylon's seizure of foreign lands (Anderson 2001, 238). But the passage could also reflect a more universal perspective (note that "earth," "humankind," and "bloodshed" are all terms found in the primeval narratives of Genesis 1-11).

The next phrase is juxtaposed without a connector (NIV and NRSV add **and**), *a city and all its inhabitants.* It is not clear if a particular *city* (*qryh*, also "town, village, settlement") is meant, although the term is applied to Jerusalem several times (e.g. Isa 1:21, 26; Mic 4:10). A tradition going back at least as far as the Aramaic Targum interprets *'rṣ* as the holy land and the *city* as Jerusalem. This would fit the context since both the Babylonians and corrupt Judean leaders had

126

caused suffering in Jerusalem. But as the capital city, the fate of Jerusalem would be symptomatic of the fate of the nation. So most interpreters and Bible translations view the singular "city" as a collective. Thus the NIV renders **cities and everyone in them** (see also NRSV, Patterson 1991, 183).

B. Woe to Those Who Build Their Houses with Plundered Wealth! (2:9-11)

■ **9** The second woe (vv 9-11) is pronounced against *the one who makes unjust profit; evil for his house*. The first phrase is literally "a profiteer of unjust profit" (*bōṣēaʿ bĕṣaʿ*, see Prov 1:19; Jer 6:13). Babylon was known for its building projects (Patterson 1991, 191-94); here it says that these are financed by the *unjust profit* of plunder and tribute (Roberts 1991, 120). **House** could include the kingdom of Babylon, the royal house of Babylon (or Judah), or the various households of rich oppressors. *Evil for his house* probably has a double meaning. On the one hand, the house is being built by *evil* (*rʿ*) means or ill-gained building materials (repeating the thought of the first line). On the other hand, the result will be *ruin* (another meaning of *rʿ*) for this house. So this statement would function as curse anticipating judgment (cp. Roberts 1991, 114; Andersen 2001, 238-40).

The next phrase indicates the use or purpose of the unjust gain, *to set (lśm) his nest on high*. The bird's **nest** can be used figuratively for one's house or home (Job 29:18). This placement **on high** is **to escape the clutches of ruin**. Having a nest built on a rock or high place is a figure of speech for a supposed secure place (Num 24:21). Since **on high** is also the abode of God (e.g., Ps 7:7 [8 HB]), it connotes the pride of those who attempt to build there. The irony is that they hope to find safety in their **nest on high**, but they will be cast down by God (Jer 49:16; Obad 3-4; Isa 14:12-19, about the king of Babylon see 14:3). The image of a high nest also suggests a fortified city built on a high place with high protective walls and towers, or the fortified garrisons of powerful rulers. The term **ruin** is the same word translated **evil** (*rʿ*) in the previous phrase. The builder commits moral **evil** to secure a house to escape the evil of **ruin**.

■ **10** The accusation shifts from the third person to the direct address of the second person. (The following comments follow the Hebrew, NIV has rearranged the word order.) From the previous verse it is self-evident that using evil to avoid evil would be destined for failure. Here that is stated more directly, *you have planned shame for your house*. There is an irony in this statement. No one would deliberately plan for failure and thus bring shame or disgrace for their house. But the accused here is essentially planning self-defeat by committing evil to escape evil.

The next phrase, *bring to an end many peoples,* explains the accompanying result. The oppressor's efforts at self-protection are at the expense of others, the destruction of *many peoples*. These would be the nations conquered by Babylon and perhaps conscripted for building projects (Nogalski 2011, 2:670). The next phrase, **forfeiting your life**, is literally "and sinning (against?) your life" or "and your life is sinning" (*wḥwṭʾ npšk*). The same expression is found in Prov 20:2 where it apparently means forfeit one's life. The sins against humanity in the name of self-preservation have resulted in the forfeiting of the life of the wicked. Although short and vague, this is the punishment threatened in this oracle.

■ 11 The offense and the punishment have already been set forth in vv 9-10. Verse 11 reminds the accused who build "nests on high" to escape evil that even the building materials of their edifices, **the stones of the wall** and the **beams of the woodwork**, will testify against them. The word **cry** (*tš'q*) (of the **stones**) is the same used in Habakkuk's opening prayer (1:2). The term **echo** (*y'nnh*) is literally "answer"; the word can also connote testimony or accusation in a lawsuit (Exod 20:16). So it could be translated *will testify concerning it*, referring to the misdeeds mentioned above. The rest of the passage (2:12-20) is best understood as the cry of the stones and testimony of the wood (cp. Calvin 1848, 104-105; Clarke 1823, 745; Roberts 1991, 122).

C. Woe to Those Who Build Cities with Plundered Wealth! (2:12-14)

■ 12 Unlike the previous woes, the third woe does not employ a figure of speech that requires interpretation. So it is shorter than the first two. Its subject is building, like the previous oracle. This verse contains two parallel lines stating the same thing in different ways. **Woe to him who builds** (*bnh*) **a city with bloodshed** (→ v 8 for comments on **bloodshed**). Babylonian city building is the subject of the prophetic condemnation (see Gen 11:1-9). The word for **injustice** (*'wlh*) often connotes violent deeds (see *HALOT* and BDB). The term is regularly translated *iniquity*. In a phrase very close to this one, Mic 3:10 condemns Jerusalem leaders who build (*bnh*) that city with **bloodshed** and **injustice**.

■ 13 The punishment for the offense follows immediately in this verse. The first phrase (*hlw' hnh m't yhwh ṣb'wt*) is awkward; literally, it reads, **Is it not, behold, from the LORD of hosts?** What is **from the LORD** may be determined from context: that God will judge Babylon for its offenses. That is to say, the punishments that will be given in the next line, and perhaps also the punishments listed in the previous oracles (vv 7, 10), come from the Lord. The rhetorical question suggests that the audience already knows this. The title LORD *of hosts* connotes God as the leader of a heavenly army who executes divine deeds of judgment and salvation (→ Nah 2:13).

The next parallel phrase completes the question begun in the first line and sets forth the punishment, *that the peoples struggle* only *to fuel the fire*, and the nations *weary* themselves for nothing? Jeremiah uses the same phrases in a passage connoting judgment against Babylon (Jer 51:58). These phrases appear to be based on proverbial wisdom (Davidson 1896, 80). The reference to *peoples*/nations applies generally to any nation who will live unjustly and hence oppose God.

The effect of the offense is intensified; Babylon has added insult to injury. Not only has Babylon conscripted foreign labor for their self-aggrandizing building projects, a crime in itself, but these projects have been slated for judgment, making the nations' efforts for nothing. Judean leaders also conscripted foreigners for works, which eventually fell under God's judgment (1 Kgs 9:15-21; cp. Jer 22:11-17).

■ **14** The concluding phrase in this oracle is hymnic and meant to provide a contrast with the futile efforts of the nations in v 13. A nearly identical phrase appears in Isa 11:9 to describe the ideal age of God's salvific reign on earth. The **glory of the** LORD connotes God's active presence (**glory** is from the root *kbd*, which means "heavy, weighty," etc.); the Lord's glory was usually thought to indwell or fill the sanctuary (Exod 29:43; 40:34-35; 1 Kgs 8:11). In this context, however, the Lord's **glory** fills **the earth**, which is manifested both directly by God's power and indirectly through the created order (e.g., Pss 24:7-10; 29:3; see Isa 6:3). **Knowledge** of the Lord's **glory** is the revelation of the Lord or the Lord's **glory** (see e.g., Isa 41:20; Ezek 20:9-12; Mic 6:5). Here it probably connotes the manifestation of God's character and deeds in creation and history.

The phrase **as the waters cover the sea** conveys the comprehensive coverage of the revelation of the Lord's glory; it is visible throughout the earth. When humans have true knowledge of (or know) God (or the Lord's glory), it results in a relationship with God that is manifested in worship of the Lord alone and a lifestyle that reflects God's love and justice. Being in the third of five oracles, this refrain stands at the midpoint of the woe oracles. It serves as a reminder that the setting right of the social order found in these oracles promotes the concerns of the God of Israel.

D. Woe to Those Who Shamefully Abuse Their Neighbors! (2:15-17)

■ **15** This oracle is difficult to interpret; it is probably best understood as a figure of speech, clarified by the restatement in v 17. Some interpreters regard it as a denunciation of drunkenness and the shameful behavior that follows (as in Gen 9:21; see Patterson 1991, 199). But here the drunken neighbors are regarded as victims; it is only the one making them drunk that is condemned. This woe is against the one **who gives drink to his neighbors** or *who causes his neighbor to drink*.

The next line indicates the intent of the one who pours out *his wrath* (from **the wineskin**)—to make his victims **drunk** so that he can look at *their nakedness*. Elsewhere making someone drunk, or pouring out a cup of **wrath** or wine, indicates mistreatment; it is applied to Babylon in Jer 25:15-29; 51:7. The exact nature of the offense here is further clarified by the interpretation of this verse in v 17 as violence committed against Lebanon, animals, humans, the earth, and cities (→ v 17). *Nakedness* refers to the stripping of conquered and exiled captives (e.g., Roberts 1991, 124; Isa 20:3-4; Lam 4:21), as well as stripping (or destroying) the land of its vegetation and other resources (Hos 2:3 [5 HB], 9-13 [11-15 HB]; see Braaten 2001, 191-93).

In summary, in this verse Babylon is condemned for acts of violence against people and lands conquered in warfare. They have stripped them of their resources and left them exposed to shame.

■ **16** The punishment will fit the crime: **You will be *sated* with shame instead of glory**. Babylon's actions have had the opposite of their intended effect (Roberts 1991, 124-25). Kings who destroy the earth, in particular who strip Lebanon of its prized cedar (see v 17), are attempting to gain **glory** for themselves and their kingdom. Instead they will have their fill of **shame** (*qlwn*)—just as they filled others by the cup of wrath. Ironically, the prophet had earlier said that endless desire is insatiable (2:5); here the same term indicates that those who seek self-glory will be *sated* (*śb't*) with shame, something they do not desire!

Once again the punishment will fit the crime; the next phrase is literally, **You too will drink, and stagger** (*hr'l*). **Stagger** follows an alternate textual tradition, and is common to this figure of speech (see e.g., Zech 12:2). The MT has the more difficult reading **let your nakedness be exposed,** literally, *show yourself uncircumcised* (*h'rl*, the difference being the transposition of two letters). The verb *'rl*, "to be uncircumcised," only appears elsewhere to connote a picked fruit tree (Lev. 19:23), which supports the stripping of vegetation motif here.

The judgment is spelled out in terms of divine punishment; **the cup *of* the LORD's right hand *will come around upon you*. The cup *of* the LORD's right hand** (or "of the Lord's wrath") connotes divine judgment (→ 2:15). According to Jeremiah, Babylon was formerly a cup of wrath in God's hand against the nations (Jer 25:15-29), but afterwards the Lord will punish Babylon and make it drink that cup (Jer 51:39, 57). The **right hand** is the place or source of God's power and authority (e.g., Exod 15:6, 12; Isa 41:10). Uncharacteristically for this series, this woe oracle links the punishment of the oppressor directly with God's action (Smith 1906, 144).

The result of the cup **coming around** is expressed in a short interjection, *filth upon your glory!* The NIV's **disgrace will cover your glory** softens the language, but conveys the meaning of the phrase which contains alliteration of k sounds, *qyqlwn 'l-kbwdk*. The word *filth* (*qyqlwn*) is rare; it appears to mean "excrement" or "dung heap" (*HALOT*). The alliteration of the phrase could be preserved with the free rendering, "Caca will crown you!" The irony is evident, by stripping the forests the Babylonians hoped to crown themselves with glory; instead it is as if they had covered themselves with a pile of dung! (cp. 1 Macc 2:62).

■ **17** The reason for God's judgment (the charge), introduced by *because* (*kî*), is stated here. Babylon has *committed violence against* Lebanon. *Violence against* **Lebanon** perhaps refers to Babylon cutting down the legendary cedars and other trees in the forest of Lebanon in order to build opulent palaces and other buildings (*ANET* 307). Violence done to Lebanon by Babylon will return upon them as their covering (v 16). Since Babylon has denuded Lebanon of its trees by **violence**, that violence will return upon them in an overwhelming manner (literally, *cover you*).

Furthermore, Babylon will suffer the consequence of the destruction of animal life. Babylon's devastation of Lebanon's forests would have destroyed important animal habitat (see Ps 104:16-18; Bruce 1993, 872). This action will come back to **shatter** (*yḥytn*) or **terrify**, that is, cause mental anguish to Babylon. Since the concluding refrain of v 8 is suitable for an oracle dealing with the destruction of creation, it is repeated here (→ v 8).

E. Woe to Idolaters and Concluding Refrain: Be Silent before the Lord (2:18-20)

■ **18** The final oracle (vv 18-20) opens with a rhetorical question, **of what value is an idol?** The implied answer is "none!" The next phrase clarifies the reason that it is useless; **for** (*kî*) **his idol he creates as a cast image, and it is a teacher of lies**. The expression translated **teacher of lies** (*wmwry šqr*) implies that idolatry is self-delusion since images cannot speak (vv 18c, 19); it is essentially self-deification (Floyd 2000, 146).

This idea is further clarified by **for** *its creator* **trusts in his own creation** *to act* (see Pss 135:18 and 115:8). This trust is misplaced (see Ps 115:9-11); it should be placed in the Lord (Ps 37:5). The word for **creator** (*yṣr*) is one of the terms used for God (e.g., Gen 2:7, 19; Isa 42:6; 45:7). Only the works of the true Creator are effective. In reality an idol says nothing, it is **a wordless worthless thing** (*'lylym 'llmym*). The phrase contains alliteration, literally "speechless vanity." **Worthless thing** (*'lylym*) is a common derogatory term for pagan gods. Both terms sound similar to Elohim (*'lhym*), "god(s)," and are plural to make better word plays on that word.

■ **19** This verse contains the woe saying, and has a number of links to the earlier woe oracles. Destruction is announced to those who think idols have life. The first two lines are parallel expressions and convey the same idea; idols of **wood** or **stone** cannot be awakened because they have no life. The word for **wake up** (*'wry*) could also be translated "stir, rouse oneself" and could be ironic since it often describes God arising to take action against enemies (e.g., see Isa 51:9; Pss 7:6 [7 HB]; 35:23). In contrast to the living God of Israel, idols cannot be stirred up to take action.

Can it give guidance? is a rhetorical question with an implied negative answer. The word **give guidance** (*ywrh*) sounds similar (by assonance) to **wake up** (*'wry*), and is meant to be a contrast to that word—it cannot wake up so it cannot guide! The text here implicitly asserts that only the Lord can offer true **guidance**. Moreover, an idol **is covered with gold and silver** (cp. Jer 10:9; Pss 115:4), indicating its only value to an image worshipper since it will not offer the guidance he craves. It is lifeless; literally, **there is** *absolutely* **no breath in it** (cp. Ps 135:17; Jer 10:14). **Breath** is *rûaḥ*, often translated "spirit," which is a synonym of *npš* found in 2:4-5. More irony is evident here; God's *rûaḥ* gives life to and renews the created order (Ps 104:29-30), but sinners destroy God's creation and create for themselves idols that have no *rûaḥ* and are totally worthless (see Braaten 2003b, 433-34).

■ **20** The concluding phrase offers a contrast to the idolatry in the current woe oracle. It also offers a presupposition for all the woe oracles: they are based on

131

divine concerns, and the violators will be punished by the Lord. The pronouncement, **The Lord is in his holy temple; let all the earth be silent before him** is probably best viewed as issuing from the heavenly court (Zech 2:13 [17 HB]; cp. Isa 6:3-10). It commands that the complaints of the prophet, the nations, and creation cease out of reverence toward God. This includes the oppressors who should become silent before the Lord, like their idols who "cannot speak" and who have "no breath" in them (vv 18-19).

In response to this decree, God will be honored in praise in Habakkuk's psalm in chapter 3.

FROM THE TEXT

This passage attests to the human pride and idolatry behind empire building. Every oracle in this passage presupposes the use of materials from God's creation at the expense of others and for the aggrandizement of self. It reveals injustices toward God's entire creation, both human and non-human, both animate and inanimate. As the concluding woe implies (vv 18-20), its source is idolatry, the worship of self over God, which results in promotion of one's own endless desires over the legitimate needs of others. Such idolatry and exploitation are most insidious when cloaked under the guise of God's work, which both the Babylonian and Judean leaders sometimes claimed. Several points can be made regarding worship, idolatry and exploitation. A few are included below.

There is only one Lord; and those who attempt to lord over others will have others lord over them (vv 6-8). Tyrants generally overreach; their rule of fear can only last so long before the majority realize that they have the power to reverse their fate. Luther saw this happen in the peasant revolt of his day, and he quotes Seneca regarding this, "The person whom many people must fear must fear many people" (Luther 1525a, 126). Tyrants seal their own destiny and prepare the instruments of their own destruction. Their overreaching carries within it the seeds of its own destruction; their "tyranny is suicide" (George Adam Smith 1906, 143-44). The example they give will eventually be followed, and they will get what they dished out.

Political leaders and clergy alike need to heed this lesson. Those who lord it over others in the name of God need to remember that there is one God and it is not them. If God's agenda needs to be forced then either it is not God's agenda, or the leader needs to back off and let God handle the situation. The Lord can arbitrate between nations and peoples without human force of arms or twisting of arms (Isa 2:4).

God's gifts are for all of creation, and those who hoard them are accruing a heavy debt to God and others (vv 6-17). Babylon was not satisfied to live on its own land and enjoy the resources of the (true) Creator; it wanted what belonged to others as well (v. 6). Babylon had the power to exploit, so it fulfilled endless desires with the goods of others. It is the age-old problem of confusing greed with need.

Very little has changed. Today a handful of nations enjoy a high standard of living because they have amassed most of the world's resources and are using up the reserves that rightfully belong to future generations, other creatures and God (see Ps 104, → next paragraph). The problem is exacerbated by the double insult of resources turned into goods destined to fill temporary needs and then disposed of and replaced by similar temporary goods. The exploited human labor helplessly looks on as they produce goods destined for the fire (v 13) and suffers from the diseases caused by the unregulated polluting by foreign industries that have conscripted them. Industrial nations occasionally decry the poverty of others and express regrets that they are not industrious enough to be like them. But the truth is that one nation's poverty supports another nation's greed, and so no real solution is sought. These exploitive nations are incurring a massive debt owed to the rest of the world, and it cannot continue long before the rest of the world decides to collect.

Creation reveals God's glory (vv 14, 18-20). Creation's flourishing is an expression of praise to the Creator, and God's people are called to join Creation in that praise (Ps 148; see Ps 150:6 and elsewhere). It is the place of humans to honor the Creator and respect this choir of creation as much as possible so that they not disturb this constant praise. They should see in creation an expression of God's love for every living thing, and so extend this love by not taking out of it what belongs to other people or other creatures. Consequently, they will only use (or not use!) creation in ways that glorify God, and reject uses which promote the idolatry of self-aggrandizing schemes. The idolaters build monuments to themselves and vainly seek a voice-bearing spirit (*rûah*) that will testify to and support their self-promoting endeavors. But they have suppressed the only voice the materials possess, the voice of creation's choir (Ps 148). This voice glorifies the Creator, not the human builder. Idolaters will find no trace of the self-confirmation they are seeking. Rather, they will be condemned for their exploitation and greed. This leads directly to the next point.

Creation testifies against human sinfulness, and the teacher of lies promotes it (vv 11-19). Creation testifies against (v 11) the injustices of those who exploit its creatures for self-promotion. Babylon symbolized these exploits with images; most industrial nations build monuments to their greed, which is every bit as idolatrous as image worship! (Col 3:5). Babylon supplied voices to its images through priests and prophets who justified Babylon's deeds. Industrial nations justify their deeds by the cultural voice of greed transmitted through CEOs, economists, politicians, and the mass media. This voice speaks as the same teacher of lies that spoke to Babylon (vv 18-19).

Creation testifies to the glory of God. But unfortunately, the prevailing voice is the cultural teacher of lies, which convinces the world to exchange the glory of God for a lie (Rom 1:23). The convincing is easy, since it speaks what our ears are itching to hear. In fact, it is the voice we invoke, or rather that we speak to ourselves, to justify our achievements. The teacher of lies tells us that creation is here just for us, that if we possess much of it then it is a sign of God's blessing and a symbol of how much God loves us. The teacher of lies says that creation has no intrinsic value; that its only worth is as a resource for disposable goods. The teacher of lies tells us that what really matters is national interest, the economy, and our way of life, and that creation should spare no expense in providing these. The teacher of lies promotes idolatrous self-worship through the unregulated exploitation of creation, and then turns around and says that those who want to preserve creation for the glory of God are worshipping creation. The teacher of lies decries the individual sins of others as displeasing to the Creator, but makes a virtue of their corporate plundering of the peoples and creatures of the Creator. The teacher of lies says what people want to hear, which is too often confused with the truth.

Most people follow the teacher of lies and refuse to take creation's voice to heart (Jer 12:11). But the consistent testimony of scripture is that God hears the testimony of creation against human sinfulness and will put human pride to shame—those who destroy the earth will be held accountable by their Creator (vv 8, 13, 17; cp. Rev 11:18). We are called to reject the teacher of lies and stand humbly before the Creator (v 20).

III. CONFIDENCE THAT THE LORD WILL SAVE THE RIGHTEOUS: A HYMNIC LAMENT: HABAKKUK 3:1-19

BEHIND THE TEXT

Habakkuk 3 is identified as a prayer (v 1). The musical directions in vv 1 and 19, as well as the refrain *selah* in vv 3, 9, 13, indicate it was written for liturgical use like many of the psalms. Habakkuk likely used this prayer in the temple as he interceded on behalf of the people. Its inclusion in the book no doubt reflects the final stage of exposition of the vision.

Although often identified as a hymn due to its long hymnic section (vv 3-15), this prayer exhibits the typical elements of the (community) lament genre found throughout the psalms (Floyd 2000, 155, 637-38). It contains address to God and petition, lament (or complaint), expression of confidence based on God's past deeds, and vow to praise in anticipation of God's help (see Westermann 1981, 170). The most telling lament psalm features are the beginning petition (v 2) and the concluding vow to praise (vv 16-19a), where the situation of the people remains unresolved. Those who identify Hab 3 as a hymn can only do so by eliminating the petition of v 2 (e.g., Hiebert 1986, 118-20). For Hab 3, the prophet's complaint is implied from vv 2 (petition) and 16 (vow to praise) through allusions to an invasion and from v 17 with mention of agricultural failures. The historic and literary contexts of Hab 3 also function as the prayer's complaint section, since Hab 1 not only contains a series of complaints, but also alludes to other complaints and petitions by the prophet.

There are several literary features in Hab 3 that make it particularly suitable for its inclusion after the concluding woes of Hab 2. The most obvious is the call to worship at the end of the chapter (2:20). A dominant connecting thread between Hab 2 and 3 is the creation motif. Hab 2:14 speaks of a time when the knowledge of God's glory will fill the earth, while Hab 3:2 asks that God's works be made known again. Then God's past glorious works are described in 3:3-15 (see also 3:2*b*). Especially significant is how the Babylonians are condemned in Hab 2 for their misuse of creation, while Hab 3 clearly shows that the Lord is sovereign over creation, and that creation is a participant in or profoundly affected by the Lord's appearing (not counting the title in v 1, only vv 2, 13, 16, and 18 lack any references to creation or creation imagery).

There are other connections between Hab 3 and Hab 1:2-2:5. The Babylonians are condemned for their self-exaltation and idolatrous pride in Hab 1-2, and Hab 3 shows the Lord as the true Exalted One. Hab 2:3 tells the prophet to wait for the appointed time for the fulfillment of the vision regarding God's intervention, while in Hab 3:2 there is a petition to revive God's work at **the approach of the year (of vindication)**. Furthermore, verbal forms of "live" (*hyh*) occur in 2:4 to describe God's work on behalf of the righteous and in 3:2 in the prophet's petition for God to make past deeds live again ("revive them") for the sake of God's people. Similarly, Hab 2:4 promises that the innocent (righteous) oppressed will live by God's faithfulness and these faithful deeds are depicted in Hab 3. The prophet speaks of the weak being oppressed by the powerful throughout Hab 1-2, and the oppressed are the object of God's deliverance in 3:13-14.

IN THE TEXT

A. Superscription (3:1)

■ **1** The first verse is a title or superscription, as found in many of the psalms. It identifies the material which follows as **a prayer** (*tplh*), a term which usually connotes a prayer of lament or intercession (see *HALOT*). **Of Habakkuk** (*lhbqwq*) is similar to the phrase "of David" (*ldwd*) found in many of the psalm titles (e.g., Pss 3; 13; 14; 15). It is literally "to," "belonging to" or "for" Habakkuk. It does not necessarily indicate authorship, although in this case it likely does.

Like the earlier chapters in the book, this prayer could have been used as a public communal lament led by Habakkuk, then appended to the vision as part of its ongoing development. The phrase **on shigionoth** (*'l šgynot*) can also be translated "according to Shigionoth" (NRSV). The term *šgyn* only occurs elsewhere in the superscription of Ps 7, and its meaning is debated. It is probably a musical term (see NIV note), which connotes a dirge or lament.

B. Petition (3:2)

■ **2** The prayer begins with a petition based on God's past salvific deeds (recounted in vv 3-15). **I have heard of your fame** is literally "I have heard what is heard about you" (*šm'ty šm'k*), or "heard the report about you." It is ironic that Habakkuk says he has **heard** about the Lord's deeds (→ below), since he complained at the beginning of the book that God has not heard his cries to act on behalf of the righteous (1:2).

I stand in awe is literally "I fear" (*yr'ty*). Although this reading is acceptable, the alternate Greek *I have seen* also provides a good contextual reading (*wr'ty*; possibly, the common *y* and *w* confusion, see *BHS*). Habakkuk joins others who see God's work and tremble (→ end of verse and v 7). This does not suggest a visionary experience. Rather, it is another way of stating that the prophet has heard about God's **deeds**. The Lord's **deeds**, literally "(your) work" (*p'lk*), are God's past deeds of salvation done on behalf of Israel (e.g., Ps 44:2 [3 HB]). These were regularly recited during the great feast days to remind Israel of how they became God's people. The prophet is providing a contrast between the Lord's past deeds of salvation for Israel and God's unfolding work (*p'l*, see 1:5), which will punish them through the Babylonians (cp. Robertson 1990, 216-17). Since "deed" is singular here, some commentators see a reference to one work of salvation, that is, the extended Exodus narrative (from the departure from Egypt to the settlement in the Promised Land). They interpret every detail in vv 2-15 as referring to the Exodus narrative (see Rosenberg 1988, 2:273-80, and the commentaries of Luther and Calvin).

The next phrase contains the threefold petition, which in the MT begins *bqrb šnym*, literally, "In the midst of years." **In our time** is one possible paraphrase. This is perhaps connected to other references to time (see 1:5; 2:3-4). We translate *as the year approaches* (reading *bqrb* as an infinitive construct of *qrb* with prefixed preposition *b*, cp. Clarke 1823, 747). So the first petition reads, *as the year approaches, repeat them*, that is, works of salvation (cp. NRSV). This asks for a deliverance from current injustices and the coming Babylonian onslaught, which will "reproduce" (Lehrman 1948, 224) past deliverances.

The second petition also begins with *as the year approaches*, then continues **make them known** (*twdy'*). The pronoun **them** (or "it") is lacking, but supplied in the NIV. The petition to **make . . . known** God's deeds requests that just as God has been revealed through deliverance of Israel in the past, so would God deliver Judah from the current and impending crises. Another implication is that God would be glorified if the nations would know that the Lord has done this (see e.g., Exod 6:7; cp. Hab 2:14).

The last petition is often translated **in wrath remember mercy**. But the term translated **wrath** (*rgz*) elsewhere means "tremble" as it does throughout this prayer (vv 7, 16a, 16b; see BDB). The unvocalized Hebrew letters for **mercy** (*rḥm*) could also be read as the noun *reḥem*, "womb." I translate *While the womb trembles, remember them* (see Margulis 1970, 412-14; cp. Haak 1992, 81-82). The trembling womb connotes labor pains (or birth pangs). It as a common figure of speech for a time of national crisis or great distress, usually due to God's judgment (e.g., Exod 15:14-16; Isa 13:8; Jer 4:31; see Bergmann 2008, 1-163). The implied pronoun *them* refers to God's works (→ above). Habakkuk implores that as Judah waits trembling under the threat of a devastating judgment (1:5-11), that God **remember** the salvific works of old. **Remember** does not suggest that God has forgotten, rather that God brings to the present and acts on former promises (see Exod 2:23-25, which is followed by God calling Moses in Exod 3-4 to implement Israel's deliverance).

C. Confidence Based on the Lord's Mighty Deeds (3:3-15)

1. Recitation of the Lord's Cosmic Deeds (3:3-7)

■ **3** Habakkuk begins by reciting God's ancient deeds upon which he is basing his petitions. He describes God coming forth from an ancient dwelling place in the south, which is traditional language found in ancient hymns recounting God's deliverance of Israel (Deut 33:2; Judg 5:4-5). This section of the prayer ends at v 7. At times it seems to retrace God's movement in the Exodus, from Sinai in the south through Midian (v 7), presumably toward and perhaps into the land of Canaan (see Hiebert 1986, 83-92).

The prophet asserts that **God came from Teman**. The word for **God** is the old term Eloah ('*ĕlôah*, see Deut 32:15 and elsewhere), which is a singular counterpart to the more common (plural) *Elohim*. **Teman** means south; it is also a territory associated with Edom, from which ancient tradition depicts the Lord as proceeding to deliver Israel (Judg 5:4-5). **Holy One** is a common epithet for the Lord (→ 1:12). **Mount Paran** is probably a mountain on the Sinai Peninsula (see Num 10:12; for a similar reference see Deut 33:2).

Selah is found after this line (see NIV note b; cp. vv 9, 13). This term is also found in the Psalms and is probably an ancient liturgical notation.

When God came forth to act, God's **majesty** [*hwd*] **covered the heavens and** God's **praise filled the earth**. The whole creation joins together to praise the God who comes forth to act for Israel. Habakkuk acknowledges that God's glorious acts had been made known through creation in the past (cp. 3:2 and 2:14).

■ **4** The description of God at his appearance and the creation's response are found in vv 4-6. The first phrase is literally "brightness was like sunlight" (cp. NRSV). The LXX is probably correct to add a pronoun, resulting in God's **brightness was like sunlight**.

The following phrases are difficult to interpret; the first is literally "two horns from his hand were his" (*qrnym mydw lw*). This could be paraphrased as God **is equipped with two horns coming from the hand**. The **horns** are understood as a (two or three) forked lightning spear, one of the weapons of ancient storm gods (Roberts 1991, 134-35, 152-53; *ANEP* 500). This imagery is similar to vv 10*b*-11, where God's shining arrows and flashing lightning replace the light of sun and moon. Some interpreters translate *qrnym* (**horns**) as **rays** (see NIV), due to the references to light in the first line, and since the verbal form of *qrn* might connote rays of light (Exod 34:29).

The verse concludes with ***and there is the hiding place of*** [God's] ***strength.*** ***Hiding place*** (*ḥbywn*) occurs only here; its meaning is a conjecture (see BDB, *HALOT*). ***Strength*** (*'z*) connotes God's power or mighty deeds, which vanquish foes and save Israel (see e.g., Exod 15:13). ***There*** probably refers to God's hand as a source of power. God's hand, lightning, and strength are mentioned in the telling of the Exodus (e.g., Exod 13:14; Deut 3:24) and these tempestuous powers are hidden in God's storehouses (e.g., Job 38:21-27; Ps 135:7).

■ **5** This verse describes the powers assisting God. **Plague went before** God. A **plague** is an uncontrollable force that is often viewed in scripture as punishment by the deity, especially for covenant disobedience (e.g., Lev 26:25; Deut 28:21). Habakkuk continues with **pestilence followed** [God's] **steps.** The word for **pestilence** (*rešep*) may literally mean "flame" and is the name for a destructive Canaanite god of war and the underworld. Like **plague,** *rešep* is sometimes depicted as an agent of God's work against disobedience (Deut 32:24). The phrase **followed** indicates the Lord's advance into battle to save Israel in v 13 (Andersen 2001, 307). Verse 5 thus depicts plague and pestilence as military attendants who assist God in battle (see Hiebert 1986, 92-94). They are not independent deities as depicted by Israel's neighbors, rather they are in the service of the Lord God of Israel.

■ **6** The response of the created order to God's appearance is depicted here. There is now a pause in the divine march; God **stood, and shook the earth.** The shaking of **the earth** indicates either the recognition of God's sovereignty over the created order (cp. Pss 97:4; 104:32) or that the earth is under judgment (Isa 24:19-20). Next, God **looked and made the nations tremble** or ***shudder,*** due to God's appearance and impending judgment. Habakkuk recounts here how in the past God **looked** (*r'h*) at **the nations** and it inspired terror in evildoers.

The response of creation continues as **the ancient mountains crumbled** or ***were shattered*** (*wytpṣṣw*). Furthermore, **the age-old hills collapsed** or ***bowed down*** (*šḥw*), which suggests homage and worship or cowering. This ancient theophany material in Habakkuk's prayer demonstrates that the Lord, and not Babylon, is master over creation.

But God **marches on forever** is literally, ***and the ancient paths*** (*hlykwt*, which the NIV reads as a verb) ***are*** God's. In Ps 68:24-27 [25-28 HB] ***paths*** indicates the joyous procession of worshipers into the temple. Here, perhaps, it connotes God marching out of the cosmic temple (2:20), accompanied by military attendants (→ v 5). Here, as elsewhere, God's coming from the south is paradigmatic of past and future deliverances of God's people (see Baker 1988, 71).

■ **7** The description of the Lord's appearance returns to the response of people (→ "nations" in v 6). The NIV follows the traditional reading of this verse, which conveys the probable meaning of the text. God's march from the south causes **distress in the tents of Cushan** and trembling in **the dwellings (*tent curtains*) of *the land of* Midian.** **Cushan** appears only here; it probably corresponds to **Midian,** mentioned in the next line. The word **anguish** (*yrgzwn* "tremble") appears in vv 2 and 16 to portray a terrified response to God's ongoing judgment. Here it indicates a response to potential divine judgment. The trembling tents represent the community that resides within them (Wesley 1754, 2561).

In the Exodus narrative, *the land of Midian* is in the wilderness near Sinai, where Moses fled from Pharaoh (Exod 2:15). The depiction here is consistent with the Lord marching from the south to act for Israel (v 3) and the nations being awed at God's work (Exod 15:14-16). Since Midian was a potential (or better, traditional) threat to Israel (see Judg chs 6-8), their trembling at the awesome sight of the Lord appearing in the storm assures Israel that their enemies will not harm them.

2. God's Wrath Is for the Sake of Deliverance (3:8-15)

■ 8 This unit depicts the Lord as the divine warrior who battles with Israel's enemies. The cosmic forces of creation are involved in a variety of ways. There are references to water in the beginning, middle, and end of the unit (vv 8, 10, 15); it also begins and ends with references to (chariots and) horses (Baker 1988, 75). The disruption of creation caused by God's appearance in the previous section and the anticipated battle (especially vv 12 and 15) naturally raises a question about God's disposition toward the created order.

Verse 8 begins by asking rhetorical questions to this effect. *Was it against the river you were angry Lord, or against the river you were wrathful?* The Hebrew has the plural rivers (*nhrym*) in both lines (NIV **rivers, streams**), but the context suggests that it should be the singular, river (*nhr*, with enclitic -*m*). The words used here for God's anger (*ḥrh*, "be hot" and *'p*, "nose") come from an expression connoting a "a hot nose" (→ Nah 1:6). The question continues: *or against the sea that you raged?* The use of **river** and **sea** suggests the Exodus event, when God's people crossed the Sea of Reeds (Exod 14-15) and the Jordan River (Josh 3). **River** and **sea** appear to be in reverse order here, unless both terms refer to the sea.

The implied answer to the series of rhetorical questions is No! The line of questioning is necessary because in Israel's cultural milieu sometimes the **river** and **sea** are depicted as hostile forces that a god must overcome to form an orderly creation (see the summary in Sweeney 2000b, 2:485). While the language here may bring to mind archaic elements of a battle with the watery forces of chaos at creation, this appears to be mixed together with the dominant motif of the crossing of the sea and the Jordan in the Exodus.

The next line explains the Lord's action, *but on the contrary* (*kî*), **you rode your horses and chariots to victory.** For this usage of *kî* (NIV **when**) as an adversative or exceptive (often after a rhetorical question or negative assertion) see *HALOT* (cp. GKC §163a-b). God is often depicted with multiple **horses** and **chariots** (e.g., 2 Kgs 2:11-12), and sometimes God rides the storm cloud like a chariot (e.g., Deut 33:26). The expression **chariots to victory** is literally *chariots of deliverance.* *Deliverance* (*yšw'h*) is God's salvation or help during a crisis, such as the Exodus (Exod 4:13; 15:2).

Assuming that Habakkuk is primarily alluding to the Exodus events (Luther 1525a, 141-42; Calvin 1848, 151-52), the verse provides an example for his own

140

time. While from one perspective it may appear that God was angry with these bodies of water, Habakkuk asserts that God's goal was the deliverance of Israel from oppression and the provision of the Promised Land. God's goal back then, as in Habakkuk's day, is **deliverance** for the oppressed (cp. Hab 3:12-13).

■ **9** This verse depicts the Lord's weapons and their initial use. The first two lines in this verse have long been considered among the most difficult to translate in the OT. Almost every word is capable of multiple meanings. It is evident that God is preparing weapons for battle, but only two words are clear, **your bow** and *clubs* (arrows), and the second has not gone unchallenged!

The first two words of the sentence (*'ryh t'wr*), a noun and a verb, convey the meaning of stripping naked; hence the translation **you uncovered your bow.** This indicates the removal of a bow from a protective case (see Roberts 1991, 155). The next line, **you called for many arrows,** is an attempt make sense of a difficult text (see Bible versions and commentaries). These two lines thus seem to convey the idea that God is equipped for the battle ahead, ready for action with **bow** and **arrows.** *Selah* appears again at the end of this line (→ v 3).

The language used in the last line and in vv 10-11 is borrowed from traditional poetic portrayals of God's defeat of the powers of chaos in creation and the Exodus (e.g., Pss 68; 74; 77; 78). Yet, it is used differently here. **You split the earth with rivers** conveys the idea of God splitting the earth with valleys where rivers can flow (see Pss 74:15; 78:15-16). This alludes to God's beneficent works in ordering and sustaining creation (see e.g., Gen 2:10-14; Pss 24:2; 65:9 [10 HB]; Isa 33:21; 41:18; see similar language in Ps 74:13, 15).

■ **10-11** Verses 10-11 portray creation's response to the appearance of the warrior God. Other passages describe nature as assisting in God's salvific work (Judg 5:20-21; Ps 114:3, 5); here, however, the Lord works alone as the cosmos is stirred by God's appearance. **The mountains saw you and writhed** connotes an earthquake. The "writhing" or quaking mountains are a warning that announces the arrival of the one who sets things right on earth (cp. Ps 18:7 [8 HB]; 114:4), which involves punishment for some and salvation for others. As one of the most ancient elements of creation (see Ps 90:2), the **mountains** are an appropriate herald of this news.

Two more announcements of God's arrival follow. **Torrents of water swept by** indicates heavy rains. Although this may seem more appropriate as a heavenly response (→ below), the term *zrm* often connotes the earthly effects of a rainstorm (e.g., Isa 25:4). **The deep roared** is literally *the deep issued its voice.* **The deep** (*tĕhôm*) indicates the cosmic waters upon which God's *rûaḥ* ("wind," "spirit") passed at creation (Gen 1:2-3; Ps 33:7). Biblical cosmology understood these primal waters to lie in the seas (Jonah 2:6 [7 HB]; Pss 71:20; 135:6) and below the surface of the earth as the source of springs (Gen 7:11). The *voice* of creation often indicates praise of the Creator (e.g., Ps 93:3); here it also announces God's coming.

The last line, **lifted its waves on high,** assumes that the deep continues to be the subject, and that "hands" (*ydym*) is poetic for **waves** (Roberts 1991, 141). However, it is also possible to translate this line as **on high** *sun lifted its hands,*

141

assuming **sun** from v 11 as the subject of the sentence (cp. NRSV; Hiebert 1986, 6, 30-31; there is no **and** between **sun** and **moon** as supplied by the NIV and many interpreters). If this reading is correct, it is assumed that sun lifting its hands is a sign of surrendering its role to God.

The NIV treats **sun** (and) **moon** as the subject of the first line of v 11. **Heavens** is literally, *lofty habitation* or *lofty residence*. Sun and moon standing in the heavens indicates inactivity or deferring of their roles to the Lord. The NIV suggests sun and moon standing still in deference to or in awe of the **lightning** (flashing) produced by God's **arrows** and **spear**. However, it is also possible that v 11 may be conveying the idea that the roles of sun and moon have been temporarily supplanted by God's **arrows** and lightning **spear**. In other words, God's weapons provide the light instead of sun and moon (*for sunlight* (*l'wr*) *your arrows pass by, for moonlight* (*lngh*) *the lightning of your spear*) (cp. Roberts 1991, 129, 141).

It was necessary for the Judeans to hear that their salvation would be from the Lord alone, since they were prone to lapse into the worship of the sun and moon (2 Kgs 23:35; Ezek 8:16). The Lord is equipped for battle like an ancient storm god (→ v 4), who is variously depicted as riding chariots (→ v 8) and armed with bow, quiver of arrows, or a lightning bolt spear (see *ANEP* 490; Hiebert 1986, 97-98). Day and night fiery weapons light up the sky, illuminating God's intentions to judge the oppressors on the earth. It is a fearful image for some, but a harbinger of hope for those who need divine protection.

■ **12** God is depicted as coming **in wrath** or *in indignation* (*bz'm*). The text says, **In wrath you strode through the earth, and in anger you threshed the nations.** The word for **strode** (*s'd*) connotes God's solemn march for the sake of deliverance in Judg 5:4 and Ps 68:7 [8 HB]. Here God's march is more universal; it is **through the earth**. These two lines convey the same idea.

Wrath (or *indignation*) and **anger** are commonly associated with God's judgment on Israel or nations that oppress Israel (e.g., Lam 2:6; Ps 78:49; Isa 10:5; Jer 10:10; Zeph 3:8). Threshing sometimes connotes conquest or divine judgment (e.g., 2 Kgs 13:7; Isa 21:10; Amos 1:3). This verse clarifies what the rhetorical question of v 8 implies: God's wrath is not against the created order nor Israel, rather, it is against disobedient **nations**. The hope implied by Habakkuk's recital of the Lord's past deeds is that God will be moved to act in similar judgment against Babylon and its allies.

■ **13** God's coming forth against the nations is further clarified here: **You came out to deliver your people, *to deliver* your anointed one.** The term **came out** (*yṣ't*) sometimes connotes going forth into battle, so it could be translated *marched forth* (see e.g., Deut 20:1). The expression **to deliver your people** (*lyš' 'mk*) is literally, "for the deliverance of your people."

The identity of the **anointed one** is the subject of debate. Since it is the Hebrew word for messiah (*mĕšîaḥ*), some identify the reference here to the ruling Davidic king (e.g., Hiebert 1986, 107), who would have been declared God's anointed one or messiah upon taking the throne (Ps 2). However, the tight parallelism of the lines would suggest that **your people** and **your anointed one** are synonymous terms (cp. Ps 105:15; also Ps 28:8). It is used figuratively here, perhaps likening the people to the anointed priests (Exod 30:30), since God's people are set apart for a special calling as a kingdom of priests (Exod 19:4-6).

Although the words of the following two parallel lines are clear, their meaning is somewhat obscure. Verses 13b-14 tell how God executed judgment on the nations mentioned in v 12 in a manner congruent with how Habakkuk hopes God will soon act against current oppressors. **You crushed the leader of the land of wickedness** is the NIV's attempt to clarify the ambiguous statement in Hebrew. It is literally *you crushed the head from the house of the wicked*. The crushing of the head of an enemy in wars of deliverance is also found in Judg 5:26 and Ps 68:21 [22 HB]. Habakkuk's woe oracles condemned the Babylonian "house" (2:10). Here the prophet recounts how God has destroyed a wicked *house* (dynasty or kingdom) in the past or its *head* (r'š), probably meaning its **leader**. So it is evident here that *house* probably connotes a dynasty represented by king and capital city, which has incurred the Lord's judgment due to the mistreatment of Israel.

The next line is literally, *laying bare the foundation up to neck;* the NIV **you stripped him from head to foot** is another attempt to clarify the Hebrew text. *Foundation* (yswd) sometimes indicates human stability or durability (or their lack of these; see e.g., Job 4:19; 22:16). *Neck* (sw'r) is a parallel image for **head**. Habakkuk again recounts God's total destruction of a kingdom that oppressed Israel in the past. The liturgical notation *selah* occurs again (→ vv 3 and 9; see also NIV note).

■ **14** The meaning of this verse is somewhat obscure, and many commentators find references to the conquest of personified chaos in some of its ambiguous details (→ v 13). The first line can be translated **You pierced his head *with his own staff.*** The pronoun **his** (with **head**) is supplied from context. *Staff* is a common translation of *mṭh*, though in this context **spear** is a possibility, since it (and not staff) would be the weapon that would be used to pierce one's head. However, if *staff* is intended here, then it implies a scepter, a sign of authority. **Head** could also refer to a king or a designated leader. Though the Lord had weapons, they were not used; rather, God destroyed the head of the enemy nation with his own symbol of authority.

When his warriors stormed to scatter us (literally, *his warriors stormed to scatter me*) links the second line with the first and explains the context of the Lord's destruction of the head. However, the second line could stand alone, since it is not a temporal clause in Hebrew. The term translated **warriors** occurs only here. The root word for **stormed** (s'r in verbal and noun forms) indicates a life-threatening wind storm, but most occurrences in the Bible are figurative. The final *to scatter me* (lhpyṣny) seems like an unusual entrance of the prophet into the scene, although something similar occurs in v 7. Some read the final *yod* as another mistake for a *waw*, which would result in **to scatter us**. Since the Babylonian crisis has not yet reached its full effect on Judah, it is likely that the prophet is identifying with the *past* scattering of his people.

The next phrase continues to depict the actions of the warriors; **gloating as though to devour the wretched who were in hiding**. The scene depicts the oppressor's ruthless pursuit of the weak, relentlessly ambushing them, showing them no mercy, and rejoicing in their oppression. God's intervention is certainly warranted.

■ **15** The final verse of the section that describes God's great deeds returns to a picture hinted at in the beginning of the section (→ v 8). It mentions the sea and God's horses: **You *tread upon* the sea with your horses, *heaping up* the great waters**. While the treading of **the sea** could be construed as reminiscent of God stilling chaotic precreation waters (cp. Job 9:8), the imagery turns to the Exodus in the last line. The ***heaping up* the great waters** recalls the standing water in that event, although different vocabulary is used elsewhere (see Exod 14:21-22; 15:8; Ps 78:13). Furthermore, Ps 77:19 [20 HB] describes the Exodus in language similar to this verse; in that verse God's "way" (*drk*, the noun form of ***tread***) was ***through the sea . . . through the great waters***. God's treading on the sea indicates that the Lord divided the waters and passed through before Israel.

Mention of this foundational salvation deed forms a fitting conclusion for the supplication section of the prayer. The Exodus, more than any other event in the OT, illustrates the Lord's saving power: against all human expectations God rescued a ragtag band of slaves from one of the world's most powerful empires.

D. Confidence in Time of Need (3:16-19*a*)

I. Trembling Silence before the Lord (3:16*a*)

■ **16*a*** This verse begins the final section, which is a vow to trust and praise God until the promises of the vision are fulfilled and Habakkuk's petitions granted. The past success of God against Israel's enemies inspires Habakkuk with confidence that God will act again. But the response is mixed.

First, we encounter his bodily reaction to the continuing adversity of God's people and the prospect of God's future judgment announced in 1:5-17. What he **heard** is the story of God's deeds, which the prophet has just recounted. Notice that the petition started the same way (v 2). The bodily response is **and my heart pounded** (literally, ***and my belly trembled***). Trembling is a key word in the prayer (→ the next line and v 7). Habakkuk's trembling corresponds to the nation trembling in birth pangs (→ v. 2, and see Bergmann 2008, 160-61, also 92). The crisis that Judah will suffer before, during, and after God's anticipated action against Babylon is a major thread in the book.

Furthermore, Habakkuk says **my lips quivered at the sound**; that is, he hears **the sound** of his own voice, and his **lips** quiver to utter such breathtaking words. The reaction continues, **decay crept into my bones**. Bones (*'ṣmym*) can signify one's inner physical and emotional wellbeing (see e.g., Pss 6:2 [3 HB]; 22:14 [15 HB]). **Decay** probably indicates Habakkuk's inner turmoil (cp. Prov 12:4; 14:30) and his

144

being on the verge of collapse. *And underneath, my footsteps tremble* is literally "and under me I tremble (*'rgz*)".

2. Waiting with Praise and Hope (3:16b-19a)

■ **16b** Despite the grim prospects of a continually unfolding crisis, the prophet states his confidence that God will act to restore order: **Yet I will wait patiently for the day of calamity to come on the nation invading us.** This is literally, *I await the day of adversity to come against the people attacking us.* The term **wait** is from a verb that usually means "rest" (*nwḥ*). The word sometimes connotes a person silently awaiting the answer to a question, that is, "wait quietly" (the NIV adds **patiently**). **The day of calamity/*adversity*** (*ywm ṣrh*) is another way to describe the Day of the Lord, a day when God intervenes to set things right. Here it implies God's punishment of Babylon; but unfortunately, it will only come after Babylon attacks Judah.

Invading (*ygwd*) indicates that the attack is continual, repeated and impending, and not a simple future event. In other words, the innocent continue to be attacked by the powerful (1:2-4), and the Babylonians will soon be attacking Judah (1:5-11). With this in view, it is clear that the term *'m* (***people***) refers to both the oppressive Judean leaders and Babylon. The NIV (**nation**) seems to limit the term to Babylon.

■ **17** Habakkuk expresses his unwavering confidence in the Lord, despite present and future adversity. Verse 17 is the beginning of a conditional sentence introduced by *kî* with an imperfect verb expressing a real or possible condition (here, of crop loss or failure). Verse 18 then expresses the consequences (GKC §159bb). Thus we have **Though** (or "supposing if," v 17) and "yet I will" (v 18).

Habakkuk assumes the loss of major crops (**fig, grapes,** and **olive crops),** which would have a devastating effect on the economy and food supply. The same can be said for the loss of **sheep** and **cattle**. Abundance of crops and livestock was counted among the Lord's blessing on an obedient Israel (Deut 28:1, 4; Lev 26:3-5). Loss of these through warfare, famine, or destructive insects is among the curses for disobedience (see e.g., Deut 28:15, 18).

In light of Habakkuk's earlier complaints about injustices, it is probable that the poor of the land were already losing their crops and livestock through unjust fines, taxes, tribute, and seizure of land and goods (→ 1:2-5). The situation would be sure to deteriorate, however, with the impending invasion of Babylon, which would continue to seize and destroy land and goods (see Jer 5:15-17). It could be claimed by the righteous that Judah's loss of crops and cattle was a sign of God's judgment against Judean oppressors and an answer to Habakkuk's prayers (1:2-17). Yet the oppressed, including Habakkuk, would not be celebrating God's intervention, for it would only worsen their own situation. This is the irony and extreme testing point of Habakkuk's faith, which makes the concluding statement (3:18-19) even more remarkable.

■ **18** This verse completes the conditional sentence begun in the previous verse and functions as the concluding (vow to) praise typical of psalms of lament. Even "though" (v 17) their way of life is threatened, Habakkuk says (on behalf of the people), **yet I will rejoice in the LORD**. The yet I (*w'ny*) is emphatic, *I, for my part*. Like many of the lament psalms, this introduces a turning point in the prayer (e.g., Ps 5:7 [8 HB]; Mic 7:7; see Keil 1868, 115). Although the first person pronouns **I** and **my** are used here and in the following verses, Habakkuk continues to represent the community and is speaking on behalf of all of God's oppressed people.

Rejoice (*'e'l ôzâ*) can be translated *exult*. Its root connotes the exultation of the oppressor in v 14 (also → below). Although the conditions listed in v 17 have already begun to affect the people, Habakkuk anticipates the Lord's deliverance and rejoices. The contrast continues, **I will be joyful**, or better *I will rejoice* (*'gylh*) **in God my Savior**. The prefixed verb forms *exult* and *rejoice* indicate continual or habitual action, and not future here (see similar usage in v 16). **Savior** is literally, "salvation, deliverance, saving help" (*yš'*). So the entire phrase is literally, *God of my deliverance* (see Ps 18:46 [47 HB]; Isa 17:10; Mic 7:7), suggesting God's *deliverance* is essentially completed. God's deliverance has been worked for God's people in the past, and it is certain for them in the future. Although deliverance has not yet occurred in Habakkuk's experience, he is certain that God will answer his petition to revive, make known, and remember the saving deeds of the past (v 2).

This concluding praise presents a significant departure from Habakkuk's opening prayer, where he stated that God does not "save" the oppressed (1:2). The prophet has come full circle. There is also an ironic contrast between the ruthless Babylonians and the beleaguered people of God. As mentioned above, forms of both words used for praise here (*'lṣ* and *gyl*) are applied to the Babylonians as they rejoice over their conquest of helpless prey. But even though the oppressor exalts when he captures and consumes the weak (1:15; 3:14), the oppressed Judeans (represented by Habakkuk) exult and rejoice in the Lord, even while they are being captured, consumed and left with nothing to eat (see v 17)!

■ **19a** Habakkuk concludes, first, with a poetic expansion on the phrase *God of my deliverance* (v 18) who can be trusted in times of adversity. **The Sovereign LORD** is literally, *Yhwh my Lord*. By articulating the divine name of God, who has the title *Lord* (*'dny*), the prophet asserts God is master of creation, and therefore will set things right for the oppressed; God is *their* (my) *Lord*.

God is also **my strength**, a word that is difficult to render exactly. The word is *ḥayil*, which generally connotes "power" or "faculty"; so the phrase could also be translated *my power*. In view of Habakkuk's mention of the decrease in flocks, herds, and harvest in this prayer (v 17), it is likely that the title *my power* also means that the Lord is the one whose power grants, or will grant, renewed fertility in livestock and agriculture (see Ruth 4:11; Prov 31:3; Eising 1980, 349).

The prophet ends with two poetic descriptions of God's deliverance for the oppressed. First, God **makes my feet like the *deer's*** (literally "doe's, female deer's"). Similar imagery is found in Ps 18:33 [34 HB]. The deer is swift and surefooted on hazardous ground, perhaps suggesting freedom and stability of body and spirit to the prophet. It is significant that this section of the prayer began with the prophet saying his feet were on the verge of giving way under him (v 16), and that it ends here with imagery suggesting confident surefootedness.

Finally, **upon my heights** (*bmwty*) God **makes me tread** (*ydrkny*). **Heights** sometimes connote Israel's battlefields where God gives them victory (2 Sam 1:19, 25), and by extension, is used figuratively for the safe places where God sets believers (Deut 32:13; Isa 58:14). The prophet's recitation of God's mighty deeds concludes with God coming down from a lofty abode and treading (*drkt*) the earthly realm to deliver the oppressed (v 15). Habakkuk here confesses that God enables the earthly oppressed to join God and once again tread on their safe places. This imagery thus suggests freedom and secure confidence granted by God to an oppressed people. While they still await their physical freedom, they are confident that they are under the watchful care of their divine deliverer.

E. Directions to Choirmaster (3:19*b*)

The last half of the verse ends with obscure musical notation, **For the director of music** (or leader), which appears fifty five times in Psalm titles (e.g., Pss 4-6; 11-14; see *HALOT*, BDB). This is its only occurrence at the end of a psalm or prayer. The phrase **On my stringed instruments** (*bngynwty*) can be rendered **with string accompaniment** (interpreting -*y* as a gentilic, see *IBHS* §5.7c).

FROM THE TEXT

Habakkuk's prayer has endured as a source of inspiration for God's people. Concerning the concluding words (vv 18-19), Adam Clarke declared, "These two verses give the finest display of *resignation* and *confidence* that I have ever met with" (Clarke 1823, 750). Several key points will be offered below, most of them focused on prayers and praise during times of adversity.

God is worthy of worship for who God is, not for what God does in the present moment for the faithful. Habakkuk's concluding praise is a testimony to this. Nothing has visibly changed since Habakkuk began his complaints (1:2) and offered his concluding praise (Hab 3, see Achtemeier 1986, 58); as a matter of fact, Habakkuk knows full well that things will get worse! Like Abraham, who was tested to follow God at the prospect of losing all of God's promises (Gen 22:1-19), Habakkuk trusts a God whose deliverance is delayed and all of God's creation blessings fail.

Habakkuk's prayer shows the proper response before God. He recites God's deeds in trembling awe; even when God's appearance seems to constantly disrupt the order of creation that is necessary for the flourishing of life! Even this unsettled creation offers an example as it shakes in awe before God! Central to Habakkuk's worship of God is a recognition of God's nature and being as the Holy one (v 3), deliverance (v 18, see vv 8, 13), light (vv 4, 10-11), and our strength (v 19). It makes no difference that we may not experience or feel these at the moment; God deserves praise for who God is.

If our dedication to God is only motivated by what God does for us, then we will not endure the trials of life (see Job 1:8-11). We need to recognize that sometimes we serve an inconvenient God. God does not move heaven and earth for the sake of our personal convenience or comfort.

Habakkuk knows that God wills the best for creation, but sometimes there is no quick and easy fix for the evil that entangles our world. Like surgery to remove life threatening cancer, God's deliverance may involve unavoidable pain on the body of creation before healing can begin. And like a good surgeon, it grieves God that pain must sometimes go before restoration. Innocents may continue to suffer, but faith in a benevolent God trusts that a greater good will eventually come.

The direction of God's work may not be easy to discern through current historical events; sometimes all we can do is pray to and praise God despite these events. While the scripture affirms we worship a God who works in history, sometimes what we see at the moment is not an accurate gauge of God's will. This was Habakkuk's dilemma from the beginning (1:2); what he thought he knew about God did not square with what he saw around him. Habakkuk could have taken the easy way out and claimed that God was causing current events. That way he would not have to worry about the suffering around him, nor the cruel actions of the oppressors. But he did not do that. Rather, Habakkuk's solution was first to challenge God, then pray in such a way that Habakkuk would hear again (3:2) what God had done in the past. By doing this he hoped to find a clearer picture of who God is and how the present moment fits into the bigger picture.

Habakkuk's questions of God's purposes and consistency were never rebuked; rather, they were the Lord's pathway to the response of praise in difficult days. While Habakkuk did not find the certainty he was seeking, he did rediscover the proper response of creation and God's people to a deliverer God. Like Habakkuk, we should not too quickly assume that whatever happens around us, especially unjust suffering, reflects God's plans. Rather, we should pray on behalf of the suffering and struggle with God in prayer over their deliverance. Only then can we learn how to praise God in the face of life's injustices.

Personal wellbeing is not always an accurate gauge of God's favor toward individuals or nations. At the prospect of an invading army and in the midst of crop failure and poverty, Habakkuk dared to rejoice in God's strength and deliverance (3:16-19). It is evident throughout scripture that God wills *shalom* or wellbeing for all of creation. But sometimes immoral people generate their own wellbeing at the expense of others; a thief can live very well on stolen goods! Once more, Habakkuk does not take the easy way out and write off the innocent as having secret faults that evoke God's judgment.

It is clear from Habakkuk that the oppressive Judean and Babylonian leaders got their power and prosperity by exploiting others. It is also clear that those who were exploited were the righteous (innocent) faithful. The same thing happens today. Yet it is surprising how often today individual or national prosperity are interpreted as a sign of God's favor, and poverty and suffering are viewed as indicators of divine judgment. This was the mistake of Job's comforters. It is even more surprising how this is sometimes used as an excuse for not helping the suffering, or even worse, as justification to further exploit the weak. Again, Habakkuk's example is to identify with and pray for the exploited.

When prayers are answered and God's deliverance finally comes, it may not include me and my circle of friends and family. Because Judah was going to endure judgment before deliverance, Habakkuk had good reason to suspect that the greater good may be for a generation other than his own. Like Jeremiah's promise of God's good plans for the exiles (Jer 29:11, see v 10, the "you" is intergenerational!), God's promises to Habakkuk (see Hab 2:4-5) were not fulfilled for two or three generations (cp. Goldingay 2009, 87).

Because these promises were not for him personally, the prophet could have easily given in to cynicism and made his own life more comfortable by joining the oppressors. But instead he held onto faith, willing to suffer in the present, even rejoicing that someday, somehow, the faithful God (see 2:4) would deliver Judah.

This offers an important prophetic corrective to cultures beset by instant gratification, who want it their way and want it now! It is always a mistake to choose present comfort or pleasure over the future greater good for our children, grandchildren, and the planet. God's deliverance takes into account a much bigger picture; we need to take this into consideration in our praises as we seek answers to our prayers.

Habakkuk's rejoicing in the time of suffering is offered as comfort for the oppressed, not as a justification for the oppressors. Supporting oppression runs counter to Habakkuk's complaints and overall message, which affirms God's concerns for the oppressed and judgment of the oppressors. As stated above, God's will is to save the oppressed, not to cause them to suffer. But sometimes people do suffer, and sometimes it is connected with God's work.

At the heart of the Gospel is a suffering Savior who calls people to follow by taking up their cross (Mark 8:31-38). Since we serve a suffering Savior we are not surprised that we, too, suffer (1 Pet 2:21). That suffering happens is a source of comfort to the suffering. But God's people need to exercise great caution before telling others that they should accept *all* suffering as God ordained. Suffering is never good for its own sake, and changes should be made if it is in one's power to alleviate it.

Therefore it is never appropriate to participate in or condone actions that cause suffering and justify it as God's will or because suffering is unavoidable. It is reprehensible to exploit others and justify it on such grounds. If a message of divinely ordained suffering is used as a tool to maintain the status quo (wealth for the powerful, suffering for the weak) and especially to quell discontent and justify the abuse of victims, then this is contrary to Habakkuk's message and to the Gospel.

Confidence in a God of deliverance despite adversity is not to be confused with denial. Habakkuk's trust in God is in the face of very real problems that threaten

149

the survival of God's people. Habakkuk's hope is realistic; it is not to be mistaken for denial of the misery he sees around him. Note that Habakkuk is trembling in his sandals over God's current and impending judgment, while at the same time expressing his confidence that God is his strength who makes his feet like a deer's (vv 16-19)! Pain, suffering, and poverty make life difficult, and cannot be casually whisked aside with a forced smile and a quick "Praise the Lord anyway."

It would be a mistake to view either the prophet's or Paul's rejoicing in the midst of suffering as saying that adversity has no effect on believers (3:18; see Phil 4:4-5; cp. 1:18-19, 2:17). Paul and Habakkuk both recognize that hardships take a toll on the believer. Both, however, were confident that God's purposes are being worked out behind the scenes (Achtemeier 1986, 59). The tension between denial and hope was captured well by Adam Clarke who wrote:

> [Habakkuk] saw that evil was at hand, and *unavoidable*; he *submitted* to the dispensation of God, whose Spirit enabled him to paint it in all its calamitous circumstances. He knew that God was merciful and gracious. He trusted to his promise, though all appearances were against its fulfilment; for he knew that the word of Jehovah could not fail, and therefore his confidence is unshaken. (Clarke 1823, 750)

Another form of denial is to reduce God's deliverance to our eternal destiny and to conclude that hardships on earth do not matter. Habakkuk does not have this option since he spoke before Israel had a clear understanding of the resurrection of the dead. The prophet is not hoping for the deliverance (or salvation) of a soul from eternal damnation and for a heaven beyond this life. Rather he is speaking of God's saving help during times of earthly crises. While we hold firm to our heavenly hope through the resurrection of Jesus from the dead, it would be a mistake to disengage from our calling to aid the suffering of this world (see e.g., James 1:27; 2:14; 1 John 3:16-17) because everything will be transformed "by and by." Contrary to a once popular hymn, this earth *is* now our home and our passing through has significance for God's kingdom on earth, as it is in heaven.

God's transforming presence is experienced in the presentation of the word. As Habakkuk remembers and retells God's past deeds of deliverance (3:2-15), the prophet's near despair is transformed to hopeful rejoicing (3:16-19). Despite the discouraging prospect of a bad situation growing worse, Habakkuk is confident that the same God who saved Israel in the Exodus and other defining moments will continue to save believers in the future. As we hear scripture proclaimed, through the Holy Spirit we encounter the same God who delivered Israel at the sea, who protected them in every crisis, and who proclaimed the coming of God's Kingdom in Jesus Christ.

ZEPHANIAH

INTRODUCTION

A. Zephaniah and His Time

Our only source of knowledge regarding the prophet Zephaniah comes through the biblical book of the same name. Zephaniah (Hebrew *ṣĕpanyâ*) means "The Lord ("Yah") has hidden (or protected, treasured)," which connotes God's special care for the faithful (see BDB under *ṣāpan*).

While Zephaniah is not explicitly identified as a prophet or visionary, his sphere of influence and message seem to place him among typical (or central) Jerusalem prophets like Isaiah, Nahum, or Habakkuk. But his message attests that he also has roots in a reforming tradition like that of Hosea and Jeremiah (Wilson 1984, 280-81). The superscription (Zeph 1:1) identifies the time of his activity as "in the days of King Josiah" (NRSV). He was probably active several years after Nahum and approximately three decades before Habakkuk.

153

The superscription also provides Zephaniah with a four generation genealogy, which is the longest given for any of the prophets in the OT. Clues to its purpose are undoubtedly found in the names of two much discussed forefathers. First, the objective of this type of linear genealogy is to connect him with Hezekiah, the prophet's great grandfather. Hezekiah's father Ahaz was an idolater who made an ill-advised Assyrian alliance (2 Kgs 16). But Hezekiah was known as a reforming king (2 Kgs 18-20), who may even have acted on the basis of an early version of Deuteronomy (McBride 2007, 115). Therefore his background was somewhat analogous to Josiah's. The prophet's pedigree perhaps explains his concern for wholehearted devotion to the Lord, something that the Manasseh branch of the family abandoned until Josiah.

Zephaniah's family ties with Josiah (they would be distant cousins) may have given him access to the royal court. It is likely that the prophet was a member of the party that inspired Josiah's reforms. Regarding the next two names in the genealogy, the fact that Hezekiah's son Amariah and grandson Gedaliah (Zeph 1:1) are not mentioned elsewhere is not unusual. Kings had multiple wives and many sons who were not widely known. Some descendants were eventually forgotten because they were not in the lineage that occupied the throne.

The second name of note in the genealogy is Zephaniah's father, Cushi. The name literally means "Cushite," and it also appears as a proper name in Jer 36:14. Cush (sometimes translated Ethiopia) or Nubia was a territory on the southern border of Egypt (see Aharoni and Avi-Yonah 1977, #15). His father's name Cushi here probably indicates African heritage, perhaps through the marriage of his grandfather Gedaliah to a Cushite woman (Rice 1979, 25, 28). During his lifetime Zephaniah would have been known as "Zephaniah ben Cushi," that is, "son of (a) Cushite." The superscription perhaps aims to clarify that Zephaniah ben Cushi was in fact an Israelite by virtue of direct descent from Hezekiah (Blenkinsopp 1996, 113-14).

The prophet's ministry is set "during the reign of Josiah" (1:1) who ruled from ca. 640-609 BC. Josiah's rise to power is understood against the backdrop of his predecessors. From the days of Isaiah, the Assyrian empire had dominated the west Asian nations, which included the conquest of Israel and reduction of Judah to a vassal state. Manasseh (r. 687-42 BC), Josiah's grandfather, was a loyal vassal of Assyria; 2 Kgs 21 portrays him as being idolatrous and a shedder of innocent blood. After his death, his son Amon (r. 642-40 BC) followed the ways of his father (2 Kgs 21:19-26). Amon was assassinated by government officials, but "the people of the land" who apparently advocated the political status quo (a pro-Assyrian view) quickly killed the assassins and placed Josiah, his eight year old son, on the throne (2 Kgs 21:23-22:1). This scenario indicates that initially Josiah's reign was under the guardianship of a pro-Assyrian party left over from the time of Manasseh (Haak 2003, 52; Kim 2008, 413). No doubt the pro- and anti-Assyrian parties were vying for control early in Josiah's reign. Zephaniah could be viewed as supporting the anti-Assyrians, who eventually won out (Haak 2003, 52, 66-67).

Zephaniah's oracles against Jerusalem (1:2-18 and 3:1-8) reflect cultic abuses very similar to those practiced during the time of Manasseh and Amon (see 2 Kgs 21). This situation was not thoroughly addressed until the eighteenth year of Josiah (622 BC), when the reported discovery of the Torah of Moses in the Temple spurred a sweeping reform (2 Kgs 22:3-23:25). According to 2 Chr 34:3-7, Josiah had already undertaken some reforms in his eighth year (632 BC). This indicates positive influences on the young king long before the discovery of the Torah scroll. Zephaniah could be characterized as one of several early voices advocating reform.

Yet, as we will see in 2:4-15, Zephaniah's later prophecies are not congruent with Josiah's supposed far-reaching move to annex surrounding nations. References to the desolate land and urban ruins that a refugee remnant will occupy after God's judgment upon Judah's neighbors (2:4, 6-7, 9) do not suggest a conquering army claiming territory for a reigning king of Judah. Furthermore, it is doubtful that Zephaniah would support the king's policy of centralizing all worship in the Jerusalem temple (→ 2:11 and 3:9-10). Indeed, the sweeping judgment against Jerusalem announced in 1:2-3:8 suggests that the temple would be destroyed with the city, although it would be considered very dangerous for the prophet to unambiguously state that (see Jer 26:6-11, 20-23). Moreover, Zephaniah does not explicitly indicate whether or not the (rebuilt) temple will play a role in Jerusalem after the restoration. The most he says is that on that day a remnant will continue to call on the name of the Lord, apparently from the Temple Mount (3:11-12).

With the above discussion in mind we can date the prophecies of 1:2-2:3 to at least before the reform of Josiah's eighteenth year (622 BC), possibly even earlier than the changes that the king implemented in his eighth year (632 BC). Zephaniah 2:4-15 appeared slightly later as an independent prophecy. It primarily focuses on the Lord's judgment on peoples and nations who have had an ongoing impact on Judah. The material in 3:1-8 is still indicative of a Jerusalem before Josiah's reform. It appears to be a slightly later reformulation of some of the threats of judgment found in 1:2-2:3, perhaps uttered in a temple setting. Zephaniah 3:9-20 addresses two facets of a post-judgment restoration hinted at in the earlier judgment oracles. The first deals with the fate of the nations who will become worshipers of the Lord (3:9-10; → 2:11). The second focuses on the future of Jerusalem occupied by a humble remnant (3:11-20; → 2:3, 7, 9). A pre-judgment and pre-reform perspective is still evident, indicating it was probably added to 3:1-8 soon after it was first proclaimed.

At a later time Zephaniah's proclamations were committed to writing and then collected into their present form. This would have happened after the abuses in Jerusalem were corrected (→ 1:2-13; 3:1-8); that is, after the reforms of Josiah were fully implemented in 622 BC. But it is more likely that it was committed to writing after the time of Habakkuk, perhaps even during the Babylonian Exile. It would have served to remind the Judeans that although many of the abuses in Jerusalem had been corrected under Josiah, Jerusalem was guilty of similar idolatry and oppression under Josiah's successors (→ Introduction to Habakkuk, Hab 1:1-

2:5 and 2:6-20). It would also have informed the Judeans that even with Josiah's corrections, the prospect of a Day of the Lord against Judah and Jerusalem had not been withdrawn (cp. 2 Kgs 23:26-27). Events such as the Babylonian Conquest and exile were therefore to be expected, since they could be interpreted as the Lord's judgment against Judah.

B. Literary Structure

The book of Zephaniah appears to have been arranged approximately in chronological order (→ above). It is divided into two major parts, 1:1-2:15 and 3:1-20. These mirror one another through the repetition of key terms, primarily "all" and "all the land" (or earth, *kl-h'rs*; → commentary).

Part one (1:1-2:15) begins with announcements of the Lord's extensive judgment against the religious, civic, and economic leaders of Jerusalem and Judah (1:2-18). It follows with a call to assemble for repentance (2:1-3) and concludes with announcements of God's judgment upon some representative peoples for the sake of God's scattered remnant (2:4-15).

Part two (3:1-20) also begins with announcements of judgment against Jerusalem and corrupt civil and religious leaders and "the whole world" (3:1-8). This is followed by God's promise to purify the lips of peoples throughout the world, enabling all peoples to worship and serve the Lord (3:9-13). The Lord promises to remove the arrogant from Jerusalem and leave the humble remnant in the city (vv 11-13). The concluding section (3:14-20) opens with an exhortation for Jerusalem to rejoice wholeheartedly and concludes with the remnant receiving praise from "all the peoples of the earth." See the detailed outline at the beginning of the commentary.

C. Message of Zephaniah

Zephaniah's message can be summarized as an announcement of the Day of the Lord as a great day of judgment upon God's people, which is followed by a restoration of a remnant. Although the Lord's actions are directed against Judah and Jerusalem, they have consequences that reach the ends of the earth. Zephaniah's proclamation of judgment and restoration is best understood against the prophet's broader theological heritage as now preserved in the scriptures (→ sidebar Cosmic Judgment in Zephaniah).

First, *the Lord demands accountability of community leaders who are called to guide God's people*. Zephaniah sees Judah under the leadership of a Jerusalem elite who fail miserably to follow its divine calling. Not only do they fail, but they have established a community that is the exact opposite of the Lord's intentions as revealed in the Torah and Psalms. Their worship of other gods is joined with self-aggrandizement, which manifests itself as abuse of power and economic exploitation (1:4-18; 3:1-5). Zephaniah hints that innocent people are suffering (1:9, 11, 12-13; 3:1, 3-4, 19). Instead of bringing worldwide honor to the Lord, corrupt leaders have brought shame upon the city and its God, both at home and abroad (2:1; 3:5, 18; cp. 2:8-10).

Second, *God's creation intentions will be accomplished even if it means judgment at the cosmic level*. God's judgment will be sweeping and it will affect both Judah and the nations in the world. In the past, Judah refused to respond to God's repeated calls for repentance and change. The Lord did not resort to punishment quickly, but instead continued to save Judah from its enemies even when the people were not wholly devoted to God (3:6). Moreover, Judah refused to accept the Lord's "correction" or disciplinary actions in the past, but continued in its sinful way of life.

Judah's vocation has cosmic significance, and therefore, its sin has cosmic effects, which can be purged only by a cosmic judgment. The prophet announces that this sweeping judgment will clear away the corrupting influences of Judah and all other nations on God's creation (1:2-2:15, → sidebar Cosmic Judgment in Zephaniah). Nations are held accountable in 2:4-15 for their idolatry and sin. Although Zephaniah mentions only Philistia, Moab, Ammon, Cush, and Assyria, these nations are symbolic of all nations who worship other gods (see 2:11). Like other great prophets (e.g., Joel 1:15-18; 2:1-11; Amos 5:18-20; Obadiah 15), Zephaniah refers to the time when God acts to set things right as the Day of the Lord (1:7-9, 14-16).

Third, *divine judgment is not the end, nor even the goal of God's work*. Zephaniah's message does not end with the announcement of a universal judgment. Rather, a humble remnant who seeks the Lord will emerge out of the ashes of judgment (2:1-3, 7, 9; 3:12-13). On the Day of the Lord God will gather this remnant and restore its fortune (3:19-20). It will become the nucleus of a new community, and Zion will have cause to rejoice over its new beginning and new status (3:14). The old corrupt Jerusalem will be replaced by a community free from fear and deceit, and sustained by God's justice (3:5, 13). The Lord who is in their midst will encourage, rule over, protect and sustain them as King, Hero, and Good Shepherd (3:5, 13, 15-17, 19-20). God will remove the shame brought by their former leaders (3:11, 18). They will no longer fear their oppressors or the Lord's judgment for the community's crimes (3:11, 15-16, 18, 19). Zion's idolatry will be a thing of the past as God enables the community to properly seek and worship the Lord (3:11-13). It will be such a happy day that even the Lord will join the celebration of this great transformation brought by God's patient love (3:17).

Fourth, Zephaniah announces that *the restoration of God's people coincides with the restoration of all peoples*. Zephaniah announces the Lord's work among distant peoples in 3:9-10. God will purify their speech, enabling them to properly call upon and worship the Lord, and bring God offerings (3:9-10). Even the offerings they present in their own temples will be considered as proper worship (3:10; cp. 2:11). The situation of idolatrous pride and self-centeredness depicted in 2:4-15 and Babel will be overcome through a gracious act of the Lord. The nations that were separated by a judgment on their speech at Babel (Gen 11:7-9) will have their speech transformed and be united to worship and serve the Lord (3:9-10). They will call on the name of the true God and honor the name of the Lord by honoring the remnant (3:9, 19-20), rather than promote their own name by their idolatrous achievements (Gen 11:4).

Fifth, *the work of the Lord is from beginning to end an act of divine grace, for which humans cannot take credit.* Zephaniah presents God as acting unilaterally in the promised restoration. We have already mentioned Israel's vocation as extending God's blessing to the nations of the world. Yet, in Zephaniah God's grace is extended to the nations without direct human intervention. While the nations witness God's judgment of Jerusalem and the restoration of the remnant (2:11; 3:8, 19-20), God appears to act directly in purifying them without human agency (2:9). Since the Jerusalem community has not been fulfilling its divine vocation, the Lord promises to essentially do it for them.

Just as the Day of the Lord is consistently depicted as an act of God alone against the sinful Jerusalem community, so the restoration will be an act of God's deliverance without human agency. The humble community that replaces the arrogant leaders on God's holy mountain (3:11) will be shepherded by the Lord alone (3:12-13, 19-20). As the community regroups, nothing is said about a human king, judges, armies, priests or a new temple. Furthermore, the remnant is an oppressed, humble, and poor people (2:1; 3:12) who are incapable of protecting themselves and inexperienced as leaders. So the Lord will be their King and Mighty Hero who saves them and dispenses justice (3:15, 17), as God has ultimately granted it in the past (3:5).

COMMENTARY
PART ONE: GOD'S JUDGMENT [AND RESTORATION] OF THE WORLD: ZEPHANIAH 1:1—2:15

I. THE LORD'S JUDGMENT ON JUDAH AND JERUSALEM: ZEPHANIAH 1:1—2:3

BEHIND THE TEXT

The superscription places the activity of Zephaniah in the reign of King Josiah of Judah (r. 640-609). The religious and ethical abuses mentioned in Zeph 1:2-18 point to a time before Josiah's reforms had taken full effect (ca. 640-622; Bennett 1996, 659-60). Since many of these abuses were addressed in this reform (2 Kgs 23:4-24), the prophet's message might have influenced the king's actions (cp. Bennett 1996, 661). It is also possible that the prophet's call for a repentance gathering in Zeph 2:1-3 was a factor in Josiah's calling an assembly for the reading of the Mosaic Torah (2 Kgs 23:1-3).

It is difficult to determine if the original occasion of this passage was a message to the royal court or if it had a more public setting. If the prophet and Josiah had a common ancestor in Hezekiah (Zeph 1:1), this family tie may have given Zephaniah access to the king, where the prophet could have proclaimed an early form of the message found here. But it is possible that the message was delivered in a variety of settings, such as in temple worship (1:4-5; 9), at the Feast of Ingathering (see Bennett 1996, 663, 665), the market place (1:11), or some specific area of Jerusalem (1:10). The message continued to be relevant after the death of Josiah when Judah quickly lapsed back into its former errors (→ Introduction and 1:5 and 8). It continued to be relevant as a justification for the Babylonian Exile and as a warning to future generations not to provoke God's wrath by repeating the sins of the ancestors.

After the superscription (1:1), Zeph 1:2-2:3 comprises the first major division in the book. This section consists of two units. The first unit contains the announcement of God's judgment on Jerusalem and Judah (1:2-18). After an introduction announcing a cosmic judgment centering on Judah and Jerusalem (1:2-6), the prophet announces the coming of the Day of the Lord as one of great wrath due to a number of cultic and ethical offenses (1:7-18). This unit is further divided into two subunits: verses 7-13 announce that the Day of the Lord will be a great sacrifice of Jerusalem's sinners and vv 14-18 piles up images of the day as one of consuming rage, devastation and horror. The second unit (2:1-3) is an unexpected continuation of the first, which ends with a surprising glimmer of hope. In these verses, the prophet invites the "humble of the land" to "seek the LORD" before "the day of the LORD's wrath comes upon" them.

IN THE TEXT

A. Superscription (1:1)

■ **1:1** The superscription gives basic information about the setting of the prophecy (→ Introduction). **The word of the LORD** characterizes the remainder of the book as God's message. The words **that came to Zephaniah** are literally "that was to Zephaniah." In superscriptions the phrase emphasizes the independent existence and authority of a divinely uttered word or message, and undergirds the authority of the prophetic book (see also Hos 1:1; Joel 1:1; Mic 1:1; Zech 1:1; Jer 1:2). **Zephaniah** means "the Lord has hidden."

The unusual four generation genealogy connects the prophet with both a royal (**Hezekiah**) and African (**Cushi**, i.e., "Cushite, Nubian") heritage (→ Introduction). Nothing is known of Hezekiah's descendants **Gedaliah** or **Amariah**. Josiah's father **Amon** was known as an idolater who continued the syncretistic policies of his father, Manasseh (2 Kgs 21). **Josiah** reigned from ca. 640-609 (2 Kgs 22-23, → Introduction for fuller details about the reigns of Manasseh, **Amon**, and **Josiah**). Note that the names of the two reformer Kings, **Hezekiah** and **Josiah**, are placed together in the genealogy.

B. God's Extensive Judgment (1:2-18)

1. Judgment as Reversal of Creation Due to Judean Idolatry (1:2-6)

■ **2** The threat of judgment in vv 2-3 form an introduction to Zeph 1:2-2:3. **I will sweep away** translates *'āsōp 'āsēp* (lit. *gathering, I will bring to an end*). The first word (*'sp*) usually connotes gathering or harvesting, but it also can connote destruction or God's judgment (see e.g., 1 Sam 15:6 and elsewhere; Roberts 1991, 169). What will be brought to an end is **everything from the face of the earth**, as further specified in v 3. The word for **the earth,** *hā'ădamâ*, often connotes ground or a specific plot of land, although it sometimes connotes "the earth." As is often observed, **everything from the face of the earth** indicates the extent of the destruction of all land creatures in the flood (see Gen 6:7; 7:4, 23; cp. 8:8). The message is indeed from God, indicated by **declares the LORD** (*n'm-yhwh)*, literally *an utterance of the Lord*).

■ **3** This verse expands the thought in the previous verse. The same verb used above, *I will bring to an end* (*'āsēp*), begins the next two lines. First, God will *bring to an end humankind and animals* ('*dm wbhmh*), then **the birds in the sky and the fish in the sea**. The mention of *humankind*, *animals*, birds and fish reminds the reader of the creation account of Gen 1:20-26, especially the dominion summary in v 26*b*. Since the list is arranged in the reverse order of their creation (cp. Hos 4:3), it suggests a reversal of creation, and perhaps loss of human dominion (De Roche 1980, 106-108). All creatures God created are faced with the threat of total destruction. Since this passage condemns false worship (vv 4-6), the implication is that Judean idolatry has already violated the order of creation by worshipping the creature rather than the Creator (see Rom 1:25).

The translation **and the idols that cause . . . to stumble** is a reasonable conjecture (see NIV note). The MT vocalizes *whmkšlwt* as a noun (**the idols**), whose only other occurrence is Isa 3:6. There it means "heap of ruins" (*HALOT*, see NIV 1984 translation of 1:3). Some interpreters connect this with the similar masculine noun (*mkšl*), which means "stumbling block" (see BDB). In that case the phrase is literally *and the stumbling blocks together with the wicked*. The *stumbling blocks* are idols patterned after earthly creatures. Whether one accepts the NIV translation or the *stumbling blocks* interpretation, it appears to be a remark condemning **the wicked** for fashioning idols from the created order.

The conclusion of the verse reformulates the introduction: **When I destroy all mankind on the face of the earth**. Death sentence is applied to one group, *humankind*, since they are the truly guilty ones (Vlaardingerbroek 1999, 61). Humans have corrupted the earth by idolatry; their wickedness results not only in their own extermination but in the destruction of all creatures.

On the surface, the disturbing judgment on the entire created order found in Zeph 1:2-3 and 18 appears to connote a literal end of the cosmos. But since the remainder of the prophecy indicates that life continues after this judgment (e.g., 2:3, 7; 3:9-20), it is clear that this is not the complete destruction of creation.

It is noteworthy that the oracle is directed against Judah and Jerusalem in vv 4-6, which narrows the extent of this "cosmic" threat to these locales. This is based on the conception that Israel's tenure on the land of promise is to be lived as a kingdom of priests (Exod 19:6), with a calling to bring God's blessing on *all the families of the land* (*'dmh*, Gen 12:3). As a people redeemed from Egyptian oppression, Israel is called to extend similar grace to others (e.g., Exod 22:21 [20 HB]; 23:9; Lev 19:33-34 Deut 5:12-15).

Sometimes the fulfillment of this vocation is focused on Jerusalem and the temple, which are depicted as the source of God's teaching, justice and blessing for all creation (Mic 4:1-4; Pss 128:5-6; 133:3). God has chosen to reside there (Pss 78:68-69; 135:21), and so it is the source from which all creation will be blessed and renewed (Pss 128:5-6; 132:13-16; 133:3; 134:3) and from which true justice will issue (see e.g., Isa 2:2-4; Ps 99:2-4; see Roberts 2009, 987-88). Jerusalem (or Zion) with its temple is depicted as the center or microcosm of God's creation. It is the source of life for creation or the "navel of the earth" (Ezek 38:12, see NRSV note; see Levenson 1984, 282-91).

When God's people do not live up to their universal vocation, then all of creation suffers and prophets announce the consequence of the failure of Israel and Judah in "cosmic" terms (e.g., Hos 4:1-3; Isa 24:1-20; Jer 4:23-28). Since Judah has failed in its universal vocation, Zephaniah presents God's judgment on Judah and Jerusalem in cosmic or universal terms (Sweeney 2003:51-52, 57). This is not actually a literal universal destruction, rather it is a refining process ultimately fulfilled through the destruction of Jerusalem and Judah going into Babylonian exile.

■ **4** The introduction has ended and specific offenses and punishments are now announced. **I will stretch out my hand against** connotes judgment (against Egypt in Exod 7:5, etc.); in the prophets the judgment is sometimes on God's people (e.g., Zeph 2:13; Isa 5:25; Jer 15:6; Ezek 6:14). Here God's judgment is **against** the southern kingdom, **Judah** and **all who live in Jerusalem**.

God's action is specified in the next line; the Lord will *cut off* or **destroy every remnant of Baal worship in this place** (NIV adds **every** and **worship** for clarification). **Baal worship** was a constant temptation for the Israelites since the early days of their settlement in the land (see e.g. Judg 2:11, 13 and elsewhere). Since **Jerusalem** is mentioned, **this place** can refer to the Jerusalem temple (see Deut 12:5, 14 and elsewhere). But the term also can mean the city and the entire holy land that extends from the temple (Jer 7:6-7, 20; and elsewhere).

God will also destroy the **names of the idolatrous priests**. The word translated **idolatrous priests** (*hkmrym*) is known from cultures around Israel, but in the Bible it connotes a type of priest who led illegitimate worship (Ben Zvi 1991,

67-68; see Hos 10:5). After the discovery of the Mosaic Torah, Josiah attempted to rid Jerusalem of **Baal worship** (revived by Manasseh) and the **idolatrous priests** installed by the kings of Judah (2 Kgs 23:4-5; see 2 Kgs 21:3). Of the two terms for priests in the Hebrew text only one occurs in the LXX; most interpreters claim that the final phrase in Hebrew, ***with the priests*** (*'m-hkhnym*), is an MT gloss (NIV omits it). The inclusion of ***priests*** probably indicates that the official priests were also engaged in (or allowed) some of the idolatrous and immoral acts listed in the following verses.

■ **5** The list of what God will destroy continues in vv 5-6. This list includes two groups in v 5 and one in v 6, each group characterized by a participle (translated **those who bow down, swear,** or "turn back"). The **starry host** (literally "host of the heavens"; see NRSV) would include the sun, moon, and stars, which were considered divine by many peoples, including the Assyrians. Israel was forbidden to worship (or "bow down to") astral bodies (see e.g., Exod 20:4-5; Deut 4:19; 17:3), yet they still venerated them from time to time (2 Kgs 17:16; 2 Kgs 21:2, 5; Jer 8:2; 7:18). The **roof** would provide a good vantage point for such astral bodies (Jer 19:13). Such idolatry was purged from the high places and temple complex under Josiah (2 Kgs 23:4, 11-12), but Jeremiah's condemnation of astral worship shows that it persisted and was widely practiced in private households (see Jer 44:15-19).

The second group in the list destined for destruction are those who declare allegiance to both **the Lord** and **Molek** (v 5). The Hebrew word *mlkm* (**Molek,** literally "their king") could be understood as a title of **the Lord** or another god (Ben Zvi 1991, 77-78). The context suggests the latter. Some minor Greek and Latin manuscripts read Melcom (i.e., Milcom, see NRSV), others read Molok (i.e., **Molek**). **Molek** worship involved child sacrifice (Lev 18:21; 20:2-4; Deut 18:10), and there is evidence that it persisted throughout Israelite history (2 Kgs 16:3; 17:17; 21:6; see Day 2009, 129-30).

The Hebrew text makes the distinction between **swear** ***to*** (*hnšb'im l-*) and **swear by** (*hnšb'im b-* see NRSV); one connoting swearing an oath of loyalty *to* a deity and the other swearing *by* a deity in everyday transactions. Since the God of Israel demands exclusive worship (Exod 20:3), it is inconsistent to **bow down and swear** *to* the Lord during occasional worship services, then to **swear by** other gods like **Molek** in one's daily life. The one whom they swear by is their de facto god. One cannot whole-heartedly serve **the Lord** unless all other gods are surrendered.

■ **6** **Those who turn back from following the Lord** are next in the list. The phrase **those who turn back from** connotes defection, disloyalty, backsliding away from, or the desertion of a commitment to someone (see Pss 44:18 [19 HB]; 53:3 [4 HB]; see Roberts 1991, 173). Since many Judeans no longer depend on the Lord in their daily conduct (→ v 5), they **neither seek the Lord nor inquire of** God. To **seek** (*bqš*) or **inquire** (*drš*) of the Lord involves determining God's will, usually by a divine oracle through a priest or prophet. Josiah provides a contrast to such behavior, since he sends his servant to "inquire (*drš*) of the Lord" (2 Kgs 22:13; NIV) regarding what Judah should do in light of the discovery of the Mosaic Torah. The action involves the priests consulting the prophet Huldah and Josiah responding humbly to her word (2 Kgs 22:11-20).

2. God's Judgment as the Day of the Lord (1:7-18)

■ **7** The next subsection (vv 7-13) begins with an ironic call to worship. The command **be silent** (or *hush*) is a call to prepare for worship (→ Hab 2:20). The next two lines convey two reasons for the call to silence: the nearness of the **Day of the** LORD and the preparation of a **sacrifice** by **the** LORD. **The day of the** LORD is the day (or time) that God goes out to battle to deliver the innocent from oppressors and punish the guilty (→ sidebar Day of the Lord on Nah 1:7). The description as **near** does not seem to convey an imminent action (see vv 8-13).

The second reason, **the** LORD **has prepared a sacrifice**, suggests the imagery of the Day of the Lord as a sacrifice of God's enemies (see e.g., Isa 34:6; Jer 46:10; see Berlin 1994, 79, and others). But as the prophet continues, the imagery takes a new turn. A **sacrifice** often included **invited** guests (1 Kgs 1:9) who ritually **consecrated** themselves for the occasion (1 Sam 16:5) and sometimes ate portions of the sacrifice with the host (1 Sam 9:13, 22-24; see Driver 1906, 115). But here it is not the guests, but the host, **the** LORD, who has **consecrated** the **invited** ones. Verse 8 clarifies the purpose of the Lord's consecration of guests.

■ **8** Verses 8-9 list the type of Judeans whom God will punish **on the day of the** LORD's **sacrifice**. Presumably, those mentioned in the list are the ones invited by the Lord. Verse 8 makes clear that they have been invited (v 7) not to *partake of* the sacrifice, but that they *are* the sacrifice (see Smith 1911, 195; cp. 2 Kgs 10:19, 25). The word translated **punish** (from *pqd* "muster, inspect, appoint, assign, visit, attend to, call to account"; see *HALOT* and BDB) can also mean the Lord's visitation of persons (or calling them to account for their sins) in the context of judgment speeches (see e.g., Isa 10:3; Hos 10:7; Jer 8:12; 10:15). The sins visited upon the people here will be discussed at the end of v 9.

The sacrificial guest list, that is, those who will be held accountable for their sins, starts with the ruling class that led Judah astray. **Officials** (*hśrym*) would include palace administrators, various types of rulers, priests, military officers, overseers, and other appointed officers throughout Judah (see e.g., 1 Kgs 4:1-6). As is often noted, the king is not singled out for judgment (but → v 9), probably because this prophecy was first pronounced before Josiah reached an accountable age (e.g., Roberts 1991, 178). Therefore, if the **king's sons** are literally offspring of the king, these would be the sons of Manasseh or Amon (Josiah's uncles or brothers), Josiah being too young to have grown children. **King's sons** could also refer to the extended royal family or special group of officials with administrative responsibilities, power, and influence within and beyond Jerusalem (see 1 Kgs 22:26; Driver 1906, 116). **All those clad in foreign clothes** could be the wealthy who preferred imported clothes; this would be a sign of an adoption of pagan culture and rejection of Israelite social and religious tradition (Vlaardingerbroek 1999, 86).

■ **9** The phrase **on that day** links with "the day of the LORD" in v 7 and "the day of the LORD's sacrifice" in v 8. The last group mentioned for punishment is described by two participial phrases: ***those who leap*** and **who fill.** Their actions are not entirely clear. One plausible ancient interpretation associates ***those who leap over the threshold*** with the ritual or taboo associated with entry into a temple of a god, as attested by an ancient Philistine custom (1 Sam 5:4-5; so the Aramaic Targum, see Gordon 1990, 166). The NIV translation, **all who avoid stepping on the threshold,** follows this interpretation. It is even possible that such a tradition was incorporated into the worship of the Lord in the Jerusalem temple (cp. Ben Zvi 1991, 98-99).

If this line of interpretation is adopted, it could also support a cultic meaning to the second line, ***those who fill the house of their lord(s)*** **with violence and deceit.** This is supported by the LXX (which paraphrases with "house of their Lord God") and also the NIV, where ***house*** is translated as **temple** and ***their lords*** (*'dwnyhm*) is paraphrased as **their gods.** If ***lords*** is understood as a title for human masters, probably the king—who is sometimes referred to by this honorific plural (e.g., 1 Kgs 1:43)—then the second line is describing the actions of the royal officials who are enriching the king and the kingdom at the expense of their subjects. They do this by practicing **violence and deceit** (see Hab 1:2, 9; 2:8-13), a clear violation of the Mosaic Torah (see e.g., Deut 16:18-20; 25:13-16). The inference here is that young Josiah prospers by the unscrupulous violations of his officials. Verse 9 is therefore a prophetic warning to the king and his guardians that Judah will be judged because of the sins committed by state officials, and that the guilt reaches as far as the palace.

■ **10** Responses to God's judgment **on that day** from various quarters of Jerusalem are anticipated in vv 10-11*a*. These verses convey a mood of intense crisis and depict this as a **day** of great mourning. Verse 10 describes responses from three sections of Jerusalem: **a cry . . . from the Fish gate, wailing from the New Quarter, a loud crash from the hills.** The word **cry** (*s'qh*) is from a root that connotes a cry of distress, anguish, desperation, or lament (e.g., Exod 12:30). The **Fish Gate** is a northwestern entrance to Jerusalem, to which Manasseh extended a new section of wall around Jerusalem (2 Chron 33:14). Its name hints at commercial activity since it probably derives from the fish brought in through this gate and sold nearby (Vlaardingerbroek 1999, 93; and others; see Neh 13:16). The **gate** complex (a small room with benches) is where ad hoc law courts were convened and justice promulgated, a form of deliverance for the oppressed (see e.g., Amos 5:15). The gates of Jerusalem are said to rejoice in the deliverance of God's people (Ps 9:13-14 [14-15 HB]) and mourn at their demise (cp. Isa 3:26; Lam 1:4; Jer 14:2).

The next section of Jerusalem, the ***Second*** or **New Quarter** (or Mishneh) is first mentioned during the time of Josiah (2 Kgs 22:14). It was probably part of the northwestern expansion of Jerusalem under Hezekiah due to the influx of Israelite refugees when the Northern Kingdom fell to Assyria. (Murphy-O'Connor 2008, 249). **Wailing** (*yllh*) is the typical cry of grief accompanying a lament in response to

165

God's judgment (Zech 11:3). Like the mourning Fish Gate (v 10), a section of the city itself appears to be mourning God's judgment on its inhabitants.

The next section, **the hills**, perhaps refers to an urban locale, that is, "The Heights" (Smith 1906, 48). It could also be a reference to the entire city since Jerusalem spans two hills (see Aharoni and Avi-Yonah 1976, p 74, #114). The phrase **loud crash** or ***great devastation*** (*šbr gdwl*) connotes a great disaster due to God's judgment in Jer 4:6; 6:1; 14:17. At other times it suggests the sound of the devastation or the wailing as a response to it (Jer 48:3; 51:54).

■ **11** The command to **wail** is given to those who live in **the market district (*the Mortar*;** see NIV note). This is the only reference to this area of Jerusalem in the Bible. Its name, "mortar bowl" (*mktš*, see Prov 27:22) suggests it was built in a low section (or "hollow") of the Central or Tyropoeon Valley (see Smith 1911, 199-200). The translation **market district** is a guess based on the merchant activity described in this verse.

The verse continues with the reason for the wailing; it is ***because*** (*kî*) **your merchants will be wiped out** (the *kî* is not translated in the NIV). **Your merchants** is literally ***the people of Canaan*** (*'m kn'n*). Since they were well-known importers and traders, "Canaanite" (*kn'ny*) also became a term for merchant (e.g., Isa 23:8). The phrase ***people of Canaan*** (*'m kn'n*) is found only here, however, and probably means not only merchant, but is also a parody on Israel as the people of the Lord (cp. Motyer 1998, 920; see Zeph 2:8-9 and elsewhere for "my people"). The calling of God's people to be a source of blessing for all peoples (Gen 12:2-3) meant that they were to be a holy people dedicated to God (Exod 19:6). As such, they were to be separated from the pagan customs of their neighbors, including the Canaanites (see e.g., Deut 7:1, 3-6; 14:2). Instead, these Judeans had become virtually indistinguishable from the Canaanites in their worship (1:4-6), adoption of a foreign and extravagant lifestyle (1:8, 12-13), and in their commerce (vv 9, 11).

These Jerusalem "Canaanites" will be treated like the Canaanites under Joshua (Luther 1525c, 330); they will be **wiped out**. Those who **trade with silver** further describes the ***people of Canaan***; the last line thus reiterates the judgment pronounced in the previous line. **Destroyed** is literally ***cut off*** (*krt*) (see Deut 12:29; 19:1; and Josh 23:4 where this same verb describes God's cutting off (*krt*) of the people who occupied the Promised Land when the Israelites entered it).

■ **12** The previous verses single out the people who are obvious offenders of God's ways. Verses 12-13 focus on a group who on the surface appear to be good citizens, but whose true nature will be discovered when God will **search Jerusalem with lamps**. The use of **lamps** suggests they dwell in darkness, perhaps symbolic of their sinful ways (see Prov 2:13; Isa 5:20, etc.). The goal of God's search is to find offenders who think they can escape (or are not worried about) God's judgment (cp. Amos 5:18-20).

God will **punish those who are complacent, who are like wine left on its dregs**. The Hebrew text is literally, ***I will punish*** (***attend to***) ***those who thicken upon their lees***. The imagery is based on wine production, which these vineyard owners would know about first hand (see v 13). **Lees** (or **dregs**, *šemer*) are the dead yeast cells which build up in the bottom of storage jars as wine ages. If wine is properly stirred and racked (i.e., decanted), a small amount of **lees** will enhance its flavor over time (Isa 25:6). But if the wine is left unattended, too many **lees** will eventually ruin it (Jer 48:11; Williams 2014, 1-2, and others). The rare verb for **thicken** or "congeal" (*qp'*; see Job 10:10; Exod 15:8) indicates the latter has occurred. A major point of the imagery is that the Jerusalem wealthy are like unattended wine that remains in storage and is of no value to anyone; they accumulate wealth for themselves and are totally indifferent to the plight of others. So ultimately, like stored wine which continues to **thicken** (Jer 48:11-12), these secluded amassers of wealth will prove to be rotten (cp. Clark 1981, 241; Baker 1988, 98). The Targum captures this with the paraphrase "lie at ease upon their wealth" (Gordon 1990, 167; cp. Amos 6:1; see NIV **complacent**).

They base their lives on the premise that **the LORD will do nothing, either good or bad (*evil*).** Apparently they think that God does not care about what happens in the world. So they act as if the Lord does not approve or bless their good actions, nor hold them accountable for mistreatment of others or for neglecting opportunities to help others. They are practical atheists who in their self-sufficiency have become their own god (cp. Pss 10:4; 14:1; see Motyer 1998, 921). But their assumptions will prove false when God searches every nook and cranny of the environs of **Jerusalem** and their palatial estates. The Lord will find them and punish them for their self-aggrandizing lifestyles (→ below).

■ **13** In v 13 the prophet announces the Lord's judgment on ***those who thicken upon their lees*** (v 12). Enemies or invading people will plunder their **wealth** and stored possessions and destroy their **houses**. The word for **wealth** (*ḥêl*) is a comprehensive term for power, worth, or resources of any sort (→ Hab 3:19). The remainder of v 13 announces the futility of their attempt to **build houses** and **plant vineyards. They will not live in them** and **they will not drink the wine** are similar to the futility curses pronounced against those who violate the Mosaic Torah (e.g., Deut 28:30).

Zephaniah may be making the point that this judgment is based on these wealthy Judeans ignoring Mosaic covenant obligations. They are building houses and planting vineyards for their own well-being without any concern for others and without any thought of God's active concern for the world (v 12). Zephaniah warns them that they will never enjoy the fruit of their labor.

■ **14** Verses 14-18 describe the horrors of that day. This is reinforced in v 14 by the twofold reiteration of the phrase **the day of the LORD** (→ v 7). Its imminence is also emphasized by the two-fold repetition of the word **near** (*qrwb*). This **day** is characterized as **great** (elsewhere only Joel 2:11, 31 [3:4 HB]; Mal 4:5 [3:23 HB]). The nearness and threatening nature of the **day** is reinforced with the words ***and hastening*** **quickly**. This is the only time that *mhr* ("to hasten, be quick") connotes the Day of the Lord.

The next line, **the cry on the day of the LORD is bitter**, reflects bitter weeping or mourning on a day of great calamity (Isa 33:7-9; Amos 8:9-10). The opening word (*qôl*, NIV **cry**) could be understood as an exclamation (**Listen!** See NIV 1984).

The line, **the Mighty Warrior shouts his battle cry**, is an attempt to make sense of the difficult phrase *ṣrḥ šm gbwr* (lit. "shouting there a warrior"). The meaning of the rare word *ṣrḥ* (a Qal participle) is difficult to determine. The verb occurs elsewhere only in Isa 42:13 where the Lord shouts out (*yṣryḥ*) a war cry like a warrior (*kgbwr*). The NIV assumes a similar meaning here; on the Day of the Lord Jerusalem will hear the battle cry of the Lord, the Divine Warrior. The bitter weeping on the Day of the Lord in the previous line could then be caused by the battle cry of the Divine Warrior. Since the text does not clearly identify the warrior as the Lord, it is possible that **warrior** functions collectively; in that case, the battle cry could be coming from an invading army.

■ **15** In a series of six appositional phrases beginning with **a day of** (repeated seven times), vv 15-16*a* list the terrors that will unfold on the Day of the Lord. The prophet begins by designating the Day of the Lord as a day of divine **wrath** (or *rage*); the context makes clear that the proud oppressors are the target of God's wrath. They will experience **distress** (*adversity*) **and anguish**, and **trouble** (*devastation*) **and ruin** on this day. The remainder of the verse uses phrases often found in theophany descriptions of the Divine Warrior; the description **a day of darkness and gloom** is similar to Amos 5:18, 20 where the people expected the Day of the Lord to be a day of light or deliverance. Instead, what they experience is darkness or God's judgment (see Deut 28:29). The **day** is also one of **clouds and blackness** (*'nn w'rpl*), terms which can characterize the day of God's intervention against oppressors on behalf of Israel (Isa 60:2; Ezek 34:12). The Judeans who were living in darkness (see Zeph 1:12) will be ironically plunged into the **darkness** of God's judgment.

■ **16** The description of the **day** continues with the demise of Judah's cities (vv 16-17*a*). It is **a day of trumpet and battle cry**. The trumpet, literally *ram's horn* (*šôpâr*), is played like a bugle to call troops to war or signal an attack (Judg 3:27; 6:34). The **battle cry** served a similar function (Num 31:6; Ezek 21:27). This cry will be against **the fortified cities**, indicating that more than Jerusalem is in view.

On that day, archers will not be able to defend their city from **corner towers** or *high places* (*gbhwt*), which are strategic structures in a city's defense system (2 Chron 26:15; Zeph 3:6; de Vaux 1965, 1:231-32). The great **fortified cities** offered protection, safety, and hope for people beleaguered by powerful enemies. When Israel entered Canaan, the Lord defeated the great fortified cities that defended the land (Deut 1:28-30; 9:1-3). It is notable that the defenses of Jericho fell at the sound of ram's horns and shouts, terms found in this passage (Josh 6:20). Since Judah has essentially become Canaanite (→ vv 4-5 and 11), God will now destroy its defenses. Once again, according to Deut 28:49-52, Israel is warned that its defenses will fall to a nation brought against them as God's discipline for their defection from the Lord.

The early use of this prophecy lent itself to multiple interpretations regarding who would come against Judah in battle. The divine warrior language here suggests it is the Lord; God's intervention seems direct in v 17. But the possibility that God's act could be through a nation like Assyria or Egypt might be anticipated by those familiar with prophets like Isaiah, Amos, or Habakkuk. It would became increasingly clear to Zephaniah's later readers that these events would occur through Babylon (→ Hab 1:5-11).

■ **17** Allusions to the curses of Deut 28 reserved for the disloyal continue with **I will bring . . . distress** *upon humankind*. The word **bring distress** may also mean to harass or besiege, as it is translated in Deut 28:52. Here it is the Lord who **will bring . . . distress**; in Deuteronomy 28 it is by a nation which God will send to besiege Israel's cities (vv 47-52). The context here also suggests that the **distress** is the besieging of Judean cities, and the notion that God will accomplish this through a foreign nation is not excluded (→ v 15). According to the broader context, the humans in view are the inhabitants of Jerusalem and Judah (→ vv 3-4) and not the entire human race (Roberts 1991, 182, 184; and others). We use the term *humankind* to translate 'ādām (as in v 3) since Zephaniah is using creation language, and he depicts God's people as a microcosm of creation (→ sidebar Cosmic Judgment in Zephaniah).

The result of the **distress** is that the people of Judah **will grope about like those who are** (*will walk about like the*) **blind** (*whlkw k'wrym*). This is a common description of the results of the judgment of God's darkness in the Exodus plague and elsewhere (→ v 15). It is also one of the curses for disloyal Israel in Deut 28:29. The phrase **because they have sinned against the LORD** stands in the center of the verse to summarize the reason for God's judgment pronounced throughout Zeph 1. In this context, to sin **against the LORD** involves rebellion or a breach of covenant with serious consequences (cp. Deut 1:41-44; 20:18). It is notable that this statement narrows God's judgment to covenant defectors (the sinners described in vv 4-6, 8-9; 11-12; see Sweeney 2003, 96). This confirms that a universal judgment is not in view here.

The death of the sinners is now described in gory detail, **their blood will be poured out [***špk***] like dust and their entrails like dung.** The usual expression is to pour out blood like water (Ps 79:3; Deut 12:16, 24; 15:23). **Poured out like dust** perhaps alludes to God's verdict that sinful humankind (Adam), made of dust, will return to dust (Gen 2:7; 3:19).

■ **18** The Judean wealthy are warned here that their wealth (**silver** and **gold**) cannot **save them on the day of the LORD's wrath.** The wealthy who claim self-sufficiency mistakenly think that their riches would sustain them during a crisis or that they can pay off their conquerors (see 2 Kgs 16:7-9; 18:13-16; Smith 1911, 207). It is also possible that idols plated with these precious metals are also in view here (cp. Isa 2:20; Watts 1975, 163).

In the fire of God's **jealousy (***zeal***) the whole earth will be consumed** is repeated in 3:8. God's **jealousy** (*qn'h*) is the divine passion (or passionate com-

169

mitment) for what belongs to God and expresses divine purposes (→ Nah 1:2). The language of divine jealousy or zeal is often found in the deliverance of God's people (e.g., Joel 2:18-27) or in judgment upon sinners (e.g., Exod 20:5). For the extent of **the whole earth** (*kl-h' rṣ*) see below and comments on v 3 above; the context still suggests it consists primarily of the land of Judah.

Verse 18 ends with the reason why there will be no deliverance. It is because God **will make a sudden end of all who live on the earth**. The prophet gives no hope to the inhabitants of Judah for their survival when the Day of the Lord comes. The concluding line of v 18 reiterates the message of vv 2-3. Again, the context makes clear that **all who live on the earth** refer to the inhabitants of the land of Judah and not of the whole earth (→ v 4).

C. God's Call for Repentance (2:1-3)

1. Call to Gather before the Day of the Lord (2:1-2)

■ **2:1** This is the beginning of the concluding unit (2:1-3) of the first section. It opens with dual commands, **gather together, gather yourselves together** (two forms of the verbal root *qšš*). The context (vv 2-3) indicates that Judah is being called to assemble in response to the impending crisis of the Day of the Lord. But *qšš* is not one of the verbal roots that would summon such an assembly (see e.g., 2 Chron 20:4; Joel 1:14). The verb *qšš* connotes gathering stubble for bricks (Exod 5:7, 12) or sticks for a fire (Numb 15:32; 1 Kgs 17:10). Here the stubble symbolism reinforces the prophet's message of "the fire of divine jealousy" that will consume the inhabitants of the land (→ 1:18). The people would have heard something like "**gather yourselves** (or be gathered) like so much straw for burning."

The prophet addresses his audience as **shameful nation** (literally, "nation who is not longed for," i.e., *undesirable nation*). This is how the Lord sees the people of Judah. They are no longer God's holy people, special possession, or a kingdom of priests, but a people who have failed to live in conformity to God's will and purpose for them (see Gen 12:2-3; Exod 19:6; Deut 4:6).

■ **2** This verse completes the sentence begun in v 1, which by itself leaves the impression that there is nothing Judah can do to avoid being totally consumed by God's fiery judgment. The threefold **before** suggests a sense of urgency (Motyer 1998, 926-27), which is the first real hint that there is something that Judah might be able to do to at least partially avert the impending crisis. The **decree** (*ḥōq*) connotes the collective disasters proclaimed as comprising the Day of the Lord in Zeph 1. Judah must act **before the decree takes effect**, that is, before the prophetic word is fulfilled.

The next half line, **and that day passes like windblown chaff**, is literally *like chaff passes the day*. The verb for passing (*'br*) can connote the wind carrying away or drying up transitory vegetation (see e.g., Ps 103:16). This is appropriate for **chaff**, which is the (discarded) light outer husk of grain that can be swiftly blown by the wind. Like stubble (→ v 1), **chaff** often signifies God's judgment. **Wind-**

blown chaff is an image of the swift disappearance of the wicked before God's judgment (Hos 13:3; Isa 29:5; see Motyer 1998, 926). The Day of the Lord will arrive quickly, it will overtake Judah so swiftly that if they wait they will not have time to respond to God's command to gather (v 1) or seek God (v 3).

The next two lines are very similar; their reiteration reinforces the message of the first line. They both begin by conveying the urgency of the situation and the need to act (**before . . . comes upon you**). The LORD's fierce anger (**burning anger**) is parallel to the LORD's wrath (**heated anger**). The imagery of the heat of judgment is found in 1:18 and is implied in the command for the Judeans to gather like stubble to be burned in 2:1.

2. Call for the Humble to Seek the Lord to Avoid That Day (2:3)

■ **3** The thought begun in v 1 is concluded here. The verse contains a threefold use of the term *bqš*, **seek**. To **seek the LORD** involves wholehearted faithfulness to God, which includes repentance and following God's ways (Hos 5:15; Ps 78:34; Jer 29:13). We have already seen that the Day of the Lord will overtake those who do not seek God (→ 1:6).

Those who are to **seek the LORD** are the **humble of the land**. The **humble** (*'nw* and the cognate *'ny*) are literally the "bowed, afflicted, poor, meek" who are abused and persecuted by the wicked (Ps 10:2; Isa 32:7; Amos 2:7). The **humble of the land** are the weakest members of the community who cannot defend themselves and need help in unfair legal cases (Amos 8:4). Since the downtrodden are likely to call upon the Lord for help, the **humble** are often synonymous with the pious or spiritually humble (Baker 1988, 103). They are also those **who do what he** (the Lord) **commands**—literally, God's *justice they practice* (*mšptw p'lw*). God's *justice* connotes decisions God makes (or supports) regarding community disputes (see e.g., Deut 25:1). It means treating the oppressed fairly, and God's people are expected to emulate it (Ps 9:5 [6 HB]; Amos 5:15, 24; Hab 1:4). The **humble** in this context are those who imitate God's righteous ways (cp. Ps 15:2); they are contrasted here with the perverse idolaters and oppressors of 1:4-13.

In the next line, the humble of the land are commanded to **seek righteousness** and **humility**. **Righteousness** characterizes the created order as rightly ordered by God, which functions harmoniously and responds properly to the Lord (Achtemeier 1962, 4:80-85; and others). To **seek righteousness** means to live justly in a relationship with God that results in a lifestyle of setting right broken communities (Isa 1:17). In this context **seek humility** (*'nwh*) connotes submission to God.

The commands to **seek righteousness** and **humility** are addressed to all who need to learn submission to the Lord, both the proud idolaters and oppressors (1:4-13) and the humble of the land (2:3). In other words, all sinners are commanded to become spiritually humble and **seek the LORD.** If this type of change (repentance) takes place, then there is hope for escape from the coming judgment.

So the prophet continues, **perhaps you will be sheltered on the day of the LORD's anger**. To be **sheltered** (*tstrw*) from the Lord is to be ***hidden*** or concealed from trouble by God's protection (see e.g., Pss 17:8; 27:5). God is sometimes likened to a shelter or hiding place (*sēter*, see Pss 32:7; 91:1). The use of **perhaps** suggests that the escape from judgment is a realistic hope, but cannot be presumed upon. It is important to note that the prophet does not hold up the possibility that **the day of the LORD's anger** will not occur, but only that when it does take place there is a possibility of escape for some. While the **perhaps** of escape is offered to the entire community, in reality only a few will **seek the LORD**; a remnant who respond to this invitation will survive by God's grace (→ 3:11-13).

FROM THE TEXT

The overall impact of reading (or hearing) Zeph 1:2-2:3 cannot be minimized. It takes the reader from a feeling of certain and deserved doom, to a surprisingly hopeful offer of a new beginning. It is easy to imagine the prophet's early audiences listening to the message of doom contained in Zeph 1 and conceding that they stood guilty as charged and would certainly bear the consequences of their sins. Perhaps the prophet paused and let the message sink in as his penetrating gaze surveyed those present. People no doubt started leaving. But the prophet was not finished and quickly brought his message to an unexpected conclusion. There is a call to assemble; there is a divine "perhaps" if they are willing to submit to the offer. Indeed, the righteous God is not satisfied to see justice served with a destructive judgment. For God, righteousness is only fulfilled when creation is set right to fulfill the Lord's intentions for the reconciliation of all things (cp. Col 1:20).

The strong emphasis on doom makes this a sobering passage. Talk of God's wrath makes us uncomfortable so we would prefer to avoid or ignore passages such as these. When we do read them, it is tempting for us to search for ways to sidestep the seriousness of their claims. We might say, "This is about someone else (ancient Israel or other religions), certainly not me (us). I (we) do not fashion or bow down to idols; that is those other groups. Today we know the God of love and forgiveness revealed in Jesus and not the harsh God taught in Zephaniah's day."

It is common to point out that there are very few clear allusions to Zephaniah in the NT, suggesting to some that later believers do not have much use for this book. Yet, it needs to be observed that much of what the early church confessed about the great judgment taking place on the Day of the Lord Jesus has been shaped by scriptures such as this one. Indeed, in a passage which may have been partially drawn from Zeph 1:14-2:3, Paul warns a group of immature Christians that if they continue in their self-centered ways, they may only barely escape the fiery judgment of the Day of the Lord (1 Cor 3:10-17). Elsewhere the NT adaptation of the Day of the Lord theme makes no attempt to soften or bypass it (see Achtemeier 1986, 73-74).

It is also important to remember that all scripture has been inspired to teach and correct God's people for "training in righteousness" in order to equip God's servants "for every good work" (2 Tim 3:16). Consequently, rather than avoid this passage, we must ask what Zeph 1:2-2:3 can say to the Lord's people today about seeking God's righteousness and how to live by it. We must also ask ourselves about the consequences that God's people and the world must bear if we fail to seek God and what the Lord requires.

Zephaniah 2:3 provides a way into the central concerns of this section. Here we see that God's faithful people are those who *seek the Lord, . . . practice [God's] justice, seek righteousness, and seek humility.* This summarizes what the people of God lack, which is the basis for the announcements of judgment in chapter 1. In their faithlessness, God's people have not sought the Lord, and they have violated the righteous order that God has established. This provides a good starting point for some comments concerning some significant elements of Zephaniah's message.

First, *God's work in the world is characterized by righteousness, and God desires that people seek the Lord and practice divine righteousness* (2:3). Righteous living is not just about being meticulous law keepers. It is expressed as an active concern to implement God's righteousness in our community. God's work has cosmic significance; all creation is the object of God's gracious ordering. God's people are called to participate in this righteous order by sustaining it and not working against it. By doing this, they share in God's cosmic work.

Second, *the righteous Creator requires exclusive and undivided worship.* Such devotion to the Lord results in the worshipper seeking to do God's will (see above). Syncretistic and idolatrous worship and life style as practiced by the Judeans (1:4-6, 8-9) divide loyalties between the living God and the gods of the surrounding nations. There is only room for one Creator in the world, so divided loyalties always result in serving the lesser and more convenient master (1 Kgs 18:21; Matt 6:24).

Idolatry is more than bowing down to a statue or confessing the name of another god; whatever has supreme sway or final say in one's life is an idol. All we need do is to put something, anything, in our life ahead of God, and that becomes our god. A thing does not need to be evil to be a false god. Anything in God's good creation can be distorted by humans and made an object of worship (Rom 1:25). Idolatry is essentially self-worship; it is our desires, our wants, and our mastery over our life projected into an object, person, desire, or ideology.

Third, *God's righteous order is promoted by those who seek God and practice divine justice* (2:3). Our acts of worship mean nothing to the Lord if they are not accompanied by a lifestyle of obedience that lives out God's concerns for a justly ordered community (see Amos 5:21-24 and Mic 6:6-8). Israel was given examples of how to do this in the Torah and Prophets. We also have the witness of the Gospels and the Epistles.

Practicing divine justice is at the heart of Jesus' concern for the poor and the weak found in the Gospels. God's people have ample opportunity and a variety of ways to help the downtrodden in their local communities. This includes rejection of greed and injustice as well as efforts to promote an equitable economic system that sustains the poor and the weak in our world. But justice will not occur as long as greed and selfishness are held up as virtues in an economic system; and it does not happen when the economy is the basis for every decision and is allowed to trump even the Gospel.

Fourth, *the created order belongs to God, and God intends its resources be shared with those in need.* The reason the wealthy are sometimes singled out for God's judgment, especially in the prophets, is because they have violated this principle. Some of the hoarders of Zeph 1:11-13 may have been implicated in the injustices hinted at in v 9. But even if some of them came by their wealth honestly, they are still reckoned among the sinners. The issue is that they have hoarded their wealth for themselves. They use it only to promote their own well-being and pleasures—they **thicken upon their lees** (v 12). While there is nothing wrong with having wealth, it is wrong to act as if it belongs to us and not to God. This is the greed that Paul considers idolatry (Col 1:5). In other words, when we place our wealth outside of God's control it becomes our god.

Some claim that wealth is a sign of God's blessing and that poverty is an indicator of God's disfavor. This is wrong on a number of levels. It sounds dangerously close to the claim that money will save one from God's wrath, which is debunked in Zeph 1:18. It fails to reckon with the fact that hoarded wealth can exacerbate the injustices associated with poverty. If wealth is to be attributed to God's blessing, then the biblical example is to share that blessing with those in need (see e.g., the two cases in Deut 15:7-11 and 12-18).

Fifth, *God entrusts leaders to guide the faithful in God's ways of righteousness.* In Israel, the priests, prophets, sages, elders, and the king were among those responsible for the welfare of God's people and for teaching and being examples of God's ways. When these leaders acted irresponsibly or idolatrously, the people under them suffered and were led astray. Their sins have greater consequences, so God holds them more accountable than others. Therefore when God's judgment is announced, it is usually first against these erring leaders (1:4-9), while the faithful humble have an opportunity of escape (2:3).

God has granted the church pastors, teachers, administrators and others to carry out the work of the Gospel and to promote the welfare of the body of Christ (see e.g., Rom 12:4-8; 1 Cor 12:27-28; Eph 4:11-14). As in Zephaniah's day, to whom much is given, much will be required (cp. Luke 12:48). If the church is going astray and working counter to God's purposes, the leaders are often ultimately accountable and will be set apart for greater judgment.

Sixth, *when God's people commit idolatry and violate God's just order of creation, repentance and humble submission before God are the proper responses.* But these are not magic wands that will suddenly avert the consequences of our misbehavior. When unrighteous structures fail, everyone connected with them, the righteous and the unrighteous, will be buried in their rubble. Everyone in ancient Israel knew this to be the case. When the judgment was announced, the righteous did not point fingers at the ungodly and smugly say "I told you so." They were fully aware that they were all in it together; they did not expect to escape the consequences of Judah's sin. "Perhaps" God might shelter the humble, but this appears entirely unexpectantly as an act of God's undeserved grace. In view of the sins announced in Zeph 1:2-18, this "perhaps" is completely unanticipated.

On the one hand, God is not to be presumed upon. This much is clear even from Zeph 2:3. But on the other hand, the ambiguity here should not leave God's people with feelings of discouragement or hopelessness. Later the prophet speaks of the humble remnant that will carry on God's work (3:12-13) and will celebrate God's acts with the rest of creation (→ 3:9-11, 14-20). Furthermore, as the time of judgment drew near, Hab 2:4 speaks of God's faithfulness toward the righteous with unqualified confidence. The judgment of God's people will not be averted, however, both prophets are in agreement on that point. Nevertheless, the righteous faithful will endure by God's grace.

Finally, *in the face of God's certain judgment, the only hope for the effectiveness of the community of God is in a God who transforms a people who then live out their divine calling.* Indeed, the hope of all creation hinges on God's people fulfilling their vocation as the bearers of God's image in a renewed creation (cp. Rom 8:18-30; 2 Cor 5:16-21; Col 3:5-15). In terms of Zephaniah's message these are the spiritually humble. They are those who seek humility (2:3) and put God first in their lives. Because they depend wholly upon God, they shun the idolatry of their surrounding culture. Therefore they avoid syncretism and self-aggrandizing behaviors such as greed and taking advantage of the weak. Without a total dependence on God, they would easily be drawn into the sins of their peers. Their righteousness (living according to God's order) and practice of justice are enabled by God's righteousness, or sustaining power. By surrendering to God's righteous work they have the power to walk in God's path. According to the Apostle Paul, this is the way of sanctification (Rom 6:1-19).

II. THE LORD'S JUDGMENT ON THE NATIONS: ZEPHANIAH 2:4-15

BEHIND THE TEXT

A change in subject signals that 2:4 begins a new section. Zephaniah 2:1-3 concludes the oracles of judgment against Jerusalem and Judah; in 2:4-15 the topic shifts to God's judgment against Philistia (vv 4-7), Moab and Ammon (vv 8-11), Cush (v 12), and Assyria (vv 13-15). This section is a continuation of Part One of the book, which comprises 1:1-2:15. The references to a Judean remnant in this passage (vv 6-7, 9) lead to the conclusion that this section presupposes the message of a catastrophic judgment of Judah; it was delivered most likely after the material found in 1:2-2:3. It is impossible to state exactly how long an interval separated the delivery of this passage from the announcement of judgment found in 1:2—2:3.

Oracles in this section fall into the category of Oracles against the Nations (OAN) (→ sidebar Oracles Against the Nations in Introduction to Nahum). Most biblical examples of OAN are prophetic adaptations announcing divine intervention against nations that are harassing God's people; or they function to get the attention of God's people who are either allied with such nations or guilty of similar offenses (see e.g., Amos 1:3-2:16). Although directed toward the nations, they are often proclaimed to God's people as a form of divine assurance that they will be freed from their enemies.

The nations in this section were chosen not only because of past or present relations with Judah, but they also serve a symbolic function. Each nation corresponds to a point on the compass in respect to Judah, which suggests the list is representative and not comprehensive. Furthermore, they are arranged in the unusual order of West, East, South and North: Philistines (West, vv 4-8); Moabites and Ammonites (East, vv 9-11), Cush (South, v 12), and Ashur and Nineveh (North, vv 13-15).

These oracles share similarities, but there are also variations. Oracles 1 and 2 name two people groups; oracle 3 has only one people group. Oracle 1 lists four capital cities of the people group, whereas oracle 4 lists the country and the capital city. Oracle 2 likens the bleak future of the people groups with two fallen cities. Oracle 3, the shortest oracle, mentions only one people group. Oracles 1, 2, and 4 announce future judgment; oracle 3 refers to past judgment (→ v 12). Oracles 1, 2 and 4 address various peoples or countries indirectly in the third person, and 3 addresses a people directly in the second person. Verse 11 concludes with a statement that is linked with v 12 and announces a universal worship of the Lord in these nations.

IN THE TEXT

A. Judah's Proximate Neighbors (2:4-11)

1. Philistines and Kerethites (2:4-7)

■ **2:4** The oracles against the nations begins with mention of four of the five major cities (**Gaza, Ashkelon, Ashdod, Ekron**), which represent the land of the Philistines (see also v 5). Only Gath is missing. Although slightly different fates are assigned to each, they are not to be strictly separated since it is likely they each represent the full destiny of Philistine territory.

Each act of judgment is described in terms of common battle imagery, without specifying who will be God's human agents. The terms **abandoned, in ruins, emptied,** and **uprooted** convey essentially the same idea; the Philistine cities will be totally destroyed and they will become unfit for human habitation. The term **abandoned** occurs often in conjunction with forsaken dwellings or towns. A city **in ruins (*desolation*)** will need to be rebuilt for human habitation.

178

At midday Ashdod will be emptied (literally, **Ashdod *at noon they will drive her out***) conveys the idea of an invading army driving out or expelling the inhabitants from Ashdod. **At midday** implies a quick battle; it will only take a half day for the invading army to finish the battle, gain control of the city, and deport its inhabitants. The term **uprooted** conveys the idea of pulling up plants (see Eccl 3:2; see Jer 1:10 for a similar idea of God's judgment uprooting Judah).

■ **5** The prophet utters a **woe**, a pronouncement of total disaster, against the Kerethites, a people **who live by the sea**, that is, the seacoast (v 5). Not much is known about the Kerethites. As is the case here, they are elsewhere associated with the coastal regions of the Philistines (e.g. in Ezek 25:16, an oracle very similar to this one). They may have been a subgroup among the Philistines.

Zephaniah's prophecy has been designated as the word of the Lord (1:1), which began as a message of God's judgment against Judah and Jerusalem (1:2-2:3). Now this **word of the LORD** is spoken against **Canaan, land of the Philistines**. Philistine territory is within the boundaries of the Canaanite land promised to Israel, but this area never came under the control of the Israelites. When the Israelites entered the land, God promised to remove the idolatrous Canaanites who occupied it. According to Zephaniah, God will first remove the idolatrous Judean "Canaanites" (1:11) and then he will finish the job among the Philistines.

The divine **word** against the nation will be implemented as a destruction of their land: **I will destroy you.** The verb **destroy** (*'bd*) does not usually have land as its object, but it is used here since land is personified. The destruction of the land thus means the destruction or the removal of the population, as indicated by the final phrase, **none will be left** (literally, ***without inhabitant***). As in the case of the comprehensive destruction announced in 1:2-3 and 1:18, this is probably an overstatement.

■ **6** The oracle continues through the next verse with a portrayal of **the land by the sea** (or, ***the seacoast***) after the judgment. The area will become **pastures** with **wells for shepherds** and **pens for flocks**. The idea is that once the land has been cleared of the sinful civilization (vv 4-5) it will revert to peaceful grazing land (cp. Jer 33:12-13).

■ **7** The prophet announces that **the remnant of the people of Judah** will possess the land that belonged to the Philistines. Zephaniah anticipates **the remnant of the people of Judah** (literally, **remnant of the *house of* Judah**) taking possession of this previously unconquered area. The **remnant** perhaps connotes the "humble" who are spared after the judgment threatened in 1:2-2:2 (→ 2:1-3). While 2:3 will only go so far to say that "perhaps" the humble might survive the judgment, this verse assumes that some certainly will. Isaiah and Jeremiah often use various cognates of **remnant** to connote the few among God's people who will survive divine judgment (e.g., Isa 10:20-23; Jer 8:1-3). Isaiah also offers hope and comfort and a renewal of God's purposes through a restored remnant (e.g., Isa 28:5-6; 37:31-32). Micah sees the remnant as an object of God's gracious protection (Mic 4:7; 5:7-8). ***House of Judah*** (*byt yhwdh*) is a designation for the tribe of Judah, apparently first adopted when it gained comparable status with Israel during the time of David (see 1 Sam 2:4-11; 1 Kgs 12:21).

The next line makes contact with the "pastures" and "shepherds" in v 6. The Judean remnant will tend their flock in the land of the Philistines, which has become pastures through God's judgment. The prophet also announces that the remnant of Judah (**they** perhaps refers to the "shepherds" in v 6) **will lie down** and find rest **in the houses of Ashkelon**. We assume that the houses here are part of the "ruins" of Ashkelon (v 4). Ironically, the once great *house of* Judah is now reduced to a **remnant** of refugees sleeping in the ruins of the **houses** of Ashkelon. **Evening** is the usual time to retire. But here it also indicates the swiftness of God's judgment: Philistine cities will be "emptied" at noon (v 4), but they will become resting places for the Judean remnant by **evening**!

Verse 7 ends with God's actions on behalf of the remnant. **The LORD their God will care for them** (literally, ***attend to them***, a positive use of the verb *pqd*); the image of God here is that of a shepherd caring for the flock.

The precise meaning of the last line, God **will restore their fortunes** (*wšb šbwtm*), is not clear. **Restore their fortunes** is a common paraphrase. The alternate translations, "will bring back their captives" (NIV note) or "restore their captivity," assumes the second term is derived from *šbh*, "to deport, take captive." It is also possible that both terms derive from *šûb* ("turn, return"). The phrase could then be translated as God "returns their turning" or "turns their turn about." In that case, God turning around their adversity may be the idea being expressed here. Though the precise meaning of this phrase is not clear, its focus is clearly on the alleviation of a crisis and return of somewhat normal life conditions for the Judeans.

2. Moabites and Ammonites (2:8-11)

■ **8** The next subunit (vv 8-11) concerns judgment against the Moabites and Ammonites, Judah's neighbors to the east. It begins with a divine speech indicating the reason for the following threats of judgment: **I have heard the insults of Moab and the taunts of the Ammonites**. **I have heard** suggests God's knowledge and awareness of human speech and actions, the basis of divine intervention in the world (see Exod 2:24; 3:7-10). The text does not give the content of the disparaging speech of the Moabites and the Ammonites. Their attempt is clearly to defame the people of Judah.

Moabites and Ammonites are reckoned as the disreputable relatives of Israel through the incestuous offspring of Lot (Gen 19:30-38). As children of Lot, they are usually mentioned together in scripture. The relationship of these peoples with Israel had always been tenuous (see Num 22:1-24:25; Judg 3:12-14; 1 Sam 14:7; 2 Sam 8:11-12; and the numerous denunciations of these nations in the prophets). Closer to Zephaniah's time (8th-7th centuries BC), they were probably working against Israel's interests by being Assyrian allies (Sweeney 2003, 137-38).

The next line states the specific charge; **they insulted my people and made threats against their land**. **My people** is the honorable title given to the Israelites in the Exodus; it also indicates the special covenantal relationship between the Lord and Israel (Exod 3:7; 5:1; 6:7; Jer 30:22; 31:1). The text implies that insulting God's people is tantamount to insulting God. **Threats against their land** (literally, "they magnified themselves upon (or against) their boundary") implies military incursions into Israelite/Judean territory for the purpose of boundary expansion by the Moabites and the Ammonites. Again, the **land** of Israel is God's land, which Israel occupies as a gift (Lev 25:23). Attack on the land of Judah is thus an attack on God's land. By attempting to invade Judean territory, they are also violating the decree of the Creator who appointed boundaries for each nation (Deut 32:8-9; see also Josh 15; see Calvin 1848, 246).

■ **9** The divine speech begun in v 8 continues with a series of solemn declarations. **Therefore** (*lkn*) introduces the threat of punishment for previously named offenses (→ v 8). The threat is prefaced with the oath formula **as I live** (*ḥy-'ny*), which almost always prefaces a divine curse (Robertson 1990, 304). The fulfillment of the pronouncement is assured by the fact that God will (always) **live** to bring it to completion (Sweeney 2003, 139).

The phrase **the LORD *of hosts* (Almighty) God of Israel** is found often in the prophets (especially in Jeremiah) as an introduction to divine speech. It is usually in oracles against Judah or the nations (e.g., Jer 16:9; 35:13; 46:25; 48:1) and occasionally in oracles of salvation (e.g., Jer 31:23; 32:14).

The Lord announces that **Moab will become like Sodom, the Ammonites like Gomorrah**. Ironically, the circumstances behind the birth of these people's forefathers (→ v 8) was directly linked with Lot's fleeing God's judgment on these cities of the plains (Gen 19:1-38). To suffer a judgment **like Sodom** and **Gomorrah** is a common figure of speech connoting a total destruction that renders the countryside infertile and uninhabitable (Deut 29:22-23 [21-22 HB]; Isa 13:19-20; Jer 49:18; see Gen 19:24-26). This is what the following half line suggests: **a place of weeds (*possession of nettles*) and salt pits, a wasteland forever (*perpetual desolation*). Nettles** are noxious stinging weeds that often take over vacant spaces or neglected farm land (Job 30:7; Prov 24:30-31; see Jørgensen 1980, 152). The tables will be turned; those who expand their boundary into the land of God's people (v 8) will lose their land to stinging weeds! As after the judgment on Sodom and Gomorrah, their territory will become so salty that it will be undesirable for farming or be filled with **salt pits** or ***salt mines***. In summary, it will become a **wasteland forever**, or a ***perpetual desolation*** incapable of sustaining human life.

After the downfall of Moab and Ammon, **the remnant of my people will plunder them**. As with the oracle against the seacoast peoples (vv 4-7), the **remnant** of Judah benefit from this divine judgment. Once again this **remnant** is called by the honorific title **my people** (→ v 8). As Israel plundered the nations when they left Egypt (Exod 3:22; 12:36) and later when they entered the Promised Land (Josh 8:27), the **remnant** would now **plunder** the descendants of Lot. But there will not be much left to take (→ below).

The survivors of my nation is synonymous with **the remnant of my people.** The land of the Moabites and the Ammonites was denied to Israel because God had granted it to them as their possession (see Deut 2:9, 19). But now it is promised to the remnant of Judah. It is clear here that possession of this territory by Judah will not happen through a conquest, but as a gift from the Lord of hosts (→ v 8). Ironically, what they are offered as their possession is not prime real estate, but an uninhabitable wasteland. Perhaps the purpose of this gift is to give assurance to Judah that they will no longer be insulted or oppressed by their enemies.

■ **10** This verse begins the conclusion of the oracle against Moab and Ammon, which is completed in v 11. It is tied to v 8 by the repetition of the charge there (→ above). The punishment stated above in v 9 is what Moab and Ammon **will get in return for their pride.** The word for **pride** (*g'wn*) here connotes an idolatrous self-exaltation asserted at the expense of others; such pride is often the reason for God's announced judgment in Isaiah (e.g., Isa 2:6-21). The last line clarifies one way Moabite and Ammonite **pride** manifests itself; they were **insulting and mocking** (literally, *they magnified themselves against*) the people of the LORD. Thus their offenses are not just against Judah, but are ultimately against the Lord (→ v 8). Although Judah is a sinful nation, since the reputation of Judah's God is at stake, the Lord will act.

■ **11** This is the key verse in this section. It functions both as a conclusion of one unit (vv 8-11) and a bridge to the next (vv 12-15). Its subject is the intended results of God's judgment.

First, **the LORD will be awesome to (*among*) them. Awesome** translates the passive participle *nwr'*, which could be literally rendered as "fearful, terrible, awe-inspiring, revered" (see BDB). The word usually describes how people respond to the Lord. God's awesome presence in a holy place evokes worship (Gen 28:17). The phrase found here, *nwr' . . . 'l*, occurs elsewhere to express how the Lord is more worthy of reverence than any other divine creature (Pss 89:7 [8 HB]; 96:4; 1 Chron 16:35) or to connote the incomparable awesomeness of God's salvific deeds among humans, including God's enemies (Ps 66:3-7). The result is that even enemies cringe and worship the Lord (cp. Ps 66:3-4). Here the self-idolatrous and proud descendants of Lot of vv 8-10 (the apparent antecedent to **them,** but as representative of the nations) will be overwhelmed by the Lord's awesome judgment on behalf of the oppressed remnant and find themselves among those who pay homage to the God of Israel (→ below).

The next clause further clarifies the effects of the divine judgment. The children of Lot will be awestruck **when (*kî*) the Lord destroys (*diminishes*) all the gods of the earth.** Throughout most of Israel's history the Hebrews believed in the existence of lesser **gods,** sometimes called "sons of the gods." These other gods were assigned to specific territories (Deut 32:8, NRSV or NIV note), but the Lord was considered the "Most High" to whom these deities were accountable (see Ps 82, which is conceptually similar to this passage; Roberts 1991, 201-02).

Here **earth** (*'rṣ*) could be translated "land," but the creation language of Zephaniah suggests that the significance of this judgment against these local gods also has cosmic significance (see 1:2-3, 18; 2:3). The God of Israel is the Creator God of the entire **earth**.

The term rendered **destroys** (*rzh*) in the NIV is rare; its cognates mean "to diminish, grow lean, disappear" (BDB, *HALOT*). The LXX translates *rzh* by a word that means "to utterly destroy." God's judgment against **the gods of the earth** is to make them ineffectual to their worshippers. Their adherents (**distant nations**, literally *all the coastlands of the nations*) will turn away from them and worship (**bow down to**) the Lord, who is revealed as the awe-inspiring God of Israel and God above **all the gods of the earth**.

All of them in their own land (literally *everyone from his own place*) implies that nations will replace their gods with the Lord God of Israel. Although *mqwm* (*place*) sometimes means **land**, it is also often shorthand for "holy place" (e.g., Gen 12:6; → 1:4). If foreign temples are meant here, then the idea is that the worship of the Lord will take place in the temples where nations once practiced idolatry. Ironically, the idolaters in the temple city of Jerusalem are bowing down to idols (v 4), yet the nations will abandon their gods and bow down the Lord from their temples.

We see here that all who deserve God's judgment may have the chance to repent and worship the Lord (cp. 2:3). Among the Moabites and Ammonites, the Philistines, and the ends of the world, by God's grace peoples may have the same experience as God's remnant. The hopeful message of this verse is that the Lord's ultimate purpose is not to destroy, but to bring all nations to worship the true God (Ben Zvi 1991, 313).

B. Judah's Powerful Neighbors (2:12-15)

1. Cushites (2:12)

■ **12** Although this oracle is linked with the previous verse, it begins a new unit ending in v 15. This short verse mentioning Cush is different from the other three oracles in the series. The grammar of the verse is awkward; **You Cushites, too, will be slain by my sword**, is literally *Also you, Cushites pierced by my sword (are) they*. The verse continues the divine speech of vv 8-11 with the opening direct address *also you*. In other words, the **Cushites** are among those who will be awe-struck and bow in worship of the Lord (see Floyd 2000, 226; cp. 3:10). **Slain by my sword** implies divine judgment executed through an earthly agent (Deut 32:41-42; Ezek 30:24-25). However, the Cushite survivors of God's judgment would join the remnant of Judah and the nations in worshipping the Lord.

This oracle is so brief and laconic that it gives the impression that it was tacked on as an appendix, perhaps shortly after the oracles first appeared in written form. Furthermore, this passage and Zeph 3:10 place Cushites in a positive light as worshippers of the Lord. One cannot help but see here an attempt to put the prophet's Cushite ancestry (1:1) in the best possible light. But it must also be noted that without this oracle there would be no mention of any peoples located south of Judah. As the center of God's cosmic work, the judgment beginning in Jerusalem and Judah radiates outward and ultimately results in peoples to the west, east, and south acknowledging the Lord in worship. The only area missing is the north, which is taken up in the next oracle.

2. Ashur and Nineveh (2:13-15)

■ 13 In the final oracle in the series against Assyria, the speech continues as a third person prophetic word. The offenses of Assyria and the threatened judgment are similar to those in the first two oracles. God **will stretch out** a **hand against** is also threatened against Judah and Jerusalem in 1:4-6.

The compass points in the other three oracles are left unnamed since their directions in relation to Judah are obvious. But the designation of Assyria as the **north** is needed since the region is often reckoned as east. The use of **north** for **Assyria** is also appropriate not only because that was Assyria's route of entry into Judah, but also because of their presence in the Assyrian controlled region north of Judah. The purpose of God's judgment is to **destroy** Assyria. The destruction of Assyria will leave **Nineveh**, the capital city, located on the Tigris River, a **desolate** and **dry** place like **the desert**.

■ 14 Verse 14 continues the picture of the desolation of Nineveh; the ruined city will become a resting place for **flocks**, a home for **creatures of every kind** (literally *every animal of the nation*). Elsewhere **flocks** connote domestic animals. Here they include wild animals. The next line names the **desert owl** and the **screech owl** as samples of the wild animals that will make Nineveh their home. These birds **will roost** (*ylynw*, "spend the night") **on her columns**, that is, on its *capitals* (cp. Isa 34:11 for the same creatures inhabiting the ruins of Edom).

The concluding lines further indicate the ruined condition of Nineveh. These three half lines are each governed by a singular verb. They appear to be a series of crisp interjections rapidly summarizing the condition of fallen Nineveh. What one hears in the city is **hooting** of the owls echoing **through the windows** of the ruined buildings (*they are singing in the window*). We may assume that human songs of joy and celebration were once heard through the windows in the city. **Rubble will fill the doorways** (*devastation is on the threshold*) suggests a city in ruins. The magnificent structures that once stood visibly in the city are now lying obscurely as ruins trampled by human feet (thresholds).

Verse 14 ends with the statement, **the beams of cedar will be exposed** (*indeed (kî) her cedar lays bare*). **Cedar** could be translated "cedar work," connoting either beams, paneling, or other decorative uses of the wood (see *HALOT*). Building with cedar was a sign of luxury and was sometimes condemned by the prophets as indicating misplaced priorities (1 Kgs 6:9-10; Jer 22:14-16). The subject of the verb *'ērāh*, **exposed** (*lays bare*), is not indicated. It is likely that the God who stretched a hand against Nineveh (v 13) is stripping bare its cedar works, its places

184

of luxury built perhaps by the stripping of the cedars of Lebanon during the Assyrian imperial expansion (cp. Hab 2:17).

■ **15** The final verse takes a post judgment perspective of Nineveh's condition. It is patterned after a lament song, which ponders how far the city has fallen from its glory days. The song begins with the reminder of its former condition: **this is the city of revelry that lived in safety.** City of revelry (*'lyzh*), literally "exultant (jubilant) city," in this context indicates celebration of military triumph. The Assyrian military strength would have given the citizens of Nineveh confidence in their safety.

She said to herself (*said in her heart*) implies self-congratulatory thinking. The content of the proud thought is **"I am the one! And there is none besides me."** This idiom expresses invincibility and incomparability, somewhat equivalent to "I am the greatest!" or "I'm invincible!" In Isa 47:8 this same statement is found in the mouth of Babylon where it suggests self-deification. Likewise, Nineveh has placed herself above the Lord (Bennett 1996, 691).

The song ends by contrasting the city's former greatness with her condition after God's judgment. The once jubilant city, full of self-confidence in her security, has become a **ruin, a lair for wild beasts. What a ruin she has become (*How she has become an appalling desolation*)** expresses disbelief about the demise of the city. The word for **ruin** or ***desolation*** (*šmh*) can mean something "horrific, a horror" (*HALOT*, BDB) or "waste" (BDB). The phrase **a lair for wild beasts (*a resting place for animals*)** links v 15 to v 14, which states flocks will lie down or rest in the midst of the city. Here *ḥyh* **(wild beasts)** probably refers to both domestic and wild animals as it seems to in v 14.

Verse 15 concludes with expressions of derision by **all who pass by** the ruined city of Nineveh. **Scoff** or ***hiss*** (*šrq*) expresses horror, sometimes mixed with scorn or hatred. **Shake their fists** is perhaps similar to the contemporary expression "shake a fist at." The oracle begins with the threat of God stretching out a hand to make sinful Nineveh into a desolation (v 13). It ends with the shaking of fists by those who pass by the city, which in this context would indicate the horrific devastation of Nineveh as a well-deserved judgment from the Lord (v 15).

FROM THE TEXT

It is easy to miss the major points of this text. On the one hand, the reader might be tempted to ignore the passage since it appears to depict an outdated view of a wrathful God bent on destroying a sinful world for their sins. Others might be inclined to embrace such a wrathful God who destroys sinners (others) so that believers (us) can prosper. Neither reading is very helpful for understanding the significant theological themes in the text. We will begin by surveying the most obvious.

This passage contains warnings against idolatrous pride. Twice in the passage we read that God will judge the proud who mock the people and purposes of God (2:8-10; 15). In every age the powerful think that their riches, political position, military strength or influence make them invincible. Yet, the pages of history are littered with examples proving otherwise. As in the case of ancient Assyria, great atrocities have been committed by peoples or nations who claim an exceptional status, often in the name of their god. Ultimately all will have to answer to the Creator for the damage they have done.

God's condemnation of powerful and proud oppressors is also a warning against those who wish to imitate them. As mentioned before in this commentary, Oracles Against the Nations are usually uttered in the hearing of God's people. When other nations are called to account for their deeds, it is an implicit message to those among God's people who are aligned with them or envy them. During the time of Manasseh and the early days of Josiah, there were many who thought submission to Assyria and adoption of Assyrian ways was the best course of action for Judah's survival and prosperity or for personal gain. But the reality was that adopting Assyrian ways did not benefit the people as a whole. The wealthy and powerful prospered by submission to Assyria while the remainder of the population bore an excessive burden in laboring to pay Assyrian tribute. The oracle against Assyria would be a warning; those who want to be like Assyria face the prospect of God's judgment and universal disdain by others (2:13-15).

But the passage contains promises that *God will turn around the adversities of the humble remnant* (v 7). A remnant of God's people will survive to occupy the land of the judged nations (2:6-7, 9). Before discussing this, however, it is important to note that we must be careful not to romanticize the promises nor claim more than the text affirms. First, the people who will move into the lands are not the entire people of God, but only those who have barely escaped the judgment threatened in 1:2-2:3.

Second, although they are innocent of the apostasy condemned by the prophet, they bear the marks of God's judgment on Jerusalem. They are to become refugees who have lost their homes and possessions, their livelihood, and perhaps their friends and families.

Third, their promised future is bare survival, not a comfortable and secure life. On the one hand, the prospect of tending their own sheep in a devastated landscape (see 2:4-7, 9) may have seemed like a hopeful new beginning for overtaxed poor shepherds from the Judean countryside. On the other hand, for Jerusalem city folk, such an existence matched neither their aptitude nor their aspirations. These urban working class folk no more yearned to leave the fortified walls of Jerusalem to become shepherds in Philistine ruins than a Boston store clerk today would aspire to live in a ghost town in Wyoming and take a job herding cattle. This certainly was not what they pictured as God's glorious future for their lives.

Fourth, in the context of the BT, the fate of the remnant appears even less promising. The total destruction of the surrounding nations found in Zephaniah's oracles is fulfilled through Babylonian intervention (Hab 1:5-11), suggesting that the remnant will now be subject to a new overlord once Assyria and their Jerusalem oppressors are gone. But the text implies this is somehow a turn for the better

(2:7). How can that be? Although it was not what they yearned for, the outcome is better than the total destruction threatened in 1:2-18.

The promises that a remnant of Judah would continue offered hope for the oppressed of a new beginning with God, and this is the major point of that promise. This hope is based on a radical expression of God's grace offered to a community that as a whole had failed to worship only the Lord and extend God's grace to others (→ below). This is indeed a move toward a better life, even if it means loss of outward security and some creature comforts. But the prospect of such an austere new beginning could only be accepted and lived out by daily dependence on the Creator. In the context of the BT, this is the answer to how the righteous ones would live by God's faithfulness (Hab 2:4), when all means of support are lost (Hab 3:17-19).

Living under the domination of others brings with it the temptation to side with the oppressors to avoid hardships and gain wealth and status. Israel had constantly been faced with this temptation before Zephaniah's day. As the reader considers the centuries after the prophet the situation changes little except that a new power replaces the old (i.e., Babylon, Persia, Greek empires, Romans). But living under the rule of others also gave Israel the chance to be God's servant, who by God's sustaining grace will be a light in a world of darkness (Isa 41:8-10; 42:1-9). This leads to the next theological themes.

The most important theme in this section is found in the key text of 2:11, which affirms that *the Lord's ultimate purpose in the world is that all peoples, nations, lands, and "gods" will submit to the awe-inspiring Lord in worship and obedience.* Zephaniah's arrangement of the nations according to the four points of the compass and the reference to "all the coastlands of the nations" (v 11) suggests a universal view. The Lord is the sovereign God over all the nations of the earth, and all are presented an opportunity to submit to the Lord in worship and obedience (2:11). As in Judah's situation (1:2-2:3), when they undergo God's judgment (2:4-12) the nations will have an opportunity to repent and submit to the only true God. This assumes that there are spiritually sensitive peoples among them who are responding to the light they have received. Unfortunately, some oppressive idolaters are so proud and hardened that they may never yield to the Lord. This appears to be the prospect for Assyria in 2:13-15, as it apparently was for the Jerusalem elite of 1:2-18. Nevertheless, the Lord's concern is that all worship the true God.

God reaches out to the nations of the world through a repentant and faithful people. The Lord has chosen a people to mediate divine blessings to all creation (Gen 12:2-3; Exod 19:3-6; 1 Pet 2:9). God's gracious calling and acts toward Israel, Judah, and the Church have this goal in mind. In the cases of the dispossessed nations in 2:4-15, it appears that the refugee remnant of Judah will carry out this vocation as a leavening influence, like the spiritually humble are an example in Jerusalem (→ 2:3). The prospect is that some among them will join the remnant of Judah as they share similar experiences. When they experience the awe-inspiring work of the Lord they will recognize the sovereign Lord in worship (2:11). The remnant of Judah will be there to articulate their experiences of the God of Israel and join them in worship of the Lord in the former temples of their gods.

God's judgment of Judah and the world in Zeph 1-2 are ultimately for the sake of this goal. God is saddened when this last resort is the only option. God is grieved when divine grace is resisted by people, whether among the faithful or unbelievers. But whether through bestowal of divine favor or exercise of divine punishment, God's gracious purposes remain; that is, to extend divine love to all and receive universal worship and obedience as a faithful response.

PART TWO: GOD'S [JUDGMENT AND] RESTORATION OF THE WORLD: ZEPHANIAH 3:1-20

III. THE LORD'S JUDGMENT ON JERUSALEM: ZEPHANIAH 3:1-8

BEHIND THE TEXT

This passage (3:1-8) begins Part Two of the book of Zephaniah, which in many ways mirrors the first half, 1:2—2:15. There are historical and literary similarities between 1:2—2:3 and the material found in 3:1-8. The social abuses mentioned in this text reflect a total disregard for the Mosaic Torah that was to become the basis for Josiah's reforms (2 Kgs 23:1-3; see 22:8-20; 23:25). It is thus possible that this text belongs to a period before Josiah began his initial reforms (ca. 640-632 BC; see 2 Chron 34:3-7), but undoubtedly not much later than 622 BC when the Mosaic Torah was discovered in the temple (2 Kgs 22:3-23:25; 2 Chron 34:8-35:19). After Josiah's death, when the former injustices returned under his son Jehoiakim (see Jer 22:13-17), the message of 3:1-8 may have found new relevance in oral or written form.

Though Zephaniah does not mention it by name, it is obvious that the city of oppression in v 1 is Jerusalem. The characterization of the city in 3:1-5 follows closely on the condemnation of Nineveh at the end of 2:13-15. Zephaniah seems to equate the two cities and suggests that Jerusalem should share Nineveh's fate. Zephaniah 3:1-5 in effect would be an indictment against the pro-Assyria party that claimed it is permissible for God's people to submit to and imitate the ways of Assyria. This party was still a dominant force before the young Josiah started implementing changes (Kim 2008, 413).

The original historical setting for the delivery of this message can only be reconstructed from literary indicators in the text (→ In the Text below). The prophet denounces here the religious and civil authorities who violate their call to administer justice through the Lord's directives. The temple setting is a likely option; the frequent references and allusions to the morning (vv 3, 5, 7) suggest the morning sacrifice, where Israel had an opportunity to meet daily with the Lord (see e.g., Exod 29:38-46; see Robertson 1990, 322; v 5). In Zeph 3 we can easily imagine Zephaniah arising during the morning sacrifice and addressing the corrupt leaders with a divine word, essentially stating that the justice lacking in the morning courts outside the temple walls will be taken up by the Lord within the temple.

Zephaniah 3:1-8 is a woe oracle that bears a striking resemblance to 1:2-2:3; it could be likened to a mirror of that passage. Both focus on Jerusalem and condemn its corrupt leaders (1:4-9, see also vv 10-13; cp. 3:1-4). Both conclude with an announcement of God's determination to consume the earth with fire on a day of judgment (1:18, see vv 14-17; cp. 3:8b) and call for an assembly to anticipate this event and perhaps to offer a chance to repent (2:1-3; 3:8a; see Floyd 2000, 232). The two passages appear to share the same basic structure and content and convey a similar message. They might be considered variations of the prophet's primary message of judgment on Jerusalem, but adapted for specific audiences and settings.

IN THE TEXT

A. Woe to the Defiled City! (3:1-5)

1. Thoroughly Corrupt Community (3:1-4)

■ 1 This verse pronounces a **woe** (*hôy*) on an unnamed city. Woe oracles are threats of divine judgment based on bereavement language. When uttered by the prophets they announce that the subject is as good as dead (→ 2:5 and sidebar Woe Oracles at Nah 3:1). As the reader continues, it becomes obvious that the unnamed city is Jerusalem, and that the oracle is not a continuation of the pronouncements against Nineveh in 2:13-15.

Verse 1 lists three corrupt characteristics of the city: **oppressors, rebellious, defiled**. The city of oppressors (*h'yr hywnh*) is literally ***the oppressor city*** or "the oppressing city" (this is found at the end of the list in MT, cp. NRSV). Oppression

190

is violence against others and disrupts human relationships. Verse 3 makes clear that oppressors are the powerful in the city. It is thus likely that the powerless are the victims of oppression. Violence against a neighbor or the marginalized in society is expressly forbidden in the Torah (e.g., in Exod 22:20 [19 HB]; Lev 19:33; 25:14) and is the subject of condemnation in the Prophets (e.g., Jer 22:3; Ezek 18:7).

Verse 1 in Hebrew begins with the characterization of the city as **rebellious** (*mr'h*); rebellion in this context is most likely a defiant revolt against God's command (Deut 1:26; Isa 1:20). Such rebellion brings doom upon God's people (Jer 4:16; 5:23-29).

The characterization of the city as **defiled** (*ng'lh* from *g'l*) indicates its unclean status. The cause of defilement is not stated; one may assume here violence and bloodshed by the powerful in the city. Uncleanness or defilement results in a disruption of relationship with God that is so severe that God no longer accepts sacrifices or delivers the community from crisis (Mal 1:7, 12-14; Isa 59:2-3).

■ **2** The city's rebellion is explained in this verse (Roberts 1991, 312). There are four things that Jerusalem does not do that she should be doing. First, **she obeys no one**. God traditionally speaks to Israel through the prophetic word, priestly instruction (see vv 3-4), or the sage's counsel (e.g., Jer 18:18). Yet Jerusalem has been disobedient to God's voice through them and others.

Second, **she accepts no correction**. The word *mwsr* can mean "discipline, warning, exhortation, punishment, training, instruction" (Branson 1990, 131-34). Learning from **correction** leads to a fulfilling life for oneself and the community (Prov 1:3; 4:13; 10:17). Not to accept such correction leads to the demise of the student and the deterioration of community wellbeing (Prov 5:23). Although not specified here, it can be assumed that the **correction** offered Jerusalem was redemptive and would lead to a closer relationship with God and the fulfillment of the city's vocation. By rejecting **correction** Jerusalem rejected the Lord (see Branson 1990, 131-32).

Third, the two half lines indicate who the city is ignoring; both begin emphatically in the Hebrew text with mention of God. The Hebrew reads *in the Lord she does not trust* (*byhwh l' bṭḥh*) (the NIV rearrangement of this and the following phrase obscures the intended emphasis). As is the case with those who accept God's correction, those who **trust in the LORD** enjoy God's blessing and security (Isa 26:3-4; Jer 17:17; Ps 37:3). Those who do not trust the Lord by finding security elsewhere will lack God's blessing and protection (Ben Zvi 1991, 188). Failure to trust in God is the source of all Jerusalem's evils (Calvin 1848, 263).

Fourth, following the Hebrew word order, the next line reads *to her God she does not draw near* (*'l-'lhyh l' qrbh*). The verb **draw near** sometimes connotes believers drawing near to the Lord for worship or instruction (Lev 9:5; Deut 5:27; 1 Sam 14:36). Jerusalem, where God dwells and is near to the faithful, has strayed far from God. But Jerusalem does not seek the Lord in worship or God's instructions for faithful living.

■ **3** Verses 3-4 focus on the misconduct of Jerusalem's leaders. Verse 3 likens the leaders to animals preying upon their own people. **Her officials within her are roaring lions.** The **officials** (*śryh*) would include an assortment of government and religious leaders (see e.g., 1 Kgs 4:1-6; → 1:8). The sound of hungry **roaring lions** stirs up terror in their prey since their destruction is certain (see Isa 5:29, Amos 3:4, 8).

Furthermore, **her rulers are evening wolves.** The Hebrew for **her rulers** (*šptyh*, which includes **judges**; see NRSV) connotes those who are responsible for implementing restorative justice (*mšpt*, Deut 16:18-20). West Asian **wolves** attack their prey at night; they are sometimes used as symbols of leaders who prey upon their own people (→ Hab 1:8; see also Ezek 22:27). The next expression, **who leave nothing for the morning,** can be translated *they do not gnaw until the morning* (*l' grmw lbqr*). The NIV's translation is based on the LXX's acceptable paraphrase of the Hebrew. The **rulers** (*judges*) are depicted as a pack of wolves who devour their prey so quickly and thoroughly that no trace is left by dawn. Zephaniah is alluding to the corruption of Jerusalem's legal proceedings. Apparently, *judges* were often bribed the **evening** before (see e.g., Isa 1:23; Ezek 22:17; Mic 3:11) and the innocent were essentially condemned long before their **morning** trial (Roberts 1991, 213).

The animal imagery in this verse may also remind the reader of how Jerusalem is compared to the imperialistic cities of oppression throughout the BT. Nahum has already likened Nineveh to a den of lions preying on the nations of the world (Nah 2:11-13 [12-14 HB]). Habakkuk has compared Babylon to a pack of threatening evening wolves (Hab 1:8). The main difference is that the imperial cities accused of conquering other nations are pagans without knowledge of the Lord, so their behavior is not completely unexpected. Jerusalem, however, is called to be the Lord's showcase of justice (Mic 4:1-4), and such behavior is contrary to Israel's divine vocation to imitate and administer the justice of the Lord (see Exod 23:6-9; Deut 10:17-19; 16:19-20; 24:17-18).

■ **4** Zephaniah now denounces corrupt religious leaders. **Her prophets are unprincipled** (*nby'yh phzym*). The latter term is rare, but apparently means *reckless*, that is, behavior characterized by lack of regard for consequences (see Judg 9:4; cp. Jer 23:32). The **prophets** are further characterized as **treacherous people** (*'nšy bgdwt*). Although this is the only occurrence of the noun *bgdwt*, the verbal form (*bgd*) sometimes connotes breach of faith in a solemn commitment between God or others (Hos 5:7; 6:7; → Hab 1:13). The **prophets** in view here are those who support political and popular policy rather than the faithful prophets who seek and speak a true word from the Lord. Those who warn about future judgment due to sins are usually unpopular or persecuted (see 1 Kgs 22:5-28; Jer 26:1-19; 27:1–28:17). The most deceitful are those who distort the word of God for personal gain and vilify those who will not enrich them (Mic 3:5-11).

Next, Zephaniah turns to Jerusalem's **priests** who violate their assigned roles (see Ezek 22:26). Priests are supposed to distinguish between the holy and profane, and teach others to keep the two separate (Lev 10:10). Instead, they do the opposite, **her priests profane the sanctuary (*defile the holy*)**. When the *holy* (*qōdĕš*, things set apart by God) are not treated according to God's instruction they are defiled (*ḥllw*, see e.g., Exod 20:25; 31:14; Lev 19:8). The word *holy* here probably functions as a general term for a variety of sacred things, rites, or commandments (see NRSV; see "holy things" in Ezek 22:26). It probably does not just refer to "the holy place," or **sanctuary** (Vlaardingerbroek 1999, 176 and others), although the term does occasionally have that meaning (e.g., Exod 28:33; 36:33).

Similar to the prophets mentioned above, the **priests** are probably modifying the standards of holiness to please the powerful and for personal gain (see Roberts 1991, 213-14). The priests' actions **do violence to the law (*torah*; *ḥmsw twrh*)**. Priests are responsible for properly handling *torah*. Although it sometimes connotes **law**, *tôrâh* has a much richer meaning than that narrow term (→ Hab 1:4). *Torah* is instruction or teaching about the Lord's gracious acts and how God requires Israel to respond to them. The *torah* suffers **violence** when the priests distort, neglect, or misinterpret it for the advantage of the powerful and the disadvantage of the weak (cp. Hos 4:6; Mal 2:6-9).

This *torah* is also issued as rulings in legal cases, since some priests acted as a court of appeals when the regular courts were incapable (see Roberts 1991, 214). As was the case with the judges mentioned in v 3, justice was being distorted by corruption and bribery. Therefore, **violence** against the *torah* often results in violence against those whom God's instruction was meant to protect (→ Hab 1:2-3).

Although prophets and priests are accused of failing in their callings to teach what is approved by the Lord, that does not necessarily take the rest of the population off the hook. Often people encourage their teachers to offer the easy way and then only approve of those who do. There are always those who prefer the easy self-justifying lie over God's demanding and generous truth (cp. Jer 5:30-31; Ps 4:2 [3 HB]; 2 Tim 4:3-4).

2. The Righteous Lord in Her Midst (3:5)

■ **5** Zephaniah contrasts the corrupt religious and civil leaders of Jerusalem with the righteous Lord who dwells in the city. The prophet asserts that **the LORD . . . is righteous** (*ṣdyq*); that is, God is committed to set right or restore order and bring justice to the oppressed in the city where there is violence, treachery, and disregard for the *torah*. In this context it may also connote innocence. Thus, God is innocent of any charge of approving or condoning the irresponsible and abusive conduct of Jerusalem's leaders (→ Hab 1:4; see Ben Zvi 1991, 206-209).

Verse 5 goes on to describe three characteristic and customary actions of God. First, God **does no wrong** or *does not commit injustice* (*l' y'śh 'wlh*); in other words, the Lord does not favor the wicked or harm the innocent (see 2 Chron 19:7; Sweeney 2003, 172-73). Instead, **every morning** God **dispenses** divine **justice** (*mšpṭw ytn*). The first phrase is repetitive and emphatic, it is literally "in the morning in the morning" (*bbqr bbqr*). The term translated **justice** (*mšpṭ*) also means "legal decision" (*HALOT*). This work is entrusted into the hands of judges (*šptym*, see v 3). Rendering justice involves the restoration of the marginalized and victimized to share in the God-granted provisions of a divinely ordered community. In contrast to the corrupt judges (and other leaders in the midst of Jerusalem) who fail to protect the innocent in the morning courts, the Lord constantly (every morning) offers justice to the community. God will not fail those who cry out for help.

Every new day God **does not fail** is parallel to the previous assertion. This line begins with a reference to light (*l'wr*), which is no doubt congruent with the idea of the dawn ("at dawn"; see *HALOT*) or a **new day**. God dispenses justice every morning with the same regularity and certainty of the dawning of light each new day.

Unfortunately, the Lord's just work is frustrated since its implementation is entrusted to leaders who have become disobedient. The concluding lines provide a contrast between the Lord and the self-serving leaders, *but* **the unrighteous know no shame** (*wl'-ywd' 'wl bšt*). The **unrighteous** ('*wl*) is a designation for those condemned in vv 2-4. They are a foil to the Lord who **does no wrong** or *injustice* ('*wl*, Keil 1868, 151). The inference of this concluding statement is that if they knew proper shame or experienced guilt, then they would not be behaving this way; rather, they would be implementing God's justice in the community (cp. Jer 6:13-15). God's will is to correct the abuses in Judah through divinely appointed leaders. Yet these leaders are ignoring God and serving their own interests. In summary, the prophet essentially announces that since justice is not being properly administered by humans in the lower courts, it will be taken up in the higher temple courts by the Lord.

B. The Lord's Past Acts Are Not Heeded So Further Judgment Is Necessary (3:6-8)

I. God's Acts Failed to Change Jerusalem (3:6-7)

■ **6** In vv 6-8 the prophet reports divine speech. Verses 6-7 indicate that God had hoped that past judgment on the nations would be a wakeup call for Jerusalem. Since it went unheeded, the Lord's threatened judgment (see 1:2-2:15) will indeed take place (v 8).

The reference to the Lord's judgment on the **nations** probably indicates God's great salvific works on behalf of Israel from the Exodus on through the monarchy (Luther 1525c, 353; Wesley 1765, 2563; cp. Smith 1984, 139-40). Since Jerusalem knows that the Lord has **destroyed** (*cut off*) **nations** (*hkrty gwym*), Jerusalem should be aware that God can and will carry out the threat in 1:4-6 to "cut off" the idolaters in Judah and Jerusalem.

The rest of v 6 describes different aspects of the Lord's destruction of the nations. **Strongholds** (*pnwt* most likely means *corner towers*) are part of the defense system of a city. When they are **demolished**, the entire city is doomed (→ 1:16). **I have left their streets deserted** indicates fleeing of the population from their defenseless cities. Although *ḥwṣwt* often means **streets** (see Nah 2:4 [5 HB]; 3:10; Jer 33:10), it sometimes connotes fields or plains (Ps 144:13; Job 5:10; and Prov 8:26; Davidson 1905, 130). It is possible then that this verse may be portraying extensive destruction that reaches from the city walls to the farmland and pastures. Regardless of the meaning of *ḥwṣwt* here, this verse depicts the total destruction of nations.

The rest of v 6 focuses on the fate of the **cities** of the nations. **They are deserted and empty** indicates fleeing of the entire population from the cities destroyed by the Lord.

■ **7** This verse indicates that the example of others has failed to teach Jerusalem the intended lesson. The NIV adds **Jerusalem** to clarify the subject of the feminine verbs and pronouns. **I thought** is a possible translation, but it is better to translate it literally, *I said* (*'mrty*; NRSV). What follows are the Lord's past admonitions to Jerusalem through prophets and other spokespersons (Luther 1525b, 353-54).

Surely you will fear me can also be understood as a command, *Just fear me* (*'k-tyr' 'wty*) (the prefix-imperfect combination in Hebrew sometimes functions as a command). Here the word **fear** (*tyr'y*) connotes awe of the Lord that results in worship and obedience. God also commanded Jerusalem to **accept correction** (*tqḥy mwsr*). The point of **correction** is often redemptive, it is to restore persons to a proper relation with God and others. **Correction** or *instruction* can be taught orally or learned by experience, either one's own experience or the example of others (e.g., Prov 24:32-34; see Branson 1990, 131-34; see on v 2 above). God had hoped that Jerusalem's leaders' inclination not to accept correction (v 2) would be changed as a result of seeing the Lord at work in the world. When the Lord subdues other nations on Israel's behalf often it serves as a warning to Israel not to follow the example of the nations (e.g., Deut 4:22-23; 6:10-15; 12:29-32). Zephaniah here accuses Jerusalem of not taking such warnings to heart.

The desired outcome of God's restorative **correction** is **then her place of refuge would not be destroyed** or *then her habitation would not be cut off* (*wl'-ykrt m'wnh*). There is probably a pun on the word translated *habitation* (*m'wn*). On the one hand, it can indicate the lair of an animal (Jer 9:10 [9 HB]; 51:37). On the other hand, the word connotes God's heavenly dwelling (Deut 26:15; Jer 25:30) or God, as a **refuge** for the distressed (Pss 71:3; 91:1; cp. Motyer 1998, 947). The point is that Jerusalem has missed its calling to find refuge in the Lord and be the city of the heavenly king that reveals God's glory to the world (Ps 47:1-9 [2-10 HB]). Instead it will be destroyed as if it were a den harboring dangerous animals. This could have been avoided if Jerusalem had paid attention to the Lord.

The next phrase is difficult. The NIV translates the negative at the beginning of the line as serving double duty, **nor all my punishments come upon her**. It is preferable to read it in apposition to the previous statement, *everything for which I called her to account* (*kl 'šr pqd 'lyh*). The root *pqd* connotes God's "visitation, calling to account, punishment" of Judah and Jerusalem. The verbal expression *pqd 'l* suggests that sins bring with them consequences, inferring that divine judgment is not arbitrary. The whole statement essentially says that Jerusalem deserved to be punished (to have her habitation cut off). She had been warned that the consequences of her sins would be visited upon her. God has done everything possible to avoid punishing the city; Jerusalem stands before the oncoming judgment without excuse.

The last phrase contains plural verbs, which probably indicate the residents of Judah and Jerusalem, or more specifically the corrupt leaders indicted in 3:2-5 and those who willingly follow them. **But they were still eager to act corruptly.** The particle *'kn* (**but . . . still**) indicates a sharp contrast with the proceeding and can be translated "however, rather, on the contrary" (BDB; *HALOT*). The phrase **eager to act** is an idiom; it is literally "rise up early" (*hškymw*). On the one hand, the Lord wills to shine forth justice with the break of every new day (v 5), yet God's people eagerly arise early **to act corruptly in all they did** or *to corrupt all their deeds* (*hšhytw kl-'lylwtm*). In other words, they behave irresponsibly and unjustly as if there were no God to call them to account (cp. Ps 14:1; Deut 32:29). Since God's justice shines forth in the morning (v 5), those who rise up early to sin can expect swift justice (see v 8).

2. Therefore Wait for Further Judgment (3:8)

■ **8** **Therefore** (*lkn*) links the grounds for judgment developed in the previous verses with this one. Because Jerusalem has not learned from the past, God will proceed with more judgment, which was also announced in 1:2-2:3. This verse contains many of the elements found in 1:14-2:3, but in abbreviated form. Since the Jerusalem community and its leaders have been warned and are without excuse, God tells the inhabitants of Judah (v 7) to **wait for me**; that is, **wait** for God's judgment to take place.

From the context it appears that the prophet is speaking to Jerusalem's corrupt leaders (see vv 3-4, 7) as the primary antecedent. The next line makes clear that they are to wait **for the day** when the Lord will **stand up to testify** (or *for the day when I arise as a witness*). **The day** is an allusion to the Day of the Lord mentioned in 1:7-18; it is **the day** when God will act to set things right (→ 1:7). The NIV **to testify** follows the LXX; the MT reads the term as "for plunder," signifying that the Lord is appearing as a Divine Warrior (see *BHS*; NIV note). In this verse, the Lord is both the witness against the corrupt Judean leaders and the judge who pronounces judgment against them. In the setting of this verse, God is also the plaintiff. In Israelite courts, plaintiffs and witnesses often functioned as judge, jury and executioner when determining justice; that is, in deciding, announcing and carrying out the verdict and sentence (see Köhler 1956, 157, and others).

The next phrase, **I have decided to** (*ky mšpty*) is literally "for my justice" or "for my judgment." The remainder of v 8 describes the judgement that carries out God's purposes. God's activity is explained in the next set of parallel lines: **to assemble the nations, to gather the kingdom.** The **nations** and **kingdoms** include the peoples mentioned in oracles against the nations, that is, the nations slated for judgment in 2:4-15. It appears that this gathering will be at a single location. The last call for an assembly of God's people before the Day of the Lord (→ below) is set in Jerusalem (see 2:1-3). Likewise, in similar passages when the nations are gathered for God's work it is usually at Jerusalem (e.g., Jer 1:15-16). Since only Jerusalem is slated for judgment (→ below), apparently the nations act as the Lord's witnesses against the sins of Jerusalem!

The rest of the verse has a near parallel in 1:18. **Pour out my wrath . . . all my fierce anger** connotes divine judgment (Ezek 21:36; 22:31; Lam 4:11). **On them** (*'lyhm*) is masculine plural, referring back to the corrupt leaders who are commanded to wait for the Lord (vv 7c-8a; see Roberts 1991, 210; 215-16). **The fire of my jealous anger** is literally, *the fire of my zeal*. God's **zeal** (*qn'ty*) is a passion to carry out divine purposes (→ Nah 1:2 and Zeph 1:18).

The consumption of **the whole *earth*** (*t'kl kl-h'rṣ*) is an exact repetition of the phrase found in 1:18. These two passages are closely linked. They both use the phrase as a conclusion to the announcement of judgment before the day of the Lord's anger. Both passages are closely connected to a call to assemble for judgment. As in 1:18, *h'rṣ* can be translated "the land." Compare this to 1:2-3 where the cosmic judgment on humans and animal life removes them from the land (*'dmh*). In each case Jerusalem and the land of Judah are depicted as a microcosm of the entire earth. Once again Jerusalem's failure to live up to its divine vocation has implications for the rest of creation. As a result, the world as Judah knows it is about to come crashing down.

FROM THE TEXT

3:1-8

The passage before us presents a gloomy picture of the fate that befalls God's disobedient people. The opening woe sets a funeral tone for the passage; death has entered the community of God. The life that had once been an option has been rejected and the end is in sight. Jerusalem's world will be consumed in fiery judgment. Yet, behind this negative depiction we can decipher God's gracious commitment to the world and the proper response expected from it.

God's acts of grace should elicit gratitude, not rebellion. In this passage we have glimpses of this grace. The Lord has acted on behalf of the people of Israel in the past, releasing them from Egyptian oppression and providing them with a homeland among hostile nations (v 6). These acts also provided warnings through examples of the fate of idolatrous nations. The Lord guided and instructed them by giving them *torah* to be taught and administered by priests, prophets, and sages (vv 2, 4, 7). God also offers positive examples of justice through sustaining the created order (v 5) and provides for a justly ordered community through rulers and judges (v 3).

The text, however, indicates that instead of fear and gratitude, the people rebelled against God. The city the Lord has chosen as the divine dwelling place among Israel has become an oppressing city. Though the Lord became a refuge for the people of God, they found security in their own "place of refuge" (v 7).

Zephaniah warns them that the Lord who delivered them in the past will rise up as a witness against them, and as their judge who will pour out a fiery wrath on them that will certainly consume them (v 8).

This dire warning about judgment itself is a display of divine grace. One cannot read this as God's final word to Judah; a key function of judgment speeches in the prophets is to persuade the audience to repent and avert the catastrophe. Thus it is possible to conclude that implicit in this oracle is a call to the Judean sinners to put an end to their rebellion and oppressive behavior and to fulfill their vocational calling.

We find a glimpse of grace in the call to "wait for me," extended to both the Judean sinners and those looking for freedom from their oppressors (v 8). This call conveys to sinners the urgency of the situation and the need to repent so that God may not carry out the threat of judgment. It also offers hope for the oppressed who wait for the day of their deliverance. The Judean sinners, by saving themselves from the coming judgment, will certainly be saving "the whole world," to which they have been called as mediators of God's grace and blessing (v 8; see Gen 12:3).

IV. THE LORD'S EXTENSIVE SALVATION: FROM THE NATIONS TO JUDAH: ZEPHANIAH 3:9-20

BEHIND THE TEXT

The tone of the message shifts radically from the focus on divine judgment announced throughout 1:2-3:8. The material in this division of the book provides a fitting conclusion to the prophecy. For the general time in which this prophecy was originally proclaimed see the discussions in Behind the Text on 1:2-3:4 and 3:1-8. This passage is very difficult to date. It is tempting to interpret it as a late text addressing Judah after it experienced the devastating judgment proclaimed elsewhere in the book. Yet, a careful reading indicates that the promises of restoration in this section continue to presuppose a time before the occurrence of this judgment.

Though judgment is announced, Zephaniah does not see evidence of repentance or an end to the Judean rebellion against God and their oppressive deeds. This oracle assumes that this judgment will take place in the future as a necessary prelude to the restoration (see vv 11-12, 15, 18-19). As with the rest of the book, it is unlikely that the reforms of Josiah have been implemented when this message first appeared. It also appears likely that this message was proclaimed after the prophecies attested in 1:2-3:8 were pronounced. The message found here probably grows out of the recognition that a proclamation based solely on divine judgment cannot sustain a community (Vlaardingerbroek 1999, 23). Once the prophet had thoroughly emphasized the coming judgment, he found it necessary to expound the hope hinted at in 2:3.

This division naturally falls into two sections. The first section (vv 9-13) contains two units, with a balanced two-pronged announcement of God's salvation and the human response among peoples of the world (vv 9-10) and the remnant in Jerusalem (vv 11-13). The second section (vv 14-20) focuses on various persons addressing Zion/Jerusalem regarding the Lord's salvation and how the community should respond. The section contains two closely related units, vv 14-17 and 18-20. The celebration of the Lord's work (vv 15, 17-18, 19-20) is emphasized throughout the passage.

IN THE TEXT

A. The Lord's Transforming Deeds on That Day (3:9-13)

1. God Purifies, Enabling True Worship by All (3:9-10)

■ **9** This passage is written in the first person as a direct word of the Lord. It is possibly a continuation of vv 6-8. The opening phrase **then** (*ky-'z*, **indeed then**) introduces God's actions after the judgment in 3:1-8 (and elsewhere in the book) has taken place.

The focus of God's action in v 9 is on restoring true worship in the world. **I will purify the lips of the peoples** or *I will give* (**change**) *for the peoples a purified* (**pure**) *lip* (**language**) conveys the idea of purified speech. **Peoples** signifies potentially all nations of the world. Since **language** (*śph*, literally "lip") is also found in the Tower of Babel narrative (Gen 11:1, 6, 7, 9), a reversal of Babel may also be assumed here (see Isa 19:18; see Motyer 1998, 951-52; and others).

Two results of their purified speech are introduced in the rest of the verse. First, **all of them may call on the name of the LORD.** To call on the Lord's name indicates the proper dependence upon the Lord in prayer and worship, which also means an end to their idolatrous worship.

Second, (**all of them**) *may* serve the Lord **shoulder to shoulder.** The phrase **all of them** (*klm*) is implied from the previous line. In this context **serve** (*'bd*) can mean anything from worshipping to obeying God (Roberts 1991, 217). Undoubtedly this purified speech issues from a purified heart. The phrase, **shoulder to shoulder** is literally, *one shoulder* (*škm 'ḥd*); it suggests the coming together of all the peoples as one worshipping community. In the only other occurrence of this phrase it connotes a portion of an inheritance (Gen 48.22). If "one portion" is the intended meaning in this context, then it suggests that the nations, who are elsewhere considered the heritage of other gods (see Deut 32:8 NRSV), now join Israel as a portion of the Lord's heritage to serve the Creator (Deut 32:9).

At the Tower of Babel people were united in a single language and purpose giving them potential for great evil against the Lord. When God's complete transformation takes place, people will be united in language and purpose to glorify God in word and deed (cp. Acts 2:1-11).

200

■ **10** This verse describes further the actions of transformed people, identified as those **beyond the rivers of Cush**. Here **Cush** likely signifies ancient Nubia (May 1984, 67). As a distant location, **Cush** is probably representative of the far corners of the earth, indicating that there is no geographical limit to God's work among foreign peoples (see Szeles 1987, 108; and others). Even distant peoples will be **my worshippers** or *my suppliants* (*'try*). Although this is the only occurrence of the noun, the verbal form of *'try* clearly means "to pray, entreat" the Lord for help (e.g., Gen 25:21; Exod 8:26 [22 HB]).

These are further identified as **my scattered people** or *my Daughter Dispersed* (*bt-'pwṣy*, literally, "daughter of my scattered ones," or "my daughter scattered ones"). In similar constructions a geographical or ethnic entity usually follows the term "daughter"; the most common is "daughter Zion/Jerusalem" (see 3:14 and elsewhere). It is difficult to determine the identity of the dispersed people. If Daughter Zion is intended here, then the prophet may be referring to the Judeans who will be scattered by the judgment. Later in this chapter the prophet speaks about the gathering of the exiles and their praise and honor "in every land where they have suffered shame" (vv 19-20). This is the view taken by many interpreters. However, the prophet's reference to God's work among "peoples" (v 9) suggests another more likely interpretation. When vv 9-10 are read together, it becomes clear that *my Daughter Dispersed* indicates the Gentile worshippers of God mentioned in v 9. If this is correct, then it is possible to find here an allusion to the Babel incident, since scattering is the judgment that came upon those who alienated themselves from the Lord (Gen 11:8-9).

They **will bring me offerings** (*ywblwn mnḥty* is literally **bring my offerings**). Zephaniah does not specify that the offerings will be brought to Jerusalem. If worshippers are the Judean exiles, then the Jerusalem temple (or temple site after its destruction) might be the intended place of worship here. However, if worshippers are the Gentiles, then their place of worship could be local holy places (see 2:11; also Isa 19:19-21).

The type of offering is a *minḥâ*, which means "gift." It often connotes a vegetable or grain offering, but can also serve as a general word for any sacrificial offering (de Vaux 1965, 2:421-22; 430-31; 452). In the Jerusalem temple this offering addressed a variety of occasions, including the thanksgiving (Lev 7:11-15) and Sabbath offerings (Num 28:9-10). It is noteworthy that it also functions as a sin offering for the poorest of the poor; those who could not afford the usual sheep or even the alternative of two doves for the impoverished (Lev 5:11-13). Therefore, this passage allows for the possibility of a ritual provision for sin for all who do not have access to Jerusalem.

Indeed, vv 9-10 indicate that the corrupt worship that Zephaniah previously denounced (1:4-9, 16) will be purified and resumed through an act of God. What is surprising is that it will occur outside of Jerusalem and will involve non-Israelites. Even more surprising is that the promise of restoration begins with these outsiders; the fate of God's people in Jerusalem is not addressed until the next unit, vv 11-13.

2. God Transforms Jerusalem (3:11-13)

■ **11** This unit addresses the humble remnant who will wait for, seek, and find refuge in the Lord (2:3, 3:8, 12-13). **On that day** and similar expressions connote the Day of the Lord as a day of divine punishment in Zephaniah (1:7-18; 2:2-3; 3:8). Here it refers to the Lord's judgment as proclaimed in 3:8; only now this has become a **day** of restoration. The common thread is that on that day God acts to set things right; the ultimate goal of divine judgment is restoration.

You . . . will not be put to shame (*l' tbwšy*) is a feminine verb, indicating that **Jerusalem** (added by the NIV for clarification) is the addressee. If Jerusalem were to live out the full consequences of its rebellion (e.g., 3:1-4) it would continue to be shamed, that is, be under the threat of God's judgment. This text indicates that divine forgiveness and transformation will release **Jerusalem** from its **shame for all the wrongs** she has **done** to the Lord (literally *on account of all the deeds by which you have transgressed against me*). This indicates a reversal of the community's character. To transgress against (*pš' b-*) God indicates a willful rebellion or revolt against God's sovereign authority, which leads to the breaking of the divine-human relationship (see e.g., 1 Kgs 12:19; and elsewhere).

The second half of the verse indicates how Jerusalem will be transformed. God will **remove** from the city **arrogant boasters** (literally *the exulting of your arrogant ones*). The word *exulting* (*'lyzy*) indicates prideful boasting in this context. The **arrogant** are essentially idolaters, they rely solely on themselves and deny that they need help from anyone, including God. They have not responded to the call to seek the Lord with righteousness and humility (→ 2:3; cp. 1:6). Verse 11 anticipates a reversal of this situation. On the day of restoration there will be a new community of worshippers on God's **holy hill**, Zion or the Temple Mount; they will be the humble who seek God. The proud and the arrogant will have no place among the restored people of God.

It is important to note that the prophet is not proclaiming here a selective removal of evil doers from the community without affecting the entire community, guilty and innocent alike. The community as a whole has been corrupted by the outward actions of its **arrogant** leaders. Therefore, Zephaniah's (as well as Habakkuk's) persistent message is that there will be a sweeping judgment against the entire community. The fires of judgment will remove the dross of the evil doers, leaving behind the purified faithful as a remnant. Yet all will endure the fire (cp. Isa 10:20-23).

■ **12-13** In vv 12-13a **the remnant** in Jerusalem is specifically named as the addressee of this prophecy. It begins **but I will leave within you** (*whš'rty bqrbk*). The verb *š'r* ("be left over, left behind") clearly conveys the idea of a remnant (*š'ryt*) (→ 2:7, 9; 3:13a).

In contrast to the haughty and corrupt leaders removed by God's judgment, the remnant will be made up of **the meek and humble** (*'m 'ny wdl* is better translated as *a people humble and powerless* or *lowly*). In 2:3 the term "humble" (*'nwy*, a cognate) connotes the oppressed faithful among God's people who might have a chance to survive divine judgment. The humble also includes those who may not necessarily be oppressed, but who seek humility (*'nwh*, → 2:3). The *powerless* (*dl*) are the helpless poor who are often exploited by the powerful (Isa 10:1-2; Amos 4:1; 5:11; and elsewhere).

In the next line (v 13), **the remnant of Israel** are the opening words in the Hebrew text. This **remnant . . . will trust** (*seek refuge*) **in the name of the** LORD, indicating the new community's total dependence on the Lord for protection and safety. The phrase **in the name of the** LORD connotes being under the Lord's power and protection; it is virtually synonymous with "in the LORD." This seeking of refuge reminds the reader of 2:3, where the humble are told that perhaps they might find protection by being hidden on the day of the Lord's wrath. It also contrasts with the community under the corrupt leaders who did not trust in the Lord (3:2). Along with the other peoples who "call on the name of the LORD"(3:9), they will find God to be trustworthy.

The description of the humble remnant continues in v 13. First, **they will do no wrong** or *they will not commit injustice* (*l' y'św 'wlh*). This repeats word for word the description of the Lord in 3:5. Empowered by divine grace, the faithful remnant completes God's work. They no longer perpetrate the injustices toward others previously committed by their corrupt leaders (see 3:1-4).

The next group of characteristics concerns their speech. **They will tell no lies**; their community life will be guided by truth telling. The parallel line, **a deceitful tongue will not be found in their mouth**, reiterates the community's commitment to honesty and truthfulness in all areas of its relationships. Justice will be preserved and promoted by this community through their actions and words. **Tongue**, like lip (see v 9) often connotes speech. As in v 9 above, this correction of false speech indicates a heart purified by God. By God's gracious acts those who have been outsiders are enabled to properly pray and worship (v 9), and the remnant people of God is empowered to form a just community (v 13).

It would probably be a mistake to separate these acts of God as if different populations will be granted different gifts. Rather, the framing of the passage by references to divinely transformed speech indicates a unified divine will for the whole community, Gentiles and Judeans alike. God will empower everyone to properly worship, pray, and articulate justice from the heart.

The passage concludes with imagery signifying the newly found security of the remnant. *Indeed* (emphatic *ky* missing in the NIV) **they will eat (*graze*) and lie down and no one will make them afraid.** The shepherding imagery includes both grazing and resting peacefully. This figure of speech suggests divine provision and protection (e.g., Isa 40:11; 49:9). The last phrase, **no one will make them afraid** (*w'yn mḥryd*, literally, *with none to terrify*) is a common expression, sometimes found in divine promises to grant peace by the removal of what inspires terror among God's people (Lev 26:6; Ezek 34:28).

The lot of the remnant has been reversed. Under God's judgment of Jerusalem, the remnant was little more than a vestige of scattered shepherds sleeping among the ruins of their neighboring peoples' cities (→ 2:7). By God's restorative grace they will be brought home and live securely in their own community. Furthermore, while formerly they had lived in fear (→ 3:15-16) under oppressive leaders within (→ 3:1-4) and the threat of divine judgment, now by God's grace they will live with freedom from terror (cp. 3:19-20; see Goldingay 2009, 129).

B. The Lord's Deliverance of Zion at That Time (3:14-20)

I. Call for Zion to Rejoice in the Lord's Coming Deliverance (3:14-17)

■ **14** This section opens with Zephaniah addressing Zion/Jerusalem (in the third person) with a call to rejoice. The general reasons for rejoicing are stated in vv 15-17, then further developed in vv 18-20. In the broader context of this passage, however, the reasons for celebration go back to v 9 and include not only what the Lord will do for the remnant, but what God will do for other peoples (cp. Zech 2:10-12 [14-16 HB]).

The terms for singing and rejoicing in this verse often occur elsewhere in calls to worship in thanksgiving and victory hymns. The word translated **Sing** (*rny*) is literally "give a ringing cry" (BDB) or *be jubilant*. It is found most often in calls for praise to the Lord for divine acts of deliverance. In the Prophets we find calls for Zion to *be jubilant* in anticipation of the Lord's future acts of salvation (e.g., Isa 12:6; 54:1; Zech 2:10 [14 HB]).

Daughter Zion and **Daughter Jerusalem** are endearing titles for Jerusalem. Although **Zion** technically signifies the Temple Mount, it is often applied to the entire city. The term **shout** in the parallel line, **shout aloud, Israel**, is often found in calls to worship where it connotes praising and rejoicing over what God has done for Israel (e.g., Pss 47:1 [2 HB]; 81:1 [2 HB]; 95:1). **Israel**, the old covenant title of God's people, is now granted to the humble and poor remnant (3:12-13).

The call **to be glad and rejoice,** together with *be jubilant* and **shout,** connote joyous celebration. The rejoicing is to be done **with all your heart.** The phrase is literally *whole heartedly* (*bkl-lb*, there is no **your** in the Hebrew), indicating resolution, inclination, or determination.

■ **15** This verse summarizes the reason for joy and the command to praise, which will be expanded throughout the remainder of the section. The first two verbs are in the perfect tense, which often connotes past time. Here they take the perspective of the community that will one day look back at what God has done.

First, **the LORD has taken away** or removed from them their **punishment.** The word **taken away** (*hsyr*) is also found in 3:11 where it connotes the removal of the arrogant from the midst of Jerusalem. The expression **your punishment** is plural (*mšptyk*); the singular form *mšpt* is often translated "justice." Here it can be literally rendered *your judgments* or "just decrees, verdicts" against the city (cp. NRSV).

Furthermore, God **has turned back** their **enemy**. The verb **turned back** (*pinnâ*) could be translated as "cleared away" (see NASB). Assuming that Zephaniah is still addressing the humble remnant, the **enemy** here could be a collective term for the haughty, unjust and oppressive leaders condemned throughout the book. The text thus anticipates the removal of the oppressors from Jerusalem as promised in 3:11 (cp. 1:3-9; 3:8, 11). Later generations could also understandably interpret this passage as a promise to remove foreign conquerors.

The remnant also receives the assurance of the Lord's presence with them; the LORD who removed the arrogant leaders from Jerusalem's midst is the self-declared **King of Israel**, the newly formed remnant community (→ vv 12, 14). The Lord's kingly rule means the end of all oppressive forces that induce fear in God's kingdom. The last line, **never again will you fear any harm**, conveys this idea of the remnant enjoying peace under the protective presence of God their king.

■ **16** This verse anticipates how Jerusalem will be addressed in the future, providing a basis for freedom from fear in the present. **On that day** is the time of restoration, a time when all oppression and fear of divine judgment that threatened **Jerusalem/Zion** in the past will be resolved for those who have anticipated God's deliverance.

The translation **they will say** is literally *it will be said*. The speech following this continues through v 17, as indicated by the quotation marks in the NIV. This indefinite passive emphasizes the message to **Jerusalem**, rather than the speakers.

The first thing spoken is **do not fear**, words which are usually attributed to God (e.g., Gen 15:1; 21:17; Judg 6:23), but are generally delivered by prophets (cp. 2 Kgs 19:6; Isa 7:4; 30:9). It is necessary to note again that this is not a blanket statement about God deciding to cancel divine punishment on the wicked in the city. It is an assurance to the faithful and repentant remnant that they will be members of a transformed community whose hope is in the Lord, despite the suffering they will endure in the judgment.

The second thing that will be said to Zion is **do not let your hands hang limp**. The feminine pronoun **your** refers back to **Jerusalem**. **Limp** or slack **hands** are a sign of discouragement or loss of courage to complete a task in the face of a crisis (2 Sam 4:1; Isa 13:7; Jer 6:24). The crisis in view here is the condition of Zion under oppressive leaders and the consequent suffering under God's judgment.

■ **17** What will be said in that day (v 16) continues through this verse. The feminine pronouns **you** and **your** indicate that Jerusalem is still being addressed. **The LORD your God** reiterates that the LORD (*Yhwh*) is Jerusalem's **God**, and no other. The prophet assures Jerusalem that the Lord will continue to be with her (*in your midst*; cp. 3:5, 8, 11 and 15).

The next half line describes the Lord as **the Mighty Warrior** [*gibbôr*] **who saves**. The term *gibbôr* (literally "mighty, strong one," → 1:14), when applied to

3:15-17

the Lord by the Israelite tradition, conveyed the idea of God as the defender of oppressed Israel from its enemies (Exod 15:3; Ps 24:8; 78:65-66). The Lord as king in Jerusalem's midst (see v 15) will be its primary defender from all harm. God will heroically defend the city and restore the community.

God also **will take great delight in you**, literally *will delight in you with rejoicing*. God delights in Israel when all the people flourish as the obedient covenant community (Deut 28:63; 30:8-10; Jer 32:40-41, and elsewhere). Here the Lord's delight will be in a restored community that reflects God's love and justice according to its divine vocation (e.g., Gen 12:2-3; Exod 19:6; Mic 4:1-4).

In his love he will no longer rebuke you is literally, God *will be silent in his love* (*yḥryš b'hbtw*). God's silence is linked here to **love** for the humble remnant of the land. It is therefore possible that this phrase conveys the idea of God withholding judgment. The NIV reflects this interpretation. Divine love is the basis of God's redemption, election, and preservation of Israel (see Deut 4:31-37; 7:6-8; also Exod 34:6-7). In v 17, God promises patient love to the remnant who will escape the full effects of the Lord's judgment.

The final line reads God **will rejoice over you with singing**. Israel (or the entire created order) is often called to rejoice over God's acts (Isa 9:3 [2 HB]; 35:1-2; Joel 2:23; Zech 9:9, and elsewhere). Here it is the Lord rejoicing over the divinely restored Jerusalem community! The word translated **singing** (*rnh*) connotes a ringing cry of either jubilation or lamentation. Although the ringing cry could be in the form of a song, the focus is on the rejoicing, so the translation *jubilation* (see BDB, *HALOT*) is preferable. The passage has come full circle: it opened with a command for Jerusalem to cry out in jubilation, it closes with the Lord's jubilation over Jerusalem.

2. The Lord Will Gather Zion for Deliverance at That Time (3:18-20)

■ **18** This verse begins a new unit, expressed in the first person as a direct word of the Lord. The Hebrew in this verse is very difficult to render into meaningful phrases.

I will remove from you all who mourn over the loss of your appointed festivals is a reasonable paraphrase of the first part of this verse. It can also be translated as *those removed because of what is appointed I gathered from you* or *those grieving because of the appointed I gathered from you.* The NIV adds the word **loss**, implying that God's judgment will remove those who grieve over the loss of Israel's festivals.

The final phrase (*hyw mś't 'lyh ḥrph*) is also difficult to translate. The NIV renders it **which is a burden and reproach for you** and links it to the preceding line, so that the appointed festivals have become a burden to those who will be removed from Jerusalem. A more literal translation is *they were a signal cloud over her of disgrace.* This combines the idea of a clearly visible cloud of disgrace of Jerusalem's leaders before the world, which also serves as a signal (*mś't*, see Judg

20:38, 40; cp. Jer 6:1; see Ben Zvi 1991, 253) for the Lord to begin judgment by removing them.

■ 19 The Lord's speech continues in v 19. The phrase **at that time** is synonymous with "on that day" in 3:11. Here it refers to the Day of the Lord when God will **deal with all who oppressed you** (→ 3:11 and sidebar Day of the Lord at Zeph 1:7). By removing the oppressors from the community, the Lord will transform it. The powerless will no longer suffer under them, and the city will no longer be under the threat of divine judgment.

The next two lines depict the Lord's work on behalf of Jerusalem as a shepherd protecting an endangered flock (see Vlaardingerbroek 1999, 217-18, and others). First, God will **rescue** or *deliver* the weak (**the lame** or *the limping*) who have suffered under divine judgment. **I will rescue** (*whwš'ty*) can be translated *I will deliver* or save (cp. 3:17). The verb indicates any type of help and sometimes connotes the redemptive acts of the Lord on behalf of Israel or the faithful (Exod 14:30; 1 Sam 10:19; and elsewhere). The term **lame** adopts the imagery of the humble remnant as God's flock (→ 3:13), with the Lord being their protective shepherd (see Isa 40:11).

I will gather the exiles (*the scattered*) connotes reversing the homelessness that will follow God's judgment (→ 2:7, 9). While scattering was due to a divine judgment that the corrupt community as a whole deserved, God's gathering of the innocent oppressed within it is an act of unmerited grace. God's scattered people are sometimes referred to as **exiles** (see Isa 27:13; Jer 40:12). Later generations could justifiably apply this passage as a promise of return from the Babylon deportation (cp. Neh 1:9), even though that was probably not the original intent of the prophet's message.

The second thing the Lord will do is reverse the contempt for the faithful by the powerful in Jerusalem and the surrounding nations (→ 2:8, 10). The phrases are difficult to translate, but they can be understood from their reformulation in v 20. **I will give them praise and honor in every land where they have suffered shame** is literally, *I will ordain for them* (*wśmtym l-*) *praise and a name in the whole earth, their shame*. It is possible that all the oppressed of Judah and the old northern kingdom of Israel are now in view as the remnant of Israel, and not just those from Jerusalem (cp. 3:12-13, 14). Wherever God's people are scattered, they will receive **praise** (*thlh*); that is, they will be well-known and honored (cp. Isa 62:7; Jer 48:2; Ps 148:14).

Stated another way, they will have a good *name* (*šm*, honor) or reputation. This is perhaps another allusion to the Babel incident (→ 3:9-10). At Babel all nations sought a name for themselves (Gen 11:4), which is considered idolatrous and inappropriate. In this passage the *name* God gives to the redeemed is dependent on their worshiping and trusting "in the name of the LORD" (v 12; cp. v 9). Therefore, this God-given *name* ultimately glorifies the Lord (→ below).

Ironically, at Babel the Lord scattered people to prevent their gaining a name through their works of pride (Gen 11:4, 6-8). In Zephaniah's reversal, after the

207

proud are judged, the dispersed remnant receives a **name** from the Lord. In this context, **praise** and **name** probably means that they will be acclaimed and honored because of what the Lord has done for them (cp. Ps 126:1-3). Therefore, it is ultimately the Lord who is honored (cp. Ps 48:9-11 [10-12]; Isa 52:10; 61:9; Jer 33:9). This will take place **in every land** or **in the whole earth** (*bkl h'rṣ*). Note that this phrase matches the extent of God's judgment due to Jerusalem's sins in 1:18 and 3:8 (*kl h'rṣ* cp. 1:2-3).

The concluding phrase, **where they have suffered shame**, is literally, **their shame** (*bštm*), which implies a meaning such as **instead of their shame**. Judgment resulted in the **shame** and reproach of God's people wherever they were scattered (2:1, 8, 10; 3:10). God promises to replace their shame with praise and honor when they are redeemed from their exile.

■ **20** This verse repeats the last half of v 19, but with slightly different language and some important expansions. This verse emphasizes the gathering of God's people in the opening parallel lines. The NIV translates **At that time I will gather you; at that time I will bring you home.** But this reverses the Hebrew word order. A literal translation is, **At that time I will bring you, at the time of my gathering you**. The third masculine plural pronouns in v 19 changes to a direct address **you** here. This shift suggests that the prophet's audience will experience the promised restoration after God's judgment. For **at that time** see comments on v 19. **I will bring you** (*'by' 'tkm*) lacks a destination. The implication is that God will bring the limping and scattered (v 19) back to Jerusalem or Judah, that is, **home**.

The next phrase reads **at the time of my gathering you** (*wb't qbṣy 'tkm*). In other words, the gathering of God's people as a flock mentioned in v 19 (cp. 3:13) is for the purpose of bringing them home. They will not be left in the nomadic and desperate state depicted in 2:7-9.

Another reformulation of verse 19 follows, but this time it is introduced by an emphatic **indeed** (*ky*, untranslated in the NIV). **I will give you honor (a name) and praise.** This reverses the order of the terms "praise" and "honor" (**name**) of v 19 and uses the more common expression **I will give** (*'tn . . . l-*) rather than **I will ordain** as in v 19.

This will take place **among all the peoples of the earth** (*bkl 'my h'rṣ*; → v 19). That these people recognize the Lord's people confirms that God's people influenced the nations' worship of the Lord in vv 9-10. Furthermore, the two "all the earth" statements in vv 19 and 20 have parallels in 1:18 and 3:8. When these verses are read together, one wonders how there can be an honoring of the remnant and their God throughout the earth (3:19-20) if that earth and its inhabitants have been destroyed, which 1:18 and 3:8 seem to suggest! This adds support to the view that the message of a comprehensive destruction of all the earth and its inhabitants in 1:2-18 and 3:8 is essentially a judgment focused on Jerusalem and Judah as the cosmic center of creation.

The restoration event is summarized in the final clause, **when I restore your fortunes before your very eyes** (*when I turn around your adversities* before your very eyes). The expression **restore your fortunes** (*bšwby 't-šbwtykm*) is literally "when I turn around your turnings" (→ 2:7). In this passage the phrase connotes a more specific hope (homecoming) than in Zeph 2. It is noteworthy that the same phrase and other terms found in 3:19-20 occur in Deut 30:3. Deuteronomy 30 depicts the Lord gathering Israel after they were scattered among the nations for disobedience as in Zephaniah (see Amos 9:11-15; Jer 30:18; 33:7-13 for specific ways God restore the fortunes of Israel).

The expression **before your very eyes** (*l'ynykm*) emphasizes certainty; the transformation will be seen by the community. In the cultural perspective of ancient Israel, the community is perceived inter-generationally. Therefore, **your eyes** may encompass what future generations will see (cp. Jer 51:24). Those who first heard Zephaniah's prophecy would not necessarily live to see its fulfillment, even if it is reinterpreted to apply to the return from Babylonian exile after 538 BC.

Says the LORD (*'mr yhwh*) indicates that the promised restoration is certain because of its divine source. Indeed, the final words reiterate what was stated by the first words of the prophecy, that the book of Zephaniah is "the word of the LORD" (*dbr-yhwh*, 1:1). From beginning to end the message of Zephaniah is God's message for Jerusalem, for Israel, for the Church; it extends to wherever God's people are found scattered and until God's work of restoration is complete.

FROM THE TEXT

This passage takes a remarkable turn in the book of Zephaniah. The threat of divine judgment against the corrupt community is still very much present. The prospect of punishment remains. But now this is only mentioned in passing as the subject of God's deliverance takes center stage. Read in context of the entire book, God's promises of deliverance can only be considered a pure act of gracious love. God does not give up on loving and winning back those who have been called to a divine vocation. The Lord finds a way to restore a people who will follow their divine calling, even if they are among the most unlikely, those whom the powerful found it easy to neglect, scorn and abuse (cp. Deut 7:7-8; 1 Cor 1:26-29). This leads us to consider some aspects of Zephaniah's message which are central not only to Zephaniah, but also to the biblical message as a whole.

First, *God's judgment upon sin is not an end in itself; the Lord's final goal is restoration.* Up to this point in the book, Zephaniah's message has been predominantly one of judgment against the corrupt culture of the Zion community. But that is not where the prophet ends, because judgment is not the ultimate intention of God's work. Rather, God wills to foster communities who will properly serve and worship the Lord. The old corrupt Zion will be replaced by a community free from fear and deceit and sustained by God's justice (v 13; → 3:5). It will consist of a humble remnant who seek the Lord (2:1-3, 7, 9) and who are granted divine protection (3:12-13, 15-17, 19-20).

God desires to sustain other communities who will offer worship purified by God's grace (vv 9-10). The Lord who is in the midst of Zion will encourage, rule

3:9-20

over, protect and sustain them as King, Heroic Savior, and Good Shepherd (3:5, 13, 15-17, 19-20). God will remove the shame brought by former leaders (vv 11, 18). The oppressed will no longer fear their oppressors or the Lord's judgment for the community's crimes (vv 11, 15-16, 18, 19). Idolatry will be a thing of the past as God enables the community to properly seek and worship the Lord (vv 9-10, 11-13; cp. 2:11). God wills to be worshipped by a rejoicing Zion (3:14; see also vv 11-12) and by others who recognize what the Lord has done for the remnant (vv 9-10, 19-20). In place of darkness, gloom, and divine anger (1:15, 18), the Lord will rejoice in a creation set right (3:17).

Second, *God chooses the excluded of the world and is pleased to be worshipped and served by them.* It seems to be a human tendency for those who enjoy God's grace to think that God only cares about people like themselves. We tend to think that others must behave, worship, or serve God exactly the way we do to be worthy of God's attention. We sometimes go a step farther and communicate to others who do not conform to *our* standards that they have been excluded by God.

This tendency was sometimes evident among the ancient Israelites who had very strict views about how worship is conducted, about who is allowed to come into God's presence and who is not. So it is completely unexpected that peoples as far away as Africa would be allowed to call on the Lord's name, serve God, and even offer acceptable sacrifices; and to top it off, this happens outside the Jerusalem temple (vv 9-10; cp. 2:11)! Yes, God must first purify their lips (3:9), but even the chosen on God's holy mountain must also submit to verbal cleansing to properly serve and worship the Lord (vv 11-13). It appears that from God's perspective neither insiders nor outsiders measure up to the divine standard; all need the same divine grace to be accepted by God and equipped for divine service. God also chooses the rejected among God's people, which is the next topic.

Third, *God is just and transforms the despised faithful to form a just community* (vv 11-13). Unfortunately, it is often the way of the world for the powerful to advance themselves by taking advantage and abusing the weak. But the Lord is a God who cares for the weak and rescues them from their oppressors (see e.g., Exod 22:23-24 [22-23 HB]; Deut 24:14-18; 27:19; → Hab 1:2-4). They may be the poor (v 12) or marked by physical and social weaknesses. They include the disabled, the homeless, and outcasts (v 19; cp. Brown 1996, 116).

But it is not enough for the Lord only to gather the causalities of a broken world and heal those wounded by the abusive oppressors. God wills to form a community where justice prevails and abuse of others is unheard of. Such a community no longer bears the mark of shame brought upon it by the bad witness of its proud and sinful leaders (vv 11, 18). In place of the former arrogant leaders, God's lowly and humble remnant will be at the center of the divine community (i.e., "in its midst," vv 11-12). Having nothing to offer God except for their inner and outer brokenness, all they can do is seek to honor the sanctity of God's holy presence (vv 11*a*) by speaking and acting with integrity in all their dealings (v 13*a*).

This can only be possible for those who seek to remain humble (→ 2:3) by taking refuge in the name of the Lord (3:12). Such a people put God's reputation (name) first as they seek divine guidance and protection (refuge). But none of this is possible without God's transforming grace.

As the Great Shepherd sustains them (vv 13b, 19), the world will see the community of God as the inauguration of the new creation (vv 19-20). Outsiders will notice a community wholly dependent on God where there is no place for the injustices perpetrated by the proud power brokers who climb to success on the backs of the weak and trustful. They will observe that justice prevails among those who are content in the provisions and rest provided for the Lord's humble flock. This community offers a refreshing alternative to those who are weary of the constant struggle to outdo others in possessions, power, position, and prestige.

Fourth, *God's power is revealed in a just love*. First, God saves the weak and oppressed. God's deliverance is not always in mighty acts of war and conquest, but in helping and gathering the weak and despised (vv 17, 19). In Zephaniah, God's rule (kingship) is expressed as a good shepherd who can help the struggling.

Second, God's power is often revealed in a quiet love (v 17). We frequently want the Lord to solve our problems quickly and boldly. We want God to rush onto the scene like a commando on a raid, carrying out a military type assault that loudly and visibly conquers evil and makes everything right again. If prayers are not answered quickly in this way, then we assume that God will not or cannot answer them. Yet contrary to common perception, God's silence is not a sign of unwillingness to act or lack of caring (cp. Hab 1:13; Ps 83:1-18 [2-19 HB]). While God sometimes appears as a conquering warrior (as in the Exodus; see Exod 15:3), in Zephaniah the Lord's heroic strength is displayed in helping the weak and withholding divine judgment (vv 13, 19). The Lord's silence is actually an expression of divine love (v 17)!

Indeed, if God were to act quickly and in ways some people expect, then more harm than good may result. We do not realize how our lives are intertwined with others. Nor do we know what effect God's judgment will have on us, for if we expect God to judge the sinful pride and disobedience of others, how can we expect the Lord to ignore our own transgressions? No, sometimes the most loving thing God can do is to be silent, to withhold judgment, to wait for a time when less damage will be sustained in the *whole* community. We need to think beyond ourselves and our community since God's loving acts of grace are not just for believers. Indeed, God's silence is often a manifestation of divine patience for a world which needs to repent (2 Pet 3:9), a world which is the Creator's handiwork and which God will pursue with every ounce of divine compassion.

Fifth, *God wills to be worshipped and served as our proper response of gratitude*. Worship is remembering, acknowledging, thanking, and rejoicing in what the Lord does (e.g., see the call to worship in Ps 105:1-6). Most frequently God's people worship by rejoicing and reciting their Redeemer's past deeds (Ps 105:7-44), which is followed by a commitment to service (Ps 105:45). As mentioned above, Zephaniah proclaims that even outsiders can become God's people (as in the case of *my Daughter Dispersed*, → v 10) and worship and serve the Lord for what they see God doing (→ vv 9-10; 19-20; cp. 2:11).

Furthermore, *God is worthy to be worshipped.* Zephaniah concludes with a call for God's people to celebrate what God does and will do for the community (vv 14-20). The prophet provides many motives for worshipping the Lord.

First, they celebrate because they are assured that God is (and will continue to be) in their midst (v 17; cp. 3:5). This is a very comforting word for a people upon whom the prophet has announced certain judgment (the main focus of 1:2-3:8). God's presence will sustain them, and will continue to be with the remnant as it emerges out of judgment (vv 11-13; cp. Jer 31:28; 32:42).

Second, God's people worship in anticipation of what God will do in the indeterminate future (vv 14-20). God's people are called to look beyond the gloomy prospect of judgment and celebrate what the Lord will do for the sake of God's people and the entire created order (→ vv 14-20). The outcome is that believers embrace a life with God free from fear (vv 13, 15-16; cp. 1 John 4:17-18). This is only possible as an act of faith in a God who has sustained them in the past, and who will continue to be with them in their future. In a sense their worship of God supports their present faith as God's deeds are anticipated in song and praise. In other words, the sustaining presence of God is made real to the believer in worship.

Furthermore, the community's celebratory faith is emboldened as the prophet announces that God anticipates rejoicing in the prospect of setting right the community (v 17). God's joyous anticipation of the deliverance of the lowly remnant confirms that this deliverance is an act of love. It assures the community that their worship, faith, and obedience will not be in vain.

Before we move to the next topic, it should be noted that the joy that God's people anticipate is not a superficial joy devoid of content. It is grounded in the Lord's future deliverance, but at the same time it does not deny present crises. The rejoicing commended here is not a sanctified denial of circumstances that urges "praise the Lord anyway," as if pain and suffering do not actually hurt or should not matter in light of spiritual realities. Nor is it an attempt to work up a spiritual high as a means of disregarding the significance of bodily suffering. Such counterfeit joy does not glorify God nor sustain the weak. It does not offer the substantive hope that the Creator wills for creation.

Sixth, *the Lord not only wills proper worship, but God also enables it.* God purifies the speech of those who would worship and serve the Lord (vv 9, 13). Speech articulates the praise that honors God (→ above). Since the fulfillment of our service to God and others is expressed in love (Luke 10:27), our speech must reflect love for both God and others. Speech expresses the intentions of the heart (Mark 7:20-23) in our web of personal and global relationships.

The corrupt leaders of Zephaniah's day were no different from those of any other time; lies and deceptive speech were a major tool for abuse, exploitation, robbery, and marginalization. If our speech promotes ourselves or our religious, social, economic, political communities at the expense or harm of others, then we fail to follow the law of love. We cannot claim to love and worship the Lord if we express ill will, contempt, or hatred of others (James 1:26; 3:5-12).

Finally, *everything that the Lord does for believers has implications that reach beyond the boundaries of the community.* That is the way it has been since God first called a community to be the bearers of divine blessing (Gen 12:1-3). God's judgment (Zeph 3:8) and restoration (vv 11-13; 15-20) convey God's work to other people and the entire created order (→ 3:9-10, 19-20). God's redemptive work is not focused on the comfort and aggrandizement of believers, but extends to benefit others, even the entire creation. When God enhances the reputation of the community of God, it is ultimately for the glory of God to be celebrated throughout creation (vv 19-20).

God's people are therefore called to look beyond themselves and their needs as they engage in their worship and exercise their spiritual gifts. Those preoccupied with personal experiences in their worship of God and who use God's gifts solely for their own enhancement end up repeating the sinful and greedy ways of corrupt leaders. Such self-centeredness only leads to the judgment announced in Zeph 1. What God gives to the community is not for self-aggrandizement (as in the case of the wealthy estate holders of 1:12-13), but to bring glory to God and to serve others.

HAGGAI, ZECHARIAH, MALACHI

Jim Edlin

DEDICATION

This portion of this work is dedicated to my wife and friend
Jo Elaine (Goodman) Edlin
whose courage and unwavering faith in the goodness of God
have been a constant source of inspiration
to me and many others.

ACKNOWLEDGMENTS

Projects such as these require a village to complete. I am grateful to the Church of the Nazarene and The Foundry Publishing for initiating this commentary series and inviting me to participate. The passion and vision of the editorial staff at Beacon Hill Press has been inspiring and encouraging.

The loving support of my family infuses me with energy like nothing else can. I am extremely grateful for my wife Jo, our two daughters Julie and Janelle, their spouses Eric and Matt, our son Jon and his wife Mindy, and our grandchildren Jacob, Daniel, Addison, Macie, Carolina, and Graham. God has given me no greater treasure than these.

Finally, I wish to honor the God of Haggai, Zechariah, and Malachi above all. Throughout this project I have found the Lord of Hosts to be the unmatched, irrepressible, indefatigable, absolutely sovereign, amazingly gracious, ever present God they said he was. Indeed, I can testify that the Lord alone strengthens his servants for kingdom tasks, supplies resources, and offers the only sure hope of new life following exile. Truly the work of God is accomplished "'not by might, nor by power, but by my Spirit' says the Lord" (Zechariah 4:6).

James Oliver (Jim) Edlin

BIBLIOGRAPHY FOR HAGGAI-MALACHI

Achtemeier, Elizabeth. 1986. *Nahum-Malachi*. IBC. Atlanta: John Knox.

Ackroyd, Peter R. 1968. *Exile and Restoration: a Study of Hebrew Thought in the Sixth Century BC*. OTL. London: SCM.

Alden, Robert L. 1985a. "Haggai," *EBC*. Vol. 7. Grand Rapids: Eerdmans.

———. 1985b. "Malachi," *EBC*. Vol. 7. Grand Rapids: Eerdmans.

Baldwin, Joyce G. 1972. *Haggai, Zechariah, Malachi*. TOTC. Downers Grove: InterVarsity.

Barker, Kenneth L. 2008. "Zechariah," *EBC: Revised Edition*. Vol. 8. Grand Rapids: Zondervan.

Boda, Mark J. 2004. *Haggai, Zechariah*. NIV Application Commentary. Grand Rapids: Zondervan.

Brown, William P. 1996. *Obadiah through Malachi*. Westminster Bible Companion. Louisville: Westminster John Knox.

Cashdan, Eli. 1957. "Haggai Introduction and Commentary," in *The Twelve Prophets: Hebrew Text, English Translation and Commentary*. Edited by A. Cohen. Soncino Books of the Bible. London: Soncino Press.

Coggins, R. J. 1987. *Haggai, Zechariah, Malachi*. OTG. Sheffield: Sheffield Academic.

Craigie, Peter C. 1984. *Twelve Prophets: Micah, Nahum, Habakkuk, Zephaniah, Haggai, Zechariah, and Malachi*. Daily Study Bible: Old Testament. Philadelphia: Westminster.

Duguid, Iain M. 2010. *A Study Commentary on Haggai, Zechariah, Malachi*. England: EP Books.

Duguid, Iain, and Matthew P. Harmon. 2018. *Zephaniah, Haggai, Malachi*. Reformed Expository Commentary. Phillipsburg, NJ: P&R Publishing.

Edlin, Jim. 2009. *Daniel: A Commentary in the Wesleyan Tradition*. Kansas City: Beacon Hill Press.

———. 2017. *Ezra/Nehemiah: A Commentary in the Wesleyan Tradition*. Kansas City: Beacon Hill Press.

Emmerson, Grace. 1998. *Minor Prophets II: Nahum, Habakkuk, Zephaniah, Haggai, Zechariah, Malachi*. Doubleday Bible Commentary. Garden City, NY: Doubleday.

Ferreiro, Alberto, ed. 2003. *The Twelve Prophets*. Old Testament. Vol. 14. ACCS. Downers Grove: InterVarsity.

Floyd, Michael H. 2000. *Minor Prophets, Part 2*. FOTL. Grand Rapids: Eerdmans.

Hanson, Paul D. 1979. *The Dawn of Apocalyptic: The Historical and Sociological Roots of Jewish Apocalyptic Eschatology*. Revised Edition. Philadelphia: Fortress.

Hill, Andrew E. 2010. *Malachi: A New Translation with Introduction and Commentary*. AB. 25D. New Haven: Yale University Press.

———. 2012. *Haggai, Zechariah and Malachi*. TOTC. Vol. 28. Downers Grove: Intervarsity.

Hill, Andrew, and Richard D. Patterson. 2008. *Minor Prophets: Hosea through Malachi*. Cornerstone Biblical Commentary. Vol. 10. Carol Stream, IL: Tyndale House.

Jones, Douglas Rawlinson. 1962. *Haggai, Zechariah and Malachi*. TBC. London: SCM.

Kelley, Page H. 1984. *Micah, Nahum, Habakkuk, Zephaniah, Haggai, Zechariah, Malachi*. Layman's Bible Book Commentary. Nashville: Broadman & Holman.

March, Eugene W. 1996. "Haggai," *NIB*. Vol. 7. Nashville: Abingdon.

Mason, Rex. 1977. *The Books of Haggai, Zechariah and Malachi*. CBC. Cambridge: University Press.

Merrill, Eugene H. 1994. *An Exegetical Commentary: Haggai, Zechariah, and Malachi*. Chicago: Moody.

———. 2008a. "Haggai," *EBC: Revised Edition*. Vol. 8. Grand Rapids: Zondervan.

———. 2008b. "Malachi," *EBC: Revised Edition*. Vol. 8. Grand Rapids: Zondervan.

Meyers, Eric M., and Carol L. Meyers. 1987. *Haggai, Zechariah 1-8: A New Translation with Introduction and Commentary*. AB. 25C. Garden City, NY: Doubleday.

Mitchell, Hinckley G. T. 1912. *A Critical and Exegetical Commentary on Haggai, Zechariah, Malachi, and Jonah*. ICC. Edinburgh: T & T Clark.

Motyer, Alec J. 1998. "Haggai." *The Minor Prophets: An Exegetical and Expository Commentary*. Edited by Thomas Edward McComiskey. Grand Rapids: Baker.

O'Brien, Julia M. 2004. *Nahum, Habakkuk, Zephaniah, Haggai, Zechariah, Malachi*. Abingdon Old Testament Commentaries. Nashville: Abingdon.

Ollenburger, Ben C. 1996. "Zechariah," *NIB*. Volume 7. Nashville: Abingdon.

Pazdan, Mary Margaret. 1986. *Joel, Obadiah, Haggai, Zechariah, Malachi*. Collegeville Bible Commentary: Old Testament Vol. 17. Collegeville, MN: Liturgical Press.

Peterson, David L. 1984. *Haggai and Zechariah 1-8*. OTL. Philadelphia: Westminster.

Petterson, Anthony R. 2015. *Haggai, Zechariah & Malachi*. Apollos Old Testament Commentary. Downers Grove: Intervarsity.

Philips, Richard D. *Zechariah*. 2007. Reformed Expository Commentary. Phillipsburg, NJ: P&R Publishing.

Redditt, Paul. 1995. *Haggai, Zechariah, Malachi*. NCB. Grand Rapids: Eerdmans.

Schuller, Eileen M. 1996. "Malachi," *IDB*. Vol. 7. Nashville: Abingdon.

Smith, Ralph L. 1984. *Micah-Malachi*. WBC. Volume 32. Dallas: Word.

Stuhlmueller, Carroll. 1988. *Rebuilding with Hope: A Commentary on the Books of Haggai and Zechariah*. ITC. Grand Rapids: Eerdmans.

Sweeney, Marvin A. 2000. *The Twelve Prophets*. Berit Olam. Collegeville, MN: Liturgical Press.

Taylor, Richard A. and E. Ray Clendenen. 2004. *Haggai, Malachi*. NAC. Nashville: Broadman & Holman.

Verhoef, Pieter A. 1987. *The Books of Haggai and Malachi*. NICOT. Grand Rapids: Eerdmans.

Walton, John H. ed. 2009. *Zondervan Illustrated Bible Backgrounds Commentary: Old Testament*. Vol. 5. Downers Grove, IL: Intervarsity.

Walton, John H., Victor H. Matthews, and Mark W. Chavalas. 2000. *The IVP Bible Background Commentary: Old Testament*. Downers Grove, IL: InterVarsity.

Williamson, H. G. M. 1985. *Ezra, Nehemiah*. WBC. Vol. 16. Dallas: Word.

Wolff, Hans Walter. 1988. *Haggai*. CC. Minnesota: Augsburg Fortress.

TABLE OF SIDEBARS

HAGGAI

INTRODUCTION

Haggai joins Zechariah and Malachi in representing an important era in the prophetic tradition of ancient Israel, the post-exilic period. These books preserve messages from prophets who ministered to God's people during a crucial moment in history. It was the time of restoration when Abraham's descendants were seeking to rebuild life in the promised land following exile in Babylon.

Haggai is the second shortest book among the Prophets, being just two chapters long and a total of thirty-eight verses. This undoubtedly explains why it is often overlooked. Yet, this little book offers many valuable insights into living faithfully in an uncertain world as well as important historical information about the early part of the restoration period.

Another reason the book of Haggai has not received much attention may be due to its exclusive interest in rebuilding the Jerusalem temple. Readers should notice, however, that underlying the prophet's concern for constructing this significant sacred space is a deep conviction that proper worship of the Lord sets the agenda for the life of God's people. More importantly, in Haggai's thinking, worship signals a life with priorities properly established. The challenge of Haggai to those who encounter his book is to find significance in life through a commitment to putting God first in every part of life. Readers of Haggai will find reverberations of Jesus' challenge to "seek first his kingdom and his righteousness" and discover that as a result "all these things will be given to you as well" (Matt 6:33).

A. The Audience

The audience that Haggai addressed consisted of Jewish exiles who returned from Babylon to Judah in the second half of the sixth century BC. Their world had been changed forever decades before when Babylonians destroyed their homeland and took survivors captive in 586 BC. The defeat of Babylon by Persia in 539 BC, however, opened the way for many exiles to return home again. The Persian king Cyrus (see Isa 45:1-6) issued a decree in 538 BC that not only allowed the Jewish exiles to come back to Judah, but also to rebuild the temple in Jerusalem (see 2 Chr 36:22-23 and Ezra 1:1-4).

The decree of Cyrus prompted an initial contingent of Jews to return to Judah under the leadership of Sheshbazzar around 537 BC (Ezra 1-2). Rebuilding the temple became one of the first orders of business for those who returned to Judah; they began by constructing an altar for sacrifices (Ezra 3:1-6). A few months later, they gathered resources and laid the foundations of the temple amidst great joy and anticipation (Ezra 3:7-13). However, lack of adequate resources and opposition from neighboring people led the Jewish community to discontinue rebuilding the temple (Ezra 4). The foundations of the temple remained untouched for over fifteen years.

Late in the year of 520 BC, Haggai began delivering messages from the Lord designed to motivate the Jewish community to begin work on the temple once again. The very specific chronological data given by Haggai indicates that his prophetic words came over a four-month period. This was during the second year of the rule of the Persian king Darius I (r. 522-486 BC), one of Persia's most efficient emperors.

Darius the Great brought stability to an empire in tumult following Cyrus' death in 530 BC. Cyrus' son Cambyses II (r. 530-522 BC) seized power by murdering his brother and began an aggressive campaign to conquer Egypt. When Cambyses mysteriously died and Gaumata laid claim to the throne, Darius stepped forward to bring the empire under control. By his own account etched on the Behistun Inscription, Darius fought nineteen battles and subdued nine kings during his first year in order to solidify his domain. Soon after Darius' successes, Haggai began encouraging the people of Judah to rebuild their temple again.

Although Haggai intended his messages for the general population of Judah, the prophet addressed Judah's leaders Zerubbabel and Joshua in particular. Zerubbabel is called "governor (*pehâ*) of Judah" (1:1), a term that implies leadership over a small area. In the case of Zerubbabel his responsibility was limited to the Judean district, making him subject to the authority of the magistrate in charge of the satrapy west of the Euphrates known as "Beyond the River." Zerubbabel was the grandson of King Jehoiachin who was exiled to Babylon in 597 BC, and thus the heir apparent to the throne of David among those who returned from Babylon.

The other individual specifically identified by Haggai is Joshua "son of Jozadak, the high priest" (1:1). His relationship to Jehozadak places him in the family line of high priests that goes back to Levi (1 Chr 6:1-15 [5:27-41 HB]). Jehozadak went into exile in Babylon along with his father, Seraiah, who was high priest at the time of the destruction of Jerusalem in 586 BC (1 Chr 6:15 [5:41 HB] and 2 Kgs 25:18).

B. The Prophet

According to Ezra 5-6, the messages of both Haggai and his contemporary Zechariah inspired the people of Judah to rebuild the temple in Jerusalem. Based on dates given to prophecies in each book, Haggai initiated the project and Zechariah joined him two months later (→ Introduction to Zechariah). Haggai completed his preaching after three and a half months, but Zechariah continued till its completion. No explanation is given as to why Haggai did not continue but many scholars conjecture that he may have died rather than just ceased preaching.

Haggai is simply identified as "the prophet" (Hag 1:1, 1:3, 1:12, 2:1, 2:10 and Ezra 5:1, 6:14). Beyond this the OT reveals little else about his background. Jewish tradition holds that Haggai had lived in exile in Babylon and returned to Judah with the first group of exiles. Some have noted though that his name does not appear in the lists of those returning from Babylon in Ezra 2 and Neh 7. This could mean that he never went into exile or that he was only a child when he returned since the lists included only the names of adults. So Haggai's status during the exile remains uncertain. A reference in 2:3 suggests that he may have seen the temple of Solomon before it was destroyed in 586 BC. If he did, he would have to be a relatively old man at the time of his ministry.

The name Haggai derives from the Hebrew word for a religious festival (*hag*) and means "my feast." This suggests that he may have been born during one of Israel's annual holy days and so named. It seems likely that he came from a priestly family. His name plus his interest in the temple and in priestly practices (Hag 2:11-14) could all support this. Further, the Septuagint connects his name, along with Zechariah's, to five psalms used in Israel's ancient worship (Pss 138 and 146-149).

Haggai the Hierocrat

One theory conjectures that Haggai represents a particular party in the restoration period labeled "hierocrats" (Hanson 1979, 173-177). According to this idea, these people envisioned the restoration of Judah within history through the reestablishment of proper worship at the temple. They supported the plan laid out in Ezek 40-48.

The hierocratic party stood in contrast to those who placed hope for Judah's future beyond human history. These might be called the "prophetic" group because they carry on visions of the God's blessings "in the last days." Isaiah 60-66 articulates this perspective.

Some scholars criticize the theory of two parties within the restoration community as overly simplistic. They sense that the situation was likely more complicated than this. But whether or not the theory is entirely accurate, it takes note of a fundamental tension between the prophetic and priestly traditions throughout Israel's history. These two great traditions, however, appear to come together in some measure in Haggai.

C. Literary Forms

Though Israel's prophets are noted for their poetry, the entire book of Haggai traditionally has been viewed as prose composition. Some scholars, however, have observed poetic features in the speeches. Thus, one might at least speak of an elevated prose, if not some poetic verse, in portions of the book (see Verhoef 1987, 17-18 and Taylor 2004, 71-73).

The predominant form of literature used throughout the book of Haggai is the prophetic speech report. This genre usually includes a description of the setting in which the speech was delivered along with the speech itself. Haggai, however, is not a collection of prophetic speeches in a manner typical of most prophetic books. Historical narrative introduces each speech laying out the prophet's work in chronological sequence. The effect is to tell the story of developments in the first four months of rebuilding the temple. The book relates four episodes in the prophet's career that argue for the significance of a worship center like the temple for a faithful community. This suggests to some scholars that Haggai represents a special kind of genre in prophetic literature that one might call an apologetic history. The function of such literature would be to argue a theological point through the mix of narrative and prophetic word (Petersen 1984, 32-36).

Haggai's speeches can be classified as royal oracles since they are addressed to Zerubbabel the governor and Joshua the high priest. They are predominantly motivational in purpose, aimed at convincing these rulers to lead their people in building the temple. Haggai uses various tactics of persuasion in order to motivate his audience. These include reasoning, threat, and promise. The word of promise sometimes comes in the form of priestly salvation oracles such as "I am with you" in 1:13 and 2:4, "I will grant peace" in 2:9, or "I will bless you" in 2:19.

The prophet also relies heavily upon divine authority to motivate. He consistently identifies his speeches as "the word of the LORD" (1:1, 13; 2:1, 10, 20). In addition, Haggai regularly employs the typical messenger formulas "this is what the LORD Almighty says" or "declares the LORD." In fact, these formulas occur 17 times in the 38 verses of the book to underscore the origin of the messages.

Haggai also makes use of rhetorical questions several times, giving his messages an element of courtroom disputation. This is particularly the mood of the first two oracles. In the third oracle a priestly inquiry takes place as the prophet asks questions to which priests provide answers.

D. Literary Structure

The book of Haggai is a well-designed unit of material. Five historical notations punctuate the book. Four of these mark the beginnings of the four prophetic messages. The fifth notation closes out the first message.

The dating formulas at the beginning of the oracles follow a clear pattern. The formulas for the first and second messages contain a reference to the year while the formulas for the third and fourth do not. This signals the paralleling structure of the book. The first two messages and the last two echo one another. Messages one (1:1-15) and three (2:10-19) recall each other by focusing upon the present economic struggles in Judah, noting the connection between their reversals and the ruined temple, and concluding with reference to laying the temple foundations. Messages two (2:1-9) and four (2:20-23) each speak about the shaking of nations and future hopes for Judah.

There is also a progression of thought that enhances the sense of parallelism between the first two and last two messages. Both sets of messages move from accusation to response to assurance.

The most significant structuring device is the alternation of challenge and promise in each of the four messages. Each message begins with a challenge to an erroneous viewpoint held by Haggai's audience. Following that challenge, Haggai delivers an encouraging promise from God. Only the last message does not contain an explicit challenge, though its promise clearly implies one. This challenge-promise pattern highlights the major theological thrust of the book. Present challenges to life are to be dealt with in light of God's promises for the future (→ outline of book in Contents).

E. Theology of Haggai

The theology of Haggai is much richer than is sometimes recognized. The prophet's challenge to build a temple for God rests upon core truths of faith. Temple building is kingdom building, which demands radical trust in the Lord who has manifested his presence in the past, is at work in the present, and will be there in the future.

The temple stands as more than a political status symbol or rallying point for community identity. It was those things, but for Haggai it represented something of far greater significance. Its construction stood as evidence of a continual movement toward God's plans for the ultimate consummation of human history. The temple signaled hope of God's new age. The promises of earlier prophets were coming true as the people responded in obedience and fully engaged in kingdom work.

The structure of the book of Haggai clarifies its theological thrust. In each of his four messages the prophet challenges the people's spiritual lethargy with promises from God that provide divine resources to a struggling community. But the struggles of that community are not so much material as spiritual, according to Haggai. They are about with misplaced priorities (1:1-15), a desire for significance (2:1-9), impurity (2:10-19), and abandoned hope (2:20-23). The promises of God to such a community is his presence, his glory, his blessing, and his messiah. These are four signature signs of the messianic age. Ezekiel 34:20-31 identifies them as essential components of the new covenant God envisioned for his people.

The messages of Haggai lift the eyes of his audience to new horizons. Their task is about more than their particular time and circumstances. It is part of the overarching scheme of redemption in this world. In the tradition of the Davidic promise in 2 Sam 7 Haggai announces that those who desire to build a house for God find out that God has something far greater in store for them. They are part of a much bigger plan that God is orchestrating for all of human history. A fine structure of stones may rise up during Haggai's time, but more importantly the kingdom of God will continue to move toward fulfilling its eternal purposes.

COMMENTARY

I. THE CHALLENGE OF PRIORITIES AND THE PROMISE OF PRESENCE: HAGGAI 1:1-15

BEHIND THE TEXT

The theological context of Haggai's message is the hopeful projections for the restoration of Judah found in Isaiah, Jeremiah, and Ezekiel. Each of these books preserves vivid images of abundant prosperity following exile and the restoration of normal life in the land of Judah. Ezekiel in particular envisioned a new temple as the central feature of God's restored community (Ezek 40-48).

Haggai's community, however, had not seen a sudden reversal of its misfortune as outlined by those earlier prophets. The community continued to live under foreign political domination; it existed with meager economic resources and with the unfulfilled dream of a new temple. The community that Haggai addresses may be best described as politically dominated, economically challenged, and theologically confused.

The logic of Haggai's message to this community rests upon the doctrine of covenant blessings and curses found in Deut 27-28. In these chapters, God promises blessings to those who follow his instructions and warns of disasters for disobedience. Haggai reminds his audience that they cannot expect to enjoy blessings from God as long the temple "remains a ruin" (1:4, 9).

231

The impact of Haggai's message also depends upon understanding the significant role of the temple in Israel. It provided a visual symbol of God's covenant promise to be with his people. Worship rituals carried out in and around the temple allowed people to affirm that the Lord was their God. As God's dwelling place, the temple was the palace for the King of the universe. From its precincts the Lord ruled over his people, the nations, and the universe. Its architecture symbolized cosmic and international sovereignty. Therefore, rebuilding the temple signaled the Lord's return to his rightful place in the world and within the community.

The temple also functioned as a symbol of local political identity. To a degree the Persian Empire tolerated such religious views. Persian policy encouraged the building of local sanctuaries as a means of developing a stronger empire (Ezra 1:1-4 and 6:1-12). They believed that more prosperous parts make for a more prosperous whole. The temple distinguished the Jewish community among the nations and provided them with a sense of particular identity. Its close association with the governing structures of the local economy affirmed the local administration of the community.

Chapter 1 is a record of a prophetic speech and its reception. It consists of three parts: the setting (v 1), the message (vv 2-11), and the response (vv 12-15). The message displays typical prophetic speech elements. It identifies the situation of the audience (vv 2-6) before delivering the challenge from God (vv 7-8) and then returning to clarify the situation further (vv 9-11). The people's response to God's message (vv 12-15) is a fairly rare feature in prophetic literature. Most prophetic books record only messages of prophets without indicating how they were received.

IN THE TEXT

A. The Setting (1:1)

■ 1 The initial verse of the book places the message of the prophet in a very specific historical context. It relates the timing, the origin, the messenger, and the recipients of the speech. Typically, Israel's prophets dated their messages in reference to their kings. Since there is no local king in Israel or Judah after the exile, the reign of the Persian king marks time. **King Darius** refers to Darius I Hystaspes, also known as Darius the Great, who ruled Persia from 522-486 BC. His **second year** ran from March 520 to February 519 BC when translated to modern calendars (→ Introduction A. The Audience).

A further time reference specifies **the first day of the sixth month**. Since the Persian year began in the spring, **the sixth month** is toward the end of summer when grapes, figs and pomegranates were harvested. **The first day** of the month would be the New Moon festival, a regular time for worshipful celebration through prescribed offerings (Num 10:10 and 28:11-15). By modern reckoning the day corresponds to August 29, 520 BC.

Haggai's message is identified as **the word of the Lord** in a manner typical of Israel's prophetic tradition (e.g., Hos 1:1, Jer 1:2, Ezek 1:3, Zech 1:1). The message originates with God and Haggai is merely the conduit through which it comes. This point is underscored further by the phrase **through the prophet Haggai** (literally, *by the hand of Haggai the prophet*). This phrase essentially conveys the same idea as the more frequently used expression "came to the prophet" (e.g., Jer 1:2; Ezek 1:3), which is also used in Hag 2:10 and 20. The latter phrase emphasizes the prophet's role as receptor of the divine message, while the former stresses his task as transmitter.

The recipients of the message are the political and spiritual leaders of Judah. **Zerubbabel** carries the title of **governor**, which identifies him as the chief political administrator for Judah. Joshua is called **the high priest**, the one in charge of the priests and Levites who directed the spiritual life of the community. Haggai recognizes the need for both political and religious leaders to be involved in God's plan for the future of his people.

The reference to the ancestors of these two men, **Shealtiel** and **Jozadak**, is more than just a note on pedigree. The family connections of both Zerubbabel and Joshua signified continuity with the past as well as hope for the future. Their link to the Davidic and Levitical lines, respectively, of the past was especially important to a community of Jews searching for identity during the restoration period (→ Introduction A. The Audience).

The arena of influence for these men was **Judah**, a relatively small region within the western satrapy of the Persian Empire. With Jerusalem at its center, Judah stretched no more than thirty-five miles in any direction from that city.

B. The Message (1:2-11)

■ **2** Haggai's message begins with the typical messenger formula, **this is what the Lord Almighty says** (v 2), indicating that the following words are of divine origin. **The Lord Almighty** (*YHWH şĕbā'ôt*) is Haggai's favorite title for God. It emphasizes the unparalleled ability of God to control circumstances of life and affect change.

The Lord Almighty

The post-exilic prophets Haggai, Zechariah and Malachi, show a marked preference for the divine name "the Lord Almighty" (*YHWH şĕbā'ôt*, literally, "the Lord of hosts;" see KJV, NASB, NRSV, and ESV). Of the 265 occurrences in the prophetic books, Isaiah and Jeremiah are responsible for the most uses of the title, employing it 137 times. By comparison, the much shorter books of Haggai, Zechariah, and Malachi utilize this term 91 times (14 times in Haggai).

The name emphasizes God's unmatched sovereignty over the powers of this world. The term *şĕbā'ôt* (hosts) can refer to groups of angelic beings, stars in heaven, or an army of warriors. So it carries militaristic connotations implying God's command over imposing forces. *YHWH* (the Lord) is the particular name of Israel's God, defined most clearly in the Egyptian Exodus experience (see Exod

3:14-15 and 6:2-8). It evokes all that event revealed about God, including his covenant faithfulness and capacity to deliver his people. Israel's prophets employed this epithet regularly in order to remind their audiences of the absolute rule of their God in a world where many deities claimed that position.

The prophet begins by quoting what he hears from the people: "**The time has not yet come to rebuild the LORD's house.**" Haggai contends that this is something they **say** repeatedly (customary perfect of *'āmar*). The people may have been saying this for over fifteen years, ever since they stopped rebuilding of the temple. Literally the sentence reads *No time has come a time the house of the Lord to be built*. The double occurrence of the word **time** (*'et*) seems strange. Early translations in Greek and Aramaic smooth out the phrase and do not repeat the word. Some scholars suggest changing the first *'et* to *'atta* and translating "not now" (BHS). Another proposal is to understand the first three words in Hebrew as the quotation and the last four as an explanation of it (Taylor 2004, 117-118). Thus the quote might be more of a popular slogan like, "The time has not come." The final words of v 2 explain that this is spoken in reference to "a time for building the house of the LORD."

There may have been several reasons why people felt **the time** was not right. They faced intense political opposition (see Ezra 4) and poor economic conditions (see Hag 1:6, 10 and 2:16-17). They may have also thought about Jeremiah's prophecy concerning the desolation of Jerusalem (Jer 25:11 and 29:10). The seventy-year period he projected would not end until around 516 BC, if Jeremiah meant the destruction of the temple in 586 BC as the beginning point of the desolation.

These people indicates a strained relationship between God and his people. It contrasts with the more endearing terms frequently used by prophets: "my people" (e.g., see Isa 1:3 and Jer 1:16) and "the remnant" (e.g., Isa 46:3 and Jer 23:3). Haggai employs the latter term after his audience responds positively (Hag 1:12, 14 and 2:2).

By calling the temple **the LORD's house** Haggai underscores the importance of God's dwelling among his people. This would be God's home in the city of Jerusalem, an important symbol of restored relationship (→ Behind the Text).

■ **3-4** The extended messenger formula in v 3 emphasizes that the way Haggai describes the people in the following statements is **the word of the Lord**, not his. Haggai is merely the messenger. The message in v 4 is a divine accusation leveled against the people that outlines a disturbing contrast. God's house **remains a ruin**, while the people live **in paneled houses** (v 4). The term for **paneled** (*sepûnîm*) basically means covered with wood. It can indicate walls finished with wood paneling such as was done in palaces and temples. This would be a luxury that common people could rarely afford. The term could also refer to roofing, which would simply mean their houses were completed. Whichever meaning was intended—and probably both were true—the point is that the people had finished building their homes but not God's.

The term **ruin** (*ḥārēb*) describes something that is either totally abandoned or in disrepair. Ezra 3:1-6 indicates that an altar for sacrifice had been erected in the temple area when the first group returned from exile. Therefore, Haggai is not saying that the temple site was not in use (see also Jer 41:5). The problem is that the temple itself remained unconstructed.

Haggai puts God's accusation in the form of a rhetorical question: **Is it a time?** (v 4). The answer is clearly no. Haggai uses the word **time** (*'et*) once again in order to highlight the contrast with the popular saying in v 3. If it is time to build their houses, why is it not time to build a house for God?

■ **5-6** The third component of Haggai's description of his audience focuses on the results of their decisions. He begins with the word **now** (literally ***and now***) in order to connect with the previous two statements (v 5). Once again Haggai interjects the messenger formula, **this is what the LORD Almighty says** (v 5), to confirm that the words are still God's and not the prophet's.

Haggai urges his audience to pause for a moment of extended reflection. **Give careful thought to your ways**, he says (v 5). Some form of this phrase occurs four other times in the book (1:7; 2:15, 2:18*a*, 2:18*b*). Literally it translates ***set your heart upon your ways***. The **heart** (*leb*) in Hebrew thinking refers to the inner person including mind, will, and emotions. It is where prudent thought takes place. **Your ways** refers to the current life experiences that Haggai is about to recount for them. The challenge is to ponder how life is going based on the decisions made in vv 2 and 3.

In five basic areas of life the people of Judah come up short: harvest, food, drink, clothing, and wages. While the shortages were undoubtedly real, the text suggests that part of the problem was their lack of satisfaction with what was available. There was adequate seed because they **planted much** (v 6). There was food to **eat,** something to **drink, clothes** to wear, and **wages** to earn. The people did not do without these things. The problem, according to Haggai, is that these things did not satisfy the people. Haggai says they **never have enough** and **never have your fill**. The term **enough** refers to having plenty or a sufficient amount of something. The word **fill** (*šākrâ*) is normally translated "drunkenness," which indicates getting more drink than needed. The last image of shortage pictures money falling through **a purse with holes in it**. This could suggest either a lack of earning power or a lack of control over spending. With a shortage of commodities prices were likely inflated.

Verses 5-6 suggest that the covenant curses of shortage and futility are at work in the lives of the people (see Deut 27-28; see in particular 28:38). By listing the current disasters Haggai implies that his audience is experiencing the judgment of God. This implication will be made explicit in vv 9-11.

■ **7-8** Haggai comes to the major point of his message in vv 7-8. They relate God's challenge to his people in light of the circumstances just described. He begins once again with an emphasis on the divine origin of the message (**this is what the LORD**

Almighty says; v 7). Then he urges his audience to pause and ponder these words (**give careful thought to your ways;** → vv 5-6).

God's action plan for Judah is punctuated with three imperatives: **go up, bring down,** and **build** (v 8). The call to **go up into the mountains and bring down timber** could be understood in one of two ways. It might be a directive to go to the forested hills west and southwest of Jerusalem in order to gather the needed lumber. Alternatively, one could think of going to the hills of Lebanon as Solomon did for choice cedar logs (see 1 Kgs 5:6). Wood was needed for scaffolding and ladders as well as roofing and paneling. Stone, the primary building material, was readily available in and around the Temple Mount.

The primary challenge of the message is to **build the house** (v 8). There is no need to explain which house God means. It is **the house** (*habbāyit*), the most important one in Judah because it is the dwelling of the most important person in the community. It is "the LORD's house" (v 2). This is the one that remained "a ruin" (v 3) and of which the people said "the time has not yet come" to build (v 2).

God's response to the question of when to build his house differs from the people's response in v 2. Now is the time, according to God. As is often the case, God's timing is not always the same as human timing.

The primary reason for building the temple is so that God might **take pleasure in it and be honored** (v 8). The verb **take pleasure** (*rāṣâ*) fundamentally means to be favorable toward something, to find it pleasing. In priestly vocabulary it conveys approval or acceptance of a person or gift for sacred use. Just as God finds pleasure in a sacrifice so he will in this building. **Be honored** (*kābēd*) can be translated either as "appear in glory" or "glorify myself." Both translations suggest that the temple is a place where God will be made known. In the second message through Haggai, God confirms that he "will fill this house with glory" (Hag 2:7). It will be, as it was before the exile (1 Kgs 7:1-3) and as promised to be afterwards (Ezek 37:27-28), a place for God to be present among his people and manifest the reality of his existence to the nations.

■ **9** With v 9 Haggai returns again to a description of the present situation in order to underscore the argument for building the temple now. What was implicit in vv 2-6 becomes explicit. Lack of resources in the community is directly linked to the ruined temple.

Several verbal features connect v 9 with vv 2-6. Repeated terms include: **much, little, ruin,** and **house.** Verses 2-6 begin with a rhetorical question and then give a list of shortages. Verse 9 inverts that order by referring to the shortages before asking a rhetorical question. These features indicate that v 9 intends to recall and clarify vv 2-6.

You expected much, but see, it turned out to be little echoes the description of shortages listed in vv 5-6. This phrase highlights the disappointment of unrealized expectations within the community. The people had hoped for more than they received. Undoubtedly the projections of Isaiah, Jeremiah, and Ezekiel about a joyful and prosperous period of restoration following exile encouraged these expectations (e.g., see Isa 51:3; Jer 33:10-11; Ezek 36:33-35). Also, those who grew up in more fertile areas of Babylon may have been surprised by the agricultural conditions around Jerusalem. They may not have been ready for the challenges of dry farming in the rocky soils of Judah.

Haggai's words also hint at the selfish motives of the people. **What you brought home** (v 9) most likely refers to the material things people accumulated and stored up in their homes to secure their future. The term **blew away** (*nāpaḥ*) and other similar terms of blowing are employed elsewhere in prophetic literature to convey divine judgment (see Isa 40:7, 24; Ezek 22:20-21).

The second part of v 9 explains the reason for God's judgment. As a result of the people allowing God's house to remain a **ruin** and giving priority to their own houses, they are experiencing the covenant curses. In Hebrew, there is a double use of **because** *(ya'an)*, which gives emphasis to the element of cause and effect *(**because of what, declares the Lord Almighty, because of my house**)*. The phrase **busy with** (active participle of *rûṣ*) literally translates ***running to***. This suggests a continuous and passionate focus upon their own houses. The bottom line is that the economic reversals in Judah are the direct consequence of the people's failure to give priority to God's temple.

■ **10-11** The final two verses of the prophetic message confirm what has just been announced. **Therefore** *('al kēn)* introduces the explanation of why judgment has come. The judgment is that **the heavens have withheld their dew and the earth its crops** (v 10). **Dew** is an important element to the agriculture of the land of Israel. During the dry summer season, such meager moisture sustains plant life. It is created when the warm humid air blows from the Mediterranean and moisture condenses on rocks cooled by night air. If these winds do not blow then **the earth** cannot produce **its crops**. The phrase, **because of you**, makes clear that God altered the regular course of nature in response to their disregard for his temple.

Verse 11 reiterates God's direct involvement in bringing judgment. Like a sovereign monarch God summoned the elements of nature to do his bidding (**I called for a drought,** v 11). He commanded them to withhold their goods as an act of judgment. The language indicates that God has set in motion the covenant curses. **Drought** is one of the main disasters to fall upon those who break covenant with God (see Deut 28:22-24). Ironically the term recalls the description of the temple in earlier verses. Both "ruin" (*ḥareb*) and **drought** (*ḥoreb*) derive from the same root. God ruins the land because his house lies in ruin.

Drought is one of the most devastating disasters for an agriculture-based economy. It affects all areas of production, both **the fields** where crops might grow **and the mountains** where vineyards and orchards might flourish (v 11). Therefore, all products of the land are impacted. **Everything else the land produces** is affected. **The grain** from wheat and barley fields, **the new wine** from grape vineyards, and **the oil** from olive groves summarizes the major products of the land of Judah. Without these food products for nourishment and trade both **men and cattle** suffer. Thus the intense **labor** of planting, cultivating, pruning, terracing, and irrigating literally prove fruitless.

C. The Response (1:12-15)

The final portion of Haggai's message relates the responses of both the audience and God to this speech. The people obey and fear God (v 12), God speaks encouragement to the people (v 13), God stirs their spirits (v 14a), and the people come to work on God's house (vv 14b-15). This kind of interaction depicts what might be expected of those in a covenant relationship with God.

■ **12** Those who responded to Haggai's message included the people of Judah as well as **Zerubbabel** and **Joshua**, the community leaders addressed in v 1. Most importantly, the people are identified as **the whole remnant of the people**. The term **remnant** (*šě'êrît*) evokes earlier prophetic traditions that designated a group in Israel who survived to carry out God's work on earth. Mention of this group sometimes indicated how extensive God's judgment might be as only a **remnant** remains (Isa 10:20-22; Jer 8:3; Ezek 5:10; Mic 5:7-8 [6-7 HB]). But more often the term emphasized the hope of a restored covenant community following judgment (Amos 5:15; Isa 10:20-21; Jer 23:3; Ezek 11:13).

The leaders and the people did two things. They **obeyed the voice of the Lord** and **feared the Lord** (v 12). These two actions describe the essential responses of submission and reverence that God asks of people who enter into covenant with him (Deut 6:24; 10:12-13; 31:13). The word **obeyed** (*šema'*) in biblical thought includes both hearing and acting upon what is heard. Thus it conveys the idea of active obedience, especially in relation to God's demands. The word **feared** (*yārē'*), in many contexts such as this one, is best understood as wholesome respect. God does not desire that people be terrified of him, but rather that they appropriately revere him (see Exod 20:20).

The point of v 12 then is to communicate that the people of Judah renewed their covenant bond with God. They did what people in covenant with God should do. The covenant relationship is implied in the identification of **the Lord** as **their God**. It evokes the classic covenant expression "They will be my people and I will be their God" (Jer 24:7; Ezek 37:27).

■ **13** God responds to the obedience of his people with the promise of presence, **I am with you** (v 13). This promise is often found in salvation oracles in the OT (see Isa 41:10, 43:2, 5; Jer 30:11). It is employed more frequently, however, in speeches of assurance from God to a chosen leader such as Isaac (Gen 26:3), Jacob (Gen 31:3), Moses (Exod 4:12), Joshua (Deut 31:23), or Jeremiah (Jer 1:19). Haggai makes clear that the people will accomplish their work for God first and foremost with the greatest resource available to them, the presence of God, which is far more important than material resources needed for building of the temple.

This promise comes directly from God through Haggai, who is identified in v 13 as **the Lord's messenger**. Prophetic books rarely designate a prophet as a **messenger** (*mal'ak*; see 2 Chr 36:15; Isa 41:27; 44:26) though that was their typical role. In general, the term identifies a person sent by a king or some authority to deliver a message (see 1 Kgs 19:2 and 2 Chr 18:12). The image is that of a runner dispatched from the heavenly throne room with a word from the King. Many times *mal'ak* also designates a heavenly messenger, an angel, sent from God (e.g., Exod 3:2).

■ **14** God's promise of presence is followed by divine action: **the Lord stirred up the spirit** of the leaders and the people of Judah (v 14). The term **stirred** (*'ûr*) calls to mind the image of a person being awakened from sleep. The word describes God moving the heart of the Persian king Cyrus to bring about the restoration of Judah (2 Chr 36:22; Ezra 1:1; Isa 41:2, 25; 45:13). God energizes, encourages, and enables people to come together to **work on the house**. Construction on the temple resumes because God empowered people for his service. This is a clear evidence of the fulfillment of the promise of God's presence with his people (v 13).

Elsewhere the term **work** (*mĕlā'kâ*) is found in the creation narrative (see Gen 2:2-3) and in the construction of the tabernacle (see Exod 35:1-36:8). The use of the same term here implies that the people of Judah are engaged in a significant act, similar to the momentous acts of creation and building the original tabernacle.

■ **15** An historical note indicates that the work began **on the twenty-fourth day of the sixth month in the second year of King Darius**, which translates to September 21, 520 BC. The message of God had come to Haggai three weeks prior on the first day of the sixth month (v 1). This amount of time may have been needed to organize the work, collect materials, and raise necessary funds for the project.

The Function and Location of 1:15

Since Haggai's first message is the only one to end with a dating formula, scholars have questioned the function and location of 1:15. Some scholars suggest that the first part of v 15 is dislocated from its original position. They conjecture that it should serve as the introduction to a supposed separate oracle in 2:15-19 (→ Behind the Text on 2:10-19).

Other scholars believe that the last part of v 15 "in the second year of King Darius" belongs to 2:1 (so NIV and NRSV). The dating formula in 2:1 lacks a year, which the introductions to the messages in 1:1 and 2:10 possess. So a consistency with these other dating formulas might be expected. The dating formula for the final message in 2:20, however, also lacks reference to the year. This feature helps to underscore the parallelism between the first and third messages and the second and fourth messages. Further, 1:15 functions well rhetorically as an inclusion feature for the first message of Haggai.

FROM THE TEXT

Some have criticized Haggai for being too superficial because he seems only concerned with material things like constructing a temple. As the exegesis has shown, however, temple building is about more than stone and timber. In truth the prophet deals with some of life's most pressing questions about human priorities, divine discipline, and divine presence.

The life of faith calls for regular reevaluation of priorities. Biblical faith demands that God and his kingdom hold sole possession of first place in the human heart. Yet, living out this conviction remains a constant challenge for every follower of God. Haggai's audience provides an example of those who forget their priorities and relegated God to second place.

The point of building the temple was not that God needed some structure of stone in which to live. What God desired was to regain first place in the hearts of his people. Constructing a place for God in this world signaled that these people had once again prioritized God and his kingdom.

So Haggai challenged his audience to "give careful thought to your ways" and consider whether or not their first allegiance was to God (v 7). Did their actions give evidence that they trusted in God alone? Was their first concern for the kingdom of God or their own kingdoms? These are questions that all believers need to ask themselves from time to time.

God alerts people to spiritual deficiencies by means of physical deficiencies. The clue that something was wrong with the priorities of Haggai's audience was their adverse circumstances. Haggai asserted that lack of prosperity indicated that they were experiencing the covenant curses promised in the law of Moses (vv 10-11). According to Deuteronomy 28, those who do not keep God first in life suffer all kinds of adversity.

The people of Judah recognized that life was not as it should be. What they did not understand though is that God allowed this reality. Haggai reminds them that they cannot expect God's faithfulness while living a life of unfaithfulness. Haggai stands firmly within biblical tradition when he labels economic reversal and natural disaster the judgment of God (see Amos 4). Of course, not every misfortunate should be viewed as God's judgment for sin, as the book of Job affirms. But when life becomes difficult, it is wise to ask about one's spiritual condition. Adversity is often the instrument of God to gain the attention of his people and to nurture spiritual development (Rom 5:3-5; James 1:2-4).

Trust reveals the power of God's presence among his people. Once people began responding to Haggai's message they received the assurance of God's presence. God confirmed, "I am with you" (v 13). As a result of his presence, God stirred the hearts of the people enabling them to do his work in this world. Obedience and the empowering presence of God go hand in hand.

II. THE CHALLENGE OF INSIGNIFICANCE AND THE PROMISE OF GLORY: HAGGAI 2:1-9

BEHIND THE TEXT

According to the opening verse, Haggai spoke these words in "the seventh month," a few weeks after work began on the temple (v 1). The seventh month, known in Israel as Ethnaim (1 Kgs 8:2) or Tishri was a busy time of concentrated religious activity among the Jews. During this month, the agricultural year came to an end with the final harvesting of fruits and nuts. Only the olive harvest remained.

Three important religious observances took place during this month: the Feast of Trumpets, the Day of Atonement, and the Feast of Tabernacles. On the first day of the month, the new moon, the Feast of Trumpets was celebrated. In late postexilic Judaism this became the New Year's Day celebration known as Rosh Hashanah. The Day of Atonement (Yom Kippur) took place on the tenth day of the month. This was the most solemn day of the Jewish calendar. It was a day of fasting and repentance for the sins of the community (see Lev 16). The third holy observance of this month, the Feast of Tabernacles, began on the fifteenth day of the month. The feast was also known as *sukkot* in Hebrew, which can be translated either as booths, tents, or tabernacles. The people lived in tents during the week of this festival as a reminder of the tent-dwelling days in the wilderness.

The Feast of Tabernacles also carried special significance for Haggai's audience because it was during this festival that Solomon dedicated his magnificent temple centuries before (1 Kgs 8:2; see also 1 Kgs 4-8; 2 Chr 3-7). The Babylonians destroyed this structure and carried off the two massive bronze pillars that stood at the front entrance to the temple along with its enormous bronze sea and other high value items (2 Kgs 25:13-17). The audience of Haggai did not possess the kind of resources needed to restore the temple to its former splendor. It is likely that a comparison of their present efforts with that of the grandeur of Solomon's temple would have disheartened the audience of Haggai (Hag 2:3, 9).

The passage of 2:1-9 is a record of a prophetic message. It is similar in structure to the 1:1-15, but lacks any reference to the audience's response. The passage identifies the setting for the message (v 1) and then records the message (vv 2-9). The message itself follows a typical pattern for prophetic speeches. Haggai describes the situation of the audience (vv 2-3) before delivering the message of God for that situation (vv 4-9). The message proper has two parts to it: words of exhortation (vv 4-5) and words of promise (vv 6-9). The relationship between these two parts is important. The promises in the second part of the message provide additional motivation for following the exhortations of the first part.

IN THE TEXT

A. The Setting (2:1)

■ 1 Once again the text begins by identifying the historical context, the origin, and the messenger of the prophetic message. Identification of the recipients of the message comes within the prophetic speech itself. The specific date for the message is **the twenty-first day of the seventh month**. Interpreters assume that "the second year of King Darius" (520 BC) in 1:15 also relates to this dating formula (so NIV; → sidebar The Function and Location of 1:15), since it is the year designated in the preceding (1:1) and following messages (2:10).

The seventh month was an extremely busy month in the religious calendar of the Jews (→ Behind the Text). **The twenty-first day of the seventh month** would be October 17 if reckoned on modern calendars and would have been the last day of the Feast of Tabernacles. So Haggai addressed the crowd just before the feast ended and work on the temple could once again commence.

This places the message just over three weeks after work on the temple began (see 1:14-15). Thus it is about seven weeks after Haggai's first message (see 1:1). During that time not much work on the temple could have been accomplished because of the final stages in the fruit and nut harvests as well as several days spent observing religious festivals. Probably only the gathering of materials and a labor force along with initial clearing of the foundation could have taken place.

As before, Haggai identifies his message as **the word of the Lord** to affirm its divine origins. The message simply comes **through the prophet Haggai**, literally, *by the hand of the prophet* (→ 1:1, 3).

B. The Message (2:2-9)

■ **2-3** The divine message begins by identifying the situation of the audience (vv 2-3). God instructs Haggai to deliver his message to the political and religious leaders (**Zerubbabel** the governor and **Joshua** the high priest) and to **the remnant of the people.** The latter designation reflects hope for those who have responded to God's previous message (→ 1:12).

The Lord sets forth three rhetorical questions that address the current discouraging situation of the people. The first question, **Who of you is left who saw this house in its former glory?** (v 3) reminds the people that not many, if any, among them had seen the glorious temple of Solomon. It had been lying in ruins for about 67 years. Yet, the **former glory** of Solomon's temple was well known in the traditions of the community (see 1 Kgs 6-7 and 2 Chr 2-4). Local legends may have even embellished its grandeur beyond what was recorded.

The second question, **How does it look to you now?** is aimed at drawing a comparison between the former splendor of the temple and its present condition. The contrast was surely great since Solomon lacked no resources and Haggai's audience possessed few.

The third question seems to answer the second. **Does it not seem to you like nothing?** This articulates the feelings of Haggai's audience; their heroic effort to rebuild the temple will seem to be **nothing,** that is, of no significance. They undoubtedly feared that their personal sacrifices, which were many, would not matter in the end.

■ **4-5** God addresses the challenge of insignificance in the community first with a word of exhortation in vv 4-5. Two imperatives of encouragement surround an imperative of instruction. The imperatives of encouragement are to **be strong** (v 4) and **do not fear** (v 5). The imperative of instruction is **work** (v 4).

The command to **be strong** calls people to firm resolve in their task (v 4). It urges them to remain committed in the face of obstacles. The imperative is repeated for each principle in Haggai's audience. The threefold repetition of this command adds intensity and urgency to the message. The two key leaders of the community, **Zerubbabel** and **Joshua**, are specifically named once again and each given this command.

The third party urged to be steadfast is the **people of the land** (*'am hā'āreṣ*). This phrase describes "the remnant" of obedient participants mentioned in 1:12, 14, and 2:2. By using this designation Haggai evokes a veiled allusion to the ancient covenant between God and Israel (Gen 12:7). Those Haggai addresses are **people of the land** that was promised to Abraham and his descendants.

The second command from God is an imperative of instruction urging the audience to continue construction on the temple. God simply orders them to **work** (*'āsâ*; v 4). This is a general term for doing or making. Usually it has an object, but in this context the temple project is simply implied. The people are to engage the task that God put before them in 1:8, "build the house."

The third imperative of this section is another word of encouragement that echoes the first. It invites Haggai's audience to **not fear** (v 5). Undoubtedly people feared both lack of resources needed to complete the project as well as political repercussions from their neighbors and the Persian government (see Ezra 4-5).

The motive for following these commands of God is the presence of God. The Lord asserts **I am with you** (v 4). This is the same phrase used in 1:13 and reaffirms the promise given in Haggai's first message (→ 1:13). It confirms that the empowering presence of God would be evident throughout the building project. The promise of presence is restated in the phrase **my Spirit remains among you** (v 5; cp. Zech 4:6). The term **remains among** (active participle of *'āmad* plus *betok*) conveys a meaningful image of God continuously standing in the midst of his people.

The background to this promise of presence is the Exodus experience when Israel **came out of Egypt**. God says it is **what I covenanted with you** at that time. The vocabulary used in v 5 evokes the pillar of cloud, which represented the presence of God leading Israel out of Egypt (Exod 14:19) or standing at the entrance to the tabernacle (Exod 33:9). The term for "pillar" (*'ammud*) derives from the same root as **remains** (*'omedet*). Otherwise God's promise to live among his people in the tabernacle could come to mind. In Exod 29:45 God promises that once the tabernacle is built he will "dwell among the Israelites and be their God." Whatever specific allusion may have been intended, Haggai deliberately connects his audience with the Exodus experience. Haggai's community can expect the same presence of God among them as they go about their task of rebuilding the temple.

The key phrases **be strong**, **fear not**, and **I am with you** also recall similar words spoken to God's people at other significant junctures (see Deut 31:6; Is 35:4). David's exhortation to Solomon as he prepared to build the temple is particularly meaningful for Haggai's audience. In that context David said, "Be strong and courageous, and do the work. Do not be afraid or discouraged, for the LORD God, my God, is with you" (1 Chr 28:20). More striking though may be God's words to Joshua just prior to the conquest of Canaan (see Josh 1:9). The people addressed by Haggai have just relived the wilderness experience during the Feast of Tabernacles. So they can identify with the people of Joshua's day as they stand ready to attempt a great task for God.

Clearly the prophetic message intends for the people of Haggai's time to see themselves within the stream of salvation history. They are reliving life with God in a manner similar to previous generations. God's encouragement and resources for the task of rebuilding the temple remain the same.

■ **6** The second part of God's response to the challenge of insignificance is a word of promise. In this portion of the message God directly addresses fears about lack of resources and possible political repercussions. God promises to subdue the nations (vv 6-7a), furnish resources (vv 7b-8), supply significance (v 9a), and give peace (v 9b). Such promises provide motivation for following the exhortations of vv 4-5. The promises articulated in these verses are at the heart of God's message to his people.

God provides a time frame for the promises to be fulfilled with the phrase **in a little while I will once more** (v 6). This is an odd poetic-like construction in Hebrew that literally reads ***yet once in a little*** (*'ôd 'aḥat me'aṭ*). It is an idiom that conveys immediate action and yet remains indefinite. The phrase **once more** communicates recurrence of the action. This is something God has done before. Based on the preceding verse, the Exodus experience is in view. God will do among the people of Haggai's time what he did at the Exodus.

What God will do is **shake the heavens and the earth, the sea and the dry land**, and **all nations** (vv 6-7). The term **shake** (*ra'ash*) connotes quivering or trembling such as experienced in earthquakes. The Hebrew Scriptures frequently associate shaking of the cosmos and nations when God takes on the role of a mighty warrior and intervenes in his world. All of creation responds to God's appearance (Exod 19:18; Isa 24:17-23; Ezek 38:18-23, Joel 3:14-16 [4:14-16 HB]; Hab 2:2-15).

God as a Mighty Warrior

People throughout the ancient Middle East frequently portrayed their deities as warriors. In Canaanite religion Baal and Anat in particular were depicted as deities of war.

Israel also pictured their God, Yahweh, this way. The Hebrew Scriptures describe God as being like "a warrior" wielding sword and leading a heavenly army (Exod 15:3; Job 16:14). Several times the Lord is called "a mighty man" (*gibbôr*), a term that identifies a person of superior strength and skill, especially in military matters (Isa 42:13; Jer 20:11).

The soldier in the ancient world held special status within society. Well-trained and equipped soldiers of great courage were essential to survival. So the image of a deity as a mighty warrior communicated special honor and accentuated its role as the ultimate protector of people.

■ **7** As a result of God shaking creation **what is desired by all nations will come** (v 7). Commentators differ in their translation and interpretation of this phrase. The phrase **what is desired** (*hemdâ*) usually refers to something coveted because it produces pleasure. It is a person or an object that someone takes delight in and values. Therefore, the word might be rendered "treasure" (NRSV and ESV) or "precious things" (NJPS). **What is desired** in this context may mean material resources needed to rebuild the temple. Therefore, God may be promising to supply adequate building materials from outside of Judah for the project. According to the book of Ezra this is exactly what happened. The Persian king Darius decreed that the cost of constructing the Jewish temple was "to be fully paid out of the royal treasury, from the revenues of Trans-Euphrates" (Ezra 6:8).

In rabbinic and Christian tradition **what is desired by all nations** has often been understood as a direct reference to the messiah. This goes back to earliest times in Christianity as reflected in Jerome's translation in the Latin Vulgate. Jerome may have been influenced by the LXX translation of **desired** with *eklectos*, the same term used in Isa 42:1 to describe the messiah in whom God delights.

Some modern English translations also encourage this interpretation by capitalizing the words and reading "the Desire of All Nations" (NKJV). Christian hymns have further supported this understanding by phrases such as "Dear desire of every nation" in Charles Wesley's "Come, Thou Long Expected Jesus."

God also promises to **fill this house with glory** (v 7). **Glory** (*kābôd*) might refer either to material wealth or to the presence of God. Its connection to the previous phrase and the reference to "silver" and "gold" in v 8 suggest that the physical impression and assets of the temple are in view. Temples in the ancient world were not only impressive structures, but also were depositories of community goods functioning somewhat like national banks. So the glory of a temple could be related to the wealth connected to it.

The idea of filling **with glory**, however, also has a long history in the OT of conveying God's presence in his sacred space, first with the tabernacle (Exod 40:34-35) and then with Solomon's temple (1 Kgs 8:11). For Ezekiel the glory of God in the temple signaled divine pleasure with the people of Judah (Ezek 10:3-4; 43:5). The promise of presence already made in Haggai's speeches (1:13 and 2:4) also supports an understanding of **glory** in this way.

The two possible meanings of this phrase may well be intentional. The **glory** of God's presence is the essential resource needed for building as indicated in 1:13 and 2:4. Yet, contributions from surrounding nations will also result in an impressive structure along with stores of riches. Thus, God may well be promising to supply both his presence as well as the riches of nations to build the temple in Jerusalem.

■ **8** God affirms that with him there are no shortages in material resources. The commodities most sought after by all nations, **silver** and **gold**, ultimately belong to God. So when the nations supply the materials for construction of the temple in Haggai's day, they will only be returning what already belonged to God.

■ **9** The message draws to a climactic conclusion in v 9. God promises to supply significance to those building the temple. He declares that **the glory of this present house will be greater than the glory of the former house** (v 9). The term **glory** (*kābôd*) can once again carry a double meaning, just as it did in v 7. It may refer to both the material wealth displayed in the building as well as the presence of God.

At the time it was finished in 520 B.C, **this present house**, the structure built by Haggai's audience, did not match the grandeur of **the former house**, Solomon's temple. The materials and workmanship in Solomon's structure far outstripped that in Zerubbabel's. Further, the store of wealth within the temple could not approach that in Solomon's temple (→ Behind the Text). Yet, in the year 19 BC Herod the Great undertook a major remodeling of the Jerusalem temple mound that eventually made it into one of the more impressive sacred complexes in the Roman world. As the center of a relatively prosperous Jewish community, it housed considerable wealth as well. One could say then that over five hundred years after the time of Haggai the physical **glory** of the Jerusalem temple did become greater than that of Solomon's day.

Along with glory God promises to **grant peace . . . in this place** (v 9). **This place** refers to the temple. The Hebrew term **place** (*māqôm*) is frequently used as a technical term for the temple (e.g., see Jer 7:3). Throughout the OT **peace** (*šalôm*) is one of God's most sought-after blessings (Num 6:26), especially in Jerusalem, the city whose name includes the word *šalôm*. Jews regularly prayed for the peace of Jerusalem (Ps 122:6-9). The Hebrew term *šalôm* expresses the idea wellbeing, harmony, and wholeness. It is more than the absence of danger or conflict. The peace of God includes elements of prosperity and fulfillment. According to this verse, it derives from God's presence. It is the gift of God with his people.

Peace is also one of the most pervasive descriptions of the messianic era (Isa 9:6-7 [5-6 HB] and 32:16-17). Thus, once again, Haggai's audience is lifted beyond its present circumstances to another time. Their significance is found not only by participating in the same story as their ancestors in the Exodus from Egypt (v 5). They as well have become part of the fulfillment of the ultimate hopes of the messiah's world, which include both glory and peace.

FROM THE TEXT

This message brings the book of Haggai to a high point. It focuses attention upon the ultimate purposes of God in his world and thereby supplies Haggai's most compelling motivation for rebuilding the temple. Haggai asserts that this project was part of the grand scheme of salvation history. In it God would repeat patterns of past redemptive activities. But even more, this building would play a key role in the future messianic era. It would be part of the grand culmination of all things, when the glory of God would be manifest on earth in measures never before experienced and the longed-for peace on earth imparted to mankind.

Kingdom work is never insignificant in the larger scheme of God's plans and purposes in the world. Haggai's audience struggled to appreciate the significance of their efforts because they knew they could not match the physical splendor of Solomon's temple. They failed to recognize though that the real splendor of the former temple had been God's presence in it (see 1 Kgs 8 and 2 Chr 6-7).

Through Haggai God promised that the new temple would be even more significant than the former temple because of God's presence there (v 9). Jesus fulfilled this promise centuries later when he entered the very temple precincts that Haggai's audience constructed. According to the Gospel of Luke, his first appearance there as an infant was momentous (Luke 2:22-38). Later, the temple area became the venue for much of his teaching, preaching, and healing ministries (e.g., see Luke 21:37 and John 10:22-23). At his death the veil to the Holy of Holies ripped apart symbolizing full access to the presence of God (Matt 27:51). The greater glory of Haggai's temple occurred when God's messiah, in the person of Jesus Christ, entered its courts.

Thus Haggai invites readers today to remain faithfully committed to God's kingdom work without comparing their contribution to the successes of others. If it is God's work, it is significant. It is part of God's grand plan to redeem the world.

God's ultimate plan is to reveal his glory so that all creation may see it and acknowledge his sovereignty as the Creator God. The language of God shaking the heavens and the earth indicates that though God invites human participation, ultimately the revealing of God's glory in the world is God's work. The shaking of the physical structure of this universe is intended to usher in the unshakable kingdom of God on earth. Referring to Hag 2:6-7, the writer of Hebrews points out that God removes "what can be shaken . . . so that what cannot be shaken may remain" (Heb 12:26-28).

Finally, Haggai reminds readers that *God's glory inhabits places where God is worshipped.* Throughout its history, the temple served to reveal the glory of God as people faithfully came to worship there. This is why Haggai urged his audience to rebuild the temple. In the temple they and all nations could encounter the presence of the living God when they worshipped there. So also today, places of worship become arenas where humans can experience God's glory. This is the purpose of such venues and the reason God leads people to build them.

III. THE CHALLENGE OF PURITY AND THE PROMISE OF BLESSING: HAGGAI 2:10-19

BEHIND THE TEXT

The first question to answer about Hag 2:10-19 is whether or not it stands as a literary unit. Some scholars believe the text has been corrupted at some point and see vv 10-14 and vv 15-19 as two distinct oracles (Wolff 1988, 59-60). They hold that during editing of the book vv 15-19 became disconnected from 1:15*a*, which stands as its proper introduction. Others maintain that 2:10-19 is a unified piece and does not need to be rearranged or emended (McComiskey 1998, 994). Clearly the canonical arrangement of the text presents these verses as one oracle beginning in v 10 and ending in v 19. The first word in v 15 "now" (*wĕ'att â*) consistently marks transition points within Haggai's oracles and does not introduce them (see 1:5 and 2:4). As the text stands, vv 10-14 and vv 15-19 are literarily connected by this term.

One of the primary reasons scholars have struggled with the integrity of the text is the reference to "when the foundation of the Lord's temple was laid" in v 18. Some commentators think this is the same time that the people "began to work on the house of the Lord" in 1:14. That event, however, took place in "the sixth month" (1:15), while the event in 2:18 takes place in "the ninth month," if the text is taken as it stands. The time for the oracle in 2:10-19 then comes at a point three months into the construction project.

"The twenty-fourth day of the ninth month" is not connected to an annual Jewish religious observance like the other dates in the book. However, it most likely marks an important religious event in the process of building the temple, a ceremony consecrating the sacred site. Throughout the ancient Near East, temple construction included solemn rituals at various junctures in the project. Several weeks after initial work began, priests and royal representatives might conduct a ceremony that involved removing a brick from the old temple and setting it in the new one. In Mesopotamia this event was known at the *kalu* ceremony (see Peterson 1984, 89-90). It symbolized continuity between the ancient sacred site and the new one. Singing, purification rites, and words of blessing accompanied this ceremony. If such an event is viewed as the background for 2:10-19, then the questions about purity in vv 10-13 make sense in connection with the promise of blessing in v 19. These questions are linked to laws concerning purity and uncleanness in Lev 11-15, 19, and 22:4-6.

This prophetic speech report follows the typical logical progression of Haggai's other oracles. The setting for the speech is identified in v 10 before a report of the speech is given in vv 11-19. The speech divides into two parts. A priestly inquiry ritual serves to provide a description of the present situation in vv 11-14. After that the divine message responds to that situation in vv 15-19.

IN THE TEXT

A. The Setting (2:10)

■ **10** As in the two previous messages (see 1:1 and 2:1), the text identifies the specific timing of the prophetic message along with its origins. **The twenty-fourth day of the ninth month in the second year of Darius** corresponds to December 18, 520 BC by modern ways of reckoning. The full significance of this day is not revealed until v 18 where Haggai identifies it as "the day when the foundation of the Lord's temple was laid." It was most likely a day of solemn ritual that set apart the sacred site of the temple for divine encounters (→ Behind the Text). In addition, **the ninth month** was the time for planting seed for next year's crops. The hope of the people must have been mixed with anxiety over the future, especially in light of the recent meager harvests noted in 1:6-8 and 10-11 and referred to again in 2:16-17.

B. The Present Situation (2:11-14)

■ **11-14** Haggai, as instructed by the Lord, employs a unique method to reveal the situation of his audience (v 11). He asks the priests two questions seeking a ruling from the law concerning the transferability of holiness and defilement (see Lev 10:10-11; Deut 17:9). His first question focuses on holiness; he wants to know if ordinary food such as **bread, wine,** etc. would become consecrated when they come into contact with consecrated food (v 12). It is possible that **someone** in v 12 is a priest who takes home **consecrated meat** from a sacrifice for his family in a **fold** in the front apron of priestly outer garment (see Lev 11:7-21 and Deut 18:8-9). This verse also assumes that the same priest may be carrying with him food that is not consecrated. The priests' answer confirms that ordinary food does not become consecrated by its contact with consecrated food; holiness is not transferrable from object to object or person to person.

The second question focuses on the issue of defilement (v 13). The priests affirm that a person defiled by **contact with a dead body** brings defilement on everything he **touches** (see Num 19). Leviticus 11-15 gives a detailed list of things that could bring defilement to the people of Israel. The second response to Haggai's question thus asserts that defilement is transferrable.

Verse 14 indicates that Haggai's questions were not intended to give his audience instruction on the law of holiness and uncleanness. They were most likely well educated on the purity laws of their tradition. Haggai's intent is to reveal to his audience that the Lord sees them as a **defiled** people and their defilement is seen in their actions and their offering to the Lord. The phrase **whatever they do** literally translates "all the work of their hands." It is possible to see here a reference to the work of both building the temple and planting seed for the new season. In life and worship, they remain defiled.

According to the laws of purity, defilement disqualifies a person from entering the presence of God until it is removed through appropriate ritual. Haggai reminds his audience that their work and their worship are unacceptable to the Lord. Though they are involved in the work of building the sacred sanctuary of the Lord, they are actually contaminating it with their defilement or uncleanness. Verse 14 thus implies that the defilement of the people needs to be removed before they can continue the work of rebuilding the temple.

C. The Message (2:15-19)

■ **15** In response to the issues raised in vv 10-14, Haggai gives a message of hope to his audience in vv 15-19. Though they remained under a curse because of their defilement, a new day will be dawning for them. God promises that their condition will change and they will be recipients of divine blessing from **this day on** (v 15; → v 18).

Haggai begins by inviting the people to carefully reflect on their condition before **one stone** was **laid on another** in the temple (v 15). The phrase might identify simply the normal construction process when stones are placed upon each other in a wall. But in the context of this speech it more likely refers to the ritual act of placing a stone from the old temple in the foundation for the new temple while purification rites were administered and blessings uttered. A typical part of the Mesopotamian *kalu* ceremony involved such a rite (→ Behind the Text). In the context of vv 10-14, it is also likely that the rituals of purification on this day included the purification of the people and the land. In other words, on this day, defilement of both the temple and the people was removed; the people could continue the work of the temple as the consecrated people of God.

■ **16-17** Haggai reminds his audience of their dismal situation before this day (v 16). They experienced severe shortage in the production and storage of grain and wine, two staples necessary for their survival. Verse 17 traces this misfortune to God's judgment. God **struck** them with natural calamities in the hope that they will return to him. The phrase, **you did not return to me**, is literally, ***and nothing of you to me*** (*wě'ên 'etkem 'ēlay*). English translations reflect the Greek rendering which is translated as, "and you did not return." The Hebrew is likely an idiomatic phrase that conveys lack of connection and loyalty. Amos uses similar words to describe Israel's failure to repent and return to God though he struck them with various calamities (see Amos 4:6-11; see also Isa 9:13).

■ **18-19** Haggai urges his audience once again to pay close attention (**give careful thought**) to how things will change from **this day on** (v 18). Instead of curses there will be blessings because the Lord promises, **From this day I will bless you** (v 19). **This day** is the day they received this message and demonstrated their commitment to the Lord by laying **the foundation of the LORD's temple**. As noted previously, this was not the day that work began, but a special day of consecration of the temple and the people (→ v 15).

So Haggai concludes this message by challenging his audience to remember their present situation and be attentive to what God will do in the future. Their current situation was extremely difficult with severe shortages in grain (**seed**) and fruit (**vine, fig, pomegranate, olive**). However, Haggai offered the hope of God's blessing in the future, a promise that their ancestors had heard since the days of Abraham (Gen 12:2-3). According to Deut 28:3-14, that promise included God's blessing upon all areas of life, including crops of the land. There would be a reversal of Judah's fortunes.

FROM THE TEXT

In this third message, Haggai clarifies that *involvement in God's mission is not a substitute for holy living.* The questions that Haggai asks the priests imply that his audience assumed they were a holy people because they were involved in building God's temple. But the question concerning the "consecrated meat" and ordinary food illustrates that holiness is not transferrable (v 12), while the question regarding "a dead body" clarifies that defilement is (v 13). These answers indicate that doing kingdom work, like building the temple, does not make people holy. On the contrary, if they are unclean, their work actually defiles God's kingdom.

On the day "when the foundation of the Lord's temple was laid" though, both the temple and the people became holy (v 18). As they consecrated their work with the laying of the stone, God consecrated them for that work. A new day dawned in their relationship with God and they received the promise of his blessing. When people commit wholeheartedly to God's kingdom, God stands ready to pour out blessings.

God calls his people to be holy, not just do good deeds. The Bible affirms this truth time and again (Lev 11:44-45; 19:2, 20:7; 1 Thess 4:3; 1 Pet 1:16). We do not become holy through our involvement in God's mission or our association with people who are holy. We must consecrated our lives to God and his purposes (Rom 12:1-2; 1 Pet 1:22). Like the audience of Haggai, people today may mistake their work for the Lord as a substitute for his call to be holy people.

The text challenges us to consecrate ourselves to God. Our cleansing does not happen through priestly rituals performed according the law of Moses, but through the Holy Spirit who purifies our hearts "by faith" (Acts 15:9). When we are cleansed from sin and defilement, the work we do to promote God's mission will become a holy task, because it is done in total obedience to the Lord. As a result, God promises, "From this day on I will bless you" (v 19).

2:10-19

IV. THE CHALLENGE OF CONTINUITY AND THE PROMISE OF MESSIAH: HAGGAI 2:20-23

BEHIND THE TEXT

The relationship between Davidic rulers and the temple is important background for understanding this oracle. According to 2 Sam 7 and 1 Chr 17, God promised to build a "house" for David in response to his desire to build a "house" for God. The rule of God symbolized in the temple advances in relationship to the rule of David's descendants who represent God's kingdom on earth (see Ps 132). The final message of Haggai indicates that rebuilding the temple during Haggai's time reignited God's covenant promise to David and the prophetic promises concerning the coming of a messianic ruler from the house of David.

The form of vv 20-23 is that of a prophetic speech report similar to the other three reports in the book. A setting (v 20) is given, then the prophetic speech (vv 21-23). The speech does not have a description of the present situation though. It only announces the message from God.

A. The Setting (2:20)

■ **20** This speech is **the second** communication from God on the same day as the previous oracle in 2:10-19. That **twenty-fourth day of the month** was special because it was "the day when the foundation of the LORD's temple" was laid in a solemn ceremony consecrating the temple precincts (→ 2:18). That celebration provided an appropriate venue for this message.

B. The Message (2:21-23)

■ **21-22** The Lord's message through Haggai is directed to **Zerubbabel governor of Judah** (v 21). As the political leader of the Jewish community, he would have played a significant role in the ceremony of laying the foundation stone (→ 2:15-19). Zechariah also had a message for Zerubbabel about laying the foundation stone (see Zech 4:6-10).

God's message begins with an announcement of dramatic actions that would affect the entire cosmos. The verbs **shake, overturn, shatter,** and **overthrow** in vv 21-22 convey the complete dominance of the Lord over those who might oppose him (see Gen 19:21-29; Exod 14:23-25; Isa 13:9-13, 24:18; Jer 20:16; Ezek 32:11-12; 38:21; Amos 4:11). The repeated use of the first person I underscores God's personal initiative in these actions. The verbs used here also echo the actions of the divine warrior in Haggai's second oracle (→ 2:6-9). The specific target of God's actions are kings and kingdoms of the nations in the world along with their war machinery (**chariots, drivers, horses, riders**).

■ **23** The climactic act of the Lord **on that day** will be to **take** Zerubbabel and **make** him like the Lord's **signet ring** (v 23). A **signet ring** was a piece of metal jewelry with the seal of a king etched on it. Its imprint in clay marked documents with a king's authority. Thus God promises to make Zerubbabel his **chosen** representative on earth, just a David and his descendants had been (1 Sam 16:12-13; 1 Kgs 8:16; Ps 89:3-4).

This divine moment will take place **on that day**, a shortened form for the Day of the Lord that is often found in the prophetic speeches (e.g., Isa 2:11-20; Jer 25:33; Amos 8:3; Zeph 1:7-18). It designates an undefined moment in the future when God will judge the wicked and vindicate the righteous. Prophets seem to speak of this event taking place in the near future, though occasionally they imply a distant future (→ Behind the Text for Zech 12:1-13:9). Since vv 21-22 belong to the context of the temple rebuilding, and since Haggai makes specific mention of Zerubbabel, it seems likely that the prophet anticipates the events of this day in the immediate future.

Some scholars think that Haggai envisions the re-establishment of the Davidic kingdom through Zerubbabel, a potential heir to the throne of David. He might naturally see the restoration of the Davidic kingdom accompanying the re-

HAGGAI

2:20-23

building of the temple. However, the message more likely intends simply to offer hope of God's sovereign rule through Zerubbabel. That is to say, in a world dominated by Persians, Zerubbabel's leadership in rebuilding the temple signals God's rule both now and forever.

Some scholars also suggest that since we do not hear anything more about Zerubbabel after these events, this message may have caused the Persians to recall him in order to squelch possible insurrection in Judah. Whether this is true, Haggai's words remain a certain promise concerning God's rule over the world through the Davidic dynasty. That promise would be ultimately fulfilled through a descendant named Jesus, the son of Mary and Joseph (Matt 1:1-17).

FROM THE TEXT

The book of Haggai concludes by affirming the rule of God in the present as well as in the future. The prophet focuses the eyes of those who are working for God upon the hopefulness of God's kingdom currently surrounding them in Zerubbabel. At the same time, he reminds them of the promise of God's ultimate victory over the kingdoms of this world. Zerubbabel's life in the days of Haggai left the impression, like a signet ring, that God is and will always be in control.

Compelling evidence for God's kingdom in this world can be seen every day. The psalmist announced, "The heavens declare the glory of God; the skies proclaim the work of his hands" (Ps 19:1). For Haggai, the heritage and position of Zerubbabel within Judah announced God with us. This local ruler was a tangible sign of the kingdom of God at work in the present age.

Haggai's message reminds us today that those who open their eyes will see the hand of God at work in this world. His kingdom remains among us though earthly kings may sit on thrones. Every day the light of God's kingdom pierces the darkness around us if we will but take notice.

Such evidence of God's present kingdom assures us that God will win in the end. These verses do not predict a particular event in the future. Rather they paint a picture of God's ultimate victory. One day God will "shake the heavens and the earth" and "overturn royal thrones" (vv 21-22). The act of a Davidic descendant laying the foundation stone of the temple fueled this hope and ensured it fulfillment. This was a foreshadowing of things to come. If God can make this happen in the desperate days of Haggai, surely God can do it again.

ZECHARIAH

INTRODUCTION

The book of Zechariah contains many memorable verses for Christians. Yet the book can puzzle modern readers for various reasons. For one thing, the meaning of certain images in its visions remains unclear. Additionally, the relationship between the oracles in the final chapters of the book and the visions in the earlier chapters poses a problem. Indeed, even determining the original historical setting for the last part of the book presents a major challenge.

Early Christians do not seem to have struggled as much with Zechariah as modern readers though. In fact, they found the book a significant source for understanding Jesus Christ and his mission in the world. When the gospel writers sought to explain the events of the final week of Jesus' life, they quoted Zechariah more often than any other prophet. The rejected shepherd portrayed in Zechariah paralleled exactly what they had experienced with Jesus. As the apostle John described scenes of his visions in the book of Revelation, he also drew heavily from the language and images of Zechariah. Paul as well employed some allusions to Zechariah in his letters (for further details on the NT use of Zechariah, see Boda 2004, 57-63 and Klein 2008, 61-63).

Undoubtedly what drew early Christians to Zechariah was its focus upon the messianic age. The book describes the character of this era, the joy that accompanies it, and its final triumph. When the Messiah comes, the Lord will establish his worldwide rule and restore a community of faithful worshipers. According to the book of Zechariah, such a world will emerge only at the end of much struggle and suffering. This includes the rejection of God's Messiah, an event the disciples of Jesus witnessed in the crucifixion. Yet God's kingdom promises to prevail in spite of all opposition giving hope to those who remain committed to it.

The prophetic words of this book originally encouraged people engaged in temple building. But they also inspired followers of Christ who struggled to build his kingdom in the first century. That has been the enduring value of the book of Zechariah for Christians throughout the ages.

A. The Prophet

According to Ezra 5:1, the prophet Zechariah joined Haggai in calling the people of Judah to rebuild their ruined temple toward the end of the sixth century BC. Three specific dates in the book relate his life to this context. These dates correspond to modern calendars as: October 520 BC (1:1), February 15, 519 BC (1:7), and December 7, 518 BC (7:1). This places Zechariah's ministry within the first two years of the temple building project in Jerusalem, which took place between 520 and 516 BC

According to the first date in 1:1, Zechariah began his ministry just after work on the temple had started in the fall of 520 BC (see Hag. 1:15). How long Zechariah continued his work is unclear. While Haggai concluded his messages in December 520 BC, Zechariah persisted at least two years beyond that. The final dated message of Zechariah occurs near the halfway point of the temple building project. Yet references to "the house of the LORD" in 9:8, 11:13-14, and 14:21 suggest that messages in these chapters were delivered after the temple was completed. Many scholars dispute, however, whether these three references, or any of chs 9-14, come from the prophet Zechariah (→ The Audience).

Zechariah, which means "the Lord remembers," was a popular name in ancient Israel. Over thirty different people in the Bible bear it. The initial verses of the book distinguish Zechariah as "son of Berekiah, the son of Iddo" (1:1, 7). Ezra 5:1 and 6:14 also identify "Zechariah the prophet" as "a descendant of Iddo," but do not mention Berekiah who was not likely as well known. Iddo was one of the priests who returned to Jerusalem with Zerubbabel, according to Nehemiah 12:4. He appears to be Zechariah's grandfather and a prominent member of the post-exilic community in Judah. In Nehemiah 12:16 Zechariah is listed as the head of Iddo's household.

Based on his family connections, Zechariah likely served as a priest in Jerusalem. The language and focus of his messages betray this background as well. His concern for rebuilding the temple, the future of Jerusalem, purity within the Jewish community, and fasting indicate priestly interests. Images of the high priest and a golden lampstand in his visions draw from this world as well.

Zechariah also shows a profound indebtedness to Israel's great prophetic tradition. Like other post-exilic prophets he draws heavily from their words and thoughts (→ Introduction to Haggai and Introduction to Malachi). He refers to "the earlier prophets" several times (1:7; 7:7, 12) and frequently alludes to messages of Amos, Hosea, Isaiah, Jeremiah, Ezekiel, and other prophets. Images from Isaiah and Ezekiel recur most often (see Klein 2008, 50-58 and Mitchell 1937, 101-102).

B. The Audience

The messages of Zechariah 1-8 address Jews living in post-exilic Judah toward the end of the sixth century BC. Judah sat within the borders of the vast Persian Empire that stretched from the Indus River to the Aegean Sea. It was a small entity located within a western satrapy of the empire known as *Eber Nahara*. The name translates to "Beyond the River," referring to the river Euphrates. Darius the Great (r. 522-486 BC), one of Persia's most able emperors, solidified control of the empire only a few months before Zechariah began his ministry around 520 BC. It was a significant time of transition in the empire (→ Introduction to Haggai: A. The Audience; also see Meyer and Meyer 1993, 16-26).

The people to whom Zechariah specifically spoke were engaged in rebuilding the temple of Jerusalem, which had suffered total destruction in 586 BC. When the first Jewish exiles returned to Jerusalem in 537 BC, work on the temple began immediately. But several discouraging circumstances eventually halted construction for over fifteen years (see Ezra 1-4). Toward the end of 520 BC Haggai motivated the people of Judah to undertake the project once again and a few months later Zechariah began his ministry.

The inhabitants of Judah faced formidable challenges to constructing a monumental building like the temple, however. In addition to meager resources Haggai identified other issues that must be overcome in order to undertake this project. These included how to deal with economic reversal, feelings of insignificance, purity within the community, and maintaining hope in the future (→ Introduction to Haggai).

Zechariah continued to address these and other issues as momentum on the building project ebbed and flowed over subsequent years. Political opposition emerged immediately after the project got underway, according to Ezra 5.

Governing officials of the Persian Empire questioned the motives and authority of the Jews for building the temple. As a result, a letter was sent to the Persian king Darius suggesting that this building represented possible rebellion among the Jews. In the end, Darius approved the project and offered support for it from the state. But awaiting an official reply from the central government must have created considerable angst among Judah's population. This may well be the context for the night visions recorded in chs 1-6.

According to Zechariah's messages in chs 1-8 spiritual issues within Judah posed the greatest obstacle to the building project. As the commentary will show, these messages speak to various problems such as: (1) lack of commitment to covenant, (2) limited trust in the Lord's ability to supply resources, (3) diminished vision for the future, and (4) religious hypocrisy.

The historical setting for the original audience of Zechariah 9-14 is difficult to determine. These chapters give no dates, names, or any clear historical allusions. References to "the house of the Lord" indicate a time after the temple was completed in 516 BC (9:8; 11:13-14; and 14:21), but this time cannot be established with any certainty. Based upon the messages in these chapters though the original audience seems to be dealing with questions of (1) God's commitment to Jerusalem, (2) purity within the community of Judah, (3) corruption among Judah's leadership, and (4) the Lord's ultimate purposes for his people.

Most modern commentators admit that discovering the precise setting for the audience of chs 9-14 is impossible. Even so, a number of scholars believe chs 9-14 relate best to a time somewhere between completion of the temple in 516 BC and the arrival of Nehemiah in 445 BC. In the opinion of these scholars, references to events related to such places as Tyre and Sidon (9:2), Ashkelon, Gaza, Ekron, and Ashdod (9:5-6), and Egypt and Assyria (10:10) can be understood best within this timeframe. Even the reference to "sons of Greece" (9:13) can make sense within this setting, though the influence of Greece increases in later centuries (see further discussions in Hill 1982, 105-134; Meyer and Meyer 1993, 26-29; Clark and Hatton 2004, 223-224; and Klein 2008, 34-40).

If the messages of chs 9-14 were given within this timeframe, they could provide encouragement for a discouraged community who sacrificed much to see the temple completed and yet continued to struggle within a world controlled by foreign powers. Still scattered throughout the empire, the Jewish faithful remained under the threat of being swallowed up by the forces of an increasingly pluralistic society. The modest structure they built in Jerusalem did not approach the grandeur of the many impressive structures that stood throughout the Persian Empire. Its seeming irrelevance within this world surely symbolized the insignificance of the people of Jerusalem and Judah. The messages of chs 9-14, however, remind such people of the Lord's keen interest in the affairs of Jerusalem and the major role it plays in his world. They enable people to see beyond their current circumstances to the grand scheme of salvation history, revealing days of struggle, but also of ultimate triumph.

The Historical Setting for Chs 9-14

In trying to account for obscure references to historical entities as well as other features of chs 9-14 scholars have suggested numerous possibilities for the setting of this material (see Smith 1984, 242-249 for details on these proposals). These range from the eighth century to the second century BC. In 1635 Joseph Mede suggested that chs 9-11 should be read in a context just prior to exile because the Gospel of Matthew attributed Zech 11:13 to Jeremiah (Matt 27:9-10). Others eventually followed his lead and ascribed all of chs 9-14 to that time period.

In the eighteenth and nineteenth centuries scholars began assigning different units to different eras in Israel's history. Benedict Flugge, for example, identified eight different historical periods represented in these chapters, while L. Berthold found just two in the pre-exilic period and J. G. Eichhorn argued for two in the post-exilic era.

In the late nineteenth century Bernard Stade developed a theory that influenced many scholars for a number of years. He held to a single author for all of chs 9-14 who worked just after the time of Alexander the Great. This material was designated Deutero-Zechariah or Second-Zechariah to distinguish it from chs 1-8.

More recently Paul Hanson put forth an interesting and widely discussed theory regarding chs 9-14. He sees these chapters deriving from the context of an ideological struggle between two groups in post-exilic Judah, which he labels visionaries and hierocrats. The hierocrats represent the conservative established guard within Jerusalem, while the visionaries come from a more progressive element that relied heavily upon the tradition of the prophet Zechariah. For Hanson, chapters 9-14 reflect the visionary party's critique of the hierocrats and puts forth a more hopeful vision of Judah's future as the center for the universal rule of the Lord (Hanson 1979, 280-401).

C. Literary Features

The book of Zechariah employs a variety of poetic and prose forms common to prophetic literature. Summons to repentance, vision reports, sign-acts, messenger speeches, woe oracles, and other such genres regularly occur in the book. These have been arranged into three distinct sections corresponding to chs 1-6, 7-8, and 9-14. The first section consists mostly of vision reports framed by a call to repentance and a sign-act. The second section organizes several prophetic speeches within a narrative question and answer framework. The third unit contains two extended collections of oracles that focus upon Judah's distant future.

Chapters 9-14 stand out from the other two sections of the book in several ways. Unlike the first eight chapters, it contains no reference to the prophet or the temple building project, no dating formulas, and no other clear references to historical persons or events. It also takes on a more definitive eschatological tone employing the phrase "on that day" multiple times throughout the six chapters.

One of the most challenging issues of Zechariah is determining the relationship of chs 9-14 to the rest of the book. These chapters most likely belong to a historical setting other than the one found earlier in the book. While some scholars relate that context to a time later in the life of the prophet Zechariah, many suggest an entirely different author and audience for the material (→ sidebar The Historical Setting of Chs 9-14). As a result, commentators often treat chs 9-14 as a distinct literary unit apart from the rest of the book of Zechariah (e.g., Meyer and Meyer 1993). A few scholars see chs 9-14 connected more directly to the book of Malachi than the rest of Zechariah. The two major sections of chs 9-14 begin with a title that identifies them as "an oracle" (*massa'*) just like Malachi. Therefore Zech 9-11 and 12-14 along with Malachi are viewed as a tripartite unit that concludes the prophetic corpus (Petersen 1995, 1-3).

Yet, in its final canonical form, chs 1-8 and 9-14 have been placed side by side to create the book of Zechariah. This suggests that all fourteen chapters should be read in relation to one another regardless of the origins of the material. The book of Zechariah is, in fact, a well-structured literary unit. Chiastic structures and other literary devices create a sense of cohesion throughout all fourteen chapters while, at the same time, marking its individual units (see Dorsey 1999, 317-320 and Hill 2012, 110-112). Prominent terms, motifs, and themes recur throughout these units integrating them into a unified work. These include: the Lord's care for Judah and Jerusalem (2:5; 9:8; 10:3; 14:11), covenant renewal language (2:11; 8:8; 13:9), divine judgment upon the nations (1:18; 9:4; 14:6), conversion of the nations (2:11; 9:7; 8:20-23; 14:16-21), and a call for purity in the community of faith (3:4-7; 5:8; 7:9-10; 8:16-17; 13:1-6; 13:9; 14:20-21). For additional literary links see Childs 1979, 482-483, Stuhlmueller 1988, 113-114, and Boda 2004, 42-45, 410-411.

One significant unifying feature of the book is its apocalyptic character. The book of Zechariah exhibits certain elements found in Jewish and Christian apocalyptic literature, which flourished between 300 BC and AD 200. Elements of this kind of literature can be found scattered throughout the OT and NT in books like Isaiah, Ezekiel, Daniel, and Revelation. Apocalyptic literature's most prominent feature is its focus upon hope for a new world order that submits to the absolute rule of the Lord.

In Zechariah the visions of chs 1-6 reflect this kind of literature. They employ a throne scene, guiding angels, symbolic animals, and images of a renewed people of God. Chapters 7-8 also envision an idyllic age, which includes the Lord's return to Jerusalem, the restoration of a vibrant community life, and all nations worshiping the Lord. In chs 9-14 apocalyptic elements intensify with end-of-the-world wars, messianic figures, cataclysmic natural events, and worldwide submission to the kingship of the Lord. These and other features mark the book as a whole as apocalyptic.

Some scholars prefer to designate Zechariah as proto-apocalyptic though, because it does not employ some elements typically found in this literature at later times. By this designation they mean it stands alongside of certain chapters in Isaiah, Ezekiel, and other prophets as a link between classic prophecy and later apocalyptic literature. A major theological difference between these two kinds of prophecy in ancient Israel is that salvation comes within human history in the former, while it arrives beyond it in the latter (see Murphy 2012, 27-65).

D. The Text of Zechariah

Extant manuscripts of the Hebrew text of Zechariah provide only a few alternate readings. Likewise the Greek, Latin, and other versions seldom stray from the MT. Most instances of variant readings in the versions are easily explained as characteristic translation principles or misunderstandings typically found in those versions. Scrolls from the Dead Sea area add little to the study of the text since the evidence consists of only small fragments of both Hebrew and Greek texts. What little there is, however, essentially supports the received text of the Masoretes. Thus the MT upon which most modern English translations rely is considered very reliable (see Meyer and Meyer 1987, lxviii and Meyer and Meyer 1993, 50-51). Those variants that carry significance will be addressed in the commentary.

The reliability of the Hebrew text of Zechariah does not mean that translation is easy however. At times the Hebrew remains obscure, especially in chs 9-14, and a confident rendering is not possible. The NJPS inserts the note "the meaning of the Heb. uncertain" twelve times in Zechariah (1:8; 2:4; 3:9; 4:10, 12; 5:3; 10:1, 12; 11:3; 12:10; 13:7; and 14:6). In addition, this translation offers numerous emendations and revocalizations in order to make sense of the text. At one point, the note on 9:15-17 simply states, "The meaning of the rest of the chapter is uncertain."

E. Hermeneutical Issues

Three important issues of interpretation arise in Zechariah. These have to do with (1) how one interprets apocalyptic elements in the text, (2) how one relates chs 9-14 to the rest of the book, and (3) how one understands possible references to a Messiah.

Interpreting apocalyptic literature presents special challenges to the modern reader. The meaning of its unusual images and terminology is not easily deciphered. Yet being aware of the purpose of apocalyptic literature and the setting out of which it typically came aides the interpreter. In general, apocalyptic literature served to raise the hopes of oppressed peoples. It emerged in settings where harsh circumstances of life curbed expectations among God's people. Fantastic and otherworldly images provided a means for viewing reality from a heavenly rather than earthly perspective. Apocalyptic literature lifted the eyes of its audience away from the present evil era to an ideal age in which the Lord rules absolute.

The dire circumstances of late sixth and early fifth century BC Judah provided fertile ground for apocalyptic style visions. As noted previously, Jews of this era faced continued political and economic struggles while seeking to rebuild the temple in Jerusalem. Images of the Lord's grand scheme of salvation culminating around Jerusalem at the end of human history supply Zechariah's audience with the encouragement and motivation needed to continue working. The struggle to complete a monumental building and maintain a vital community of faith would prove worthwhile in light of God's ultimate purposes.

Whether chs 9-14 emerged out of this context or a later time of oppression remains an important debate for interpreting Zechariah. As noted in the discussion of the book's literary features above, the apocalyptic elements intensify in these chapters. The reason for this could be that the circumstances of its audience had grown more oppressive. Whether this occurred soon after the temple completion in 516 BC or centuries later is impossible to say. The obscurity of the historical references in these chapters allows for multiple options (→ sidebar The Historical Setting of Chs 9-14).

Regardless of its original setting, chs 9-14 stand in relation to chs 1-8 in their present canonical location. This literary connection indicates that interpreters should read these materials in relationship to one another. The ancient editor who placed these chapters together must have seen a connection between them, though the reason for this is not entirely clear to people today. Whether that was because they derive from a common author such as Zechariah the prophet cannot be definitively determined at this point in time. Nevertheless modern interpreters will do well to take a cue from the ancient compiler and look for ways that chs 1-8 and 9-14 interface with one another.

One way in which chs 1-8 and 9-14 relate is in their consistent projection of hope in a messianic age. How one interprets the messianic figure that occurs in relation to these passages constitutes another hermeneutical challenge for the interpreter. The first clear reference to this individual comes in Zechariah's vision of the high priest Joshua in ch 3. There the Lord promises, "I am going to bring my servant, the Branch" (3:8). In reference to this person the Lord projects that he "will remove the sin of this land in a single day" (3:9). Later in ch 9 Jerusalem's "king comes . . . riding on a donkey" proclaiming "peace to the nations" (9:9-10). A more cryptic reference to the Messiah may appear in ch 10 when the prophet projects that "from Judah will come the cornerstone," "the tent peg," "the battle bow," and "every ruler" (10:4). If these images represent the Messiah they convey the stability his reign will bring.

As the portrait of the Messiah in this book unfolds, it takes a surprising twist. Those to whom the Messiah comes reject his rule. A drama in ch 11 portrays the Lord's Messiah as a shepherd who is paid "thirty pieces of silver" and dismissed (11:12). Following this 12:10 alludes to this Messiah as being "the one they have pierced," while 13:7 describes him as being struck down and his sheep "scattered."

Centuries after Zechariah Christians identified the messianic figure portrayed in the book with Jesus Christ. Both Matthew and John associate Zech 9:9 with Jesus entering Jerusalem on Palm Sunday (Matt 21:5; John 12:15). The gospel writers also relate the rejected and wounded shepherd in Zech 11-13 to Jesus (Matt 26:31, 27:9-

10; Mark 14:27; and John 19:34-37). They saw the story of a rejected Messiah whose flock scatters after he is struck down paralleling the events of Jesus' life. With these quotations and allusions NT writers established a precedent for modern interpreters. A messianic reading of these passages in Zechariah can follow the same path taking by the gospel writers.

F. The Theology of Zechariah

The many messages and images of the book of Zechariah highlight one central theological truth: the presence of the Lord among his people transforms life. This forms the heart of Zechariah's motivation for rebuilding the temple. As the locus of God's special presence on earth, the temple represents God with his people in all his power and glory. When that takes place, God's people return home, God's covenant is renewed, God's laws are lived out, and God's blessings abound. All this foreshadows the ultimate hope of salvation in the new age of the Messiah.

The Lord coming to dwell among his people is the central promise of the book of Zechariah (1:3, 16; 2:5, 10-12; 8:3; 9:9, 14; 14:5). The Lord plans to "return to Zion and dwell in Jerusalem" (8:3). He assures Zechariah's audience, "I am coming and I will live among you" (2:10). This is why construction of the temple in Jerusalem is so vital. As the special dwelling of the Lord on earth it is the ultimate symbol of divine presence among people. Moreover, this building and those who serve in it are "symbolic of things to come" (3:8). They foreshadow the era toward which all human history is moving, the age of the Messiah. By constructing the temple Zechariah's audience was participating in God's grand scheme of salvation history. As a result, they could be certain that every resource needed would be supplied. Kingdom building is accomplished "'not by might, nor by power, but by my Spirit' says the LORD" (4:6).

Thus the book of Zechariah envisions the coming of the messianic age, its character and the process by which it will come about. The Lord announces, "I am going to bring my servant, the Branch" (3:8). He is "your king" who "comes to you, righteous and having salvation, gentle and riding on a donkey" (9:9). While his arrival is a time for great rejoicing, his kingdom does not come about without great struggle. The Messiah "will proclaim peace" (9:10), but only after he defeats the enemies of his kingdom who reside both within and without the covenant community.

The Lord is passionate about his people, "very jealous for Jerusalem and Zion" (1:14; 8:2). "Whoever touches you," the prophet says, "touches the apple of his eye" (2:8). But this passion moves the Lord to anger when people break covenant with him. The prophet reminds his audience that the Lord became "very angry" with their ancestors for ignoring his covenant guidelines (1:2-6). He "scattered them with a whirlwind among the nations" (7:14). In exile they experienced the covenant curses promised long ago in the law of Moses (1:6 and 7:13-14).

This same passion also moves the Lord to deal decisively with the enemies of his people. Zechariah tells his audience that even though God punishes them, he also intends to protect them. The Lord says, "Just as I had determined to bring disaster upon you . . . so now I have determined to do good again to Jerusalem and Judah" (8:14-15). As a result, the Lord moves forward like a divine warrior, sword in hand, determined to "defend my house against marauding forces" (9:8). He will make himself like "a wall of fire" around Jerusalem (2:5) and his people "like mighty men" who excel on the battlefield (10:5-7). One day he plans to gather all the nations to Jerusalem and then "go out and fight against" them (14:3). In the end, Judah's enemies will suffer utter defeat at the hand of the Lord.

The goal of divine punishment for covenant people as well as the destruction of their enemies is to restore them to genuine relationship with the Lord. God plans to "pour out on the house of David and the inhabitants of Jerusalem a spirit of grace and supplication" (12:10a). This is a spirit of repentance in which people will "mourn" and "grieve bitterly" over their spiritual condition (12:10b). In particular, they will grieve their rejection of God's Messiah, "the one they have pierced" (12:10), the one they "detested" (11:8) and paid an insulting wage of "thirty pieces of silver" (11:13).

In response to genuine repentance the Lord pledges renewal. He promises "a fountain will be opened . . . to cleanse them from sin and impurity" (13:1). He will "refine them like silver and test them like gold" until he can say of them "they are my people" (13:9). At that point the fortunes of God's people will be reversed. With Jerusalem secure and covenant renewed the Lord projects that his people will flock to the promised land where life will flourish. They will come from every direction to live in the holy city and worship the Lord. Remarkably, even people from other nations will become part of the worshiping community (2:11; 8:20-23; 14:16-21). According to the Lord's vision for the future, "many nations will be joined to the LORD in that day and will become my people" (2:11).

The beauty of this new community will be its complete consecration to the Lord. Everything and everyone in it will be set apart for the Lord's service. They will become an entirely sanctified community of worshipers. Even bells on horses will be inscribed with "Holy to the LORD" like the high priest's turban and the common cooking pot will be used for sacred purposes (14:20-21). The Lord will lay claim to the entire land as his "holy land" (2:12) and designate the place of his dwelling as "the Holy Mountain" (8:3). As a result, the Lord promises that "my towns will again overflow with prosperity" (1:17) and "the city streets will be filled with boys and girls playing there" (8:5). The richness of God's covenant blessings will once again flow to his people as God originally intended.

The Lord will do all this because he plans to "strengthen," "save," "restore," and "have compassion" on his people like an ideal shepherd (10:6). The Lord, in fact, can do all this because he remains sovereign over his world. He is "the LORD Almighty" (so designated 53 times), the God who displayed unmatched military prowess when he rescued his people from bondage in Egypt. He is "the Lord of all the earth" (4:14; 6:5) whose eyes range throughout the world (4:10) and whose attendants patrol all of creation (1:10, 11; 6:7). In the end, the Lord will be acknowledged as exclusive "king of all the earth" by all nations (14:9).

COMMENTARY

I. CHARACTER OF THE MESSIANIC AGE: ZECHARIAH 1:1—6:15

A. Call to Repentance (1:1-6)

BEHIND THE TEXT

The initial verse of the book sets Zechariah's first message within the time frame of Haggai's brief four-month ministry. **The eighth month of the second year of Darius** occurred between Haggai's second and third messages (cp. Hag 2:1; 2:10). Zechariah's audience had responded to Haggai's preaching and just begun rebuilding the Jerusalem temple despite numerous challenges both economically and politically (→ Hag 1:1-15; and Ezra 4). **The second year of Darius** refers to Nisan 519 to Adar 520 BC when Darius the Great finally solidified control over the Persian Empire (→ Introduction to Haggai: A. The Audience).

This passage does not refer to any geographical location. But Ezra 5:1 records Zechariah's ministry taking place in Jerusalem. Several references to Judah and Jerusalem in subsequent visions further confirm that this is the setting for this oracle as well (1:12, 14, 16, 17, etc.).

273

The speech recorded in this passage reflects several elements of the traditional penitential prayer in ancient Israel (see Pss 6, 32, 51; Ezra 9; Neh 1, 9; Dan 9). Such prayers frequently refer to former generations refusing to listen to the prophets. They speak of turning toward God and away from sin, while confirming God's justice in holding his people accountable. These kinds of prayers typically serve as an important first step in God's program of restoration (cp. Lev 26:40-42, Deut 30:1-10, and 1 Kgs 8:22-53; see Boda 2004, 174-176).

Within the context of prophetic literature Zechariah's speech can be classified as a summons to repentance. The first verse identifies the setting and speaker as well as the origins of the message (v 1). The prophetic speech (vv 2-6) begins with a motivation for repentance (v 2) before the prophet exhorts his audience to repent (v 3). Then further motivation is given through a lesson drawn from Israel's history (vv 4-6a). The passage concludes with what appears to be a response from the prophet's audience (v 6b).

IN THE TEXT

■ **I** The first verse of Zechariah establishes the historical setting for the beginning of the prophet's ministry. The **second year** of **Darius** I Hystaspes (r. 522 to 486 BC) marked the end of a tumultuous period when numerous rebellions throughout the empire had to be contained following Darius' succession. **The eighth month** corresponds to late October through early November on current calendars. It follows the intensely religious seventh month that included observance of the Feast of Trumpets, the Day of Atonement, and the Feast of Tabernacles (→ Behind the Text for Hag 2:1-9). Zechariah's message picks up on several themes in these holy days, which challenged people to recall their past and confess their sins as the cycle of the agricultural year drew to a close. This date also sets Zechariah's message within the time frame of Haggai's ministry (→ Behind the Text).

Zechariah is connected to the priestly family of **Iddo**. This was one of several clans that returned from Babylonian exile to Judah with Zerubbabel (see Neh 12:1-7; → Introduction to Zechariah: A. The Prophet). Though Zechariah eventually served as head of this important family (Neh 12:16), he is identified simply as **the prophet**, one called out to speak on behalf of God.

■ **2** Zechariah begins with the assertion, **the LORD was very angry with your ancestors** (v 2). The term **very angry** (*qāṣap*) expresses God's loving response toward those who break covenant with him. God allows covenant curses to fall upon his people so that they might return to him (see Deut 29:25-28 [24-27 HB]). The **ancestors** are not the distant generations from Israel's early history, but those from more recent history who have failed to give attention to the message of "earlier prophets" (→ v 4). Their disobedience to God resulted in the judgment of the Babylonian exile.

■ **3** A series of imperatives follows in vv 3-4. The invitation to **return** (v 3) is found frequently in prophetic speeches. The term **return** (*šûb*) conveys repentance, the idea of changing direction entirely, of completely reorienting life. This is not only a change of mind and practices, but also of relationship. The Lord urges his people to stop pursuing their self-centered ways and decide to reconnect with him (**return to me**).

The call here is for the renewal of their covenant relationship with God. When the people of Judah do so, the Lord promises, **I will return to you.** This promise is the primary motivation for repentance. The Lord's return to his people is Judah's best hope for receiving God's blessings and securing the future (→ 1:16 and 8:3).

Zechariah emphasizes the author of this message by repeating a messenger formula three times in v 3: (1) **this is what the Lord Almighty says,** (2) **declares the Lord Almighty,** and (3) **says the Lord Almighty.** The divine name **the Lord Almighty** (*YHWH ṣĕbā'ôt*) is the prophet's favorite designation for God throughout the book. The name emphasizes the superior power and sovereignty of Judah's God in the midst of a religiously pluralistic Persian world. Both Haggai and Malachi, other prophets of the restoration period, favor this name as well (→ Hag 1:2).

■ **4** In v 4, Zechariah warns his audience not to follow the example of their **ancestors,** who **would not listen or pay attention** to God's invitation through **earlier prophets.** This description of their **ancestors** fits those who lived during Israel's monarchy. So the **earlier prophets** would be pre-exilic prophets like Amos, Hosea, Isaiah, Jeremiah and Ezekiel.

Those prophets consistently called people to **turn from** their **evil ways** and **evil practices** (see Jer 18:11; 35:15; Ezek 14:6; 18:30; 33:11). Jeremiah and Ezekiel, who frequently employed these same phrases, maintained that such conduct came about because people turned away from the Lord and followed after other gods (e.g., see Jer 25:5-6).

The Hebrew terms for **listen** (*šema'*) and **pay attention** (*qāšab*) are nearly synonymous. They convey the idea of hearing something and acting upon it, obeying or heeding what is said. The combination of these terms emphasizes Israel's total lack of response to God.

■ **5-6a** The goal of Zechariah's message is to convince his audience to recommit themselves to a covenant relationship with God. In order to drive home this point, the prophet poses three rhetorical questions that underscore the impact of the exile. The first question, **where are your ancestors now?** (v 5a) reminds his listeners that they are either dead, still in exile, or struggling to recover from it. The second question, **Do they live forever?** (v 5b) confirms that they have forfeited the covenant promise of long life in the land. The third question, **did not my words and my decrees . . . overtake your ancestors?** (v 6a) affirms the fulfillment of God's warning concerning the curses of the covenant. The term **overtake** (*nāśag*) conveys an image of pursuing or hunting something until it is caught. The covenant curses of Deut 28 caught up with their ancestors.

■ **6b** The last part of v 6 is most likely the response of Zechariah's audience (see Boda 2004, 176-177), though some interpret it as referring to their ancestors (see NLT). Regardless of who spoke these words, they model what God desires to hear from those who have truly **repented** (*šûb*; → v 3). They express complete agreement with the Lord's judgment, **the LORD Almighty has done to us what our ways and practices deserve**. This statement acknowledges two things: (1) that they have sinned and (2) that God's punishment for their sin was fair.

FROM THE TEXT

The initial message of Zechariah sets the tone for the book. Like other prophets in ancient Israel Zechariah challenges his audience to look to the past in order to fully understand the present and move into the future. Two important ideas emerge from this message.

First, Zechariah reminds us that *the road to spiritual renewal begins with genuine repentance.* The prophet opens with a call to repentance before delivering messages that encourage people to build the temple. He knew that before God's people could restore the temple they must return to the Lord (v 3). Temple building was not just about laying one stone on top of another. More importantly it was about building a community that was living in covenant fellowship with God. The most pious endeavors, even building a temple, require complete surrender to God.

Second, *genuine repentance agrees with the Lord about sin.* Whether the words of repentence recorded in v 6 come from Zechariah's audience or their ancestors, they stand as a model of genuine repentance. They confess that God's assessment and handling of sin is right. Such a posture opens the way for fruitful service to God.

B. Visions about Rebuilding the Temple (1:7—6:8)

Overview

Through a series of eight visions Zechariah offers hope to people engaged in a daunting task for God. Construction of the Jerusalem temple was beyond the resources of the small struggling community in Judah. Yet, these visions affirm that this task will be accomplished within the lifetime of Zerubbabel.

The eight visions of 1:7—6:8 consist of paralleling couplets arranged in an overall chiasmic structure. Three groups of visions (2-3, 4-5, and 6-7) are framed by two corresponding visions (1 and 8). Visions six and seven recall ideas in visions two and three, while visions four and five serve as the fulcrum of the chiasm. The relationship of the visions can be seen in the following layout:

A Vision 1 (1:7-17)
   B Vision 2 (1:18-21)
   B Vision 3 (2:1-13)
      C Vision 4 (3:1-10)
      C' Vision 5 (4:1-14)
   B' Vision 6 (5:1-4)
   B' Vision 7 (5:5-11)
A' Vision 8 (6:1-8)

Thematically, the first and last visions focus upon God's control over the world. The second and third visions declare judgment upon enemies of God's people and God's plan to dwell in Zion. Visions four and five serve as a fulcrum to the series emphasizing God's provision and empowerment of Judah's leadership. The sixth and seventh visions recall visions two and three as they relate God's war on sin.

Thus, the visions confirm that the Lord (1) will exert his sovereignty over this world, (2) bring rest from enemies, (3) purify his people, and (4) supply resources to establish his kingdom on earth. These are the marks of the messianic age, which Zechariah invites his audience to participate in by building the temple.

Each of the visions follows the format of a vision report. This genre typically includes three elements: a description of what is seen, a dialogue with an angel, and a divine message based upon the things described in the vision.

I. First Vision: Four Horsemen (1:7-17)

BEHIND THE TEXT

Zechariah's vision begins with a dating formula that introduces the first vision as well as the entire series of visions. "The eleventh month . . . in the second year of Darius" indicates that these visions occurred within the early months of the Jerusalem temple building project (v 7). Haggai's ministry had come to an end in the ninth month on the day the foundation stone of the temple was laid (Hag 2:10-23). Work had begun on the temple only three months before that (Hag 1:15). Both of these events, as well as Zechariah's visions, took place precisely on "the twenty-fourth day" of their respective months (Hag 1:15, 2:10, and Zech 1:7), only a few days before new moon.

The second year of Darius I Hystaspes (r. 522-486 BC) saw the beginning of some stability and relative peace in the Persian Empire after the tumultuous first year of his reign (→ Introduction). Yet the Jews may have still felt anxiety over the Persian advance planned toward Egypt in the spring of that year.

Also that spring, on the first day of Nisan, the traditional New Year Akitu Festival would be celebrated in Babylon. Its rituals, including the recital of the creation myth Enuma Elish, would affirm the sovereignty of Mesopotamian gods over the world. Priests would legitimize the ruling monarch and proclaim destinies, which the gods had determined, for the empire in the coming year. Within such a context, Zechariah received visions that express the will of the Lord for the people of Judah in the following year and beyond.

Following an introduction to the vision (v 7), the prophet gives an initial description of what he sees (v 8) before a dialogue with an angel ensues (vv 9-10). A unique feature of this vision report is that a dialogue between characters within the vision is recounted (vv 11-12). This includes conversations between heavenly beings (v 11) and between God and an angel (v 12). Finally, the meaning of the vision is conveyed through a divine message (vv 13-17).

■ **7** The twenty-fourth day of the eleventh month . . . in the second year of Darius would be February 15, 519 BC in current calendars (v 7). This is about three months after Zechariah's first message in 1:1-6, exactly five months after work began on the Jerusalem temple in response to Haggai's preaching (Hag 1:14-15), and two months after a ceremony for laying the foundation stone of the temple took place (Hag 2:18). **Shebat** is the Babylonian name for **the eleventh month**. Its use reflects the continued influence of Babylonian culture upon the Jews, even though the exile along with the Babylonian Empire had ended nearly twenty years earlier. The identity of Zechariah as a **prophet** underscores his credibility as a spokesperson of the Lord who has received **the word of the LORD** in a vision.

■ **8** Zechariah describes his experience as that of having **a vision** (v 8). More literally the Hebrew simply says, *I saw* (*rā'iti*). This is technical terminology for Israel's prophets when they seek to relate the experience of receiving divine revelation (e.g., see Amos 9:1 and Hab 3:7). The prophet notes that the vision came **during the night.** This notation adds further mystery to the experience since night visions are typically viewed as especially ominous throughout the OT (Gen 46:2; Job 33:15-18; Dan 7:2).

Zechariah sees a secretive meeting of horsemen taking place **among myrtle trees in a ravine.** Commonly found throughout the land of Judah, **myrtle trees** are actually evergreen bushes that can grow as high as eight feet. Their branches were often used during the Feast of Tabernacles to construct booths in commemoration of the wilderness experience (Neh 8:15). Their thick foliage, along with their location in a **ravine**, provides an ideal place for clandestine meetings at night.

Within this setting **a man mounted on a red horse** encounters other riders. Though the text only mentions other **horses**, one may assume they are mounted with riders based on the conversation that takes place in v 11. The different colors of **horses** do not carry any special symbolism except to represent variety among the horsemen. **Red** might be better understood as deep reddish brown or chestnut color, while **brown** could convey a lighter brown, almost pinkish color. The number of four horses, however, does seem significant. This likely signifies full coverage of the earth in all directions of the compass.

■ **9** A dialogue between the prophet and an angel in vv 9-10 clarifies details of the vision. The prophet initiates the conversation with a being he describes as **the angel who was talking with me** (v 9). This **angel** appears to be someone other than the "man mounted on a red horse" in v 8, though both enter into dialogue with the prophet. He is the prophet's companion who will reappear later in the following visions to help interpret their meanings (1:19; 2:3; 4:1,4; 5:5,10; 6:4).

Zechariah asks a question that he will repeat in three other visions (1:19; 4:4; 6:4). He wants to know, **What are these, my lord?** He is probing for an explanation of the meaning of the vision. The angel promises, **I will show you what they are.**

Literally, he says, *I will cause you to see* (causative form of *rā'â*). In other words, the angel will enable the prophet to grasp the divine meaning behind this scene.

■ **10** **The man standing among the myrtle trees,** that is the "man mounted on a red horse" in v 8, actually answers the question of the prophet rather than "the angel" (v 10). He explains that the group of horsemen has been on a divine mission. The Lord commissioned them **to go throughout the earth.** The term **go throughout** (causative form of *hālak*) conveys the idea of moving back and forth, suggesting intense scrutiny. Thus several English translations render the term with "patrol" (NRSV, NASB, ESV; notice also KJV "walk to and fro"). The description of horsemen moving across the landscape evokes military images familiar during the Persian period. Persian armies employed cavalries and chariot forces extensively with great effectiveness. They also developed a highly efficient system of communication throughout the empire by means of relay horses.

■ **11** At this point, a dialogue within the vision is described. The riders report that they have **found the whole world at rest and in peace** (v 11). The phrase **at rest and in peace** connotes an image of a settled state. Literally, one might translate *sitting down and quiet*. This reflects the circumstances of the Persian Empire in "the second year of Darius" (v 7). According to the Behistun Inscription, Darius subdued nineteen rebellions that broke out at his succession. These major threats to the stability of the empire had been extinguished by the end of his first year.

The riders give their reconnaissance report to the **man standing among the myrtle trees,** that is the "man mounted on a red horse" in v 8. At this point, he is further described as **the angel of the LORD.** Thus, two angels are identified in this vision: the one who rides a red horse and the one who acts as Zechariah's interpreter. Both serve as "messengers" of the Lord to Zechariah and his people, which is the fundamental task of an **angel** (*mal'ak*), as their name suggests.

Angels in the Old Testament

Angels appear frequently throughout the Bible. They are heavenly beings whose primary role is to convey a message to humans from the divine world. Hence, the Hebrew term most often used to designate them is *mal'āk*, which fundamentally means "messenger." In addition to this role, angels execute the judgment of God (Ps 78:49), give protection to his people (Ps 91:11-12), and offer praise to God (Ps 148:2).

A special type of angel is the interpreting angel, like the one found in Zechariah's visions of chs 1-6. Throughout these visions Zechariah identifies this being as "the angel who was speaking with me" (1:9, 13, 14, 19; 2:3; 5:5, 10; 6:4). This kind of angel acts as a companion to the human observing the vision and engages in conversation in order to draw out the meaning of the vision. Interpreting angels appear elsewhere in the OT in the visions of Ezekiel 40-48 and Daniel 7-12. Such creatures are regular features of extra-canonical apocalyptic literature as well. In the NT an interpreting angel accompanies the apostle John during his visions recounted in the Revelation.

■ **12** The report of the horsemen is not good news to the people of Judah. The stabilization of the Persian Empire means that hopes for Judah's independence and reestablishment of the Davidic monarchy have been delayed. They will remain under domination of a foreign state for a while longer.

So the man riding the red horse, who is once again called **the angel of the LORD**, abruptly turns to complain to God (v 12). He articulates the question burning within the hearts of many in Zechariah's audience, **how long will you withhold mercy from Jerusalem?** The question, **how long**, is not about God's ability to act. It is about God's timing. **How long** is a frequent question of those lamenting their lot in life and waiting for God to act (see Ps 79:5; 80:4 [5 HB]; 94:3).

This question implies that the compassionate care of the Lord has been absent from Judah for an extended period. To **withhold mercy** is another way of saying that the Lord is **angry** with his people (see 1:2). **Mercy** (*rāḥam*) can be translated "compassion" and refers to the unmerited favor that a superior confers on an inferior. Though underserved, it is part of the blessing promised to those who keep covenant with the Lord (see Deut 13:17-18 [18-19 HB]; Exod 34:7).

The reference to **seventy years** symbolizes a period of extended punishment, not a precise calculation of years. The actual time from the destruction of Jerusalem in 586 BC to this vision in 519 BC is sixty-seven years. In ch 7 Zechariah once again refers to **seventy years** as the time from the destruction of the temple till the time of an oracle given in 518 BC, which is sixty-eight years. This symbolic use of **seventy years** is found elsewhere in the Bible (see Jer 25:11-12 and 29:10; see also Dan 9:2 and 2 Chr 36:21; Isa 23:15-17). It is worth noting, however, that the time from the destruction of the temple in 586 BC to the dedication of the rebuilt temple in 516 BC was almost exactly 70 years.

■ **13** The Lord responds with words that are **kind** (*ṭôb*) or "good" to the ears of God's people and **comforting** (*niḥûm*) or "consoling" to them (cp. Isa 40:1). The content of the Lord's **comforting words** in this vision will be conveyed in the divine message given in vv 14-17. These words are spoken **to the angel who talked with** Zechariah. This is the interpreting angel rather than the one who articulated the question. God speaks to the angel so that he might communicate the divine message to Zechariah.

■ **14-15** In vv 14-17, the interpreting angel relates the Lord's message to Zechariah with the command to **proclaim** it to the people, like a herald announcing a king's decree (vv 14, 17). The message begins with strong expressions of divine emotion: God is **very jealous for Jerusalem and Zion** (v 14) and **very angry with the nations** (v 15). The text literally reads, *I am very jealous (with) a great jealousy . . . and (with) a great anger I am angry*. Throughout the OT, the term **jealous** (*qānā'*) conveys God's intensely passionate protective love for his people (see Exod 20:5, 34:14; Joel 2:18; Nah 1:2; also see Zech 8:2). Some scholars suggest "zealous" as a possible translation for this word.

Though **Jerusalem and Zion** often function as synonyms, here they designate the holy city more broadly and the temple site in particular within it. They are the objects of God's passionate concern. By contrast, the Lord's intense anger is focused upon **the nations that feel secure** (v 15). These are the many people groups that constituted the vast Persian Empire of the time. As v 11 indicates, peoples of the empire had come to **feel secure** with the "rest and ... peace" that came over the land following Darius' successful ascendance to the throne. The term translated **feel secure** (*šā'an*) sometimes connotes an inappropriate self-reliance or arrogance (Amos 6:1; Isa 32:9, 11; Ps 123:4) and probably does so here.

The Lord clarifies the reason for his intense anger against the Persian world. **They went too far with the punishment** of Judah (v 15). The Lord in his anger sent the nations to punish his people (see e.g., Jer 1:15-16), but they went too far; their ruthless treatment of Judah exceeded what God had in mind. This likely refers to the Babylonian's ruthless destruction of Jerusalem, its temple, and its people in 586 BC (2 Kgs 25).

■ **16** God's message of comfort and hope to Judah conveys his commitment to **return to Jerusalem with mercy** (v 16). Though in Zech 1:3, the Lord's return to his people is connected to the people's **return** to God, here there are no conditions. God's return is an act of **mercy** (*rāḥam*) extended to his people. God's unearned favor will be expressed through his involvement in rebuilding the temple. **My house will be rebuilt** is a solemn promise from God. The promise also includes rebuilding the city of Jerusalem (see 2:1-13).

■ **17** The message attached to the first vision ends with the promise of **prosperity** in the land of Judah, **comfort** for **Zion**, and the election of **Jerusalem**. The Lord claims the towns of Judah as his towns (**my towns**) and promises they will **overflow** (*pûṣ*) **with prosperity** (*ṭôb*; goodness), like springs of water bubbling over (cp. Prov 5:16). Evidence of divine **prosperity** would include an abundance of food, animals, and people in the land (see Deut 28:1-14).

The **comfort** promised for **Zion** (the temple mount) will come through the Lord's decision to **choose Jerusalem** once **again** as the city of his dwelling. The term **again** (*'ôd*) punctuates this final verse four times in the Hebrew text in order to highlight a sense of renewal. The people of Judah likely regarded the Babylonian destruction of the city as a sign that God had abandoned the city. But in this message God assures them that the city still belongs to him and will continue to be a favored place in this world. Such words reaffirm God's covenant with David, which included the selection of Jerusalem as God's special dwelling place (1 Kgs 11:13, 32, 36; 14:21; Ps 132:13).

FROM THE TEXT

The first of Zechariah's eight visions establishes the Lord's intention to build his kingdom in this world. Like the pronouncement of divine destinies at the spring Akitu festival in Babylon, the prophetic word in this vision proclaims Judah's destiny for the coming year and beyond. The people of God will build the Lord's temple in Jerusalem (v 16).

The Lord's kingdom will advance even in the midst of opposition from the world. The horsemen in the vision report a world that is "at rest and in peace," confident in its own resources and accomplishments (v 11). But this self-sufficient and self-reliant world of the Persians is disconnected from God and even opposes God's plans and purposes.

The vision, however, offers comfort to God's people who feel anxious and despondent in such a world. God does not abandon his people, neither in the past nor today. God is passionate about those he loves and intentionally chooses to dwell among them. Just as God chose to dwell in the Jerusalem temple in the past, he chooses to dwell in those who have become "a holy temple in the Lord" today (see Eph 2:21-22).

This destiny for God's people emerges from the heart of a passionately loving God. In this vision we find a God who speaks "kind and comforting words" (v 13). He is "very jealous" for his people as well as "very angry with the nations" (vv 14-15). God returns to Jerusalem "with mercy" (v 16) and brings "comfort" and "prosperity" to it (v 17). This is the sort of God whose "compassions never fail" (Lam 3:22) and remains the same today as he was in Zechariah's day.

2. Second Vision: Four Horns (1:18-21 [2:1-4 HB])

BEHIND THE TEXT

Zechariah's second vision builds upon the first. It describes some of the "comfort" (1:17) that the Lord promised to Judah. Those nations with which the Lord was "very angry" (v 15) will be judged. In this vision Zechariah sees these nations as four horns that are destroyed by four craftsmen.

Two common images from the biblical world form the background for this vision: horns and craftsmen. Because horns on animals convey the impression of prowess and strength, they frequently served as symbols of status and power. The Bible picks up on this imagery and frequently communicates the military might of a person or nation with the symbol of a horn (Deut 33:17; I Sam 2:1, 10; Dan 7:24; 4:21-22 [18-19 HB]). Even the Lord is said to be "the horn of my salvation, my stronghold" (Ps 18:2 [3 HB]). Ancient artists also depicted both kings and gods wearing headpieces containing horns.

Various kinds of craftsmen were part of daily life in the ancient world. Some persons possessed skills in working stone and wood, while others had abilities to craft items from metal, leather, gems, and cloth. Archaeologists have discovered that various craftsmen formed guilds and tended to live in the same section of a city or in a particular village. These kinds of skilled workmen would have been employed in the construction of the Jerusalem temple.

Some interpreters view 1:18-21 [2:1-4 HB] as part of the vision in 1:7-17. This reduces the total number of visions to seven and allows for a chiastic structure that highlights 4:1-14 as its central vision (Dorsey 318 n.5 and 37.2). Most commentators, however, see 1:7-17 and 1:18-21 [2:1-4 HB] as two separate visions. The introductory phrase "Then I looked up" in v 18 [2:1 HB] signals a new vision several other times in chs 1-6. Also, the Hebrew Bible indicates vv 18-21 [2:1-4 HB] represent a distinct vision since it begins an entirely new chapter with these verses.

This vision contains typical elements of the vision report. But there are two cycles of these elements since two things are seen. The report begins with a description of what the prophet sees (v 18 [2:1 HB]). This is followed by the prophet's request for clarification (v 19*a* [2:2*a* HB]) and the angel's explanation (v 19*b* [2:2*b* HB]). Then the prophet sees a second item (v 20 [2:3 HB]). A request for clarification once again follows (v 21*a* [2:4*a* HB]) and the angel provides such to complete the report and convey the meaning of the vision (v 21*b* [2:4*b* HB]).

IN THE TEXT

■ **18-19 [2:1-2 HB]** The vision report begins with the appearance of **four horns** before the prophet. Based on the context of the rest of the vision, these are animal horns. But there is no indication they were attached to an animal. The prophet asks for the meaning of the horns or their identity by simply asking, **what are these?** (v 19 [2:2 HB]; see also 1:9; 4:4; 6:4).

The angel explains that the horns represent the nations that **scattered Judah, Israel, and Jerusalem.** The word **scattered** (*zārâ*) is an agricultural term that refers to planting seeds or separating grain from chaff. Jeremiah and Ezekiel used this term to describe the exile of Abraham's descendants from their land (see Jer 9:16 [15 HB]; 13:24; 18:17; and Ezek 5:2, 10, 12; 6:8). Assyria deported the population of the northern kingdom Israel in the eighth century BC and Babylon did the same to the people of Judah at the beginning of the sixth century BC. The **four horns** symbolize these nations and others who supported them. The number **four** may be a symbolic number signifying totality, indicating all the nations involved in the exile of Israel and Judah.

Some interpreters relate the **four horns** of this vision with the images of four kingdoms in Dan 2 and 7. They suggest that the **four horns** represent Babylonia, Persia, Greece and Rome, or some other combination of empires that Dan 2 and 7 evoke. Such interpretation pushes the meaning of the vision far beyond the time of Zechariah and may read more into the text than is intended (see Edlin 2009, 181).

■ **20 [2:3]** Following the explanation of the angel, the prophet sees **four craftsmen** in his vision (v 20 [2:3 HB]). The term **craftsmen** designates persons of special skill in working with a variety of materials. This might include metalworkers, stonemasons, or any of a number of skilled laborers (→ Behind the Text). The reason there are **four** craftsmen may be so that they match the number of horns.

■ **21 [2:4]** Zechariah does not inquire about the identity of the craftsmen. He simply asks about their mission, **what are these coming to do?** (v 21 [2:4 HB]). The angel explains that **the craftsmen have come to terrify . . . and to throw down these horns.** The term **terrify** (*ḥārad*) fundamentally means to cause trembling or anxiety. The term **throw down** (*yādâ*) is an intensive form of a word that essentially means to cast something aside. Their mission is to destroy the horns, the nations that scattered the people of God.

Who the **craftsmen** represent in this vision is difficult to determine. Since their role is to bring down the nations that humiliated Judah, one might suggest that the **craftsmen** are the Persians. If this is accurate, then the number **four** may represent the multicultural nature of that empire, as reliefs at Persepolis suggest. Otherwise the craftsmen might simply be artisans working on the temple whose work reverses the destruction caused by the horns. Regardless of who the craftsmen might signify, the message seems to be clear. The Lord comforts the humiliated people of Judah with the promise that he will judge their enemies who scattered them from their land.

FROM THE TEXT

The second vision of Zechariah affirms that *God is the sovereign judge of all nations and will deal with the enemies of his people.* The Lord announces that those who attempt to destroy Judah, "the horns," will be brought to judgment by others that God chooses, "the craftsmen" (v 21 [2:4 HB]). All nations are accountable to God. They will be judged on the basis of their treatment of other nations in the world, especially how they treat God's people. The latter chapters of Zechariah will envision fulfillment of this promise in even greater detail (see chs 9, 12, and 14).

This message fulfills a promise of covenant blessing and becomes a message in which believers today can find comfort. For those who live faithfully in covenant relationship with God Deut 28:7 promises, "The LORD will grant that the enemies who rise up against you will be defeated before you." Someday all of God's faithful servants will be able to praise the Lord with the psalmist and declare, "I am saved from my enemies" (Ps 18:3).

3. Third Vision: Man with Measuring Line (2:1-13 [2:5-17 HB])

BEHIND THE TEXT

The strategy of wall building in the ancient world lies behind the point of Zechariah's third vision. Walls around cities signified security and prosperity as well as self-sufficiency and community strength. Unprotected cities were often the target of attacks by bandits and organized armies in the ancient times. So people involved in building the temple in Jerusalem would have likely raised questions about the security of the temple and the city. Though some of Jerusalem's walls remained after the destruction of 586 BC, they continued in disrepair until the time of Nehemiah, several generations after Zechariah (Neh 1:3; 2:11-14).

Some commentators identify 2:1-5 [2:6-9 HB] as a report of a third vision and then treat 2:6-13 [2:10-17 HB] as separate prophetic speeches by Zechariah (see Peterson 1984, 174 and Clark and Hatton, 2002, 107). Thus, the prophetic speeches would function as a sort of interlude within the series of vision reports.

As such, they highlight features in the first three visions providing a summary of key points made in them.

Other scholars, however, sense that the interrelationships between the prophetic oracles and the report warrant treating 2:1-13 [2:5-17 HB] as a complete unit (see McComiskey 1998, 1057). The oracles flow out of the vision experience. The primary message of the vision is that the Lord will secure Jerusalem. Thus the oracles invite people still in exile to return to the city because it is safe for habitation.

This vision report is heavily weighted with prophetic oracle. It begins in typical fashion with an identification of what the prophet sees (v 1 [5 HB]) before dialogue ensues between the prophet and a being in the vision (v 2 [6 HB]). Then an angel explains the meaning of the vision by means of a prophetic message (vv 3-13 [7-17 HB]). The prophetic speech begins with identification of the heavenly speaker (v 3 [7 HB]). Then the speech itself divides into three components: (1) a proclamation regarding Jerusalem's security (vv 4-5 [8-9 HB]), (2) an invitation for exiles to return to Jerusalem (vv 6-9 [10-11 HB]), and (3) a hymn of praise for the renewal of Jerusalem (vv 10-13 [12-17 HB]).

IN THE TEXT

■ **1 [5 HB]** The phrase **then I looked up** (v 1 [5 HB]) signals a new vision (see 1:18; 5:9; 6:1). This time Zechariah sees **a man with a measuring line in his hand**. A **measuring line** is a construction tool used to layout buildings and streets in straight lines as well as to mark lengths. Ezekiel 40-42 also envisioned a man measuring the various components of the temple complex (see also Jer 31:38-39).

■ **2 [6 HB]** As is typical in these visions, Zechariah asks a question in order to flesh out the meaning of the vision. But this time the question is addressed to the man in the vision and not to the interpreting angel. The man explains that he is going **to measure Jerusalem to find out how wide and how long it is** (v 2 [6 HB]). This is the task of a builder preparing for or involved in construction as well as of a surveyor identifying land to be inherited. The concern here is not only with the temple area, but also with the dimensions of the entire city of **Jerusalem**.

■ **3 [7 HB]** The rest of the vision deals with a conversation between two angels. Zechariah's companion throughout the vision experience, whom he designates **the angel who was speaking to me**, encounters another heavenly being he calls **another angel** (v 3 [7 HB]). Through their conversation, the angels relay the meaning of the vision and the Lord's message for his people.

■ **4 [8 HB]** The angel who has just arrived instructs Zechariah's interpreting angel to **run, tell that young man** a message from the Lord (v 4 [8 HB]). **That young man** is most likely "the man with the measuring line" since the intent of the angel's message is to stop the man from measuring Jerusalem. He does not need to layout plans for city walls because they will not be necessary. The urgency of this message is conveyed through the double imperatives **run** and **tell**. The message is clear. **Jerusalem** will become a safe place filled with a bustling population. It will be like a rural village, whose inhabitants spread out so far it will be as if it is **without walls**. There will be **a great number of people and animals in it**. Jeremiah and other prophets projected a similar picture of Jerusalem in the future (Jer 33:10-13; Isa 49:18-20). Such a portrait implies economic and political prosperity.

■ **5 [9 HB]** There is no need for a city wall because the Lord himself will be **a wall of fire** (literally, *I, I will be for you a wall of fire*) around the city (v 5 [9 HB]). This evokes images of the Exodus experience when the Lord guided and protected his people with a pillar of fire (Exod 13:21-22, 14:19-20).

Moreover, the Lord himself will be **its glory within**, filling the city with his presence. **Glory** (*kābôd*) is the weighty manifestation of God's presence. It also filled the tabernacle (Exod 40:34-35), Solomon's temple (1 Kgs 8:11), and the new temple in Ezekiel (Ezek 43:5).

■ **6-7 [10-11 HB]** At this point the oracle turns to address those Jews who live outside of Judah. There are still many who are left in **the land of the north** (v 6 [10 HB]) and the Lord invites them to come home to **Zion** or the city of Jerusalem (v 7 [11 HB]).

The repeated imperatives, **come, come, flee, come, escape** throughout vv 6-7 [10-11 HB] convey the urgency of this call. **Come** translates the Hebrew term *hoy*, which is often rendered "woe" to convey feelings of utter ruin. Here the term has a positive connotation evoking emotion and excitement. The term **flee** (*nûs*) denotes a quick exit, an immediate response to God's urgent call. The term **escape** (*mālaṭ*) connotes the idea of slipping away from a dangerous situation. The implication is that the place where they live is risky and unsafe, most likely for their spiritual health.

The land of the north (v 6 [10 HB]) from which people are urged to escape is **Babylon**, the land of exile (v 7 [11 HB]; see Jer 1:15; 6:1; 22, etc.). The designation **Daughter Babylon** might intend to convey the attractiveness of Babylon. Jews who opted to remain in Babylon likely thought of it as a good place to live because of its robust economy (see NJPS, "fair Babylon").

The One who calls his people to come home is the God who **scattered** them **to the four winds of heavens** (see 1:21 [2:4 HB]), that is, throughout the world. The Babylonian exile earlier in the century displaced the survivors of Judah to various places in the ancient Middle East, including into Egypt (see Jer 40:11-12; 43:7).

■ **8-9 [12-13 HB]** The Lord now gives the motivation for accepting his invitation. The primary reason is that the **nations that have plundered** Judah (v 8 [12 HB]) will soon be humiliated by **their slaves** who plunder them (v 9 [13 HB]). The image of those conquered and made captives (**slaves**) plundering their oppressors was a sign of dramatic reversal in the ancient world, even political chaos. It recalls Israel's Exodus experience when they took goods from the Egyptians as they left (Exod 12:36; see also Ezek 39:10; Zech 14:14). The **nations that have plundered** refer to Babylonians and other people groups responsible for Judah's exile (see 1:18-21).

The phrase **after the Glorious One has sent me against the nations** is difficult (v 8 [12 HB]; see Clark and Hatton 2002, 110-111 and Klein 2008, 119-122 for different options for translation). The NIV suggests that the Lord is **the Glorious One** who **has sent** the prophet to speak words of judgment **against the nations** (cp. NJPS, MSG). Other translations, however, indicate that **me** refers to someone other than the prophet, perhaps a messianic or heavenly being (cp. NASB, HCSB).

Regardless of how v 8 might be understood, the key idea of the Lord's message at this point is that he will deal decisively with Judah's enemies (**raise my hand against them**) because of a deep personal connection to his people (v 9). The phrase, **whoever touches you touches the apple of his eye** (v 8), plays off of a similar expression of God's care for his people in Deut 32:10. **The apple of his eye** is literally the gate or pupil of the eye, the most sensitive and significant part of the eyeball. The Lord regards the damage done to his people by their enemies as an attack on himself.

This part of the message ends with Zechariah expressing confidence in the fulfillment of God's word of judgment. He is also certain that when the Lord fulfills his word, the people will acknowledge him as a prophet **sent** by the **LORD Almighty** (v 9 [13 HB]; see Deut 18:21-22).

■ **10-11 [14-15 HB]** The final portion of the divine speech shifts attention to God's coming. Verses 10-12 [14-16 HB]) follow the typical pattern of a hymn. A call to praise (v 10a [14a HB]) is followed by reasons for praise (vv 10b-12 [14b-16 HB]). The imperatives **shout and be glad** exhort God's people to enter into exuberant and joyful worship of the Lord (v 10 [14 HB]).

Those addressed are called **Daughter of Zion**, a term that reflects God's special love for people currently living in Jerusalem as well as in exile. The reason for joy is that the Lord is **coming** to Jerusalem and **will live among** his people (v 10 [14 HB]). To **live among you** implies the glory of God filling the temple (cp. v 5 [9 HB]). The Lord's coming to Jerusalem will prompt the nations to **be joined with the LORD** in Jerusalem (v 11 [15 HB]). They will also become **my people**, which implies the nations have entered into covenant relationship with God just like Israel.

That day alludes to the Day of the Lord. In the prophets, that day is often eschatological, the final day of both God's judgment of his enemies and the salvation of those who have a covenant relationship with him (→ Behind the Text at 12:1-13:9). In this oracle God welcomes his scattered people into his house along with the nations who also have become the Lord's people (cp. 14:16). When these remarkable things take place, Zechariah will once again be validated as a prophet **sent** by the Lord (see v 9 [13 HB].

■ **12 [16 HB]** In the next verse the prophet announces another reason for joy: the Lord plans to claim **Judah** as his **portion in the holy land** and to **choose Jerusalem** as the city of his dwelling (v 12 [16 HB]; cp. 1:16-17). The vision portrayed a man with the measuring line laying out boundaries for lands to be inherited (→ v 2 [6 HB]). Now the Lord claims that area, the entire land of Judah, as his inheritance (**portion**). It is reserved entirely for God (cp. 14:20-21).

The text further locates the boundaries of Judah in **the holy land** ('*adamat haqodes*). This is the only place in the Hebrew Bible that this term appears. The reference is most likely to the land promised to Abraham and his descendants (Gen 12:1-3), which included the land of Judah in the south and the land of Israel in the north. Together this area is called **the holy land** because God's dwelling place is located within its boundaries. This term seems to expand upon the frequently used term "holy mountain" (*har qodesh*; Pss 2:6; 15:1; Isa 27:13), referring to the Temple Mount set apart exclusively for God's purposes.

■ **13 [17 HB]** The prophet's announcement of God's coming ends with a call extended to all mankind to **be still before the** LORD (v 13 [17 HB]). The prophet describes the Lord's coming from his **holy dwelling** like a mighty warrior awaking from sleep and stirring into action. The **holy dwelling** most likely refers to God's heavenly abode (see Deut 26:15). The call to **be still** is a call to remain silent out of respect and awe, because the stirring of the Lord from heaven is about to have significant impact on all who dwell on earth.

FROM THE TEXT

The third vision of Zechariah reaffirms the messages of the two previous visions and expands upon them. In particular it answers an important question about the advisability of building a temple in a city without walls. The answer to that question is that the Lord will be "a wall of fire around it" (v 5 [9 HB]).

Security for the people of God comes from the presence of God among them. In this vision God promises not only to protect Jerusalem from enemies, he also promises to fill the city with his presence (v 5 [9 HB]). People might desire to build walls for protection. But these may be more a sign of self-sufficiency and self-reliance. The people of God can trust that wherever God is, they are secure.

As a result, *the place God occupies becomes a welcoming place for all peoples.* In this vision God announces that one day "many nations will be joined with the LORD" and "become my people" (v 11 [15 HB]). This is the hope to which God's people can lay hold, a time when there will be no walls, no war, no division, no conflict, no domination, and no exploitation. Someday there will be no claims of national, ethnic, or religious superiority. The kind of community Paul imagined will finally come about where "there is neither Jew nor Gentile, neither slave nor free, nor is there male and female, for you are all one in Christ Jesus" (Gal 3:28).

4. Fourth Vision: New Garments for Joshua (3:1-10)

BEHIND THE TEXT

The fourth vision focuses on the purification of Joshua the high priest. As head of the priesthood, he oversaw the spiritual life of the Jewish community and filled a prominent leadership role alongside the governor Zerubbabel (Hag 2:2; → Introduction to Haggai: A. The Audience). During the rebuilding of the temple his role likely expanded considerably. He undoubtedly found himself in charge of fundraising as well as general oversight of the entire construction project.

In order to lead the community spiritually, priests needed to remain pure. Exodus 29 describes various rituals required for the consecration of priests for their service. To attempt to lead worship without being properly consecrated resulted in death (Lev 10:1-11). A sense of the Lord's holy otherness demanded cleanliness and separation from defilement. Thus the Lord directed priests as well as the entire community to "be holy, because I am holy" (Lev 11:44, 19:2, 20:8, 26).

The focus of this vision upon Judah's spiritual leader connects it to the next vision, which focuses upon Judah's political leader Zerubbabel. Together visions four and five form a couplet that stands at the center of the chiastic structure of the eight visions (→ Overview of 1:7-6:8). As the center of this collection they emphasize the significance of God inspired leaders in the community of faith.

This vision departs from the typical vision report genre used previously. It includes no questions from Zechariah that lead to a dialogue explaining the meaning of the vision. Rather, Zechariah describes a scene that includes dialogue between members of the heavenly courts (vv 1-5). Then an angel relays a divine message that reveals the vision's meaning (vv 6-10).

IN THE TEXT

■ 1 The vision report begins with an introduction of **Joshua the high priest, the angel of the** LORD, and **Satan** (v 1). The scene depicted reflects a legal setting. **Joshua** is **standing before the angel of the** LORD as if in a courtroom. **Joshua** is the defendant, **Satan** the prosecutor, and **the angel of the** LORD represents the Lord who functions as judge.

The text identifies **Joshua** as **the high priest,** the leader of the priesthood in Judah. As **high priest,** he was not only the spiritual leader, but his influence also extended into the political and cultural life of the people. **The angel of the** LORD in this vision may be the interpreting angel who accompanies Zechariah throughout the vision experience in chs 1-6. But this is unclear since the typical identification of that angel, "the angel who spoke with me," is not used in this vision. **The angel** is the principal actor in this vision. It gives orders to other heavenly beings (v 4*a*), explains the meaning of actions in the vision (v 4*b*), oversees the investiture of Joshua (v 5), and speaks on behalf of the Lord (v 6).

Satan serves as a prosecutor whose role is **to accuse** Joshua of some misdeed. The content of his accusation is not specified. But based on what unfolds in the rest of the vision one might assume that he accuses Joshua of being unfit to carry out his role as spiritual leader in Judah. Some commentators link this accusation with a list of iniquities of the priests in Lam 4:11-13 that provoked God to destroy Jerusalem.

Satan in the Bible

Many scholars believe that the being called **Satan** in this vision may not be the same personage known by that name in the NT. The Hebrew word *śāṭān* means "adversary" and is used in reference to humans (2 Sam 19:22; 1 Kgs 5:4; 11:14, 23, 25; Pss 71:13; 109:6, 20, 29) as well as non-humans. The angel of the

Lord who confronted Balaam, for example, literally "stood in the road as an adversary to him" (Num 22:22, 32). Here, as well as in Job 1:6, the term *śāṭān* occurs with a definite article, which indicates it is not a proper name but rather a label for a type of individual, "the adversary". Hebrew rarely attaches definite articles to proper names.

In both Zechariah and Job, *haśśāṭān* stands among the council of angels in heaven. He levels accusations against persons who are, in a sense, on trial. A person with a similar type of role functioned in Old Babylonian courts, the *rabisu* official who was responsible for preliminary examination of defendants (van der Toorn 2001, 682-83). This same practice may be reflected in Ps 109:6 when the psalmist prays that his enemy will have "an accuser stand at his right hand" and question him.

By NT times, the supernatural being who opposes God is known as Satan (*satanas*) as well as the devil (*ho diabolos*). Jesus calls his tempter in the wilderness Satan though the narrative in Matthew calls him the devil (Matt 4:10). Over thirty times NT writers designate the major adversary to God and his kingdom as Satan.

In the OT, the noun "Satan" may be understood as a proper name in 1 Chr 21:1. There it appears with no definite article. The text reads, "Satan rose up against Israel." But one could also translate "an adversary rose up against Israel." The parallel passage in 2 Sam 24:1 reads, "the anger of the LORD increased against Israel."

■ **2** The Lord speaks to Satan, most likely through the angel, who relays all other words from the Lord. He strongly reprimands Satan with a double **rebuke** because God has decidedly **chosen Jerusalem** (v 2). This is the third time God refers to his choosing Jerusalem in the vision series (see 1:17 and 2:12). The emphasis on the divine choice of Jerusalem in the context of God's rebuke of Satan suggests the vital role Joshua is destined to play in restoring the city.

Joshua is also divinely chosen, for the Lord rhetorically asks, "**Is not this man a burning stick snatched from the fire?**" This question may imply that pagan influences had corrupted Joshua in some way. It is also possible that the question implies the divine rescue of Joshua from death as a young man when Jerusalem fell and throughout his exile in Babylon. His grandfather Seraiah and other priests did not fare so well (see 2 Kgs 25:18-21). In Amos 4:11, the prophet uses a similar expression to describe those whom God spared from catastrophic destruction. In either case, Joshua has been selected for a significant role in the community.

■ **3** Though Joshua has been chosen and rescued from death, he is still unfit to serve God because he is wearing **filthy clothes** (v 3). Such clothing may symbolize either his own or the community's corruption, since as high priest he represented the entire community before God. According to Mosaic law, priests could not serve God with soiled clothing. They must be properly consecrated in order to come before the Lord (see Exod 29).

■ **4** So the angel initiates the consecration and reinstatement of Joshua as high priest. He orders **those who were standing before him** to **take off his filthy clothes** (v 4). **Those who were standing before him** seem to be other heavenly beings, perhaps even Satan who was also located **before him**. The angel explains that this action means his **sin**, and thus the **sin** of the community, has been **taken away.** The word for **sin** here is *'āwôn*, which is often translated "iniquity" or "guilt" (so NRSV and ESV). It fundamentally connotes the idea of crookedness and conveys a state in which one stands out of alignment with God's will and, thus, under the judgment of God. The term **taken away** (*'ābar*) means "pass over" or "move from one place to another." Here it connotes the sense of overlooking, which is one way the OT expresses the idea of forgiveness, though it is rarely used in this way (see Mic 7:18).

In exchange for **filthy clothes** the angel orders **fine garments** for Joshua. According to Exod 28:5, these **fine garments** were made with "gold, and blue, purple and scarlet yarn, and fine linen." These signify his purity and thus his fitness for leading the community in worship.

■ **5** Once Joshua is clothed, Zechariah calls for the final item of the high priest's dress, **a clean turban on his head** (v 5). The term used for **turban** (*sānîp*) is different from the one typically employed in Exodus and Leviticus (*miṣenepet*). It carries associations with headpieces of especially prominent persons, even of royalty (Isa 3:23, 62:3; Job 29:14). Thus this **turban** may be intended to convey additional status to Joshua. Following the vision reports, Joshua will receive a royal crown from Zechariah in a dramatic symbolic action (6:9-15).

■ **6** The remainder of the vision report that unfolds in vv 6-10 contains the divine message delivered through **the angel of the Lord** (v 6). It begins with what is called a **charge to Joshua** in v 7 and is followed by a promise of future blessings in vv 8-10.

■ **7** Successful execution of the high priest's office is contingent upon obedience. So the Lord exhorts Joshua to **walk in obedience to me and keep my requirements** (v 7). If this is done, then Joshua will fulfill his divinely ordained role as high priest, which is to **govern my house** and **have charge of my courts**. In other words, Joshua will lead the community in worship and teach them the ways of the Lord. In addition, he **will have a place among these standing here**. This suggests that he will have access to the heavenly council, **a place** where the will of God for people may be known (see Jer 23:22).

■ **8** As a result of the high priest—and by proxy the people of Judah—assuming his rightful role in this world, certain blessings can be expected in the future. The angel signals the significance of his announcement at this point with an urgent appeal to **listen**. Then he reminds the **high priest** and his fellow priestly **associates** that they are actually **symbols of things to come** (v 8). They point toward God's activities on behalf of his people that are yet to take place, which include ushering in the messianic age.

The work of the priesthood testifies to the fact that someday the Lord is **going to bring my servant, the Branch**. This is the angel's important announcement: the Messiah is coming to his people one day. Two messianic titles found in other prophets combine here in Zechariah. The books of Isaiah and Ezekiel identify the future Messiah as **my servant** (Isa 42:1; 52:13; Ezek 34:23, 37:24-25), while both Isaiah and Jeremiah refer to him as a **Branch** or shoot from the family of David (Isa 11:1; Jer 23:5, 33:15). These titles connect the Messiah to Israel's most celebrated king, David, who is also frequently called **my servant** (2 Sam 3:18, 7:5, etc.). Thus these terms evoke all the grandeur and hopes wrapped up in that glorious era of Israel's history.

■ **9** The angel continues his important announcement about the future. He begins with a strong interjection **see** (*kî hinneh*; translated "surely" in 2:9 [2:13 HB]), which alerts the audience to pay careful attention to what he is about to reveal (v 9).

What the angel shows them is a **stone** with **seven eyes** on which the Lord **will engrave an inscription**. This **stone** is another image of the Messiah. The message does not specify exactly what this **stone** looks like. However, it is located **in front of Joshua**, like the high priest's breastplate. The high priest's garments contained two engraved stones on the shoulders and twelve on the breastplate (see Exod 28:9-21). Perhaps one of these is the **stone**.

The meaning of the **seven eyes** on the stone may be explained in the next vision in 4:10. There "the seven eyes of the LORD" signify God's sovereign oversight of his world since they "range throughout the earth." The number **seven** typically conveys the idea of perfection. Thus the **seven eyes** may symbolize the total sovereignty of the Lord over creation.

Verse 9 ends with God's promise to **remove the sin of this land in one day**. This dramatic statement recalls the cleansing of Joshua in v 4. Deliverance from **sin** is one of the prominent features of God's ideal future (Isa 1:26; 4:3-4; Jer 31:33-34; Dan 9:24). The element of God accomplishing this **in one day** adds a new twist to the hope. This phrase implies that the coming of the Branch and forgiveness of sin will coincide. The Messiah will initiate the messianic age with forgiveness.

■ **10** Finally, the angel identifies the era about which he has been speaking as **that day** (v 10; → 2:11). Zechariah anticipates that peace and prosperity will characterize life in the messianic era (see also Jer 33:6-7; Mic 4:4). **Neighbor** inviting neighbor conveys the picture of peaceful relationship among people in the world, while **vine and fig tree** symbolize prosperity.

FROM THE TEXT

This vision highlights the significance of spiritual leadership within the community of faith. Those who lead God's people must remain free from the pollution of sin because they point to something beyond themselves. They stand as images of the coming Messiah and the hope of his new world.

God calls spiritual leaders to stand apart from a life of sin. Elements in the surrounding culture can contaminate God's leaders like they did Joshua and his people. But the Lord desires to cleanse his leaders from such pollution. So also Paul urged early Christians to clothe themselves in righteousness and "put on the new self" (Eph 4:24 and Col 3:10). He challenged the Corinthians, "let us purify ourselves from everything that contaminates body and spirit, perfecting holiness out of reverence for God" (2 Cor. 7:1). Especially those who lead others in spiritual formation Paul calls to be "above reproach" (2 Tim 3:2).

As representatives of Christ on earth, Christians point to a greater reality. Their commitment to Christ and to living apart from sin provides an image of the age to come. Those who fully surrender to the Lordship of Christ signify the day that "the Branch" will be restored to his rightful rule over the hearts of all persons. Sanctified followers foreshadow the age when "every knee should bow . . . and every tongue confess that Jesus Christ is Lord" (Phil 3:9-10).

5. Fifth Vision: Golden Lamp Stand (4:1-14)

BEHIND THE TEXT

This vision highlights the role of Zerubbabel in bringing the temple project to its completion. Haggai identifies Zerubbabel as the "governor of Judah" (Hag 1:1), which means he administered the political affairs of Jews around Jerusalem (→ Introduction to Haggai: A. The Audience). According to Ezra 3:8-13, Zerubbabel was present at the laying of the temple foundation in 537 BC. Nearly twenty years later, Haggai directed each of his messages to Zerubbabel, along with Joshua the high priest. This, however, is the only message Zechariah addresses to him.

The primary image in this vision is that of a lampstand. Both the tabernacle and Solomon's temple contained gold lampstands. The tabernacle had only one lampstand with seven lights (Exod 25:31-39), while the temple included ten (1 Kgs 7:29). These served a practical function of providing light inside windowless structures. Yet they also symbolized the special presence of the Lord within sacred space (Pss 27:1; 89:15 [16 HB]; Isa 2:5; 60:1, 19).

Since Zechariah's report of this vision flows awkwardly at times, scholars have questioned its literary unity. The dialogue between the prophet and the angel seems disrupted by the oracles in vv 6-10. Some commentators treat vv 1-6*a* along with vv 10*b*-14 as the original vision and consider vv 6*b*-10*a* as a later insertion (Peterson 1984, 238-244). The entire chapter can be viewed as a unified piece, however, because of the thematic relationships between the oracles and the vision (Meyer and Meyer 1987, 265-268). These will be noted in the commentary below.

The structure of this vision report varies from others, although it contains most of the same elements found in each of other visions in this series. Following a unique introduction to the vision (v 1), a dialogue unfolds between the prophet and an angel that describes what is seen (vv 2-5). Then divine messages (vv 6-7 and vv 8-10) provide explanation of the meaning of the vision. Finally, a concluding dialogue between the angel and the prophet clarify one final point of the vision (vv 11-14).

■ **1** **The angel who talked** with Zechariah plays a prominent role in Zechariah's visions except for the one reported in ch 3 (1:9, 13, 14, 19; 2:3; 5:5, 10; 6:4). Here the angel resumes his normal activity (**returned**) after playing only a limited role in the previous vision (ch 3). The prophet reports that the angel **woke me up.** This does not necessarily mean he had fallen asleep. Zechariah explains that he was simply **like someone awakened from sleep.** The point is that the angel broke his focus and contemplation upon the previous vision and shifted to another visual experience.

■ **2** The question, **what do you see?,** is also found in other vision reports (v 2; see Jer 1:11, 13). Zechariah responds with a detailed description of **a gold lampstand.** The design of this **lampstand** differs from the menorah of later Judaism as well as earlier versions of lampstands in the tabernacle and temple. Zechariah's description suggests a cylindrical pedestal with **a bowl** sitting on top of it and **seven lamps** arranged around the top at the edge of the bowl. Typically **lamps** were clay saucers containing oil and pinched in one or several places where wicks could be laid to draw oil when lit. Whether the **seven channels** feeding the lamps are conduits to separate oil lamps or simply grooves in the bowl is unclear. Some commentators suggest that each lamp had seven channels, which means seven lamps with seven flames, thus a total of forty-nine lights for the lampstand (see NLT; also Meyer and Meyer 1987, 229-238 and Petersen 1984, 217-223). In that case, the light emitted from the lampstand would be extremely bright.

■ **3** Another detail related to the lampstand includes **two olive trees** standing on each side of it (v 3). Zechariah provides further detail about these trees toward the end of the vision report. He sees them connected to the lamp stand through "two gold pipes that pour out golden oil" (v 12). Verse 14 reveals that these **two olive trees** represent Joshua and Zerubbabel (→ vv 12 and 14).

■ **4-5** As in previous visions, the prophet asks, **what are these, my lord?** (v 4; see also 1:9, 19; 6:4). He seeks insight into the meaning of the vision. The angel, however, delays answering Zechariah's inquiry by asking him, **Do you not know what these are?** (v 5).

■ **6-7** Two oracles (vv 6-7 and 8-10) seem to interrupt the conversation between Zechariah and the angel, but they actually answer both Zechariah's and the angel's questions indirectly. They reveal the overall meaning of the vision, though not the specifics of its various components.

The first oracle is a **word of the LORD to Zerubbabel** (v 6) and contains one of the most memorable verses of the OT: **Not by might nor by power, but by my Spirit, says the LORD Almighty.** The term **might** (*hayil*) connotes exceptional expertise, often within military contexts. The word **power** (*kōah*) conveys the idea of more basic human strength or talent. These words combine, like a hendiadys, to express the concept of the very best resources humans can muster.

ZECHARIAH

4:1-7

The poignant message of the oracle is that the essential resource for building the temple will not be human strength or ability but the **Spirit** of **the** LORD **Almighty**. This **Spirit** was an empowering force in the work of creation (see Gen 1:2; Ps 33:6) and for various persons doing the work of God throughout Israel's history (e.g., see Exod 31:3; Num 11:25; Judg 6:34; 13:25). The title **the** LORD **Almighty** further emphasizes the unlimited capacities of Judah's God (→ sidebar The Lord Almighty at Hag 1:2). Zerubbabel's God is capable of providing all resources needed for building the temple.

The rhetorical question addressed to a **mighty mountain** (v 7) implies that it holds no threat to the completion of the temple. This **mighty mountain** may represent the many economic and political obstacles that Zechariah's audience faced in building the temple. But it could also simply refer to the mountain of rubble created by the destruction of the temple in 586 BC. Clearing this heap of rubble would have been a very difficult task. Regardless of whether the **mighty mountain** is physical or symbolic, the oracle promises that **before Zerubbabel** it will **become level ground**, because of the Spirit's work. This image recalls the leveling of terrain at the coming of the Lord in Isa 40:4, 41:15, and 49:11.

The oracle also promises that Zerubbabel will see the temple project to completion. One day he will set in place the final stone of the temple, **the capstone**. This **capstone** (*hā'eben hārō'šâ*) was likely the last item placed in an arch or some other significant place in the structure. Workers probably set aside this stone from the previous temple and reserved it for this final moment in order to emphasize continuity between the old and new temples.

Placing the **capstone** to mark the temple's completion will be an act of worship, with people shouting **God bless it! God bless it!** These words, which translate literally *grace, grace to it* (*hēn hēn lāh*), acknowledge the fulfillment of the Lord's promise in v 6. This scene recalls the emotional celebration that took place when the foundation for the temple was first laid (see Ezra 3:10-13) as well as the pageantry when Solomon's temple was dedicated (1 Kgs 8).

■ **8-10** A second oracle recorded in vv 8-10 clarifies the first one. The Lord confirms that **the hands** that **laid the foundation of this temple . . . will complete it** (v 9). These **hands** refer to the **hands** of Zerubbabel. Ezra 3 confirms that Zerubbabel was present at the laying of **the foundation of this temple** almost twenty years earlier. According to Haggai, his **hands** also laid a ceremonial foundation stone just a few months before in a ritual celebrating the restart of construction once again (→ Hag 2:15-18). When Zerubbabel lays that final stone, it will confirm that Zechariah truly was a prophet sent by God (v 9; see also 2:9, 11).

The oracle ends with a challenge to those who **despise the day of small things** (v 10). These are people who scoff at the modest design of the temple compared to Solomon's magnificent edifice (→ Hag 2:3). Such criticism will eventually turn to rejoicing as Zerubbabel sets **the chosen capstone** in its place. The Hebrew text does not make clear who will rejoice; some translations identify scoffers as the subject while others see **the seven eyes of the** LORD as the subject (cp. NIV with NRSV; see

Clark and Hatton 2002, 142-144 and McComiskey 1998, 1089-1099 for extended discussions on the translation of v 10).

The Hebrew words translated **chosen capstone** (*hā'eben habbedîl*; literally, "the tin stone") are very difficult to understand. The translation **chosen capstone** derives from rendering *habbedil* as "distinction" instead of "tin." Thus this is "the stone of distinction" (NJPS), meaning the specially selected final **capstone** in a building. This would be another way to designate "the capstone" (*hā'eben hārō'šâ*, literally "the headstone") mentioned in v 7.

During a ritual dedication ceremony Zerubbabel will set **the chosen capstone** in full view of **the seven eyes of the** Lord. Throughout the OT the **eyes of the** Lord metaphorically express God's presence and his knowledge of everything that happens in this world (see Prov 15:3). **Seven** symbolically represents perfection or completeness and suggests there are no gaps in God's knowledge of this world. Nothing and no one escape the watchful eyes of the Lord. The **seven eyes of the** Lord further may provide a clue to understanding the "seven lamps" of the lampstand in v 2. If the light from lampstands in the temple and tabernacle symbolized the presence of God among his people, then the seven lamps might represent **the seven eyes of the** Lord and thus God's omnipresence and omniscience.

■ **11-14** The question and answer format between prophet and angel returns in vv 11-14. The prophet asks for clarification about the second main feature of the vision, **the two olive trees** (v 11). He articulates the same question twice, but with different details in the second question. These details give greater insight into the meaning of the various elements in the vision.

The prophet identifies **two olive branches, two gold pipes,** and **golden oil** (v 12). The **two olive branches** represent the two trees that stand **on the right and on the left of the lampstand**. The **two gold pipes** are conduits through which **golden oil** flows. Presumably one pipe connects to each branch or tree. The words **golden oil** translate the Hebrew word *hazzāhāb*, which simply means "the gold." Because of the context of olive trees, which serve as the primary source for lamp oil, interpreters have understood *hazzāhāb* to be indicating oil for the lamp stand.

These three elements fill in details about how the trees and the lampstand interrelate in this vision. They suggest that the **golden oil** flows from **two olive branches** by means of **two gold pipes** to the lampstand. The vision thus provides an image of a perpetual supply of oil for the lampstand. In such case, the lamp would never go out.

In v 13, the angel prods the prophet once again with the question **Do you not know what these are?**. The prophet's response of **No** confirms that the interpretation of this vision must come from heaven. Finally, the angel answers the prophet's question directly, yet still somewhat cryptically. The two olive trees represent **the two who are anointed to serve the** Lord **of all the earth** (v 14). **The two** the angel has in mind must be Zerubbabel and Joshua, the governor and the high priest of Judah respectively.

296

The angel designates Zerubbabel and Joshua as persons **who are anointed.** Literally the angel calls them ***sons of new oil*** (*bĕnê hayyiṣhār*). The use of the word *yiṣhār* to designate **new oil**, emphasizes the sense of new beginnings associated with these two persons. In ancient Israel both priests and kings went through an anointing ceremony where oil was poured on their heads. The oil symbolized God's Spirit resting upon them as they performed the duties of their offices. Joshua likely underwent such a ceremony at his inauguration as high priest. But Zerubbabel surely did not for fear of raising suspicions among Persian authorities of a Jewish rebellion. Though Zerubbabel came from the line of David, he was only a local magistrate, not a king. The angel's reference to him as one of the **anointed** acknowledges a spiritual appointment for Zerubbabel.

The function of Zerubbabel and Joshua as the anointed ones of the Lord is to **serve the Lord of all the earth** (v 14). The designation, **Lord of all the earth,** emphasizes the universal sovereignty of Judah's God. This is a remarkable assertion given Judah's insignificant status within the vast Persian Empire.

FROM THE TEXT

This vision encourages people who are challenged to complete an overwhelming task for God. The central theological claim of this text is found in v 6, one of the most well-known statements in the Bible. This verse affirms that *the Spirit of God is the only adequate resource for accomplishing kingdom work.* Human "might" and "power" are never enough. Zechariah's audience apparently recognized this. They knew they faced significant opposition from neighboring peoples and did not have adequate resources to construct a monumental building like the temple. Yet, Zechariah announced that God's Spirit would empower Zerubbabel to bring the temple building project to completion. The prophet affirmed that humans can accomplish great things for God as the Holy Spirit empowers them.

When we submit ourselves to God's plans and purposes, his Spirit enables us to do his work. Like the oil that flows into the lamps in the vision of the lampstand, God's Spirit flows into our lives. This is the empowering Spirit that makes it possible for God's people to become God's light in the world. Whether we are constructing buildings or proclaiming his word to a lost world, the Spirit of God makes all the difference. God's followers continue to hold on to the hope that the Lord will "pour out" his Spirit upon them and transform the world in which they live (Joel 2:28-29 [3:1-2 HB]; Acts 2:1-4).

6. Sixth Vision: Flying Scroll (5:1-4)

BEHIND THE TEXT

The sixth vision speaks of a curse from God coming over the land. Curses were dreaded in the ancient world because they expressed divine disapproval, which people knew did not bode well for one's life. They had particularly significant consequences in the context of a Israel's covenantal relationship with God. A curse blocked blessing, the positive benefits of covenant, and thus affected prosperity and general wellbeing (see Deut 27:15-26; 28:15-68).

The curse in this vision falls upon those who steal and swear falsely, violations of two basic commandments in Mosaic law. By singling out violators of these commandments, the prophet undoubtedly indicates a problem that emerged in relationship to the temple building project. During biblical times, people typically made pledges of financial and other support for construction of temples. Donors took an oath before the god of that temple and their promised gift became a sacred trust. Persons who backed out on those pledges would be guilty of making a false oath in the deity's name as well as theft (see Mal 3:8-10). As a result, they would fall under a curse from the deity whose temple was affected.

This brief vision report begins with an initial description of what the prophet sees (v 1). A dialogue between the prophet and an angel further clarify what is seen (v 2). Then the angel explains the meaning of the vision (v 3) and conveys a divine word regarding it (v 4).

IN THE TEXT

■ **1** The phrase **I looked again** signals a new vision experience, using words similar to those that introduce visions two and three (1:18 and 2:1). The object Zechariah sees in this vision is **a flying scroll**, something like a large banner in the sky. A **scroll** was one of the primary means of preserving texts in the ancient world. People made scrolls from animal skins (either sheep or goat), papyrus, or even metal such as copper or tin. The fact that this scroll was **flying**, like a bird or cloud, marks it as unique. Such mobility may intend to symbolize the universal application of its contents.

■ **2** The question-answer style continues in this vision report. The question, **what do you see?**, most likely comes from the interpreting angel. Zechariah's answer includes the length and width of the scroll, **twenty cubits long** (thirty feet) **and ten cubits wide** (fifteen feet). The length of the scroll is not unusual, but its width is, since a typical scroll would be only about six to twelve inches wide. The dimensions of the scroll match those of the front porch to Solomon's temple (1 Kgs 6:3). So the scroll would be the same width and depth as the colonnaded entrance to Solomon's temple and, perhaps, the one under construction.

■ **3-4** The angel reveals that the writing on the scroll is a **curse that is going over the whole land.** Because of two kinds of covenant breakers, thieves and liars, **the whole land** has been placed under a curse. A **curse** is the withdrawal of God's covenant blessings (→ Behind the Text).

In the context of the Sinai covenant, a **thief** is a person who breaks the eighth commandment (Exod 20:15) and the one who **swears falsely** in God's name breaks the third commandment (Exod 20:7). These two acts of covenant violation may identify those who pledged resources toward the temple project and then reneged on that commitment (→ Behind the Text). In so doing they would be guilty of trivializing God's name as well as stealing from God and the community.

Both kinds of covenant violators would become social outcasts according to the scroll. They would be **banished** from the land (v 3) and have their homes destroyed (v 4). The verb **banished** (*nāqâ*), literally "purged" (NASB) or "cleaned out" (ESV), conveys the idea of forceful removal of criminals from the community in order to purify it. The destruction of their homes suggests the Babylonian and Persian practice of punishing people by pulling **timbers** from their houses and turning the **stones** from their walls into piles of rubble (see Dan 2:5; 3:29; Ezra 6:11).

The angel personifies the curse as an unwelcome visitor, entering houses and bringing destruction (v 4). This reflects the Hebrew belief in the power of a divine word. God's spoken word takes on a life of its own and accomplishes whatever God intends for it to do (Gen 1:3; Isa 55:11).

FROM THE TEXT

Along with visions two, three, and seven, this vision promises God's judgment upon the enemies of Judah. Visions two and three speak of God dealing with external oppressors like Assyria, Babylon, and Persia. Visions six and seven, however, focus on people within the community of faith.

In order to build his kingdom, the Lord will deal with enemies within the community as well as those outside it. Though Zechariah's audience faced many external threats, this vision reveals that corruption within the community also threatened construction of the temple. As in the days of the judges, Judah discovered that the biggest obstacle to accomplishing God's plans for them was their own sin, not that of others.

Lawbreakers within the community of faith disrupt God's purposes. According to 4:6, God does not need their resources to build the temple anyway. Their deception and lack of commitment distracts from the business of God. So God releases his curse upon those whose lifestyle shows a lack of commitment to what God intends to do. The message of the scroll reminds us that God calls his people to holy living so that his kingdom might go forth into this world.

7. Seventh Vision: Woman in a Basket (5:5-11)

BEHIND THE TEXT

Zechariah's seventh vision, like the sixth vision, portrays the removal of sin from Judah. The action in this vision recalls the ritual displacement of sin performed on the Day of Atonement in Lev 16. Part of the ritual included placing the sin of the people on a goat and removing it from the community. Other ancient Middle Eastern religions had similar rituals that sent the sin from a local site to enemy lands (Floyd 1996, 64).

A woman in a basket represents the sin that is removed from Judah and has evoked considerable discussion among scholars as to what she might represent. Some see her as symbolizing evil in general (see Petersen 1987, 257), while others have identified her more specifically with the foreign wives in the community who worshiped other gods (see Meyer and Meyer 1987, 301-302; see Ezra 10:10-12; Neh 13:23-27; Mal 2:10-17). Still others argue that the woman symbolizes idolatry in the land. She could be a figurine of Asherah or some other deity since sacred objects of this kind were frequently transported by means of ceremonial baskets (Meyer and Meyer 1987, 296-303). If this is true, then the vision would be dealing with the problem of idolatry in the Jewish community. As such the vision would confront the violation of the first and second commandments (Exod 20:3-6) and would suggest that the judgment of exile did not completely eliminate idolatry among Jews. This had been one of the primary causes for God's judgment of exile (1 Kgs 9:6-9; 2 Kgs 17:7-12; Jer 1:15-16; 5:18-19).

This vision report includes the elements typically found in the other seven visions of this series: dialogue between angel and prophet, description of the visual experience, and explanation of its meaning. What is unique to this vision is the arrangement of these elements. The vision unfolds in three movements with each stage providing greater description of what is seen and more clarification as to what it means.

The first section of the vision (vv 5-6) opens with the angel's invitation to view something new, which evokes the prophet's question and the angel's response to it. The second section (vv 7-8) provides additional description of details about the vision and more of the angel's explanation. The third section (vv 9-11) gives yet further details of activity in the vision, which evokes another question from the prophet and a final explanation from the angel. The structure of sections one and three parallel one another forming a frame around the central section. This literary feature tends to highlight the words and actions of the angel in the middle part of the vision.

IN THE TEXT

■ **5** An **angel** draws the attention of Zechariah to a new experience with a command to **look up and see** (v 5). This is the same **angel** who has accompanied the prophet in other visions where it is also designated **the angel who was speaking to me** (1:9, 19; 2:3; 4:1,4; 5:10; 6:4).

The angel instructs the prophet to observe **what is appearing**. The word **appearing** ($y\bar{a}\d{s}\bar{a}$') might be better translated *going out* (see NASB, NRSV, and ESV), a term that appears in some form four times in this vision. This is the only vision in which the angel commands the prophet to take notice of what is happening. The reason for the angel's command may be that this scene is on the move and its action is more important than the identity of its objects.

■ **6** Zechariah seems uncertain about what he sees, so he asks **what is it?** (v 6). The angel's reply, **it is a basket,** is literally, *it is an ephah,* which is a unit of dry measure and refers to a container size. The *ephah* in ancient Israel held about two thirds of a bushel or about five gallons. Thus, the **basket** would be a rounded container suitable for one or two persons to carry from a field, roughly twelve to eighteen inches wide and eighteen to twenty-four inches tall. Typically, such containers would have been clay pots, but baskets of woven reeds or palms are also known.

The angel further explains that the basket contains **the iniquity of the people throughout the land**. The Hebrew text reads *'ayin* ("eye") instead of *'awon* (**iniquity**). Most English translations follow the LXX reading (*adikia* "unrighteousness"), which makes better sense. The Hebrew reading may be a scribal error caused by the confusion of *yod* and *waw*, two similar looking consonants in Hebrew. The Hebrew term *'awon* connotes a state of crookedness, being bent away from God's straight path. In vision four, the Lord takes away the **iniquity** of Joshua and Judah (3:4 and 9). The same thing will happen to **the iniquity of the people** of Judah in this vision.

■ **7-8** A second development in the vision takes place as **the cover of lead was raised** from the basket (v 7). **The cover of lead** is not a typical feature for a basket. Its extra weightiness suggests that **the cover** secures the contents of the basket firmly.

With the lid raised the prophet notes that the basket contains **a woman** (v 7). This **woman** appears to be an idol, since a normal sized human could not fit within an *ephah* basket. The angel calls this woman **wickedness** (*riš'â*), a Hebrew term used for actions that violate God's standards for community relationships (Num 16:26; Deut 31:18; Jer 6:7; Ps 37:21). The Hebrew term for **wickedness** (*riš'â*) evokes the fertility goddess Asherah (*'ašērâ*) because these two terms are anagrams.

To prevent such evil from escaping, the angel pushes her **back into the basket** and puts **the lead cover down on it** (v 8). This forceful action graphically illustrates God's desire to keep wickedness from spreading among his people.

■ **9** The final stage of the vision sees **two women** with **wings like those of a stork** carry away the basket with the woman inside (v 9). The wickedness of the land of Judah is transported to another land. The description of the **two women** as winged creatures recalls the two-winged cherubim in Solomon's temple (1 Kgs 8:6-7; see also Isa 6:2; Ezek 1:11). The **stork** is a long-legged migratory bird in Israel with a large wingspan. Its Hebrew name *ḥasîdâ* relates to the word *ḥasîd*, which means faithfulness or loyalty. It is possible that the two women with wings represent the faithful in the community who are expected to play a role in removing wickedness from the land.

The phrase, **the wind in their wings**, implies the empowerment of the faithful by the Spirit of God. The term for **wind** (*rûaḥ*) is also the word for "spirit" in Hebrew. In the fourth vision, the temple rebuilding will be done by the empowerment of the Spirit (4:6). In this vision, removal of wickedness from the land also will be accomplished by the power of the Spirit.

■ **10-11** In response to the prophet's question **"Where are they taking the basket?"**, the angel identifies **the country of Babylonia** (vv 10-11). The Hebrew text says "the land of Shinar" (*'ereṣ šin'ār*), which is the ancient name for **Babylonia**. The choice of "Shinar" to designate **Babylonia** is purposeful because this is where prideful humanity attempted to make a name for themselves by building a tower that reaches the heavens (Gen 11:1-9). The land of Shinar is the home of human arrogance and idolatry. Wickedness has no place in God's holy land. So the Lord removes it from his land and relocates it where it belongs.

The basket will be placed in **a house**, a temple, in Babylon (v 11). The vision thus makes a clear contrast between the temple in Jerusalem and a temple in Babylon. The former will be the house of the holy God of the people of Judah, but the latter will be the house where all wickedness on earth dwells.

FROM THE TEXT

This vision, along with the previous one, focuses on the removal of sin from the community of faith so that God's purpose can be accomplished. In particular, this vision deals with one of humanity's most persistent and crippling sins, idolatry.

Idolatry tempts the people of God in every generation. According to the vision, an idol is like a seductive person who can be placed in a basket and transported wherever needed. Though a supposedly powerful force, it can be packaged in a manageable size for human manipulation. An idol is the essence of "iniquity," the twisting of reality (v 6), and "wickedness," the disruption of the life God intended (v 8). Its rightful place is not among God's people, but in a land where false gods abound (v 11).

Thus, *idolatry must be removed from among those who would attempt to build God's kingdom.* God does not tolerate any sin. But idolatry is especially revolting to God (Ezek 11:18). It violates "the most important" commandment to love the Lord with all of one's being (Mark 12:31). The Lord intends to wipe it from the land completely one day (Zech 13:2; Dan 9:24).

According to ch 1, God's plans for Judah included renewing covenant relationship with his people and setting up residence in their midst. The Lord envisioned his Spirit flowing through community leaders who would model God's ideal for this world (ch 3) and light the lamp of his grace in it (ch 4). But these dreams cannot take place unless the community keeps the Lord first in life. All that God plans for his people will never unfold as long as idolatry remains among them. So God calls his people to remove anything that distracts people from the Lord and his kingdom purposes. A holy God calls his people to be holy in order to live the whole life he has planned for them (Lev 19:2).

8. Eighth Vision: Four Chariots (6:1-8)

BEHIND THE TEXT

The key image in this vision, the chariot, played a major role in military life of the ancient world. It was essentially a mobile platform from which to launch spears and arrows and to wield swords. The lightweight, two-wheeled chariot, developed in Egypt during the Late Bronze Age (ca. 1550-1200 BC), became the model for rapid attack on plains areas. Typically drawn by two to four horses, war chariots usually included a driver and a fighter. At times a shield bearer might be included. Persians added the scythe element to the chariot wheel, which enabled them to level enemies on the field. Chariots were also used in victory parades, hunting expeditions, and travel.

Several OT passages picture the Lord possessing chariot forces (Ps 68:17 [18 HB]; Hab 3:8) and riding in his own chariot of clouds (Ps 104:3). Other gods throughout the ancient Middle East, such as the Babylonian sun-god Shamash, also rode chariots.

This final vision report includes elements typically found in the other visions of this series. It begins with the prophet describing what he sees (vv 1-3). Then he engages an angel in a dialogue about the vision, which helps explain the meaning of its images (vv 4-6). Additional details of activity within the vision (v 7) lead into a final message about its key point (v 8).

IN THE TEXT

■ **I** The introduction to this vision report, **I looked up again and there before me** (v 1), is similar to that of five other previous visions (see 1:8, 18; 2:1; 5:1, 9). The prophet sees **four chariots coming out from between two mountains**. The **four chariots** evoke an image of elite military troops swiftly moving to attack (→ Behind the Text). The chariots come from the presence of God, as v 5 clarifies. The **two mountains** made of **bronze** might symbolize the gates of heaven, which may have been clad with **bronze**, as ancient city gate often were. In the OT, the abode of God is frequently associated with **mountains**, especially Mount Sinai (Exod 19:20; Judg 5:4-5) and Mount Zion (Pss 48:1-3 [2-4 HB]; 132:13-14). Solomon's temple sat atop Mount Zion and its entrance included two giant pillars of bronze (1 Kgs 7:15-22). Perhaps this is part of the symbolism evoked here. At times Mesopotamian religions also imagined their gods coming from the mountains riding in chariots .

■ **2-3** Zechariah notices the colors of the horses pulling each of the four chariots. He describes them as **red, black, white**, and **dappled** (vv 2-3). These colors recall the four horses of different colors in the first vision (see 1:8). This detail assures the connection between the first and last vision alerting the reader to the literary frame they create. Though Rev 6:1-8 assigns meaning to the colors of horses in that vision, Zechariah's vision does not indicate what significance these colors have in this context, if any.

The prophet further describes the horses as **powerful**. The term **powerful** derives from a verb (*'āmēṣ*) that means "stout" or "strong." Verse 7 will affirm this same description of the horses a second time. It is what one might expect of horses on a heavenly mission.

■ **4-6** The angel answers Zechariah's question (**what are these, my lord?**) by explaining the meaning of the chariots and the horses. The angel explains that the four chariots are **the four spirits of heaven going out from standing in the presence of the** LORD (v 5). The charioteers are divine emissaries sent out from heaven on a mission, as the term **going out** implies (see v 6). They have been commissioned to patrol the entire earth. The word **spirits** (*ruḥôt*) can be translated "winds" (so NRSV, NJPS, ESV). So **the four spirits** or "winds" represent the four points of the compass from which wind blows across the earth.

The angel explains that these messengers have been **standing in the presence of the Lord of the whole world** (v 5). This describes a scene of a heavenly council gathered around God's throne, similar to the one depicted in vision three (3:1-10). The divine title **the Lord of the whole world** occurs for the second time in these visions (see 4:14) emphasizing once again the Lord's range of sovereignty over all earthly kingdoms.

Each chariot moves out to its destination on the compass. **Black horses** head **north, white horses . . . west,** and **dappled horses . . . south** (v 6). In each case the chariots are said to be **going** (*yāṣa'*), though the NIV only translates this verb once. It is a key term for this vision. Aside from the three occurrences in this verse, *yāṣa'* is used four more times ("coming out" v 1; "going out" v 5; "went out" v 7; and "going" v 8). Combined with the three occurrences of "go throughout" (*hālak*) in v 7, the term connotes decisive movement on behalf of God. The chariots are on a divine mission.

Presumably the "red horses" went east, though the text does not say this. Perhaps the angel assumed this understanding by process of elimination. Some scholars, however, suggest ancient scribes lost this line during transmission. But no manuscript evidence exists to support such as supposition.

■ **7-8** The threefold use of the phrase, **go throughout the earth,** emphasizes the worldwide scope of the mission of the horses once again (v 7). No nation is outside the sovereign rule of the Lord.

Finally, the angel tells Zechariah the main focus of this vision in v 8. His concern is not so much with the chariots that went east, west, or south. Rather he notes the impact of the black horses **going toward the north country** (v 8). That is the direction from which Judah's primary oppressors have come in recent centuries, including the Assyrians and Babylonians as well as the Persians. The assault of the heavenly chariot did its work there. It gave God's **Spirit rest.** That is to say, the chariot force subdued Judah's enemies **in the land of the north.**

This promise applies to Judah's current oppressors, the Persians. The resting of God's **Spirit . . . in the land of the north** implies that Persia remains under God's control as well. The account of temple construction in Ezra confirms that this happened. Persian authorities cooperated with the Jews and even contributed significantly to the temple's completion (Ezra 6). So Zechariah's audience could rest because God's Spirit was at rest.

FROM THE TEXT

With the last vision of the series the chiastic structure of the eight visions comes full circle returning to where it began. This vision proclaims the sovereign rule of the Lord with military images just as the first vision did. Thus the vision series is framed with a strong reminder that the God who calls Zechariah's audience to build a temple remains in absolute control over all the earth.

All nations of the world remain under the sovereign reign of the Lord. In this vision, "the Lord of the whole world" sends his chariot forces throughout the entire world (v 5). They can go wherever they please because all the earth is God's domain. The importance of this point for Zechariah's audience as well as for people today is that God's people can rest in God's sovereign rule though their worlds may be in tumult.

Because God is sovereign only the Lord can truly give rest to this world. In the first vision, God's patrol "found the whole world at rest and in peace" as a result of the Persian hegemony (1:11). But this was only an allusion and certainly not good news to God's people. The good news in the first vision as well as in this one is that God's emissaries "have given my Spirit rest in the land" (6:8). Though earthly powers can offer their version of rest, only the Spirit of God can provide the rest that truly satisfies the heart of God and his people. This evokes an image of the messianic age when Jesus promises rest to those who come to him (Matt 11:28) and peace that only he can give (see Luke 2:13; John 14:27; 16:33; Acts 10:36; Rom 5:1).

C. Symbolic Act: Crowning Joshua (6:9-15)

BEHIND THE TEXT

In this passage God instructs Zechariah to perform a symbolic act: the crowning of Joshua the high priest. Coronations in the ancient world conferred legitimacy upon community leaders signifying both popular acclaim as well as divine approval (see 1 Kgs 1:38-40; 2 Chr 23:1-11). Such ceremonies were normally reserved for kings, but priests also underwent rituals of ordination that included placing a priestly turban upon the head (see Exod 29; Lev 8).

During the time of Zechariah Judah had no king since the Persian emperor ruled. On the local level, Zerubbabel the governor of Judah remained primarily responsible to Persian magistrates for civil order and economic progress while Joshua the high priest carried responsibility for the spiritual life of the community under the authority of God. Their roles were distinct, yet complimentary. Since Joshua's position carried significant influence in the community, his appointment was subject to the approval of the Persians. The offices of civil and religious leadership in Judah combined sometime after the Persian period when the Hasmonean Simon became both high priest and king around 142 BC (1 Macc 14:41-44).

Prophetic books frequently report symbolic actions of Israel's prophets. While details vary in these reports, the most typical elements include: (1) a divine instruction to the prophet and (2) a divine message explaining the meaning of the action (e.g., see Jer 19:1-15). The account of Zechariah's symbolic action in this passage follows these typical features. First, the prophet describes the instructions that the Lord gave to him (vv 9-11). Then he conveys the message that the Lord directs him to relay to his audience regarding the action (vv 12-15). As with other reports of symbolic actions, the prophet's obedience is not indicated. It may be assumed though, since the prophet recorded what the Lord commanded.

IN THE TEXT

■ **9-11** The introductory formula, **The word of the LORD came to me** (v 9), indicates the divine origin of the commands, **take, go, take, make, and set** (vv 10-11). None of these verbs is actually an imperative, but each carries the force of such in this context. Six verbal commands actually appear within the Hebrew text because **go** is repeated twice for emphasis in v 10.

The Lord commands Zechariah to **take silver and gold from the exiles** (v 10). A group had recently **arrived from Babylon** with gifts for the temple project, a typical practice for people returning from exile (Ezra 2:68-69). These are Jews who continued to live in Babylon and are only now returning to Judah or, perhaps, just visiting. Four prominent men lead them, **Heldai, Tobijah, Jedaiah,** and **Josiah.** The last of these may be the most influential since his ancestry is given and Zechariah goes to his **house.** The great-grandfather of **Josiah** may have been the high-ranking priest **Zephaniah** who was put to death by Nebuchadnezzar at the fall of Jerusalem in 586 BC (2 Kgs 25:18). None of these individuals can be identified with persons of the same name in other parts of the OT (see Jedaiah in Ezra 2:36 and Tobijah in Ezra 2:60).

The Lord directs Zechariah to use some of the **silver and gold** this group brought to **make a crown for the high priest, Joshua** (v 11). Crowns were typically fashioned from **gold**, not **silver**. The addition of the rarer metal **silver** signifies something important. The word **crown** (*'ăṭārôt*) refers to a royal headdress and not the traditional turban of high priests. The word **crown** is actually plural, which may suggest multiple crowns. Ancient monarchs frequently wore several crowns at once to indicate the various domains they controlled. Since Zechariah mentions two metals, one crown may have been made of silver and the other of gold.

In what could only be a very dramatic moment, Zechariah was to **set** the crowns fashioned from gold and silver **on the head of the high priest, Joshua.** In the role of **high priest, Joshua** functioned as the spiritual leader of the Jewish community in Judah (→ Behind the Text and 3:1). His role was primarily religious, not political. Yet, this coronation implies expansion of that role to include civil leadership like a king. The oracle from the Lord in the following verses explains what that means.

■ **12** The Lord instructs Zechariah to **tell** Joshua **what the LORD Almighty says** (v 12). The Lord begins the message by identifying Joshua with the messianic title **the Branch** (*ṣemaḥ*). In Jeremiah this term refers to a descendant of David who would lead Judah in future days (Jer 5:5-6; 33:15-16; see also Isa 4:2; 11:1) and the vision of Zech 3 promises a Messiah named **the Branch** who is prefigured by Joshua and his fellow priests (→ 3:8). This vision suggests that the Lord calls Joshua **the Branch** not to identify him as the Messiah himself. Rather Joshua points toward the future Messiah by fulfilling his role as high priest in the community.

During the time of Zechariah, one of the high priest's primary tasks centered round overseeing temple construction. So playing upon the word **Branch** the Lord announces that Joshua **will branch out from his place and build the temple of the LORD**. In vision five, the Lord promised divine empowerment for Zerubbabel to complete the building project (4:6-10). Now the Lord assures that Joshua, the religious authority, will stand alongside Zerubbabel, the civil authority, throughout this task. The promise that Joshua **will branch out** evokes Isaiah's statement about the Messiah who sprouts up "like a tender shoot and like a root out of dry ground" (Isa 53:2).

■ **13** For emphasis the Lord asserts a second time that Joshua **will build the temple of the LORD** (v 13). In this role he will be like a king. Along with the crown that Zechariah places upon his head, Joshua **will be clothed with majesty and will sit and rule on his throne**. He could not function as an actual king since that would be a challenge to Darius' absolute authority over the Persian Empire. But Joshua will function under the greater authority of the Lord Almighty, God of Judah. **He will be a priest on his throne**. This is the emphasis of this message. Joshua is not simply a royal figure sitting **upon his throne** as kings do. He is first and foremost **a priest** ruling from a royal throne. In this way he reflects the mysterious Melchizedek who functioned as priest and king in the days of Abraham (Gen 14:18-20). Further, he prefigures the messianic figure of Ps 110 who rules with a "scepter from Zion" and yet is also "a priest forever in the order of Melchizedek" (Ps 110:2-4).

At this point, the significance of Joshua's multiple crowns comes into focus. The silver and gold used to make these crowns may represent the two domains of leadership in Judah, the secular and the religious. These come together in this symbolic act as both are set upon Joshua's head according to v 11. So in Joshua **there will be harmony between the two** offices of religious and civil authority in Judah.

■ **14** The Lord stipulates that **the crown will be given to Heldai, Tobijah, Jedaiah and Hen son of Zephaniah** for its placement **as a memorial** in the newly constructed temple. The placement of **the crown** in the temple **as a memorial** highlights the significance of Joshua's coronation for generations to come. The point is that within the community of God's restored people secular and spiritual leaders must function as one. The spiritual aspect will take precedence as the coronation of Joshua suggests.

■ **15** The divine message ends with the promise that **those who are far away will come and help to build the temple of the LORD** (v 15). **Those who are far away** includes Jews still living in exile in Babylon and other places. But it also could include non-Jews contributing toward the temple effort. Support from the nations is alluded to in Zechariah's third vision (see 2:11). Haggai also envisioned them helping with the temple building project (Hag 2:7-9; see also Ezra 6:8-10).

Zechariah also expresses his confidence that when these events unfold, his audience **will know that the LORD Almighty has sent** him to do what he just did (v 15; see 2:9, 11, and 4:9; see also Deut 18:21-22). Zechariah's ministry and authority as a prophet will be validated by the fulfillment of his prophetic word.

Verse 15 ends with Zechariah's reminder to his audience that **this will happen if you diligently obey the LORD your God**. In other words, the fulfillment of God's words rests upon Judah's faithful commitment to the Lord. This recalls the opening call to repentance in 1:2-6 and reminds Zechariah's audience that their positive response to God's word is critical the success of the building project.

FROM THE TEXT

The account of Zechariah's eight visions concludes with a report of a dramatic symbolic action that refocuses attention on the two central visions of the series (chs 3 and 4) and recalls the opening summons to repentance (ch 1). This report reminds us that the success of kingdom work always depends upon the spiritual health of the community and its leaders. It gives one more message highlighting the significant role of Judah's spiritual and civil leaders in building the temple and assures Zechariah's audience that the temple will be completed. It also reminds them that their work is part of something much bigger than they might have imagined. The temple will become a significant sign of the Lord's presence in their world. But its completion will also foreshadow the age of the Messiah.

Spiritual leaders fill the most important role within a community of faith. God directed Zechariah to place crowns on the head of the priest representing both political and spiritual authority. This act signaled the preeminence of the office of the priest over that of the king and reminds us how significant spiritual leadership is for God's people. While administration of civil life remains important, leading people to know and worship God stands above it. No role within a community is more vital than nurturing the spiritual life of people.

God's people are part of something much bigger than their immediate tasks. The coronation of Joshua reminded Zechariah's audience of the greater significance of their work. Constructing the temple involved them in God's grand plans of redemption that will come to final fulfillment in the messianic age. Kingdom work in any era signals the Lord's sovereignty over this world both in the present as well as in the age to come.

In Jesus Christ the combination of priestly and kingly roles finds ultimate fulfillment. According to the NT, Jesus served as both priest and king, after the order of Melchizedek (Heb 5:5-6; 7:1-3, 15-22). Because of this "a better hope is introduced by which we draw near to God" (Heb 7:19). People gain access to God through Jesus Christ (Rom 5:1) and at the same time live under his benevolent lordship both now and into eternity (Phil 2:9-11).

II. JOY OF THE MESSIANIC AGE: ZECHARIAH 7:1—8:23

BEHIND THE TEXT

The spiritual discipline of fasting forms the background for these chapters. Though the law of Moses required fasting only on the Day of Atonement (Yom Kippur), the Israelites practiced it on other occasions as well. These included during times of national crisis (2 Chr 20:3), as an act of repentance (Neh 9:1-2), during a period of mourning (2 Sam 1:12), or for other special reasons (Ps 35:13). The time of a fast could vary from one (1 Sam 14:24) to forty days (Exod 34:28).

During the exile to Babylon the Jews set aside four additional times for community fasting. These were: (1) for the fall of Jerusalem on the ninth day of the fourth month Ab (2 Kgs 25:3-4), (2) for the destruction of the temple on the tenth day of the fifth month Elul (Jer 52:12-13), (3) for the murder of Gedaliah on the second day of the seventh month Tishri (2 Kgs 25:25), and (4) for the beginning of the Babylonian siege of Jerusalem on the tenth day of the tenth month Tebet (2 Kgs 25:1). Each of these is alluded to in 8:18. The second fast serves as the basis for the initial question of this section.

Chapters 7-8 form a complete literary unit, though the connection of 8:1-17 to the rest of the materials in chs 7-8 is difficult to discern at first glance. Some commentators prefer to treat chs 7 and 8 separately for this reason. Often scholars assert that ch 8 consists of an edited collection of various oracles from different times in the life of the prophet (see Klein 1984, 219-220). Whether this analysis of the early history of these oracles is accurate, they are now clearly connected to ch 7 and function as an important part of it (see Boda 2004, 379).

The discussions of fasting in the opening section of 7:1-3 and the closing section of 8:18-23 form an *inclusio* for the unit. This is strengthened by repetition of the phrase "entreat the LORD" in 7:2 and 8:21 and by the call for social justice in 7:9-10 and 8:16-17. Further analysis of the chapters reveals a simple structure of question and answer. The people pose a question about fasting in 7:1-3 and the rest of the material in 7:4-8:23 constitutes the Lord's answer through Zechariah.

The divine response further breaks down into four sections: 7:4-7, 7:8-14, 8:1-17, and 8:18-23. The same messenger formula "the word of the LORD came" introduces each of these sections. The first section questions the questioners about their motives for fasting. The second section reminds the people of their past and why they have been fasting. The third section turns attention to what the Lord has been doing in recent years and urges people of Judah toward a more coura- geous and optimistic lifestyle in light of these mercies. Finally, the fourth section imagines a new day of transformation from fasting to feasting in God's new world.

Chapters 7-8 act as a bridge between the other two major parts of the book, chs 1-6 and chs 9-14. They reiterate some of the themes already sounded in the vi- sions of chs 1-6. These include: (1) the concern for community justice (7:9-10 and 8:16-17), (2) the stubbornness of previous generations (7:11-14), (3) the passion of the Lord for Jerusalem (8:2), (4) the coming of the Lord to Jerusalem (8:3), (5) the building of the temple (8:3, 9), and (6) the drawing of other nations to Jerusalem (8:20-23). Several of these themes will recur in chs 9-14. In particular the coming of the Lord to Jerusalem and the cleansing of the community from injustice will become important subjects in chs 9-14. A new theme that emerges in chs 7-8, the joy of life in the New Jerusalem (8:4-13, 19), will be taken up in chs 9-14.

IN THE TEXT

A. People's Question about Fasting (7:1-3)

■ 1 The time frame for chs 7-8 is **the fourth year of Darius . . . the fourth day of the ninth month**, which translates to December 7, 518 BC in contemporary calendars (v 1). This date places the events of chs 7-8 almost two years after the visions of chs 1-6 (see 1:1). It has been over two years since the temple rebuilding started, and it will continue for another two years. The **word of the LORD came to Zechariah** formula conveys the divine origin of the message that follows; it appears four other times in chs 7-8 marking the major sections of the Lord's response to the people's inquiry (7:4, 7:8, 8:1, and 8:18).

■ **2-3** The message is a divine response to a question asked by a delegation from **Bethel**, an important religious center located about twelve miles north of Jerusalem (v 2). The patriarchs worshiped God at Bethel (see Gen 12:8 and 35:1-15) and it was the site of the Northern Kingdom's temple, erected by Jeroboam I (1 Kgs 12:28-30; see also Amos 7:10-13). Ezra reports that a number of people who returned from Babylon made Bethel their home (2:28). The Bethel delegation was led by **Sharezer and Regem-Melech**, two men who were either religious or political leaders from that area.

The Hebrew text of v 2 is difficult to translate. Literally it reads: ***And he sent Bethel Sharezer and Regem-melech and his men***. The first noun after a verb is usually the subject in Hebrew, but **Bethel** is an awkward subject. The NIV adds **the people of** before **Bethel** in order to make better sense in English. Some scholars take **Bethel** as the first element in a compound name Bethel-sharezer (Baldwin 1972, 141-143). In this way it corresponds to the second compound name. Thus the phrase would be translated "Bethel-sharezer sent Regem-melech together with his men" (REB) or "Bethel-sharazer and Regem-melech and his men sent" (NJPS). Either of these translations could imply that the delegation sent to Jerusalem came from a Babylonian Jewish community rather than Bethel (Stuhlmueller 1988, 102). However, most English translations treat Bethel as the origin of the delegation.

Worshipers typically inquired of the Lord **by asking the priests . . . and the prophets** for a divine judgment (v 3). These two religious leaders functioned as the Lord's mouthpiece on various matters. **Priests** provided answers from the law of Moses (Lev 10:10-11) and the Urim and Thummim in the high priest's breastplate (Ex 28:30). **Prophets** received their response more directly from the council of God (Jer 23:22) or the Spirit of God (Zech 7:12).

The delegation wanted to know if they should continue to **fast in the fifth month**, a practice initiated after the destruction of Jerusalem in 586 BC in order to recall that event (→ Behind the Text). The question arises most likely because of the progress being made on the temple rebuilding project. The priests had undoubtedly been conducting sacrifices and other rituals around the temple precincts for some time (Ezra 3:1-6). Now a fully functioning temple appeared to be on the horizon soon.

B. God's Answer to Question about Fasting (7:4—8:23)

I. God's Questions about Fasting (7:4-7)

■ **4-7** The Lord responds with three rhetorical questions that probe the people's reason for fasting and give them a history lesson in vv 4-7. The Lord's questions are addressed to both the people and their religious leaders, **all the people of the land and the priests** (v 5).

The Lord's first question asks about the motivation for fasting. **When you fasted and mourned . . . was it really for me that you fasted?** This question implies that the people did not fast in the past for the right reason. The focus of their fast was not on God and their relationship with him, but on making them feel good about themselves. The Lord's response also mentions the fast on **the seventh month**, which was most likely in remembrance of Gedaliah's assassination (2 Kgs 25:25; → Behind the Text).

Seventy years approximates an actual sixty-eight years since Jerusalem's destruction in 586 BC and the time of this oracle in 518 BC. **Seventy years** is the general timeframe that Jeremiah announced for the duration of Babylonian oppression (Jer 25:11 and 29:10).

The second question shifts to the issue of feasting, most likely during festival days such as Passover, Pentecost, Tabernacles, and New Moons (v 6). The question, **when you were eating and drinking, were you not just feasting for yourselves?**, is a clear indictment of the people's selfish interests. Whether fasting or feasting, they sought to please themselves rather than God.

The Lord's third question reminds his audience that the point of the two previous questions is nothing new and creates a bridge to the next part of the Lord's answer in vv 8-14. The Lord asks, **Are these not the words the LORD proclaimed through the earlier prophets?** (v 7). These **earlier prophets** are the ones Zechariah refers to in 1:4 and alludes to later in this unit (7:7, 12; 8:9). Zechariah most often borrows the thoughts and words of Isaiah, Jeremiah, and Ezekiel, though he alludes to others as well. These prophets lived before the exile **when Jerusalem and its surrounding towns were at rest and prosperous, and the Negev and the western foothills were settled.** The geographical references suggest that the dry area to the south, **the Negev**, as well as the fertile region to the west of Jerusalem, **the western foothills**, were still sparsely settled in Zechariah's time. During the restoration period most settlement of Judah took place in the hill country around Jerusalem (see Ezra 2:21-35).

2. Lessons from the Past (7:8-14)

■ **8-10** In vv 8-16 Zechariah reminds his audience the real reason for fasting by recalling events from the past. Verses 9-10 provide one of the Bible's best summaries of prophetic preaching before the exile with its particular concern for social justice. Four features of this preaching are highlighted, two positive and two negative.

First, the prophets regularly called people to **administer true justice** (v 9; see Amos 5:24; Isa 1:16-17; Jer 7:5-7). Within the biblical context, **justice** (*mišpāṭ*) means living up to the demands of covenant relationship with God. These demands include fair treatment of other people within clans as well as the larger community (see Exod 20:12-17; 21:1-23:9). The verb **administer** (*šāpaṭ*), which could be translated *judge*, focuses upon the act of rendering proper judgments in legal settings. The qualifier **true** (*'emet*) emphasizes consistent or faithful application of justice regardless of a person's status or kinship (see Exod 23:2-3, 6-7).

True justice emerges from a desire to **show mercy and compassion to one another** (v 9). The term **mercy** (*ḥesed*) denotes a commitment to kindness. A merciful person determines to display care without regard for how that is received. **Compassion** (*rāḥam*) refers to a passionate feeling to share good things with others. According to biblical writers, **mercy and compassion** lie at the heart of God's character (Exod 34:6-7; Ps 103:8-13).

Following two positive expressions of justice, the prophet describes justice with two negative commands. On a practical level doing justice means a person should **not oppress the widow or the fatherless, the alien or the poor** (v 10). These four classes of people struggled to survive in the ancient world. So biblical religion always called for their care (Deut 14:28-29). **The widow, the fatherless,** and **the alien** all lacked family protection and support. **The poor** are those afflicted with unfortunate circumstances of life that cause them to lack adequate resources. The prophets frequently indict people for ignoring or trying to do away with **the poor** (Ezek 16:49; Amos 8:4). This is one way they might **oppress** (*'āšaq*) them. The term means to exploit or mistreat people in some way.

Finally, the prophetic summary notes that the origin of true justice comes from within. The prophets often warned about the impact of inner attitudes (Jer 17:9-10) and offered hope for changing the heart (Jer 31:33-34; Ezek 36:26-27). They admonished **in your hearts do not think evil of each other** (v 10). They knew that every injustice begins in the **hearts** of people who **think evil** of others.

This summary of the prophetic call to justice makes an important point related to fasting. The Lord desires more than performance of religious duties. Of greater importance is how people treat one another. Isaiah 58 makes the same connection between social justice and fasting when it asserts that genuine fasting will "loose the chains of injustice" (Isa 58:6).

■ **11-12b** The Lord reminds Zechariah's audience that their ancestors did not listen to the prophetic call for justice. In fact, **they refused to pay attention** and **stubbornly . . . turned their backs**, like an ox refusing to take a yoke (v 11). They even **stopped up their ears,** which suggests they intentionally covered their ears so they could not hear the prophets speak.

The reason for such stubborn behavior is their hearts. **They made their hearts as hard as flint** (v 12). Perhaps "the heart of stone" Ezekiel spoke about is in view here (Ezek 36:26). Once again, the Lord focuses upon the inner person as the seat of the human problem (see v 10). An unresponsive heart made people so that they **would not listen to the law,** the very foundation for life (Ps 19:7-11 [8-12 HB]). It also kept them from hearing the **words that the LORD Almighty had sent by his Spirit through the earlier prophets.** The divinely inspired word of God had been ignored.

■ **12c-14** As a consequence of Israel's refusal to listen, the Lord became **very angry** (v 12c). The anger of the Lord affects three major aspects of Abraham's covenant promise: relationship to God, descendants, and land (see Gen 17:7-8). First, the promise of relationship became strained when God determined he **would not** listen to them **when they called** (v 13). Communication between God and people is essential to covenant relationship. Isaiah, Jeremiah, and Ezekiel all warned this would happen when people break covenant (Isa 1:15; Jer 11:10-11; Ezek 8:18).

Next, the promise of descendants is threatened. The Lord says he **scattered them with a whirlwind among all the nations** (v 14). The verb **scattered** (*sā'ar*) means to blow something around in a storm (see Isa 40:24). Prophets frequently used this image for Israel's exile picturing the dispersion of Abraham's descendants like seed or chaff strewn about in the wind (Jer 13:24; Ezek 22:15).

Third, the dispersion of Israel's people left **the land desolate**. A **desolate** (*šāmēm*) place connotes something that is horrifying to look at as opposed to a **pleasant land** "flowing with milk and honey" (Deut 6:3). The people **made the pleasant land desolate** because they refused to listen to the prophets (see 2 Kgs 17:13-15). Both Leviticus and Deuteronomy warned that covenant violators would be **scattered** and have their land left **desolate** (Lev 26:33-34; see also Deut 28:36-37, 64).

3. Restoration in the Present and Future (8:1-17)

■ **1-3** Following the recital of Israel's past history of disobedience and subsequent destruction, Zechariah relates a series of messages on future blessings from the Lord in 8:1-17. Each message is introduced by an introductory formula, **This is what the LORD Almighty says** (see vv, 3, 4, 6, 7, 9, 14), which indicates that several originally independent oracles may have been combined to form this larger unit.

In vv 2-3, the Lord announces his return to Jerusalem (see 1:7-17; see also 9:1-17; 12:1-9; 14:1-15). The divine motivation for this return is God's passion for the city. The Lord confesses, **I am very jealous for Zion; I am burning with jealousy for her** (v 2). In Hebrew these lines are arranged in a chiasm and convey great emotional intensity. Literally they read ***I am jealous for Zion with great jealousy and with great wrath I am jealous for her.*** The term **jealous** (*qānā'*) means passionate zeal. The three uses of *qānā'* (two verbs and one noun) increase the impact of this idea. The descriptor ***with great wrath*** only adds to it. The first vision of Zechariah also made connection between God's **jealousy** and **wrath**, which combine to express God's intense emotional involvement with his people (see 1:14-15, 9:1-8, 9:14-17, 12:1-9, 14:3-5, and 14:12-15; see also Ezek 36:5-6). Appropriately in this context, Jerusalem is called **Zion**, a term reflecting the Lord's long history with this city (→ 1:15; see also 2 Sam 5:7; 1 Kgs 8:1).

The purpose of the Lord's return is to **dwell in Jerusalem** (v 3; see also 1:3, 16; 2:5, 10-12; 9:9, 14; 14:5). The coming of the Lord to live among his people is a key promise of the book of Zechariah (1:3, 16; 2:5, 10-12; 9:9, 14; 14:5). To **dwell** (*šākan*) implies settling in and taking up extended residence, as in establishing an encampment (see Num 24:2).

The city will be transformed upon God's arrival. It will be called by a new name, **the Faithful City,** and the mountain on which the temple is located will be called **the Holy Mountain.** The term **Faithful** (*'emet*) implies that the inhabitants of the city will live in a committed relationship with God and with one another. Zion will be known as **the Holy Mountain** because it is set apart as the dwelling of God on earth.

■ **4-5** Following the Lord's return to Jerusalem, people will return to it. Zechariah utilizes several images to describe this repopulation of Jerusalem. He envisions **men and women of ripe old age . . . in the streets of Jerusalem** along with **boys and girls playing there** (vv 4-5). People of all ages inhabiting the city implies the end of war and the coming of new era of peace and prosperity in the land, a foreshadowing of the messianic age (see Isa 11:6-8; 65:13; Joel 2:28 [3:1 HB]; see also Jer 33: 10-11). They are experiencing the promises of long life and multiplication of descendants for those faithful to covenant with God (Deut 28:1-14).

■ **6** Such a scene may seem too **marvelous** (wonderful) for **the remnant** who survived the horrors of exile (v 6). How could Jerusalem ever become so peaceful again? But to God, such radical transformation is never impossible, because "nothing is too hard" for the Creator of the Universe (Jer 32:17).

■ **7-8** The Lord promises to save his people **from the countries of the east and the west** (v 7) and **bring them back to live in Jerusalem** (v 8). The word **save** (*yāša'*) connotes rescuing from danger and bringing into a safe environment. **The countries of the east and the west** represent the many places to which the people of Judah were scattered during exile, in particular Egypt to **the west** and Babylon to **the east**. The Lord's act to **bring them back** reverses the scattering that he did in the exile (→ 7:14).

Moreover, Jerusalem will become the home for both the Lord and his people. For God the ultimate goal of this return to Jerusalem is so that **they will be my people, and I will be faithful and righteous to them as their God** (v 8). The phrases, **my people . . . their God** summarizes the covenant relationship (Jer 24:7; 31:33; 32:38; Ezek 11:20; 14:11; 34:30; 37:23, 27; see also Zech 13:9). The Lord promises to be **faithful and righteous** in his relationship with his people. **Faithful** (*'emet*) conveys the idea of unwavering consistency and trustworthiness, while **righteous** (*ṣĕdāqâ*) evokes the high standard of ethical treatment stipulated in the Law. The Lord holds himself to the same standard he demands of his people.

■ **9-13** At this point, the Lord begins urging his people to continue rebuilding the temple and living in covenant faithfulness with him and one another. In turn, the Lord promises to bless them.

The Lord admonishes Zechariah's audience to remain **strong** (firm) in their commitment to rebuild the temple (v 9). This same appeal came through **the prophets who were present when the foundation of the temple was laid** about two years before (v 9; Hag 2:4). These **prophets** are Haggai and Zechariah who were present December 520 BC when this event took place (→ Hag 2:18 and Zech 4:9; also see Ezra 5:1-2).

Much like Haggai's message on the day the foundation stone of the temple was laid (Hag 2:15-19), this message contrasts life before temple building began and life now. Before temple construction began both **people** and **animals** suffered due to weak economy (v 10). No one felt safe to do **business** for fear of **their enemies**, which might include both those outside as well as those within the community (see Hag 2:3 and Zech 4:10).

But the Lord promises to reverse this curse on the land and send his blessings as a result of the temple being rebuilt (vv 11-13). God will not deal with his people in the way he did **in the past** (v 11). The desolate land will be transformed and it will become a fertile and productive place. As anticipated in the covenant blessings, the **seed, the vine, the ground,** and **the heavens** will all cooperate in producing a good harvest (v 12; see Deut 28:11-12; see also Ezek 34:26-27). This will be like an **inheritance** from the Creator, just as the land had been (Gen 32:13).

The Lord also promises to reverse the curse on the people of **Judah and Israel** (v 13). The destruction of Jerusalem and the expulsion of the people from the land made them an example **among the nations** of what it means to be cursed by God. Now, the Lord promises to **save** them from their humiliation and make them **a blessing.** They will fulfill their destiny in the world as the descendants of Abraham (Gen 12:3). They need not **be afraid** of their enemies. They can **be strong** and continue rebuilding the temple. As blessed people, they are assured of the Lord's protection and prosperity.

■ **14-17** As this series of messages draw to a close, the Lord once again makes a contrast between former and present circumstances. This time it is between the past judgment upon ancestral disobedience and the good that the Lord intends to do to Jerusalem (cp. Jer 31:28 and 32:42).

The exile was a **disaster** (evil) that the Lord **determined** (*zāmam*) **to bring . . . on his people** for their continual disregard of the covenant (v 14). The Lord **showed no pity** (*nāḥam*) and let the full weight of the curse fall upon his people. Yet, the Lord is just as **determined** (*zāmam*) to do good to his people (v 15). The repetition of *zāmam* in these verses emphasizes that the same resolve God displayed in bringing disaster, he will employ in doing **good again to Jerusalem and Judah.** In view of this promise to do good, the Lord urges his people, **Do not be afraid.**

The Lord lists four things people should do as they continue their work and anticipate his blessings. First, they should **speak the truth to each other** (v 16), an admonition to be honest in conversations. Next, they should **render true and sound judgment.** Such **judgment** follows the law consistently without showing favoritism to the rich or poor, and thus promotes the wellbeing of the community (Exod 23:2-3). The word **sound** (*šālôm*) is the Hebrew term for peace or wholeness. The terms **truth** and **true** derive from the same root *'emet*. Some form of this word appears six times in chs 7-8. It is translated **true** here and in 7:9, "faithful" in 8:3 and 8:8, and **truth** here and in 8:19. Such repetition highlights God's deep concern for integrity within the community of faith. **In your courts** is literally *in your gates*, which denotes the place where people carried out their daily business and settled their legal disputes. The level of integrity found in the gates reflected on the character of the entire city.

Following two positive admonitions, the Lord lists two negative prohibitions for his people. First, they should **not plot evil against each other** (v 17). The Hebrew conveys the idea of planning schemes in one's heart (see NASB, NRSV, ESV, and HCSB), underscoring the Bible's regular concern that inner motives lead to harmful action (Prov 4:23; Luke 6:45).

Finally, the people of Judah should **not love to swear falsely** (v 17). The term love (*'āhab*) means to prioritize something. Thus the Lord admonishes people not to put falsehood before truth. **All this**, including both plotting evil and swearing falsely, are behaviors that the Lord passionately dislikes (→ Mal 1:2-3).

4. Transformation of Fasting (8:18-23)

■ **18-23** The Lord's answer to the question of fasting in 7:3 concludes in vv 18-23. The Lord announces that one day **fasts . . . will become joyful and glad occasions and happy festivals for Judah** (v 19). The three terms **joyful, glad occasions,** and **happy festivals** characterize events of great celebration, even things associated with the messianic era (Isa 65:13-14; Jer 33:9-11).

The Bethel delegation's question was about the fast in the **fifth** month (7:3). The Lord's answer, however, includes three other fasts: one in the **fourth** month commemorating the breach of Jerusalem's walls, another in the **seventh** month commemorating Gedaliah's assassination, and one more in the **tenth** month commemorating the arrival of the Babylonian army. As festivals of joy replace these fasts, the Lord reminds Zechariah's audience to remain committed to the covenant. They must **love truth and peace** (v 19), actions that promote a healthy community of faith and justice admonished in vv 16-17 (see also 7:9-10).

The reversal of Judah's fortunes creates a community so transformed that it will attract **many peoples and the inhabitants of many cities** (v 20). Though this might refer to other dispersed Jews, it most likely speaks primarily of non-Israelites as v 23 clarifies (see Isa 60:1-3; Micah 4:2-5; Zech 14:16-19).

Verse 21 projects a conversation between pilgrims on their way to Jerusalem. **The inhabitants of one city** invite people in another city to **go at once to entreat the** Lord **and seek the** Lord **Almighty.** The phrase **go at once** conveys urgency. These foreigners are anxious to **entreat the** Lord. This is the identical phrase used at the beginning of this unit to describe the purposes of the Bethel delegation. It connotes seeking favor from the Lord, which is essentially the same idea denoted by the phrase **seek the** Lord. These pilgrims entice their fellow Gentiles to join them by confessing **I myself am going.** This is persuasion by personal example.

Verse 22 parallels v 21 reaffirming this stunning development in the world order. It reiterates that **many peoples and powerful nations will come to Jerusalem to seek the** Lord **Almighty and to entreat him.** This time the foreign worshippers include not just **many peoples**, but also **powerful nations**, which would undoubtedly include Judah's recent oppressors, the Babylonians and Persians.

The unit ends with another scene of a pilgrimage of Jews and Gentiles to Jerusalem (v 23). The phrase **in those days** implies that the pilgrimage envisioned here is a future event, perhaps in the messianic age. The scene portrays **ten people from all languages and nations** pleading with **one Jew.** The ratio of **ten to one** symbolizes a new status for Jews among the nations. Instead of being an object of scorn (8:13) the **Jew** has become someone admired and respected. The act of grabbing **the hem of his robe** further underscores this honored position.

The request of the foreign worshipers ends this unit on an important thought. They asked to **go with** the Jew because they **have heard that God is with you** (v 23). Nations are eager to experience God because they have witnessed the presence of God among his people. They want to be part of the covenant community.

FROM THE TEXT

In these chapters, the Lord's answer to a question about fasting provides helpful instruction about the benefits of the spiritual discipline of fasting. It is more than a religious ritual of self-denial and mourning over adversity. Fasts should be times of refocusing upon God, recalling the past, recommitting to covenant, and re-orienting toward the future.

Fasting should refocus our attention upon God. The Lord asked a pointed question to the delegation who inquired about fasting, "was it really for me that you fasted?" (v 5). Apparently these people thought fasting was about them and not God. They did not understand the difference between a holy day, a day dedicated to God, and a holiday, a day dedicated to people. Genuine fasting can help people rediscover the difference.

In order to help people refocus upon God, *fasting should include a time of recalling the past.* In 7:8-14 the Lord rehearsed the painful experience of the Judah's exile. This included recounting their sins and the consequences they brought. Though unpleasant, these memories allowed God's people to assess the progress of their spiritual journey. We can only move forward with God once we know where we have been.

Once sin is revealed, *fasting should lead to recommitment to covenant with God.* While the Lord rehearsed the past failures of Judah, he also urged them to rededicate themselves to the demands of the covenant relationship. At the heart of these demands was the call to justice because treating people fairly matters a great deal to God. The Lord urged them to "love truth and peace" (8:19).

Finally, *fasting should reorient people toward a hopeful future.* It should enable people to see beyond their past and present circumstances into a new reality. Chapter 8 paints a glorious picture of a day when the Lord will come to dwell with his people and fasting will turn into feasting (8:19). Zechariah anticipates a day when the genuine fasting of God's people will pave the way for all who are lost in this world to find their true home in God (8:23).

III. TRIUMPH OF THE MESSIANIC AGE: ZECHARIAH 9:1—14:21

A. Promise and Struggle of the Messianic Age (9:1—11:17)

The oracle in chs 9-11 portrays both the hopes and disappointments associated with the messianic age. It begins by describing the coming of the messianic king as God, the Divine Warrior, vanquishes Israel's enemies (ch 9). This is followed by a picture of Israel's hopeful future under the care of the divine shepherd (ch 10). Finally, the oracle closes with the promise of the messianic age thwarted by the rejection of God's shepherd (ch 11).

I. The Promise of a Coming King (9:1-17)

BEHIND THE TEXT

The portrait of the Lord as a warrior dominates ch 9. This image of God emerges in the Exodus and conquest narratives (see Exod 15:3-4; Josh 3:10-11; 24:11-13). Other ancient Near Eastern religions also maintained a similar view of their gods. For example, Baal of the Canaanites, Ishtar of the Assyrians, and Marduk of the Babylonians, all were believed to possess exceptional military prowess.

In prophetic literature, the warrior image of the Lord is often associated with collections of oracles against other nations (e.g., see Amos 1:1-10; Isa 23, Jer 47; 49:23-27; Ezek 25:15-17; 26:1-28:26). Zechariah 9 shares several features that are typical of this genre. These include: (1) a description of the nation's offense, (2) a proclamation of judgment from the Lord, and (3) an analysis of the effects of judgment. At times the genre also includes words of salvation for Israel and Judah. Their primary function seems to be comfort and encouragement for God's people since they affirm the Lord's sovereignty over the nations (→ sidebar Oracles Against Nations at Nah 1:1).

Chapter 9 divides into two major sections: (1) the conquest of enemies in preparation for the coming king in vv 1-8 and (2) the arrival of the king and his kingdom in vv 9-17. The scenes depicted in these sections alternate between images of war and peace. In the first section, an initial conquest of enemies (vv 1-7) gives way to a picture of the Lord's protection of Jerusalem (v 8). The second section begins with the glory of the king's peaceful kingdom (vv 9-12), then shifts to images of divine war (vv 13-15) before turning back to the beauty of God's rescued people (vv 16-17).

IN THE TEXT

a. Preparation for the Coming King (9:1-8)

■ **1-3** A prophecy: **the word of the** LORD identifies the material in chs 9-11 (v 1). These same words also designate the genre of chs 12-14 as well as the book of Malachi. The term **prophecy** (*massā'*) is often translated "oracle" (NASB, HSCB) or "burden" (NRSV, ESV) in English versions. It denotes a prophetic word that carries an ominous message. Thus it is a "burden" to deliver and to receive (→ Mal 1:1).

The prophecy begins with the Lord's word of judgment against **Hadrak, Damascus,** and **Hamath,** three regions north of Judah in modern Syria (vv 1-2*a*). These names represent key cities within the Persian satrapy known as *Eber Nahara* ("Beyond the River"), the political region west of the Euphrates in which Judah was located. **Hadrak,** not mentioned elsewhere in the OT, refers to Hatarikka, a city situated along a main trade route between Mesopotamia and Canaan. **Damascus** controlled movement along this same trade route further south. **Hamath** was located about 130 miles northeast of Damascus along the Orontes River. Israel had a long history of hostility and war with **Damascus** and **Hamath** reaching back to the time when David subdued them and made them part of his empire (2 Sam 8:5-10; 1 Kgs 15:18; Isa 7:1).

The statement **the eyes of all people and all the tribes of Israel are on the LORD** (v 1) describes other nations, not just the tribes of Israel, watching what God is doing (cp. Isa 17:7). They look to the Lord for his righteous judgments, which are about to be described in vv 4-8.

The word of the Lord is spoken against two more places north of Judah, **Tyre and Sidon** (v 2b). These great cities dominated the Phoenicia coast and controlled western Mediterranean maritime trade for centuries. Verse 3 notes the wealth these cities amassed through their trade and other natural resources. The **stronghold** (*māṣôr*) of Tyre refers to the city's island fortress, which proved impregnable for centuries until Alexander the Great conquered it in 332 BC by building a sea wall out to the island from the mainland.

■ **4** This message predicts the destruction of Tyre, its wealth (**possessions**) and **power,** by means of **fire** (v 4; cp. Amos 1:9-10; Jer 49:27; Isa 23; Ezek 26-28). Alexander the Great's conquest of this region may have fulfilled these predictions, but something beyond his time is also in view.

■ **5-7a** The fall of Tyre will unsettle the powerful Philistine cities of **Ashkelon, Gaza, Ekron** and **Ashdod** located further south along the Mediterranean coast (vv 5-6). They will experience **fear, agony** and loss of **hope.** This is how the people of Canaan felt when the Israelites began conquest of the promised land (Deut 2:25; Josh 2:9). These cities represent some of Israel's most despised enemies because they frustrated occupation of the promised land until the time of David (Josh 13:2; 1 Sam 4:1-10; 31:1-7).

The specific predictions about Gaza's king and the desertion of **Ashkelon** implies a similar fate for all other Philistine cities. Likewise, the humiliation of Ashdod—having undesirable **mongrel people** occupy it—suggests the mortification of all the **Philistines.**

God's judgment upon the Philistines includes the removal of pagan practices that were detestable to the Jews (v 7a). **Blood from their mouth** may refer to eating meat with blood in it, a practice **forbidden** in Mosaic law (Lev 7:26-27).

■ **7b** In the last part of v 7, this message takes a turn and anticipates the incorporation of **those who are left** among the Philistines into the Jewish community (v 7b). They will become one of its clans, and thus a people who **belong to our God.** The phrase **those who are left** alludes to "the remnant" (*še'erit*), a special term that identifies the Jews who survived exile (Hag 1:12, 14; 2:2; Zech 8:6, 11, 12). The Philistines, represented by the city of **Ekron,** will assimilate into the life of Israel **like the Jebusites** did after David's conquest of Jerusalem (Josh 15:63).

■ **8** While the great cities of Syria, Phoenicia, and Philistia fall, the Lord **will encamp at my temple to guard it** (v 8). This action anticipates the coming of the Messiah in vv 9-17. The terms **encamp** and **guard** convey the image of an army setting up tents in and around a city for protection. **My temple** is literally *my house* (so NASB, NRSV, ESV). Here it most likely refers to the entire land of Judah and the people

321

in it, rather than just the **temple** (cp. Jer 12:7). Like a warrior, the Lord stands guard **against marauding forces** and any other **oppressor**.

The reason no one can touch God's people is because the Lord is **keeping watch** over them. This phrase literally translates *now I see with my eyes*. It recalls "the seven eyes of the LORD that range throughout the earth" in Zechariah's fifth night vision (→ 4:11). The watching eyes of God connote care as well as sovereignty (see Deut 11:12; Ps 33:18).

b. Arrival of the King (9:9-17)

■ **9** Following the defeat of Judah's enemies in vv 1-8, the way is cleared for the coming of Judah's king in vv 9-17. His arrival brings peace, but also war as he leads his people in battle to secure the land and bring about the blessings of the messianic age.

The announcement of the king's arrival calls for celebration. The prophet urges people to **rejoice greatly** and **shout**, the kind of sounds that might be heard on a battlefield as well as in the temple courts (v 9; see Josh 6:10; Ps 60:8). People **rejoice** during worship especially when they reflect upon God's salvation (Ps 9:14; 35:9).

Those urged to celebrate are called **Daughter Zion** and **Daughter Jerusalem**, parallel terms referring to inhabitants of the holy city (v 9). Prophets sometimes applied the affectionate term **Daughter** to **Zion** and **Jerusalem** to indicate God's special relationship to the city (→ 1:15).

See, your king comes to you indicates that the king's coming is already happening and that everyone in Judah will see his arrival. In the ancient world, parades and other pageantry usually accompanied the arrival of a king to his royal city, especially when returning from victory on the battlefield.

The king who comes is described as **righteous** and **victorious**, but also **lowly** and **humble**, **riding on a donkey**. Being **righteous** is an essential quality of good kings throughout the OT and, in particular, of the Lord's Messiah (2 Sam 8:15; 1 Kgs 10:9; Isa 9:7 [6 HB]; 11:4; Jer 23:5). It has to do with conforming to God's standards for fairness and honesty in all aspects of life, including business, administration, and legal decisions.

The term **victorious** translates a passive participle of *yāša‘* ("save"), which implies that the king has been rescued and, for that reason, has triumphed over his enemies. **Lowly** (*‘ānî*) designates someone who exudes a modest and unassuming attitude or behavior. It indicates that the king acknowledges his victory derives from the hand of God and not his own. The word **lowly** also denotes an afflicted person, and thus subtly foreshadows the experience of the rejected shepherd king in ch 11.

This king expresses his humility by **riding on a donkey** (v 9). In the ancient world, the **donkey** commonly transported goods and worked in fields. But it also served as a dignified mount for royalty on occasion (Judg 10:4; 1 Kgs 1:33). Kings might display military prowess by riding a horse or chariot, the most advanced weapons of war, into a city. But they could signify a state of peace by **riding on a donkey**.

The description of this **donkey** as **a colt, the foal of a donkey** highlights a hopeful future. **A colt** is a young animal newly trained for its task in the world. Mention of **the colt** also connects this passage to Jacob's prediction regarding a Judean king who ties his donkey colt to a tree (Gen 49:11). In the NT, the gospel writers note that Jesus rode into Jerusalem on a donkey just before his death (Matt 21:1-11; Mark 11:1-11; Luke 19:28-40; John 12:12-15). Both Matthew and John quote Zech 9:9 indicating that this prophecy was fulfilled in Jesus' triumphal entry (Matt 21:5; John 12:15).

■ **10** The purpose of the coming king is to establish a peaceful kingdom on earth, which he will do through actions and spoken word. First, he will remove instruments of war, **chariots, warhorses,** and **the battle bow** from the entire land of Israel, represented by **Ephraim** and **Jerusalem** (v 10; cp. Isa 2:4).

Then the coming king will **proclaim peace to the nations**. Unlike Cyrus who issued a proclamation of peace after conquering Babylon in 539 BC, this king will proclaim peace following unilateral disarmament. **Peace** (*šālôm*) connotes wholeness and wellbeing, and thus far more than cessation of war. All **nations** of the world will fall under the king's peaceful domain because **his rule will extend from sea to sea** (the cosmic waters enveloping the earth) **and from the River** (Euphrates) **to the ends of the earth** (see Ps 72:8). The prophet anticipates world-wide peace because of the coming king (see Isa 9:6-7 [5-6 HB]; Mic 5:4-5 [3-4 HB]).

■ **11-12** The following verses (vv 11-13) address those who may have been perplexed by the fate of the Jews still dispersed in exile. They announce that the king will liberate the exiles and bring them to Zion once again. The promise of peace in the preceding verses shifts to the promise of a war though, which will be necessary to accomplish the restoration of the remaining exiles.

The Lord's speech begins with the promise to free Judah's **prisoners from the waterless pit**. The image of **the waterless pit** pictures the hopelessness Jews faced in exile (see Gen 37:24; Jer 38:6). The Lord promises not to forget them or leave them in the land of their exile because they are his **covenant** people. **The blood of my covenant** refers to God's covenant with Israel ratified through the slaughter of animals (see Exod 24:5-8; see also Mark 14:24).

Instead of being imprisoned in a **waterless pit** (v 11), they will become **prisoners of hope** (v 12). They will return to the protection of their **fortress** temple in Jerusalem and receive **twice as much** as they had before.

■ **13** Deliverance of the exiles comes at the price of conflict. The Lord will employ the people of Israel as weapons of war: **Judah** will act like **a bow** in God's hands and **Ephraim** as its arrow (v 13). The Lord will also brandish them like **a warrior's sword**.

Some commentators have linked the battle against **Greece** in this verse to the Maccabean defeat of Seleucid armies in the second century BC. Others, however, see here the liberation of the Jews who were sold to the Greeks by Tyre, Sidon, and the Philistines (see Joel 3:6-7 [4:6-7 HB]). Isaiah 66:19-20 lists Greece among the distant lands in the west, which suggests that it may be symbolic of the farthest places in the known world. What is certain here is that the peace the coming king brings will be total and that he will leave no one in bondage or in exile.

■ **14-15** The Lord promises to lead his people into battle with the force of a powerful storm. He **will appear over them** (v 14) and **shield them** (v 15), perhaps like he did in the pillar of fire that surrounded Israel at the Red Sea (Exod 14:19-20). Appearing **over them** could allude to the banner typically carried into battle by troops to remind them of their deity's presence (Isa 11:10; 30:17; 31:9).

In vv 14-15, the language of theophany (**lightning, storms**) is mixed with weapons of war (**arrow, trumpet, shield, slingstones**). These portray the Lord as a warrior engaged in battle (→ Hab 3:11; see also Pss 18:5 [6 HB]; 144:5-8). Thus the prophet employs the names **the Sovereign Lord** (*'ădônay YHWH*) and **the Lord Almighty** (*YHWH ṣĕbā'ôt*) to accentuate God's military prowess (→ sidebar The Lord Almighty at Hag 1:2). The Lord not only leads, but also empowers his warriors to **destroy and overcome with slingstones**, which underscores divine assistance. While **slingstones** were vital weapons in ancient warfare, they were not necessarily the most effective (see 2 Chr 26:14).

The latter part of v 15 describes a raucous victory celebration following battle. Soldiers become so full of plundered **wine** that they are **like a bowl used for sprinkling the corners of the altar**. This **bowl** is the one priests used for the ritual of catching blood from a sacrifice and sprinkling it on the altar (see Exod 24:6-8; Lev 1:5).

■ **16-17** Summarizing what has just been described in vv 13-15, the prophecy declares that **the Lord their God will save them on that day** (v 16). To **save** (*yāša'*) means to rescue from danger and open up new possibilities (→ 8:7). **That day** refers to the Day of the Lord, a time designated by Israel's prophets when the Lord intervenes in exceptional ways to rescue his people. (→ 2:11 and Behind the Text at 12:1-13:9).

The Lord will rescue his people from their oppressors like a **shepherd saves his flock** (v 16). The image of God as a shepherd is frequently found in the Bible (Gen 48:15; Ps 23:1, etc.). Likewise, Israel is often compared to a flock of sheep (Jer 23:1; Ezek 36:37). Both of these images become important in chs 10 and 11 (→ Behind the Text at 11:1-17).

As a result of God's salvation, his people will **sparkle . . . like jewels in a crown** (v 16) and be **attractive and beautiful** (v 17). Both images convey the idea of a bright and glorious future for God's people in their land. They will enjoy the provisions of plentiful **grain** from the fields and **new wine** from the vineyards. These crops will energize both **young men** and **young women** so that they do not just live life, but **thrive**. Other prophets also envisioned such bountiful blessings in store for God's people in the future (Isa 4:2; 30:23; Ezek 34:26-27; Joel 3:18 [4:18 HB]; Amos 9:13).

This passage provides a vivid picture of one of the Bible's most important assertions about the future: *the Lord plans to bring worldwide peace through his messianic king.* In this prophecy, the Lord's victorious Messiah humbly rides into Jerusalem bringing justice and proclaiming peace (vv 9-10). He protects his people against oppressors (v 8), takes away weapons of war (v 10), frees captives from exile (v 11), brings them home (v 12), and causes them to flourish in the land (v 17). This is the world toward which the Lord is moving all of creation. It is good news not only for ancient Israel but for people today.

Zechariah stands in the tradition of Israel's other great prophets who also anticipated a messianic kingdom of peace and justice. They too envisioned a world in which pride, hostility, and aggression have no place (see Isa 9:6-7 [5-6 HB]; 11:7: Jer 33:15: Mic 5:5 [4 HB]).

Yet this passage also reminds us that *the Lord must engage the enemies of his people in order to establish this kingdom.* The arrogant of this world must come down (vv 1-7) and those who hold his people captive neutralized (vv 11-15). So the Lord fights for his people and purposes like a mighty warrior (v 14) and empowers those who would join him in that battle (vv 13 and 15). Peace comes at a price. But the king who finally arrives victorious in Jerusalem ultimately proclaims peace, not war.

NT writers did not miss the importance of this prophetic hope. All four Gospels allude to Zech 9:9 in their portrayal of Jesus' triumphal entry into Jerusalem (Matt 21:5-9; Mark 11:9-10; Luke 19:38; John 12:13-15). Their profile of Jesus emphasizes that he was "gentle and humble in heart" (Matt 11:29). Yet, he fully engaged the enemies of peace in this world in order to establish his kingdom. Ironically though, he did not bring it about through war or military strength but through submission and suffering (Isa 52:13-53:12; 1 Pet 2:21-25). He knew that "our struggle is not against flesh and blood, but against the rulers, against the authorities, against the powers of this dark world and against the spiritual forces of evil in the heavenly realms" (Eph 6:12).

2. The Hope of Divine Care (10:1-12)

BEHIND THE TEXT

This chapter develops the image of the Lord as a shepherd and his people as sheep. This idea was briefly introduced in ch 9 when it says, "God will save his people . . . as a shepherd saves his flock" (9:16). Chapter 11 will take this image further in a story about a rejected shepherd.

Several commentators and translations see 11:1-3 as a fitting conclusion to ch 10. The verses continue in rhythmic poetic lines like the rest of ch 10 and 11:4 starts a prose section. Yet the tone and subject matter of 11:1-3 moves away from that of ch 10. The call to mourning in these verses functions better as an introduction to the rejected shepherd in ch 11. These verses also connect to the last verse of ch 11, which returns to poetic verse and the theme of remorse. Thus the poetic sections of 11:1-3 and 11:17 form a literary inclusion that frames the story of the rejected shepherd (see Smith 1984, 267 and Hanson 1979, 334-337).

The prophetic words in ch 10 display typical features of the messenger speech. In the opening verses the prophet creatively describes the situation God addresses (vv 1-2). Then the remainder of the chapter relates the divine message for that situation (vv 3-12). This message alternates between divine declaration and human implications. Thus the message consists of a series of five couplets announcing what God will do followed by the effects of those actions (vv 3-5, 6-7, 8-9, 10-11, 12*a-b*). The entire message concludes with a messenger formula (v 12*c*).

IN THE TEXT

■ **1-2** The first two verses describe the situation to which the message of this chapter is addressed: God's people **wander like sheep . . . for lack of a shepherd** (v 2). The ancient world often used the image of a **shepherd** as a metaphor for both spiritual and political leaders. So the point is that Judah's leaders either are absent or have not fulfilled their roles of guiding people toward God. As a result, people are **oppressed** (*'ānâ*), meaning they have become objects of violence for predators, as wandering sheep are prone to be.

The prophet's opening statement indicates why people have become so vulnerable. They have been seeking divine help from fertility gods, perhaps the Canaanite gods Baal or Asherah, for **rain in the springtime** (v 1). Some people believed these gods controlled rainfall and brought fertility to the ground. But the prophet urges them to **ask the Lord** instead, because he is truly the one **who sends the thunderstorms, showers of rain,** and **plants of the field to everyone** (see Gen 7:4; Exod 9:33; 1 Kgs 18:1; Job 38:22-30; Jer 14:22; Ezek 13:13).

Spiritual leaders in the community apparently directed people toward **idols** and **diviners** for divine guidance (v 2). **Idols** (*terāpîm*) probably refers to household images that represent fertility gods or ancestors. **Diviners** were highly trained professionals who believed they could determine the will of the gods by observing unusual natural phenomena, examining sheep livers, or mixing oil and water. The prophet reminds his audience that both of these **give comfort in vain**, because they **speak deceitfully, see visions that lie,** and **tell dreams that are false.** The term **vain** (*hebel*) is used throughout Ecclesiastes to describe that which evaporates and gains nothing (Eccl 1:2).

■ **3** Verses 3-12 convey the Lord's reaction to Judah's lack of faithful shepherds. The Lord begins by expressing his intense ire **against the shepherds** (v 3). The idiom **anger burns** (*ḥārâ 'ap*) evokes the image of a hot, raging fire. This is God's response toward those who break covenant with him by pursuing other gods (Deut 6:14-15). The book of Zechariah begins by announcing God's intense anger toward his people (→ 1:2) and then toward the nations who mistreated them (→ 1:15).

Such emotion moves God both to **punish the leaders** and to **care for his flock** (v 3). Both actions, **punish** and **care for,** derive from the same rood *pāqad*, which literally means to attend to or visit. As in this verse, the Lord might visit someone in judgment (Amos 3:2) or with care (Exod 3:16). **Leaders** (*'attûdîm*) is literally "male goats," an appropriate image for those who would lead a flock astray.

With the Lord's care Judah will become **like a proud horse in battle** (v 2), confident and victorious. The contrast between a powerful mounted steed and a sheep that wanders without a shepherd conveys a significant transformation that awaits Judah.

■ **4** The Lord announces the coming of a new kind of leader who will strengthen the community rather than weaken it as the "leaders" in vv 1-3 did. The new leader will be like **the cornerstone, the tent peg,** and **the battle bow,** all metaphors that convey stability (v 4). **The cornerstone** was a large cut stone placed in a foundation to provide orientation for the rest of a building. **The tent peg** secured the ropes of a tent, while a **battle bow** served as a basic weapon for ancient armies.

This new leader derives **from Judah** (the Hebrew literally reads "from him," but the NIV appropriately supplies **Judah** as the antecedent from the previous verse). Many interpreters, beginning as earlier as the Aramaic Targums, have understood this new leader to be one particular descendent of Judah, the Messiah. Other OT passages connect the Messiah to the image of a cornerstone (Isa 28:16; Ps 118:22) and NT writers see a similar relationship with Jesus (Matt 21:42; Acts 4:11; Rom 9:30; Eph 2:20; 1 Pet 2:6-8). Yet, no other biblical passage connects the Messiah to a tent peg or battle bow. Since the next verse begins with a plural pronoun, several rulers could be in view rather than one (see Boda 2004, 441-442 and Klein 2008, 293-295).

■ **5** As a result of the stabilizing influence of the new leader, Judah will be like elite **warriors in battle** (*gibbōrîm*), a term that connotes superior soldiers of war (v 5). Such men constituted David's crack troops, his "mighty men," in a previous era (2 Sam 23:8-39). They will be **trampling their enemy into the mud of the streets** as they press forward in battle. They will also **put the enemy horsemen to shame,** which could imply hamstringing their horses so they cannot be used again. Both images portray Judah's troops as victorious combatants, though their success is not due to their abilities. They win because **the LORD is with them.** Once again the book of Zechariah highlights the profound difference God's presence makes for Judah and her leaders (→ 4:6; see also 1:16; 2:10; 8:3; 9:14).

■ **6** The Lord announces that he will be the shepherd of all Israel, both **Judah** and the **tribes of Joseph,** here a designation for the northern Israel (v 6). Once again the text anticipates a united Israel as in the days of David (see 8:13, 9:10 and 9:13).

God promises to **strengthen, save,** and **restore** Israel (v 6). **Strengthen** (*gābar*) connotes the idea of equipping men for warfare. **Save** (*yāša'*) regularly describes God's activity of rescuing and providing new opportunity for life as he did in the Exodus from Egypt (→ 9:16). **Restore** (*šub*) implies not just reclaiming lost possessions but also returning to covenant relationship with God (Jer 30:3).

327

This means people will know the Lord as **their God** and he **will answer them**, phrases that characterize Israel's covenant experience with the Lord (Jer 31:33; → Zech 8:8).

God's **compassion** for his people is the primary motive that underlies this promise (v 6), because by nature the Lord is a merciful God (Exod 34:7; Ps 103:8; Jer 42:12). Such compassion realigns Israel's relationship to God so that **they will be as though I had not rejected them**. Exile had been a sign of God's rejection (Lam 2:7). But this will fade into past memory as the Lord restores his people.

■ **7** Further signs of restoration include **the Ephraimites** becoming **like warriors** celebrating victory (v 7). **The Ephraimites** designates the old northern kingdom of Israel just as "the tribes of Joseph" did in v 6. The tribe of Ephraim was the most dominant group in Israel with the capitol of Samaria located within its boundaries. These also **become like warriors** (*gibborîm*), men of exceptional military prowess, like the troops of Judah in v 5.

Words like **glad**, **joyful**, and **rejoice** express a victorious celebratory mood among God's people (v 7). Such joy springs from deep within, from **their hearts**. It also comes from the most vulnerable of society, **their children**, which indicates that life is truly good.

■ **8** The last five verses of this unit describe the final stage of Israel's restoration, the return of those who remain in exile. The promise of exiles returning recurs throughout Zechariah, in the visions as well as the oracles (2:6-7; 8:4-8; 9:12).

Three things the Lord will do to bring his people home are **signal, gather,** and **redeem** (v 8). The **signal** God sends to his people is a whistle, like shepherds might do in order to herd their flocks. This will help **gather** those exiles that were scattered like seeds throughout the nations (→ 7:14). To **redeem** (*pādâ*) means to pay a price in order to obtain something, such as freedom from slavery. This term describes what the Lord did when he delivered his people from Egypt (Deut 15:15; 24:18).

These divine acts will result in God's people becoming **as numerous as before** (v 8). Since Babylonian invasions and deportations had drastically reduced the population of Israel, this is a significant promise. It recalls God's promise to Abraham to multiply his descendants and make them "as numerous as the stars in the sky and as the sand on the seashore" (Gen 22:17).

■ **9-10** The Lord also promises **they will remember me** (v 9*a*), even though several generations had passed since Israel first went into exile in 722 BC. God anticipates **they and their children will survive and they will return** (v 9*b*), because God will personally **bring them back from Egypt** and **Assyria** (v 10*a*). These were two of the main areas where Israel's population went into exile and most likely represent many other regions where Jews settled.

The Lord plans to **bring them to Gilead and Lebanon** (v 10*b*), areas located along the fringes of the promised land to the east and north respectively. If returning exiles must settle in these regions, it means **there will not be room enough for** them within the traditional boundaries of Israel. The blessings of Israel's restoration will be so great that the land "will be too small" for its population (Isa 49:19).

■ **11** Israel's return means that obstacles must be overcome, such as **the sea of trouble, the surging sea,** and **the depths of the Nile** (v 11). These water barriers indicate that the experience of the returning exiles will be similar to that of their ancestors whom the Lord led out of Egypt (see Exod 15:1-18). They too will witness a dramatic display of divine power that will make it possible for them to reenter the promised land (cp. Isa 11:11-16). **Assyria** and **Egypt** receive special mention here because they are the two national super powers that oppressed Israel in the past. If the Lord can subdue the **pride** and **scepter** (a symbol of power in a king's hand) of these two, then no enemy can stand in the way of the Lord when he comes to save his people.

■ **12** In a final word of encouragement, the Lord promises once more to **strengthen** his people (v 12). This is the second time in this unit that the Lord has specifically promised strength (see v 6). They will **live securely** in the land because of the strong **name** of the Lord, not because of their own strength or power (cp. 4:6). The phrase **live securely** extends the normal meaning of the Hebrew word *hālak*, which literally means "to walk." Often in the OT walking metaphorically describes living in covenant commitment to God (Deut 10:12; 30:16; Mic 6:8). Therefore, v 12 implies that walking in the covenant way of life is what makes a secure life in the promise land possible for Israel.

FROM THE TEXT

Several truths about God ordained leadership within the community of faith emerge from this passage and give hope to believers in every generation.

First and foremost, *the Lord provides the ideal model of a caring leader of people.* As sovereign sustainer of creation the Lord sends "showers of rain to all people" and makes things grow (v 1). Then like a shepherd who truly cares for his flock the Lord empowers people to become as confident as "a proud horse in battle" (v 3) and expert "warriors" able to defeat their enemies (v 5). Driven by deep "compassion," the Lord strengthens, rescues and restores his people (v 6). He "redeems" them and brings them home where they can "live securely" once again as a complete family that includes Judah as well as "the tribes of Joseph" (vv 8-12).

Without strong leadership people languish. They become like lost sheep who are vulnerable to predators (v 2). Desperate for life sustaining resources like rain for crops, they will turn to popular sources like "idols" and "diviners" who can only lie and "give comfort in vain" (v 2).

So the LORD promises a leader from Judah who will be a stabilizing force among his people. He will provide orientation for life like a "cornerstone," grounded direction like a "tent peg," and secure protection like a "battle bow" (v 4). This person is God's Messiah, the kind of leader for whom godly people in every generation long. From the perspective of the early Christians, Jesus Christ was such a leader for his followers. He was the good shepherd who laid down his life for his sheep (John

10:1-18). In so doing, he became the "cornerstone" upon which the community of faith was built (Eph 2:20; 1 Pet 2:6-8).

3. The Rejection of the Lord's Shepherd (11:1-17)

BEHIND THE TEXT

The oracle of chs 9-11 ends on a sad note. The joy of the king's coming in ch 9 and the hope of divine care in ch 10 turn bleak in ch 11. God's people reject their appointed shepherd and bear the consequences of that decision as a worthless shepherd replaces the rejected one.

The ancient world frequently compared leaders such as kings, priests, and even deities to shepherds in order to highlight their role as providers and protectors of people. This occurred as early as the third millennium BC when a Sumerian king named Lugalzagessi applied the terminology to himself. Various Egyptian and Mesopotamian texts in subsequent centuries continued using this metaphor for leaders as well. OT writers also compared Israel's leaders to shepherds (see Num 27:17; 2 Sam 5:2; 7:8; Ps 78:71) and even described the Lord as a shepherd on several occasions (see Gen 48:15; Ps 23:1; 95:7; Isa 40:11). Israel's prophets frequently employed shepherd imagery to highlight the role of the Messiah as a provider and protector of people, a task that Israel's rulers often failed to carry out (Jer 23:1-6; 25:34-38; Ezek 34:1-31; Mic 5:4 [3 HB]; see Ryken 1998, 782-785).

Chapter 11 employs three distinct genres. The first three verses constitute a prophetic taunt song (vv 1-3), which conveys a message of judgment by mocking its recipient. This is followed by an autobiographical prose section (vv 4-16) reporting symbolic actions of the prophet, a genre used throughout prophetic literature (e.g., Ezek 4:1-5:17 and Jer 43:8-13) and found earlier in Zech 3:1-10 and 6:9-15. Finally, the chapter ends with a poetic woe oracle that laments God's coming judgment (v 17). The two poetic units form a frame around the prose section, which tends to highlight the theme of God's judgment upon Judah's foolish shepherds/rulers for abandoning their flock.

IN THE TEXT

a. A Taunt Song (11:1-3)

■ 1-3 This short poetic unit is a taunt song that imagines the deforestation of **Lebanon**, **Basham** and the **Jordan** valley in order to picture God's judgment on Judah's rulers (v 1). These three areas represented some of the most fertile regions in and around Israel.

The song begins with an urgent call to **Lebanon** to **open your doors** (v 1). These words evoke the image of a royal processional when a triumphant king returns to his capital city (see Ps 24:7-10). **Lebanon** sits north of the land of Israel and was noted for its densely forested mountains of **cedars**, a highly valued tree for construction of palaces and temples (1 Kgs 5:6). In a dramatic twist to the celebratory procession theme, the prophet announces that **fire** will enter the gates instead of a victorious king and **devour** (*'ākal*) its vegetation like an animal eating its prey. The irony of the verse is that Lebanon is urged to invite destruction upon itself.

As fire ravishes the forest, the song turns to a lament and invites **juniper** trees, which grow alongside the cedar, to **wail** over the **fallen** cedars, the **stately trees** in the forest (v 2). If mighty cedars fall, other trees do not stand a chance. **Wail** (*hêlēl*) is an expression of deep sorrow, even despair, and accordingly prophets frequently used this term to announce divine judgment (see e.g., Isa 23:1 and Jer 25:34).

The **oaks of Bashan** should also wail, because destruction is coming to them as well (v 2). The region of **Bashan** sits east of the Sea of Galilee and was known for its tree groves and lush pastoral lands for grazing sheep and cattle (Amos 4:1). The fertile areas of both **Lebanon** and **Bashan** stood as symbols of pride to the prophets of Israel (Isa 2:13).

The song ends by announcing a third area of rich vegetation marked for destruction, **the Jordan** valley (v 3). **The Jordan** carries water from the Sea of Galilee to the Dead Sea. Though not large, the river provides **rich pastures** for sheep and **lush thickets** for wildlife along its banks. The term **rich pastures** (*'eder*) denotes extra fertile fields for grazing. The song asks the reader to **listen** for the sounds of mourning coming from **the shepherds** who tend sheep and **the lion** who hunts his prey there. The ruin of this area symbolically expresses God's judgment upon the pride of Judah's leaders.

b. The First Commission and Its Execution (11:4-14)

■ **4-5** The autobiographical report in vv 4-14 begins with a divine command to the prophet to perform a symbolic act: **shepherd the flock** (v 4). The reference to the Lord as **my God** implies the personal relationship between the Lord and the prophet. It may also imply that the leaders and the people mentioned in the following verses do not enjoy the same kind of relationship with God.

The **flock** the prophet must tend is the people of Judah. They have been **marked for slaughter,** which might initially suggest they were like sheep in the temple flocks dedicated to the Lord for sacrifices. But v 5 indicates that the phrase actually means they were like sheep that owners might sell off to for profit. The market place scene of **buyers** and **those who sell** presents an image of a community that is being exploited by its leaders, **their own shepherds.** These local political and religious rulers **do not spare** the flock. Literally, they have "no pity" on the flock (see NRSV, ESV). There is corruption and self-enrichment at all levels among Judah's leadership.

■ **6** The next verse can be understood as an explanation as to why Judah suffered at the hands of its leaders. It is because the Lord withheld his favor. As God explains, **I no longer have pity on the people** . . . and **I will give everyone into the hands of their neighbors and their king** (v 6). As such, this verse would allude to

331

past judgments in which the Lord delivered Israel into the hands of their enemies, the Assyrian, the Babylonian, and the Persians.

Another way to understand this verse, however, is to view it as the Lord anticipating his response to the rejection of the prophet/shepherd in v 8. The Lord is explaining how the symbolic act will play out. God **will no longer have pity** (*hāmal*; v 6) because Judah's leaders "do not spare (*hāmal*; have pity on) them" (v 5). So when the people of Judah refuse to receive God's shepherd, the Lord will respond like Judah's shepherds.

Without the Lord's protective care Judah will be at the mercy of **their neighbor and their king** (v 6). The Hebrew word for **neighbor** (*rēa'*) sounds similar to the word for shepherd (*ro'eh*). This play on words highlights the change that takes place in the Judah as neighboring authorities seize control of the Judah instead of local leaders. This became Judah's destiny for centuries as Persians, then Greeks directed the affairs of Judah. For a brief century following the Maccabean revolt in 164 BC Judah regained control of local affairs under the Hasmonean family. But Romans eventually came to dominate once again and other foreign powers followed until the independent state of Israel emerged in the mid-twentieth century AD.

The Lord projects that these foreign rulers **will devastate** (*crush*) **the land** and he will not intervene to **rescue anyone from their hands.** The people of Judah will become like helpless sheep without a shepherd to save them from violent enemies (cp. Matt 9:36). The Roman destruction of Jerusalem in AD 70 is one event that matches this description.

■ **7** In vv 7-14, the prophet reports his efforts to accomplish the Lord's instruction in v 4 to act as a shepherd to **the flock marked for slaughter** (v 7). He gave special attention to **the oppressed of the flock** as a good shepherd would. **The oppressed** (*'ani*) are those who have become injured either by accident or violence. As Ezekiel indicates, an ideal shepherd looked after "the weak ... the sick . . . the injured . . . the strays . . . the lost" (Ezek 34:4; see also Zech 11:16).

Alternate Translation of Verse 7

Translators have taken different approaches to understanding the Hebrew text behind the phrase **particularly the oppressed of** (*lāken 'ăniyyê*) in v 7. The question is whether the two words *lāken 'ăniyyê* should be understood as one word *likna'aniyye*, which would mean "for the merchants of." This requires a slight change in vowels and a different word division from the MT. It makes the verse refer to the marketplace buyers and sellers of v 6 and indicates that they employ the shepherd and that he served their interests. The Septuagint rendered it this way. But the Latin Vulgate followed the MT. Modern English translations divide similarly. The NRSV and ESV agree with the Septuagint, while NIV, NASB, NJPS, and HCSB take the approach of the Latin. The same issue arises in v 11 (see Clark and Hatton 2002, 289-290).

The prophet reports three other actions he performed in the following verses. First, he took **two staffs** and called one **Favor** and the other **Union.** A shepherd's staff is a stick of wood used as a weapon for protecting the flock and a prod for guiding it. The names of these **two staffs** symbolize important ideas to God's people. The staff called **Favor** (*nō'am*) refers to that which is delightful or pleasant; v 10 clarifies that this staff signifies God's **favor** in establishing a covenant with all the nations.

The other staff named **Union** represents the unification of the northern and southern kingdoms of Israel according to v 14. This staff recalls Ezekiel's symbolic act of writing on two sticks to signify Israel and Judah reuniting under one Davidic king (Ezek 37:15-28). Part of the prophetic vision for Israel's ultimate restoration in the messianic age includes the reconciliation of all of Jacob's descendants (Isa 11:11-13; Zech 8:13; 9:13; 10:7-12). The prophet may well be symbolically performing the tasks of the Messiah with his two staffs. Thus he portrays what one might call a Shepherd-Messiah.

■ **8** The prophet/shepherd moves decisively to protect the flock in v 8. In a relatively brief time of **one month**, the prophet reports that he **got rid of the three shepherds** (v 8). The text does not identify who these **three shepherds** represent or why they were dismissed. They were undoubtedly the kind of leaders who mistreated people like those mentioned earlier in v 5 and later in v 16. Not enough detail exists to connect these leaders to any particular historical figure either past, present, or future (see Baldwin 1972, 181-183 and Klein 2008, 329-332 for a survey of various views). Since the number **three** can symbolize completeness, the text may intend to say that he dismissed every unfit leader.

According to the NIV, **the flock** did not appreciate the work of God's appointed shepherd (v 8). The word **flock** does not actually appear in the Hebrew text however. Instead "their soul" (*napšām*) occurs, which is a poetic way of saying "they" and could be a reference either to the people of Judah, the merchants, or the three shepherds. The NIV interpretation makes good sense because v 9 mentions being "your shepherd," a statement better addressed to the flock rather than either the merchants or the three shepherds. But compare the NASB, NRSV, NJPS, NKJV and HCSB who take the three shepherds as the antecedent of *napšām*.

The second part of v 8 indicates that the flock **detested** their shepherd who was concerned for their well-being. This is likely the reason why the shepherd **grew weary** of the flock. The phrase **grew weary of them** literally translates "my soul became short with them," which is an idiom expressing impatience. It appears that the flock preferred to be led by **three shepherds** who did not care for them rather than by the shepherd who did care about their well-being.

■ **9** In response to his rejection, the prophet announces **I will not be your shepherd** (v 9). To add emphasis to this ominous pronouncement, the prophet utters a curse of relinquishment and breaks a staff to symbolize termination of his shepherd role. The curse poetically calls for death to the flock: **Let the dying die, and the perishing perish. Let those who are left eat one another's flesh** (v 9). He abandons the flock to death and destruction, an outcome anticipated in v 6.

■ **10** After announcing the curse, the prophet breaks the **staff called Favor** (v 10). This symbolized termination of **the covenant** the Lord had **made with all the nations**. A divine covenant with all the nations is not mentioned anywhere else in the OT, though it could reflect the promise to Abraham that "all peoples on earth" would be blessed through him and his descendants (Gen 12:3). However, in light of other OT passages, it is not likely this verse announces the termination of that promise. Rather, this verse could be more appropriately linked to God's "covenant of peace" with Israel, which promises restoration to the promised land following exile (see Ezek 34:25-28; 37:24-26). This covenant assures Israel of protection and safety from predatory nations. With this covenant broken though, Judah will suffer at the hands of other nations (as v 6 suggests).

Thus, the shepherd who was detested by the flock not only dismisses himself from his duty, but also abandons his flock to attacks from invading nations. They will no longer be protected or guided by the shepherd's staffs.

■ **11** The dramatic act of breaking the staffs drew the attention of **the oppressed of the flock** (v 11). **The oppressed** could also be translated "the sheep merchants" as in v 7 (so NRSV and ESV; → sidebar Alternate Translation of Verse 7). They, either **the flock** or the merchants (or perhaps both), **were watching** the prophet act out the role of the rejected shepherd. They saw this symbolic action as **the word of the** LORD. The context favors "the sheep merchants" in this verse, because it is likely that they would have recognized this symbolic act as the Lord's decision to let them prey on the flock and enrich themselves as they have done before (see v 5). Verse 12 makes more sense if this reading of v 11 is followed.

■ **12** The prophet asks the merchants for his **pay**, if they thought he deserved wages for abandoning the flock (v 12). Their payment of **thirty pieces of silver** indicates that they saw his action benefitting them in some way. **They paid** is literally, "they weighed out" (NASB), which reflects the ancient system of weighing bits of metal rather than using minted coins.

■ **13** The amount paid the prophet is described as a **handsome** (*'eder*) **price** (v 13), a "magnificent" or "lordly" price (see NASB, NRSV, ESV). This might be taken as a significant amount since Exodus 21:32 cites "thirty shekels of silver" as compensation for a slave being gored to death by a bull. But many commentators take **handsome price** as sarcastic. They interpret it as an insulting wage in light of the Lord's next instruction.

The Lord instructs the prophet to **throw it to the potter ... at the house of the** LORD. The term **throw** (*šalak*) connotes intense action of casting or flinging something, perhaps in frustration. The term **potter** (*yôşēr*) could be translated "treasury" (NRSV), if one alters the letters slightly and follows the Syriac version. But the MT reads **potter** or artisan, meaning one who works with either clay or metal. This was a low-level employee retained at the temple for smelting metal offerings or crafting sacred pottery.

In obedience to the Lord's command, the prophet performed the symbolic action. He **threw them to the potter** as a way of emphasizing his rejection of Judah

334

for rejecting him. Matthew alludes to the **thirty pieces of silver** when Judas receives payment for his betrayal of Jesus (Matt 26:15; see also Matt 27:9-10).

■ **14** The prophet performs one more symbolic act of rejection when he breaks **the second staff called Union** (v 14). This act symbolizes that **the family bond between Judah and Israel** is broken. In other words, the rejection of God's appointed shepherd suspends the promise of the reunification of Jacob's descendants. The promise projected that Israel and Judah would be restored from the lands of their exile into a unified nation under one Davidic shepherd (Ezek 37:19-24).

c. The Second Commission to the Prophet (11:15-16)

■ **15** The Lord commands the prophet to perform one more deed that will illustrate the consequences of rejecting the Lord's shepherd. He directs him to **take again the equipment of a foolish shepherd** (v 15). The term **foolish** (*'ĕwilî*) occurs frequently in wisdom literature to designate those who live contrary to God's direction for life. They despise wisdom (Prov 1:7), spurn parental advice (Prov 15:5), are quarrelsome (Prov 20:3), and become easily insulted (Prov 12:16). Basically the word means to be thick, as in thickheaded. A **foolish shepherd** then does not understand his true role; he is functionally "worthless" in his job as v 17 indicates.

The **equipment of a foolish shepherd** evidently does not include items that shepherds typically carried. Ordinarily a shepherd would possess a staff with a bent end for prodding and rescuing sheep, a pipe for calling the sheep (Judg 5:16), a horn of oil to tend injuries (Ps 23:5), and a weapon such as a club or a slingshot with stones (1 Sam 17:40). Based on what follows **the equipment of a foolish shepherd** might include cooking pots and eating utensils, for this shepherd preys upon his flock rather than nurtures them.

Thus this unfit shepherd **will not care for the lost, or seek the young, or heal the injured, or feed the healthy** (v 16). **The lost, the young,** and **the injured** represent the most vulnerable in a flock. They must have the shepherd's care to survive. Instead of caring for his sheep though, the unfit shepherd **will eat the meat of the choice sheep, tearing off their hoofs**. Eating **the meat of the choice sheep** threatens the future of the flock since these are the healthy ones that need to be used for breeding, not for food. **Tearing off their hoofs** connotes avarice and brutality through hyperbole. This action exaggerates the image of a person greedily consuming a sheep.

These actions describe the kind of cruel leader no one desires. Yet, the Lord promises to **raise up** such a person to rule **over the land** of Judah. Since people rejected his caring shepherd, the Lord designates a "foolish shepherd" who exploits rather than protects his people.

d. Curse for the Worthless Shepherd (11:17)

■ **17** The prophet finishes his report of symbolic actions by announcing a poetic **woe to the worthless shepherd** (v 17). Woe (*hoy*) is an expression of mourning that one might hear at a funeral and recalls the plea to "wail" in v 2. Prophets frequently introduce laments and judgments with these words (Amos 5:18; Hab 2:6-19; see "woe to the shepherds" of Judah in Jer 23:1 and Ezek 34:2).

The foolish shepherd of v 15 is now called **the worthless shepherd** (v 17). Worthless (*'ĕlîl*) connotes something that is weak or deficient. **He is useless because he deserts the flock** leaving them vulnerable to the dangers of the field.

So the prophet pronounces a curse that calls for this shepherd to become powerless, like a wounded soldier. After being struck with a **sword**, the shepherd will find **his arm . . . completely withered** and **his right eye totally blinded** (v 17). He will not be able to fight effectively since his **arm** would normally wield a sword or spear and his **right eye** aim an arrow. As a result, he will no longer be able to ravage the flock under his care.

FROM THE TEXT

Zechariah 11 is a powerful commentary on Israel's leaders throughout its history. As such it reminds us that the role of leaders in the community of faith and the responses of people to them carry significant impact in ancient as well as modern times.

From this text we see that *the Lord desires community leaders who will truly care for and protect those they lead*. God's first instructed the prophet to "shepherd the flock marked for slaughter" (v 4). In this role the prophet took particular care of "the oppressed" and employed staffs that represented grace and unity (v 7). He eliminated uncaring shepherds (v 8) and undoubtedly became the kind of ideal leader described in chs 9-10 who would "care for his flock" (10:3).

Such a person reflects the character God desires to see in all leaders. In addition, the profile of this good shepherd also provides an image of the promised Messiah in the OT. Along with Ezekiel, Zechariah envisioned a time when the Lord "will place over them one shepherd . . . and he will tend" the flock of God's people (Ezek 34:22-23 and 37:24; see also Mic 5:4 [3 HB]).

Unfortunately, *people tend to reject God's plans for them and suffer the consequences of that decision*. The flock "detested" the good shepherd and, as a result, he "grew weary of them" (v 8). The prophet stopped being a shepherd to the flock and broke his staffs of grace and unity (vv 9-10). Then the Lord instructed the prophet to perform a second symbolic act and take on the role of "a foolish shepherd" (v 15). This shepherd exploited his flock and essentially destroyed them (v 16). At this point the text seems inspired by the images of Israel's unfaithful shepherds in Ezek 34:1-10 and the unruly flock in Ezek 34:17-19. The sad irony is that the people of God would rather have leaders who enrich themselves at the expense of their flock, than shepherds who are concerned for their well-being.

The image of the rejected shepherd in ch 11 clarifies why NT writers turned to Zechariah for understanding Jesus Christ. They saw in Zech 11 a portrait of Jesus, rejected by the religious leaders and the Jewish people of his day. John says, "He came to that which was his own, but his own did not receive him" (John 1:11).

Matthew saw a connection between the "thirty pieces of silver" in Zech 11:12-13 and the money paid Judas received for betraying Jesus (Matt 26:15; 27:5-10).

The story of this rejected shepherd continues to unfold in subsequent passages of Zechariah. In 12:10 the prophet speaks of "the one they have pierced" and 13:7 identifies a shepherd who is struck with a sword and his flock scatters. The gospel writers relate these passages to Jesus as well (→ 12:10 and 13:7). For early Christians, these passages in Zechariah portrayed the rejection of God's Messiah that culminated in Jesus' crucifixion and death.

B. Final Triumph of the Messianic Kingdom (12:1—14:21)

1. Spiritual Transformation of God's People (12:1—13:9)

BEHIND THE TEXT

The concluding oracle of the book (chs 12-14) assures its audience that the messianic kingdom will prevail. Judah's rejection of their Messiah in the previous oracle (ch 11) is not the final word. The ultimate salvation of Jerusalem, which represents the kingdom of God, will happen according to the Lord's designs. God's covenant people will be fully restored one day.

The phrase "on that day" is found sixteen times in the forty-four verses of the final three chapters of Zechariah. It is a shorter form of the longer designation the Day of the Lord, which is found in 14:1 and regularly in other prophetic literature (e.g., see Zeph 1:7 and 14; see other variations of this phrase in Isa 2:2; Jer 23:5; Joel 3:1 [4:1 HB]; Amos 5:18; Mal 3:17).

The Day of the Lord is a moment in time when God manifests his presence in his world in dramatic ways. On this day the Lord judges his enemies and brings salvation to his people. Thus for those opposed to God it becomes a dreadful day of wrath, trouble, and gloom (Isa 13:6-9; Joel 2:1-2; Zeph 1:14-18). Yet the people of God can expect deliverance, purification, and blessing (Isa 4:2-4; Hos 2:16-23 [18-25 HB]; Mal 3:2-4), including the outpouring of God's Spirit (Joel 2:28-32 [3:1-5 HB]). While this day frequently describes a time beyond human history, it can also occur within it. When the phrase occurs in conjunction with "and it will be," as it regularly does in chs 12-14, the focus is eschatological, a time beyond the present age.

The object of the Lord's saving actions in these chapters is "the house of David and the inhabitants of Jerusalem" (12:7, 8, 10; 13:1) or simply the city of Jerusalem (12:2, 3, 6, 9, 11). Judah and its leaders are also frequently designated (12:2, 4, 5, 6, 7). These entities refer to the place where the Lord's temple was located along with its leadership and local population. But they represent much more than a particular geographical location or historical persons. In the eschatological context of these chapters, they symbolize the people of God that the Lord intends finally to restore.

337

The oracle contained in chs 12-14 is a tightly woven speech with a number of overlapping patterns used to bind its parts. As a result, scholars differ on their analysis of the literary structure of the oracle. Most scholars recognize ch 14 as a meaningful, stand-alone literary unit that describes the ultimate victory of the Lord at the end of human history. But how chs 12 and 13 divide remains debated (see Clark and Hatton 2002, 307 for a survey of various options). In the end, the most meaningful approach is to view chs 12 and 13 together as one continuous description of Jerusalem's spiritual transformation. That transformation unfolds in four parts beginning with Jerusalem's inhabitants experiencing deliverance (12:1-9). This is followed by the people's repentance (12:10-14), their cleansing (13:1-6), and finally their refining (13:7-9).

IN THE TEXT

a. Deliverance (12:1-9)

■ **1** Zechariah introduces the content of chs 12-14 as a **prophecy** (*massā'*), the same label used for chs 9-11 (→ 9:1). It is **the word of the LORD**, which indicates the divine origin of the message of these chapters. It concerns all the descendants of Abraham, the people of **Israel,** not only the people of Judah (v 1).

The introduction to the speech affirms God's universal authority as Creator of the world. The Lord is the one **who stretches out the heavens** like a tent over a frame and **lays the foundations of the earth** like a craftsman setting stones for a building (cp. Ps 104:2, 5). Additionally, like a potter the Lord **forms the human spirit within a person**. The term **forms** (*yāṣar*) suggests the image of shaping something with one's hands as a potter would do (see Gen 2:7; Ps 33:15; 139:13-16). The Creator's domains include all of creation, **the heavens, the earth**, and **the human spirit**. The Hebrew text employs participles to express the divine actions of stretching, laying, and forming, which implies ongoing creation. The Lord who continually and purposefully designs creation will move it toward the final goal that he deems fit in the following verses.

■ **2** The language that exalts the Lord as creator in v 1 is appropriate, since in the following verses he is the one who directs the destiny of Judah and the nations. The Lord asserts emphatically (**I** [*'ānōkî*] plus "behold" [*hinnēh*]) that he will personally act to make Jerusalem **a cup** of intoxicating drink that **sends all the surrounding peoples reeling** (v 2). Other prophets also use the image of nations or Jerusalem drinking from the cup of the Lord's wrath (see Isa 51:17; Hab 2:16; Jer 25:15; cp. seven bowls of wrath in Rev 16). The language of **reeling** conveys a state of drunkenness, which pictures the nations stumbling over each other as they attempt to enter the besieged city and plunder it.

■ **3** Though v 1 anticipates massive destruction and plundering of Jerusalem, the Lord effectively turns the nations' drunkenness to the benefit of Jerusalem. Though surrounded by enemies, the Lord announces that he will **make Jerusalem an immovable rock for all the nations**. This **immovable rock** evokes an image of the massive limestone rocks used to construct the foundation of monumental buildings like the temple. Thus no foreign power will be able to penetrate Jerusalem's defenses. Those who attempt to do so **will injury themselves**.

■ **4** The Lord intends to completely demoralize and weaken the elite troops of enemy nations. The Lord will strike them with **panic** and **madness** and blindness, thus making them totally incapable of carrying out an attack against Judah (v 4). In contrast to the blinded eyes of **the horses**, the Lord's eyes are **watchful**, literally "open" (*pākaḥ*), **over the house of Judah** (cp. 9:8).

■ **5** The Lord's actions will generate spiritual conviction among Judah's **clans** (*'alupîm*) or perhaps its "leaders" (v 5). The term *'alupîm* could have either meaning (see "governors" in NKJV; "leaders" in HCSB). The point is that people within Judah will recognize God's hand in the deliverance of Jerusalem. They will acknowledge that the people of Jerusalem remain **strong** during this crisis **because the LORD Almighty is their God** (see NRSV, "The inhabitants of Jerusalem have strength through the LORD of hosts, their God"). This affirmation echoes Zech 4:6 in which the Lord's proclaims, "Not by might, nor by power, but by my Spirit." It also fulfills the Lord's promise in 10:6 and 12 to strengthen his people.

■ **6** Two more images describe the strength of God's people during enemy attack. They have already been compared to a cup of strong drink (v 2) and a heavy stone (v 3). Now they are like **a firepot in a woodpile** and **a flaming torch among sheaves** (v 6). A **firepot** is a metal pan used to carry hot coals during temple rituals (Lev 10:1-2). **A flaming torch** might be made of oil-soaked rags on a stick or of twigs bunched together. Both could set a **woodpile** or bundles of grain ablaze with fire. An ancient audience might envision fire sweeping across a field during the dry season of harvest.

The fire generated by God's people is controlled burning though. It consumes **all the surrounding peoples**, that is, the enemies that came to attack (see vv 2, 3, 9). **But Jerusalem**, the prized possession of the Lord and his people, **will remain intact in her place**. Like Ps 48 and other passages, this verse affirms that "God makes her [Jerusalem] secure forever" (Ps 48:8; see also Ps 46; Isa 37:35).

■ **7** People living throughout Judah will share the honor of victory alongside those in Jerusalem. Typically, invading armies subdued villages and cities of a region before attacking its central city. Sennacherib, for example, "attacked all the fortified cities of Judah and captured them" prior to laying siege to Jerusalem in 701 BC (2 Kgs 18:13). But in this oracle the Lord promises to **save the dwellings of Judah first** (v 7). As a result, the ruling family of **the house of David** and the rest of **Jerusalem's inhabitants** will receive no more credit for the triumph than the outlying areas of Judah. The **first** victories will occur outside the holy city.

Tension between city and rural dwellers existed throughout Israel's history, particularly in the restoration period. The divine act announced in this verse affirms the value of all Jews who populate the land of Judah. While people living in Jerusalem might have felt more important because of their immediate connection to the temple and political structures, others in the holy land held just as much significance to God.

■ **8** As enemies advance against Jerusalem the Lord promises to act as a shield-bearer for the city (v 8). An aide often accompanied a premier warrior in ancient times, especially a king, in order to **shield** him from incoming arrows or spears (see e.g., 1 Sam 17:41; 31:4-6). Under this protection the inhabitants of Jerusalem rise to new levels of effectiveness in battle. **The feeblest among them will be like David**, Judah's legendary warrior king (v 8). Even more, members of the ruling **house of David will be like God,** in the sense that they will lead their people to safety **like the angel of the** LORD did in the Exodus from Egypt (Judg 2:1) or as it did in destroying Sennacherib's army in 701 BC (Isa 37:36).

■ **9** Once again the Lord reiterates his determination to **destroy all the nations that attack Jerusalem** (v 9). This affirmation recalls promises made earlier in the book in 1:18-21, 2:7-9, and 9:1-9. It also foreshadows the final triumph of Jerusalem portrayed in ch 14.

b. Repentance (12:10-14)

■ **10** One would have expected the people of Judah to respond to the promise of Jerusalem's deliverance with joy and celebration. However, in the next segment of ch 12, the mood of the people is that of contrition, sorrow and mourning. The Lord who defends and protects his people promises to **pour out** on them **a spirit of grace and supplication** (v 10).

The recipients of this promise are the elite rulers, **the house of David**, as well as the ordinary people, **the inhabitants of Jerusalem**. No one is excluded from this promise. They will all receive a **spirit,** an inclination that is receptive to spiritual things. **Grace** (*hēn*) and **supplication** (*taḥănûnîm*) derive from the same Hebrew root. **Grace** denotes the gift of underserved favor, while **supplication** conveys the search for God's favor. Both of these come from the Lord who envisions this **spirit** like a liquid that one might **pour out** of a vessel. It evokes images of an anointing ceremony when oil is poured upon the head as a symbol of God's Spirit coming upon the individual (see 1 Sam 10:1 and 16:13; see Joel 2:28-32 [3:1-5 HB]).

The reason for this growing spiritual sensitivity is an awareness of sin. **They will look on me, the one they have pierced,** implies that the people of Judah have inflicted a deep wound on the Lord (v 10).

Alternate Interpretations of 12:10

Scholars offer various identifications for "the one they have pierced" in v 10. To avoid the implication that God is somehow wounded some modern scholars emend the Hebrew text to read "they will look on him" (*'ēlô*) instead of "on me" (*'ēlay*; see Meyers and Meyers 1993, 336). Thus the NRSV translates "when they look on the one whom they have pierced." Such a reading relieves the tension created by a shift to third person in the following phrase "they will mourn for him" where one might have expected "they will mourn for me." It also allows for persons other than God to be identified as the one pierced. Since there is no manuscript or version evidence for this change, however, it remains a tenuous option.

Nevertheless, many commentators have sought to identify "the one they have pierced" with particular historical characters whose deaths evoked special mourning. These include the prophet Zechariah son of Jehoida murdered by Joash (2 Chr 24:20-21), the high priest Onias III assassinated in 170 BC (2 Macc 4:33-34), and Simon the Maccabee killed in 134 BC (1 Macc 16:14-17). Other suggestions include groups of persons such as Jews who died defending Jerusalem (Cashdan 1957, 321) or prophetic visionaries oppressed by temple hierocrats (Hanson 1979, 365-366). See Klein 2008, 366-368 for a survey of various proposals.

The text does not explain how the people of Jerusalem might have **pierced** or wounded the Lord. This could refer to the effects of sinful behavior in general. But within the context of Zechariah, it most likely refers either to Judah's idolatry mentioned in 13:2 or their rejection of the Lord's appointed shepherd in 11:7-14.

As the sorrowful response of the people continues, the pronoun changes from **me** to **him** in the phrase **they will mourn for him**. In divine speeches, the shift from first person to third person is not unusual. Some scholars have attempted to explain this shift by linking **the one they have pierced** with the shepherd struck by a sword in 13:7, who is also identified with the rejected shepherd of 11:4-14. Since the Lord closely identifies with this shepherd in 13:7, it is possible to say that wounding the shepherd is the same as wounding the Lord (→ 13:7).

NT writers understood a link between the rejected shepherd in 11:4-14, the pierced one in 12:10, and the shepherd struck by a sword in 13:7. They relate all three to Jesus (→ 11:14-17 and 13:7). The Gospel of John, in particular, connects the pierced one in this verse to Jesus at his crucifixion. When soldiers thrust a spear into the side of Jesus on the cross, it quotes Zech 12:10 (John 19:34-37). The Revelation also alludes to this verse when it announces that Christ "is coming in the clouds, and every eye will see him, even those who pierced him; and all peoples of earth will mourn because of him" (Rev 1:7).

The language of v 10 recalls that of Isaiah 53, which speaks of a suffering servant. This servant "was pierced for our transgressions" (Isa 53:5). Though the terms for "pierced" in these verses are different, the image of killing by means of stabbing relates the two passages. NT writers also identify the suffering servant of Isaiah with Jesus Christ (Acts 8:32-35; 1 Pet 2:21-25).

Verse 10 ends by comparing the grief of people who have wounded the Lord to that of someone who lost **an only child** or a **firstborn son**. The language utilized here evokes the image of an ancient funeral procession, which was typically accompanied by loud expressions of intense sorrow (v 10). The loss of **an only child** or a **firstborn son** was especially devastating in the ancient world because the future of a family depended upon their survival.

■ **11** The depth of mourning in Jerusalem is also compared to the **weeping of Hadad Rimmon in the plain of Megiddo** (v 11). The meaning of **Hadad Rimmon** is not clear since this is the only time the term occurs in the OT. It can be understood as either the name of a place or a Canaanite god. If it refers to a village near **the plain of Meggido**, then the weeping caused by the death of Josiah in 609 BC may be in view since he was killed by Egyptian troops there (2 Kgs 23:28-30; 2 Chr 35:20-25).

■ **12-14** Widespread mourning among Judah's elite illustrates further the depth of remorse felt for the sin of piercing the Lord. These verses anticipate the mourning of various family groups in the land, which include the royal **house of David** and the priestly family of **the house of Levi** (vv 12-13). The houses of **Nathan** and **Shimei** also likely represent prominent families. But their precise identity is not known since these were common names in OT times. To underscore the extent of mourning the list includes **the rest of the clans**

c. Cleansing (13:1-6)

■ **1-2** The Lord's response to Judah's mourning is to **cleanse** both **the house of David** and **the inhabitants of Jerusalem** from their **sin and impurity** (v 1; cp. Ezek 36:25). The reference to opening **a fountain** recalls the springs of water used in priestly purification rituals for disease (Lev 14:5). **Opened** is a participle in Hebrew, which indicates that water from this fountain will flow continuously. The term for **sin** (*hata'*) connotes actions that fall short of God's standards, while **impurity** (*niddâ*) denotes things people do that make them unfit to approach a holy God (see Lev 20:21; Lev 15:19).

■ **2-3** According to v 2, idolatry is the "sin and impurity" in the land (cp. Ezek 36:25). The Lord promises not only to cleanse his people from it, but also to **banish the names of the idols from the land** (v 2). This implies that those who returned from exile continued to worship idols even though idolatry had been a primary reason for God's judgment on their ancestors. The removal of idols from the land will be total and permanent in the future though, and it will be so effective that the coming generations will have no memory of the names of idols their ancestors worshipped.

The second part of v 2 suggests that the impurity of idols in the land was promoted by false **prophets**. So the Lord's promise includes removing those prophets who fostered **the spirit of impurity** in the land by giving prophetic oracles in the name of idols. Parents of **anyone who still prophesies** after the Lord banishes idolatry will follow the instructions given in Deut 13:6-9 [7-10 HB] (v 3). These commands directed Israelites to kill anyone who tried to persuade them to worship other gods, even if that person is a friend or close relative (see also Deut 18:20). Such radical action by parents would be appropriate since the prophets told **lies in the LORD's name**. Unauthorized prophecy was a problem that Jeremiah and Ezekiel had to deal with in their day (Jer 14:14; 23:16; 27:15; Ezek 13:6-8).

■ **4-6** The outcome of the Lord's strong stance against false prophets is that they will become so **ashamed of their prophetic visions** that they will disavow any connections to them (v 4). They will not dress in the traditional garb of a prophet, which apparently included **a garment of hair** like the cloak Elijah wore (2 Kgs

2:13-14). They will not even admit that they are prophets. If asked, a false prophet will prefer to identify himself as a **farmer** rather than a prophet, which normally held more status (v 5). Further, they will deny the true source of the scares from **wounds** that marked them as prophets (v 6). Such **wounds** were likely self-inflicted during ecstatic rituals designed to demonstrate sincerity before a pagan idol (as in 1Kgs 18:28; see also Lev 19:28; 21:5; Deut 14:1; Jer 16:6; 41:5; 48:37).

d. Refining (13:7-9)

■ **7** The text shifts to poetry in vv 7-9 to portray further cleansing of the community through a process of refining. It begins with a startling command to strike down a **shepherd** (v 7). The Lord addresses a **sword** as if it is a slumbering person, calling it to come **awake** from its sheath and go into action (cp. Isa 34:5-6 and Jer 9:16 [15 HB]; also Jer 47:6 and Ezek 21:16). The target of the attack is **my shepherd**, also described as **the man who is close to me**. The latter phrase translates *geber 'amîtî*, which occurs elsewhere only in Leviticus where it refers to a neighbor within the community of Israel (Lev 6:2 [5:21 HB]; 18:20; 19:15). The phrases **my shepherd** and **close to me** indicate that the **shepherd** is someone with a special connection to the Lord. Of the shepherds mentioned in Zechariah, this is most like the rejected shepherd of 11:4-14. This might also be "the one they have pierced" in 12:10. According to the gospels of Matthew and Mark, Jesus recognized the parallel between himself and this **shepherd**. He quoted this verse to describe the events that were about to unfold on the night of his arrest (Matt 26:31; Mark 14:27). He would be fatally wounded on the cross, as with a blow from a sword, and his disciples would scatter.

The next command, **strike the shepherd,** does not seem to be addressed to the sword, since the imperative **strike** is a masculine form and **sword** is a feminine noun (v 7). The phrase **strike the shepherd and the sheep will be scattered** seems best understood as a general or proverbial statement of truth. Whenever one strikes down a shepherd, then the leaderless flock will wander off. The term **scattered** (*pûṣ*) can convey the image of wandering sheep.

Verse 7 ends with the Lord's announcement that he will turn his **hand against the little ones** (v 7). This phrase could be read either positively or negatively. The hand of God turned **against** someone often connotes judgment (see Amos 1:8). If this is the meaning, then no one is spared; even the young and the vulnerable of the flock will be scattered (see Jer 49:20; 50:45). However, the preposition **against** (*'al*) can also mean "upon" and thus convey protection and care (see Isa 1:25). The statement, **one-third will be left** in the land (v 8), seems to support God's protective care of **the little ones**.

The Shepherd in 13:7

Scholars have offered several options for the identity of the shepherd in 13:7. Most frequently mentioned is the worthless prophet of 11:15-17, who is also struck with a sword (Boda 2004, 514-515 and Smith 1984, 283). But the difficulty of identifying the shepherd of 11:15-17 with 13:7 is the Lord's relationship to each. The worthless shepherd clearly does not please the Lord. He is an evil shepherd who devours his flock. The shepherd of 13:7, on the other hand, is "the man who is close" to God.

The question of why the Lord would strike his good shepherd with a sword is best answered by reference to Isaiah 53. In that passage "it was the LORD's will to crush" his servant and "cause him to suffer" (Isa 53:10). Salvation comes through the suffering of God's servant. Thus the prophet explains, "The punishment that brought us peace was on him and by his wounds we are healed" (Isa 53:5).

■ **8** Striking the shepherd causes the sheep, those who live **in the whole land** of Judah, to scatter into two groups (v 8). A large group of **two-thirds will be struck down and perish**, while a smaller group, half the size of the other, **will be left**. The term **struck down** (*kārat*) often connotes a consequence for breaking covenant regulations. It conveys the idea of being cut off from the covenant community either by excommunication or death (see Lev 7:20-21). The main point is that the population will be drastically reduced in the land; only **one-third** of the people will remain in the land (see Ezek 5:1-12).

■ **9** The **third** that remains is the remnant of God's people that are preserved in order to carry on the covenant community (v 9). Israel's prophets consistently promise that the Lord will preserve such a group (1 Kgs 19:18; Isa 6:13, 10:20-21; Jer 23:3; Hag 1:12; Zech 8:6-13). The Lord announces that he **will refine them like silver and test them like gold** (cp. Isa 1:25, 4:4, and 48:10). The image of refining comes from the industry of metallurgy where metal ore is heated in a crucible until it becomes liquid and impurities can be skimmed off (see Mal 3:1-3).

The end result of this refining process is a restored covenant between the Lord and those who survive. The Lord promises to **answer** this community when they **call** on his **name** (see 1 Kgs 8:22-61). He will address them as **my people** and they will address him as **our God** (see Exod 19:5; Hos 2:23 [25 HB]; Jer 30:22). This summarizes the essential hope of the book of Zechariah, that a genuine committed relationship between God and his people will be reestablished (1:16; 2:5, 10-11; 8:3, 23).

FROM THE TEXT

Zechariah 12-13 reveals how the Lord will restore a covenant relationship with his people some day in the future. It is a process that involves deliverance, repentance, cleansing, and refining.

The Lord initiates salvation by delivering his people from their enemies. As always God takes the first step in redeeming his people. In this passage, the Lord makes his people like "a cup" of intoxicating liquid that renders warriors ineffective drunkards (12:2), "an immovable stone" that gouges workmen who try to lift it (12:3), "a firepot" that sets woodpiles afire (12:6), and "a torch" that ignites harvest fields (12:6). The Lord strengthens his people in the day of battle so that even "the feeblest" are like Israel's greatest warrior and the strongest like the protective "angel of the LORD" (12:8). In other words, the Lord works through his people to fight their enemies and rescue them from those who oppose his kingdom (cp. Exod 14:14).

The Lord's deliverance, then, leads to the people's repentance. This outcome is unexpected since triumphant armies normally celebrate. But once God eliminates external threats his people can see more clearly the inward threat to life. With victory secured, the Lord pours out "a spirit of grace and supplication" that produces mourning for sin (12:10*a*). His people look upon "the one they have pierced" (12:10*b*) and feel profound remorse for what they have done when they rejected God's good shepherd (→ ch 11). When the battle smoke clears people can see that their efforts apart from God wound the very heart of God (see Acts 9:4).

The Lord responds to genuine repentance by cleansing his people from their sin. A holy God demands a holy people. So the Lord rids his people of those things that displease him, which in ch 12 includes idolatry and false prophets. This passage imagines cleansing from sin like a ritual "fountain" that prepares sacrifices for worship (13:1). As water washes away impurities from an animal to make it acceptable before God, so the Lord "will banish the names of idols from the land" and "will remove the prophets and the spirit of impurity from the land" (13:2). God undoubtedly desires to cleanse the hearts of his people today also, banishing anything that seeks to replace God as well as any words that are false about him (2 Cor 7:1).

The Lord further refines his people so that they can fully enter into covenant with him. The work of cleansing people continues in this passage as the Lord strikes down the shepherd and scatters people like a flock of sheep (13:7) until only "one-third" is left (13:8). Then, the Lord further "refine(s) them like silver and test(s) them like gold" until no impurity remains in them (13:9). Only then is full covenant relationship with God restored for the Lord calls this purified remnant "my people" because he has become their God (13:9; cp. Heb 10:19-22).

In these chapters, the key figures in the process of salvation are the pierced one in 12:10 and the shepherd struck down in 13:7. As noted in the exegesis, NT writers identify Jesus with both of these persons. In so doing they help tie together the oracles of chs 9-11 and 12-14, because they also relate the coming king of ch 9 and the rejected shepherd of ch 11 to Jesus. These four passages reflect the story of God's Messiah as it plays out in the life of Jesus Christ and his followers. He comes riding on a donkey like a conquering king who brings God's salvation to his people (9:9-10). But people rejected him and thus his offer of renewed life with God (11:7-14). They not only pay him off with an insulting wage (11:13), they kill him by piercing him on a cross (12:10). When he is struck down, those who had followed him scatter in all directions like sheep without a shepherd (13:7). They experience cleansing and refining until a portion is finally restored to full covenant relationship (13:8-9). For early Christians this drama unfolded in the crucifixion of Christ and the subsequent Roman destruction of Judah.

2. Ultimate Victory of the Lord (14:1-21)

BEHIND THE TEXT

The key phrase "on that day" continues to dominate ch 14 as it has the two previous chapters. In chs 12-13 it designates momentous events when the Lord dramatically intervenes in the history of Judah and the nations in the world. Throughout ch 14, however, the Day of the Lord is consistently eschatological, referring to an era when the current world order transforms into another. It is a day when the topography of Israel is altered (vv 4, 8, and 10), cosmic upheavals occur (vv 6-7), Jerusalem becomes secure forever (v 11), and all nations recognize the Lord as their king (vv 9 and 16-21). These elements describe a time beyond the present age.

The language of this chapter reflects some elements characteristic of Jewish apocalyptic literature. In general, it projects a movement from an evil age to an ideal good age because of a dramatic intervention of God. Its images of splitting mountains (v 4), continuous daylight (vv 6-7), and water flowing out of Jerusalem (v 8) approach the kind of symbolism typically found in apocalyptic literature. These images, however, are not as fantastic as those found in later apocalyptic works. Nor do other elements of the apocalyptic genre appear here. For these reasons scholars often refer to Zechariah as proto-apocalyptic, meaning that it represents a stage of development between earlier classic prophecy in Israel and later apocalyptic literature.

This chapter is the last section of the oracle contained in chs 12-14. This oracle proclaims the final triumph of the messianic kingdom. In chs 12-13 the Lord acts to renew his people spiritually and reestablish covenant relationship with them. In ch 14 the Lord assumes his rightful place among the nations as their king. This description of the Lord's enthronement unfolds in four major movements. The Lord gathers the nations against Jerusalem and then rescues the city (vv 1-5). Then a description of the remarkable transformation of the holy city and its environs follows (vv 6-11) with the salvation of Jerusalem sharply contrasted to how the Lord's enemies fare (vv 12-15). The final climactic segment of this chapter pictures nations streaming to Jerusalem to honor the Lord as king of the world (vv 16-21).

IN THE TEXT

a. Rescue of Jerusalem (14:1-5)

The story of the Lord's ultimate victory begins with the nations of the world attacking Jerusalem. Chs 12-13 of this oracle began in the same manner, but here the nations overrun Jerusalem. Yet, at the right moment, as 12:1-9 similarly portrays, the Lord arrives to deliver his people.

■ **1** The prophet announces to Jerusalem that her **possessions** will be **plundered** and **divided up** on **a day of the LORD** (v 1). Though **Jerusalem** does not occur in the Hebrew text, the NIV supplies it based on the mention of the city in v 2. This **day** is a critical moment when the Lord takes full control of earth's affairs and manifests his sovereignty over them. In the rest of the chapter, this day is called "that day" (vv 4, 6, 8, 9, 13, 20, 21), which indicates that it refers to the final days of human history.

Israel's prophets typically spoke of "the Day of the LORD" (*yôm YHWH*; → Behind the Text at 12:1-13:9). In verse 1, however, the Hebrew reads *yôm bā' la-YHWH*, which literally translates as "a day is coming for the LORD" (NRSV, NASB, ESV). This emphasizes that the day belongs to the Lord and no one else; it is the Lord's time to take full control of all affairs in creation.

■ **2** The Lord **will gather all the nations** to Jerusalem and cause them to plunder and divide up possessions of the city (v 2). Thus the prophet begins with a description of the nations executing the Lord's judgment on Jerusalem. The picture of the Lord gathering the nations against Jerusalem is also found in 12:3, Ezek 38-39, Joel 3:1-16 [4:1-16 HB], and Mic 4:11-13 (see also Rev 19). The devastating effects of this attack on Jerusalem will be several: **the city will be captured, houses ransacked, women raped**, and people taken into **exile**. The only good news here is that only **half of the city will go into exile**. The scene recalls Babylon's brutal destruction of Jerusalem in 586 BC (see 2 Kgs 25).

■ **3-5** The scene changes in vv 3-5. The Lord, who summons the nations to come against Jerusalem, becomes the divine warrior who will go out and fight against the nations that came against Jerusalem (v 3; see ch 9; 12:1-9). The magnitude of the Lord's military prowess is conveyed by an image of God standing **on the Mount of Olives** and causing it to **split in two from east to west** (v 4). **The Mount of Olives** is a steep ridge running north and south for over two miles immediately **east of Jerusalem**. It rises a few hundred feet higher than the city. The deep Kidron Valley that runs between this ridge and the hills of Jerusalem creates a natural defense for the city's east side.

A **mountain valley** formed by the Lord provides an escape route from Jerusalem (v 5). It allows refugees to **flee** the battle as far as **Azel**. This is most likely a place east of Jerusalem toward the Dead Sea. Though its exact location is unknown, **Azel** appears to be a safe distance from the conflict. Those who run there will do so with the same urgency and anxiety as the people who **fled from the earthquake in the days of Uzziah king of Judah.** This famous earthquake occurred somewhere around 760 BC just two years before Amos prophesied (see Amos 1:1).

The salvation of Jerusalem happens when the Lord arrives. The prophet summarizes this momentous event by simply saying **the LORD my God will come, and all the holy ones with him** (v 5). The term **holy ones** (*qĕdōšîm*) designates God's heavenly attendants (Ps 89:5-7 [6-8 HB]), who might also be understood as an angelic army (Isa 13:3). The Hebrew text actually says **the holy ones** are "with you" (*'immāk*) rather than **with him** (*'immô*). Most modern versions prefer to follow the Greek along with other ancient versions and translate the third person pronoun however.

b. Transformation of Jerusalem (14:6-11)

■ **6-7** The following verses announce radical changes in the cosmos and Jerusalem as a result of the Lord's arrival. Creation's ordered pattern of **sunlight**, **cold**, **darkness**, and **day and night** will come to an end (vv 6-7). The word **unique**, literally, "one day" (*yôm 'eḥād*), can also mean "one continuous day" (see NRSV). It is **a day known to the Lord**, which suggests God alone determines its timing (see Isa 60:22 and Matt 24:36).

Translation of 14:6

The Hebrew text of 14:6 is difficult to understand and therefore considered a scribal error by many scholars (see Meyer and Meyer 1993, 432). The second half of the verse literally translates "splendid ones will contract" (*yĕqārôt yĕqippā'ôn*). In this context, this could be a poetic way of saying that stars will dim (see NASB; Boda 2004, 525; Baldwin 1972, 203).

The Greek, Latin, and Syriac versions translate these two words as "cold and ice" apparently on the basis of Hebrew terms that look similar to what is in the MT. Modern scholars, however, cannot reconstruct with certainty the Hebrew words the ancient versions might have translated. Nevertheless, most modern English translations prefer to follow the ancient versions rather than the Hebrew since they seem to make more sense.

■ **8** The Lord's arrival will also transform Jerusalem into a source of **living water** that will flow out to the **Dead Sea** and the **Mediterranean Sea** (v 8). The term **living water** (*mayim ḥayyîm*) is actually a Hebrew idiom for running water; it conveys the idea of a fresh and constant supply of water. This stream will provide water both in **summer** and **winter** as well as to the **east** and **west** of Jerusalem, implying abundant fertility throughout the entire promised land. This scene recalls Ezekiel's vision in which a river flows from Jerusalem in the last days. That river will pour forth from the temple threshold toward the east and grow deeper as it flows. All along its banks vegetation will flourish and the Dead Sea will teem with fish (Ezek 47:1-12; see also Isa 33:21; 35:6-7; 41:18-19; 43:19-20; Joel 3:18 [4:18 HB]).

■ **9** The most significant aspect of the Day of the Lord is the establishment of the universal kingship of the Lord. **The whole earth** will recognize Israel's God as sovereign and his name will be **the only name** on earth designated as king (v 9). The enthronement songs in the book of Psalms convey this same hope (e.g., see Pss 93 and 95).

■ **10** The Day of the Lord will also change the topography of Judah. **Jerusalem will be raised up** while the surrounding towns in the Judean hills will become like **the Arabah**, the low lying valley extending south from the Dead Sea. **Geba**, about six miles north of Jerusalem, and **Rimmon**, most likely a site about thirty miles south of the city, are part of the Judean hills. The area between them will become flat and Jerusalem raised up, so it will become visible to every city and village in the land. Isaiah and Micah also envisioned "the mountain of the Lord's temple . . . established as the highest of the mountains . . . exalted above the hills" (Isa 2:2 and Mic 4:1). References to several gates and other Jerusalem landmarks (**Tower of Hananel**, etc.) indicate elevation of the entire city, not just the hill on which the temple is located.

■ **11** The arrival of the Lord will bring an end to the history of the city's destruction and deportation of its population, a promise also found in 8:4-5. Repopulation of Jerusalem is possible because it will **never again be destroyed** (v 11). The term **destroyed** (*ḥerem*) refers to something that has been devoted to destruction for religious purposes, traditionally called "the ban" (see Josh 6:17-18; Deut 7:1-2; see also Isa 43:28). Verse 11 announces the reversal of this ban. Thus the city **will be secure** for human habitation. The term **secure** (*beṭaḥ*) suggests physical safety as well as divine protection and blessing like that envisioned by Ezekiel (Ezek 34:25-29). Living safely in the land is a reward for keeping covenant with the Lord (Lev 25:18-19; 26:3-5).

c. Judgment on Hostile Nations (14:12-15)

■ **12-14** The focus of the Lord shifts to the enemies of Jerusalem in vv 12-15. The Lord had gathered the nations to fight against Jerusalem (v 2), but now they become the object of the Lord's judgment. He will afflict them with a severe **plague** that causes their bodies and their organs to **rot** (v 12). God will also strike them with **great panic** that will lead enemy soldiers to turn against their fellow soldiers (v 13). The disorientation of the enemy will embolden people from the outer lying regions of **Judah** and they will join the **fight at Jerusalem** (v 14; cp. 12:7). Together they will gain victory and plunder **the wealth of all the surrounding nations**. So instead of being plundered (v 1) Jerusalem will become the plunderer.

Alternate Translation of Verse 14

The ESV translates the first line of v 14 as "even Judah will fight against Jerusalem." This is a possible rendering since the preposition "against" (*bĕ*) is often rendered this way. The Vulgate and Targums understood it in this manner. But most modern English translations follow the Greek and Syriac in translating the preposition as either "at" or "in."

Though it may seem strange to speak of Judah fighting against Jerusalem, the idea could make sense in this context. Judah attacking Jerusalem may be another example of the great panic that caused soldiers in v 13 to fight one another (see Clark and Hatton 2004, 361).

■ **15** The impact of the plague extends to **animals** in the enemy camps. These animals are essential to the transportation of soldiers, war equipment, and food supplies. With the destruction of these animals, the enemy will become ineffective.

d. Universal Worship of the Lord (14:16-21)

■ **16** The climactic feature of the Day of the Lord is the universal worship of the Lord. Though the nations came up to Jerusalem to fight against the city (v 2), Zechariah anticipates that **survivors** from those battles will one day make annual pilgrimages to Jerusalem **to worship the King, the LORD Almighty** (v 16; cp. 8:20-23). Just as there will be survivors of Judah (13:8), there will be **survivors** among the nations. Both v 16 and 13:8 use the Hebrew root *yātar* to speak of those who are left after the Lord's judgment.

The term **go up** (*'alâ*) is a technical term for participating in a religious pilgrimage to Jerusalem (cp. Ezra 1:3; see Edlin 2017, 44-45). The word **worship**, an intensive reflexive form of *šāḥāt*, connotes bowing oneself down in total submission. Recognition of Israel's God as the King who reigns over the world is thus the primary purpose of the nations' pilgrimage to Jerusalem.

Israel has always confessed the Lord as the sovereign ruler of the world (e.g., see Pss 93:1, 95:3; 96:10-13, etc.). Someday **all the nations** will confess this faith along with Israel at **the Festival of Tabernacles**, one of ancient Israel's three annual pilgrimage feasts (v 16; see Exod 23:14-17 and Lev 23:33-36). This festival occurs in the seventh month of the religious calendar at the end of harvest season and celebrates the Lord's provision for the year. It also recalls the Lord's care during Israel's wilderness experience. According to Deut 16:14, foreigners were welcome at this feast, and during the post-exilic era, the festival became a time for reading the law aloud. So the coming of nations to Jerusalem for this feast seems to indicate a commitment to learn the laws of the Lord and live in obedience to them (see Isa 2:3; Mic 4:2; Jer 3:17).

■ **17-19** In vv 17-19, the Lord threatens to punish **the peoples on the earth** who **do not go up to Jerusalem to worship the King.** They will suffer economically because their crops will have **no rain,** the curse for covenant breaking in Deut 28:22-24. The Feast of Tabernacles was a time to pray for rain, since it marked the end of the dry season in Israel.

The Egyptians are mentioned in particular in vv 18-19 as a representative of nations that refuse to make the pilgrimage to Jerusalem. Egypt may be singled out here because it was home for a number of Jewish communities following the Babylonian destruction of Judah and Jerusalem in 586 BC (see Jer 41:16-43:13). Since Egypt relied heavily on the Nile and not seasonal rain for its agriculture, the threat of **no rain** may seem pointless. However, without rains at its headwaters, the Nile could not fertilize fields with its floodwaters.

Lack of rain is called a **plague** (v 18), which evokes the plagues that the Lord inflicted upon Egypt during the Exodus (Exod 7-11). It is also **the punishment** for those who **do not go up to celebrate the Festival of Tabernacles** (v 19). The term for **punishment** (*ḥaṭṭā't*) is the regular word for sin in Hebrew, which connotes not living up to divine standards. It can also convey **punishment** received for deviating from God's will.

Translation of Verse 18

Translating the Hebrew text of v 18 is challenging. It can be understood to say that Egypt "shall not be visited by the same affliction" as the other nations (NJPS). In this case, the verse would be saying that Egypt will receive a different plague, other than drought. The translation found in the majority of modern English translations either follows the Greek rendering of the verse or supplies the words "no rain" as an ellipsis from the previous verse (see Clark and Hatton 2004, 364-365 and Meyer and Meyer 1993, 476-477).

■ **20** The final two verses of the book anticipate everything in Judah and Jerusalem being completely dedicated to God someday. When the Lord arrives in Jerusalem and establishes himself as the sovereign king, Judah and Jerusalem will be totally transformed to reflect his holiness. **Horses** and **cooking pots**, examples of what is ordinary and unclean, will become sacred (v 20). **HOLY TO THE LORD,** words reserved exclusively for the diadem on the high priest's turban (Exod 39:29-30), will be inscribed on **the bells of the horses.**

The transformation of the ordinary into the sacred means there will no longer be any distinction between secular and sacred. Moreover, this transformation will bring an end to the special degree of holiness assigned to those who serve the Lord and the cultic objects in the temple. **Cooking pots in the LORD's house** will be just as acceptable for God's service as **the sacred bowls in front of the altar.** All and everything will be dedicated to the Lord. Such an egalitarian view of holiness is a radical concept for ancient Israel.

■ **21** The text ends with the announcement that **there will no longer be a Canaanite in the house of the LORD Almighty** (v 21). The term **Canaanite** can refer to the original inhabitants of the land of Israel, who were known for their idolatry. However, most commentators see here a reference to merchants or traders (see Isa 23:8) who sold utensils and animals approved for use in the temple worship. An entire industry of selling such items to worshipers flourished around the temple in the post-exilic period. Since all things will be holy with the arrival of the Lord, the book anticipates the end of all commercial activities in the temple area. Such a scene recalls the story of Jesus driving the sellers and money changers from the temple courts (Mark 11:15-17).

The final verses of Zechariah, then, emphasize the holy character of those who worship the Lord on that eschatological day of his coming. A holy people will offer holy worship to a holy God.

FROM THE TEXT

This final chapter serves as a fitting conclusion to the book of Zechariah. It concludes the book by emphasizing major themes found in both the visions and the oracles. This chapter highlights the Lord's care for his people in defeating their enemies and coming to dwell in their midst, the main focus of messages recorded in 1:18-21; 2:1-12; 8:1-8; 9:1-17; 10:1-12; and 12:1-9. In addition, the important theme of purifying God's people so that they might become a holy worshipping community recurs in this chapter. This was stressed earlier in 3:1-10; 5:1-4; 5:5-11; 13:1-7; and 13:7-9. These themes interweave among two primary theological points of this chapter: (1) the Lord's universal kingship and (2) the world's transformation when the Lord takes full control.

Zechariah 14 affirms that *the Lord will one day manifest his absolute sovereign rule over this world*. In the end, the Lord will reign, and the Lord will win. The prophet announces the Lord's universal kingship not only in the way he gathers the nations to fight against Jerusalem but also in his deliverance of the city. The Lord plans to "gather all the nations to Jerusalem" (v 2), and yet, he will rise up to "fight against those nations" (v 3). In other words, the Lord orchestrates a final showdown with world powers in order to display his sovereign rule over them. Such a scene conveys comfort to ancient as well as modern audiences because the Lord, rather than earthly rulers, determine the outcome of world affairs. In the end "the LORD will be king over the whole earth" (v 9). This is the same hope expressed in the NT when the "KING OF KINGS AND LORD OF LORDS" appears (Rev 19:16).

The day the Lord takes full control of this world is the day everything changes. When the Lord finally manifests his sovereign rule the natural order of planet earth will be transformed as well as its social and spiritual dimensions. Cataclysmic cosmic changes will unfold as the Mount of Olives splits in two (v 4), light from the sun, moon, and stars becomes unnecessary (vv 6-7), living water flows out of Jerusalem (v 8), and the surrounding region flattens into a low lying plain leaving the Jerusalem raised up high (v 10). These are marks of a new age. They symbolize a time when new pathways to the Lord open up, when the Lord's light becomes all that is needed, when the resources for life flow from the Lord's dwelling, and the Lord becomes the focus for all the earth. This is also the vision of the writer of Revelation who saw "the river of the water of life . . . flowing from the throne of God" in the city of Jerusalem that "will not need the light of a lamp or the light of the sun, for the Lord God will give them light" (22:1-5).

Major spiritual transformation also accompanies these dramatic cosmic changes. The Lord plans for "survivors from all the nations" to join the people of Israel in worship (v 16). The universal kingship of the Lord will desegregate worship. All peoples of earth will rejoice with the psalmists and shout, "The LORD reigns, let the earth be glad; let the distant shores rejoice" (Ps 97:1).

Further, all who worship the Lord in that day will be holy; they will be fully consecrated to the Lord and his kingdom. Holiness will erase all boundaries so that access to God will not be determined by one's social or economic status. "There will no longer be a Canaanite in the house of the LORD Almighty" (v 21), only those who submit to the kingship of the Lord. All people who worship the Lord as king will be accepted regardless of where they come from or who they are. This is the kind of world the Lord originally envisioned and to which all his salvific acts lead.

MALACHI

INTRODUCTION

The location of the book of Malachi within the sacred scriptures of both Christianity and Judaism should signal its significance. In the Christian canon, Malachi stands last among the prophetic books, which ends the OT section of the Bible. For the Jewish tradition it marks the completion of the second major section of the Hebrew Scriptures known as the Prophets.

Within the world of literature endings are always important. Writers typically seek to bring fitting closure to their works. They highlight important themes, summarize, bring resolution, and prompt readers to further thought. Malachi accomplishes all this and more.

For Christians, Malachi serves as a bridge into the NT. It reminds readers of some of the most salient themes in the OT and then leads them toward important ideas that will unfold in the NT. In particular, Malachi highlights the coming of the Lord and his forerunner, John the Baptist. For this and many other reasons the book of Malachi is worthy of careful study.

A. The Prophet

The prophet behind the messages of the book is usually referred to as Malachi. This is not a typical personal name in ancient Israel, so scholars have questioned whether or not it denotes his name or describes his function. Malachi means "my messenger" and might simply refer to the role of a courier from God, which is an appropriate description of a prophet. The Hebrew term *mal'ākî* occurs twice in the book. In 3:1 it is clearly not the name of a person but a title. It refers to the individual who will prepare the way for the coming of the Lord sometime in the future.

In 1:1, however, *mal'ākî* appears within the typical formula for identifying the speaker of oracles in a prophetic book. This verse introduces the collection by describing it as "the word of the LORD to Israel through *mal'ākî*." This occurrence of the term is most naturally taken as a personal name. Scholarly arguments for and against understanding Malachi as a proper name continue without a consensus however (see Verhoef, 1987, 154-156). In the final analysis, certainty on the matter may not be possible. Most scholars hold to Malachi as a personal name, but are open to the alternative view.

More important for understanding the book are the character and historical circumstances of the prophet. Clearly the prophet behind the book sees himself as a mediator of divine messages. The typical prophetic messenger formulas, in various forms, punctuate the oracles of the prophet more intensely than is normally found in prophetic books. Some form of the messenger formula "says the LORD" occurs 26 times in the 55 verses of the book.

This persistent appeal to divine authority may derive from the prophet's confrontational style. Like other prophets Malachi was called by God to defend and project the enforcement of covenant curses. His extensive knowledge of Deuteronomic law made him acutely aware of the reason for present hardship and future potential disasters. They were experiencing covenant curses (2:2, 14; 3:9). This uncomfortable observation brought significant opposition, as his oracles indicate. So Malachi adopted an argumentative approach to delivering his oracles (→ Literary Forms below).

Though polemical in manner, Malachi was not without compassion for his audience. He reveals a clear understanding of God's profound grace toward them in his statements about the Lord's love (1:2) and his pleas for repentance (2:2, 15-16; 3:7). So, genuine concern for his audience undergirds all his preaching.

B. The Audience

The messages of Malachi were originally delivered to people living in Judah sometime in the middle of the fifth century BC. The book contains few historical references, so precise dates for the prophet and his audience are not possible. A profile of the audience, however, can be pieced together from comments made in the text.

References to Israel, Judah, and Jerusalem locate those addressed geographically within the holy land (1:1, 1:5, 2:11, 3:4, and 4:4). Mention of "governor" (pehāh) in 1:8 along with the "temple" in 1:10 sets the time frame within the postexilic era during the rule of the Persians (539-330 BC). At that time the homeland of Abraham's descendants consisted of a small region surrounding Jerusalem known as Yehud. Its borders stretched no further than thirty miles in any direction from the holy city. It was one of several political entities that comprised the western satrapy of the Persian Empire known as Eber-Nahara, that is, "beyond the river" Euphrates.

The reigns of Darius I (r. 521-486 BC), Xerxes I (r. 486-465 BC), and Artaxerxes I (r. 464-424 BC) provide the broader historical background for Malachi's ministry. Throughout this period, Persian power peaked and brought relative stability to the region in spite of strong resistance from Greek city-states in the west. Early in the reign of Darius, the Jews completed rebuilding the Jerusalem temple, a significant achievement both spiritually and politically. Xerxes is the Persian king of the book of Esther. So sometime during his reign Jews throughout the empire experienced a dramatic challenge to their existence and a miraculous deliverance from God. Not long after these events, Artaxerxes I commissioned Ezra and Nehemiah to go to Jerusalem to help secure and rebuild the community. What motivated him to help the Jews is not clear from a human perspective, but the biblical writers clearly saw it as the hand of God (Ezra 7:6; Neh 2:8b). So both Ezra and Nehemiah carried out significant spiritual and economic reforms in Jerusalem and Judah during the mid-fifth century BC.

The mention of sacrifices and priests indicates ongoing worship in the newly rebuilt temple during Malachi's ministry. However, Malachi gives ample evidence of the community's lack of commitment to God. They try to get by with substandard sacrifices (1:7-8) and partial tithing (3:8). They raise questions about God's love (1:2) and justice (2:17) and whether serving God is even worthwhile (3:14). Malachi blames the priests for the people's disloyalty to God; they do not set an example for the people by honoring God and giving proper guidance to them (2:2, 8). Malachi sees lack of commitment to God as the root cause of the moral failures of the people, such as Jewish men marrying non-believers (2:11) and breaking faith with their Jewish wives (2:14). He also speaks of people who commit perjury in the courts, defraud workers of their wages, oppress widows and orphans, and deny justice to foreigners (3:5).

To be fair to Malachi's contemporaries, this spiritual apathy had roots in a legitimate theological dissonance. Similar to the situation of Haggai and Zechariah, the restoration community in Judah continued to struggle with unfulfilled promises even into the mid-fifth century BC. The grand hopes of new life proclaimed by Judah's earlier prophets did not match with Judah's realities. They had not seen God "overturn royal thrones and shatter the power of the foreign kingdoms" (Hag 2:22). Neither had "the glory of this present house" become "greater than the glory of the former house" (Hag 2:9). The people of the restoration longed for God to "go out and fight against those nations" (Zech 14:3) and become "king over the whole earth" (Zech 14:9). But that had not happened. Thus a certain amount of theological disillusionment surely existed within Judah.

Certain characteristics of Malachi's audience resemble those of Ezra and Nehemiah's contemporaries. The marriage issues, in particular, recall similar challenges faced during the reforms mentioned in Ezra 10 and Nehemiah 13. In addition, these reformers speak about lack of contributions to the temple treasury and corruption in the priesthood, two other issues addressed by Malachi.

These similarities suggest a relationship between the ministries of these three men. But the exact connection between Malachi and the two reformers is difficult to determine. Many scholars hold that Malachi must have been working alongside of Ezra and Nehemiah, since their concerns are so similar. But Malachi never mentions Ezra and Nehemiah and vice versa. So others scholars suggest that Malachi preceded Ezra and Nehemiah or, perhaps, followed them. If Malachi preached before Ezra and Nehemiah arrived, then his messages would appear to have been relatively ineffective. On the other hand, if Malachi followed Ezra and Nehemiah, the reforms reported in their books would not have been as successful as indicated. In the final analysis, definitive evidence for determining the interrelationship between the three is lacking (see Hill, 1998, 77-84).

C. Literary Forms

The book of Malachi is a record of prophetic speeches that the book itself designates as a *massā'*, a term most often translated either "oracle" or "burden" (1:1; → Zech 1:1). This term conveys the serious nature of the speeches and elevates interest in them. Because these speeches are punctuated with various forms of the phrase "this is what the LORD says," they are fundamentally messenger speeches. As such they contain the basic elements of the messenger styled speech found throughout prophetic literature. They provide (1) an indication of the situation of the audience and (2) a divine message relevant to that situation.

Malachi employs a particular type of prophetic speech that creates an argumentative mood throughout the book and evokes a legal setting. The prophet's speeches take on the form of a disputation with the audience that includes projected dialogue between people and God. In its simplest structure, the two typical elements of each speech are: (1) opening statements and (2) arguments. This style is found occasionally in other prophets (see Isa 40:27-31 and 49:14-21). But Malachi uses it almost exclusively.

The opening statements in each speech usually include a projected dialogue between God and the people addressed. Whether these statements were actually spoken is difficult to say. They may simply reflect the attitudes of each. The exchange typically proceeds logically from (a) accusation to (b) protest to (c) clarification. God begins by uttering a statement reflecting the condition of the people. Since these statements are negative in character, they carry the weight of an accusation. Those addressed typically protest the accusation by questioning it. The nature of these questions is such that they convey a sense of denial or rebuttal. At this point God responds with further clarification stating more directly the divine indictment of the audience.

The argument section in this speech form continues to explain reasons for God's accusation. The prophet amasses evidence in support of God's indictment. Within the accusation section some argument has already been presented, but this section establishes the case further. It also conveys a message from God regarding the future. Most often this is a threatening judgment, but an element of hope is mixed in as well. The prophet infuses words of exhortation throughout his speeches in order to offer hope to his audience, particularly toward the end of the book.

To further enhance the argumentative mood of his oracles, Malachi displays a marked use of the rhetorical question. He employs it in some manner in nearly every oracle. These questions with an obvious answer help make a point more forcefully. Thus Malachi asks, for example, "Was not Esau Jacob's brother?" (1:2) and "If I am a father, where is the honor due me?" (1:6; see also 2:10, 15; 3:2, 8, 14).

Scholars have debated the poetic nature of Malachi. His speeches are rhythmic and include a number of literary devices. Parallelism, alliteration, assonance, lexical repetition, and other kinds of wordplay occur regularly. Yet these features can be found in prose as well. The density of relative pronouns, the object marker 'et, and the definite article mark Malachi's speeches as primarily prose compositions (see Hill 1998, 23-26).

D. Literary Structure

The literary structure of the book of Malachi can be observed on several levels. Like most literature, it possesses a number of structuring devices that mark distinction as well as cohesion within the work. In the case of Malachi, no one outline of the material has gained overwhelming support from scholars. This factor testifies to the skillful weaving of its various interconnecting features. Clearly the book is an intentionally designed unit and not a random collection of prophecies (see Hill, 1998, 26-34).

Many commentators recognize six distinct pericopes in the book. Yet there is disagreement at points about them. For example, opinions vary as to whether or not 3:6 concludes or introduces a passage. The final three verses of the book 4:4-6

[3:22-24 HB] are usually taken as separate a conclusion to the book, but some see them as an essential part of the final message that begins in 3:13. The function of the first verse of the book has also been questioned. Most see it as a superscription to the entire book, but a few have taken it as part of the first oracle that extends to 1:5.

More serious is the varied analyses of 1:6-2:9. Frequently commentators treat this as one message with two distinct units because of the close association of subject matter. Yet the speech clearly takes a major turn at 2:1. So some scholars identify 1:6-14 and 2:1-9 as two separate, though closely related, units. They maintain then that the book contains seven distinct pericopes (Dorsey 1999, 321-322).

Connections between the seven messages are accomplished in several ways. Key words, phrases, and motifs run throughout the book. For example, the idea and terminology of honor and respect, which begins in 1:6, reappears again in 1:11, 14, 2:2, 5, 3:5, 16, and 4:2 [3:20 HB]. The language of covenant keeping is also pervasive.

Key words and ideas further link the messages into a chain of progressive thought. For example, the greatness of the Lord among the nations mentioned at the conclusion of 1:2-5 gains more focus in the following message of 1:6-14. Likewise, the concept of God acting as a witness for marriages in Judah in 2:10-16 is followed up with God witnessing against evildoers in Judah in 2:17-3:5.

Because of these associations some commentators have attempted to group the messages thematically. For example, one scholar sees 1:2-2:9 as exhortations calling priests to honor God, 2:10-3:6 as exhortations calling Judah to faithfulness, and 2:7-4:6 [2:7-3:23 HB] as exhortations calling Judah to return and remember (Clendenen 2004, 227-231). This outline follows the lead of the three-part division of the book found in the MT. It also takes note of the chiastic structuring of three key elements in each division: situation, command, and motivation.

More commonly commentators identify the structure of the book in terms of the six or seven oracles of the prophet, as is done in this commentary. These oracles are bound together by a chiastic pattern wherein oracles toward the end of the book recall elements of oracles in the first part of the book. Working with the seven-oracle structure a chiastic pattern can be observed as follows (see Dorsey 1999, 321-324):

Superscription (1:1)
    I. God's Distinction Between Jacob and Esau (1:2-5)
        II. God's Curse Upon Defective Sacrifices (1:6-14)
            III. God's Curse Upon the Levites (2:1-9)
                IV. God's Challenge to Judah's Unfaithfulness (2:10-16)
            V. God's Purification of the Levites (2:17-3:5)
        VI. God's Blessing Upon the Whole Tithe (3:6-12)
    VII. God's Distinction Between the Righteous and the Wicked (3:13-4:3 [3:13-21 HB])
Conclusion: (4:4-6 [3:22-24 HB])

As this structure shows, the book begins with a brief introductory super-scription in 1:1 and concludes with a summary exhortation and promise in 4:4-6 [3:22-24 HB]. The opening oracle of 1:2-5 is echoed again in the final oracle of 3:13-4:3 [3:13-21 HB] with the topic of God distinguishing between people in his judgment. Then the second oracle of 1:6-14 is recalled in the sixth oracle of 3:6-12 with its focus upon worship rituals, while the third oracle of 2:1-9 resonates with the fifth oracle of 2:17-3:5 with its concern for the Levites. This leaves the fourth oracle of 2:10-16 as the fulcrum of the chiasm centering particular attention upon its message regarding Judah's betrayal of their covenant commitments.

Confirmation of the significance of the central oracle in 2:10-16 comes in the concluding verses of the book. In the very last verse Malachi returns to the theme of familial covenant commitment one last time. He announces that Elijah "will turn the hearts of the parents to their children, and the hearts of the children to their parents" (4:6 [3:24 HB]). Thus, faithful relationships in the family stands as the primary way one prepares for the coming Day of the Lord and lives out the covenant commitment that Malachi urges upon his audience. This is the primary focus of Malachi's preaching.

Regardless of how one identifies the structure of the book, the element of hope emerges more strongly toward the latter half of it. This is typical of prophetic books. The final shape of Malachi ends on a note of hopeful future with God. As such it provides a fitting conclusion to the Christian OT preparing readers for the hope filled words of the stories about Jesus Christ in the NT.

E. Relationship to Haggai and Zechariah

Malachi stands alongside of Haggai and Zechariah as the last three books in the collection of the Minor Prophets, known as the Book of the Twelve in the Hebrew Scriptures. These three all derive from the post-exilic period and thus constitute a major unit in the larger collection.

As a literary unit The Twelve speak to the dramatic story of Israel's experience with the land. The first six prophets, Hosea to Micah, identify the sins of the Assyrian period that bring about judgment in the Babylonian period. They answer the question of why disaster struck and the land was lost. Habakkuk, Nahum, and Zephaniah relate the devastating judgment brought on by the Babylonians and provide insight into how one might live though such times. Haggai, Zechariah, and Malachi then speak of the restoration that takes place in the Persian period. These three provide instruction for a people seeking to reestablish themselves as an authentic community of faith.

A major theory among modern scholars posits the idea that Malachi along with Zechariah 9-11 and 12-14 were originally three independent anonymous collections appended to Zechariah 1-8. Each of these collections describes themselves as an "oracle" or "burden" (*massā'*) in their superscriptions. The theory states that an unknown compiler attached the name "Malachi" to the last collection because of its usage in the text (Mal 3:1). This editor distinguished the Malachi collection from the other materials in order to arrive at a group of twelve prophetic books corresponding to the number of tribes in Israel (see Petersen 1995, 1-6).

Lack of manuscript evidence, arguments for the literary unity of the book of Zechariah, and other factors challenge the viability of this theory (see Childs 1979, 489-492). In point of fact, too much uncertainty surrounds the early history of the text to establish a sound theory of its origins.

F. The Text of Malachi

For the most part the MT of Malachi appears to be carefully preserved and readable. The most challenging verses to translate are 2:15-16. Yet even here none of the early versions or alternate Hebrew texts provide any compelling reason to emend the MT in any significant manner.

The earliest witness to Malachi comes from Qumran fragments known as 4QXIIa and date to around 150-125 BC. These fragments contain about 38 per cent of 2:10-4:6 in four columns. They provide perspective on obscure verses. But their readings do not call for any important alterations to the MT. The same may be said of the LXX, which generally follows the MT closely while providing some interesting variations at times. Most of its alternate readings are easily explained by its typical expansionistic and Midrashic tendencies. The LXX stands by itself among textual witnesses in rearranging the last three verses and placing 4:4 [3:22 HB] after 4:5-6 [3:23-24] (see Hill 1998, 3-12).

The verse numbering of the Hebrew text differs from all other versions, including the English. The Hebrew text of Malachi has no fourth chapter. Rather it continues to number 4:1-6 in the English Bible as verses 19-24 of chapter 3. From a literary standpoint, the Hebrew versification is preferable since it does not disrupt the flow of the final oracle with a chapter division like other versions do.

G. Hermeneutical Issues

Two key hermeneutical issues emerge from the texts of Malachi. The first has to do with the principle of retribution, an issue not unfamiliar to other prophets and the Deuteronomistic writings in the OT (→ Hermeneutical Issues in Haggai). Malachi blatantly asserts that tithing produces rewards (3:10). To heighten the drama Malachi quotes God as daring people to "test" him in this to see if it does not work. The blessings described do not appear to be spiritual, but rather material. Crops and fields will be productive and Judah will gain recognition within the world community (3:11-12).

Read apart from the rest of the book, this assertion and challenge appears superficial and self-serving. But understood within the context of covenant relationship, a spiritual depth becomes apparent. Tangible blessing in response to tangible actions provides hard evidence of genuine relationship, according to Malachi. Earlier in this same oracle God calls Judah to "return" to him. If they do so, God promises to "return" to them (3:7). When asked to define the details of this returning, God calls for a tangible display of heart change by bringing "the whole tithe"

(3:10). In like manner, God promises tangible evidence of his return to them by blessing their land. This shows not only God's change of heart. It also proves God's faithfulness to covenant promises such as those found in Deut 28:1-14.

The issue is that of character not simply physical rewards. Both the character of the people and that of God are proved by visible activity. Biblical religion is not just about giving and getting. It is about the integrity of the covenant partners involved. Visible actions display the condition of the heart.

The other major hermeneutical issue in Malachi has to do with interpretation of the Day of the Lord. In particular scholars have asked about the feature of the forerunner that Malachi introduces. The prophet not only projects such a figure (3:1), he names him (4:5). Did the prophet actually expect Elijah to return to earth centuries after being transported to heaven by chariot? (2 Kgs 2:11).

Several elements in Malachi's presentation of the Day of the Lord suggest that Elijah must be taken more symbolically than literally (see Hill 1998, 384). The NT identification of Elijah with John the Baptist confirms this approach (Matt 11:14; 17:10-13; Luke 1:17). In addition, Jesus leaves the door open for further expectations of another Elijah-like prophet coming before the final Day of the Lord. Using both present and future tenses he declares, "Elijah is indeed coming and will restore all things" (Matt 17:11 NRSV). Jesus allows for application of Malachi's text to his first advent as well as to a future event.

Such reapplication of Malachi's words provides perspective for interpreting other elements of the Day of the Lord. The various features associated with that day must be permitted to apply to different situations. The Day of the Lord surely points to the ultimate closing out of human history, but also to other key moments prior to that time.

H. Theology of Malachi

The primary image of God in the oracles of Malachi is that of covenant partner. This understanding of God forms the essential context for hearing Malachi's message. The logic of Malachi's preaching rests upon the Lord's covenant with Abraham. As descendants of Abraham, Malachi's audience stands in covenantal relationship with the Lord and thus receives both the privileges and consequences of that relationship. Because of this covenant bond, the prophet challenges his audience to live up to their part of the agreement.

As a covenant partner, God fulfills a number of roles. God is the Lord Almighty, the faithful partner in the relationship, the ideal father, the covenant enforcer, the final judge of all humanity, and the sovereign king of the world.

The Lord Almighty. The most frequently used name for God in Malachi is the covenantal name "the Lord Almighty" (*YHWH ṣebā'ôt*). It occurs 24 times in the 55 verses of the book, with 16 additional uses of "the Lord" without the title "Almighty." This name evokes the history of Judah's covenant with God, especially the seminal Mosaic era. In the story of Israel's deliverance from Egypt, God reveals that he is the powerful Lord Almighty who remembers his covenant with Abraham

(Exod 2:24). God brings his people out of bondage in order to reestablish relationship with them. At Sinai the Lord articulates the stipulations of the covenant agreement detailing how that relationship can work.

Faithful Covenant Partner. God has been a faithful covenant partner throughout the history of this relationship, according to Malachi. The Lord does "not change" in his commitment to it (3:6). God's fundamental obligation to the covenant is to love his people. According to Malachi, God has done this faithfully.

The initial oracle of the book confirms the constancy of God's love for Jacob's descendants. The Lord says, "I have loved you," with the implication that it has always been so (1:2). This fact is proven by his treatment of Israel. In contrast to Edom, they have not been destroyed (1:3-4 and 3:6). On the day of judgment those who fear the Lord within Israel will be spared disaster. The religious leaders will be refined so that true worship can be restored according the stipulations of the covenant (3:2-4). God will claim those who fear him as his "treasured possession" and write their names in "a scroll of remembrance" (3:16-17). But before that final day, God promises to extend grace once more and send a prophet to persuade them to live in the covenant (4:5-6 [3:22-24 HB]).

Ideal Father. In the context of the covenant, God is like an ideal father to his people (2:10). On the day of judgment God treats those who keep covenant as a good son (3:17). But God also expects them to act like sons and to honor him appropriately as their father (1:6).

Covenant Enforcer. The Lord enforces the covenant by administering the curses (1:14; 2:2; 4:6) and blessings (3:10-12) stipulated in the law. In this vein God acts as a "witness" against those who break covenant regulations (2:14; 3:5). God urges his people to honor the covenant demands (2:2), not to break faith (2:15-16), and to return to a faithful relationship with him (3:7). The Lord lays out a challenge to the people of Judah to "test" him to see if he will not enforce the promised blessings when they live out their obligations to the covenant (3:10).

Final Judge. In the end, the Lord will sit as the final arbiter of human decisions and distinguish between those who live in covenant and those who do not (3:18). Malachi promises that "the day is coming" when God will punish covenant breakers severely and vindicate the covenant keepers (4:1-3 [3:19-21]).

Sovereign King. The Lord does not function as an equal partner in the covenant bond. Judah's God is "the great king" whose "name is to be feared among the nations" (2:14). Typically in ancient Middle Eastern treaties, covenants were struck between a greater and a lesser party. The more dominant partner, called the suzerain, viewed himself as king of the world. So also Malachi presents the Lord as the suzerain in Israel's covenant agreement.

As such the prophet urges the descendants of Abraham to live out covenant stipulations so that the King is given his proper due. By fulfilling the obligations of covenant worship and community commitments the people honor the Lord as their sovereign ruler. Pleasing sacrifices and generous giving (1:6-14; 3:6-12), faithful spiritual leadership (2:1-9; 2:17-3:5), and strong family commitments (2:10-16) give the Lord the honor he should have.

Regardless of how well people might fulfill their side of the pact though, Malachi knew that the Lord's "name will be great among the nations, from where the sun rises to where it sets" (1:11-12). In the end, God's status does not depend upon Judah's response to the covenant agreement. The Lord stands apart from and above this relationship. God created the covenant and the covenant people (2:10). Therefore, the Lord remains absolutely sovereign over all whether or not humans respond. So any overtures to heal the covenant relationship come from the grace filled heart of the Covenant Partner who begins his appeal with the words, "I have loved you" (1:2).

COMMENTARY

I. FIRST DISPUTE: GOD'S DISTINCTION BETWEEN JACOB AND ESAU: MALACHI 1:1-5

BEHIND THE TEXT

The history of the Edomites provides important background for understanding this oracle. The land of Edom was located south of the Dead Sea and Moab, extending just over a hundred miles (about 175 km) to the Gulf of Aqaba. Red sandstone ranges appropriately characterize the region since the name Edom derives from the Semitic root for red. During ancient times one of the most important north-south trade routes, the King's Highway, ran through Edom. This roadway, along with extensive copper mining, provided economic stimulus for the region.

According to biblical tradition the inhabitants of Edom descended from Esau the twin brother of Jacob and son of Isaac. The familial hostility between these brothers reflected in Gen 25-36 continued throughout the history of their descendants. When Israel was making its way to the promised land under the leadership of Moses the Edomites did not permit them to pass through their land (Num 20). Later Saul engaged the Edomites along with other enemies in his struggle to establish the state of Israel (1 Sam 14).

.During the monarchy David subdued the Edomites and incorporated them into his empire (1 Chr 18). But after Solomon, Edom regained its independence until the time of Jehoshaphat (r. 873-849 BC). For a time, Jehoshaphat controlled the rich resources of Edom and the port of Ezion-geber (1 Chr 20) before his son Jehoram lost it (2 Kgs 8). During the reigns of Amaziah (r. 800-783 BC) and Uzziah (r. 783-742 BC) Judah once again exerted a level of control over Edom (2 Kgs 14). After Edom reclaimed its freedom at the time of Ahaz (735-715 BC) though, they never again came under Judah's sovereignty. By the seventh century BC, Edom prospered as a vassal of the Assyrian Empire and became an increasing nemesis to Judah. When Judah finally fell to the Babylonians in 586 BC, the Edomites swept in and added to the destruction of Jerusalem (Ps 137:7; Ezek 35:1-15; Obad 10-14).

Judah's prophets regularly predicted the demise of Edom for its hostility toward God and his people (see Amos 1:11-12; Joel 3:19 [4:19 HB]; Isa 21:11-12; Jer 49:7-22; Ezek 25:12-14). Their role in the plunder of Judah in 586 BC was particularly odious to them. The Edomites, in fact, came to symbolize all the enemies of God who were destined for destruction in the messianic age (Isa 34; 63:1-6; Ezek 36:1-7).

The many prophecies against Edom eventually came to fulfillment. The Babylonians continued to reduce Edom's strength and influence after destroying Judah. Arabian tribes appear to have infiltrated the mountains of Edom over the next few centuries gradually wresting control of the region from them. By late fourth century BC inscriptions indicate that Nabateans had displaced the Edomites from their ancient homeland. All that remained of these people was an area south of Judah in the Negev called Idumea by the Greeks.

This initial prophecy of Malachi can be viewed as an oracle of judgment against a foreign nation, intended to encourage Judah. The present situation is identified in vv 2-4a while the message of judgment comes in vv 4b-5. That message is introduced with the typical messenger formula "this is what the LORD Almighty says."

The style of the prophecy is disputational, which characterizes the prophetic speeches of Malachi as a whole (→ Introduction: C. Literary Forms). It begins with opening statements by God and the people of Judah (v 2a-b). Then God lays out the evidence for his case against Judah (vv 2c-5).

The verses of this oracle display poetic elements, though no major English translation formats them as poetry. There are numerous parallel lines and chiastic structures within these lines. The language is concise and rhythmic as it employs numerous colorful images and wordplays.

IN THE TEXT

A. Superscription (1:1)

■ **1** The superscription identifies the book of Malachi as **a prophecy** (*massā'*) and **the word of the LORD** (*dĕbar YHWH*). The term **prophecy** (*massā'*), which is translated "oracle" or "burden" in some English translations, labels certain kinds of prophetic material in the OT (→ Zech 9:1; cp. Nah 1:1; Hab 1:1; Zech 12:1; Isa 13:1; 15:1; 17:1). The noun *massā'* derives from the verb *nāsā'* ("lift up" or "carry"), which has led to the suggestion that the term means the lifting up of the prophetic voice, and thus a pronouncement. It may also mean that the message from the Lord is heavy with ominous words, and thus a burden; the prophet must unload it or deliver it to its intended audience (see Muller, 2003, 20-24; Weis, 1994, 28-29).

The phrase **the word of the LORD** is frequently found in the prophetic books to indicate the divine origin of messages from prophets (see Isa 1:10; Jer 1:2; Ezek 1:3, etc.). **Israel** is the intended audience of this prophetic word. Later in the book they are also called "Judah" (2:11 and 3:4), "Jacob" (2:12), and "descendants of Jacob" (3:6). These terms convey their continued existence as the covenant people of God, though they possess a distinct political identity as residents of Yehud, a part of the western satrapy within the Persian Empire.

The superscription identifies **Malachi** as the messenger of the word of the Lord. The name Malachi is meaningful, but unusual as a personal name; it simply means "my messenger" and may be a shortened form of *Malakiyahu*, which means "messenger of the Lord" (→ Introduction: A. The Prophet)

B. Opening Statements (1:2a-b)

■ **2a** Malachi's message begins with a bold declaration of God: **I have loved you** (v 2a). The form of the verb **loved** (*'āhabti*) expresses simple complete action that can encompass past, present, and future. One could communicate its meaning by rendering ***I have loved you and will always love you*** (see NLT). The Hebrew word **loved** (*'āhab*), usually found in the context of family relationship, conveys God's special connections with Israel through his covenant and his choosing of this people to be mediators of his blessing to "all peoples on earth" (see Gen 12:3). Deuteronomy 10:15 also links God's love for Israel and his election of them.

■ **2b** The people of Judah challenge God's claim with the question, **How have you loved us?** (v 2b). This could also be rendered ***In what manner have you loved us?*** More of what lies behind this question is revealed by other questions spoken by Malachi's audience later in the book. They want to know "Where is the God of justice?" (2:17) and "What did we gain by carrying out his requirements?" (3:14). At this point in their history, they do not see much evidence of God's love for them and their election as a special people in the world (→ Introduction: B. The Audience).

C. Argument (1:2c-5)

■ **2c** God responds to the people's question with a rhetorical question: **Was not Esau Jacob's brother?** (v 2c). The people know the story of the twin brothers, **Esau and Jacob.** Esau, the elder brother, should have received the birthright blessings as the firstborn in the family. Yet, even prior to birth, God declared that "the older (Esau) will serve the younger (Jacob)" (Gen 25:23). Later at Bethel, God made Jacob heir to covenant promises (Gen 28:13-15).

God's assertion **yet I have loved Jacob** implies the manner in which God has chosen (**loved**) Jacob, and by extension, the manner in which he continues to love the audience of Malachi. He has set aside the customs and traditions of the world and bestowed his favor on the less privileged in the society. Thus, **I have loved Jacob** is the same as **I have loved you**. Both Jacob and his descendants continue to be the chosen ones to mediate God's blessings to the world.

■ **3** God emphasizes his love (election) of Israel when he announces, **Esau I have hated** (v 3). In certain contexts, the term **hated** (*sānē'*) means "detested" or "intensely disliked" (Gen 37:4) and in other places it means "less loved" (Gen 29:31; Deut 21:15-17). Here it is the opposite of "loved" in v 2. So **hated** means "not chosen" for special relationship with God, to be heir to the covenant promises, and to mediate God's blessing to the world. This does not mean God did not care for Esau or that Esau could not have a relationship with God and receive his blessing (see Gen 33:16, 36:7, 31-42; see also Ezek 35:9, 15).

The second part of v 3 indicates that Edom had often been the subject of God's judgment. The scene of God turning the impressive mountains of Edom **into a wasteland** fit for **desert jackals** most likely refers to the devastation brought by the Babylonians in the mid-sixth century BC. It could also refer to more recent incursions from Arabian tribes during the early fifth century BC.

■ **4** Ironically, as evidence of God's love for Jacob, Malachi announces the utter ruin of Edom and gives no hope for its rebuilding. Total devastation of Israel's enemies and their lands is a common theme in the prophetic oracles against the nations (see Ezek 35:9; also Ezek 26:4-5). The Lord will continue to frustrate Edom's attempts to **rebuild the ruins** and will give them the infamous reputation as **the Wicked Land.** This name stands in stark contrast to Judah's label "the holy land" in Zech 2:12 [16 HB] and "a delightful land" in Mal 3:12. The Edomites are destined to become **a people always under the wrath of the Lord.** The words **under the wrath** translate *zā'am*, a term that means "denounced" or even more strongly "cursed." The NIV **always** (*'ad 'ôlām*) simply means "for a long time." It does not necessarily imply that the curse upon Edom cannot ever be lifted.

■ **5** God anticipates that when Judah witnesses God's judgment on Edom, an expression of God's love for them, they will confess, **Great is the Lord—even beyond the borders of Israel** (v 5). The phrase **Great is the Lord** echoes throughout the Psalms asserting the sovereignty of God both in present and future ages. Those who speak these words love God's salvation (Pss 35:27; 40:16 [17 HB]; 48:1

[2 HB]; 70:4 [5 HB]) and affirm God's profound love for them (Ps 145:3-9). It is a word of praise that confesses God's ultimate victory over the nations of the world (Ps 99:2).

FROM THE TEXT

The first oracle of the book sets the stage for the rest of Malachi's messages. It confronts Judah's fundamental struggle with their identity. Undoubtedly because of contemporary political, religious, social, and economic problems, they failed to believe they were a people loved by God.

History reveals evidence of God's love for people. From time to time people need to pause and revisit their history to rediscover the truth of God's love. Malachi's audience needed to reflect on how God had chosen their ancestor Jacob, though he was the younger brother and possessed no special merit or spiritual qualities. It was simply an act of God's grace. As Deut 7:7-8 states, the Lord "set his affection" on Israel and chose them because he "loved" them and was faithful to his covenant with Abraham. The selection of Israel as the covenant people says more about God than it does about Israel. God loves because that is who God is.

The statement that God hated Esau underscores God's love for Jacob, as Paul understood when he quoted Mal 1:2 in Rom 9:13. It cannot be taken to mean that Esau was chosen for eternal damnation as some have supposed. The point is that God did not choose Esau and his descendants as a covenant people to carry out his mission in the world. The OT clarifies that Esau and his descendants made their own choices and resisted relationship with God (see Gen 25, Amos 1:11-12; Isa 34:1-17; Jer 49:7-22; Ezek 35:1-36:7). Yet, God offers them opportunity to join his mission just as any other people of the world can. They are part of "all nations" that God wants to include in his kingdom (Matt 28:19).

Beginning the book of Malachi with this oracle suggests that *grasping the depth of God's love forms the foundation of a healthy spiritual life.* The first point Malachi's audience needed to hear was God's consist love for them. Once they embraced this truth they could confess, "Great is the LORD—even beyond the borders of Israel" (v 5). A realization of their true identity in God would empower them to act in accord with their calling. They can proclaim the sovereign rule of God in this world and "be a blessing" to the nations (Gen 12:3).

So it is with all who by faith become one of Abraham's descendants (Rom 9:8). Once seized by the depth of God's love, people become free to be who God has made them to be. They are the elect who have allied themselves with God in order to redeem the world. Their identity in God clarifies their purpose and destiny in this world. They become the ones through whom God chooses to fulfill his promise to Abraham.

II. SECOND DISPUTE: GOD'S CURSE UPON DEFECTIVE SACRIFICES: MALACHI 1:6-14

BEHIND THE TEXT

The logic of this message rests upon the social concepts of honor and shame. Ancient cultures placed significant value upon honor. Israel shared with her neighboring cultures the conviction that those in authority, such as kings (1 Kgs 10:24), parents (Exod 20:12), elders (Lev 19:32), as well as deities (Ps 29:1-2), must be accorded the honor due them. Offering appropriate sacrifices provided one significant way people could honor God in ancient Israel. Leviticus 22:17-25 and other passages lay out specific requirements for acceptable sacrifices, and the law stipulates severe consequences, even death to priests, for failure to follow these requirements (see Lev 10:1-3). Offering unacceptable sacrifices breached the covenant relationship and showed disrespect for God.

373

This oracle is linked to the previous one by means of cause and effect. Judah's false perception of God in 1:2-5 (not believing in God's love for them) leads to the kind of worship in 1:6-14 that disrespects God. Failing to receive love results in withholding it.

The message in 1:6-14 is a self-contained unit, though it is closely connected to the following message in 2:1-9. These two messages are so tightly associated thematically and verbally that commentators regularly treat them as one extended message with two parts. The rhetorical feature of inclusion, however, marks the unit's boundaries. The questions posed in v 6 receive a direct response in v 14. The questions are answered earlier in v 11, but the text continues to restate the argument of vv 8-10 in vv 12-14 for the sake of emphasis. Thus the passage has three primary structural sections. Opening questions and statements introduce the topic (vv 6-7). Then the topic is clarified and argued (vv 8-10). The final section (vv 12-14) parallels the argument made in the previous section and expands on it. This double presentation of the argument balances the double questions at the beginning of the oracle.

IN THE TEXT

A. Opening Statements (1:6-7)

■ **6** God's opening statement is a reminder of basic social values held by nearly all cultures in the ancient world. Almost universally people expected authorities such as a **father** and a **master** to be honored by those under them (v 6). Clan-centered cultures like Judah insisted upon appropriate respect for a **father** who functioned as head of the family as well as the entire extended household.

The word **honors** (*kabad*) comes from a Hebrew root meaning "heavy" or "weighty." So by extension the term expresses the weight of worth or value of someone or something. **Respect** (*mora'*) is closely related to the idea of honor. It comes from the verb meaning "fear" (*yara'*) and is often used to connote appropriate reverence or awe of someone or something.

In this verse God identifies himself as both **father** and **master** of Judah. The image of God as **father** recurs throughout the Bible (see e.g., Deut 32:6; Hos 11:1-11; Jer 31:9, 20; Matt 6:6; Rom 1:7; 1 Cor 1:3). God is also frequently called **master**. But when God is designated as such the term normally carries an intensifying ending and is spelled *'ădônai*. In those cases, it is usually translated "Lord" in the sense of absolute sovereign, as it is in Mal 1:12, 14, and elsewhere in the OT.

God's questions indicate that people have failed to show appropriate respect for God and his authority over them. Those accused of disrespecting God in particular are **you priests**. In Malachi **priests** refers to all those functioning in leadership roles in the temple, not just descendants of Aaron (→ Behind the Text at 2:1-9). God charges that they dishonor him by their **contempt** for his **name**. The word translated **show contempt** (*bāzâ*) means to "treat lightly" or "despise."

God's **name** denotes the character and reputation of God, including his holiness and authority.

Following the disputation style, Malachi presents the response of the priests to God's charge against them; they ask, **How have we shown contempt?** Implicit in this question is a denial of the accusation. But on the surface, at least, it conveys a desire to know more specifics.

■ **7** God responds to the priests' question with a charge that they have dishonored his name by **offering defiled food on** his **altar** (v 7). The term **defiled** (*gā'al*) identifies things that were not acceptable for worship of the Lord. Further details of these kinds of offerings will be given in vv 8 and 13.

A second question from the priests, **How have we defiled you?**, seeks clarification. But it may also indicate that they were either clueless or in a state of denial. God's response to this question is essentially the same as before. By their actions the priests announce that **the LORD's table is contemptible**, that is, despised or worthless. The word **contemptible** (*bāzâ*) is the same word used in the initial accusation in v 6. So the dialogue has come back to the original issue; they are dishonoring God.

The phrase **the LORD's table** refers either to the altar of sacrifice or the tables where priests prepared sacrifices. If it means the altar, which makes sense in this context, then the designation is a rare occurrence in the Hebrew Scriptures (see Ezek 44:16 for another possible reference to the altar as the table of the Lord).

Throughout this speech the prophet uses the participial form of verbs ("showing contempt" and "offering") in order to emphasize repeated action. Dishonoring God was not a one-time error in judgment. For the priests, this was a way of life.

B. Argument (1:8-14)

■ **8-9** These verses present further evidence of how the priests dishonor God. They defile the altar by sacrificing **blind, lame,** and **diseased animals**. The law very clearly forbids the sacrifice of such animals (see Deut 15:21; Lev 22:17-25). Malachi's rhetorical question, **is that not wrong** (*ra'*, "evil")?, affirms that such sacrifices not only violate the law, but they promote all that is contrary to God (evil).

At this point Malachi puts forth two challenges to his audience. First, he encourages them to offer these sorts of offerings to the local political leader of Judah, their **governor**. The prophet asks if he would **be pleased** and **accept you**. The answer, of course, is no. Such offerings would be an insult.

The second challenge is to **plead with God to be gracious to us** (v 9). Literally this phrase reads *appease the face of God that he may be gracious to us*. The prophet is playing with the image of looking into a face. He asks, **Will he accept you?** This is the same phrase in v 8 that literally means to *lift up your face*. Malachi undoubtedly has in mind the well-known Aaronic blessing in Num 6:24-26. He alludes to it several times in this oracle and the next. The point of the two challenges is clear. God will not accept second-rate sacrifices any more than a political leader would.

■ **10** The prophet calls for extreme measures to drive home the point of just how deplorable such sacrifices are. He pleads for someone to **shut the temple doors** and end temple sacrifices all together (v 10). The flames of the altar are called **useless fires** because the sacrifices do not accomplish their intended purposes. Other prophets of Israel expressed similar sentiments when worship at the temple became too repugnant (Amos 5:21-23; Isa 1:11-15).

At this point, God finally states his judgment on the situation directly. **I am not pleased with you . . . I will accept no offerings from your hands** (v 10). Such words are haunting to anyone but especially to priests whose primary job was to please God and to take the lead in sacrifices.

■ **11** Though Judah's priests do not show God proper respect, God announces that the nations will honor him. They will bring **incense and pure offerings** to him (v 11). The word **pure** (*tĕhôrâ*) refers to that which is ceremonially clean according to Israel's law codes. Some scholars suggest that v 11 speaks of present circumstances rather than future ones. They identify those who offer pure offerings as either Jews or non-Jews living in other areas of the Persian Empire. But there is very little evidence to indicate that Jewish communities outside Judah were any more faithful than those within. In fact, the archaeological evidence of Egyptian Jewish communities reveals considerable syncretism (see Verhoef, 1987, 225-231).

The idea of nations one day honoring God is repeated twice (vv 11 and 14). These statements, coupled with the phrases **from where the sun rises to where it sets** and **in every place,** emphasize that Israel's God will be honored from places "beyond the borders of Israel" (1:5). This is a reversal of the roles of Israel and the nations. Those whom Israel considers as outsiders to the covenant will bring acceptable offerings to the Lord. They will teach Israel, the covenant people, the proper way to honor God. Thus among the nations, God's **name will be great**. They will preserve God's reputation and character. The picture of the universal worship of the Lord portrayed here is consistent with the hopes of other prophets as well as the psalmists in Israel (see Isa 2:2-4; Zech 14:16; Ps 22:27-28 [28-29 HB]; 47:1-2 [2-3 HB]).

■ **12** A second cycle of arguments begins with v 12, which recalls the words of Malachi's audience at the end of v 7. The Lord accuses the priests of speaking against **the LORD's table** (the altar) and **its food** (the sacrifices). They call them **defiled** (*gāʼal*) and **contemptible** (*bāzâ*), words used previously in the oracle in vv 6-7. They are nearly synonymous in conveying the idea of showing disregard for the importance of something or someone. Thus they **profane** the altar of the Lord. The term **profane** (*ḥālal*) stands as the antonym to "make holy" (*qādaš*). It conveys the idea of treating something as ordinary, removed from the realm of the sacred. The verbal form of this word is once again a participle, which emphasizes continuous action.

■ 13 The Lord also brings the accusation that priests regard the whole business of offering sacrifices **a burden** and **sniff at it contemptuously** (v 13). These expressions convey boredom and frustration with their priestly tasks. Once again God lists the particular unacceptable sacrifices the priests are offering and asks if it makes any sense for God to approve them. Clearly **injured, lame or diseased animals** should not be accepted, as the rhetorical question implies (→ v 8).

■ 14 While judgment is communicated implicitly in the rhetorical question of v 13, God pronounces a direct verdict upon one specific case in v 14. That is the case of a person who **vows** to give **an acceptable male** for sacrifice and offers a **blemished animal** instead (v 14). Worshipers often made **vows** to do something once prayer was answered (see Ps 54:6-7 [8-9 HB]). The law of Moses issues a strong warning to those who do not following through on a vow (Deut 23:21-23 [22-24 HB]). God calls the one who reneges on his vow a **cheat** (*nôkēl*), a label that identifies the person as one who deceives with intent to do harm. The Lord pronounces his curse on those who deceive him with vows they do not intend to fulfill (see Deut 28:15-68).

The oracle concludes by recalling v 11 and returning to the theme of God's honor. God affirms that his **name is to be feared among the nations**. This phrase parallels "my name will be great among the nations" in v 11. The word **feared** (*yārē'*) also connects back to the word "respect" in v 6, which derives from the same root. Thus this statement responds to the second question of v 6, "where is the respect due me?" The answer given is the same one given in v 11. It will be found **among the nations** when, in a future era, they will worship the Lord as their **great king** (cp. Zech 14:16).

FROM THE TEXT

This message teaches the importance of proper worship. How we honor God matters to God as well as to us.

God is clearly worthy of all the honor people might give him. Malachi's message reminds the people of Judah that God is like "a father" to his people and "a master" of the covenant (v 6). It also notes that one day all nations will recognize the Lord as "the great king" of the world (vv 11 and 14). If sons, slaves, and nations can express proper respect, surely God's people can honor "the LORD Almighty" whose very name reminds them of his worth. Indeed, God is worthy of being exalted above all names and given the very best his people can possibly offer.

Yet, Malachi's audience failed to honor God with their worship activities. They offered unacceptable, second rate sacrifices (v 10) and felt that these activities had become a "burden" to them (v 13). The reason for this attitude is likely related to the previous oracle in the book. According to Malachi's first message (vv 2-5), Judah did not realize that God loved them. As a result, their worship of God suffered. Failure to grasp God's love caused them to fail to grasp God's worth.

What people believe about God affects their worship of God. This oracle invites its readers to reflect on the relationship between their beliefs and their worship. Do we have a proper theology, a correct understanding of God's love for us? Do we worship God in such a way that everything we do in the name of worship is consistent with our theology? Is honoring God the primary goal of our worship? Truthful responses to these questions can lead us to a life of covenant faithfulness to the great King who is worthy of all honor and praise.

III. THIRD DISPUTE: GOD'S CURSE UPON THE LEVITES: MALACHI 2:1-9

BEHIND THE TEXT

The third message of Malachi is closely tied to the previous oracle (→ Behind the Text at 1:6-14). The focus of this message is on the failure of priests to honor God's covenant with Levi, the ancestor of the priestly tribe. In Israel, members of the priesthood originally came from the house of Aaron of the tribe of Levi. Those who belonged to the rest of the families of the tribe of Levi were known as Levites. In Israel's early history, there was a clear distinction between priests and Levites. Priests were privileged with the responsibility to offer sacrifices and offerings, while Levites played a secondary role in the temple as assistants to the priests and custodians of the temple vessels and other furnishings. Later in Israel's history, particularly in the postexilic era this distinction became obscured. Ezra and Nehemiah indicate that Levites became more and more involved in performing many of the duties originally assigned exclusively to Aaron's descendants. In Malachi, the term "priests" does not refer only to the descendants of Aaron, but to all descendants of Levi.

379

The "covenant with Levi" mentioned in v 4 provides the essential background for understanding this oracle. This is the agreement God made with the descendants of Levi that they would serve as spiritual leaders to the community of Israel. During the time of Moses God "set apart the tribe of Levi to carry the ark of the covenant of the Lord, to stand before the Lord to minister and to pronounce blessings in his name" (Deut 10:8). Under this covenant God promised them "peace" and "a lasting priesthood" (Num 25:10-13; see also Jer 33:20-22). In return the descendants of Levi were obligated to act as trustees of the covenantal directives given by God at Sinai. They were responsible for preserving, teaching, and applying the Mosaic law in Israel. Their ultimate purpose was the same as the law's purpose, which was to guide people in maintaining a strong relationship with a holy and loving God. This required the priests to have extensive knowledge of the Laws of Moses (Deut 33:9-10; Lev 10:11), a function that is particularly emphasized in Mal 2:1-9.

Priests and Levites in Israel

The history of priests and Levites in Israel is one of the most vexing problems of OT studies. The roles and relationships between these two groups changed over the course of Israelite history. The biblical texts, however, are not entirely clear on when or how things developed. Julius Wellhausen's famous historical reconstruction of the priesthood identified the time of Josiah as the point when Levites were relegated to a secondary role in the temple. Much of Wellhausen's thesis has been modified in recent scholarship, but it continues to hold considerable influence over discussion about the priesthood (see Garrett, 2003, 519-522 and Duke, 2003, 646-655).

This speech is stylistically and structurally different from most of the others in the book. It does not make use of the typical projected dialogue in which God states a concern and the audience protests. Yet the mood of courtroom disputation remains. God levels accusations against the priests and argues his case with supporting evidence. In this message though, we do not hear the protest of the audience. The passage begins with a pronouncement of judgment that functions as the opening statement of accusation (vv 1-4). This is followed by a description of the situation that contains argument for the accusation (vv 5-9).

IN THE TEXT

A. Opening Statements (2:1-4)

■ 1 The opening phrase **and now** introduces the transition from accusations in 1:6-14 to a pronouncement of judgment in 2:1-9. The Lord announces a **warning** for the priests (v 1). The NIV translation of *miṣwâ* as **warning** might be rendered better "decision" or "verdict." It regularly appears along with "law" (*tôrâh*), "regulations" (*mišpāṭ*), or "decrees" (*ḥoq*) in the Pentateuch to describe the stipulations of the Mosaic law (see Lev 26:15). Its usage in Malachi evokes this covenantal context.

■ **2** The prophet uses a conditional sentence to announce judgment. The condition is stated twice in parallel phrases: **if you do not listen and if you do not resolve to honor my name** (v 2). These two statements express the same thought, with the last line clarifying the first. Throughout the OT **listen** (*šāmaʿ*) carries the idea of active hearing or obedience. What must be obeyed is the command to **resolve to honor my name**. **Resolve** translates the Hebrew phrase *sîm ʿal leb*, which is literally *put upon a heart*. Thus some English translation render the phrase "take it to heart" (NASB, HCSB). It conveys the idea of a person's passionate determination to do something. The focus of determination is **honor** for God's **name**, meaning carefully protecting and acknowledging God's character and reputation (→ 1:6). This was a fundamental obligation of priests according to v 5.

In poetic fashion, two other parallel statements balance the first two and relate the consequence for dishonoring God. God threatens to **send a curse** upon the priests, not simply place one upon them. The word **send** (*šālaḥ*) is an intensive form that carries the force of "let loose" or "commission" (see Amos 4:10; Num 21:6: 2 Kgs 17:25), like a king sending out a messenger (Isa 6:8).

Deuteronomy 28-32 identifies a variety of disasters that might occur when the covenant is not kept and Israel's prophets regularly evoked them in judgment speeches. Malachi will identify the specifics of the curses coming upon the priests in vv 3 and 9. Here, however, God threatens to **curse** the **blessings** they might offer during worship. Instead of bestowing the Lord's protection, grace, and "peace" on people (Num 6:24-26), their words tragically brought about the opposite. One of their primary ministries had been rendered ineffectual.

Verse 2 ends with the assertion that God has **already** carried out his threat. The priests are under God's curse as Malachi speaks because they **have not resolved to honor** the Lord.

■ **3** Though Israel's priesthood was hereditary, God announces that he will suspend that tradition and reject their descendants as priests. **I will rebuke** (*gōʾer*) is a strong statement of rejection (v 3). The LXX translates the phrase with *aphorizo*, which means "separate" or "cut off." Additionally, God announces that the priests will suffer humiliation because they dishonor him (v 3). Smearing **dung** on one's **face** would be as offensive to ancient audiences as it is to modern ones. This was especially repugnant for Israel's priests because of their concern for the laws of purity and uncleanness. Contamination with unclean things would render priests unserviceable in the temple (see Lev 10 and 21). **Dung** refers to the internal parts of animals sacrificed during festivals. Such waste would normally be taken out of the temple area to be burned (Lev 4:11-12).

Nothing could be more devastating than the two curses put forth in this message. God drives home his message in the strongest terms possible most likely to shake the priests out of their complacency.

■ 4 The pronouncement of judgment closes with a statement of its desired effect. The Lord wants the priests to **know** (*yāda'*, acknowledge) that this **warning** comes from God and as a result continue his **covenant with Levi** (v 4). Acknowledging that this message comes from God implies that the priests have decided to honor the Lord and return to their covenantal relationship with him. **The covenant with Levi** is the agreement God made with the tribe of Levi that they would function as the spiritual leaders of Israel (Num 25:10-13; Jer 33:19-22). Some of the specific elements involved in this ministry are described in the following verses (→ Behind the Text).

B. Argument (2:5-9)

■ 5 The message shifts in v 5 toward a description of the present situation, a typical element in prophetic speeches. God begins by reminding Malachi's audience what his "covenant with Levi" entailed and how this covenant was kept by the priests in the past. That covenant produced **life and peace** (v 5), two gifts only God can give (see Gen 2:7 and Num 6:26; see Prov 3:2). **Life** (*ḥayyîm*) ranges in meaning from simple physical existence (as opposed to death) to continual vitality accompanied by blessedness and wellbeing. Likewise, **peace** (*šālôm*) conveys the sense of the good life that includes wholeness, wellbeing, and prosperity as well as tranquility. The two terms function together to express the abundant life involved in the blessing of God.

The covenant required Levi and his descendants to show **reverence** to God through their life and ministry. The previous generations of priests, unlike the present one, had fulfilled their covenant obligations because they truly **revered** God. The term **revered** (*yara'*) regularly connotes deep respect (→ 1:6). But the term **stood in awe** (*ḥātat*) expresses more the idea of terror or overwhelming dread. The two terms combine to convey a sense of profound respect for the otherness of God.

■ 6 Priests in the past fulfilled their covenant obligation as follows: (1) they provided **true instruction**, (2) **walked** with God, and (3) **turned many from sin** (v 6). Giving **true instruction** from the words of Moses was an essential task of the priesthood (Lev 10:10-11; Deut 17:9). Saying **nothing false** implies the priests applied the law appropriately. Throughout the OT the image of walking with God communicates the idea of maintaining a personal relationship with God (Gen 17:1; Mic 6:8). This is demonstrated by obeying God's commands (Deut 10:12), which they did consistently, as the phrase **in peace and uprightness** suggests. Through their teaching and their way of life, priests **turned many from sin**. This was the primary purpose of the priesthood, to guide people toward a life with God.

■ 7 **The lips of a priest** play a critical role in communicating as well as preserving **knowledge** of God's **instruction** for life (v 7). **People seek instruction** (*tôrâh*) from priests because they are messengers of divine truth. Only in Malachi do we find the label **the messenger of the LORD Almighty** applied to the priests. This label is more frequently used of heavenly beings and a few times of prophets (Hag 1:13;

but also see Mal 3:1). Malachi applies this label to the priests because they were couriers of the codified revelation of God preserved in the law.

■ **8** After emphasizing the responsibility of priests as teachers of God's laws, the Lord indicts them for failing in this role. First, they themselves had **turned from the way** of life put forth in the law (v 8). This personal failing impacted their **teaching**, which **caused many to stumble**. They had made the law of God more of an obstacle than a path to life, as it was intended to be (see Ps 19:7-11; 119:9, 105). Finally, God says the priests had **violated the covenant with Levi**. The word **violated** (*šāḥat*) means "spoiled" or "ruined" like a devastated vineyard (Jer 12:10) or a wasted building (Lam 2:6). God's **covenant with Levi** to act as Israel's spiritual leaders was ruined. Rather than giving "true instruction" (v 6), turning "many from sin" (v 6), and acting as a "a messenger of the LORD" (v 7), the priests of Malachi's time had done exactly the opposite.

■ **9** The final sentence of the oracle restates God's judgment and the reasons for it. The priests who thought the Lord's table was "contemptible" (*bāzâ*; 1:7, 12) are now **despised** (*bāzâ*) **and humiliated before all the people**. The extent of their humiliation has already been described in v 3. For such degrading things to happen **before all the people** intensifies the punishment in a culture where personal status is highly valued.

A summary of the indictments given in v 8 is that the priests **have not followed** God's **ways**. The **ways** of God are the ways of life articulated in the laws of Moses (see Deut 31:15-20). The participial form of the verb **followed** conveys regular mishandling of the law.

One additional accusation is that the priests **have shown partiality in matters of the law**. This explains one way in which the priests "caused many to stumble" by their teaching (v 8). The term **shown partiality** literally translates "lifting faces," an idiom for extending favor or honor toward someone (→ 1:9; cp. Ps 82:2). The indictment is that the priests were not applying the law equitably among the people. By showing partiality, they failed to truly represent God "who shows no partiality" (Deut 10:17) and is known for his justice (Pss 9:16 [17 HB]; 11:7; 33:5).

FROM THE TEXT

This message provides a theology for leadership within the community of faith and challenges those who aspire to serve in this way. It lays out God's ideal for spiritual leaders and reminds them that God holds them accountable to fulfill their God ordained vocation.

God's leaders must show as well as teach the community of faith how to live before God. First of all, leaders personally need to "resolve to honor" God (v 2) and stand in awe of him (v 5). They are models for those who would follow the Lord. Then, they must instruct people how to live by speaking nothing but the truth about God so that people turn away from sin (v 6). Spiritual leaders need to understand their role as that of a "messenger of the LORD Almighty" (v 7). In a sense, they have become part of the tribe of Levi and entered into "a covenant of life and peace" that draws people into the very life of God (vv 4-5).

Because the responsibilities of spiritual leadership are so significant, *God holds spiritual leaders accountable for fulfilling their roles.* When they fail to give "true instruction" (v 6), people stumble in their walk with the Lord (v 8). As a consequence, the Lord humiliates his servants before those they were called to serve (vv 3, 9). Their ministry becomes like a ruined vineyard (v 8). When a leader becomes a stumbling block for people instead of a steppingstone to spiritual maturity, God will "send a curse" upon that leader's ministry (v 2).

This message reminds readers today that the call to be a minister before God is a high calling that comes with great responsibility. To be in a covenant with God to lead people to him is a special honor. But it demands much, because the stakes are so high.

IV. FOURTH DISPUTE: GOD'S CHALLENGE TO JUDAH'S UNFAITHFULNESS: MALACHI 2:10-16

BEHIND THE TEXT

Marriage practices in ancient Judah provide the background for understanding Malachi's fourth message. In biblical times parents typically arranged marriages for their children while they were still young. So a person could very meaningfully refer to "the wife of your youth" in such a context (v 14). Marriage agreements typically involved the exchange of money and gifts. The bridegroom paid the bride's father for the loss of her services in the home. He also gave gifts to his bride. The bride's father provided a dowry for his daughter to bring into the marriage. In the post-exilic era families increasingly drew up marriage contracts and signed them in order to legalize the agreement and protect their monetary investments. Marriage was also a religious event in Israel, since Israel considered God as a witness of the union (v 14; see also Prov 2:16-17).

Mosaic law forbade Israelites to marry outside the covenant community (Exod 34:12-16). The reason for this was not ethnic purity, but rather covenant fidelity (Deut 7:4-6). This commandment, however, did not preclude all marriage to non-Israelites. If the foreigner embraced the God of Israel, then marriage was permitted. Boaz, for example, married Ruth the Moabite who had committed herself to following the Lord (Ruth 1:16). Ezra and Nehemiah indicate that they responded to the problem of mixed marriages during their day by demanding the Israelite men send away their foreign wives (Ezra 10:2-17; Neh 13:23-28).

This oracle has the character of a summons to repentance. It admonishes the audience to change its practices with a command that is repeated twice "guard yourself in your spirit and do not break faith" (vv 15c and 16c). The rest of the speech provides the motivation for this exhortation by pointing out the people's offenses and why they displease God. Implicitly the oracle functions as a message of judgment since it also conveys God's displeasure with the people's actions.

The passage is difficult to outline because of the interweaving of supporting arguments with accusations and commands. The accusations and initial arguments are made in the opening statements of vv 10-14 and the commands are given with additional arguments in vv 15-16.

IN THE ℟ TEXT

A. Opening Statements (2:10-14)

■ **10** In these verses Malachi engages his audiences with a series of questions that focus on Judah's unfaithfulness **to the covenant of our ancestors** (v 10). He then identifies marriage to "women who worship a foreign god" as the specific violation of that covenant (vv 11-12).

The first two questions of this section assert the familial bond and interconnectedness his audience enjoyed through a common **Father** and Creator. The NIV treats **one Father** in the first question as parallel to **one God** who **creates us** in the second question (see Deut 32:6). However, it is possible that **Father** could be translated as a lowercase "father" and be a reference to Abraham or Jacob or both. If Judah's ancestors are intended here, then Malachi would be emphasizing a family bond through their common ancestors. The point of the questions then would be to affirm that God has created them to be his chosen family through this covenant; this identity for the audience is fundamental to Malachi's argument.

Malachi's third question is a strong accusation that **by being unfaithful to one another**, his listeners have desecrated the **covenant** of their **(our) ancestors**. As a result, they have violated their historic family bond and have betrayed one another by not fulfilling the commitment they made. The term **being unfaithful** is the key phrase of the speech (see vv 10, 11, 14, 15, and 16). The Hebrew word translated **being unfaithful,** *bāgad*, conveys the idea of betrayal. It means not carrying through on a commitment. The term can also include the connotation of willful misleading or pretense. Persons who break faith with God might act as if they are being faithful when in reality they are not (see Jer 3:10).

■ **11** Malachi identifies two specific ways in which his audience has broken covenantal bonds in vv 11-14. Marriage to foreign **women who worship a foreign god** is the charge in v 11. This phrase literally translates as ***daughter of a foreign god*** (*bat 'el nēcār*) and can be read as an allusion to the female goddess Asherah. If so, it would be a direct indictment of idolatry in Judah (see Petersen 1995, 198-200). The phrase, however, most likely refers to non-Jewish women who honor deities other than Israel's God. Marriage to such women could have led husbands to abandon their allegiance to the Lord and thus violate the first commandment (Exod 20:3). King Solomon stands as the most famous example of the disastrous consequences of marriage to foreign women (see 1 Kgs 11:1-13).

Malachi calls such marriages **a detestable thing** (*tô'ēbâ*, v 11), something that is particularly offensive to God and for which people should feel shame (see Deut 7:25-26). According to Malachi, **the sanctuary the L**ORD **loves** (the Jerusalem temple) was deeply impacted by mixed marriages. Men who married foreign women and become worshippers of foreign gods would bring their defilement with them when they came to worship the Lord and thus contaminated that sacred sphere.

■ **12** The prophet pronounces a curse on those who defile the sacred sanctuary by their marriage to foreign women (v 12). Though they may bring an offering to God and thus claim to be worshippers of God, their allegiance to foreign gods has brought a death penalty upon them. When God removes them **from the tents of Jacob**, the covenant community of Israel, they will be cut off from their primary social and economic support group. This was a devastating prospect in ancient times.

No one seems exempt from this curse. The phrase **whoever he may be** implies both priests and ordinary worshippers. However, the phrase is difficult to translate since it literally reads, "one awaking and one answering" (see NASB, "everyone who awakes and answers"; NRSV "any to witness or answer"). It appears to be an idiom that expresses totality (see Hill 1998, 234-235).

■ **13-14** Malachi introduces a second example of Judah's unfaithfulness in vv 13-14. He states the consequence of the offense first and follows with its description (in vv 11-12 the order is reversed). The consequence is that people **weep and wail** because God **no longer looks with favor or accepts** their offerings (v 13). The prophet assumes that his audience would want to know "**why**" the Lord is not pleased with them (v 14). So he gives the reason: they have offended the Lord by being **unfaithful** to their wives. Malachi explains that the Lord has functioned as **the witness** to their marriages, a designated member of the wedding party in ancient Israel who not only observed the exchange of vows, but also became responsible to ensure that they were kept.

Malachi further reminds his audience that a husband's unfaithfulness to his wife becomes a serious offense because of the important roles she occupies in the marriage relationship. For a husband, she is (1) **the wife of your youth,** (2)

387

your partner, and (3) **the wife of your marriage covenant**. Each of these highlights the deep levels of commitment involved in marriage. The designation **the wife of your youth** alludes to the longevity of relationship and, perhaps, earlier passions. The phrase **the wife of your marriage covenant** emphasizes the legal and contractual nature of marriages in ancient Israel. Marriage brought not only a man and a woman, but also their families, into a covenant relationship (→ Behind the Text). Calling the wife **partner** (*ḥăberâ*) raises her status. The term identifies a person who is bound to another in special friendship. It implies equality between husband and wife that makes a breach of covenant more serious.

B. Argument (2:15-16)

■ **15** The oracle moves toward its main purpose in the final two verses. In the first part of v 15, Malachi puts forth key arguments for keeping marriage vows. Unfortunately, he does so in such cryptic language that it is difficult to translate clearly. Regardless of its difficulty, most translations recognize God's sovereign purposes for marriage in the four clauses of this verse. The first clause is a rhetorical question: **has not the one God made you?** (v 15). This clause literally reads, *And did not one he make*. The verb **made** does not have an object so translators supply various options (**you** NIV; "her" NRSV; "them" ESV; "all" NJPS). The NIV also supplies **God** as the subject, perhaps based on the reference to "one" in Deut 6:4. But the word **one** could be understood as the object rather than the subject of the clause, which would produce an alternate question "did not he make them one" (ESV; see KJV, "And did not he make one"). This rendering plays off of Gen 2:24, which emphasizes that a man and a woman become "one flesh" when united in marriage.

The second clause of v 15 is extremely difficult to interpret. Literally, it reads *and a remnant of spirit to it (him)*. The NIV adopts an emendation for the word "remnant" (*šě'ār*) and reads *šě'ēr* **body**, a change that involves vowels. The NIV also supplies the preposition **in** and the conjunction **and**, which produces the reading **in body and spirit**. This alteration to the text is an attempt to clarify the phrase **remnant of spirit**. The Hebrew text as it stands seems to suggest that a residue of (God's) spirit is in a marriage (see the ESV, "with a portion of the Spirit in their union").

The third clause asks another question **and what does the one God seek?** Again, a cryptic Hebrew phrase leaves open alternate translations. Literally the Hebrew reads, *and what the one seeking*. If **one** refers to God, then the question is about what God seeks. If **one** refers to the unity of a man and a woman in marriage, then the question is about the purpose of such a union. In either case the answer is the same. God's goal in marriage is **godly offspring**, children who are committed to a covenant relationship with God.

The fourth clause admonishes men in the audience to diligently keep the marriage covenant (**be on your guard**) and **not be unfaithful** to their wives. This is the fourth of five references to unfaithfulness in this oracle (vv 10, 11, 14, 16; → v

10). Malachi insists on faithfulness to the marriage covenant because it reflects on one's commitment to covenant with God.

Translation of Malachi 2:15-16

The possibilities for translating Mal 2:15-16 are numerous and have not been exhausted in this commentary. For excellent discussions of the alternative translations for these verses, including the contributions of ancient versions and the Dead Sea scroll fragments, see Hill 1998, 243-249, Clendenen 2004, 349-357, and Hugenberger 1994, 48-83 and 124-167.

■ **16** Translation of God's speech in v 16 is also very difficult. Literally it reads, *If he hates [and] sends away, says the Lord God of Israel, then he spreads violence upon his clothes*. Many English versions have traditionally translated the verse as the NRSV, "For I hate divorce, says the LORD, the God of Israel, and covering one's garment with violence, says the LORD of hosts." (cp. NASB, NLT, NCV, KJV, NJPS, and NIV[1984]). This translation does not account for the third person form of the verb "hate" in Hebrew. Translators assume that since God speaks these words, he refers to himself in the third person. However, one might expect a first person verb (with a first person pronoun) if God wanted to express his hatred of divorce as compellingly as the NRSV translation connotes.

The NIV translation, **The man who hates and divorces his wife . . . does violence to the one he should protect,** is a satisfactory rendering of the Hebrew text (cp. ESV and HCSB). The words **his wife** are not in the Hebrew text, but implied. The phrase **violence to the one he should protect** in Hebrew is literally *spreads violence upon his clothes*. This phrase may allude to the wedding custom of a groom spreading his garment over his bride as a symbol of his claim to her and his promise to protect her. If this is the case, then the Lord's speech describes a man's unfaithfulness to his wife as a violent act committed against her, the one whom he has promised to protect. **Violence** (*hāmās*) connotes harsh, even brutal, treatment that injures someone severely.

The term **divorces** translates the infinitive form of *šallaḥ*, which functions as an explanation of the finite verb **hates**. It clarifies the extent to which a man dislikes his wife, that is, enough to divorce her. The verb *šallaḥ* is not necessarily a technical term for divorce, however. It basically means "to send away" and describes only one portion of the divorce proceedings (cp. KJV "putting away"). Divorce involved several distinct steps including: (1) writing a certificate of divorce, (2) returning dowry, and (3) sending the wife back to her family. It is possible that God may be chiding men of Judah for sending wives away without following proper customs, especially giving monetary compensation. In order to avoid repayment of the dowry, some men may have simply separated from their wives and sent them away. Such injustice surely would be labeled "being unfaithful" (v 10). If this is the issue with which Malachi is dealing, then the broader concern of mishandling marriage commitments is the primary problem, not only the actual act of divorce.

The prophet ends the message by reiterating the challenge given in v 15. He once again urges his audience to be diligent in keeping the marriage covenant (do not be unfaithful). The phrase "the wife of your youth" is not repeated from v 15. Hence, the challenge could have a wider application. The prophet may be challenging his audience to maintain fidelity in all relationships in the community.

FROM THE TEXT

This central oracle of the book focuses upon the major concern throughout the book: lack of faithful commitment to God. The five references in the oracle to "being unfaithful," including the twice-repeated admonition "do not be unfaithful," make sure the point is not missed. While the topic of the prophetic speech is dysfunctional marriage practices the deeper concern is dysfunctional covenantal relationship with God. By addressing the problems of marriage in Judah Malachi is able to remind his audience that social relationships expose the reality of one's relationship with God. They also allow him to highlight the sacredness of the marriage bond.

Community and family relationships reveal the depth of a person's spiritual commitments. The two most important social spheres of life are the family and one's neighbors. Infidelity in these relationships invariably signals betrayal of commitments in the spiritual realm, because commitment to God involves commitment to those with whom we live.

So the prophet calls the people of Judah to loyalty in human relationships. He chides them for "marrying women who worship a foreign god" (v 11) and for being "unfaithful" in their marriage commitments (v 14). The first offense subjects the community to those who hold allegiance to other gods. Malachi calls this "a detestable thing" (v 11), a gross corruption of one's worship of God. There are to be no other gods (Exod 20:3) among those who have "one Father" and "one God" who created them (v 10). The other offense also violates the first as well as "the second" of the two greatest commandments (Mark 12:31). Loving God and loving neighbors mean loving one's spouse.

God designed marriage to be a sacred relationship. Marriage is more than a secular contract between two persons and their families. According to Malachi, men and women come together as equal partners before God (v 14). Covenant commitments are made in the presence of heaven as God stands alongside the rest of the community on earth as a "witness" to these commitments (v 14). He takes his role seriously and actively intervenes when husbands betray wives. He no longer accepts their acts of worship (v 13) and flatly exhorts them, "Do not be unfaithful to the wife of your youth" (v 15). According to the voice of God in Malachi, a man's infidelity in marriage is a brutally violent action against his wife, "the one he should protect" (v 16).

This oracle invites the listening community today to reflect on the sacredness of the marriage relationship. Our world is not unlike the world of Malachi. We too live in a world where marriage has lost its covenantal character and believers enter into marriages with non-believers without regard for the impact upon their relationship with God. Malachi reminds us that the crisis in marriages within our communities of faith often can be traced to loss of relationship with God. The prophet invites his audience, both then and now, to return to covenant fidelity, which is critical for the restoration of broken relationship with God and with others.

V. FIFTH DISPUTE: GOD'S PURIFICATION OF THE LEVITES: MALACHI 2:17—3:5

BEHIND THE TEXT

The fifth oracle of the book addresses the age-old issue of God's justice. Malachi's audience thinks that God is on the side of those who do evil in their world. This perspective can be traced to the theological disillusionment of the Jewish community in the restoration period. The promises of Isaiah and other prophets that God would bring justice to Israel and to the nations still remained unfulfilled (see e.g., Isa 30:18; 42:1-4; 61:8).

Malachi responds to the despondency of his audience by announcing the coming of the Lord to establish justice through his refining judgment. Malachi uses two common images from the ancient world to describe God's refining work. The first of these is the refining of metals, an image utilized by other prophets to speak of God's judgment (see Isa 1:25; Jer 6:29-30; Ezek 22:17-22; Zech 13:9). On a daily basis metal workers might be observed extracting pure metals such as silver or gold by placing ore in a crucible and heating it over a fire. These ancient craftsmen were highly skilled at selecting the right materials for crucibles, monitoring temperatures of their furnaces with bellows, and skimming off impurities. Silver was especially challenging to process and attain complete purity. This may be why Malachi speaks of God as doing the work of "a purifier of silver" in 3:3. A craftsman determined the silver had reached a pure state when he saw his face reflected in the metal.

The other image used in the message is that of clothes laundering. Again, women and children washed clothing almost daily in whatever water was available, rinsing and pounding the material on rocks. An alkali powder derived from ice plants provided a detergent substance that helped remove stains and brighten clothing.

This message revisits the problem of corrupt priesthood in Judah. It corresponds to the condemnation of priests in the third message (2:1-9) and provides an additional response to it. This oracle employs the familiar disputation form of previous oracles. The prophet projects an exchange of opening statements between God and the audience (2:17). Then God presents his argument in response to the complaint of injustice (3:1-5).

IN THE TEXT

A. Opening Statements (2:17)

■ **17** Malachi begins this oracle with the accusation that the people of Judah have **wearied the L**ORD with things that they say (v 17). The word **wearied** (*yāga'*) is used metaphorically of God to indicate the burden he feels because of their complaints (cp. Isa 43:24). They think the Lord does not make a clear distinction between good and evil. They claim that **all who do evil are good** in his sight and that **he is pleased with them.** Clearly, such a view distorts the traditional faith of Israel that sets God apart from anything that is evil (Ps 5:4 [5 HB]; Deut 12:25, 21:9; 1 Kgs 15:5, 22:43; 2 Kgs 12:2 [3 HB]; 2 Chr 14:2 [1 HB]). The people are likely responding emotionally to the kind of things listed in v 5. Ironically, Malachi's audience has set themselves up for judgment, because Isaiah warned, "Woe to those who call evil good and good evil." (Isa 5:20)

The question, **Where is the God of justice?**, echoes the cry of troubled believers throughout the OT (e.g., see Job 21:7-15; Ps 73:2-14; Hab 1:2-4; Jer 12:1-2). This question implies that God may be just, but he is delaying his action against the unjust or even letting them go unpunished.

B. Argument (3:1-5)

■ **1** God responds to questions about his justice in vv 1-5. He confirms that he will come (v 1) and bring justice (vv 2-5). But God must deal first with the religious leaders (vv 2-4) before judging others who do not fear him (v 5).

The promise of God coming in judgment reflects the elaborate pomp surrounding the arrival of an ancient monarch. Prior to this momentous event, the divine king **will send** a forerunner to **prepare the way** for his royal entourage (v 1). The term **prepare** (*pānâh*) literally means "make clear" and suggests removing any obstacles that would hinder the arrival (cp. Isa 40:3-4). The forerunner is called **my messenger** (*mal'ākî*), which is the same word as the name of the prophet of this book (→ Introduction A. The Prophet). This is the second time Malachi has played upon his name to add impact to his words (see 2:7; see also "the messenger of the covenant" later in this verse). Though God sometimes sent an angelic being as his messenger (Exod 23:20-33), the forerunner in this verse is most likely a human prophetic figure as in 4:5-6 [3:23-24 HB]. Jesus and the NT writers confirm this interpretation when they identify John the Baptist fulfilling this role (Matt 11:10; Mark 1:2; Luke 1:76, 7:27).

Malachi announces that **suddenly the Lord . . . will come to his temple** following the preparation of the way by the forerunner. That **the Lord** comes **suddenly** adds an ominous element to the event; it accentuates the significance and efficiency of the divine monarch. The title **the Lord** (*ha'adôn*) conveys the idea of a magistrate who possesses authority to judge. **The temple**, the royal palace of Israel's God on earth, is the place where he will hear cases and render decisions. The term **the messenger of the covenant** in the next line is another name for **the Lord** and underscores his role as covenant enforcer. He will hold his people accountable to their covenant with him and distribute both blessings and curses of the covenant.

Scholars have debated the identity of the three persons mentioned in 3:1, "my messenger," "the Lord," and "the messenger of the covenant." Some scholars suggest that all three titles refer to the same person (Peterson 1995, 210-212). Most, however, understand that the verse delineates two different persons, because two titles seem to refer to the same person and the third to another. In the context of this verse, it is likely that **the messenger who will prepare the way** is someone other than **the Lord you are seeking** and **the messenger of the covenant whom you desire**. The latter two seem to refer to the same person (see Hill 1998, 286-289 and Clendenen 2004, 384-385).

The relative clauses, **you are seeking** and **whom you desire**, most likely refer to the question, "where is the God of justice?" in 2:17. There is irony in these phrases. As the following verses reveal, the judge they long for will in fact exact judgment upon them. Like the people of Amos' time they seem unaware that the Day of the Lord they desire "will be darkness and not light" for them (Amos 5:18).

■ **2-4** Malachi calls the advent of God's judgment **the day of his coming** (v 2). This is the Day of the Lord mentioned often in the prophetic messages (→ Behind the Text at Zech 12:1-13:9). Two parallel rhetorical questions announce the unpleasant effects of God's judgment day. God asks, **who can endure** and **who can stand?** The terms **endure** (*kûl*) and **stand** (*'āmad*) evoke the scene of a soldier standing his ground on a battlefield, an image often associated with the Day of the Lord (e.g., see Zeph 1:14). The implied answer to the questions is that no one, or perhaps only a few, will be able to hold their ground when the Lord advances. Whenever God **appears** (*rā'â*) elsewhere in the OT, it always overwhelms people (Exod 33:20; Ezek 1:28; Dan 10:7-9).

Two familiar images of the ancient world, metalworking and laundering, describe the nature of God's judgment. God is likened to **a refiner's fire** as well as the **refiner** or **purifier** of metals. In the ancient world, a metalworker removed impurities from ore by means of heating it over fire. God is also compared to **a launderer's** soap, an alkali powder used to scrub clothing clean (→ Behind the Text). The point of these two analogies is to highlight God's goal in judgment. God seeks to **purify** people, not simply punish them (v 3). The word **purify** (*ṭahēr*) comes from a family of words that describe what must take place for something or someone to function in God's service. Both people and things used in the tabernacle and temple must be cleansed of anything that is unacceptable to God (see Lev 14-15; Num 8 and 19). This is an essential part of the process that prepares them to be set apart (made holy) for their task.

The first group God purifies in his judgment is the **Levites**, literally *the sons of Levi* (v 3). In Malachi this refers to the entire priesthood, those especially entrusted with the responsibility of being spiritual leaders in Judah (→ 1:6-14; 2:1-9). The effects of a purified priesthood will be authentic worship of God. The priests **will bring offerings in righteousness** that **will be acceptable to the LORD** (vv 3*b*-4). That is to say they will present the right kinds of sacrifices in the right spirit according to the directives laid out in the laws of Moses (see Lev 21-22 and Ezek 44). The phrases, **in days gone by** and **as in former years,** refer to the days when worship was carried out in faithfulness to God (cp. 2:5-6). Although no particular time is identified, the prophet may be thinking about worship during the days of David or Josiah.

■ **5** The message ends with the announcement of God's judgment on evildoers in the land. God promises to put them **on trial** and **to testify against** such people (v 5). This envisions a trial where God acts as witness, prosecutor, and judge.

The seven evildoers listed are representative of those who disrupt community life by taking advantage of people, especially the vulnerable in society. **Sorcerers** prey on the simple minded and desperate through their appeal to magic arts. **Adulterers** betray spouses; in most cases wives abandoned by their husbands were among the most helpless in ancient Israelite society. **Perjurers** deceive neighbors by swearing false oaths. Unfair employers **defraud laborers of their wages**, while people of power **oppress the widows and the fatherless**. Finally, dishonest judges **deprive foreigners of justice**. The last three victims mentioned were some of the most helpless in the ancient world. Crimes against them are especially abhorrent to the Lord (see Exod 22:22-24 [21-23 HB] and Deut 27:19).

In sum, these are people who **do not fear** God. That is, they do not respect God enough to follow the laws he gave for living in community (see Exod 22:18 [17 HB] and Lev 19:11-13). Those who truly **fear** the Lord "walk in all his ways" and "observe the LORD's commands and decrees" (Deut 10:12-13).

FROM THE TEXT

This text speaks about God's justice as well as God's determination to purify his people. It reminds us that God is always fair and will eventually make things right. As the Lord administers justice though, we see that his ultimate goal is purity, not simply punishment. What God seeks is transformed, holy people who are led by transformed, holy leaders.

Someday God will make everything right again. Like so many people throughout history, Malachi's audience was disturbed by injustice in this world. This oracle assures them though that justice will be done eventually. God promises, "The Lord you are seeking will come" (3:1). Therefore, God's people need "not fret because of those who do evil or be envious of those who do wrong; for like the grass they will soon wither, like green plants they will soon die away" (Ps 37:1).

According to the Gospels, Jesus fulfilled Malachi's message. John the Baptist was his forerunner "messenger" and Jesus "the Lord" and "the messenger of the covenant" who comes to his temple (Matt 11:10, Mark 1:2, Luke 1:76, and 7:27). In his first coming, Jesus did not sit as judge like "the Lord" in this passage does (John 3:17-18). Yet, "all authority in heaven and on earth" was given him following his resurrection (Matt 28:18). At his second coming, Jesus will take on the role of final judge of all mankind (Dan 7:14-15; Phil 2:9-11; Rev 19:11-20:15). So the word of Malachi in this passage awaits a complete fulfillment at the end of time.

The final goal of God's judgment is a transformed community. God's judgment is never only about punishment. The ultimate outcome that the Lord seeks is transformed people living in conformity with his laws for life. In other words, God desires a holy people (Exod 19:5-6; Lev 19:2). As Zephaniah proclaimed, God brings the dark day of judgment so that he can "purify the lips of the peoples, that all of them may call on the name of the LORD and serve him shoulder to shoulder" (Zeph 3:9).

A transformed community begins with transformed leaders. In Malachi's message, the Lord envisions a time when he "will purify" the spiritual leaders of the community "and refine them like gold and silver" (3:3). Then they will return to their calling, "bring offerings in righteousness" (3:3), and lead their community to bring offerings that are "acceptable to the LORD" (3:4). These will be the kind of offerings God most desires, "a broken and contrite heart" (Ps 51:17). Purity of life leads to God-pleasing worship and the kind of world we most desire. Someday the Lord will fulfill our longing for justice (2:17) with a pure life that pleases him (3:3-4). Though the process of purifying may be intense, like smelting fire and abrasive soap, in the end it will transform God's people.

VI. SIXTH DISPUTE: GOD'S BLESSING UPON THE WHOLE TITHE: MALACHI 3:6-12

BEHIND THE TEXT

The first question to decide about this oracle is what verse serves as its beginning. Most modern commentators and English translations mark v 6 as the initial verse. Yet some versions and scholars view v 6 as the appropriate conclusion to the previous oracle (see NASB, HCSB). For them it provides a more hopeful ending to the message about the day of God's judgment in 3:1-5 (Achtemeier 1986, 183-187; also Clark and Hatton 2002, 435-436; Clendenen 2004, 399-401). This commentary views v 6 as the beginning of a new message, because it introduces the God who calls his people to repentance in v 7.

The subject of this oracle is "tithes and offerings" (v 8). These were the primary means for supporting the temple personnel and its operations. More importantly though, they served as tangible expressions of a person's dedication to God (see Deut 12:4-7). Throughout the ancient world, the tithe (*ma'ăśēr*), literally "a tenth part," was a way of acknowledging divine ownership and blessing. In Gen 14:20 Abraham reflects the practice of surrounding cultures when he gave a tenth of his plunder to Melchizedek as a way of recognizing God's hand in overcoming his enemies (see also Jacob's vow in Gen 28:20-22). The laws of Israel prescribed a tenth of all produce from fields and flocks be set aside each year as "holy to the LORD" (Lev 27:30-32). While this act recognized God's goodness, it also functioned to support the priesthood. The tithe was the Levites "inheritance," that is, their means of livelihood, since they did not own land (Num 18:21-24, 31). It provided "food" for them and their families (Mal 3:10). In addition to an annual tithe, the laws of Moses called for another tithe every three years for support of widows, orphans, and foreigners as well as the Levites (Deut 14:28-29).

The "offering" (*těrûmâ*) is a generic term designating a wide variety of contributions made to God at different times, either voluntarily or by law. Its root (*rûm*) suggests that the term refers to anything "lifted up" before the Lord. This might include harvest products, clothing, construction materials, or precious metals (see Exod 25:1-7). The tithe seems to be one special type of offering. In Num 18:25-28, the Levitical tithe of the tithe is another offering designated with the term *těrûmâ*. This is the tithe that Levites take from the general tithe given them and present to the Lord as their offering. Several scholars believe this is the particular kind of offering Malachi speaks of in 3:8 (see Peterson 1995, 216 and Hill 1998, 306).

This oracle is integrally connected to what goes before and what comes after it. Both the preceding (2:17-3:5) and following oracles (3:12-4:3) deal with questions about God's justice. These oracles defend the integrity of God's righteousness by announcing the day of judgment. Between these two oracles Malachi appropriately calls his audience to repentance in order to prepare them for that day.

Though this oracle functions primarily as a call to repentance, it still follows the familiar disputation format found in other speeches within the book. Accordingly, Malachi begins with opening statements in vv 6-8 before moving toward the argument in vv 9-12. Both of these sections place challenges before the audience in the form of imperatives. In vv 6-8 God puts forth a general call to "return to me." In vv 9-12 this calling is given specificity as God urges people to "bring the whole tithe" and "test me in this."

IN THE TEXT

A. Opening Statements (3:6-8)

■ **6** God's speech begins with the declaration, **I the LORD do not change,** which asserts the consistency of his character (v 6). The self-identifying phrase, **I the LORD** (*'ănî YHWH*, better translated "I am the LORD"; so KJV), conveys a sense of absolute authority over those addressed along with the complete adequacy of the Lord. Israel's God stands alone, apart, and above all.

The assertion, **I . . . do not change,** is not necessarily a metaphysical statement about the nature of God. The term **change** (*šānâ*) carries the meaning of "going back on one's word." In the context of this oracle, the point is that God remains committed to his covenant with **the descendants of Jacob.** On the one hand, God's covenant is an "everlasting" covenant with Israel (see Gen 17:6-8). God remains faithful to this covenant by being merciful and compassionate to the descendants of Abraham when they sin against him (see Exod 34:6-7).

On the other hand, the covenant curses in the Mosaic law call for Israel's punishment for breaking covenant (see Deut 28:15-68). Along with other prophets, Malachi proclaims that Israel deserves to be **destroyed** (see Isa 1:28; Jer 5:6; Ezek 5:11-12). However, his message also implies that God's covenant promises to the patriarchs override the just requirements of the law.

■ **7** The Lord cites Israel's long history of disobedience as the reason why the nation deserves destruction (v 7*a*). **Your ancestors** refers to any prior generation, including the ones that brought about the exile. The phrases, **you have turned away from my decrees and have not kept them,** specify the charges being leveled against the people. Deuteronomy repeatedly warns Israel against these two ways of covenant breaking. The Lord implies that Malachi's audience has participated with their ancestors in the history of the nation's rebellion against the **decrees** given at Sinai.

The Lord invites Malachi's audience to **return** to him and thus bring an end to the long history of covenant breaking. The term **return** (*šûb*) is the most frequent word for repentance in the OT. It means to "turn around" or "reorient," which includes turning away from something as well as turning toward something. In the context of covenant making it carries the connotation of changing allegiances. Thus God calls the people of Judah to realign themselves to God and his ways. This is a frequent summons throughout the prophets (Isa 55:7; Jer 25:5; Ezek 33:11; Hos 14:1-2 [2-3 HB]; Joel 2:12-13; Zech 1:3-4).

God promises to **return** to Israel when the nation returns to him (v 7*b*). This promise does not mean that God has been disloyal to Israel or walked away from his people. Instead, it expresses his commitment to renew the covenant that the people broke (see Jer 31:31-34). An important aspect of this covenant renewal is the enjoyment of God's blessings by the people (see vv 10-12).

Malachi's audience responds with a question, **How are we to return?** (v 7*c*), whose mood is difficult to determine. The people may be (1) puzzled about how to proceed, (2) pessimistic that it could be done, or (3) protesting the implication that they need to repent. Any of these indicates the same kind of spiritual insensitivity displayed by the people elsewhere in the book (cp. 1:2, 6-7, 12-13; 2:14, 17; 3:14-15).

■ **8** God responds with a rhetorical question, **Will a mere mortal rob God?** (v 8). The idea of a **mere mortal** (*'ādam*), a created being, robbing **God** the Creator produces the obvious answer of no. Such a thing seems unthinkable. The LXX translates the verb **rob** (*hǎyīqbaʿ* from *qābaʿ*) in this verse with *pternizo*, which means "deceive" or "cheat." Some scholars believe this reflects an alternate Hebrew text containing *hayaʿǎqōb* (BHS). This would be a play on the name Jacob (*yaʿǎqōb*) in v 6. Thus the NLT renders the question, "Should people cheat God?"

At first this question seems like a shift away from the topic of repentance in v 7. But it actually leads to the main accusation of the oracle, which is that they were robbing God **in tithes and offerings**. This is the specific way by which the people "turned away" and the reason they needed to "return" to God (v 7). Withholding **tithes and offerings** revealed a significant spiritual lapse in the community. Such gifts sustained the temple and its personnel, but more importantly they expressed gratitude and honor to God (→ Behind the Text). This same problem emerged during Nehemiah's time (see Neh 10:37-39 [38-40 HB]; 12:44; 13:5, 10-13).

B. Argument (3:9-12)

■ **9** Throughout the rest of this oracle God announces the adverse effects of the people's actions (v 9) as well as the possibilities for reversing them (vv 10-12). The **whole nation** is under **a curse** because the people withhold their tithe (v 9). According to vv 10-11, this curse consists of agricultural, and thus economic, hardship.

The participle form of the verb **robbing** indicates repeated action; withholding tithes and offerings had become the regular practice in Judah. **You are robbing me** indicates that the offended party is God, though not paying tithes and offerings also resulted in shortages for temple personnel.

■ **10** The Lord's remedy for Judah's sin is set forth in two compelling challenges. With imperatives, **bring** and **test** (v 10), God answers the question of v 7 about how one can return to God. The imperative **see** has been added by the NIV, but helps express the God's challenge to **test** him.

God's first challenge to Judah is to **bring the whole tithe into the storehouse**. The emphasis on **whole** suggests a partial keeping of the laws by the people, which would have resulted in insufficient resources in the temple. This parallels the kind of substandard sacrifices mentioned in the second oracle (1:6-14). **The storehouse** refers to storage rooms built around the temple in Jerusalem. These rooms held large pottery jars designed to keep grain, fruit, wine, and oil brought for offerings (Neh 10:37-39). Solomon's temple boasted three stories with thirty storerooms on each (1 Kgs 6:5-8; see also Ezek 41:5-11).

The motive for following God's challenge is so **that there may be food in my house**. This alludes to the functional purpose of tithes and offerings. They provided **food** for the priests and worshipers as well as the destitute of society (Lev 18:31; Deut 14:26-29).

God's second challenge adds weight to the first. The Lord urges the people to **test me in this** (v 10*b*). Ordinarily the Bible does not encourage humans to **test** God (Deut 6:16). But that is in the sense of arrogantly provoking God with disobedience. Here the Lord challenges Judah to prove his faithfulness by means of their faithfulness in tithes and offerings. He invites them to "taste and see that the LORD is good" (Ps 34:8).

The result of such a test will be an abundance of divine provision for Judah (v 10c). Rain will enliven crops as God throws **open the floodgates of heaven**. This image reflects a cosmology that views the earth surrounded by waters held back only by a sky and dry ground (cp. Gen 1:6-8). Rain comes when the deity opens portals in the sky to allow the flow of water upon the earth. The blessing of rain is God's promised response to faithful living (Deut 28:12; also Deut 11:13-14 and Isa 41:18).

■ **11** God promises to respond to the people's faithfulness with productive harvests. He will protect crops from **pests** and keep **fruit** on vines until they are ready to be picked. These promises reverse the effects of curses prescribed for covenantal disobedience in Deut 28:38-39 (see also Lev 26:18-20).

The Hebrew text of vv 10-11 emphasizes God's action on behalf of his people. The prepositional phrase *for you* (*lakem*) is repeated five times, once after each verbal form. Thus, the text literally reads, *I will throw open for you . . . I will pour out for you . . . I will prevent for you . . . pests will not destroy for you* and *vines will not miscarry for you.*

■ **12** God's bountiful blessing is not for Judah alone however. It will distinguish them in the eyes of the world and make them a witness to God's goodness. **All the nations** will recognize the favorable hand of the Lord upon them and pronounce them **blessed** (v 12). Thus the promise to Abraham in Gen 12:1-3 will be fulfilled (cp. Isa 61:9). They will be marked as **a delightful land,** a place that brings joy to its inhabitants and God. This is the kind of land that experiences the rich blessing of God envisioned in Deut 28:3-14.

FROM THE TEXT

This oracle is best known for its provoking statements about robbing God and tithing. But its message encompasses much more. The tithing problem among God's people indicates a much bigger issue, that of commitment to covenantal relationship with God. In contrast to humans, God remains unwaveringly loyal to the covenant. So the Lord calls his covenant partners to the same kind of fidelity. Both God and people express their loyalty tangibly. People do so by tithing while God does so by blessing the land. When people demonstrate faithfulness to God, they provide further opportunity for God to prove faithful.

God remains unchanging in his commitment to people. Some of the most comforting words in Malachi are "I the LORD do not change" (v 6). Some theologians take the statement as a maxim expressing the absolute immutability of God in all things. They say that nothing about God ever changes in any way. But this stands in tension with the text itself. The Lord's promise to return once the people return (v 7) imply that God will change the way he relates to them according to their response. This is the fundamental premise of the call to repentance in prophetic preaching.

403

The unchanging aspect of the Lord in this oracle relates to his consistent commitment to a loving relationship with people. "The descendants of Jacob" were "not destroyed" because of this commitment (v 6). From a theological perspective, the statement "I the LORD do not change" affirms the truth that God can be trusted to act consistently toward us in all circumstances. God's love for people does not change. Neither does his commitment to righteousness and justice.

God calls for tangible evidence of repentance. When Malachi's audience asked how they should go about returning to God, the Lord commanded them to "bring the whole tithe into the storehouse" (v 10). This might be interpreted as a kind of legalism. But that would miss the intensely personal mood of the oracle. God invites people to "return to me" not simply to religious activities (v 7). The payment of tithes is only one way to demonstrate that people truly desire a relationship with God and trust him enough to follow his instructions for life. Repentance is first of all about a change of heart and mind. But a change of heart can be seen in one's actions. As James noted, "Faith by itself, if it is not accompanied by action, is dead" (Jas 2:17).

While tithing is not required by any NT verse, some believe it is assumed. If not that, then at the very least Paul admonishes Christians to be generous in financial contributions (2 Cor 9:6-8). He recognizes that giving to the church "is not only supplying the needs of the church but is also overflowing in many expressions of thanks to God" (2 Cor 9:12). As with the OT tithe, NT offerings are a way of acknowledging God's ownership of all things and expressing serious commitment to a relationship with him. For Christians, tithes and offerings are a significant statement of faith. The essence of the divine challenge, "test me in this," is to abandon self-sufficiency (v 10). Giving to God's kingdom puts the worshiper at risk of scarcity. Those resources might be used for daily sustenance, especially in hard economic times. So giving a portion of one's resources demonstrates one's trust in the adequacy of God's provisions for life.

The text reiterates a fundamental spiritual truth echoed throughout scripture: *God blesses the faithful.* This is not a prosperity gospel in which people give so that they might receive material goods from God. Rather it is a gospel of God's goodness. God expresses his commitment to his covenant with people just as tangibly as humans do. The psalmist knew that those who trust God "will see the goodness of the LORD in the land of the living" (Ps 27:13). So also Paul believed that God would respond to the generosity of Philippian Christians by meeting all their "needs according to the riches of his glory in Christ Jesus" (Phil 4:19).

VII. SEVENTH DISPUTE: GOD'S DISTINCTION BETWEEN THE RIGHTEOUS AND THE WICKED: MALACHI 3:13—4:3 [3:13-21 HB]

BEHIND THE TEXT

The concept of the Day of the Lord forms an important backdrop for this oracle. This is one of the frequent themes found throughout Israel's prophetic literature (→ Behind the Text at Zech 12:1-13:9). It speaks of a moment in time, or perhaps beyond time, when God settles all accounts. On that day God displays his justice both by punishing evil and by vindicating righteousness. Thus, for those opposed to God, it is a day of God's wrath, distress, anguish, trouble, ruin, darkness, and gloom (Zeph 1:14-18; see also Is 2:12-18, 13:6-13; and Amos 5:18-20). But for the righteous it is a day of vindication and renewal (Zeph 3:16-20; see also Amos 9:11-15; Mic 4:6-8). Earlier in the book Malachi spoke of this day as one of purification for his people (3:1-5). This day often denotes an eschatological reality; but many times prophets seem to include both immediate and distant future in their vision of that day (e.g., see Hos 2:16-23 [18-25 HB]). The difference between these often remains blurred.

Another important image related to this oracle is that of written records in heaven. The "scroll of remembrance" mentioned in v 16 evokes practices of ancient royal courts. Persian kings, for example, recorded deeds done by their subjects and kept them for future reference. This is why King Ahasuerus honored Mordecai at one point in the book of Esther (Esth 2:23 and 6:1). This practice may provide the background for other biblical references to heavenly books (Jer 22:30;

405

Ezek 13:9). Some contain information about future events (Ps 139:16; Dan 10:21), while others preserve the names and deeds of the righteous (Exod 32:32-33; Pss 56:8 [9 HB]; 69:28 [29 HB]) as well as the wicked (Isa 65:6; Dan 7:10). These will be used at the final judgment so that rewards are appropriately distributed (Dan 12:1-4). NT writers also knew about a "book of life" that served to identify the righteous and the wicked (Luke 10:20; Phil 4:3; Heb 12:23; Rev 3:5, 13:8, 17:8, 20:12-15, 21:27).

This last oracle corresponds to the first oracle (1:2-5). The distinction between the righteous and the wicked in 3:13-4:3 echoes the distinction between Jacob and Esau in 1:2-5. Both oracles emphasize God's great compassion for his chosen ones while speaking of God's decisive judgment upon those who do not respond rightly toward him.

The English and Hebrew texts differ in their numbering of verses within this oracle. The final three verses of 4:1-3 in English are verses 19-21 in the Hebrew Bible. The reason for English versions, as well as Greek and Latin, beginning a new chapter at 4:1 is difficult to defend. Perhaps the announcement that "the day is coming" seemed to warrant a fresh chapter. In any case, the Hebrew tradition of versification is more accurate in viewing the divine speech as a complete unit.

This prophetic speech completes the cycle of disputations in the book and adopts the typical pattern seen throughout. In the opening statements (vv 13-15) God accuses the people of misconduct, the people protest the accusation, and God clarifies what he means. An argument section (3:16-4:3 [3:16-21 HB]) follows, establishing God's case more firmly and communicating a message of both warning and hope. A unique feature of this oracle is the third-person interlude in v 16, which provides context to the divine speech.

IN THE TEXT

A. Opening Statements (3:13-15)

■ **13** This message begins with God's accusation and the people's protest, just as oracles one and five did (see 1:2 and 2:17). God says the people of Judah have **spoken arrogantly against** him (v 13). Literally the Lord says, *Your words are strong against me.* These kinds of words might include the many high-handed words spoken by the people throughout the book (see 1:2, 6-7, 12-13; 2:14, 17). But the particular arrogance on God's mind at this point is explained in vv 14-15.

In typical fashion, the people protest by asking, **What have we said against you?** The NJPS tries to catch the passive and reflexive aspects of the verb **said** by rendering the question, "What have we been saying among ourselves against you?"

■ **14** God quotes the arrogant words of Malachi's audience to them. In summary, they have said that **it is futile to serve God** (v 14). This terse three-word saying (šāwĕ' 'ābōd ĕlōhîm) makes a shocking assertion. The people feel that covenant relationship with God is meaningless. **Futile** (šāwĕ') refers to something that is "worthless" or "comes to nothing." The term **serve** ('ābōd) is the typical word used to describe the actions of a person submitting to the authority of another, like a priest or worshiper before the Lord.

The reason people felt it was futile to serve God was because God did not seem to reward them for their pious acts (v 14). They felt they were **carrying out his requirements** (*šāmarnû mišmartô*), the covenant stipulations. Also, they were **going about like mourners**, meaning that they performed penitential rituals such as fasting, weeping, and wearing sackcloth (see Neh 9:1-2 and Ps 35:13-14). Their rhetorical question (**What do we gain . . . ?**) implies a strong negative answer. The people claim that their religious efforts do not result in any **gain** (*beṣa'*, literally "profit"). They are not seeing the blessings mentioned in Deut 28:1-14 for those who keep the law.

■ **15** To make matters worse, Malachi's audience felt as though the **arrogant** and **evildoers** enjoy the blessings they should have (v 15). They claim that God does not take any action against such people even when they put him **to the test**. Malachi's audience suggests that covenant blessings and curses have been reversed. So it seems better to be a covenant breaker than a covenant keeper.

B. Argument (3:16—4:3 [3:16-21 HB])

■ **16** The Lord responds to the people's complaint with a speech about the Day of the Lord (3:17-4:3 [3:17-21 HB]). But first, the prophet prepares for that speech by highlighting a group in Judah **who feared the LORD** (v 16). This group contrasts sharply to the complainers of vv 13-15. The term **those who feared** (*yir' ê*) designates people who show a healthy respect for God by living according to his laws. When they spoke, **the LORD listened** because he was pleased with what he heard. They **honored his name**, so the Lord wrote their names in the **scroll of remembrance**, apparently a record of those who have done good deeds (→ Behind the Text).

■ **17** The divine speech begins with the Lord announcing what will happen **on the day** when he acts (v 17). Those just described in v 16 will become God's **treasured possession** (*sĕgullâh*). This term refers to private property of a king (1 Chr 29:3). While the Lord owns everything within his domain, those who fear him remain his uniquely favored possession. In Exod 19:5-6 the *sĕgullâh* are also known as God's "kingdom of priests" and "holy nation" (see also Deut 26:18).

The Lord also promises to **spare them** from the horrible fate of the wicked described in 4:1 and to treat them with **compassion**. The **father . . . son** language in this verse underscores the truth that God's people are not just subjects in a kingdom, but family.

■ **18** God's compassionate treatment of those who fear him is clear evidence of **the distinction** he makes **between the righteous and the wicked** (v 18*a*). Here is God's response to the complaints of vv 14-15. God will make a distinction between **those who serve God and those who do not** (v 18*b*). **Those who serve God** as obedient servants are **the righteous**, who align their lives with God's law. They follow Moses' instruction "to fear the LORD your God, to walk in obedience to him, to love him, to serve the LORD . . . and to observe the LORD's commands" (Deut 10:12-13).

■ **4:1 [3:19 HB]** The divine speech continues in vv 1-3 [3:19-21 HB] to elaborate on the different outcomes for the righteous and the wicked on **the day** of God's judgment (v 1 [3:19 HB]). First, God describes his judgement upon the wicked. They will become like **stubble** that burns up rapidly in a **furnace**. God promises to take care of the **arrogant** and **evildoer** that bothered Malachi's audience so much in v 15. Reference to the destruction of the **root** and **branch** indicates the effect of judgment on the families of the wicked. They are given no hope of a future, a devastating prospect in the ancient world.

■ **2 [3:20 HB]** God pronounces a much different reward for those **who revere** his **name** (v 2). The Lord promises that **the sun of righteousness will rise**, which evokes an image of a morning sunrise bringing the light and warmth a new day. Over the centuries some interpreters have seen this as a metaphor either for God or his Messiah (see "Sun" capitalized in KJV and NLT; → sidebar The Lord and the Sun Metaphor). In spite of this traditional interpretation, this image may simply intend to picture a world where everything has been made right. **Righteousness** (*ṣĕdāqâ*) denotes conformity to God's standards. Its spreading over the earth like rays of the sun suggests God's justice permeating every part of this world.

As righteousness spreads over the land it will bring **healing** (*marpē'*) and new life to God's people. They will become energized like **well-fed calves** frolicking in the field. Such an image vividly conveys the kind of relief and freedom the righteous will experience on judgment day.

The Lord and the Sun Metaphor

The Hebrew Scriptures rarely use the sun as a metaphor for God. This is probably because biblical writers wished to avoid confusion with sun gods worshiped in other cultures of the ancient world, such as Amun-Ra in Egypt or Shamash in Mesopotamia.

A few OT passages, however, do compare God to the sun (Ps 84:11 [12 HB]) and his actions to a sunrise (Deut 33:2; Isa 60:1-3). In the NT Jesus declared himself "the light of the world" (John 8:12) and early Christians thought of him being like "the rising sun" coming "from heaven to shine on those living in darkness" (Luke 1:78-79; see also John 1:4-9; 3:19; 12:35-36; 2 Cor 4:6). This has led to a long Christian tradition of applying "the sun of righteousness" to Jesus (see Ferreiro 2003, 308-311).

■ **3 [3:21 HB]** Finally, when the day of judgment comes God will reward the righteous with complete victory over evil. God promises that the righteous **will trample on the wicked** like a victorious soldier (v 3 [3:21 HB]). By contrast, **the wicked**, who seemed to be doing so well in this world, **will be ashes under the soles of your feet**. This pictures the righteous like a triumphant army marching over the slain on a battlefield or, perhaps, standing with their foot on the neck of a defeated enemy (see Josh 10:24). In any case, the righteous ultimately win and the wicked finally lose.

FROM THE TEXT

In the final oracle of the book the prophet draws together some emotional images in order to help his audience deal with their critical identity crisis. They have not been able to tell who is righteous and who is wicked by outward appearances. So the prophet affirms the indisputable reality of a day for God's judgment when the righteous and the wicked will be clearly delineated. While describing the horrific incendiary results of this day for the wicked, the prophet also highlights God's fatherly compassion for the righteous. All of this clarifies a fundamental practical point of the oracle that real religion is judged on the basis of relationship and not ritual.

Someday the Lord will clearly distinguish between believers and non-believers. Like Malachi's audience, God's people are often frustrated by the injustices of this world. It feels "futile to serve God" when those who honor him seem to gain little by doing so (3:14). In addition, too often "evildoers prosper" and "get away" with challenging God (3:15). But Malachi announces a defining moment in history that will be like a furnace for the wicked and a morning sunrise for the righteous (4:1-2 [3:19-20]). On that day the difference between the wicked and the righteous will become crystal clear. Malachi does not stand alone in heralding a such a day. This is a theme found in both testaments (e.g., see Ps 96:13; Isa 11:4; Matt 13:41-43).

The day of God's judgment is a day God demonstrates his love for people. Often God's justice and love are viewed in tension. Malachi, however, brings them together. While making clear the finality of God's punishment for unbelievers, the prophet highlights the blessed state of believers. God extends compassion toward those who fear him and lays claim to them as his special favored possession (3:17). He spreads righteousness over this world like rays of sunshine (4:2 [3:20 HB]). Whether the "sun of righteousness" should be understood as God's Son who came to shine his light into this world is unclear. Certainly this could be one application of this oracle (see Luke 1:78-79 and John 1:4-9). But undoubtedly it awaits a final fulfillment at the end of time.

The nature of God's judgment in this oracle clarifies that *religion is not about rigid rituals, but about relationship.* When the day of accountability arrives, relationship counts, not performance of duties. Those who honor the Lord by following his instruction for covenant relationship will know his blessings. The people of Malachi's audience felt as though "carrying out his requirements and going about like mourners" could earn them status with God (3:14). They believed their piety entitled them to blessing. But God requires more than pious actions. Performance of religious duty, even perfect performance, is not what God seeks. God wants people "to act justly and to love mercy and to walk humbly with" him (Mic 6:8).

VIII. CONCLUSION: MALACHI 4:4-6 [3:22-24 HB]

BEHIND THE TEXT

The last three verses could serve as a conclusion to the previous oracle that begins in 3:13. But for several reasons most commentators view them as a fitting conclusion to the entire book. For one thing, the previous oracle comes to an appropriate end in 4:3 [3:21 HB]. Also, ancient Hebrew texts, including both the Leningrad and Aleppo Codices, mark a significant break between vv 3 and 4 [3:21 and 3:22 HB]. Most importantly, though, the topics addressed in 4:4-6 [3:22-24] broaden beyond those of 3:13-4:3 [3:13-21 HB]. These verses focus on two key themes that resonate with the other oracles of the book. These themes, the law of Moses and the judgment of God, form a foundation upon which other topics of the book rest. They restate the fundamental challenge and motivation of the seven disputations and thus provide a meaningful conclusion to the entire book.

Moses and Elijah, two central figures in Israel's history, play a significant role in these concluding verses of Malachi. Each represents one of the great traditions of Israel's faith. Moses personifies the law tradition and Elijah the prophetic. The effect of their appearance together unites these essential elements in Israel's story and connects Malachi to each. As such they bring fitting closure not only to the book of Malachi, but also to the entire prophetic corpus. The Prophets (*Nebi'im*) stand as the second major section of the Hebrew Scriptures following the Law (*Torah*). Malachi's concluding emphasis on Moses and Elijah links these two fundamental portions of the Hebrew Scriptures. Significantly, both Elijah and Moses also appear at the transfiguration of Jesus in the NT (Matt 17:3-4).

The stature of Moses within Judaism is hard to overstate. Through him God dramatically delivered his people from foreign bondage and mediated his covenant. This covenant formed the basis for all of life in Israel. Within himself Moses brings together the two great traditions of law and prophet, being remembered as a key player in both arenas (Deut 34:10-12). Yet, Malachi focuses upon his role as lawgiver in 4:4 [3:22 HB] urging his audience to adopt the covenant life outlined in the law.

Elijah stands as the archetypical prophet in Israel calling people to repentance and changing the course of a nation (1 Kgs 17-19). A certain mystery surrounds him because he appears with no ancestors and disappears with no death (1 Kgs 18 and 2 Kgs 2). He performed amazing miracles and, in many ways, addressed a people just as ambivalent about the Lord as Malachi's audience. In later Judaism Elijah remained a prominent figure being referenced regularly in prayers at meals and on the Sabbath (see Smith 1984, 342).

Once again, the verse numbering differs between the Hebrew Bible and other versions. In English, Greek, Latin, and other translations 4:4-6 corresponds to 3:22-24 in Hebrew texts. Jewish tradition has called for the rereading of v 4 [3:22 HB] after v 6 [3:24 HB]. This emphasizes the central challenge of Malachi while also allowing for a more hopeful conclusion to the book. The LXX, perhaps in deference to this ancient tradition, rearranged the text and places v 4 [3:22 HB] after vv 5-6 [3:23-24 HB].

The concluding verses of the book of Malachi are a direct speech from the Lord consisting of a command (v 4 [3:22 HB]) and a motivation (vv 5-6 [3:23-24 HB]). Though the typical disputation format is no longer used, the argumentative mood remains. The latter section justifies the challenge put forth in the former in hopes of persuading change in the audience.

IN THE TEXT

■ **4 [3:22 HB]** Malachi's book concludes with God's command to **remember the law**, which had been given through his **servant Moses** (v 4 [3:22 HB]). The imperative **remember** urges people to do more than simply recall or recite something. It includes a call to act upon what is remembered, to live in compliance with covenant guidelines. The designation of Moses as **my servant** highlights his role as an obedient subject of the divine King. Other heroes of the faith shared this title as well (Abraham Gen 26:24; Jacob Deut 9:7; David 2 Sam 3:18).

The reference to **all Israel** as the recipients of the law may be intended to remind Malachi's audience that they were present, in a sense, at **Horeb** when God gave the law through Moses (cp. Deut 5:2-3). **Horeb**, instead of Sinai, may be used here because both Moses and Elijah experienced divine encounters there (see Exod 3:1-4:17; 1 Kgs 19:8-18).

Scholars debate what might have been the content of **the law** of Moses during Malachi's time. Based on allusions throughout the book, it seems likely that the bulk of the legal material recorded in Exodus through Deuteronomy is in view. These are the guidelines for people living in covenant relationship with the Lord. The totality of this material is emphasized with the phrase **the decrees and laws**. In this verse Malachi uses three key words to identify the covenant stipulations: **law** (*tôrâh*), **decrees** (*ḥuqqim*) and **laws** (*mišpaṭim*). They do not necessarily designate different types of laws, though some scholars have tried to make such distinctions. Rather, they occur together regularly throughout the OT to designate all covenantal legislation (Lev 26:46; Deut 4:8; 2 Chr 33:8; Ezra 7:10; Neh 9:13-14).

■ **5 [3:23 HB]** These verses offer motivation for heeding the Lord's command in the previous verse. Malachi reminds his audience that **the great and dreadful day of the LORD** is coming (v 5 [3:23 HB]). Malachi has already spoken about the unbearable nature of this day in 3:1-5 and 3:17-4:3 [3:17-21 HB]. Remembering and keeping the law is what enables one to escape the destruction this day brings on the earth.

Though the Day of the Lord is dreadful, the Lord offers another opportunity for escape for those who refuse to remember and keep the law. He promises to **send the prophet Elijah** before this day comes (v 5 [3:23]). The "messenger" of 3:1 now is specifically identified as the prophet Elijah. The naming of Elijah most likely intends to identify a person of his character and not the historical person himself. The messenger who comes from God will possess the kind of tenacity of the prophet who fearlessly challenged Israel to show loyalty to God (see 1 Kgs 18; → Behind the Text). According to the NT, John the Baptist was a prophet like Elijah (Matt 11:14, 17:11-13; Luke 1:17).

■ **6 [3:24 HB]** The mission of the Elijah-like messenger from God is to **turn the hearts** of parents and children toward one another (v 6 [3:24 HB]). The word **turn** (*šûb*) is the causative form of the OT word for repentance, which might be rendered literally as "cause to turn around" (→ 3:6). The phrase **turn the hearts** conveys the idea of reconciliation, which includes turning toward someone while turning away from that which disrupts relationship. Malachi anticipates the formation of a unified inter-generational community that will pave the way for restoring covenant with God. This connection between family and covenant community recalls a key point of the central oracle of the book (→ 2:10-16).

But there is also the threat of **total destruction** (*ḥerem*) on that day (v 6). Those who reject the messenger from the Lord and his message are given the warning that the Lord will **come and strike the land**. The verb **strike** (*nākâ*) recalls God's judgment on Egypt with the plagues (Exod 12:12). The word *ḥerem* means something set apart for destruction. This term is used for the complete devastation of Jericho and Ai during Israel's conquest of Canaan (Josh 6:21, 8:26). Thus Malachi ends his message with a solemn warning that resistance to the Lord's efforts to bring people back to covenantal faithfulness will have disastrous consequences.

FROM THE TEXT

The concluding verses of Malachi revisit key themes that are central to the message of the book and relevant to all generations.

God urges people to remain faithful to their covenant commitment. The first note sounded in the concluding verses of the book is "remember the law" (v 4 [3:22 HB]). This law provides guidance for living in relationship with God and others as the Creator intended. They are the covenant guidelines. The imperative "remember" urges people not only to recall the various laws, but to live them out.

Remembering the covenant demands has been the fundamental challenge of Malachi's preaching throughout the book. He has challenged people to live like they are truly in a committed relationship with God. This can reveal itself in the kinds of offerings they bring (1:7-8; 3:8-10), the kinds of things religious leaders teach (2:6-8), the kinds of family relationships people maintain (2:10-16), and the kinds of things they say about God (2:17-3:5 and 3:13-4:3 [3:13-21 HB]).

4:4-6   *Commitment to community, particularly family, indicates covenant faithfulness to God.* According to Malachi, the preaching of the Elijah-like prophet before the Day of the Lord will bring about reconciliation in families (v 6). Of all the results that might precipitate from prophetic preaching Malachi notes this one. This is because the issue of community faithfulness is pivotal in the book. As the central oracle of the book (2:10-16) affirms, family allegiance impacts the community contract and reveals one's level of devotion to covenant with God. This connection is reflected in the Ten Commandments (Exod 20:1-17), which focus upon how to live faithfully with people as well as with God. Biblical religion calls people to faithful covenantal living with both God and fellow humans.

God continues to hold out hope for the restoration of covenant faithfulness. According to Malachi, God remains committed to seeing covenant restored among his people. He will send a prophet "before the great and dreadful day of the LORD" (v 5 [3:23 HB]) who will hopefully "turn the hearts" of people (v 6 [3:24 HB]). In the time of Jesus, John the Baptist fulfilled this role (Matt 11:14, 17:11-13; Luke 1:17). Perhaps when Jesus comes again "witnesses" will accomplish this task (Rev 11:3-6). Regardless of how that may be, believers can be sure that God will continue offering mercy to people. This is the affirmation of Malachi as well as other prophets of the Bible. The Lord who says, "I have loved you" (1:2), will keep offering grace until the final day of judgment arrives.